Program Authors

Dr. Diane August
Dr. Donald Bear
Dr. Janice A. Dole
Dr. Jana Echevarria
Dr. Douglas Fisher
Dr. David J. Francis
Dr. Vicki Gibson
Dr. Jan Hasbrouck
Margaret Kilgo
Dr. Scott G. Paris
Dr. Timothy Shanahan
Dr. Josefina V. Tinajero

Mc
Graw
Hill
Education

Also Available from McGraw-Hill Education

 TextEvaluator.

ETS and the ETS logo are registered trademarks of Educational Testing Service (ETS).
TextEvaluator is a trademark of Educational Testing Service.

Cover and Title Pages: Nathan Love

www.mheonline.com/readingwonders

Send all inquiries to:
McGraw-Hill Education
2 Penn Plaza
New York, NY 10121

ISBN: 978-0-07-678341-0
MHID: 0-07-678341-3

Printed in the United States of America.

1 2 3 4 5 6 7 8 9 RMN 20 19 18 17 16 15   A

66 *The students love their books. With this curriculum, we have fantastic informational text and a variety of genres.* *99*

— Becky Boyle, Campbell Elementary, Lincoln, NE

66 *I feel that my students are lucky to be exposed to Wonders. It makes a world of difference. The online piece has made my job easier and allowed me to become a better teacher.* *99*

— Todd Kimmel, Horatio B. Hackett School, Philadelphia, PA

66 *Students are able to do more than we thought they could. We have raised the rigor and they want more. The conversations that are happening between my students are more sophisticated.* *99*

— Heather Griffith, Lakeside Farms Elementary, Lakeside, CA

PROGRAM AUTHORS

Dr. Diane August
American Institutes for Research,
Washington, D.C.

Managing Researcher
Education Program

Dr. Donald R. Bear
Iowa State University

Professor, Iowa State University
Author of *Words Their Way, Words
Their Way with English Learners,
Vocabulary Their Way,* and *Words
Their Way with Struggling Readers, 4–12*

Dr. Janice A. Dole
University of Utah

Professor, University of Utah
Director, Utah Center for Reading and
Literacy
Content Facilitator, National Assessment
of Educational Progress (NAEP)
CCSS Consultant to Literacy Coaches,
Salt Lake City School District, Utah

Dr. Jana Echevarria
California State University, Long
Beach

Professor Emerita, California State University
Author of *Making Content Comprehensible
for English Learners: The SIOP Model*

Dr. Douglas Fisher
San Diego State University

Co-Director, Center for the Advancement
of Reading, California State University
Author of *Language Arts Workshop:
Purposeful Reading and Writing Instruction,
Reading for Information in Elementary
School;* coauthor of *Close Reading and
Writing from Sources, Rigorous Reading: 5
Access Points for Comprehending Complex
Text,* and *Text-Dependent Questions,
Grades K-5* with N. Frey

Dr. David J. Francis
University of Houston

Director of the Center for Research
on Educational Achievement and
Teaching of English Language
Learners (CREATE)

Consulting Authors

Kathy R. Bumgardner
National Literacy Consultant

Strategies Unlimited, Inc.
Gastonia, NC

Jay McTighe
Jay McTighe and Associates

Author of *Essential Questions: Opening
Doors to Student Understanding,
The Understanding by Design Guide
to Creating High Quality Units* and
*Schooling by Design: Mission, Action,
Achievement* with G. Wiggins,
and *Differentiated Instruction and
Understanding By Design* with C.
Tomlinson

Dr. Doris Walker-Dalhouse
Marquette University

Associate Professor, Department
of Educational Policy & Leadership
Author of articles on multicultural
literature, struggling readers, and
reading instruction in urban schools

Dinah Zike
Educational Consultant

Dinah-Might Activities, Inc.
San Antonio, TX

(Dole) Patrick Brennan; (Echevarria) Victoria Sanchez, CSULB; (Fisher) Courtesy of Douglas Fisher; (Gibson, Hasbrouck) Roger Pelissier; (Kilgo) Courtesy of Margaret Kilgo; (Paris) Courtesy of Scott G. Paris; (Shanahan) Courtesy of Timothy Shanahan; (Tinajero) Courtesy of Josefina V. Tinajero; (Bumgardner) Courtesy of sixcentsphotography; (Walker-Dalhouse) Dan Johnson, Marquette University; (others) McGraw-Hill Education

Dr. Scott G. Paris
Educational Testing Service,
Vice President, Research Professor,
Nanyang Technological University,
Singapore, 2008–2011
Professor of Education and Psychology,
University of Michigan, 1978–2008

Dr. Timothy Shanahan
University of Illinois at Chicago
Distinguished Professor, Urban Education
Director, UIC Center for Literacy Chair,
Department of Curriculum & Instruction
Member, English Language Arts Work
Team and Writer of the Common Core
State Standards
President, International Reading
Association, 2006

Dr. Josefina V. Tinajero
University of Texas at El Paso
Professor of Bilingual Education &
Special Assistant to the Vice President
of Research.

Dr. Vicki Gibson
Educational Consultant Gibson
Hasbrouck and Associates
Author of *Differentiated Instruction:
Grouping for Success, Differentiated
Instruction: Guidelines for Implementation,*
and *Managing Behaviors to Support
Differentiated Instruction*

Dr. Jan Hasbrouck
J.H. Consulting
Gibson Hasbrouck and Associates
Developed Oral Reading Fluency Norms for
Grades 1-8
Author of *The Reading Coach: A How-
to Manual for Success* and *Educators as
Physicians: Using RTI Assessments for
Effective Decision-Making*

Margaret Kilgo
Educational Consultant
Kilgo Consulting, Inc., Austin, TX
Developed Data-Driven Decisions
process for evaluating student
performance by standard
Member of Common Core State
Standards Anchor Standards
Committee for Reading and Writing

National Program Advisors

Mayda Bahamonde-Gunnell, Ed.D
Grand Rapids Public Schools
Rockford, MI

Maria Campanario
Boston Public Schools
Boston, MA

Sharon Giless Aguina
Waukegan Community Unit School District #60
Waukegan, IL

Carolyn Gore, Ph.D.
Caddo Parish School District
Shreveport, LA

Kellie Jones
Department of Bilingual/ESL Services
Brockton, MA

Michelle Martinez
Albuquerque Public Schools Curriculum and
   Instruction
Albuquerque, NM

Jadi Miller
Lincoln Public Schools
Lincoln, NE

Matthew Walsh
Wissahickon School District
Ambler, PA

CONNECTED LITERACY TOOLS

Weekly Concept and Essential Question

The Keys to Unlock the Week

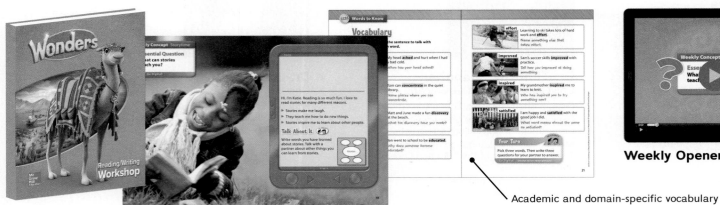

Reading/Writing Workshop

Academic and domain-specific vocabulary

Weekly Opener Video

Teach and Model

With Rich Opportunities for Collaborative Conversations

Reading/Writing Workshop

All building on the week's Essential Question

Collaborative Conversations PD

Practice and Apply

Close Reading, Writing to Sources, Grammar, Spelling, and Phonics

Literature Anthology

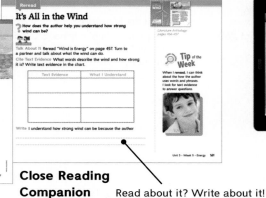

Close Reading Companion

Read about it? Write about it!

Digital Practice

Build Knowledge and Skills at Every Level

Differentiate to Accelerate

Move students ahead as soon as they're ready

Over 6500 more leveled readers online!

Nonfiction Leveled Readers

Fiction Leveled Readers

Also available:
- WonderWorks
- Wonders for English Learners
- Wonders Adaptive Learning

Adaptive Learning

Integrate Understanding

Writing across texts, research and inquiry

Performance task practice throughout the year

Writer's Workspace

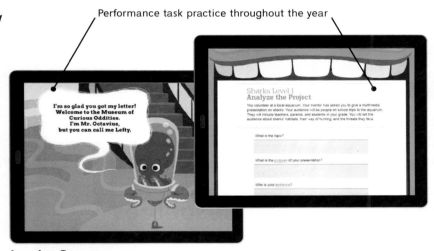

Inquiry Space

Assess

Specific skills and standards for every student, assignment, and class

Specific recommendations for every skill and standard.

Weekly, Unit, Benchmark Assessments

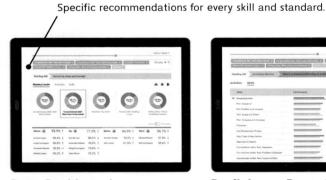

Data Dashboard

Proficiency Report

PROGRAM COMPONENTS
Print and Digital

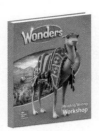

Reading/Writing Workshop

Literature Anthology **Close Reading Companion**

Leveled Readers

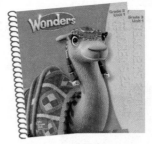

Teacher Editions

Classroom Library Trade Books

Your Turn Practice Book

Visual Vocabulary Cards

Leveled Workstation Activity Cards

Sound-Spelling Cards

High-Frequency Word Cards

Response Board

Weekly Assessment

Unit Assessment

Benchmark Assessment

Additional Digital Resources

For You

Plan
Customizable Lesson Plans

Teach
Classroom Presentation Tools
Instructional Lessons

Manage and Assign
Student Grouping and Assignments

Assess
Online Assessments
Reports and Scoring

Collaborate
Online Class Conversations
Interactive Group Projects

School to Home
Activities and Messages

Professional Development
Model Lessons and PD Videos

Additional Online Resources
• Leveled Practice
• Grammar Practice
• Phonics/Spelling
• ELL Activities
• Genre Study
• Reader's Theater
• Tier 2 Intervention
• Instructional Routine Handbook

For Your Students

My To Do List
Assignments
Assessment

Read
e Books
Interactive Texts

Write
Interactive Writing

Words to Know
Build Vocabulary

Play
Interactive Games

School to Home Support
• Activities for Home
• Messages from the Teacher

www.connected.mcgraw-hill.com

viii

Think It Over

Unit Planning

Weekly Lessons

Writing Process — Genre Writing: Informative Text

Model Lesson — Extended Complex Text

Close Reading Routine

Program Information

(t to b) John Lund/Marc Romanelli/Blend Images/Getty Images; Ryan McVay/Lifesize/Getty Images; Vladimir Rys/Stringer/Getty Images Sport/Getty Images; Peter Dazeley/Photographer's Choice/Getty Images; Bob Elsdale/Photonica/Getty Images

UNIT OVERVIEW

Text Complexity Range for Grades 2–3

Lexile

420   *TextEvaluator*™   820

2   35

	Week 1	Week 2	Week 3

READING

TREASURES	WEATHER	LEARNING TO SUCCEED

TREASURES

ESSENTIAL QUESTION
How do you decide what's important?

Build Background

CCSS Vocabulary
L.3.6 *alarmed, anguish, necessary, obsessed, possess, reward, treasure, wealth*
Root Words

CCSS Comprehension
RL.3.2 Strategy: Make, Confirm, and Revise Predictions
Skill: Theme
Genre: Myth/Drama

CCSS Phonics
RF.3.3a Prefixes, Roots in Related Words

CCSS Fluency
RF.3.4c Expression

WEATHER

ESSENTIAL QUESTION
How can weather affect us?

Build Background

CCSS Vocabulary
L.3.6 *argue, astonished, complained, conditions, forbidding, forecast, relief, stranded*
Idioms

CCSS Comprehension
RL.3.2 Strategy: Make, Confirm, and Revise Predictions
Skill: Theme
Genre: Historical Fiction

CCSS Phonics
RF.3.3b Consonant + *le* Syllable, Latin Suffixes

CCSS Fluency
RF.3.4a Phrasing

LEARNING TO SUCCEED

ESSENTIAL QUESTION
Why are goals important?

Build Background

CCSS Vocabulary
L.3.6 *communicated, essential, goal, motivated, professional, research, serious, specialist*
Greek and Latin Roots

CCSS Comprehension
RI.3.3 Strategy: Reread
Skill: Text Structure: Problem and Solution
Genre: Biography

CCSS Phonics
RF.3.3c Vowel-Team Syllables, Greek and Latin Roots

CCSS Fluency
RF.3.4c Accuracy

LANGUAGE ARTS

Week 1	Week 2	Week 3

CCSS Writing
W.3.1a Write to Sources: Opinion

CCSS Grammar
L.3.1a Adjectives and Articles

CCSS Spelling
L.3.2f Prefixes

CCSS Vocabulary
L.3.4c Build Vocabulary

CCSS Writing
W.3.3a Write to Sources: Narrative

CCSS Grammar
L.3.1g Adjectives That Compare

CCSS Spelling
L.3.2f Consonant + *le* Syllables

CCSS Vocabulary
L.3.5a Build Vocabulary

CCSS Writing
W.3.2a Write to Sources: Informative

CCSS Grammar
L.3.1a Adverbs

CCSS Spelling
L.3.2f Vowel-Team Syllables

CCSS Vocabulary
L.3.4c Build Vocabulary

 Genre Writing: Informative Text Feature Article T344–T349

(l to r) John Lund/Marc Romanelli/Blend Images/Getty Images; Ryan McVay/Lifesize/Getty Images; Vladimir Rys/Stringer/Getty Images; Peter Dazeley/Photographer's Choice/Getty Images; Bob Elsdale/Photonica/Getty Images

Think It Over

Review and Assess

Week 4	Week 5	Week 6
ANIMALS AND YOU	FUNNY TIMES	

Week 4 — ANIMALS AND YOU

ESSENTIAL QUESTION
How can learning about animals help you respect them?

Build Background

CCSS **Vocabulary**
L.3.6 *endangered, fascinating, illegal, inhabit, requirement, respected, unaware, wildlife*
Paragraph Clues

CCSS **Comprehension**
RI.3.8 Strategy: Reread
Skill: Text Structure: Compare and Contrast
Genre: Expository Text

CCSS **Phonics**
RF.3.3b *r*-Controlled Vowel Syllables, Latin Suffixes

CCSS **Fluency**
RF.3.4b Phrasing

Week 5 — FUNNY TIMES

ESSENTIAL QUESTION
What makes you laugh?

Build Background

CCSS **Vocabulary**
L.3.6 *entertainment, humorous, ridiculous, slithered*
Idioms

CCSS **Comprehension**
RL.3.6 Genre: Narrative Poem
Skill: Point of View
Literary Elements: Rhythm and Rhyme

CCSS **Phonics**
RF.3.3a Suffixes *-ful, -less, -ly,*
Frequently Misspelled Words

CCSS **Fluency**
RF.3.4b Phrasing and Expression

Week 6

CCSS **Reader's Theater**
RF.3.4b Focus on Vocabulary
Fluency: Accuracy, Rate, and Prosody

CCSS **Reading Digitally**
SL.3.2 Notetaking
Evaluate Sources
Navigating Links

CCSS **Research and Inquiry**
W.3.6 Using Technology for Research
Unit Projects
Presentation of Ideas

Unit 6 Assessment

Unit Assessment Book
Fluency Assessment
pages 172–181

CCSS **Writing**
W.3.2d Write to Sources: Informative

CCSS **Grammar**
L.3.1g Adverbs That Compare

CCSS **Spelling**
L.3.2f *r*-Controlled Vowel Syllables

CCSS **Vocabulary**
L.3.4a Build Vocabulary

CCSS **Writing**
W.3.3b Write to Sources: Narrative

CCSS **Grammar**
L.3.1i Prepositions

CCSS **Spelling**
L.3.2e Suffixes *-ful, -less, -ly*

CCSS **Vocabulary**
L.3.5a Build Vocabulary

CCSS **Writing**
W.3.10 Publishing Celebrations
Portfolio Choice

 Genre Writing: Informative Text Research Report T350–T355

UNIT OPENER

Think It Over

Diamond in the Rough

Dad called it a diamond in the rough,
A big, old field outside of town
Now just a dumping ground
A ton of trash
    A mile of mess
"No way!" my friends say.

But I just shake my head and smile.
I know.

I can clean it. Make it green.
Polish up that diamond in the rough.

I go each day,
Pick up trash,
Haul away sack after sack
    After sack.

My friends follow,
    Watching, watching,
Then roll up their sleeves.
They see it too—
    A diamond in the rough.

Together we yank up weeds,
    Rake things smooth,

Until finally, finally
    A baseball field.

Not the biggest
Not the best

But OURS
    A diamond in the rough.

— By Maureen Wong

The Big Idea How do we decide what's important?

Reading/Writing
Workshop

READING/WRITING WORKSHOP, pp. 400–401

The Big Idea *How do we decide what's important?*

COLLABORATE

Talk About It

Have students read the Big Idea aloud. Ask students how they decide whether something is important or not. Students should think about questions, such as how a decision might affect their futures or the lives of people around them.

Ask: *What are some things that are important to you?* Have students discuss with partners or in groups and then share their ideas with the class.

Music Links Introduce a song at the start of the unit. Go to www.connected.mcgraw-hill.com **Resources Media: Music** to find audio recordings, song lyrics, and activities.

Read the Poem: "Diamond in the Rough"

Read aloud "Diamond in the Rough." Ask students questions to explore the theme.

- What does the narrator want to do?
- How does the narrator go about his plans?
- What does the narrator think is important?

Metaphor Ask students what they think "the diamond in the rough" is. Explain that "a diamond in the rough" is a phrase used to describe something valuable hidden in an unlikely place.

Repetition Have students read the lines "Haul away sack after sack / After sack." Ask students: What word is being repeated? Why do you think the author repeats it?

RESEARCH AND INQUIRY

Weekly Projects Each week students will produce a project related to the Essential Question. They will then develop one of these projects more fully for the Unit Research Project. Through their research, students will focus their attention on:

* comparing information across sources.
* recalling, paraphrasing, and presenting information they have found.

Shared Research Board You may wish to develop a Shared Research Board. Students can post questions, ideas, and information about the unit theme. Students can post articles, facts, and other information they gather. They can also post lists and plans describing steps they think need to be taken in order to make an important decision.

WEEKLY PROJECTS
Students work in pairs or small groups.

Week 1 Interview a Classmate, T38
Week 2 Extreme Weather Summary, T102
Week 3 Setting Goals Interview, T166
Week 4 Create Illustrations, T230
Week 5 Write a Humorous Poem, T294

WEEK 6
Students work in small groups to complete and present one of the following projects.

* Quality They Value Essay
* Weather Disaster News Story
* Goal Setting Plan
* Fantasy Story with Animal Character
* Health Slide Show

WRITING

Write to Sources As students read and reread each week for close reading of text, they take notes, cite text evidence to support their ideas and opinions, and write short analytical responses. After reading, students build writing fluency, analyze model responses, craft longer responses incorporating text evidence, and focus on writing traits. Each week, students first write to one source and then write to two sources.

WEEKLY WRITING TRAITS
Week 1 Sentence Fluency, T28
Week 2 Word Choice, T92
Week 3 Organization, T156
Week 4 Organization, T220
Week 5 Word Choice, T284

Writing Process: Focus on Informative Text

Over the course of the unit, students will develop one or two longer informative texts. Students will work through the various stages of the writing process, allowing them time to continue revising their writing, conferring with peers and teacher.

GENRE WRITING: INFORMATIVE TEXT
Choose one or complete both 3-week writing process lessons over the course of the unit.

Feature Article, T344–T349

Week 1 Expert Model, Prewrite
Week 2 Draft, Revise
Week 3 Proofread/Edit and Publish, Evaluate

Research Report, T350–T355

Week 4 Expert Model, Prewrite
Week 5 Draft, Revise
Week 6 Proofread/Edit and Publish, Evaluate

 **COLLABORATE** Post student questions and monitor student online discussions. Create a Shared Research Board.

 **WRITER'S WORKSPACE** Ask students to work through their genre writing using the online tools for support.

Go Digital! www.connected.mcgraw-hill.com

WEEKLY OVERVIEW

Build Knowledge
Treasures

? Essential Question:
How do you decide what's important?

Teach and Model
Close Reading and Writing

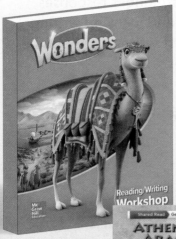

Reading Writing Workshop

"Athena and Arachne," 406–409
Genre Myth/Drama **Lexile** N/A **ETS** *TextEvaluator* N/A

Practice and Apply
Close Reading and Writing

Literature Anthology

King Midas and the Golden Touch, 462–475
Genre Drama/Myth **Lexile** N/A **ETS** *TextEvaluator* N/A

"Carlos's Gift" 478–481
Genre Realistic Fiction **Lexile** 640 **ETS** *TextEvaluator* 36

Differentiated Texts

APPROACHING
Lexile N/A
ETS *TextEvaluator* N/A

ON LEVEL
Lexile N/A
ETS *TextEvaluator* N/A

BEYOND
Lexile N/A
ETS *TextEvaluator* N/A

ELL
Lexile N/A
ETS *TextEvaluator* N/A

Leveled Readers

Extended Complex Texts

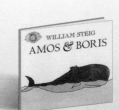

The Hurricane Mystery
(Boxcar Children)
Genre Fiction
Lexile 580

Amos and Boris
Genre Fiction
Lexile 810

Classroom Library

Student Outcomes

Close Reading of Complex Text
- Cite relevant evidence from text
- Determine theme
- Make, Confirm, and Revise Predictions

RL.3.1, RL.3.2

Writing
Write to Sources
- Draw evidence from literature
- Write opinion texts
- Conduct short research on qualities people value

Writing Process
- Prewrite a Feature Article

W.3.1a, W.3.8, W.3.10

Speaking and Listening
- Engage in collaborative discussions about treasures
- Paraphrase portions of "Pandora Finds a Box" and presentations on treasures
- Present information on treasures

SL.3.1b, SL.3.2

Language Development
Conventions
- Distinguish adjectives and articles

Vocabulary Acquisition
- Acquire and use academic vocabulary

alarmed	anguish	necessary	obsessed
possess	reward	treasure	wealth

- Use root words as clues to the meaning of a word

L.3.1a, L.3.4c, L.3.5b, L.3.6

Foundational Skills
Phonics/Word Study
- Prefixes *un-, re-, pre-, dis-*
- Roots in related words

Spelling Words

disagreed	dislike	disappear	prepaid
preschool	precook	previous	rebuild
return	resell	reprint	unwrap
unlucky	untied	unbeaten	

Fluency
- Expression

RF.3.3a, RF.3.4b, RF.3.4c

Ken Karp/McGraw-Hill Education

Professional Development
- See lessons in action in real classrooms.
- Get expert advice on instructional practices.
- Collaborate with other teachers.
- Access PLC Resources.

Go Digital! www.connected.mcgraw-hill.com.

1 Talk About Treasures

Guide students in collaborative conversations.

Discuss the essential question: *How do you decide what is important?*

Develop academic language.

Listen to "Pandora Finds a Box" and discuss the story.

2 Read "Athena and Arachne"

Model close reading with a short complex text.

Read

"Athena and Arachne" to learn why valuing a talent can cause problems, citing text evidence to answer text-dependent questions.

Reread

"Athena and Arachne" to analyze text, craft, and structure, citing text evidence.

3 Write About "Athena and Arachne"

Model writing to a source.

Analyze a short response student model.

Use text evidence from close reading to write to a source.

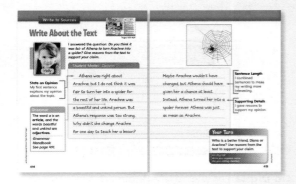

4 ## Read and Write About
King Midas and the Golden Touch

Practice and apply close reading of the anchor text.

Read

King Midas and the Golden Touch to learn how King Midas discovers what he values most.

Reread

King Midas and the Golden Touch and use text evidence to understand how the author uses text, craft, and structure to develop a deeper understanding of the story.

Write a short response about *King Midas and the Golden Touch*.

Integrate

Information about people who changed their values in other stories you have read.

Write to Two Sources, citing text evidence from *King Midas and the Golden Touch* and "Carlos's Gift."

5 ## Independent Partner Work

Gradual release of support to independent work

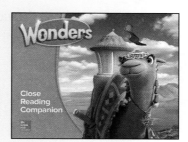

- Text-Dependent Questions
- Scaffolded Partner Work
  Talk with a Partner
  Cite Text Evidence
  Complete a sentence frame.
- Guided Text Annotation

6 ## Integrate Knowledge and Ideas

Connect Texts

Text to Text Discuss how each of the texts answers the question: How do you decide what is important?

Text to Photography Compare character traits in the text read and the photograph of a boy walking with a friend on crutches.

Conduct a Short Research Project

Interview a classmate about the things he or she values.

DEVELOPING READERS AND WRITERS

Write to Sources

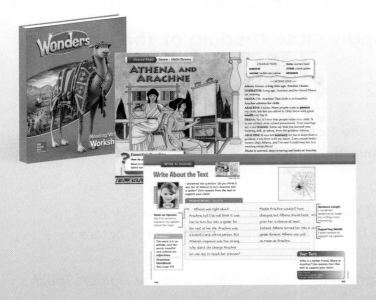

Day 1 and Day 2

Build Writing Fluency

- Quick write on "Athena and Arachne," p. T28

Write to a Source

- Analyze a student model, p. T28

- Write about "Athena and Arachne," p. T29

- Apply Writing Trait: Vary Sentence Lengths, p. T28

- Apply Grammar Skill: Adjectives and Articles, p. T29

Day 3

Write to a Source

- Write about *King Midas and the Golden Touch*, independent practice, p. T25P

- Provide scaffolded instruction to meet student needs, p. T30

Day 4 and Day 5

Write to Two Sources

- Analyze a student model, pp. T30–31

- Write to compare *King Midas and the Golden Touch* with "Carlos's Gift," p. T31

Writing Process

Go Digital

Writer's Workspace

Genre Writing: Informative Text

Feature Article
Expert Model

• Discuss features of informational writing

• Discuss the expert model

Prewrite

• Discuss purpose and audience

• Plan the topic

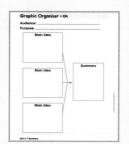

Expert Model • Summary • 101

A Summary of "Animals in the Extreme"
by Jessica K.

You might think that nothing could live in climates that are extremely cold or extremely hot. That isn't true. This article tells about the adaptations of two animals—the Siberian husky and the fennec fox. Both animals have features that help them live in places where the temperatures are extreme.

The Siberian husky has two-layered fur that sheds the rain and keeps the dog warm in Siberia. Its tail is long enough to cover its face when the dog sleeps. The dog's paws are thick and furry, too. They help the dog run on snow and ice.

The paws of the fennec fox are furry as well, but this animal lives in the extreme heat of the Sahara Desert. The fur on its feet protects it from the burning sand. The animal digs with its feet, too. The fox's fur is thick to block the extreme heat. It wraps its tail around it body, too, as it sleeps during the day.

Unit 6 • Summary

Expert Model

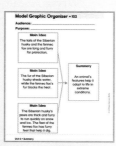

Features of a Feature Article

Model Graphic Organizer

Graphic Organizer

Grammar and Spelling Resources

Online PDFs

Reading/Writing Workshop Grammar Handbook p. 491

Online Spelling and Grammar Games

Grammar Practice, pp. 126–130

Phonics/Spelling Practice, pp. 151–156

SUGGESTED LESSON PLAN

READING		DAY 1	DAY 2
Teach, Model and Apply *Wonders* Reading/Writing Workshop	Core	**Introduce the Concept** T10–T11 **Vocabulary** T14–T15 **Close Reading** "Athena and Arachne," T16–T17	**Close Reading** "Athena and Arachne," T16–T17 **Strategy** Make, Confirm, or Revise Predictions, T18–T19 **Skill** Theme, T20–T21 **Vocabulary Strategy** Root Words, T24–T25
	Options	**Listening Comprehension** T12–T13	**Genre** Myth/Drama, T22–T23

LANGUAGE ARTS			
Writing **Grammar** **Spelling** **Build Vocabulary**	Core	**Grammar** Adjectives and Articles, T34 **Spelling** Prefixes *un-, re-, pre-,* and *dis-,* T34 **Build Vocabulary** T36	**Write About the Text** Model Note-Taking and Write to a Prompt, T28–T29 **Grammar** Adjectives and Articles, T32 **Build Vocabulary** T36
	Options	**Write About the Text** Writing Fluency, T28 **Genre Writing** Feature Article: Read Like a Writer, T344	**Genre Writing** Feature Article: Discuss the Expert Model, T344 **Spelling** Prefixes *un-, re-, pre-,* and *dis-,* T34

Whole Group

(Writing Process) **Writing Process: Informative Text** Feature Article, T344–T349   Use with Weeks 1–3

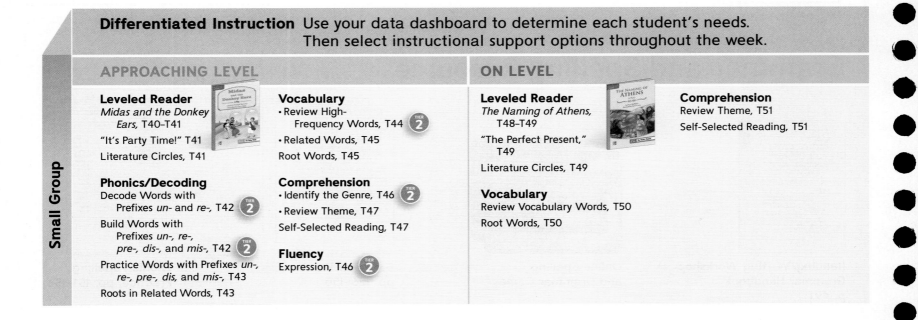

Differentiated Instruction Use your data dashboard to determine each student's needs. Then select instructional support options throughout the week.

Small Group

APPROACHING LEVEL

Leveled Reader
Midas and the Donkey Ears, T40–T41

"It's Party Time!" T41

Literature Circles, T41

Phonics/Decoding
Decode Words with Prefixes *un-* and *re-,* T42 (TIER 2)

Build Words with Prefixes *un-, re-, pre-, dis-,* and *mis-,* T42 (TIER 2)

Practice Words with Prefixes *un-, re-, pre-, dis,* and *mis-,* T43

Roots in Related Words, T43

Vocabulary
• Review High-Frequency Words, T44 (TIER 2)
• Related Words, T45

Root Words, T45

Comprehension
• Identify the Genre, T46 (TIER 2)
• Review Theme, T47

Self-Selected Reading, T47

Fluency
Expression, T46 (TIER 2)

ON LEVEL

Leveled Reader
The Naming of Athens, T48–T49

"The Perfect Present," T49

Literature Circles, T49

Vocabulary
Review Vocabulary Words, T50

Root Words, T50

Comprehension
Review Theme, T51

Self-Selected Reading, T51

DAY 3	DAY 4	DAY 5
Close Reading *King Midas and the Golden Touch,* T25A–T25P	**Fluency** T27 **Close Reading** "Carlos's Gift," T25Q–T25T **Integrate Ideas** Research and Inquiry, T38–T39	**Integrate Ideas** T38–T39 • Text Connections • Research and Inquiry **Weekly Assessment**
Phonics/Decoding T26–T27 • Prefixes • Roots in Related Words	**Close Reading** *King Midas and the Golden Touch,* T25A–T25P	

Grammar Adjectives and Articles, T33	**Write About Two Texts** Model Note-Taking and Taking Notes, T30	**Write About Two Texts** Analyze Student Model and Write to the Prompt, T31 **Spelling** Prefixes *un-, re-, pre-* and *dis-*, T35
Write About the Text T30 **Genre Writing** Feature Article and Prewrite, T345 **Spelling** Prefixes *un-, re-, pre-,* and *dis-*, T35 **Build Vocabulary** T37	**Genre Writing** Feature Article: Teach the Prewrite Minilesson, T345 **Grammar** T33 **Spelling** Prefixes *un-, re-, pre-,* and *dis-*, T35 **Build Vocabulary** T37	**Genre Writing** Feature Article: Choose Your Topic and Plan, T345 **Grammar** T33 **Build Vocabulary** T37

Writing Process: Informative Text Feature Article, T344–T349   Use with Weeks 1–3

BEYOND LEVEL

Leveled Reader
Odysseus and King Aeolus, T52–T53
"Darla's Dream," T53
Literature Circles, T53

Vocabulary
Review Domain-Specific Words, T54
• Root Words, T54
• Dialogue, T54

Comprehension
Review Theme, T55
• Self-Selected Reading, T55
• Independent Study, T55

ENGLISH LANGUAGE LEARNERS

Shared Read
"Athena and Arachne," T56–T57

Leveled Reader
The Naming of Athens, T58–T59
"The Perfect Present," T59
Literature Circles, T59

Phonics/Decoding
Decode Words with Prefixes *un-* and *re-*, T42
Build Words with Prefixes *un-, re-, pre-, dis-,* and *mis-*, T42
Practice Words with Prefixes *un-, re-, pre-, dis-,* and *mis-*, T43
Roots in Related Words, T43

Vocabulary
• Preteach Vocabulary, T60
• Review High-Frequency Words, T44
Review Vocabulary, T60
Root Words, T61
Additional Vocabulary, T61

Spelling
Spell Words with Prefixes *un-, re-, pre-, dis-,* and *mis-*, T62

Writing
Writing Trait: Vary Sentence Lengths, T62

Grammar
Adjectives and Articles, T63

DIFFERENTIATE TO ACCELERATE

   **Scaffold to** **A**ccess **C**omplex **T**ext

| IF | the text complexity of a particular selection is too difficult for students |
| THEN | see the references noted in the chart below for scaffolded instruction to help students Access Complex Text. |

Qualitative / Quantitative / Reader and Task
TEXT COMPLEXITY

	Reading/Writing Workshop	Literature Anthology	Leveled Readers	Classroom Library
			 Approach · On Level · Beyond · ELL	

Quantitative

Reading/Writing Workshop

"Athena and Arachne"

Lexile N/A
TextEvaluator™ N/A

Literature Anthology

King Midas and the Golden Touch

Lexile N/A
TextEvaluator™ N/A

"Carlos's Gift"

Lexile 640
TextEvaluator™ 36

Leveled Readers

Approaching Level

Lexile N/A
TextEvaluator™ N/A

Beyond Level

Lexile N/A
TextEvaluator™ N/A

On Level

Lexile N/A
TextEvaluator™ N/A

ELL

Lexile N/A
TextEvaluator™ N/A

Classroom Library

The Hurricane Mystery

Lexile 580

Amos and Boris

Lexile 810

Qualitative

What Makes the Text Complex?

• **Prior Knowledge** Greek Mythology T17
• **Genre** Features of Drama T23

A C T *See Scaffolded Instruction in Teacher's Edition T17 and T23.*

What Makes the Text Complex?

• **Genre** Features of Myth/ Drama T25A, T25D, T25E, T25I, T25M
• **Sentence Structure** T25C, T25K
• **Connection of Ideas** Synthesize T25H, T25S
• **Organization** Sequence T25G; Cause and Effect T25J
• **Specific Vocabulary** Synonyms T25Q

A C T *See Scaffolded Instruction in Teacher's Edition T25A–T25T.*

What Makes the Text Complex?

• **Specific Vocabulary**
• **Sentence Structure**
• **Connection of Ideas**
• **Genre**

A C T *See Level Up lessons online for Leveled Readers.*

What Makes the Text Complex?

• **Genre**
• **Specific Vocabulary**
• **Prior Knowledge**
• **Sentence Structure**
• **Organization**
• **Purpose**
• **Connection of Ideas**

A C T *See Scaffolded Instruction in Teacher's Edition T360–T361.*

Reader and Task

The Introduce the Concept lesson on pages T10–T11 will help determine the reader's knowledge and engagement in the weekly concept. See pages T16–T25 and T38–T39 for questions and tasks for this text.

The Introduce the Concept lesson on pages T10–T11 will help determine the reader's knowledge and engagement in the weekly concept. See pages T25A–T25T and T38–T39 for questions and tasks for this text.

The Introduce the Concept lesson on pages T10–T11 will help determine the reader's knowledge and engagement in the weekly concept. See pages T40–T41, T48–T49, T52–T53, T58–T59, and T38–T39 for questions and tasks for this text.

The Introduce the Concept lesson on pages T10–T11 will help determine the reader's knowledge and engagement in the weekly concept. See pages T360–T361 for questions and tasks for this text.

Monitor and *Differentiate*

✔ Quick Check

To differentiate instruction, use the Quick Checks to assess students' needs and select the appropriate small group instruction focus.

Comprehension Strategy Make Predictions T19
Comprehension Skill Theme T21
Genre Myth/Drama T23
Vocabulary Strategy Root Words T25
Phonics/Fluency Prefixes, Expression T27

If No → | Approaching Level | **Reteach** T40–T47
| **ELL** | **Develop** T56–T63
If Yes → | On Level | **Review** T48–T51
| Beyond Level | **Extend** T52–T55

Using Weekly Data

Check your data Dashboard to verify assessment results and guide grouping decisions.

Level Up with Leveled Readers

IF → students can read their leveled text fluently and answer comprehension questions

THEN → work with the next level up to accelerate students' reading with more complex text.

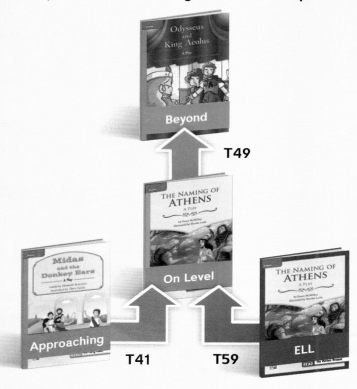

Beyond

T49

On Level

Approaching   *ELL*

T41   T59

ELL ENGLISH LANGUAGE LEARNERS

Small Group Instruction

Use the ELL small group lessons in the Wonders Teacher's Edition to provide focused instruction.

Language Development
Vocabulary preteaching and review, additional vocabulary building, and vocabulary strategy lessons, pp. T60–T61

Close Reading
Interactive Question-Response routines for scaffolded text-dependent questioning for reading and rereading the Shared Read and Leveled Reader, pp. T56–T59

Writing
Focus on the weekly writing trait, grammar skills, and spelling words, pp. T62–T63

Additional ELL Support

Use *Reading Wonders for English Learners* for ELD instruction that connects to the core.

Language Development
Ample opportunities for discussions, and scaffolded language support

Close Reading
Companion Worktexts for guided support in annotating text and citing text evidence. Differentiated Texts about the weekly concept.

Writing
Scaffolded instruction for writing to sources and revising student models

Reading Wonders for ELLs Teacher Edition and Companion Worktexts

→ Introduce the Concept

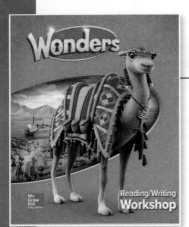

Reading/Writing Workshop

OBJECTIVES

 Engage effectively in a range of collaborative discussions (one-on-one, in groups, and teacher-led) with diverse partners on grade 3 topics and texts, building on others' ideas and expressing their own clearly. Follow agreed-upon rules for discussions (e.g., gaining the floor in respectful ways, listening to others with care, speaking one at a time about the topics and texts under discussion).
SL.3.1b

ACADEMIC LANGUAGE
- *treasure, wealth*
- Cognate: *tesoro*

Build Background

ESSENTIAL QUESTION

How do you decide what is important?

Have students read the Essential Question on page 402 of the **Reading/Writing Workshop**. Tell them that the things we value are things we feel are important.

Discuss the photo with students. Focus on how the girl's opportunity to spend time with her grandfather is something that she values.

- Spending time with people and learning new things can be more valuable than **treasure** to many people.
- **Wealth** is not always money or jewels. Sometimes wealth is the people we know and the things we learn.
- Healthy habits and sharing with others are important too.

Talk About It

Ask: *What is valuable to you? What are some treasures in your life?* Have students discuss in pairs or small groups.

- Model using the Concept Web to generate words and phrases related to what is valuable and why it is important.
- Have partners continue the discussion by talking about how they decide what they value. They can complete the Concept Webs, generating additional words and phrases.

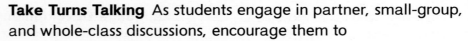

Collaborative Conversations

Take Turns Talking As students engage in partner, small-group, and whole-class discussions, encourage them to

- wait for a person to finish before they speak. They should not speak over others.
- raise their hand to let others know they would like a turn to speak.
- ask others in the groups to share their opinions so that all students have a chance to share.

Go Digital

Discuss the Concept

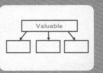
Watch Video

Use Graphic Organizer

Weekly Concept Treasures

? Essential Question
How do you decide what's important?

Go Digital!

WHAT WE VALUE

Spending time with my grandfather is important. He shares what he knows and helps me learn new things. He values spending time with me, too.

► Spending time with people and learning new things are valuable to me.

► Healthy habits and sharing are important, too.

Talk About It

Write words you have learned about what's valuable. Talk with a partner about the things that you value.

Valuable

402 | 403

READING/WRITING WORKSHOP, *pp. 402–403*

ENGLISH LANGUAGE LEARNERS
ELL SCAFFOLD

Beginning	**Intermediate**	**Advanced/High**
Use Visuals Point to the picture. Say: *Look at the picture. The girl is with her grandfather. This is important to her. She values being with him.* Have pairs of students ask and answer questions about a few things they value. Correct students' pronunciation as needed.	**Describe** Have students describe the picture. Ask: *What is important to the girl? ____ is important. Why is this important? This is important because ____.* Elicit details to further develop students' responses. Have pairs of students ask and answer questions about a few things they value.	**Discuss** Have partners discuss what is valuable to them. Ask: *What is valuable in your life?* Have students write down three things that are valuable to them and discuss their lists with a partner. Encourage students to explain why each thing is valuable to them.

GRAPHIC ORGANIZER 51

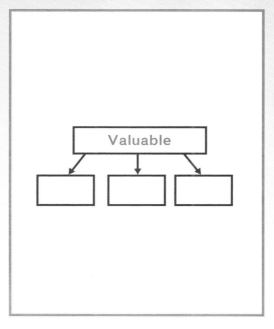

Valuable

→ Listening Comprehension

MINILESSON
10 Mins

Interactive Read Aloud

OBJECTIVES

CCSS Ask and answer questions to determine understanding of a text, referring explicitly to the text as the basis for the answers. **RL.3.1**

CCSS Recount stories, including fables, folktales, and myths from diverse cultures; determine the central message, lesson, or moral and explain how it is conveyed through key details in the text. **RL.3.2**

CCSS Determine the main ideas and supporting details of a text read aloud or information presented in diverse media and formats, including visually, quantitatively, and orally. **SL.3.2**

• Listen for a purpose.

• Identify characteristics of a myth.

ACADEMIC LANGUAGE

• *myth; make, confirm, and revise predictions*

• Cognates: *predicciones, mito*

Connect to Concept: Treasures

Tell students that our actions reveal what we value in life. Let students know that they will be listening to a passage about a woman who decides it is more important to satisfy her own curiosity rather than obey instructions. As students listen, have them think about how the story answers the Essential Question.

Preview Genre: Myth

Explain that the story you will read aloud is a myth. Discuss features of a myth:

• occurs in an ancient time and place

• often teaches a lesson or explains something in nature

• may use gods and goddesses as characters, as well as humans

Preview Comprehension Strategy: Make, Confirm, and Revise Predictions

Point out that readers can use prior knowledge along with story clues to make logical predictions about what might happen next. As readers continue, they may confirm or revise their predictions and make additional ones based on new information.

Use the Think Alouds on page T13 to model the strategy.

Respond to Reading

Think Aloud Clouds Display Think Aloud Master 3: *I predicted _____ because . . .* to reinforce how you used the Make, Confirm, and Revise Predictions strategy to understand content.

Genre Features With students, discuss the elements of the Read Aloud that let them know it is a myth. Ask them to think about other texts that you have read or they have read independently that were myths.

Summarize Have students briefly retell the story "Pandora Finds a Box" in their own words to determine the main idea and identify the supporting details of the myth.

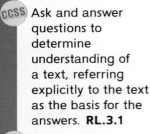

View Illustrations

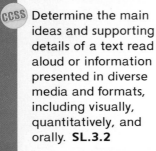

I predicted _____ because...

Model Think Alouds

Genre	Features

Fill in Genre Chart

Pandora Finds a Box

In a time and place long ago, there lived a young woman named Pandora. One day, as she sat by the seashore, a box washed up onto the sandy bank. She picked it up and saw it was finely decorated and had a strong lock on its latch. She also saw that there were three words carved into the top of the box: *Do Not Open!* **1**

Pandora wondered what could be in the box. Could it be filled with gold, silver, and jewels? "Why can't I open this box?" she said aloud. She shook it to see if whatever was inside made a noise.

"I'm sure it's filled with treasure, but it's not mine," she said. "I should follow the instructions and leave it for its rightful owner."

Try as she might, Pandora could not ignore the box. She was curious about what was inside and confident it was treasure. Pandora looked around to find something with which to open the box. She found a rock and began hitting it against the heavy lock. She heard a deep rumbling inside and again thought she should probably leave the box alone.

She touched the words carved into the lid: *Do Not Open!* **2**

However, curiosity once again caused her to pick up the rock. With one final blow, the lock broke and the latch was free. Pandora slowly lifted the top. Suddenly, the top flew open with such force that Pandora fell back upon the sand. Out of the box swirled dark, smoky wisps. They rose into the sky and flew off in four directions. Pandora looked into the box, expecting to find it empty.

Inside was a scroll of paper and a dandelion. Pandora read the scroll: *You have just let loose terrible things in the world: sadness, greed, pain, and hunger. The dandelion contains the seeds of hope. Blow the seeds and let the winds carry them away. This will make certain that there will always be hope.* **3**

Pandora blew the dandelion seeds of hope and watched them float away. She wondered if they would be enough. Feeling the heavy burden of what she had done, Pandora crept home alone.

Stockbroker/SuperStock

1 **Think Aloud** I wonder what's inside the box. I **make a prediction** that Pandora will try to open it. After I read, I can **confirm my prediction**.

2 **Think Aloud** My first prediction was correct. Pandora is trying to open the box. But now I think she might be afraid. I **predict** that she will finally leave the box alone.

3 **Think Aloud** My second prediction was incorrect. Pandora kept working at the lock until it broke. Now that she knows what's inside the box I **predict** that Pandora will feel terrible about what she did and will blow the dandelion seeds as the scroll instructed her to do.

Vocabulary

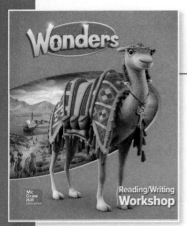

Reading/Writing Workshop

OBJECTIVES

CCSS Demonstrate understanding of word relationships and nuances in word meanings. Identify real-life connections between words and their use (e.g., describe people who are *friendly* or *helpful*). **L.3.5b**

CCSS Acquire and use accurately grade-appropriate conversational, general academic, and domain-specific words and phrases, including those that signal spatial and temporal relationships (e.g., *After dinner that night we went looking for them*). **L.3.6**

Learn meanings of new vocabulary words.

ACADEMIC LANGUAGE

• *treasure, wealth*

• Cognate: *tesoro*

 MINILESSON 10 Mins

Words in Context

Model the Routine

Introduce each vocabulary word using the **Vocabulary Routine** found on the **Visual Vocabulary Cards**.

Visual Vocabulary Cards

Vocabu...

Define:

Example:

Ask:

Vocabulary Routine

Define: **Wealth** is a great amount of money or valuable things.

Example: We are counting our money and will share our wealth by donating it.

Ask: What is another word for *wealth*?

Definitions

• **alarmed**   **Alarmed** means afraid or frightened.
   Cognate: *alarmado*

• **anguish**   **Anguish** is a great suffering of the mind, or agony.

• **necessary**   Something that is **necessary** needs to be done or is required.
   Cognate: *necesario*

• **obsessed**   When you are **obsessed**, you think about one thing all the time and nothing else.

• **possess**   When you **possess** something, you have or own it.

• **reward**   A **reward** is something given or received in return for something done.

• **treasure**   A **treasure** can be money, jewels, or other things that are valuable.
   Cognate: *tesoro*

Talk About It

 COLLABORATE

Have students work with a partner to look at each picture and discuss the definition of each word. Then ask students to choose three words and write questions for their partner to answer.

Go Digital

Wealth

Use Visual Glossary

Words to Know

Vocabulary

Use the picture and the sentence to talk with a partner about each word.

alarmed
Jess was **alarmed** as he watched the barber cut his hair.

Show how you would look if you were alarmed by something.

anguish
Andy felt **anguish** when he realized his bike was missing.

What is another word that means the same as anguish?

necessary
Food is **necessary** for all living things.

What other things are necessary for living things?

obsessed
Paul is **obsessed** with space and wears his astronaut suit all the time.

Name something you are obsessed with.

possess
Dan and Meg **possess** a huge bunch of colorful balloons.

Tell about something you possess.

reward
Dad took us on vacation as a **reward** for getting good grades in school.

What reward would you like to get?

treasure
Lila found a real **treasure** at the book sale.

Tell about a treasure you have.

wealth
We are counting our money and will share our **wealth** by donating it.

What is another word for *wealth*?

Your Turn

COLLABORATE

Pick three words. Write three questions for your partner to answer.

Go Digital! Use the online visual glossary

404

405

READING/WRITING WORKSHOP, pp. 404–405

ELL ENGLISH LANGUAGE LEARNERS SCAFFOLD

Beginning

Use Visuals Say: *Let's look at the picture for* wealth. *The children have lots of money. They will share the wealth.* Hold up a handful of coins. *Do people with wealth have money?* (yes) Provide the sentence frame: *People with ____ have a lot of money.* Have students repeat the sentence with you. Correct students' pronunciation and meaning as necessary.

Intermediate

Describe Point to the picture for *wealth* and read the sentence. Ask: *What are two kinds of wealth?* Have students complete the frame: *Two kinds of wealth are ____ and ____.* Elicit details to develop students' responses.

Advanced/High

Discuss Ask students to talk about the picture with a partner and write a definition. Then challenge pairs to use each vocabulary word in a sentence. Correct the meaning of students' responses as needed.

ON-LEVEL PRACTICE BOOK p. 251

| possess | necessary | treasure | alarmed |
| obsessed | reward | anguish | wealth |

Use the context clues in each sentence to help you decide which vocabulary word fits best in the blank. Possible responses provided.

"Guess what I just read?" said Mary. "It was an exciting story about two friends looking for a secret ___treasure___, something of great value hidden in a jungle. Finding it was all they could think about. They were ___obsessed___!"

"Well, do they find it?" asked Charlene.

"I won't tell you the end. It's ___necessary___ for you to read the book to find out. I will tell you, though, that the two friends go on a great adventure. They want to ___possess___ the valuable item to have it for their own. So they follow a map."

"That sounds exciting!" said Charlene.

"It is! But little do they know that someone else has seen their map, someone who wants all the ___wealth___ and money that the map promises."

"Oh, no!" said Charlene. She sounded ___alarmed___, worried about what might happen in the story.

"The two friends soon find out that someone else is following their map. They think someone else might find the ___reward___ at the end of the map before they do. But they want the prize for themselves!"

"Oh, my goodness," said Charlene. "After following the map and going on such an adventure, it must fill them with ___anguish___ to think that someone might find the prize before them. They must be so worried. What happens next?"

Mary handed the book to Charlene. "Like I said, you have to read it!" Charlene raced home, eager to read about the adventure Mary described.

| APPROACHING p. 251 | BEYOND p. 251 | ELL p. 251 |

Shared Read | Genre • Myth/Drama

ATHENA AND ARACHNE

Essential Question

How do you decide what's important?

Read a myth that shows why valuing a talent can cause problems.

Jenny Reynish

CHARACTERS

NARRATOR

ARACHNE: (uh-RAK-nee) a weaver

DIANA: Arachne's friend

ATHENA: a Greek goddess

MESSENGER

⟝⟝⟝ SCENE ONE ⟝⟝⟝

Athens, Greece, a long time ago, Arachne's home.

NARRATOR: Long ago, Arachne and her friend Diana sat weaving.

DIANA: Oh, Arachne! That cloth is so beautiful.

Arachne admires her cloth.

ARACHNE: I know. Many people want to **possess** my cloth, but few can afford it. Only those with great **wealth** can buy it.

DIANA: Yes, it's true that people value your cloth. It is one of their most valued possessions. Your weavings are a real **treasure**. Some say that you learned your weaving skill, or talent, from the goddess Athena.

ARACHNE: It was not **necessary** for me to learn from a goddess. I was born with my talent. I am a much better weaver than Athena, and I'm sure I could beat her in a weaving competition!

Diana is worried, stops weaving and looks at Arachne.

DIANA: Ssshhh! I hope Athena isn't listening, or you're in big trouble!

ARACHNE: Nonsense! There's no reason to be **alarmed** or worried. Athena is much too busy to come down from Mount Olympus to compete with me.

406 / 407

READING/WRITING WORKSHOP, pp. 406–407

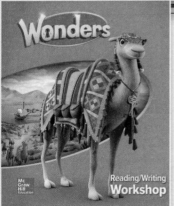

Shared Read

CLOSE READING

Close Reading Routine

Read DOK 1–2

- Identify key ideas and details about Treasures.
- Take notes and summarize.
- Use **A C T** prompts as needed.

Reread DOK 2–3

- Analyze the text, craft, and structure.
- Use the Reread minilessons.

ELL

See pages T56–T57 for Interactive Question-Response routine for the Shared Read.

Integrate DOK 4

- Integrate knowledge and ideas.
- Make text-to-text connections.
- Use the Integrate lesson.

Read

Connect to Concept: Treasures Tell students that they will read about how valuing your own talent too much may cause trouble.

Note Taking Read page 407 together. As you read, model how to take notes. *I will think about the Essential Question as I read and note key ideas and details.* Encourage students to note words they don't understand and questions they have.

Scene One: Reread Scene One. Ask *Why is Diana worried?* Model how to cite text evidence. Diana hears Arachne boast that she is a better weaver than the goddess Athena. She is worried Athena will be angry.

SCENE TWO

Mount Olympus, home of Athena. A messenger arrives.

MESSENGER: Goddess Athena! I have news from Athens. The weaver Arachne says she can beat you in a weaving competition. She's **obsessed** with her skill and thinks she is the best weaver in Greece!

ATHENA: I'll show her who weaves the finest cloth! Her obsession with weaving must end. Please get me my cloak. *Messenger hands Athena her cloak.*

ATHENA: Arachne cannot talk about me that way! If she refuses to apologize, I will make her pay for her boastful words. Her **anguish** will be great!

SCENE THREE

Arachne's home. There is a knock at the door.

ARACHNE: Who's there?

ATHENA: Just an old woman with a question.

Athena is hiding under her cloak. She enters the room.

ATHENA: Is it true that you challenged the goddess Athena to a weaving competition?

ARACHNE: Yes, that's right. *Athena drops her cloak.*

ATHENA: Well, I am Athena, and I am here to compete with you!

DIANA: Arachne, please don't! It is unwise to compete with a goddess!

Arachne and Athena sit down at the empty looms and begin to weave furiously.

408

ARACHNE: I am ready to win and get my **reward**!

ATHENA: There's no prize if you lose!

NARRATOR: Arachne and Athena both wove beautiful cloths. However, Arachne's cloth was filled with pictures of the gods being unkind.

ATHENA: Arachne, your weaving is beautiful, but I am insulted and upset by the pictures you chose to weave. You are boastful, and your cloth is mean and unkind. For that, I will punish you.

Athena points dramatically at Arachne. Arachne falls behind her loom and crawls out as a spider.

ATHENA: Arachne, you will spend the rest of your life weaving and living in your own web.

NARRATOR: Arachne was mean and boastful, so Athena turned her into a spider. That's why spiders are now called arachnids. Arachne learned that bragging and too much pride can lead to trouble.

THE END

Make Connections

What does Arachne value? How does it cause her trouble? ESSENTIAL QUESTION

What do you value? Why do you value it? TEXT TO SELF

409

Jenny Reynish

READING/WRITING WORKSHOP, *pp. 408–409*

Scene Two: Ask: *What happens in this scene?* **Model how to summarize.** The messenger tells Athena about Arachne's boasts and says that Arachne thinks she is the best weaver in Greece. Athena says that she will make Arachne pay if her boasting does not stop.

Make Connections

COLLABORATE

Essential Question Encourage students to work with a partner to discuss Arachne's boasting and the trouble it causes. Ask them to cite text evidence. Use these sentence frames to focus discussion:

> Arachne boasts . . .
> Athena threatens . . .

A C T **A**ccess **C**omplex **T**ext

▶ **Prior Knowledge**

Point out that "Athena and Arachne" is based on a Greek myth. Discuss the following:

- Athena is the Greek goddess of wisdom and the arts. She is known for her weaving.

- In Greek mythology, gods and goddesses were worshipped by humans. However, Greek gods and goddesses interacted with humans and displayed human qualities, such as anger, envy, and jealousy.

→ Comprehension Strategy

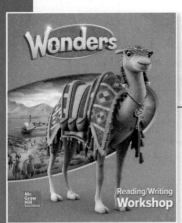

Reading/Writing Workshop

Make, Confirm, and Revise Predictions

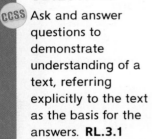 MINILESSON 10 Mins

1 Explain

Explain that when students read a drama, they should pay attention to the clues given in the text to make predictions. Tell students that making predictions will help them better understand what is happening in the story.

- Good readers know how to find clues in the story's text and its illustrations to make a prediction.

- Students may stop to confirm or revise their predictions if necessary.

- Making predictions will help students understand why a character says certain things and acts in certain ways.

Point out that making predictions will help students follow and remember the events in a story.

2 Model Close Reading: Text Evidence

Model how to use clues from page 407 of "Athena and Arachne" to make a prediction about Arachne. Point out the clues that help support the prediction.

3 Guided Practice of Close Reading

Have students work in pairs to discuss what they thought would happen when Athena went to see Arachne. Direct them to tell what clues in the text led to their predictions. Have partners reread page 408 to confirm or revise their predictions.

Go Digital

View "Athena and Arachne"

Make Predictions

Use details in the story to predict what happens next. Was your prediction right? Read on to check it. Change your prediction if it is not right.

 Find Text Evidence

You may have made a prediction about Arachne at the beginning of "Athena and Arachne." What clues on page 407 helped you guess what might happen?

> page 407
>
> **DIANA:** Oh, Arachne! That cloth is so beautiful.
> *Arachne admires her cloth.*
> **ARACHNE:** I know. Many people want to **possess** my cloth, but few can afford it. Only those with great **wealth** can buy it.
> **DIANA:** Yes, it's true that people value your cloth. It is one of their most valued possessions. Your weavings are a real **treasure**. Some say that you learned your weaving skill, or talent, from the goddess Athena.
> **ARACHNE:** It was not **necessary** for me to learn from a goddess. I was born with my talent. I am a much better weaver than Athena, and I'm sure I could beat her in a weaving competition!

I predicted that Arachne and Athena would compete. I read that Arachne says she is a better weaver than Athena and could beat her in a contest. I will read on to check my prediction.

Your Turn

What did you predict would happen when Athena went to see Arachne? Reread page 408 to check your prediction. Remember to make, confirm, and revise predictions as you read.

Jenny Reynish

410

READING/WRITING WORKSHOP, *p. 410*

ELL ENGLISH LANGUAGE LEARNERS SCAFFOLD

Beginning

Monitor Help students reread the dialogue on page 407. Say: *Arachne is sure she can beat Athena. Diana is worried.* Gasp and demonstrate being worried. *Do you think Athena is listening?* (yes) Ask students to predict how they think Athena feels about Arachne's boasts. Allow them to respond nonverbally with gestures, and help them form a verbal response.

Intermediate

Describe Have students reread page 407. Ask: *What is Arachne's talent?* (weaving) *Who else is good at weaving?* (Athena) Point out why this text is confusing. *This text is here for a reason. It is a clue about what will happen. What do you think will happen next?* Elicit details to develop students' predictions.

Advanced/High

Discuss Have students reread page 407. Elicit from students why the text is confusing. Say: *Arachne says she is sure she could beat Athena in a competition. What do you think will happen next?* Have students work with partners to discuss. Elicit details to develop their responses.

Monitor and *Differentiate*

 Quick Check

Do students predict what would happen when Athena went to see Arachne? Do they confirm or revise their predictions as necessary?

⬇

Small Group Instruction

If No → | Approaching Level | Reteach p. T40
| ELL | Develop p. T56
If Yes → | On Level | Review p. T48
| Beyond Level | Extend p. T52

ON-LEVEL PRACTICE BOOK pp. 253–254

Read the passage. Use the make predictions strategy to check your understanding as you read.

> **Prometheus Brings Fire to Humans**
>
> Cast:
> 1   Narrator | Prometheus | Zeus | Human 1 | Human 2
> 8   Scene 1
> 10   *Setting: Mount Olympus, the home of the ancient Greek gods.*
> 20   *Zeus sits on a throne in the middle of the stage. There is a*
> 34   *fireplace with a roaring fire in it to his left. Prometheus enters.*
> 46   **Zeus:** Prometheus! Welcome to my throne room! I trust
> 55   everything is good.
> 58   **Prometheus:** I'm afraid not, Lord Zeus. I have been to Earth
> 69   and lived among the people. They are miserable. They live in
> 80   caves and eat raw meat. When winter comes, they die of cold and
> 93   starvation. I would like to ask you to share fire with them.
> 105   I believe it would help them keep warm and cook their meat.
> 117   **Zeus:** Absolutely not! If humans have fire, they might become
> 127   strong and wise like the gods. They could force us from our
> 139   kingdom. I am happy to keep them cold and uninformed. That
> 150   way we gods can rule the world unthreatened and happy.
> 160   **Prometheus:** *(under his breath)* But I am not a god. I am a
> 173   Titan. If you will not help them, I will! *(he exits)*

| APPROACHING pp. 253–254 | BEYOND pp. 253–254 | ELL pp. 253–254 |

→ Comprehension Skill

MINILESSON 10 Mins

Theme

Go Digital

1 Explain

Explain to students that authors often have a message for the reader. This is the theme of a story. It tells what the author thinks is important to learn from the story.

- To identify the theme, students should look for details in the actions and words of the characters.

- Students can recount the story to determine the central message, lesson, or moral and explain how it is conveyed through details in the text.

- Students can then make inferences about the theme based on the details found in the text.

2 Model Close Reading: Text Evidence

Identify the key details in the actions of the characters in "Athena and Arachne." Then model using the graphic organizer to determine the theme supported by the details.

 Analytical Writing **Write About Reading: Summary** Model for students how to use the notes from the graphic organizer to write a summary of the theme of "Athena and Arachne."

3 Guided Practice of Close Reading

 COLLABORATE Have students work in pairs to complete the graphic organizer for "Athena and Arachne," going back into the text to find details that support the theme.

Analytical Writing **Write About Reading: Summary** Have pairs work together to write a summary about the theme of "Athena and Arachne" using the information in the graphic organizer. Encourage students to include additional details that support the theme.

Present the Lesson

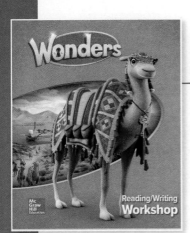

Reading/Writing Workshop

OBJECTIVES

CCSS Recount stories, including fables, folktales, and myths from diverse cultures; determine the central message, lesson, or moral and explain how it is conveyed through key details in the text. **RL.3.2**

Identify the theme in a myth or drama.

ACADEMIC LANGUAGE

theme, details

SKILLS TRACE

THEME

Introduce Unit 2 Week 1

Review Unit 2 Weeks 2, 6; Unit 3 Week 6; Unit 4 Weeks 5, 6; Unit 6 Weeks 1, 2, 6

Assess Units 2, 4, 6

Comprehension Skill

Theme

The theme of a story is the author's message. Think about what the characters do and say. This will help you figure out the theme.

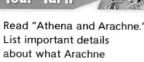 **Find Text Evidence**

In "Athena and Arachne," Arachne learns that bragging and too much pride can lead to trouble. This is the story's theme. I can reread to find details that help me figure out the theme.

> **Detail**
> Arachne said that many people want to possess her cloth, but few can afford it. Only those with great wealth can buy it.
>
> ↓
>
> **Detail**
>
> ↓
>
> **Detail**
>
> ↓
>
> **Detail**
>
> ↓
>
> **Theme**
> Bragging and too much pride can lead to trouble.

Your Turn COLLABORATE

Read "Athena and Arachne." List important details about what Arachne says and does in your graphic organizer. Be sure the details tell about the theme.

Go Digital!
Use the interactive graphic organizer

411

READING/WRITING WORKSHOP, *p. 411*

 **Monitor and *Differentiate***

 Quick Check

As students complete the graphic organizer for "Athena and Arachne," are they able to identify details that support the theme?

↓

Small Group Instruction

If No → | Approaching Level | Reteach p. T47
| ELL | Develop p. T57

If Yes → | On Level | Review p. T51
| Beyond Level | Extend p. T55

ELL ENGLISH LANGUAGE LEARNERS SCAFFOLD

Beginning

Recognize Reread the dialogue on page 407. Point out important details, and explain how they tell about the theme of the story. Have students complete the sentence frame: ____ *is an important detail that tells about the theme.* Correct students' responses for meaning and pronunciation as needed.

Intermediate

Describe Reread Arachne's first lines on page 407. Ask: *What is an important detail that tells about the theme? How do you know? Explain to a partner.* Then have partners describe the important detail that tells about the theme. ____ *is an important detail because ____.* Elicit details to develop students' responses.

Advanced/High

Discuss Have students review the details in "Athena and Arachne" that help them discover the theme of the story. Ask: *Based on these details, what might be the theme of "Athena and Arachne"?* Have partners discuss how these clues support the theme. Encourage them to use vocabulary words.

ON-LEVEL PRACTICE BOOK pp. 253–255

A. Reread the passage and answer the questions.
Possible responses provided.

1. **How does Prometheus describe humans to Zeus?**
   He says they are miserable. They live in caves and eat raw meat. They die of cold and starvation.

2. **What does Prometheus want to do to help humans?**
   He wants to share fire with them.

3. **List some ways Prometheus thinks fire will help improve the lives of humans.**
   They can use fire to cook their meat; fire will keep humans warm; fire will allow humans to explore the world.

4. **What is the theme of this story?**
   It is good to help those who are less fortunate.

B. Work with a partner. Read the passage aloud. Pay attention to expression. Stop after one minute. Fill out the chart.

	Words Read	–	Number of Errors	=	Words Correct Score
First Read		–		=	
Second Read		–		=	

APPROACHING pp. 253–255	BEYOND pp. 253–255	ELL pp. 253–255

→ **Genre: Literature**

Reading/Writing Workshop

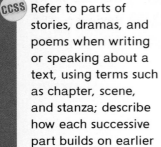

OBJECTIVES

CCSS Refer to parts of stories, dramas, and poems when writing or speaking about a text, using terms such as chapter, scene, and stanza; describe how each successive part builds on earlier sections. **RL.3.5**

Recognize the characteristics and features of myths and drama.

ACADEMIC LANGUAGE
- *myth, drama, scene, stage directions, dialogue*
- Cognates: *mito, drama, escena, diálogo*

 10 Mins **Myth/Drama**

Go Digital

Present the Lesson

1 Explain

Explain to students that a **myth** tells how something came to be. Share with students the following characteristics of a **drama**.

- A drama tells a story through dialogue and can be performed.
- A drama is divided into parts called acts or scenes.
- A drama provides stage directions that tell the actors what to do.

2 Model Close Reading: Text Evidence

Model identifying and using literary elements and characteristics of myths and dramas on page 408 of "Athena and Arachne" that show that it is both a myth and a drama.

Scene A scene is a part of the play. Scenes tell the story in time order. Remind students that they can identify which scene they are reading by looking for the scene number.

Stage Directions Stage directions tell what the characters do and how they move. Remind students that they can identify stage directions by looking at the typeface, which is different than the typeface of the dialogue.

Dialogue Point out the dialogue in "Athena and Arachne." Remind students that they can identify who is speaking by the characters' names in capital letters before each section. When they read a drama, they learn about the action mostly from what the characters say.

3 Guided Practice of Close Reading

Have students work with partners to find more examples of dialogue and stage directions in "Athena and Arachne." Partners should discuss how these features work together to tell the story. Then have them talk about why "Athena and Arachne" is both a myth and a drama, using details from the text.

Myth/Drama

"Athena and Arachne" is a myth and a drama, or play. A **myth** tells how something came to be. A **drama**:

- Tells a story through dialogue and is performed
- Is separated into scenes and has stage directions

Find Text Evidence

I see that "Athena and Arachne" is a myth and a play. It is divided into three scenes. It uses dialogue and stage directions to tell how spiders came to weave webs.

page 408

— SCENE TWO —

Mount Olympus, home of Athena. A messenger arrives.
MESSENGER: Goddess Athena! I have news from Athens. The weaver Arachne says she can beat you in a weaving competition. She's **obsessed** with her skill and thinks she is the best weaver in Greece!
ATHENA: I'll show her who weaves the finest cloth! Her obsession with weaving must end. Please get me my cloak. *Messenger hands Athena her cloak.*
ATHENA: Arachne cannot talk to me that way! If she refuses to apologize, I will make her pay for her boastful words. Her **anguish** will be great!

— SCENE THREE —

Arachne's home. There is a knock at the door.
ARACHNE: Who's there?
ATHENA: Just an old woman with a question. *Athena is hiding under her cloak. She enters the room.*
ATHENA: Is it true that you challenged the goddess Athena to a weaving competition?
ARACHNE: Yes, that's right. *Athena drops her cloak.*
ATHENA: Well, I am Athena, and I am here to compete with you!

Scene A scene is a part of a play. Scenes tell the story in time order.

Stage Directions Stage directions tell what the characters do and how they move.

Dialogue Dialogue is the words the characters speak.

Your Turn COLLABORATE

Find more examples of scenes, dialogue, and stage directions in "Athena and Arachne." Tell your partner how they help tell the story.

412

Jenny Reynish

READING/WRITING WORKSHOP, *p. 412*

A C T Access Complex Text

▶ Genre

Students may need help understanding that the Narrator is not a character who is present within the action on the stage.

- *The Narrator is listed in the character list. Does the Narrator interact with Arachne, Diana, or Athena?* (no)

- *Who does the Narrator talk to throughout the play?* (the audience, the reader)

- *What kind of things does the Narrator say?* (The Narrator provides information about what is happening and why.)

Monitor and *Differentiate*

✔ Quick Check

Are students able to identify features of myths and drama in "Athena and Arachne"?

⬇

Small Group Instruction

If No → | Approaching Level | Reteach p. T40
| ELL | Develop p. T56

If Yes → | On Level | Review p. T48
| Beyond Level | Extend p. T52

→ Vocabulary Strategy

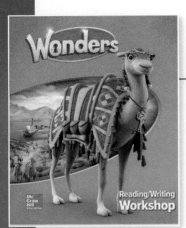

MINILESSON
10 Mins

Root Words

1 Explain

Remind students that they can often figure out the meaning of an unknown word by examining its root word.

- A root word is the simplest form of a word.

- No prefixes, suffixes, or inflectional endings have been added to the root word.

- Knowing the meaning of a root word can help clarify the meaning of an unfamiliar word.

2 Model Close Reading: Text Evidence

Model using the root word *compete* to figure out the meaning of *competition* on page 407. Write the word *competition* then cross out the suffix to show how you determined the root word was *compete*.

3 Guided Practice of Close Reading

COLLABORATE

Have students work in pairs to figure out the meanings of *possessions* and *obsession* in "Athena and Arachne." Have partners identify the root words and use them to figure out the meanings of the words.

Use Reference Sources

Dictionaries Have students use a print or digital dictionary to clarify the meaning of the root words *possess* and *obsess*. Ask if knowing the dictionary definitions of the root words changes what they think about the meanings of *possessions* and *obsession*. Have them revise the definitions they created, if necessary, and then use the dictionary to confirm the definition of each.

OBJECTIVES

CCSS Determine or clarify the meaning of unknown and multiple-meaning words and phrases based on grade 3 reading and content, choosing flexibly from a range of strategies. Use a known root word as a clue to the meaning of an unknown word with the same root (e.g., *company, companion*). **L.3.4c**

ACADEMIC LANGUAGE
root words

SKILLS TRACE

ROOT WORDS

Introduce Unit 3 Week 4

Review Unit 3 Week 5; Unit 4 Weeks 1, 2; Unit 5 Weeks 1, 2; Unit 6 Weeks 1, 2

Assess Units 3, 4, 5, 6

Go Digital

Present the Lesson

Vocabulary Strategy

Root Words

A root word is the simplest form of a word. It helps you figure out the meaning of a related word.

 Find Text Evidence

In "Athena and Arachne," I see the word competition. I think the root word of competition is compete. I know compete means "to be in a contest." I think a competition is "a contest where people try to win."

> I am a much better weaver than Athena, and I'm sure I could beat her in a weaving competition!

Your Turn

Find the root word. Then use it to figure out the meaning of each word.
possessions, *page 407*
obsession, *page 408*

413

READING/WRITING WORKSHOP, *p. 413*

Monitor and *Differentiate*

 Quick Check

Do students use root words to figure out the meaning of the words *possessions* and *obsession*?

Small Group Instruction

If No →	Approaching Level	Reteach p. T45
	ELL	Develop p. T61
If Yes→	On Level	Review p. T50
	Beyond Level	Extend p. T54

ENGLISH LANGUAGE LEARNERS SCAFFOLD

 ELL

Beginning

Understand On the board, write the word *possessions*. Cross out the suffix. Define the root word, and explain that adding *-ion* changes it to mean "something owned." Repeat with the word *obsession*. Use the words in sentences, and help students replace them with words they know.

Intermediate

Define Write the words *possessions* and *obsession* on the board. Cross out the suffixes. Define the root words for students. Say: *Reread the sentence with the word* possessions. *What does it mean?* Repeat with *obsession*. Finally, have pairs write a sentence for each word.

Advanced/High

Write Have students work in pairs to define the root words *possess* and *obsess*. Have them find context clues to explain the meanings of *possessions* and *obsession* and then use them in sentences. Correct students' sentences for meaning as necessary.

ON-LEVEL PRACTICE BOOK p. 257

Read each sentence below. Write the root word of the word in bold on the line. Then write the definition of the word in bold.
Possible responses provided.

1. I have been to Earth and lived among the people. They are **miserable**.
   misery; unhappy

2. When winter comes, they die of cold and **starvation**.
   starve; suffer from hunger

3. I am happy to keep them cold and **uninformed**.
   inform; not having information

4. That way we gods can rule the world **unthreatened** and happy.
   threat; safe

5. I have brought you the secret to your **empowerment**!
   power; getting the power to do something

6. I only ask that you also help those less **fortunate** when you have the chance.
   fortune, having luck

| APPROACHING p. 257 | BEYOND p. 257 | ELL p. 257 |

King Midas and the Golden Touch

Literature Anthology
Lexile and TextEvaluator scores are not provided for non-prose selections, such as poetry and drama.

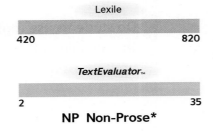

Text Complexity Range

Lexile

420   820

TextEvaluator™

2   35

NP Non-Prose*

What makes this text complex?
▶ **Genre**
▶ **Sentence Structure**
▶ **Connection of Ideas**
▶ **Organization**

Close Reading Routine

Read   DOK 1–2

• Identify key ideas and details about Treasures.
• Take notes and summarize.
• Use A C T prompts as needed.

Reread   DOK 2–3

• Analyze the craft, text, and structure.
• Use *Close Reading Companion,* pp. 166-167.

Integrate   DOK 4

• Integrate knowledge and ideas.
• Make text-to-text connections.
• Use the Integrate lesson.

Genre • Drama/Myth

? Essential Question
How do you decide what is important?
Read about how King Midas discovers what he values most.

Go Digital!

462

A C T   Access Complex Text

▶ Genre

Help students connect the title and illustration with the selection they are about to read.

• *Who do you think the main character of this selection is?* (King Midas)

• *Based on the illustration, what can you tell about King Midas?* (He is rich. He likes to count his money.)

KING MIDAS AND THE GOLDEN TOUCH

by Margaret H. Lippert

illustrated by Gail Armstrong

CHARACTERS

Storyteller

King Midas

Princess Marigold, King Midas's daughter

Nikolas, King Midas's servant

Rosie, a gardener's daughter

Rex, King Midas's horse

Mysterious Traveler

463

LITERATURE ANTHOLOGY, *pp. 462–463*

Read

Tell students that they will be reading a myth about a king who loved gold. Ask students to predict how the selection will help them answer the Essential Question.

Note Taking: Use the Graphic Organizer

Remind students to take notes as they read. Have them fill in the graphic organizer on the **Your Turn Practice Book** page 252. Ask them to record details related to the theme of the story. They can also note words they don't understand and questions they have.

Reread

Genre: Drama

How can you tell that the selection is a drama? Turn to a partner and discuss. (There is a cast of characters, which is usually part of a drama. I can read this list to see who the main characters will be.)

Read

1 Skill: Theme

Things that the characters do and say often provide details about the theme. What details do the characters of Midas and Marigold provide about King Midas's love of gold? Give specific evidence from the text. (King Midas says, "So much gold. So much wealth. I love it!" Marigold says, "You spend more time with your gold than with me.") Add these details about King Midas's love of gold to the first detail section of your graphic organizer.

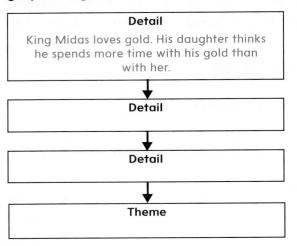

Detail
King Midas loves gold. His daughter thinks he spends more time with his gold than with her.

↓

Detail

↓

Detail

↓

Theme

SCENE ONE

In the palace. Early morning.

Storyteller: The story of King Midas takes place long ago and far away, in the country of Greece. King Midas **possessed** more gold than anyone in the world. One morning, he is counting his gold in his treasure chamber.

King Midas *(tying the last bag of gold)*: So much gold. So much wealth. I love it!

Marigold: *(calling from off stage)* Papa! Where are you?

King Midas: *(calling)* Here, Marigold.

(Marigold enters.)

464

A C T Access Complex Text

▶ Sentence Structure

Point to the text in parentheses on pages 464 and 465. Explain that this text is the stage directions. It tells the actors what they should be doing. Point out that these words should not be read aloud, but students should read them silently to help them picture what the characters are doing.

- *On page 464, when Marigold calls "Papa! Where are you?" is she on stage or off stage?* (She is off stage.)

- *On page 465, what is King Midas doing when he says, "Of course! I have a roomful of gold, but only one Marigold"?* (He is laughing because he thinks it is silly that Marigold believes he loves gold more than her.)

Marigold: Counting your gold again? You spend more time with your gold than with me. **1**

King Midas: I'm locking it up because I'm leaving on a journey.

Marigold: I'll miss you, Papa.

King Midas: I'll miss you too, Marigold.

Marigold: More than your gold? **2**

King Midas: *(laughing)* Of course! I have a roomful of gold, but only one Marigold! *(He looks out the window)* I see your friend Rosie is playing in the garden. Run along now. I'll say goodbye before I leave.

(Marigold exits.)

King Midas: *(calling)* Nikolas!

(Nikolas enters.)

Nikolas: Yes, your Majesty?

King Midas: Saddle my horse.

Nikolas: As you wish.

(Nikolas exits. King Midas puts the bags of gold into the trunk and locks it. He exits.)

465

LITERATURE ANTHOLOGY, *pp. 464–465*

Read

2 Skill: Make Inferences

What inference can you make about Marigold's feelings about her father? Paraphrase evidence from the text to support your inference. (She loves him but she wants him to spend more time with her. She says he spends more time with his gold than with her. She also questions whether he will miss her or his gold more.)

Reread   *Close Reading Companion*

Author's Craft: Character Development

How does the author help you visualize how much King Midas loves gold? (The play begins with a description of King Midas counting his gold in his treasure chamber. In King Midas's first lines of dialogue, he exclaims about how much he loves gold.)

How does the author show Midas's feelings for Marigold? (Midas tells Marigold that he loves her and says that he has lots of gold but only one Marigold.)

▶ Genre

Tell students that plays often have a storyteller or narrator who is not a character in the play, but gives information about the narrative elements.

- *Where does the story take place?* (in the country of Greece) *What information does the storyteller give about King Midas?* (King Midas possessed more gold than anyone in the world.)

ELL Demonstrate the stage directions, such as *off stage, enters,* and *exits.* Then check understanding of the characters by asking:

- *What does King Midas like?* (gold)

- Help students complete this frame: *Marigold is King Midas's _____* (daughter).

LITERATURE ANTHOLOGY   **T25D**

Read

3 Skill: Theme

Why does Marigold give King Midas a stone in the shape of a heart? (Marigold gives King Midas a stone in the shape of a heart so he will be reminded that she loves him.) **What might Marigold's actions tell you about the theme?** (Marigold's actions demonstrate that love and showing people that you love them is valuable. The theme may be related to love.) Add the detail to your organizer.

Detail
King Midas loves gold. His daughter thinks he spends more time with his gold than with her.

↓

Detail
Marigold gives King Midas a stone in the shape of a heart so that he will be reminded that she loves him.

↓

Detail

↓

Theme

Build Vocabulary page 466

rhythm: repeated pattern of sound or movement

SCENE TWO

Storyteller: A few minutes later, in the palace rose garden, Rosie is jumping rope.

Rosie: *(chanting in rhythm to her jumping)*
Roses are red, Violets are blue,
Sugar is sweet, And I AM TOO!
Roses are red, Violets are blue,
Sugar is sweet, And —
(Marigold runs in, twirling her jump rope.)

Marigold and **Rosie:** I AM TOO!

(They stop jumping and Marigold stoops down.)

Rosie: What are you doing?

Marigold: Hunting for a stone to give Papa.

Rosie: *(picking up a stone)* How about this one?

Marigold: I want to find one that looks like a heart.

466

A C T Access Complex Text

▶ Genre

Point to the words "Scene Two" at the top of page 466. Explain that dramas can be divided into scenes. A new scene usually begins when the setting changes. Tell students to refer to the different scenes to discuss the settings.

- *What is the setting at the beginning of the play?* (Scene One takes place in the King's palace.)

- *What is the setting for Scene Two?* (Scene Two takes place in the palace rose garden.)

Tell students that when a new scene begins, they should look for how the time and place of the play has changed and think about how that change influences the characters' actions.

Author's Craft: Word Choice

When authors write stage directions, they must choose precise verbs to tell the actors exactly what to do. Reread the stage directions for Marigold on page 466. What precise verb can you find? (*twirling*) Why does the author's stage direction say she runs in *twirling her jump rope* rather than saying she runs in *with her jump rope*? (*Twirling* is a more precise verb that helps the reader picture precisely what Marigold is doing and tells the actor playing Marigold exactly what she should be doing.)

(*Marigold picks up several stones and tosses them down again, then picks up a heart shaped stone and shows it to Rosie.*)

Marigold: I found one!

(*King Midas enters. Marigold runs to him and gives him the stone.*)

Marigold: Here, Papa. A heart, to remind you that I love you.

(*King Midas puts the stone in his pocket.*)

King Midas: Thank you, my darling.

467

LITERATURE ANTHOLOGY, *pp. 466–467*

ELL Point to *Scene Two* at the top of page 466. Discuss the cognate *escena.* Have students point to the new setting for this part of the play—the rose garden. Ask:

- *What shape is the stone that Marigold finds in the rose garden?* (a heart)

- *To whom does she give the stone?* (King Midas)

Read

4 Ask and Answer Questions

COLLABORATE

Generate a question of your own about the text and share it with a partner. To find the answer, try rereading and paraphrasing the text. For example, you might ask, "What happens to the traveler?" Then you can reread and paraphrase the traveler's lines. (The traveler fell off his horse and hurt his leg. Then his horse ran away.)

5 Strategy: Make, Confirm, and Revise Predictions

Teacher Think Aloud As I read, I **make predictions** about what I am reading and then I look for story details that help me **confirm** or **revise** them. On page 469, I read that King Midas helps a hurt traveler. I know that this is a myth, as well as a play, and that in myths, characters are often rewarded for their deeds. I predict that King Midas will receive some type of reward for helping the hurt traveler.

(Nikolas enters.)

Nikolas: Rex is saddled, Your Majesty.

King Midas: *(to Marigold)* I must go now.

Marigold: Is it really **necessary**?

King Midas: Yes. *(He picks a rose and gives it to Marigold.)* But here is a gift for you. I will return in seven days, before it wilts.

Marigold: *(smelling the rose)* Mmmmm. I love the smell, almost as much as I love you.

King Midas: Farewell, my daughter.

Marigold: Farewell, Papa.

(King Midas and Nikolas exit.)

Marigold: *(to Rosie)* I'll put this rose in a vase by my bed. Come with me.

(Marigold and Rosie exit.)

468

A C T Access Complex Text

▶ Organization

Explain that stories told in sequence sometimes skip over events and move forward in time. Read aloud the storyteller's lines in Scene Three on page 469.

- *How much time has passed between Marigold putting the rose in a vase and this scene?* (Scene Three takes place one week later.)

- *Why do you think the author includes the storyteller's lines?* (to show readers that time has passed between when King Midas left on his journey and when he is returning home)

SCENE THREE

Storyteller: One week later, early in the morning, King Midas rides Rex through a forest. He is returning home from his journey.
(Traveler moans offstage.)
King Midas: Hark! Someone is hurt.
(Traveler moans again.)
King Midas: *(stops and looks around.)* Am I dreaming?
(Traveler moans louder.)
Rex: *(Neighs)*
King Midas: *(patting Rex)* Calm down, Rex. Don't be **alarmed**.
(Traveler enters limping and falls to the ground.)
King Midas: What ails you, Traveler?
Traveler: My leg. I fell off my horse.
King Midas: You need help. My palace is just over the hill.
Traveler: My horse ran away. **4**
King Midas: Then ride with me.
(King Midas and Traveler ride Rex together.)
Rex: *(Neighs.)*
King Midas: Good boy, Rex. We're almost home. **5**
(They exit.)

469

LITERATURE ANTHOLOGY, *pp. 468–469*

Build Vocabulary page 469

moans: long, low sounds as from pain

ails: hurts

Reread   *Close Reading Companion*

Author's Craft: Character Development

Reread pages 468 and 469. How does the author show that King Midas is not just interested in gold? (King Midas gives Marigold a flower and tells her good-bye before he leaves. Midas also helps the injured traveler.) How does the author contrast Midas's love of gold and his caring for other people? (The author has established that Midas loves his gold, but he also shows Midas's love for Marigold and his kindness in the way he helps others.)

Author's Craft: Text Structure

The phrase "almost as much" is used to signal a comparison. What two things are being compared? (Marigold is comparing her love for the smell of the rose with her love for her father.)

▶ Connection of Ideas

Have students connect what they learn about King Midas in Scene Three to what they already know.

- *How does Midas feel about gold?* (He loves it.)

- *Think about how Midas behaves in Scene Three. How does this add to what you know about King Midas?* (It shows you that he is also kind and helps those in need.)

 Read the storyteller's lines aloud with students. Point out the phrase *one week later.* If necessary, use a calendar to visually show how much time has passed. Guide students to identify similar time and order words and phrases throughout the selection to help them keep track of the order of events.

Read

6 Strategy: Confirm and Revise Predictions

COLLABORATE

Teacher Think Aloud There is information on page 470 that we can use to confirm or revise the prediction we made about King Midas. Was our prediction confirmed?

Prompt students to apply the strategy in a Think Aloud by rereading the traveler's lines on page 470 and paraphrasing them to a partner.

Student Think Aloud I can confirm the prediction by rereading the traveler's lines. We predicted that King Midas would be rewarded for his kindness to the traveler and he is. The traveler offers to grant King Midas a wish.

STOP AND CHECK

Make Predictions What do you think will happen when King Midas gets his wish? (I predict he will be happy at first but then he will realize there are some things that he will not want to turn into gold.)

Build Vocabulary page 470
  dismount: to get off a horse

SCENE FOUR

Storyteller: Soon they arrive back at the rose garden.
(King Midas and Traveler dismount.)
King Midas: Here we are. I'll call my servant.
Traveler: Wait. As a **reward** for your kindness to a poor Traveler, I will grant you a wish.

6

King Midas: You grant wishes?
Traveler: Make a wish, and see if it comes true.
King Midas: Well, I love gold! So I wish that everything I touch turns to gold!
Traveler: Your wish is granted.
King Midas: Really? I'll try it on the stone Marigold gave me!
(He takes the heart stone out of his pocket. It turns to gold.)

STOP AND CHECK

Make Predictions What do you think will happen when King Midas gets his wish?

470

A C T Access Complex Text

▶ Genre

Remind students that even though stage directions are not read aloud, they should read them silently to better understand what is happening.

- *How does King Midas turn the heart stone into gold?* (He takes it out of his pocket.)

- *What happens to Marigold's face when she sees the gold rose?* (Her smile turns to shocked surprise.)

- *What does Marigold's face tell you about her feelings?* (She is upset and unhappy about what she sees.)

King Midas: Incredible! This stone has turned to gold! *(He picks a rose. It turns to gold.)* Fantastic! This is gold too! What a perfect gift for Marigold!

Marigold: *(offstage)* Papa will be home today, Rosie. We can watch for him over the garden wall.

(Marigold and Rosie enter. King Midas holds the rose out to Marigold.)

King Midas: Look, my daughter. A gold rose for you!

(Marigold's happy smile turns to shocked surprise.)

Marigold: Oh Papa, how terrible. *(She smells it.)* It doesn't smell sweet.

471

LITERATURE ANTHOLOGY, *pp. 470–471*

Read

⑦ Skill: Theme

How does Marigold feel about the gold rose? (She thinks it is terrible.) What might her point of view tell you about the theme? (Gold doesn't make everything more valuable. Some things are valuable just the way they are.)

Reread   *Close Reading Companion*

Author's Craft: Literary Device

How does the author show that something will happen to Marigold later in the story? (King Midas thinks she will like his gift of a golden rose. But Marigold is shocked and stops smiling. She says, "Oh Papa, how terrible." She is sad that the gold flower no longer smells sweet.)

▶ Organization

Point out that dramas, like other kinds of texts, can have causes and effects.

- *What causes King Midas to be able to turn things into gold?* (The traveler grants his wish to turn everything he touches into gold.)

- *What are two effects of King Midas's wish?* (He turns a stone and a rose into gold.)

ELL Point out cognates on page 471: *incredible/increíble, surprise/sorpresa, terrible/terrible*. Have students use these words to act out and then explain how King Midas and Marigold react when the king turns things into gold.

Read

8 Skill: Theme

What happens when King Midas takes Marigold's hand? (Marigold turns to gold.) Add the detail to your organizer.

Detail
King Midas loves gold. His daughter thinks he spends more time with his gold than with her.

↓

Detail
Marigold gives King Midas a stone in the shape of a heart so that he will be reminded that she loves him.

↓

Detail
Marigold turns to gold.

↓

Theme

472

A C T Access Complex Text

▶ Sentence Structure

Point out that authors sometimes use type styles, such as words in all capital letters, to create emphasis. Have students find and read aloud the words in all capital letters on page 473.

- *Why does the author emphasize the word wonderful?* (to show how excited King Midas is about turning everything into gold)

- *Why does the author emphasize the word everything?* (Putting *everything* in all capital letters shows that King Midas can't pick and choose what he turns to gold. Everything he touches, including Marigold, will turn to gold.)

King Midas: Terrible? No, it is WONDERFUL! I can turn everything to gold! (He reaches out to take her hand. She freezes in place as if turned to gold.) Oh no! My precious daughter has turned to gold!

Traveler: As you wished. You said, "I wish EVERYTHING I touch will turn to gold."

King Midas: But—

Traveler: No buts. You wished, and your wish came true. You were so obsessed with gold that all you wanted was more.

King Midas: (He gives an anguished cry.) But now all I want is Marigold, alive again. I wish I could undo my foolish wish.

Traveler: I can see by your anguish that now you realize true wealth is not gold, but life. So I will grant you one more wish. **9**

King Midas: I wish that everything I have turned to gold becomes real again.

Traveler: Your wish is granted. Fill that watering can with water from the pond. Pour it on all you wish to be real again. (King Midas fills the watering can and pours water over Marigold. She comes back to life.)

STOP AND CHECK

Confirm Predictions What happened when King Midas got his wish? Was your prediction correct?

473

LITERATURE ANTHOLOGY, *pp. 472–473*

Read

9 Skill: Make Inferences

What can you tell about the traveler, based on what he says to King Midas and what he does? (He is wise because he wants King Midas to learn a lesson. He is also sympathetic because he is willing to grant King Midas another wish.)

STOP AND CHECK

Confirm Predictions What happened when King Midas got his wish? Was your prediction correct?

Reread page 473 and look for details that confirm your prediction or help you revise it. Turn to a partner and paraphrase the text that you used to confirm or revise your prediction.

Student Think Aloud I can confirm my prediction by rereading King Midas's first part on page 473. At first he thinks it is wonderful to be able to turn everything into gold. Then he says "Oh no! My precious daughter has turned to gold." He is very upset and doesn't think turning things into gold is good anymore, which is what I predicted.

ELL Chorally read the traveler's line, "No buts." Explain that "No buts" is another way of saying "no exceptions." Point out that it is similar in meaning to the Spanish idiom "No hay pero que valga."

The traveler wants King Midas to understand that when he wished for everything to turn to gold, EVERYTHING, including his daughter, would turn to gold.

Read

10 Skill: Theme

What is the theme of this selection? Use the details you've recorded in your organizer to help you. (Life is more precious than gold, and each living thing has its own value.) Add the theme to your organizer.

Detail
King Midas loves gold. His daughter thinks he spends more time with his gold than with her.

↓

Detail
Marigold gives King Midas a stone in the shape of a heart so that he will be reminded that she loves him.

↓

Detail
Marigold turns to gold.

↓

Theme
Life is more precious than gold, and each living thing has its own value.

Build Vocabulary page 474

appreciated: understood the importance of something

King Midas: Oh how wonderful! You're alive again!
(King Midas takes her hands and joyfully swings her around.)
Marigold: What happened, Papa? Did I fall in the pond?
King Midas: (laughing) Oh no, my treasure. Come inside and dry off, and I will tell you the story.
Marigold: What story, Papa?
10 King Midas: The story of how I learned that my obsession with gold almost cost me what is truly precious. (He takes the heart stone out of his pocket and pours water over it.) I never noticed before how beautiful a real stone is. (He pours water over the gold rose and smells it.) I never appreciated how sweet a rose smells.

474

A C T Access Complex Text

▶ Genre

Explain that myths often involve a character with a weakness. The character may learn a lesson as a result of this weakness.

- *At the beginning of the story, what is King Midas's weakness?* (He is greedy. He values gold so much that he doesn't pay enough attention to the people and things around him.)

- *How does King Midas's weakness cause trouble?* (He wishes that everything he touches will turn to gold. As a result, his daughter turns to gold.)

- *What lesson does he learn?* (He learns that there are things more valuable than gold.)

(Nikolas enters.)

Nikolas: Breakfast is ready, Your Majesty.

King Midas: (to Traveler) Come, join us at breakfast.

Traveler: Thank you, but I must be on my way. My leg is better and I have other wishes to grant. Farewell.

(He exits.)

King Midas: (calling after him) Farewell, and thank you!

Marigold: "Thank you?" For what, Papa?

King Midas: For showing me what is more valuable than gold. At breakfast I will tell you the story of my foolish wish, and how you got wet without falling into the pond! **⑪**

(King Midas takes Marigold's hand, and Marigold takes Rosie's hand.)

Marigold: Rosie, come with me to hear Papa's story.

Storyteller: So ends the story of King Midas and the Golden Touch.

(All exit.)

> **STOP AND CHECK**
>
> **Summarize** What happened at the end of the story? Tell the important events in order.

475

LITERATURE ANTHOLOGY, *pp. 474–475*

---

⑪ Vocabulary Strategy: Roots

What is the root word of *valuable*? (value) What do you think *valuable* means? (something that has worth or importance)

Return to Purposes Review students' predictions and purposes for reading. Ask them to use text evidence to answer the Essential Question. (We can decide what is important by thinking about who and what we value and what makes our life meaningful and happy.)

STOP AND CHECK

Summarize What happened at the end of the story? Tell the important events in order. (King Midas poured water on his daughter so that she would become alive again. He learned that there are things more valuable than gold. He thanked the traveler for teaching him this lesson and planned to tell Marigold the story at breakfast.)

Read

About the Author and Illustrator

Margaret H. Lippert and Gail Armstrong

Have students read the biographies of the author and illustrator. Ask:

- Why do you think the author was excited to write this play?

- Why are Gail Armstrong's illustrations an important part of this play?

Author's Purpose

To Entertain

Remind students that authors who write to entertain can also have a message they want to share with readers. Students may say the author wanted to tell readers that the people we love are worth more than all the gold in the world.

Reread

Author's Craft

Explain that specific verbs convey action precisely and descriptively. Discuss what this adds to the writing. Reread to find examples of specific verbs in stage directions. (Answers may vary. Answer may include *chanting in rhythm to her jumping* on page 466 and *Traveler moans offstage* on page 469.) **Why are these verbs important to actors and readers?** (They let actors know what they should do on stage. They help readers visualize the action.)

ABOUT THE AUTHOR AND ILLUSTRATOR

Margaret H. Lippert is a teacher, a storyteller, and an award-winning author of children's books. She has traveled around the world sharing stories. Margaret has written many books in which she retells folktales and stories from different cultures. She was excited to write a play about King Midas because his story is one of her favorite myths. She had fun naming the characters in the play. She says, "I thought a king who loved gold might name his daughter Marigold."

Gail Armstrong has been a paper sculptor for more than twenty years. She uses the traditional craft of paper folding, or origami, to create people, animals, flowers, and castles, then turns these paper sculptures into illustrations for books on a computer. Gail says, "I find it fascinating how something as ordinary as a piece of paper can be transformed with a simple cut or fold."

AUTHOR'S PURPOSE
What message was the author trying to tell in this play?

476

LITERATURE ANTHOLOGY, *pp. 476–477*

Respond to the Text

Summarize

What are the most important events in this story? Information from your Theme chart may help you summarize.

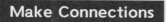

Detail
Detail
Detail
Theme

Write

How does the author help you understand the theme of this play? Use these sentence frames to help you organize text evidence.

> The author uses sensory language to describe how King Midas . . .
> She also compares . . .
> This helps me understand the theme because . . .

Make Connections

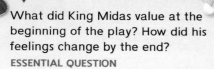

What did King Midas value at the beginning of the play? How did his feelings change by the end? **ESSENTIAL QUESTION**

Why is it important to value family friends? **TEXT TO WORLD**

477

Integrate

Make Connections

COLLABORATE

Essential Question <u>Answer:</u> At first, the king valued gold and Marigold. At the end of the story, the king valued Marigold and other living things much more than gold. <u>Evidence:</u> On page 474, the king tells Marigold that his obsession with gold almost made him lose what is most important.

Text to World Responses will vary. After students list and share some ideas, have them share examples of specific ways that they have shown or could show appreciation.

Respond to the Text

Read

Summarize

Tell students they will use the information from their Theme charts to summarize the story. As I read, I collected the key details about the theme of the story. To summarize, I will paraphrase these details in a logical way.

Reread

Analyze the Text

After students summarize the selection, have them reread to develop a deeper understanding of the text and answer the questions on **Close Reading Companion** pages 166–168. For students who need support in citing text evidence, use the Reread prompts on pages T25B–T25J.

Write About the Text

Review the writing prompt and sentence frames. Remind students to use their responses from the **Close Reading Companion** to support their answers. For a full lesson on writing a response using text evidence, see page T30. **Answer:** The author repeatedly compares and contrasts the king's love of gold with his love of other, more precious things, such as his daughter. **Evidence:** As King Midas counts his gold, he tells Marigold that he loves her more than gold (page 465). The king gives Marigold a rose as a present and also shows his kindness by helping the traveller (pages 468–469). The king is thrilled with the solid-gold stone and rose, but Marigold is sad that the rose is not the same (page 471).

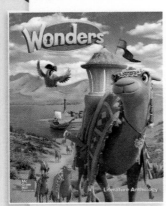

"Carlos's Gift"

Literature Anthology
Complex vocabulary and connections of ideas place this selection above TextEvaluator range. Content is grade-level appropriate.

Text Complexity Range

Lexile

420 ▲ 820
640

TextEvaluator™

2 35 ▲ 36
*36

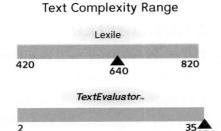

What makes this text complex?
▶ **Specific Vocabulary**
▶ **Connection of Ideas**

Compare Texts *Analytical Writing*

As students read and reread "Carlos's Gift" encourage them to take notes and think about the Essential Question: *How do you decide what is important?* Tell students to think about how this text compares with *King Midas and the Golden Touch*.

Genre · Realistic Fiction

Compare Texts
Read about a boy who learns to value something different.

Carlos's Gift

Carlos wanted a puppy in the worst way. He dreamed about puppies—big ones, little ones, spotted ones, frisky ones. Now it was his birthday, and Carlos had one thing on his mind. A puppy! When Mama handed him a flat, square box, Carlos almost started to cry.

It was a book about caring for dogs.

Papa smiled, "You need to learn how to care for a puppy before you get one."

Carlos read the book that night. He found a photograph of the exact kind of bulldog puppy that he craved. He eagerly showed Mama the next morning.

① "That kind of dog is too expensive," said Mama. Noticing his crestfallen expression, she added, "Try earning some money. Ask our neighbors if they have jobs you can do."

478

A C T Access Complex Text

▶ Specific Vocabulary

Point out *crestfallen* on page 478.

- *What is a synonym for* crestfallen*? Think about how Carlos is feeling?* (very disappointed) Have students use a dictionary to confirm their answer.

- *What is a synonym for* optimistic*? Look for paragraph clues on page 479 to help you.* (hopeful)

Mama's suggestion made Carlos more optimistic. He could save up for the puppy of his dreams!

After two weeks, Carlos had saved twenty-six dollars. It seemed like a **treasure**, but it was not enough to buy a puppy. Then Papa pointed out a poster at the store: City Animal Shelter Needs Your Help!

"The shelter takes care of abandoned pets," Papa said. "Carlos, you can learn a lot by working there. Let's visit."

At the shelter, Miss Jones, the manager said, "We only take volunteers who work for free. All our money is devoted to helping animals."

"You'll learn a lot about dogs," Papa urged Carlos.

Carlos's shoulders drooped. How was he ever going to accumulate enough money for a puppy? Finally, he agreed to give it a try. **2**

479

LITERATURE ANTHOLOGY, *pp. 478–479*

 Read

1 Skill: Cause and Effect

What does Carlos want? Why can't he have it? (Carlos wants a bulldog puppy. He can't have one because they are too expensive.)

2 Strategy: Summarize

Summarize Carlos's reasons for not wanting to work at the City Animal Shelter. (The position is not paid. Carlos is not sure how he will earn enough money to buy the puppy he wants.)

Reread

Author's Craft: Character Development

Reread pages 478 and 479. What details in the text tell you about Carlos's character? (Carlos really wants a puppy, and he is excited to get a book about caring for them. He is "crestfallen" and sad to learn that the kind of puppy he wants costs too much, but he is hopeful and happy about earning money to buy the puppy. When he finds out he will not be paid if he works at the shelter, he is sad. His shoulders droop. But he is willing to try. That tells me that Carlos is open to new ideas and experiences.)

ELL Restate more complex words, such as *crestfallen* and *optimistic* as "disappointed" and "hopeful." Then have students find the word *volunteers* in paragraph 4 on page 479.

- *What is a context clue that can help us find the meaning of* volunteers? (work for free)

- *What is a volunteer?* (a person who works for free)
- *Where does Carlos volunteer?* (at City Animal Shelter)

Read

3 Skill: Theme

What discovery does Carlos make as he works at the shelter? (He discovers that he enjoys the job because of the time he spends with the dogs, especially Pepper.) **How does this experience change Carlos?** (He realizes he values the uniqueness of the dogs, or one special dog, more than just the idea of owning a dog.)

Reread   *Close Reading Companion*

Author's Craft: Dialogue

How does the author use dialogue to show how Carlos feels about Pepper? (On page 480, Miss Jones tells Carlos that they are having trouble finding a home for Pepper. These words make Carlos realize his feelings. He replies that he wishes he could buy Pepper. At the end of the story, Carlos says, "I thought I wanted a bulldog puppy, but I got Pepper instead.")

Carlos started working at the shelter on Saturday. His assignment was sweeping. Afterwards, the dogs scampered out to play. One dog named Pepper had a funny curly tail that never stopped wagging. She was fully grown but as playful as a puppy. When Pepper leaped in the pile of sticks and leaves that Carlos had just swept up, he laughed.

Carlos went to the shelter every weekend. He began to treasure his time with the dogs, especially Pepper. One day Carlos asked why Pepper was still at the shelter.

Miss Jones sighed, "We've had trouble finding a home for Pepper. Most people don't want such an energetic dog."

Carlos suddenly realized he didn't want a bulldog puppy. He wanted Pepper. "I wish I could buy her," he replied.

480

A C T Access Complex Text

▶ Connection of Ideas

Remind students to think about what Carlos had to do to get a dog.

- *What did Carlos's parents want him to do before he could get a dog?* (They wanted him to learn how to care for dogs.)

- *How does Carlos's work at the shelter help him get Pepper, even though he isn't paid for working there?* (He already has enough money to adopt Pepper, and working at the shelter has proved that he is responsible enough to take care of her.)

Miss Jones smiled, "You can't buy her, but you can adopt her. There's a fifteen-dollar fee, and your parents must complete a form proving that you can give Pepper a good home."

Both Mama and Papa agreed that Carlos had learned enough about dogs to adopt Pepper. Carlos was so thrilled that he ran all the way to the shelter to get Pepper.

Carlos used part of his hard-earned **wealth** to pay the fee. And he decided to donate the rest of his puppy fund to aid more shelter dogs. "I thought I wanted a bulldog puppy, but I got Pepper instead." Pepper barked with joy. **3**

Make Connections

What does Carlos value at the story's beginning? How have his feelings changed at the end of the story? ESSENTIAL QUESTION

What other stories have you read about how people changed their values? TEXT TO TEXT

481

LITERATURE ANTHOLOGY, *pp. 480–481*

Read

Summarize

Guide students to summarize the selection.

Reread

Analyze the Text

After students read and summarize, have them reread to develop a deeper understanding of the text by annotating and answering questions on pages 169–171 of the **Close Reading Companion.**

Integrate

Make Connections

Essential Question <u>Answer:</u> At the beginning of the story, Carlos values a bulldog puppy. At the end of the story, Carlos values Pepper and the other shelter dogs. <u>Evidence:</u> On page 478, Carlos decides he wants a bulldog puppy. On page 480, Carlos realizes that he wants Pepper, a playful dog. He gives up the idea of having a bulldog puppy.

Text to Text Responses may vary, but encourage students to cite text evidence from each source.

ELL Clarify the difference between adopting a puppy and buying one. Then ask:

- *Who does Carlos adopt?* (Pepper)
- *Does Carlos still want a bulldog puppy?* (no)

- *Show me or tell me how Carlos feels at the beginning of this story. Now show me or tell me how he feels at the end.* (He is upset and disappointed at the beginning of the story. He is thrilled at the end.)

$\rightarrow$ Phonics/Fluency

MINILESSON **20** Mins

Prefixes

OBJECTIVES

 Identify and know the meaning of the most common prefixes and derivational suffixes. **RF.3.3a**

CCSS Create engaging audio recordings of stories or poems that demonstrate fluid reading at an understandable pace; add visual displays when appropriate to emphasize or enhance certain facts or details. **SL.3.5**

 Use a known root word as a clue to the meaning of an unknown word with the same root (e.g., *company, companion*). **L.3.4c**

Rate: 97–117 WCPM

ACADEMIC LANGUAGE

• *expression*

• Cognate: *expresión*

Refer to the sound transfers chart in the **Language Transfers Handbook** to identify sounds that do not transfer in Spanish, Cantonese, Vietnamese, Hmong, and Korean.

1 Explain

Remind students that a prefix is a word part added to the beginning of a word to make a new word. Identifying prefixes and understanding their meanings can help readers figure out the meanings of unfamiliar words. The prefixes *un-* and *dis-* mean "not", *pre-* means "before", *re-* means "again", and *mis-* means "wrong."

2 Model

Write the word *review* on the board. Draw a line between the two word parts (re/view). Model how to say the word, pronouncing each word part and then running your finger under the word as you sound out the whole word. Tell students that *view* means "to look at or see." Explain that to *review* means "to look at again."

3 Guided Practice

Write the following words. Help students identify the prefixes and base words and then pronounce each whole word. Guide them to use the prefixes and base words to figure out the meanings of the words.

unfold	rebuild	prepay
disappear	misspell	unkind
reread	preheat	dislike

Read Multisyllabic Words

Transition to Longer Words Give students practice with reading longer words with prefixes. Draw a T-chart. In the first column write *agree, arrange, lucky,* and *understand.* In the second column, write *disagree, rearrange, unlucky,* and *misunderstand.* Point to the words in the first column and model how to read each word. Have students repeat.

Explain that the words in the second column contain a base word from the first column. Have students identify the prefix in each word and draw a line between the prefix and base word. Point to each word and have students read the words chorally. Write simple sentences with words from the second column, for example, *I disagree with her.* Have students read the words with prefixes in sentences.

Roots in Related Words

1 Explain

Words that share a common root or base word are called related words. The words *viewer, viewing, review,* and *preview* share the common root *view*.

- Identifying the common root word and determining its meaning can help readers figure out the meanings of unfamiliar words.

2 Model

Write and say the words *heater, preheat,* and *reheat*. Have students repeat the words. Model identifying the root word and using the root word to figure out the meaning of each word.

3 Guided Practice

Write the related words *useful, misuse, reuse; coverage, recover, uncover, discover, discovery*. Guide students as they identify the common root in each set of words and then figure out the meaning of each word.

 FLUENCY

Expression

Explain/Model Explain that part of reading with expression is using your voice to add dramatic meaning to a passage. Point out that reading dialogue the way the character would have said it is a way to use expression when reading.

Model reading page 407 of "Athena and Arachne." Emphasize expression when reading the dialogue between Diana and Arachne.

Practice/Apply Have students create audio recordings of the passage to demonstrate fluid reading. Remind students to use appropriate expression. Offer opportunities for students to listen to their recordings and provide feedback to students as needed.

Daily Fluency Practice FLUENCY

Students can practice fluency using **Your Turn Practice Book.**

Monitor and *Differentiate*

✓ Quick Check

Can students decode words with prefixes and use the prefixes to determine the meanings of the words? Can students read related words and use the root words to determine the meanings of the words? Can students read fluently?

⬇

Small Group Instruction

If No → | Approaching Level | Reteach pp. T40, T42

| ELL | Develop p. T58

If Yes → | On Level | Review p. T48

| Beyond Level | Extend p. T52

ON-LEVEL PRACTICE BOOK p. 258

A. Read each sentence. Underline the word that has a prefix. Write the meaning of the word on the line.

1. My model ship fell off the table, and now I have to rebuild it.
   build again

2. Of all the vegetables on the table, I dislike peas the most.
   do not like

3. Before my sister started kindergarten, she went to preschool.
   before school

4. When I fell into the mud puddle, I knew I was having an unlucky day.
   not lucky

5. I lost my copy of the story, so I need to reprint it before class.
   print again

B. Related words have a common root or base word. Read each set of words. Circle the words that have a common root or base word.

1. alike · unlike · click
2. precook · pretty · cooking
3. halfway · unhappy · happily
4. review · viewing · voting
5. unlucky · cluck · luckily

| APPROACHING p. 258 | BEYOND p. 258 | ELL p. 258 |

→ Write to Sources

Reading/Writing Workshop

OBJECTIVES

CCSS Write informative/ explanatory texts to examine a topic and convey ideas and information clearly. Introduce a topic and group related information together; include illustrations when useful to aiding comprehension. **W.3.2a**

ACADEMIC LANGUAGE

rhythm, attention

Go Digital

U6W1 Sentence Fluency: Varying Sentence Lengths

DAY 1

Writing Fluency

Write to a Prompt Provide students with the prompt: *Write about Arachne's character traits.* Have students share their descriptions of the traits. *How would you describe Arachne?* Have students write continuously for fifteen minutes in their Writer's Notebook. If students stop writing, encourage them to keep going.

COLLABORATE When students finish writing have them work with a partner to compare ideas and make sure that they both have a clear understanding of the story.

Genre Writing

Feature Article pp. T344–T349

First Week Focus: Over the course of the week, focus on the following stages of the writing process:

Expert Model: Discuss the Expert Model found online at Writer's Workspace. Work with students to find the features of a feature article.

Prewrite: Explain a feature article to students. Teach the minilesson on organization. Distribute the Sequence Chart found online at Writer's Workspace, and have students use it to start planning their own feature articles.

DAY 2

Write to the Reading/Writing Workshop Text

Analyze the Prompt Read aloud the first paragraph on page 414 of the **Reading/Writing Workshop**. Ask: *What is the prompt asking?* (to state and support an opinion) Say: *Let's reread to see what happened between Athena and Arachne. We can note text evidence.*

Analyze Text Evidence Display Graphic Organizer 51 in Writer's Workspace. Say: *Let's see how one student, Holly, took notes to answer the prompt. She notes how Athena responded to Arachne's boasts.* Guide the class through the rest of Holly's notes.

Analyze the Student Model Explain how Holly used text evidence from her notes to write a response to the prompt.

- **State an Opinion** Stating a clear, focused opinion helps readers know what your writing is about. Holly clearly stated her opinion on the topic in her first sentence. Trait: Organization

- **Sentence Length** Using sentences of different lengths helps build interest in your writing. Holly combined two short sentences to make a longer sentence. Trait: Sentence Fluency

- **Supporting Details** It is important for writers to provide text evidence and other details to support their opinions. Holly included details from the selection to support each of her points. Trait: Ideas

For additional practice with sentence fluency and varying sentence lengths, assign **Your Turn Practice Book** page 259.

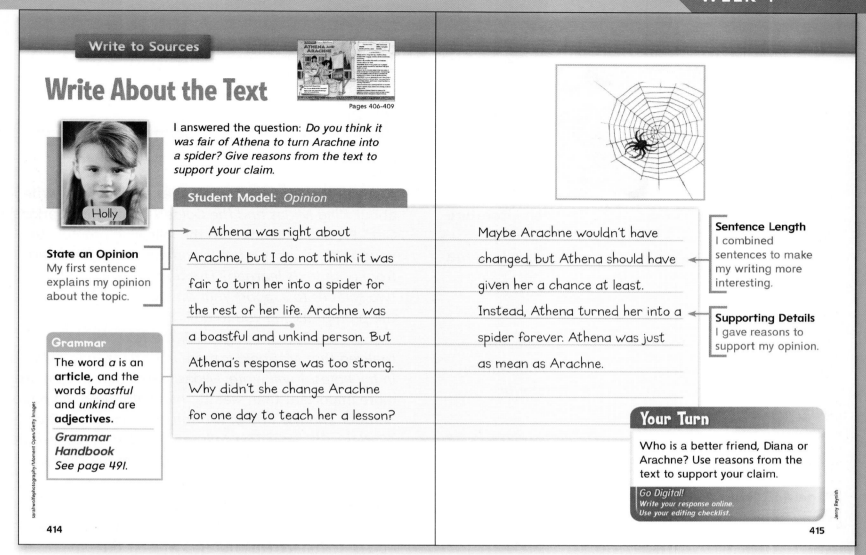

Write to Sources

Write About the Text

Pages 406–409

Holly

I answered the question: *Do you think it was fair of Athena to turn Arachne into a spider? Give reasons from the text to support your claim.*

Student Model: *Opinion*

State an Opinion
My first sentence explains my opinion about the topic.

Athena was right about

Arachne, but I do not think it was

fair to turn her into a spider for

the rest of her life. Arachne was

a boastful and unkind person. But

Athena's response was too strong.

Why didn't she change Arachne

for one day to teach her a lesson?

Maybe Arachne wouldn't have

changed, but Athena should have

given her a chance at least.

Instead, Athena turned her into a

spider forever. Athena was just

as mean as Arachne.

Grammar
The word *a* is an **article,** and the words *boastful* and *unkind* are **adjectives.**

Grammar Handbook See page 491.

Sentence Length
I combined sentences to make my writing more interesting.

Supporting Details
I gave reasons to support my opinion.

Your Turn
Who is a better friend, Diana or Arachne? Use reasons from the text to support your claim.

Go Digital!
Write your response online.
Use your editing checklist.

414

415

READING/WRITING WORKSHOP, *pp. 414–415*

Your Turn Writing Read the Your Turn prompt on page 415 of the Reading/Writing Workshop aloud. Discuss the prompt with students. If necessary, review with students that good writers vary the length of their sentences to give their writing a pleasing rhythm and to keep their readers' attention.

Have students take notes as they look for text evidence to answer the prompt. Remind them to include the following elements as they craft their response from their notes:

• State an Opinion

• Sentence Length

• Supporting Details

Have students use **Grammar Handbook** page 491 in the Reading/Writing Workshop to edit for errors in articles and adjectives.

ELL ENGLISH LANGUAGE LEARNERS SCAFFOLD

Beginning

Write Help students complete the sentence frames.
As a friend, Diana _____.
As a friend, Arachne _____.

Intermediate

Describe Ask students to complete the sentence frame. Encourage students to provide details.
_____ was the better friend because _____.

Advanced/High

Discuss Check for understanding. Ask: *Which woman was the better friend? What evidence supports your claim?*

Write to Sources

DAY 3 For students who need support to complete the writing assignment for the Literature Anthology, provide the following instruction.

DAY 4

Write to the Literature Anthology Text

Analyze the Prompt Explain that students will write about *King Midas and the Golden Touch* on **Literature Anthology** pages 462–475. Provide the following prompt: *How does the author help you understand the theme of this play?* Ask: *What is the prompt asking you to do?* (to analyze how the author conveys the theme of the play to the reader)

Analyze Text Evidence Help students note evidence.

Page 465 Read the page. Ask: *How does the author show how Midas feels about gold and about his daughter, Marigold?* (The author shows Midas counting his gold. He also spends time with Marigold and tells her that he loves her.) *How does this relate to the theme of the play?*

Page 468 Read the page. Ask: *How does the author compare and contrast Midas's love of gold and his feelings for other people?* (Even though we know King Midas loves gold, he also is caring and helps the traveler.) *Why is this important?*

Encourage students to look for more text evidence about the play's theme. Then have them craft a short response. Use the conference routine below.

Write to Two Sources

Analyze the Prompt Explain that students will write about *King Midas and the Golden Touch* and "Carlos's Gift." Provide students with the following prompt: *In your opinion, what is the lesson the main characters from both texts learned? Use text evidence from two sources to support your answer.* Ask: *What is the prompt asking you to do?* (to state and support an opinion) Say: *On page 475, the text says Midas realized that Marigold is more important than gold. So in my notes, I will write:* Midas learns that people are more important than wealth. *I will also note the page number and the title of the source. On page 480 of "Carlos's Gift," the text tells me that Carlos realized he wanted a dog he had played with from the shelter. I will add this to my notes.*

Analyze Text Evidence Display online Graphic Organizer 52 in Writer's Workspace. Say: *Let's see how one student took notes to answer the prompt. Here are Holly's notes.* Read through the text evidence for each selection and have students point out lessons the main characters learn.

Teacher Conferences

STEP 1

Talk about the strengths of the writing.

Your sentences are well written and their length varies. This kept me interested as I read through your ideas about the theme of the play.

STEP 2

Focus on how the writer uses text evidence.

Most of the text evidence you cited supports your topic sentence. You could include more details from the text to support your idea that Marigold is precious beyond gold.

STEP 3

Make concrete suggestions.

You used supporting details, but some could relate more closely to the topic. Rewrite this portion with more specific and focused details.

DAY

5

Share the Prompt Provide the following prompt to students: *Which character is a better person, King Midas or Carlos? Use text evidence from King Midas and the Golden Touch and "Carlos's Gift" to support your answer.*

Find Text Evidence Have students take notes. Find text evidence and give guidance where needed. If necessary, review with students how to paraphrase. Remind them to write the page number and source of the information.

Analyze the Student Model Review the prompt and Holly's notes from Day 4. Display the student model on page 260 of the **Your Turn Practice Book**. Explain to students that Holly synthesized her notes to write a response to the prompt. Discuss the page together with students or have them do it independently.

Write the Response Review the prompt from Day 4 with students. Remind them that they took notes on this prompt on Day 4. Have students use their notes to craft a short response. Tell students to include the titles of both sources and the following elements:

• State an Opinion

• Sentence Length

• Supporting Details

COLLABORATE

Share and Reflect Have students share their responses with a partner. Use the Peer Conference routine below.

Suggested Revisions

Provide specific direction to help focus young writers.

Focus on a Sentence
Read the draft and target one sentence for revision. *Rewrite this run-on sentence by breaking it into two shorter sentences.*

Focus on a Section
Underline a section that needs to be revised. *I want to know more about ____. Try using more supporting details to show ____.*

Focus on a Revision Strategy
Underline a section. Have students focus on a specific revision strategy, such as combining. *This section has many short sentences. Combine two of the related short sentences into one longer sentence.*

Peer Conferences

Focus peer responses on varying sentence length and using supporting details. Provide these questions:

• Is the opinion stated clearly?

• Are the sentences different lengths?

• What other details would support the opinion?

Grammar: Adjectives and Articles

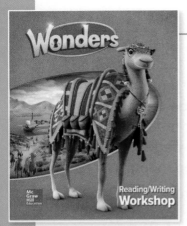

Reading/Writing Workshop

OBJECTIVES

 Explain the function of nouns, pronouns, verbs, adjectives, and adverbs in general and their functions in particular sentences. **L.3.1a**

- Distinguish adjectives and articles
- Identify when to use adjectives and articles
- Proofread sentences for mechanics and usage errors

In small groups, have students examine an illustration or a photograph of a person. One student describes the clothing the person is wearing. The other students listen for adjectives and the articles *a, an,* and *the.* Students take turns being the student who describes the clothing.

DAY 1

DAILY LANGUAGE ACTIVITY

Dr purcell studied at school. He is the most smart doctor I know.
(1: Dr.; 2: Purcell; 3: studied; 4: smartest)

Introduce Adjectives

- An **adjective** describes a noun. An adjective usually comes before the noun it describes:
    I have a **blue** jacket.

- Some adjectives are descriptive. They tell *what kind* of person, place, or thing the noun is:
    We have a **small** dog.

- Some adjectives tell *how many:*
    Jack has **five** guitars.

- Some adjectives are limiting, such as *this, that, these,* and *those:*
    These cookies are delicious.

Have partners discuss adjectives using page 491 and 492 of the Grammar Handbook.

DAY 2

DAILY LANGUAGE ACTIVITY

We have a busy day, we has to get the house ready and then we will cook dinner.
(1: day.; 2: We; 3: have; 4: ready,)

Review Adjectives

Review descriptive and limiting adjectives. Have students give several examples of each.

Introduce Articles

Present the following:

- The **articles** *a, an,* and *the* are special adjectives:
    We have **a** party every year.

- Use *an* before an adjective or a nonspecific singular noun that begins with a vowel:
    I ate **an** apple for my snack.

- Use *the* before singular and plural nouns when referring to something specific:
    We are going to **the** grocery store.

 TALK ABOUT IT

COLLABORATE

DESCRIBE WITH ADJECTIVES

Have small groups write down five things that are important to them. Have students take turns choosing an item and creating a simple, compound, or complex sentence using adjectives about why this item is valuable.

NAME THE ARTICLE

Have small groups write sentences with articles about why certain things are valuable. Then have each student read a sentence aloud, and have the other students name the article used in the sentence.

DAY 3

DAILY LANGUAGE ACTIVITY

Jen was'nt home so I leave her package by the door. I hope she see it.
(1: wasn't; 2: home,; 3: left; 4: sees)

Mechanics and Usage: Commas in a Series and in Dates

- Use commas to separate three or more words in a series.
- Use a comma between the day and the year in a date.
- Use a comma after introductory words.

As students write, refer them to Grammar Handbook pages 491 and 503.

DAY 4

DAILY LANGUAGE ACTIVITY

Martin Luther King, Jr.'s birthday is January 15 1929 I read about him at the library. (1: 15,; 2: 1929. I)

Proofread

Have students correct errors in these sentences.

1. I need potting soil seeds and a flower pot. (1: soil,; 2: seeds,)

2. The U.S. Constitution was signed on september 17 1789. (1: September; 2: 17, 1789.)

3. Jane has an small brown short-haired puppy. (1: a; 2: small,; 3: brown,)

4. After today I only have one test left. Im so relieved. (1: today,; 2: I'm)

Have students check their work using Grammar Handbook pages 491, 502, and 503 on adjectives, articles, and commas in sentences and letters.

DAY 5

DAILY LANGUAGE ACTIVITY

Do you know who lived at 221B baker Street London England? He is my favorit detective. (1: Baker; 2: Street,; 3: London,; 4: favorite)

Assess

Use the Daily Language Activity and Grammar Practice Reproducibles page 130 for assessment.

Reteach

Use Grammar Practice Reproducibles pages 126–129 and selected pages from the Grammar Handbook for reteaching. Remind students that it is important to use descriptive and limiting adjectives correctly as they read, write, and speak.

Check students' writing for use of the skill and listen for it in their speaking. Assign Grammar Revision Assignments in their Writer's Notebooks as needed.

See Grammar Practice Reproducibles pages 126–130.

PLACE THE COMMA

Ask partners to select a paragraph from a book. Taking turns, have one partner read the sentences in the paragraph to the other partner. The second partner will identify where the commas should be in the sentences.

CREATE A SENTENCE

Have students in small groups write articles *a*, *an*, and *the*, and adjectives *this*, *that*, *these*, and *those* on cards. Each student picks a card and creates a sentence using the article or adjective in a sentence about the qualities that give an item value.

GUESS THE ITEM

Have each group member write the name of an item they value and use and keep it private. All the other students will take turns asking questions to guess the item. Group members should use descriptive and limiting adjectives in their questions and answers.

Spelling: Prefixes *un-, re-, pre-,* and *dis-*

 DAY 1

 DAY 2

OBJECTIVES

CCSS Use spelling patterns and generalizations (e.g., *word families, position-based spellings, syllable patterns, ending rules, meaningful word parts*) in writing words. **L.3.2f**

CCSS Consult reference materials, including beginning dictionaries, as needed to check and correct spellings. **L.3.2g**

Spelling Words

disagreed	dislike	disappear
prepaid	preschool	precook
previous	rebuild	return
resell	reprint	unwrap
unlucky	untied	unbeaten

Review robot, tiny, label
Challenge unknown, recover

Differentiated Spelling

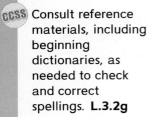

Approaching Level

dislike	prepaid	precook
prevent	review	resell
rebuild	return	reprint
redo	unhappy	unfold
unkind	untied	unlucky

Beyond Level

dislike	disappear	precook
previous	recover	rearrange
rebuild	reread	reenter
unwrap	untied	unafraid
unknown	unbeaten	unlucky

Assess Prior Knowledge

Display the spelling words. Read them aloud, drawing out and slowly enunciating the prefixes.

Model for students how to spell the word *unbeaten*. Draw lines between the syllables: *un/beat/en*. Point out the base word and identify its prefix.

Demonstrate sorting the spelling words by pattern under key words *unwrap, resell, prepaid,* and *dislike.* (Write the words on index cards or the IWB.) Sort a few words by prefixes. Have students say each word and identify the prefix in each word.

Then use the Dictation Sentences from Day 5. Say the underlined word, read the sentence, and repeat the word. Have students write the words.

Spiral Review

Review the open syllables in the words *robot, tiny,* and *label*. Have students find words in this week's readings with the same sounds. Use the Dictation Sentences below for the review words. Read the sentence, say the word, and have students write the words.

1. This <u>robot</u> operates with wheels.
2. The <u>tiny</u> mouse raced under the lion's legs.
3. Blake read the <u>label</u> with care.

Have partners check the spellings.

Challenge Words Review this week's spelling words, pointing out the prefixes. Use these Dictation Sentences for challenge words. Read the sentence, say the word, have students write the word.

1. The owner of that boat in the bay is <u>unknown</u>.
2. Wilbur will <u>recover</u> from his fall.

Have students write the words in their word study notebook.

 WORD SORTS

COLLABORATE

OPEN SORT

Have students cut apart the **Spelling Word Cards BLM** in the Online Resource Book and initial the backs of each card. Have them read the words aloud with a partner. Then have partners do an **open sort**. Have them record the sort in their word study notebook.

PATTERN SORT

Complete the **pattern sort** using the key words, pointing out the prefixes. Have students use Spelling Word Cards to do their own pattern sort. A partner can compare and check their sorts.

DAY 3

Word Meanings

Have students copy the words below into their Writer's Notebooks. Have them figure out the spelling word that goes with each definition.

1. to sell again (resell)
2. to come back (return)
3. vanish from view (disappear)
4. gave money ahead of time (prepaid)
5. uncover something (unwrap)

Challenge students to come up with clues for other spelling, review, or challenge words.

See Phonics/Spelling Reproducibles pp. 151–156.

SPEED SORT

Have partners do a **speed sort** to see who is faster. Then have partners write sentences for each spelling word, leaving blanks where the words should go. Have them trade papers and fill in the blanks.

DAY 4

Proofread and Write

Write these sentences on the board. Have students circle and correct each misspelled word. Remind students they can use print or electronic resources to check and correct spelling.

1. Please inrap and procook the food. (unwrap, precook)
2. I dissagreed, but did not disliek the idea. (disagreed, dislike)
3. When you wreturn, we must rebilled this sand castle. (return, rebuild)
4. When he arrived at preskool, he untyed his scarf and hung it up. (preschool, untied)
5. The team was unbeeten for the whole year. (unbeaten)

Error Correction Remind students that prefixes can never be repeated within a word and that a prefix is often its own syllable. If they say the word syllable by syllable as they spell it, this will help them.

BLIND SORT

Have partners do a **blind sort**: one reads a spelling word card; the other tells under which key word it belongs. Have them take turns until both have sorted all their words. Then have students explain how they sorted the words.

DAY 5

Assess

Use the Dictation Sentences for the Posttest. Have students list misspelled words in their word study notebooks. Look for students' use of these words in their writings.

Dictation Sentences

1. He <u>disagreed</u> with her answer.
2. Some people <u>dislike</u> spiders.
3. The magician made the rabbit <u>disappear</u>.
4. My family <u>prepaid</u> before pumping gas.
5. Little children go to <u>preschool</u>.
6. Did you <u>precook</u> the carrots?
7. This song sounds like the <u>previous</u> song.
8. Danielle wanted to <u>rebuild</u> the tree house.
9. Jason will <u>return</u> later.
10. The store will <u>resell</u> used books.
11. You must <u>reprint</u> your name.
12. I want to <u>unwrap</u> my presents.
13. She was <u>unlucky</u> at the chess match.
14. The child <u>untied</u> the string.
15. Our team is still <u>unbeaten</u>.

Have students self-correct the tests.

→ Build Vocabulary

DAY 1

DAY 2

OBJECTIVES

CCSS Use a known root word as a clue to the meaning of an unknown word with the same root (e.g., *company, companion*). **L.3.4c**

CCSS Identify real-life connections between words and their use (e.g., describe people who are *friendly* or *helpful*). **L.3.5b**

Expand vocabulary by adding inflectional endings and suffixes.

Vocabulary Words

alarmed	possess
anguish	reward
necessary	treasure
obsessed	wealth

Provide sentence frames to help students practice using the different forms of this week's vocabulary words they generate on Day 2. Review verb tenses as needed.

Connect to Words

Practice this week's vocabulary.

1. Describe feeling **alarmed**.
2. How can you get over feelings of **anguish**?
3. Do you think it's **necessary** to be organized?
4. Have you ever felt **obsessed** about a movie or book?
5. Do you **possess** anything that you can't live without?
6. Describe a **reward** you have received.
7. Describe kinds of **treasure**.
8. Describe a way a person can gain **wealth**.

Expand Vocabulary

Help students generate different forms of this week's words by adding, changing, or removing inflectional endings.

- Draw a four-column chart. Write *obsess* in the left column. Then write *obsessed, obsessing,* and *obsession* in the other columns. Read aloud the words and discuss the meanings

- Have students share sentences with each form of *obsess*.

- Students can fill in the chart for other words, such as *possess*.

- Have students copy the chart in their word study notebook.

 BUILD MORE VOCABULARY

COLLABORATE

ACADEMIC VOCABULARY

Discuss important academic words.

- Display the terms *finance* and *currency* and discuss the meanings.

- Display *finance* and *financial*. Have partners look up and define related words.

- Write the related words on the board. Have partners ask and answer questions using the words. Repeat with *currency*. Elicit examples from students.

HOMOPHONES

- Remind students that homophones are words that sound the same but have different meanings. Write the following sentences and discuss each meaning of *rose: I picked a pretty rose. I rose from my chair.*

- Have partners find other homophones using the reading selections or a dictionary.

- Write the examples on the board and discuss as a class.

DAY 3

Reinforce the Words

Review this week's vocabulary words. Have students orally complete each sentence stem.

1. Jenny was <u>alarmed</u> when she saw the big ____.
2. Tommy felt <u>anguish</u> over the loss of ____.
3. It's <u>necessary</u> to ____ every day.
4. Leo was <u>obsessed</u> with a book called ____.
5. She doesn't <u>possess</u> a lot of ____.
6. If you find the missing ____, you may get a <u>reward</u>.

DAY 4

Connect to Writing

- Have students write sentences in their word study notebooks using this week's vocabulary.
- Tell them to write sentences that provide information about the words and their meanings.
- Provide the Day 3 sentence stems for students needing extra support.

Write About Vocabulary Have students write something they learned from this week's words in their word study notebook. For example, they might write about how a myth might teach lessons about *possessions* and *wealth*.

DAY 5

Word Squares

Ask students to create Word Squares for each vocabulary word.

- In the first square, students write the word. (example: *wealth*)
- In the second square, students write their own definition of the word and any related words. (examples: *riches, gold*)
- In the third square, students draw a simple illustration that will help them remember the word. (example: *piles of money*)
- In the fourth square, students write non-examples. (examples: *poverty, poor*)
- Have students share their Word Squares with a partner.

ROOT WORDS

Remind students that identifying root words can help them determine the meanings of unfamiliar words.

- Display **Your Turn Practice Book** pages 253–254. Read Scene 1 and model figuring out the meaning of *miserable*.
- For additional practice with root words, have students complete page 257. Discuss with students how the root words helped them figure out the meanings of the words.

SHADES OF MEANING

Help students generate words related to *anguish*. Draw a synonym/antonym scale.

- Begin a discussion about the word *anguish*. Discuss synonyms, such as *sadness* and *sorrow* and write them on the scale. Then discuss antonyms, such as *joy* and *elation* and write them on the scale.
- Have partners work together to add words to the scale.
- Ask students to copy the words in their word study notebook.

MORPHOLOGY

Use the word *possession* as a springboard for students to learn more words.

- Write the word *possess* and discuss the meaning.
- Write the suffix *–ion*. Discuss how adding this suffix changes the meaning of the word.
- Ask partners to list other words with the suffix *–ion*, such as *objection* and *creation*.
- As a class, discuss the meanings of the words.

Integrate Ideas

Close Reading Routine

Read   DOK 1–2

- Identify key ideas and details about Treasures.
- Take notes and summarize.
- Use **A C T** prompts as needed.

Reread   DOK 2–3

- Analyze the text, craft, and structure.
- Use the **Close Reading Companion.**

Integrate   DOK 4

- Integrate knowledge and ideas.
- Make text-to-text connections.
- Use the Integrate lesson.
- Use *Close Reading Companion,* p. 172.

TEXT CONNECTIONS

Connect to the Essential Question

Write the essential question on the board: How do you decide what's important? Divide the class into small groups. Tell students that each group will compare the information that they have learned about how to decide what is important. Model how to compare this information by using examples from this week's **Leveled Readers** and "Athena and Arachne," **Reading/Writing Workshop** pages 406–409.

Evaluate Text Evidence Have students review their class notes and completed graphic organizers before they begin their discussions. Encourage students to compare information from all the week's reads. Have each group pick one student to take notes. Explain that each group will use a Layered Book Foldable® to record their ideas. You may wish to model how to use a Layered Book Foldable® to record comparisons.

Things that People Value

Dinah Zike's
FOLDABLES
Study Organizer

Valuable Qualities

Go Digital

Collaborate

Research Roadmap

Resources: Research and Inquiry

RESEARCH AND INQUIRY

Interview a Classmate

Explain that students will work with a partner to complete a short research project to collect information about qualities that they admire. They will collect their information by interviewing one another about the things they value. Discuss the following steps:

❶ **Brainstorm** Begin a discussion about valuable qualities in people. As students begin thinking about valuable qualities, have them consider their own experiences and the weekly reading selections.

❷ **Interviewing Skills** Discuss effective interviewing skills with students. Explain that interviewers often write down their questions before an interview. Review the six basic question words (*who, what, when, where, why, how*). Have students use the Interview Form for help.

Text to Photography

As students discuss the information from all the week's reads, have them include the photograph on page 172 of the **Close Reading Companion** as a part of their discussion. Guide students to see the connections between the photograph of the boys and text. Ask: *How does the photograph connect to what you read this week?*

Present Ideas and Synthesize Information

When students finish their discussions, ask for a volunteer from each group to read his or her notes aloud.

OBJECTIVE

CCSS Refer to parts of stories, dramas, and poems when writing or speaking about a text, using terms such as chapter, scene, and stanza; describe how each successive part builds on earlier sections. **RL.3.5**

③ **Guided Practice** Have students use the six basic question words to write a list of questions to ask one another.

④ **Create the Project: Interview** Have students use their list of questions to interview one another about the things they value. Encourage them to take notes and keep the interview focused on the topic.

Present the Interview

Have students use their notes to reenact their interviews for the rest of the class. Explain that they can publish a print or audio version of the interview. Afterward, have the class discuss the main ideas and details presented in the interviews. Have students use the online Presentation Checklist 3 to evaluate their presentations.

OBJECTIVES

CCSS Conduct short research projects that build knowledge about a topic. **W.3.7**

CCSS Determine the main ideas and supporting details of a text read aloud or information presented in diverse media and formats, including visually, quantitatively, and orally. **SL.3.2**

• Conduct interviews.
• Collaborate with others.

ACADEMIC LANGUAGE
interview, qualities, value

→ Approaching Level

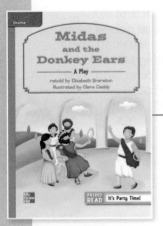

Lexile N/A
TextEvaluator™ N/A

 OBJECTIVES

CCSS Recount stories, including fables, folktales, and myths from diverse cultures; determine the central message, lesson, or moral and explain how it is conveyed through key details in the text. **RL.3.2**

CCSS Use a known root word as a clue to the meaning of an unknown word with the same root (e.g., *company, companion*). **L.3.4c**

• Make and confirm or revise predictions.
• Identify the theme of a story.

ACADEMIC LANGUAGE
make, confirm, revise predictions, theme, play, root words, realistic fiction

Leveled Reader:
Midas and the Donkey Ears

Before Reading

Preview and Predict

Have students read the Essential Question. Then have them read the title and the table of contents of *Midas and the Donkey Ears*. Have students make a prediction about the plot of the play and share it with a partner.

Leveled Readers

Review Genre: Play

Review with students that a play is a story told through dialogue and is meant to be performed. A play also includes stage directions and scenes. As they preview *Midas and the Donkey Ears*, have students identify features of a play.

During Reading

Close Reading

Note Taking Have students use their graphic organizer as they read.

Pages 2–4 *What do you learn about King Midas from the Townsperson on page 3?* (He is vain and foolish and obsessed with wealth.) *Why is Apollo upset on page 4?* (It seems like Midas has already made up his mind to choose Pan as the winner.)

Fill in the Graphic Organizer

Pages 5–6 *Why does Apollo give King Midas donkey ears?* (Apollo says that the reason Midas picked Pan is because his ears must be too small.) *Turn to a partner and make a prediction about what Midas will do now that he has donkey ears.*

Pages 7–8 *Did you predict that King Midas would try to hide his ears? What detail helped you confirm or revise your prediction?* (Page 8: *It is necessary for you to give me a new hairstyle that will hide these ears.*)

Pages 9–11 *Who does the barber tell about King Midas?* (Mother Earth) *Make a prediction about whether or not Mother Earth will keep his secret.*

Pages 12–13 *Did you predict that Mother Earth would tell the secret? What detail helped you confirm your prediction?* (Pages 12–13: *Mother Earth says "King Midas has donkey ears!" three times.*)

Page 14 *Apollo says that he punished Midas because he was an unfair judge. What happens as a result of Midas not learning his lesson?* (Midas is sent to live with donkeys.) *What lesson do we learn?* (Possible Response: There will be consequences if we do not act fairly.)

Page 15 *What is the root of the noun* laughter *on page 15?* (laugh) *Use the root word to help you define the word.* (*Laughter* means "the act of laughing.") *What is the theme of the story?* (Possible Responses: judge fairly; learn from your mistakes.)

After Reading

Respond to Reading Revisit the Essential Question, and ask students to complete the Text Evidence questions on page 16.

Analytical Writing **Write About Reading** Have students work with a partner to write a short paragraph about the lesson the story was intended to teach. Make sure they include details from the text.

Fluency: Expression

Model Model reading page 5 with expression. Next, reread the page aloud, and have students read along with you.

Apply Have students practice reading with a partner.

PAIRED READ

"It's Party Time!"

Make Connections: Write About It • *Analytical Writing*

Before reading, have students note that the genre of this text is realistic fiction, which means it contains characters and events that could exist or happen in real life. Then discuss the Essential Question.

After reading, have students make connections between how the characters learn lessons in "It's Party Time!" and *Midas and the Donkey Ears.*

Leveled Reader

✏ *Analytical Writing*

COMPARE TEXTS

• Have students use text evidence to compare a play to a story.

Literature Circles

Ask students to conduct a literature circle using the Thinkmark questions to guide the discussion. You may wish to have a whole-class discussion on other well-known characters in literature who have learned lessons.

Level Up

Level-up lessons available online.

IF students read the Approaching Level fluently and answered the questions

THEN pair them with students who have proficiently read On Level and have approaching-level students

• echo-read the On Level main selection with their partner.

• use self-stick notes to mark a detail to discuss in each section.

A C T Access Complex Text

The On Level challenges students by including more **domain-specific words** and **complex sentence structures**.

→ Approaching Level

Phonics/Decoding

DECODE WORDS WITH PREFIXES *un-, re-*

OBJECTIVES

 Know and apply grade-level phonics and word analysis skills in decoding words. Decode multisyllable words. **RF.3.3c**

Decode words with prefixes *un-, re-*.

 I Do Remind students that understanding the meaning of a prefix will help them find the meaning of an unknown word. Review the meanings of *re-*: "again" or "back," and *un-*: "not" or "opposite of." Write and say the word *repay*. Draw a line between *re* and *pay*, and model how to determine the meaning of the word. Repeat with *unfair, redo, undo, recount,* and *unsafe*.

 We Do Write *unlock, rewrite, untie, unmask, remake* on the board. Model identifying the prefix in *unlock*, decoding the word, and then defining the word. Guide students as they decode the rest of the words then use the meanings of the prefixes to define the words.

 You Do Add *unkind, resend, restart, unpack, rematch*. Have students read the words aloud, identify the prefix, and give a short definition for each. Then point to the words in random order for students to read chorally.

BUILD WORDS WITH PREFIXES *un-, re-, pre-, dis-, mis-*

OBJECTIVES

 Know and apply grade-level phonics and word analysis skills in decoding words. Decode multisyllable words. **RF.3.3c**

Build words with prefixes *un-, re-, pre-, dis-,* and *mis-*.

 I Do Tell students that they will be building multisyllable words with the prefixes *un-, re-, pre-, dis-,* and *mis-*. Review the meaning of each prefix, then display these **Word-Building Cards** one at a time: *dis, un, pre, re, mis, made, read, ties, trust,* and *new*. Model sounding out each syllable.

 We Do Have students chorally read each syllable. Repeat at varying speeds and in random order. Next, display all the cards and syllables. Work with students to combine the Word-Building Cards and the prefixes to form multisyllable words. Have students chorally read the words: *premade, misread, distrust, renew, unties*.

 You Do Display these Word-Building Cards one at a time: *try, sold, read, sent, able,* and *block*. Then write these syllables on the board: *un, re, pre, dis, mis*. Have students work with partners to build multisyllable words using the prefixes. Then have partners share the words they built.

PRACTICE WORDS WITH PREFIXES *un-, re-, pre-, dis-, mis-*

OBJECTIVES

CCSS Know and apply grade-level phonics and word analysis skills in decoding words. Decode multisyllable words. **RF.3.3c**

Read words with prefixes *un-, re-, pre-, dis-,* and *mis-*.

 I Do Remind students that they can use their knowledge of the prefixes *un-, re-, pre-, dis-,* and *mis-* to help decode an unfamiliar word. Write the word *discover* on the board, and draw a line between *dis* and *cover*. Model how to decode the word. Repeat for the words *unhappy, recycle, preheated, disconnect,* and *misinformed.*

 We Do Write the words *untested, researching, preseason, disbelief,* and *misdirect* on the board. Model how to decode the first word, then guide students as they decode the remaining words. Help them divide each word into syllables using the syllable-scoop technique to help them read one syllable at a time.

 You Do Point to the words in random order for students to chorally read.

ROOTS IN RELATED WORDS

OBJECTIVES

CCSS Use a known root word as a clue to the meaning of an unknown word with the same root (e.g., *company, companion*). **L.3.4c**

Decode words with related root words.

 I Do Review that related words share a root word. Tell students that by determining the meaning of the root word, they can figure out the meaning of an unknown word. Write and say: *heater, preheat, heated, reheat. Model identifying the common root heat,* determining its meaning, then finding the meaning of each word.

 We Do Write and say: *replace, displace, replaceable, misplace, placement.* Have students read the words. Guide students in identifying the common root word *place* and then finding the meaning of each word.

 You Do Afterward, write the words *misprint, printer, footprint, reprint,* and *fingerprint* on the board. Have students read each word, identify the common root word *print,* and then find the meaning of each word.

ELL ENGLISH LANGUAGE LEARNERS

For the students who need **phonics**, **decoding**, and **fluency** practice, use scaffolding methods as necessary to ensure students understand the meaning of the words. Refer to the **Language Transfers Handbook** for phonics elements that may not transfer in students' native languages.

Approaching Level

Vocabulary

REVIEW HIGH-FREQUENCY WORDS

 TIER 2

OBJECTIVES

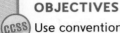 Use conventional spelling for high-frequency and other studied words and for adding suffixes to base words (e.g., *sitting, smiled, cries, happiness*). **L.3.2e**

Review high-frequency words.

 I Do Use Word Cards 201–210. Display one word at a time, following the routine:

Display the word. Read the word. Then spell the word.

 We Do Ask students to state the word and spell the word with you. Model using the word in a sentence, and have students repeat after you.

You Do Display the word. Ask students to say the word then spell it. When completed, quickly flip through the word card set as students chorally read the words. Provide opportunities for students to use the words in speaking and writing. For example, provide sentence starters such as *James and Hilary built the treehouse _____*. Ask students to write each word in their **Writer's Notebook**.

REVIEW VOCABULARY WORDS

TIER 2

OBJECTIVES

 Acquire and use accurately grade-appropriate conversational, general academic, and domain-specific words and phrases, including those that signal spatial and temporal relationships. **L.3.6**

Review vocabulary words.

 I Do Display each **Visual Vocabulary Card** and state the word. Explain how the photograph illustrates the word. State the example sentence and repeat the word.

 We Do Point to the word on the card and read the word with students. Ask them to repeat the word. Engage students in structured partner talk about the image as prompted on the back of the vocabulary card.

 You Do Display each visual in random order, hiding the word. Have students match the definitions and context sentences of the words to the visuals displayed. Then ask students to complete **Approaching Reproducibles** page 251.

IDENTIFY RELATED WORDS

OBJECTIVES

CCSS Demonstrate understanding of word relationships and nuances in word meanings. Identify real-life connections between words and their use (e.g., describe people who are *friendly* or *helpful*). **L.3.5b**

Identify word with similar meanings.

 I Do Display the *alarmed* **Visual Vocabulary Card**, and say aloud the word set *alarmed, calm, anxious.* Point out that the word *calm* does not belong, and explain why.

 We Do Display the vocabulary card for the word *obsessed.* Say aloud the word set *obsessed, distracted, preoccupied.* With students, identify the word that does not belong and discuss why.

 You Do Using the word sets below, display the remaining cards one at a time, saying aloud each word set. Ask students to identify the word that does not belong.

wealth, poverty, riches	*possess, have, lose*
treasure, fortune, hardship	*anguish, joy, misery*
reward, prize, punishment	*necessary, unimportant, essential*

ROOT WORDS

OBJECTIVES

CCSS Use a known root word as a clue to the meaning of an unknown word with the same root (e.g, *company, companion*). **L.3.4c**

Use root words as clues to words with the same root words.

 I Do Display the Comprehension and Fluency passage on **Approaching Reproducibles** pages 253–254. Read aloud Prometheus's first lines on page 253. Point to the word *starvation.* Explain to students that they can figure out the meaning of an unfamiliar word by determining the meaning of the root word. Remind students that a root word is a word in which no prefixes, suffixes, or inflectional endings have been added.

Think Aloud I do not know the word *starvation,* but I see that it contains the root word *starve* and the suffix *-ation.* To starve means "to suffer because you are hungry." The suffix *-ation* refers to a process or a state of being. I think that *starvation* refers to suffering because you have nothing to eat.

Write the definition of *starvation.*

 We Do Ask students to point to the words *miserable* and *kingdom* in the passage. With students, discuss how to break each word down into its root word and suffix to determine its meaning. Write the definitions of the words.

 You Do Have students find the meanings of *uninformed, unthreatened, empowerment,* and *fortunate* using their knowledge of root words.

Approaching Level

Comprehension

EXPRESSION

OBJECTIVES

CCSS Read on-level prose and poetry orally with accuracy, appropriate rate, and expression on successive readings. **RF.3.4b**

Read fluently with appropriate expression.

 I Do Remind students that good readers use expression to add dramatic meaning to a passage. Tell students that they should read dialogue the way a character would say it. Read the first scene in the Comprehension and Fluency passage on **Approaching Reproducibles** pages 253–254.

 We Do Read the second scene aloud, and have students repeat each line after you, emphasizing certain words to add meaning. Point out that reading dialogue the way the characters say it is one way to use expression.

 You Do Have partners take turns reading dialogue from the Approaching Reproducibles passage. Remind them to focus on their expression. Listen in and provide corrective feedback as needed by modeling proper fluency.

IDENTIFY THE GENRE

OBJECTIVES

 CCSS Refer to parts of stories, dramas, and poems when writing or speaking about a text, using terms such as chapter, scene, and stanza; describe how each successive part builds on earlier sections. **RL.3.5**

Identify elements of a play.

 I Do Tell students that "Prometheus Brings Fire to Humans" is a myth. A myth explains how something, such as fire, came to be in the world. Explain to students that the story of Prometheus has been written as a drama, or play. Plays include scenes, stage directions, and dialogue, and they are created to be performed on a stage. The scenes in the play tell the story through dialogue. Stage directions tell the actors what actions they should be doing.

 We Do Preview the Comprehension and Fluency passage in the **Approaching Reproducibles**. Ask: *How many scenes does the play have? Who are the characters? How can you tell that Prometheus is the main character?* Explain to students that the narrator, Zeus, Prometheus, Human 1, and Human 2 are listed as part of the cast, but Prometheus appears in the title of the play, and the narrator describes his actions.

 You Do Have students read the stage directions in the play following the word *Setting*. Ask students: *Where does the myth take place? Which words and phrases in the stage directions help you understand what is happening in the first scene?*

REVIEW THEME

OBJECTIVES

CCSS Recount stories, including fables, folktales, and myths from diverse cultures; determine the central message, lesson, or moral and explain how it is conveyed through key details in the text. **RL.3.2**

Determine the theme of a selection.

 I Do Remind students that the theme of a story is the author's message. The author reveals the theme through details about the characters. Tell students they should think about what the characters say and do. These details tell them about the theme of the story. As they read, students should ask: *What is the author's message?*

 We Do Read the first scene of the Comprehension and Fluency passage in **Approaching Reproducibles** together. Pause to point out details that show what the characters do and say in each line. With students, describe what Zeus and Prometheus think of humans. Have them explain how Prometheus reacts when Zeus tells him not to give humans fire. Model how to decide which details point to the theme. Use details from each paragraph to determine the theme of the passage.

 You Do Have students read the rest of the selection. Ask students to discuss which details showed that Prometheus was going to disobey Zeus. *What does Prometheus ask humans to do after he gives them fire? What do Prometheus's words to the humans tell you about the theme of the story?*

SELF-SELECTED READING

OBJECTIVES

CCSS Recount stories, including fables, folktales, and myths from diverse cultures; determine the central message, lesson, or moral and explain how it is conveyed through key details in the text. **RL.3.2**

• Determine the theme of a selection.
• Make and confirm or revise predictions.

Read Independently

Have students choose a myth, preferably in the form of a play, for sustained silent reading. Remind students that:

- The characters' actions and words provide details about the theme.
- students should make predictions as they read the story and then confirm or revise those predictions as they gain more information.

Read Purposefully

Have students record details that support the theme on **Graphic Organizer 148** as they read independently. After they finish, they can conduct a Book Talk, each summarizing the myth they read.

- Students should share their organizers and answer these questions: *What is the theme of the selection? Which details helped you determine the theme?*
- Students should tell what their predictions were and which ones they were able to confirm and which ones they had to revise.

→ On Level

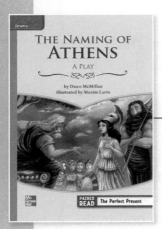

Lexile N/A
TextEvaluator™ N/A

OBJECTIVES

 Recount stories, including fables, folktales, and myths from diverse cultures; determine the central message, lesson, or moral and explain how it is conveyed through key details in the text. **RL.3.2**

 Use a known root word as a clue to the meaning of an unknown word with the same root (e.g., *company, companion*). **L.3.4c**

• Make and confirm or revise predictions.
• Identify the theme of the story.

ACADEMIC LANGUAGE
make, confirm, revise predictions, theme, play, word parts, root words, realistic fiction

Leveled Reader:
The Naming of Athens

Go Digital

Before Reading

Preview and Predict

Have students read the Essential Question. Then have them read the title and the table of contents of *The Naming of Athens.* Have students make a prediction about the plot of the play and share it with a partner.

Review Genre: Play

Review with students that a play is a story told through dialogue and is meant to be performed. A play also includes stage directions and scenes. As they preview *The Naming of Athens*, have students identify features of a play.

Leveled Readers

During Reading

Close Reading

Note Taking Have students use their graphic organizer as they read.

Pages 2–3 *What is the root of the word* civilization *on page 3?* (*civil*) *Tell students* civil *refers to a citizen, someone who belongs to a country. Have students use this information to define the words* civilize *and* civilization. (*To civilize* is to make people citizens; *a civilization* is a group of citizens, people who have formed a developed human society.)

Pages 4–7 *Turn to a partner and make a prediction about which god the citizens will choose to name their city for. Why?* (Possible Response: Athena, because we know by the title and the beginning of the play that the city is named Athens.)

Pages 8–11 *What is wrong with Poseidon's gift?* (His supply of water is salty, so people cannot drink it.) *How do the stage directions in Scene Two help you understand the action?* (They tell me how Poseidon gets the water flowing and also help me see how the citizens react badly to the salty water.)

Pages 12–13 *What makes the people choose Athena?* (Her gift is useful and will bring the city wealth.) *What does Athena's gift provide?* (Her gift provides food, oil, firewood; all the things necessary for a good life.)

Fill in the Graphic Organizer

Pages 14–15 *Turn to a partner and summarize the theme of the play.*
(The best gifts are those that help people live a good and healthy life.)
Was your prediction about the city's name correct? Confirm or revise it.
(Possible Response: Yes, because the people chose Athena's gift, and
Cecrops decides the city will be named Athens.)

After Reading

Respond to Reading Revisit the Essential Question, and ask students
to complete the Text Evidence questions on page 16.

Analytical Writing **Write About Reading** Have partners write a short version of
the story in which Poseidon wins. Have students describe what would
be different using details about Poseidon from the play.

Fluency: Expression

Model Model reading page 13 with expression. Next, reread the page
aloud, and have students read along with you.

Apply Have students practice reading with a partner.

PAIRED READ

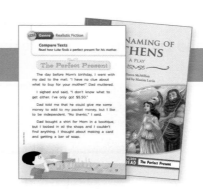

Leveled Reader

"The Perfect Present"

Make Connections: Write About It ✎ *Analytical Writing*

Before reading, have students note
that the genre of this text is realistic fiction, which means it contains
characters and plot events that could exist or occur in real life. Then
discuss the Essential Question.

After reading, have students make connections between the choices
characters made in "The Perfect Present" and *The Naming of Athens.*

✏️ *Analytical Writing*

COMPARE TEXTS

• Have students use text evidence to compare a play
to a story.

Literature Circles

Ask students to conduct a
literature circle using the
Thinkmark questions to guide
the discussion. You may wish to
have a whole-class discussion
on other well-known characters
in literature who have learned
lessons.

Level Up

Level-up
lessons
available
online.

IF students read the `On Level` fluently
and answered the questions

THEN pair them with students who
have proficiently read `Beyond Level` and
have on-level students

• partner-read the `Beyond Level` main
selection.

• list difficult words and look them up
with their partner.

A C T Access Complex Text

The `Beyond Level` challenges students by
including more **domain-specific words**
and **complex sentence structures**.

On Level

Vocabulary

REVIEW VOCABULARY WORDS

OBJECTIVES

 Acquire and use accurately grade-appropriate conversational, general academic, and domain-specific words and phrases, including those that signal spatial and temporal relationships (e.g., *After dinner that night we went looking for them*). **L.3.6**

Review vocabulary words.

I Do Use the **Visual Vocabulary Cards** to review key vocabulary words *alarmed, anguish, necessary, obsessed, possess,* and *reward.* Point to each word, read it aloud, and have students chorally repeat it.

We Do Help students choose a vocabulary word for the sentence frames.

• Caroline did not think it was ____ to buy a new coat.

• One thing I would like to ____ is a new bike.

• The actor expressed his ____ by crying quietly.

You Do Have student pairs complete the frames and explain their answers.

• Were they ____ when the car stalled on the highway?

• Sabrina received a ____ for returning the wallet to its owner.

• Craig and Lucy are ____ with taking photographs.

ROOT WORDS

OBJECTIVES

 Use a known root word as a clue to the meaning of an unknown word with the same root (e.g., *company, companion*). **L.3.4c**

Determine the meaning of unknown words using root words.

I Do Remind students that they can figure out the meaning of an unknown word by identifying the root word, which is the simplest form of a word. Use the Comprehension and Fluency passage on **Your Turn Practice Book** pages 253–254 to determine the meaning of *starvation.*

Think Aloud The root word is *starve.* When you *starve,* you suffer because you are very hungry. The prefix *-ation* means "process" or "state of being." I think *starvation* means "suffering from being very hungry."

We Do Have students continue reading the selection. When they encounter the words *miserable* and *kingdom,* have students figure out the definition of the words by looking at the root words and suffixes. Ask students to think of other words with the root words *king* and *misery.*

You Do Have students work in pairs to determine the meanings of the words *unthreatened, empowerment, fortunate,* and *uninformed* as they read.

Comprehension

REVIEW THEME

OBJECTIVES

 Recount stories, including fables, folktales, and myths from diverse cultures; determine the central message, lesson, or moral and explain how it is conveyed through key details in the text. **RL.3.2**

Determine the theme of the selection.

 I Do

Remind students that the theme of a story is the author's message. The author reveals the theme by providing details about the characters. Tell students to focus on what the characters say and do to find the theme. If the theme is not stated clearly by the narrator or a character, students can identify what it is from other details. As they read, students should ask: *What is the author's message?*

 We Do

Have a volunteer read the first scene of the Comprehension and Fluency passage on **Your Turn Practice Book** pages 253–254. Have students name details about what Prometheus and Zeus say and do. Help them identify which details are key. Then, model explaining how these details support the author's message. Ask: *What reason did Prometheus give Zeus for helping humans? Why do you think it was important for a Titan to help humans?*

 You Do

Have partners identify key details and the author's message in the rest of the play. Then have them come up with the theme of the whole play.

SELF-SELECTED READING

OBJECTIVES

 Recount stories, including fables, folktales, and myths from diverse cultures; determine the central message, lesson, or moral and explain how it is conveyed through key details in the text. **RL.3.2**

• Determine the theme of a selection.

• Make and confirm or revise predictions.

Read Independently

Have students choose a myth, preferably in the form of a play, for sustained silent reading.

• Before they read, have students preview the myth, viewing any illustrations that tell more about the myth.

• As students read, tell them to make predictions about the story. Have them confirm or revise their predictions as they read.

Read Purposefully

Encourage students to read different myths from various cultures.

• As students read, have them fill in **Graphic Organizer 148**. Students should share their organizers and answer these questions: *What was the theme of the myth? Which details helped you determine the theme?*

• They can use their organizer to help them write a summary of the myth.

• Have students share their reactions to the myth with classmates. Ask them if they agree with the message of the myth and explain why.

Beyond Level

Lexile N/A
TextEvaluator™ N/A

OBJECTIVES

 Recount stories, including fables, folktales, and myths from diverse cultures; determine the central message, lesson, or moral and explain how it is conveyed through key details in the text. **RL.3.2**

CCSS Use a known root word as a clue to the meaning of an unknown word with the same root (e.g., *company, companion*). **L.3.4c**

• Make and confirm or revise predictions.
• Identify the theme of the story.

ACADEMIC LANGUAGE
make, confirm, revise predictions, theme, play, word parts, root words, realistic fiction

---

Leveled Reader:
Odysseus and King Aeolus

Before Reading

Preview and Predict

Have students read the Essential Question. Then have them read the title and table of contents of *Odysseus and King Aeolus*. Have students make a prediction about the plot of the play and share it with a partner.

Review Genre: Play

Review with students that a play is a story told through dialogue and is meant to be performed. A play also includes stage directions and scenes. As they preview *Odysseus and King Aeolus*, have students identify features of a play.

During Reading

Close Reading

Note Taking Have students use their graphic organizer as they read.

Pages 2–5 *What is the meaning of* offering *on page 4?* (An *offering* means "something given freely.") **What gives you a clue?** (The root word *offer* means "to give freely," and the use of this word *offering* is a noun.) *How does the author make the dialogue sound realistic?* (The children interrupt their grandfather. Grandfather takes a long time getting to the actual story of Odysseus.) *What story does he end up telling?* (one of the adventures Odysseus had on his trip home)

Pages 6–10 *Make a prediction about what will happen as a result of the sailors' opening the bag. What information are you using to make your prediction?* (Possible Response: Something bad will happen when they open the bag because, on page 8, King Aeolus told Odysseus not to open the bag.)

Page 11 *Was your prediction correct? What helped you confirm or revise your prediction?* (Possible Response: I can confirm my prediction; it says that *the winds caused havoc,* and *the ship was blown farther and farther away from Ithaca.*) *Make a prediction about whether Odysseus will find his way home.* (Possible Response: I think Odysseus will find a way to stop or catch the winds.)

Go
Digital

Leveled Readers

Fill in the
Graphic
Organizer

Pages 12–15 *Was your prediction correct? What helped you confirm or revise your prediction?* (Possible Response: I have to revise my prediction, because Odysseus and the sailors end up back on Aeolia, and they do not get help from King Aeolus.) *Why does King Aeolus not help Odysseus and his crew?* (King Aeolus thinks the gods must be angry with Odysseus to let such a disaster occur.) *Summarize the theme of the play to a partner.* (Possible Response: Without trust, the journey is long and dangerous.)

Literature Circles

Ask students to conduct a literature circle using the Thinkmark questions to guide the discussion. You may wish to have a whole-class discussion on other well-known characters in literature who have learned lessons.

After Reading

Respond to Reading Revisit the Essential Question, and ask students to complete the Text Evidence questions on page 16.

Analytical Writing Write About Reading Have students work with a partner to write a version of the story in which the sailors did not open the bag. Make sure they include details that are different from the story.

Fluency: Expression

Model Model reading page 13 with expression. Next, reread the page aloud, and have students read along with you.

Apply Have students practice reading with a partner.

PAIRED READ

Leveled Reader

"Daria's Dream"

Make Connections: Write About It ✎ *Analytical Writing*

Before reading, have students note that the genre of this text is realistic fiction, which means it contains characters and plot events that could exist or happen in real life. Then discuss the Essential Question.

After reading, have students make connections between the choices characters made in "Daria's Dream" and *Odysseus and King Aeolus*.

Gifted and Talented

Synthesize Challenge students to write about another adventure of Odysseus during his 10-year journey home. Have them write about another time in which Odysseus must make a difficult choice. Invite students to share their stories with the class.

✎ *Analytical Writing*

COMPARE TEXTS

- Have students use text evidence to compare a play to a story.

Beyond Level

Vocabulary

REVIEW DOMAIN-SPECIFIC WORDS

OBJECTIVES

 Produce simple, compound, and complex sentences. **L.3.1i**

Review and discuss domain-specific words.

Model Use the **Visual Vocabulary Cards** to review the meanings of the words *reward* and *possess*. Write social studies related sentences on the board using the words.

Write the words *obsessed, brainstorm,* and *hospitality* on the board, and discuss the meanings with students. Then help students write sentences using these words.

Apply Have students work in pairs to discuss the meanings of the words *generous, honestly,* and *opportunity*. Then have partners write sentences using the words.

ROOT WORDS

OBJECTIVES

 Use a known root word as a clue to the meaning of an unknown word with the same root (e.g., *company, companion*). **L.3.4c**

Determine the meanings of unknown words using root words.

Model Read aloud the first scene of the Comprehension and Fluency passage on **Beyond Reproducibles** pages 253–254.

Think Aloud I want to understand the word *starvation*. I know that the root word is *starve*. When you *starve*, you suffer because you are hungry. The suffix *-ation* means "process" or "state of being." From these clues, I can tell that *starvation* means "suffering from being very hungry."

With students, read the rest of the first page. Help them figure out the meanings of *miserable, kingdom, uninformed,* and *unthreatened* using the root words.

Apply Have pairs of students read the next scene. Ask them to determine the meanings of *empowerment, fortunate,* and any other unfamiliar words.

 Dialogue Have students think of what life would be like without computers. Have students write a scene in which two students discuss the necessity of computers. Students should use two of the following words in the dialogue: *necessary, alarmed, possess, obsessed, wealth,* and *treasure*.

Comprehension

REVIEW THEME

OBJECTIVES

 Recount stories, including fables, folktales, and myths from diverse cultures; determine the central message, lesson, or moral and explain how it is conveyed through key details in the text. **RL.3.2**

Determine the theme of a selection.

 Model Explain that the theme is the author's message. The author reveals the theme through what the characters do and say. If the theme is not stated by the narrator or a character, they can infer it from other details. As they read, students should ask themselves: *What is the author's message?*

Have students read the Comprehension and Fluency passage on **Beyond Reproducibles** pages 253–254. Ask questions to facilitate discussion, such as *How do Prometheus and Zeus feel about humans? What reason does Prometheus give Zeus for helping humans? Why do you think it was important for a Titan to help humans? Which details in the text show why?*

 Apply Have students fill in **Graphic Organizer 148**. Then have partners summarize the author's message. Ask: *Do you agree with the theme? How can you tell the author thinks it is important to help less fortunate people?*

SELF-SELECTED READING

OBJECTIVES

 Recount stories, including fables, folktales, and myths from diverse cultures; determine the central message, lesson, or moral and explain how it is conveyed through key details in the text. **RL.3.2**

• Determine the theme of a selection.

• Make and confirm or revise predictions.

Read Independently

Have students choose a myth for sustained silent reading.

• As students read, have them fill in **Graphic Organizer 148**.

• Remind them to make predictions about the story. Students should confirm or revise their predictions as they read.

Read Purposefully

Encourage students to keep a reading journal. Ask them to read different myths and plays from various cultures.

• Students can write summaries of the stories in their journals.

• Ask students to share their reactions to the stories with classmates. Ask: *What is the theme of the story? Which details support the theme?*

 Independent Study Challenge students to discuss how the stories relate to the weekly theme of deciding what is important. Have students discuss the decisions the main characters make in the stories. Tell students that we make decisions based on what we value. Ask students: *What do you value?* Then have them compare and contrast what is important to them with what is important to the main characters in the stories.

English Language Learners

**Reading/Writing
Workshop**

 OBJECTIVES
Recount stories,
including fables,
folktales, and myths
from diverse cultures;
determine the central
message, lesson, or
moral and explain
how it is conveyed
through key details in
the text. **RL.3.2**

• Use root words
to determine the
meanings of words.

• Make and confirm
or revise predictions.

**LANGUAGE
OBJECTIVE**
Identify the theme of
a story.

**ACADEMIC
LANGUAGE**
• predictions, theme,
myth, drama, root
words

• Cognates:
predicciones, tema,
mito, drama

Shared Read
Athena and Arachne

**View "Athena
and Arachne"**

Before Reading

Build Background

Read the Essential Question: How do you decide what's important?

• Explain the meaning of the Essential Question. Show a picture of
something you value, like a family heirloom. *What do you own that is
most important to you? Why is it important?*

• **Model an answer:** *This quilt is important to me because it reminds
me of my grandmother. When I see it, I think about her sewing it.*

• Ask students a question that ties the Essential Question to their own
background knowledge: *Think about things that are important to you.
Draw a picture of one of those things and share it with a partner. Tell
why it is important to you.* Call on several pairs and have students
present their partner's item.

During Reading

Interactive-Question Response

• Ask questions that help students understand the meaning of the text
after each paragraph.

• Reinforce the meanings of key vocabulary.

• Ask students questions that require them to use key vocabulary.

• Reinforce strategies and skills of the week by modeling.

Page 407

Read the list of characters. Point out that italic text tells about the setting or action in the play.

Scene One

Find the stage directions on the page. Tell a partner one thing you learn from reading them. (The story is set in Greece a long time ago.)

Look at the beginning of Scene One. Who speaks first? (the Narrator) Read Diana's first line, and point to the cloth in the picture. *How does Diana feel about the cloth?* (She is excited.)

Explain and Model Root Words *The root of* beautiful *is* beauty. *It is the word without suffixes or prefixes.* Beauty *means "the quality of being pleasing to the eye."* Demonstrate the meaning of the word by pointing out something beautiful in nature. *The suffix,* -ful, *means "full of." Use this information to figure out what* beautiful *means.* ("full of beauty")

Explain and Model Making Predictions Model making predictions on the first page. *As I read a play, I make guesses about what will happen next based on what I have read. Who does Arachne think she could beat in a weaving competition?* (Athena) *Who is Athena?* (a Greek goddess) *Why does Diana want Arachne to be quiet?* (She is afraid Athena is listening.) *Based on this information, I predict that Athena will ask Arachne to compete. Let's read on to confirm or revise this prediction.*

Page 408

Scene Two
Look at the words in italic at the beginning of Scene Two. Where does it take place? (Mount Olympus, home of Athena) *What does the messenger tell Athena?* (that Arachne is saying she can beat Athena in a weaving competition)

Take turns reading Athena's dialogue, and imitate her reaction to the messenger's news. Help students with vocabulary.

Scene Three
How does Athena look when she knocks on Arachne's door? (She is hiding under a cloak.)

Explain and Model Confirming or Revising Predictions *Now that we know more about the story, let's check our prediction. Was the prediction about the weaving competition correct?* (yes) *How do you know?* Have a student read Athena's line after she drops her cloak on page 408. *Make another prediction about who you think will win.*

Page 409

What does Arachne's cloth show? (pictures of the gods being unkind) *To be* boastful *means "to tell others how great you are." What is Arachne* boastful *about?* (her weaving skills) *How does Athena punish Arachne?* (Athena turns Arachne into a spider.)

Model Theme *The narrator gives us clues to the theme of the play. What does the narrator say about why Athena turned Arachne into a spider?* (because she was mean and boastful) *Fill in the sentence frame to explain the theme: Being mean and boastful can lead to____* (trouble).

Why did Athena punish Arachne this way? (Spiders weave webs.) *Talk to a partner about how you feel about Arachne's punishment.*

After Reading

Make Connections

- Review the Essential Question: How do you decide what's important?

- Make text connections.

- Have students complete the **ELL Reproducibles** pages 253–255.

English Language Learners

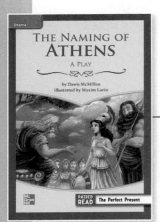

Lexile N/A
TextEvaluator™ N/A

OBJECTIVES

(CCSS) Recount stories, including fables, folktales, and myths from diverse cultures; determine the central message, lesson, or moral and explain how it is conveyed through key details in the text. **RL.3.2**

• Make and confirm or revise predictions.

• Use root words to determine the meanings of words.

LANGUAGE OBJECTIVE
Identify the theme of the story.

ACADEMIC LANGUAGE

• *make, confirm or revise predictions, theme, play, root words, realistic fiction*

• Cognates: *confirmar, revisar, predicciones, tema*

Leveled Reader:
The Naming of Athens

Go Digital

Leveled Readers

Before Reading

Preview

• Read the Essential Question: How do you decide what's important?

• Refer to What We Value: *What is one thing that you value?*

• Preview *The Naming of Athens* and "The Perfect Present": *Let's read about how characters make choices that benefit others.*

Vocabulary

Use the **Visual Vocabulary Cards** to preteach the ELL vocabulary: *beginnings, miracle.* Use the routine found on the cards.

During Reading

Interactive Question-Response

Note Taking Have students use their graphic organizer on **ELL Reproducibles** page 252. Ask the following questions after reading each section. Use visuals or pictures to define key vocabulary.

Pages 2–3 Read the *Reader's* first lines. *What is this play about?* (how Athens got its name)

Page 4 *Why does Poseidon think the city should have his name?* Have one student complete the sentence frame and another verify the answer. *Poseidon says that the city should be named after him because* _____ (he is the god of the sea and the city is surrounded by the ocean).

Page 5 *Look at the word* wisdom *on page 5. The root of this word is* wise. *The suffix* -dom *means "the quality of." Use this information to define* wisdom. *Fill in the sentence frame: Wisdom means* _____ (the quality of being wise).

Pages 6–8 *How will the citizens decide which name to pick?* (The best gift wins.) *What gift do you predict Poseidon and Athena will give the city?* (Possible Response: I predict Poseidon will give a gift from the sea and Athena will give something useful.) *Why?* (Poseidon is god of the sea, and Athena is goddess of wisdom.)

Fill in the Graphic Organizer

Pages 9–11 *Why do the people not like Poseidon's gift?* Have one student answer and another elaborate on the answer. (The water was salty, so people could not drink it.)

Pages 12–15 *Was your prediction about the city's gifts correct? What information helps you confirm or revise your prediction?* (Possible Response: Yes, Poseidon did give a gift from the sea, and Athena did give something useful.) Guide students to what Cecrops says on page 14. *Fill in the frame to find the theme: The best gifts are those that _____* (help you lead a happy life).

After Reading

Respond to Reading Help students complete the graphic organizer. Revisit the Essential Question. Have student pairs summarize and answer the Text Evidence questions. Support students as necessary and review all responses as a group.

Analytical Writing **Write About Reading** Have students work with a partner to write a new ending to the play in which Poseidon is the winner.

Fluency: Expression

Model Model reading page 13 with expression. Next, reread the page aloud, and have students read along with you.

Apply Have students practice reading with a partner.

PAIRED READ

"The Perfect Present"

Make Connections: Write About It · *Analytical Writing*

Leveled Reader

Before reading, have students note that the genre of this text is realistic fiction, which means it has characters, events, and plots that could occur in real life. Then discuss the Essential Question.

After reading, have students make connections between the choices characters made in "The Perfect Present" and *The Naming of Athens*.

Analytical Writing

COMPARE TEXTS

- Have students use text evidence to compare a play to a story.

Literature Circles

Ask students to conduct a literature circle using the Thinkmark questions to guide the discussion. You may wish to have a whole-class discussion on other well-known characters in literature who have learned lessons.

Level Up

Level-up lessons available online.

IF students read the ELL Level fluently and answered the questions

THEN pair them with students who have proficiently read On Level and have ELL students

- echo-read the On Level main selection with their partner.
- list difficult words and discuss them with their partner.

A C T Access Complex Text

The On Level challenges students by including more **domain-specific words** and **complex sentence structures**.

→ English Language Learners
Vocabulary

PRETEACH VOCABULARY

OBJECTIVES
Acquire and use accurately grade-appropriate conversational, general academic, and domain-specific words and phrases, including those that signal spatial and temporal relationships. **L.3.6**

LANGUAGE OBJECTIVE
Use vocabulary words.

 I Do Preteach vocabulary from "Athena and Arachne" following the Vocabulary Routine found on the **Visual Vocabulary Cards** for *alarmed, anguish, necessary, obsessed, possess, reward, treasure,* and *wealth.*

 We Do Complete the Vocabulary Routine for each word, and point to the word on the Visual Vocabulary Card. Next, read the word with students. Ask students to repeat the word. Act out the word using gestures and actions.

 You Do Have students work with a partner to use four words in sentences and draw a picture describing one word. Have each pair read the sentences aloud.

Beginning	Intermediate	Advanced/High
Help students write the sentences and read them aloud.	Ask students to explain the difference between *possess* and *obsessed.*	Challenge students to explain how *treasure* and *wealth* are different.

REVIEW VOCABULARY

OBJECTIVES
Acquire and use accurately grade-appropriate conversational, general academic, and domain-specific words and phrases, including those that signal spatial and temporal relationships. **L.3.6**

LANGUAGE OBJECTIVE
Review vocabulary words.

 I Do Review the previous week's vocabulary words over a few days. Read each word aloud and point to the word on the **Visual Vocabulary Card**. Ask students to repeat after you. Then follow the Vocabulary Routine on the back of each card.

 We Do Act out two vocabulary words for students. Ask students to guess each word you act out. Provide students with a clue, such as a synonym or an antonym, if they cannot guess the word.

 You Do In pairs, have students act out three words. Help students with the clues and suggest appropriate gestures or actions. Have student pairs act out the words for other pairs.

Beginning	Intermediate	Advanced/High
Help students think of ways to act out two of the words.	Have students write a synonym and antonym for each word they act out.	Ask students to write three clues using complete sentences.

ROOT WORDS

CCSS

OBJECTIVES

Use a known root word as a clue to the meaning of an unknown word with the same root (e.g., *company, companion*). **L.3.4c**

LANGUAGE OBJECTIVE

Determine the meanings of unknown words using root words.

 I Do Read aloud the first scene in "Athena and Arachne" on page 407 as students follow along. Point to the word *competition*. Tell students that a root word can often be used to determine the meaning of a word with the same root.

Think Aloud The root word of *competition* is *compete*. I know that *compete* means "to have a contest between people to see who wins." The suffix *-ition* shows an action or process. In the story, Arachne says she could "beat" Athena at weaving. So *competition* means "a contest between two people."

 We Do Have students find the word *possessions* on page 407. Help them find the meaning of the word using its root word. Write the meaning on the board.

 You Do In pairs, have students reread page 408 and find the word *obsession*. Have them figure out its meaning by determining the root word.

Beginning	Intermediate	Advanced/High
Help students determine its meaning by acting out the root word *obsess*.	Ask students to act out and find a synonym for *obsession*.	Challenge students to find an antonym for *obsession* and to use it in a sentence.

ADDITIONAL VOCABULARY

CCSS

OBJECTIVES

Use conventional spellings for high-frequency and other studied words and for adding suffixes to base words (e.g., *sitting, smiled, cries, happiness*). **L.3.2e**

Discuss concept and high-frequency words.

LANGUAGE OBJECTIVE

Use concept and high-frequency words.

 I Do List concept and high-frequency words from "Athena and Arachne": *value, boastful, time;* and *The Naming of Athens: wisdom, to, two*. Define each word for students: A *boastful* person is someone who is not modest, or humble. *Natasha was* boastful *about being the best student in her class.*

 We Do Model using the word *time* for students in a sentence: *Richard uses his free time to help less fortunate people.* Then provide a sentence frame and complete it with students: *At what time would you like to ____?*

 You Do Have pairs write two sentence frames using *to* and *two*. Have students present their sentence frames to the class.

Beginning	Intermediate	Advanced/High
Help students copy the sentence frames correctly.	Have students write sentence frames and provide clues for the class.	Have students also write sentence frames with the words *value* and *wisdom*.

→ English Language Learners
Writing/Spelling

WRITING TRAIT: VARY SENTENCE LENGTHS

OBJECTIVES

CCSS With guidance and support from peers and adults, develop and strengthen writing as needed by planning, revising, and editing. **W.3.5**

Vary sentence lengths.

LANGUAGE OBJECTIVE

Write dialogue using sentences that vary in length.

 I Do Remind students that good writers use long and short sentences to add rhythm to their writing. Varying sentence lengths makes writing more interesting to read. Read the Student Model passage as students follow along, and point to short and long sentences.

 We Do Read aloud scene 1 from "Athena and Arachne" as students follow along. Model identifying and listing various sentence lengths. Have students focus on the rhythm when long and short sentences are both used.

 You Do Have student pairs write a short dialogue in which they discuss a skill they both have. Students should include short and long sentence lengths.

Beginning	Intermediate	Advanced/High
Help students write the edited dialogue.	Have students revise their dialogue checking for varying sentence lengths.	Have students revise sentence lengths and edit for errors.

SPELL WORDS WITH PREFIXES *un-, re-, pre-, mis-, dis-*

OBJECTIVES

CCSS Use spelling patterns and generalizations (e.g., word families, position-based spellings, syllable patterns, ending rules, meaningful word parts) in writing words. **L.3.2f**

LANGUAGE OBJECTIVE

Spell words with prefixes *un-, re-, pre-, mis-,* and *dis-*.

 I Do Read the Spelling Words on T34 aloud, modeling how to pronounce the words. Say and write the word *dislike* on the board. Draw a line between the word parts in *dislike*. Tell students the prefix *dis-* means "not" or "opposite of." Spell out each prefix, and have students repeat.

 We Do Read the Dictation Sentences on page T35 aloud for students. With each sentence, read the underlined word slowly, modeling how to identify and define the prefix. Have students repeat after you and write the word.

 You Do Display the words. Have students exchange their lists with a partner to check the spelling and write the words correctly.

Beginning	Intermediate	Advanced/High
Help students copy the words with correct spelling and say the words aloud.	Have students circle the prefix in each word.	After students correct their words, have them sort the words by prefix.

Grammar

ADJECTIVES AND ARTICLES

OBJECTIVES

 Explain the function of nouns, pronouns, verbs, adjectives, and adverbs in general and their functions in particular sentences. **L.3.1a**

Identify adjectives and articles.

LANGUAGE OBJECTIVE

Use adjectives and articles.

Language Transfers Handbook

Hmong, Spanish, and Vietnamese speakers usually place adjectives after the noun they modify. Have these students describe what they are wearing and model the correct placement of adjectives. Build on the number of adjectives gradually.

 I Do Remind students that an adjective is a word that describes a noun. It usually comes before a noun. Some adjectives tell what kind or how many there are of a person, place, or thing: *We walked through the lovely garden. There are eight boys in the class.* Then explain that limiting adjectives include the words *this, that,* and *those*: *Those waves are strong.* The words *a, an,* and *the* are special adjectives called articles. Use *the* before specific singular and plural nouns: *The man threw the ball.* The articles *a* and *an* are used with nonspecific singular nouns. If the noun or adjective begins with a consonant, use *a*: *A dog ran in the yard.* If the noun or adjective begins with a vowel, use *an*: *It was* an *amazing day.*

We Do Write the sentence frames below on the board. Have volunteers use an adjective or article to complete the sentences.

> We ran out of the ____ house.
>
> ____ cashier put our purchases in ____ bags.
>
> I asked the clerk for ____ interesting book.
>
> ____ painting was sold at an auction.
>
> Jane had a ____ singing voice.

 You Do Have student pairs write sentences describing characters and illustrations in "Athena and Arachne." They should use adjectives and articles.

Beginning	Intermediate	Advanced/High
Describe the illustrations in "Athena and Arachne" using adjectives and articles. Ask: *What do you see in these illustrations?* Have students repeat the sentences.	Ask students to describe the characters in "Athena and Arachne" using adjectives and articles. Have students use complete sentences to describe the characters.	Challenge students to use an adjective and an article in the sentences they write to describe the characters in "Athena and Arachne."

For extra support, have students complete the activities in the **Grammar Practice Reproducibles** during the week, using the routine below:

- Explain the grammar skill.
- Model the first activity in the Grammar Practice Reproducibles.
- Have the whole group complete the next couple of activities, then the rest with a partner.
- Review the activities with correct answers.

PROGRESS MONITORING

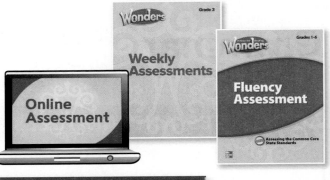

Unit 6 Week 1 Formal Assessment	Standards Covered	Component for Assessment
Text Evidence	RL.3.1	• *Selection Test* • *Weekly Assessment* • *Approaching-Level Weekly Assessment*
Theme	RL.3.2	• *Weekly Assessment* • *Approaching-Level Weekly Assessment*
Root Words	L.3.4c	• *Selection Test* • *Weekly Assessment* • *Approaching-Level Weekly Assessment*
Writing About Text	W.3.8	*Weekly Assessment*
Unit 6 Week 1 Informal Assessment	**Standards Covered**	**Component for Assessment**
Research/Listening/ Collaborating	SL.3.1d, SL.3.2, SL.3.3	• *RWW* • *Teacher's Edition*
Oral Reading Fluency (ORF) **Fluency Goal:** 97–117 words correct per minute (WCPM) **Accuracy Rate Goal:** 95% or higher	RF.3.4a, RF.3.4b, RF.3.4c	*Fluency Assessment*

Using Assessment Results

Weekly Assessments Skills and Fluency	If . . .	Then . . .
COMPREHENSION	Students score below 70% . . .	. . . assign Lessons 34–36 on Theme from the *Tier 2 Comprehension Intervention online PDFs*.
VOCABULARY	Students score below 70% . . .	. . . assign Lesson 155 on Word Parts: Roots, Prefixes and Suffixes from the *Tier 2 Vocabulary Intervention online PDFs*.
WRITING	Students score below "3" on constructed response . . .	. . . assign Lessons 34–36 and/or Write About Reading Lesson 194 from the *Tier 2 Comprehension Intervention online PDFs*.
FLUENCY	Students have a WCPM score of 89–96 . . .	. . . assign a lesson from Section 1, 7, 8, 9 or 10 of the *Tier 2 Fluency Intervention online PDFs*.
	Students have a WCPM score of 0–88 . . .	. . . assign a lesson from Sections 2–6 of the *Tier 2 Fluency Intervention online PDFs*.

Using Weekly Data

Check your data Dashboard to verify assessment results and guide grouping decisions.

Data-Driven Recommendations

Response to Intervention

Use the appropriate sections of the *Placement and Diagnostic Assessment* as well as students' assessment results to designate students requiring:

 Intervention Online PDFs   **WonderWorks Intervention Program**

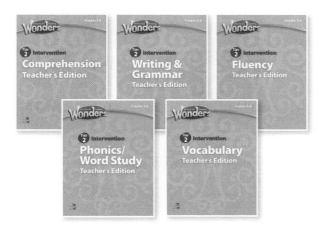

WEEKLY OVERVIEW

Build Knowledge
Weather

? **Essential Question:**
How can weather affect us?

Teach and Model
Close Reading and Writing

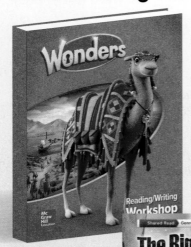

Reading/Writing Workshop

"The Big Blizzard," 420–423
Genre Historical Fiction **Lexile** 690 ETS *TextEvaluator* 43

Practice and Apply
Close Reading and Writing

Literature Anthology

Nora's Ark, 482–501
Genre Historical Fiction **Lexile** 740
ETS *TextEvaluator* 35

"The Wind and the Sun," 504–505
Genre Fable **Lexile** 570 ETS *TextEvaluator* 43

Differentiated Texts

APPROACHING
Lexile 470
ETS *TextEvaluator* 30

ON LEVEL
Lexile 610
ETS *TextEvaluator* 31

BEYOND
Lexile 630
ETS *TextEvaluator* 35

ELL
Lexile 490
ETS *TextEvaluator* 5

Leveled Readers

Extended Complex Texts

The Hurricane Mystery
(Boxcar Children)
Genre Fiction
Lexile 580

Amos and Boris
Genre Fiction
Lexile 810

Classroom Library

Student Outcomes

Close Reading of Complex Text

- Cite relevant evidence from text
- Determine theme
- Make, Confirm, and Revise Predictions

RL.3.1, RL.3.2

Writing

Write to Sources

- Draw evidence from literature
- Write narrative texts
- Conduct short research on the effects of extreme weather

Writing Process

- Draft and Revise a Feature Article

W.3.1a, W.3.8, W.3.10

Speaking and Listening

- Engage in collaborative discussions about weather
- Paraphrase portions of "Joshua's Odd Neighbor" and presentations on weather
- Present information on weather

SL.3.1b, SL.3.1d, SL.3.3

Content Knowledge

- Summarize how scientists record patterns of weather so they can make predictions.

Language Development

Conventions

- Identify and use comparative and superlative adjectives

Vocabulary Acquisition

- Acquire and use academic vocabulary

argue	astonished	complained	conditions
forbid	forecast	relief	stranded

- Demonstrate understanding of idioms

L.3.1g, L.3.5a, L.3.5b, RL.3.4

Foundational Skills

Phonics/Word Study

- Consonant + *le* syllable
- Latin suffixes

Spelling Words

able	purple	riddle	handle
eagle	puzzle	castle	little
pickle	towel	nickel	camel
travel	tunnel	squirrel	

Fluency

- Phrasing

RF.3.3b, RF.3.3c, RF.3.4a

Professional Development

- See lessons in action in real classrooms.
- Get expert advice on instructional practices.
- Collaborate with other teachers.
- Access PLC Resources.

Go Digital! www.connected.mcgraw-hill.com.

INSTRUCTIONAL PATH

1 Talk About Weather

Guide students in collaborative conversations.

Discuss the essential question: *How can weather affect us?*

Develop academic language.

Listen to "Joshua's Odd Neighbor" and discuss the story.

2

Read "The Big Blizzard"

Model close reading with a short complex text.

Read

"The Big Blizzard" to learn how a blizzard affects the Hernandez family in New York City, citing text evidence to answer text-dependent question.

Reread

"The Big Blizzard" to analyze text, craft, and structure, citing text evidence.

Write About "The Big Blizzard"

3

Model writing to a source.

Analyze a short response student model.

Use text evidence from close reading to write to a source.

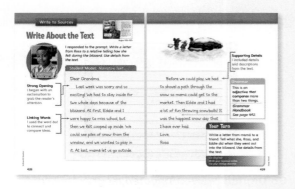

4 Read and Write About *Nora's Ark*

Practice and apply close reading of the anchor text.

Read

Nora's Ark to learn about a farm family that survives a storm and a terrible flood.

Reread

Nora's Ark and use text evidence to understand how the author uses text, craft, and structure to develop a deeper understanding of the story.

Write a short response about ***Nora's Ark***.

Integrate

Information about this story to other stories about the weather.

Write to Two Sources, citing text evidence from ***Nora's Ark*** and "The Wind and the Sun."

5 Independent Partner Work

Gradual release of support to independent work

- Text-Dependent Questions
- Scaffolded Partner Work
  Talk with a Partner
  Cite Text Evidence
  Complete a sentence frame.
- Guided Text Annotation

6 Integrate Knowledge and Ideas

Connect Texts

Text to Text Discuss how each of the texts answers the question: How can weather affect us?

Text to Fine Art Compare how the theme in the texts read is illustrated in the 19th century painting.

Conduct a Short Research Project

Write a summary about the effects of extreme weather.

DEVELOPING READERS AND WRITERS

Write to Sources

Day 1 and Day 2
Build Writing Fluency
- Quick write on "The Big Blizzard," p. T92

Write to a Source
- Analyze a student model, p. T92
- Write about "The Big Blizzard," p. T93
- Apply Writing Trait: Linking Words and Phrases, p. T92
- Apply Grammar Skill: Adjectives That Compare, p. T93

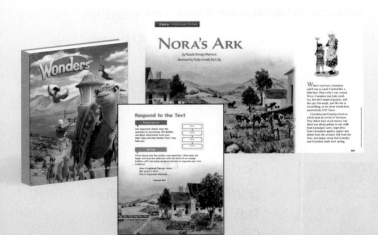

Day 3
Write to a Source
- Write about *Nora's Ark*, independent practice, p. T89V
- Provide scaffolded instruction to meet student needs, p. T94

Day 4 and Day 5
Write to Two Sources
- Analyze a student model, pp. T94–T95
- Write to compare *Nora's Ark* with "The Wind and the Sun," p. T95

WEEK 1: PREWRITE | **WEEK 2: DRAFT AND REVISE** | WEEK 3: PROOFREAD/EDIT, PUBLISH, EVALUATE

Writing Process

Go Digital

Writer's Workspace

Genre Writing: Informative Text

Feature Article
Draft

* Discuss the student draft model
* Students write their drafts

Revise

* Discuss the revised student model
* Students revise their drafts

Revised Student Model

Student Draft

Revised Checklist

Grammar and Spelling Resources

Online PDFs

Reading/Writing Workshop Grammar Handbook p. 492

Online Spelling and Grammar Games

Grammar Practice, pp. 131–135

Phonics/Spelling Practice, pp. 157–162

READING		DAY 1	DAY 2
Teach, Model and Apply	Core	**Introduce the Concept** T74-T75 **Vocabulary** T78-T79 **Close Reading** "The Big Blizzard," T80-T81	**Close Reading** "The Big Blizzard," T80-T81 **Strategy** Make, Confirm, or Revise Predictions, T82-T83 **Skill** Theme, T84-T85 **Vocabulary Strategy** Idioms, T88-T89
Reading/Writing Workshop	Options	**Listening Comprehension** T76-T77	**Genre** Historical Fiction, T86-T87

LANGUAGE ARTS			
Writing **Grammar** **Spelling** **Build Vocabulary**	Core	**Grammar** Adjectives That Compare, T98 **Spelling** Consonant and *le* Syllables, T98 **Build Vocabulary** T100	**Write About the Text** Model Note-Taking and Write to a Prompt, T92-T93 **Grammar** Adjectives That Compare, T96 **Build Vocabulary** T100
	Options	**Write About the Text** Writing Fluency, T92 **Genre Writing** Feature Article: Draft, T346	**Genre Writing** Feature Article and Teach the Draft Minilesson, T349 **Spelling** Consonant + *le* Syllables, T98

Writing Process | **Writing Process: Informative Text** Feature Article, T344-T349   Use with Weeks 1–3

Differentiated Instruction Use your data dashboard to determine each student's needs. Then select instructional support options throughout the week.

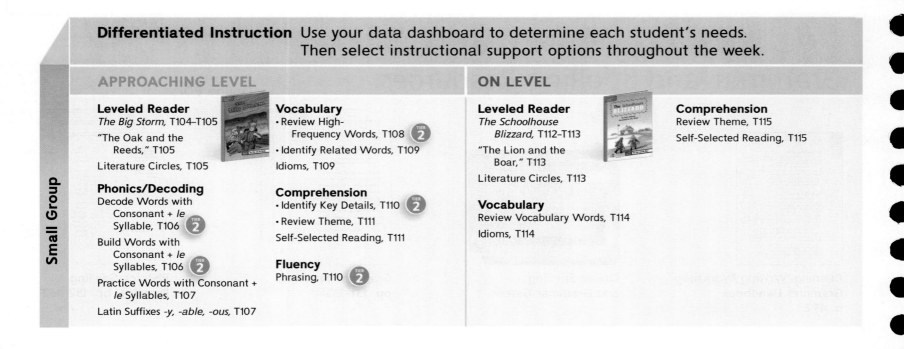

APPROACHING LEVEL

Leveled Reader
The Big Storm, T104-T105
"The Oak and the Reeds," T105
Literature Circles, T105

Phonics/Decoding
Decode Words with Consonant + *le* Syllable, T106 **TIER 2**
Build Words with Consonant + *le* Syllables, T106 **TIER 2**
Practice Words with Consonant + *le* Syllables, T107
Latin Suffixes *-y, -able, -ous,* T107

Vocabulary
• Review High-Frequency Words, T108 **TIER 2**
• Identify Related Words, T109
Idioms, T109

Comprehension
• Identify Key Details, T110 **TIER 2**
• Review Theme, T111
Self-Selected Reading, T111

Fluency
Phrasing, T110 **TIER 2**

ON LEVEL

Leveled Reader
The Schoolhouse Blizzard, T112-T113
"The Lion and the Boar," T113
Literature Circles, T113

Vocabulary
Review Vocabulary Words, T114
Idioms, T114

Comprehension
Review Theme, T115
Self-Selected Reading, T115

DAY 3	DAY 4	DAY 5
Close Reading *Nora's Ark,* T89A–T89V	**Fluency** T91	**Integrate Ideas** T102–T103
	Close Reading "The Wind and the Sun," T89W–T89X	• Text Connections
		• Research and Inquiry
	Integrate Ideas Research and Inquiry, T102–T103	**Weekly Assessment**
Phonics/Decoding T90–T91	**Close Reading** *Nora's Ark,* T89A–T89V	
• Consonant + *le* Syllables, T90		
• Latin Suffixes, T91		

Grammar Adjectives That Compare, T97	**Write About Two Texts** Model Note-Taking and Taking Notes, T94	**Write About Two Texts**
		Analyze Student Model and Write to the Prompt, T95
		Spelling Consonant + *le* Syllables, T99
Write About the Text T94	**Genre Writing** Feature Article: Teach the Minilesson, T348	**Genre Writing** Feature Article: Peer Conferences, T347
Genre Writing Feature Article: Revise, T348	**Grammar** Adjectives That Compare, T97	**Grammar** Adjectives That Compare, T97
Spelling Consonant + *le* Syllables, T99	**Spelling** Consonant + *le* Syllables, T99	**Build Vocabulary** T101
Build Vocabulary T101	**Build Vocabulary** T101	

Writing Process

Writing Process: Informative Text Feature Article, T344–T349   Use with Weeks 1–3

BEYOND LEVEL

Leveled Reader
The Hottest Summer,
T116–T117
"The Swallow and
the Crow," T117
Literature Circles, T117

Vocabulary
Review Domain-Specific Words, T118
• Idioms, T118
• Plan of Action, T118

Gifted and Talented

Comprehension
Review Theme, T119
• Self-Selected Reading, T119
• Independent Study, T119

ENGLISH LANGUAGE LEARNERS

Shared Read
"The Big Blizzard," T120–T121

Leveled Reader
The Schoolhouse Blizzard,
T122–T123
"The Lion and the Boar," T123
Literature Circles, T123

Phonics/Decoding
Decode Words with Consonant + *le*
Syllable, T106
Build Words with Consonant + *le*
Syllables, T106
Practice Words with Consonant + *le*
Syllables, T107
Latin Suffixes -*y,* -*able,* -*ous,* T107

Vocabulary
• Preteach Vocabulary, T124
• Review High-Frequency Words, T108
Review Vocabulary, T188
Idoims, T125
Additional Vocabulary, T125

Spelling
Words with Consonant + *le* Syllables, T126

Writing
Waiting Trait: Word Choice, T126

Grammar
Adjectives That Compare, T127

DIFFERENTIATE TO ACCELERATE

 **Scaffold to Access Complex Text**

IF the text complexity of a particular selection is too difficult for students

THEN see the references noted in the chart below for scaffolded instruction to help students Access Complex Text.

Qualitative Quantitative
Reader and Task
TEXT COMPLEXITY

	Reading/Writing Workshop	Literature Anthology	Leveled Readers		Classroom Library
Quantitative	 **"The Big Blizzard"** **Lexile** 690 *TextEvaluator*™ 43	 ***Nora's Ark*** **Lexile** 740 *TextEvaluator*™ 35 **"The Wind and the Sun"** **Lexile** 570 *TextEvaluator*™ 43	 **Approaching Level** **Lexile** 470 *TextEvaluator*™ 30 **Beyond Level** **Lexile** 630 *TextEvaluator*™ 35	**On Level** **Lexile** 610 *TextEvaluator*™ 31 **ELL** **Lexile** 490 *TextEvaluator*™ 5	***The Hurricane Mystery*** **Lexile** 580 ***Amos and Boris*** **Lexile** 810
Qualitative	**What Makes the Text Complex?** • **Genre** Historical Factor T81 • **Specific Vocabulary** Idioms T89 **ACT** *See Scaffolded Instruction in Teachers Edition T81 and T89.*	**What Makes the Text Complex?** • **Specific Vocabulary** Unfamiliar Words T89B, T89F, T89G, T89O • **Connection of Ideas** Synthesize T89C, T89E, T89G, T89I, T89K • **Genre** Fables T89W–T89X • Sentence Structure T89M • **Prior Knowledge** Story of Noah's Ark T89Q • **Organization** Foreshadowing T89C–T89D; Sequence T89S **ACT** *See Scaffolded Instruction in Teachers Edition T89A–T89X.*	**What Makes the Text Complex?** • **Specific Vocabulary** • **Sentence Structure** • **Connection of Ideas** • **Genre** **ACT** *See Level Up lessons online for Leveled Readers.*		**What Makes the Text Complex?** • **Genre** • **Specific Vocabulary** • **Prior Knowledge** • **Sentence Structure** • **Organization** • **Purpose** • **Connection of Ideas** **ACT** *See Scaffolded Instruction in Teachers Edition T360–T361.*
Reader and Task	The Introduce the Concept lesson on pages T74–T75 will help determine the reader's knowledge and engagement in the weekly concept. See pages T80–T89 and T102–T103 for questions and tasks for this text.	The Introduce the Concept lesson on pages T74–T75 will help determine the reader's knowledge and engagement in the weekly concept. See pages T89A–T89X and T102–T103 for questions and tasks for this text.	The Introduce the Concept lesson on pages T74–T75 will help determine the reader's knowledge and engagement in the weekly concept. See pages T104–T105, T112–T113, T116–T117, T122–T123, and T102–T103 for questions and tasks for this text.		The Introduce the Concept lesson on pages T74–T75 will help determine the reader's knowledge and engagement in the weekly concept. See pages T360–T361 for questions and tasks for this text.

Monitor and *Differentiate*

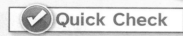

✓ Quick Check

To differentiate instruction, use the Quick Checks to assess students' needs and select the appropriate small group instruction focus.

Comprehension Strategy Make Predictions T83
Comprehension Skill Theme T85
Genre Historical Fiction T87
Vocabulary Strategy Idioms T89
Phonics/Fluency Consonant + *le*, Phrasing T91

If No →	Approaching Level	**Reteach** T104–T111
	ELL	**Develop** T120–T127
If Yes →	On Level	**Review** T112–T115
	Beyond Level	**Extend** T116–T119

Using Weekly Data

Check your data Dashboard to verify assessment results and guide grouping decisions.

Level Up with Leveled Readers

IF → students can read their leveled text fluently and answer comprehension questions

THEN → work with the next level up to accelerate students' reading with more complex text.

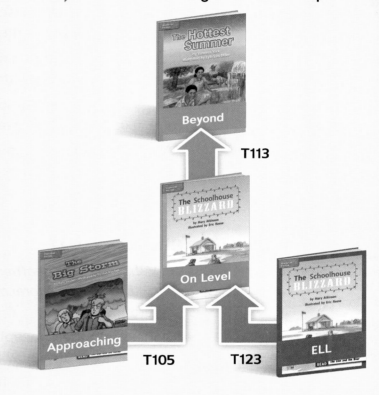

Beyond

T113

On Level

Approaching   T105   T123   ELL

ELL ENGLISH LANGUAGE LEARNERS

Small Group Instruction

Use the ELL small group lessons in the Wonders Teacher's Edition to provide focused instruction.

Language Development
Vocabulary preteaching and review, additional vocabulary building, and vocabulary strategy lessons, pp. T124–T125

Close Reading
Interactive Question-Response routines for scaffolded text-dependent questioning for reading and rereading the Shared Read and Leveled Reader, pp. T120–T123

Writing
Focus on the weekly writing trait, grammar skills, and spelling words, pp. T126–T127

Additional ELL Support

Use *Reading Wonders for English Learners* for ELD instruction that connects to the core.

Language Development
Ample opportunities for discussions, and scaffolded language support

Close Reading
Companion Worktexts for guided support in annotating text and citing text evidence. Differentiated Texts about the weekly concept.

Writing
Scaffolded instruction for writing to sources and revising student models

Reading Wonders for ELLs Teacher Edition and Companion Worktexts

→ Introduce the Concept

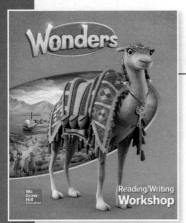

Reading/Writing Workshop

MINILESSON 10 Mins
Build Background

ESSENTIAL QUESTION
How can weather affect us?

Have students read the Essential Question on page 416 of the **Reading/Writing Workshop**. Tell them that a *forecast* tells about the weather.

Discuss the main idea and details in the photo with students. Focus on how weather *conditions* affect us.

• How's the weather outside? You can look out the window to find out, or you can look at the weather forecast.

• Weather conditions can change and affect us every day. They can affect how we dress. They can affect what we do. They can also affect the way we live.

Talk About It

Ask: *What are the weather conditions like outside? Why is it important to know the weather forecast?* Have students discuss in pairs or small groups.

• Model using the Concept Web to generate words and phrases related to the weather and how it affects us. Add students' contributions.

• Have partners continue the discussion by talking about how the weather has affected them in the past. They can complete the Concept Webs, generating additional words and phrases.

Collaborative Conversations

Listen Carefully As students engage in partner, small-group, and whole-class discussions, encourage them to

• always look at the person who is speaking.

• respect others by not interrupting them.

• repeat peers' ideas to check understanding.

• speak in complete sentences when you are clarifying or adding details.

Go Digital

Discuss the Concept

Watch Video

View Photos

Use Graphic Organizer

BLAST BACK!

studysync
Assign Blast

Weekly Concept Weather

Essential Question
How can weather affect us?

Go Digital!

WEATHER AFFECTS US

How's the weather? Turn on the weather report or look outdoors to find out. Is it sunny? Is it raining? It's important to know what the weather is. What's today's forecast? Warm and rainy with a side of fun.

▶ Weather is what is happening outdoors right now.
▶ It affects how we dress and what we do.
▶ Sometimes severe weather affects the way we live.

Talk About It

Write words you have learned about weather. Talk with a partner about how weather affects you.

Weather

416
417

READING/WRITING WORKSHOP, pp. 416–417

BLAST BACK! studysync

Share the Blast assignment. Point out that you will discuss students' responses during the **Integrate Ideas** lesson at the end of the week.

 ENGLISH LANGUAGE LEARNERS SCAFFOLD

Beginning	Intermediate	Advanced/High
Use Visuals Point to the picture. Say: *It is rainy in the picture. The weather conditions affect the way the children dress. How are the children dressed?* (they wear raincoats and rain boots) Have students ask one question about the weather. Correct students' pronunciation as needed.	**Describe** Have students describe the picture. Ask: *What are the weather conditions in the picture?* (rainy) *How does this affect the children?* (they wear raincoats) Elicit details to further develop students' responses.	**Discuss** Have partners discuss what the weather is like outside. Ask: *What are the weather conditions like outside?* Encourage students to use the concept words in their discussions. Correct their responses for meaning as needed.

GRAPHIC ORGANIZER 62

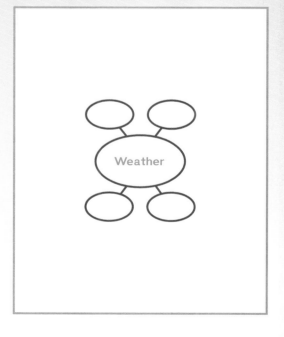

Weather

→ Listening Comprehension

MINILESSON
10 Mins

Interactive Read Aloud

OBJECTIVES

CCSS Recount stories, including fables, folktales, and myths from diverse cultures; determine the central message, lesson, or moral and explain how it is conveyed through key details in the text. **RL.3.2**

CCSS Determine the main ideas and supporting details of a text read aloud or information presented in diverse media and formats, including visually, quantitatively, and orally. **SL.3.2**

• Listen for a purpose.
• Identify characteristics of historical fiction.

ACADEMIC LANGUAGE
• historical fiction; make, confirm, and revise predictions
• Cognates: ficción histórica, predecir

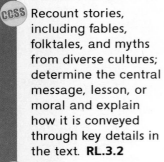

Connect to Concept: Weather

Tell students that weather is around us every day and can affect people and what they do. Let students know that you will be reading aloud a story about a boy who witnesses a historic event in the middle of a storm. As students listen, have them think about how the story answers the essential question.

Preview Genre: Historical Fiction

Explain that the story you will read aloud is historical fiction. Discuss features of historical fiction:

• is based on a historical event
• contains a mix of fiction and historical fact
• is set in a real time and place in history

Preview Comprehension Strategy: Make, Confirm, and Revise Predictions

Point out that readers can use clues in the story to make logical predictions about what might happen next in a text. As they continue to read, they may confirm or revise their original predictions and make new ones based on what they have learned.

Use the Think Alouds on page T77 to model the strategy.

Respond to Reading

Think Aloud Clouds Display Think Aloud Master 3: *I predicted ____ because . . .* to reinforce how you used the make, confirm, and revise predictions strategy to understand content.

Genre Features With students, discuss the elements of the Read Aloud that let them know it is historical fiction. Ask them to think about other texts you have read aloud or they have read independently that were historical fiction.

Summarize Have students determine the key details and explain how they convey the central message of the story. Then, have them briefly recount "Joshua's Odd Neighbor" in their own words.

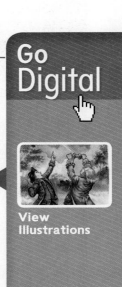

Go Digital

View Illustrations

I predicted ____ because...

Model Think Alouds

Genre	Features

Fill in Genre Chart

Joshua's Odd Neighbor

Joshua sat in the window seat on the third floor of his house. It was his favorite place to read and think. But, he had to admit, it was also the perfect place to spy on his rather odd neighbor, Mr. Benjamin Franklin.

Joshua knew this wasn't a nice thing to do, but Mr. Ben Franklin was always up to something. And it was always so interesting! Just then heavy rain began to pelt the window. "Too bad!" Joshua thought as he looked up at the dark clouds. I don't suppose my neighbor will be outside in this storm. **1**

Suddenly, Joshua saw the back door fly open. Mr. Franklin, along with his son, William, ran out onto the lawn. Mr. Franklin was holding a kite. "They're going to fly a kite! In this weather!" thought Joshua. He pressed his nose even closer to the window and looked down onto his neighbor's backyard.

And that's when Ben Franklin saw the boy. He gave a wave and made a motion for him to open his window. "Hello, Joshua!" shouted Ben Franklin above the howl of the wind. Joshua waved back, feeling ashamed that he had been caught spying.

"Prepare to see history!" Mr. Franklin shouted over the rumble of thunder. "It is my belief that lightning is no more than electricity! I hope to prove it today when lightning strikes the key on my kite!" **2**

Joshua saw the kite fly as high as the treetops, trailing a silk tail. Attached to the kite string was a metal key. Suddenly, the sky lit up in a blazing flash of lightning. Mr. Franklin quickly pulled down the kite. "When I touch the key," he shouted, "I should feel an electric shock. This will prove that lightning is electrical." Joshua was certain that his mouth was hanging open as Mr. Franklin grabbed the key. The man winced and quickly dropped it. "It's true! My experiment is a success!" shouted Ben Franklin. **3**

Just as quickly as they had run outside, Mr. Franklin and his son ran back into the house. Joshua sat shaking his head, wondering if he had really just witnessed history as his neighbor had said.

1 Think Aloud I can think about what Joshua is doing and **make a prediction** about what might happen. I **predict** Joshua will see Ben Franklin even though a storm is coming. After I read, I can **confirm my prediction**.

2 Think Aloud My first **prediction** was correct. Now I wonder if Ben Franklin's experiment will be a success. I predict it will not be successful, because I don't understand how a kite and a key can tell anything about electricity.

3 Think Aloud My second **prediction** was incorrect. Ben Franklin proved that lightning was electricity. After lightning struck the key on the kite, Franklin was able to feel an electric shock when he touched the key. Now I understand why he attached a key to his kite.

Yellow Dog Productions/Digital Vision/Getty Images

→ Vocabulary

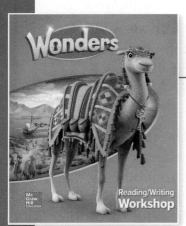

Reading/Writing Workshop

OBJECTIVES

CCSS Determine the meaning of words and phrases as they are used in a text, distinguishing literal from nonliteral language. **RL.3.4**

CCSS Identify real-life connections between words and their use (e.g., describe people who are *friendly* or *helpful*). **L.3.5b**

• Learn meanings of new vocabulary words.

• Write questions using new words.

ACADEMIC LANGUAGE
• *forecast, conditions*
• Cognate: *condiciones*

MINILESSON 10 Mins

Words in Context

Model the Routine

Introduce each vocabulary word using the Vocabulary Routine found on the **Visual Vocabulary Cards.**

Visual Vocabulary Cards

Vocabu...
Define:
Example:
Ask:

> **Vocabulary Routine**
>
> <u>Define:</u> **Conditions** are the state or circumstances something is in.
>
> <u>Example:</u> Mark's umbrella was ruined by the windy conditions.
>
> <u>Ask:</u> What are the weather conditions today?

Go Digital

conditions

Use Visual Glossary

Definitions

• **argue**   To **argue** means to express a difference of opinion or to disagree.

• **astonished**   When people are **astonished**, they are surprised or amazed.

• **complained**   When people **complain**, they make an accusation or a charge.

• **forbidding**   **Forbidding** means prohibiting or ordering someone or something to not do something.

• **forecast**   A **forecast** is a statement that tells what will or may happen.

• **relief**   **Relief** is the freeing from discomfort or pain.

• **stranded**   When people are **stranded**, they are left in a helpless position.

Talk About It

COLLABORATE

Have students work with a partner and look at each picture and discuss the definition of each word. Then ask students to choose three words and write questions for their partner to answer.

Words to Know

Vocabulary

Use the picture and the sentence to talk with a partner about each word.

argue James and his grandfather sometimes discuss movies and **argue** about them.

What are some words that mean the opposite of *argue*?

astonished Tammy and Kim were **astonished** and amazed at the big bug they found.

What is another word for *astonished*?

complained Ben **complained** about his dinner because he didn't like peas.

Tell about a time when you complained about something.

conditions Mark's umbrella was ruined by the windy **conditions**.

What are the weather conditions today?

418

forbidding This sign is **forbidding** us to swim in the pond.

Think of some words that mean the same as *forbidding*.

forecast The weatherman says that the **forecast** today is sunny and warm.

Why do you look at a weather forecast?

relief It was a **relief** that Mom found my dog, and he was okay.

Tell about a time when you felt relief.

stranded Patricia was **stranded** at home during the rainstorm.

Why might you be stranded in bad weather?

Your Turn

COLLABORATE

Pick three words. Write three questions for your partner to answer.

Go Digital! Use the online visual glossary

419

READING/WRITING WORKSHOP, *pp. 418–419*

ELL ENGLISH LANGUAGE LEARNERS SCAFFOLD

Beginning

Use Visuals Say: *Look at the picture. The wind ruined Mark's umbrella. The weather conditions are windy.* Point out the window. *What are the weather conditions today?* Have students repeat after you: *The weather conditions are ____.* Correct pronunciation as needed.

Intermediate

Describe Point to the picture for *conditions* and read the sentence. Ask: *What are the weather conditions today?* Have students complete the frame: *The weather conditions are ____ and ____.* Elicit details to develop students' responses.

Advanced/High

Discuss Ask students to talk about the picture with a partner and write a definition. Then have pairs use each vocabulary word in a sentence and share one sentence with the class. Correct the meaning of students' responses as needed.

ON-LEVEL PRACTICE BOOK p. 261

| forecast | relief | forbidding | stranded |
| argue | astonished | conditions | complained |

Finish each sentence using the vocabulary word provided.
Possible responses provided.

1. **(stranded)** When the bus wouldn't start, we were *stranded* three miles away from school

2. **(conditions)** During the winter months the *conditions* are often icy and cold

3. **(argue)** It is not polite to *argue* with someone who has a different opinion

4. **(forbidding)** There was a large sign *forbidding* people from walking their dogs on the beach

5. **(complained)** After the terrible movie everyone *complained* and wished they had gone to see something else

6. **(relief)** When the long race ended we were filled with *relief,* especially since we won

7. **(astonished)** My classmates were *astonished* when I brought my pet snake to the picnic

8. **(forecast)** This week the *forecast* calls for rain on Friday

| APPROACHING | BEYOND | ELL |
| p. 261 | p. 261 | p. 261 |

Shared Read | Genre • Historical Fiction

The Big Blizzard

Essential Question

How can weather affect us?

Read how a blizzard affects the Hernandez family in New York City.

420

Rosa and Eddie Hernandez huddled close to the radio and listened carefully to the scratchy voice of the news announcer.

"The blizzard of 1947 is the biggest snowstorm in New York City history! Tremendous amounts of snow and terrible weather **conditions** caused the city's subway system to shut down yesterday from Wall Street to Spanish Harlem. Parents are even **forbidding** their children to go outside because it is so dangerous. The weather **forecast** for today predicts that the snow will stop. In the meantime, Mayor O'Dwyer's message to all New Yorkers is this: Help each other in the face of this disaster."

"Oh, mamá!" whispered Rosa. "Will papá ever get home from work?"

Mamá gave Rosa a big hug. "He must be stuck at work and unable to get home," she said. "He is **stranded**, but don't worry. The snow is slowing down now, and I'm sure he will make it home soon."

Mamá went into the kitchen to make lunch. She came out carrying her coat and scarf.

"We are out of milk and bread, so I need to try to get to Maria's Market," said mamá.

Rosa and Eddie jumped up and begged to go with her. Mamá had kept them inside for two days because it was snowing too hard to go out.

"No," said mamá. "It's too cold."

421

READING/WRITING WORKSHOP, *pp. 420–421*

Shared Read

CLOSE READING

Lexile 690   *TextEvaluator*™ 43

Wonders

Reading/Writing Workshop

Reading/Writing Workshop

See pages T120–T121 for Interactive Question-Response routine for the Shared Read.

Close Reading Routine

Read   DOK 1–2

• Identify key ideas and details about Weather.
• Take notes and summarize.
• Use **A C T** prompts as needed.

Reread   DOK 2–3

• Analyze the text, craft, and structure.
• Use the Reread minilessons.

Integrate   DOK 4

• Integrate knowledge and ideas.
• Make text-to-text connections.
• Use the Integrate lesson.

Read

Connect to Concept: Weather Tell students that they will read about how a family deals with a snowstorm in 1947.

Note Taking Read page 421 together. As you read, model how to take notes. *I will think about the Essential Question as I read and note key ideas and details.* Encourage students to note words they don't understand and questions they have.

Paragraph 2: Reread page 421 together. Ask: *What is happening in New York City?*

There is a blizzard in New York City. It is dangerous, so children have to stay indoors. The forecast says the snow will stop, but the mayor wants everyone to help one another.

Rosa and Eddie knew they shouldn't **argue** with mamá, but they were tired of being indoors.

"Oh please, take us outside! We can all go to the store together!" said Eddie.

"Okay," said mamá with a sigh. "But we have to stick together and stay close to each other."

Mamá helped Rosa and Eddie bundle up in their uncomfortable, but warm, wool clothes. When they got outside, they were **astonished** and amazed to find a wall of snow several feet high! Luckily, their neighbor Mr. Colón arrived with two metal shovels.

"Who wants to help dig out?" he asked.

Mamá, Rosa, and Eddie took turns shoveling snow. It was hard work, but no one fussed or **complained**. When they were done, they looked across the street. Maria's Market was still snowed in. Mrs. Sanchez, the owner, was trying to clear the snow with a small broom.

"Mr. Colón, may we borrow your shovels, *por favor*?" asked Rosa. "I think we need to give Mrs. Sanchez a hand."

422

Shoveling the walk in front of the store was easy. It was a piece of cake for Rosa and Eddie. They laughed and threw snowballs, too. Mrs. Sanchez was grateful for their help. "*Gracias*," she said, and gave mamá milk and bread from her store as thanks.

As Rosa and Eddie crossed the snowy street with mamá to go home, they heard a deep, familiar voice.

"Is that my Rosa and Eddie?"

"Papá!" they shouted and ran over to him. Rosa told him breathlessly about how they helped Mr. Colón and Mrs. Sanchez.

"It is such a **relief** and a comfort to finally be home," said papá. "I am so proud of you for helping our neighbors."

Make Connections

? How does the weather affect the Hernandez family? ESSENTIAL QUESTION

Tell about a time when you or your family helped out in bad weather. TEXT TO SELF

Stacey Schuett

423

READING/WRITING WORKSHOP, *pp. 422–423*

Page 422: Model how to summarize page 422. Remind students that retelling a character's actions can help you understand the story.

Rosa and Eddie ask Mamá if they can go with her to the store. There is a big wall of snow outside. Mr. Colón digs them out. They see that Maria's Market is snowed in, so Rosa asks Mr. Colón if she can borrow his shovels to help Mrs. Sanchez.

Make Connections
COLLABORATE

Essential Question Encourage students to work with a partner to discuss how the weather affects the Hernandez family. Ask them to cite text evidence. Use these sentence frames to focus discussion:

> *The weather outside was . . .*
> *Mamá, Rosa, and Eddie went to . . .*

A C T Access Complex Text

▶ **Genre**

Some students may have difficulty distinguishing between real and fictional elements in historical fiction.

- *Point out that the blizzard of 1947 really happened. The entire New York City subway system was shut down. Total snowfall measured 26.4 inches.*

- *Mayor O'Dwyer, who is mentioned in the story, was the mayor at the time of the blizzard. The Hernandez family and their neighbors are fictional.*

→ Comprehension Strategy

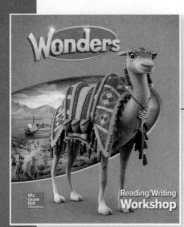

Reading/Writing Workshop

Wonders
Reading/Writing
Workshop
McGraw Hill Education

OBJECTIVES

CCSS Ask and answer questions to demonstrate understanding of a text, referring explicitly to the text as the basis for the answers. **RL.3.1**

CCSS Recount stories, including fables, folktales, and myths from diverse cultures; determine the central message, lesson, or moral and explain how it is conveyed through key details in the text. **RL.3.2**

Use text clues to make, confirm, and revise predictions.

ACADEMIC LANGUAGE

prediction, details, illustrations

MINILESSON 10 Mins

Make, Confirm, and Revise Predictions

1 Explain

Explain that when students read a story they should pay attention to the clues given in the text to make predictions. Tell students that making predictions will help them better understand what is happening in the story.

- Good readers use details and clues from the story's text and its illustrations to make predictions.

- Students may stop to confirm or revise their predictions if necessary.

- Making predictions will help students understand why a character says certain things and acts in certain ways.

Point out that making predictions will help students follow and remember the events in a story.

2 Model Close Reading: Text Evidence

Model how to use details from page 421 to make a prediction about *Papá*. Point out the details that help support the prediction.

3 Guided Practice of Close Reading

Have students work in pairs to discuss the predictions they made after Mr. Colón arrived with two metal shovels. Direct them to tell what clues in the text led to their predictions. Have partners reread page 422 and discuss whether their original predictions had been confirmed or if they needed to revise their predictions. Have students discuss how the details they used to confirm their predictions added to their understanding of the story's main lesson.

Go Digital

View "The Big Blizzard"

Comprehension Strategy

Make Predictions

Use details in the story to tell, or predict, what happens next. Was your prediction right? Read on to check it. Change it if it is not right.

Find Text Evidence

You may have made a prediction about *papá* as you read "The Big Blizzard." What details on page 421 helped you tell what might happen?

page 421

Street to Spanish Harlem. Parents are even forbidding their children to go outside because it is so dangerous. The weather **forecast** for today predicts that the snow will stop. In the meantime, Mayor O'Dwyer's message to all New Yorkers is this: Help each other in the face of this disaster."

"Oh, mamá!" whispered Rosa. "Will papá ever get home from work?"

Mamá gave Rosa a big hug. "He must be stuck at work and unable to get home," she said. "He is **stranded**, but don't worry. The snow is slowing down now, and I'm sure he will make it home soon."

Mamá went into the kitchen to make lunch. She came out carrying her coat and scarf.

I predicted that papá would come home soon. I read that the radio announcer said the snow would stop. Mamá told Rosa that she was sure he would make it home soon. I will read on to check my prediction.

Your Turn

COLLABORATE

What did you predict would happen when Mr. Colón arrived with two metal shovels? Read page 422. Was your prediction correct? Did it need to be revised?

Stacey Schuett

424

READING/WRITING WORKSHOP, *p. 424*

Monitor and *Differentiate*

✓ Quick Check

Did students make predictions when Mr. Colón arrived? Did they confirm or revise their predictions as necessary?

⬇

Small Group Instruction

If No → | Approaching Level | Reteach p. T104

ELL | Develop p. T120

If Yes → | On Level | Review p. T112

Beyond Level | Extend p. T116

Read the passage. Use the make predictions strategy to check your understanding as you read.

Warm Enough for Wheat

I live on a farm in the Middle Colonies. Living here is
12 what I have always known. I was the first of my family born
25 here. My parents and two sisters came here from England,
35 though. I often ask Father what life was like before I was born.
48 He's always so proud to tell me. My family was brave to leave
61 all they knew to start a new life here. Strangely enough, it was
74 the weather that helped my family decide where they would live
85 in this new land.
89   My father likes adventure. Mother says that if he isn't
99 exploring, Father is at sixes and sevens and he doesn't know
110 what to do with himself! So when my Uncle Charles moved to
122 New England, Father knew it was time for a change, too. Moving
134 to New England would mean adventure and a new life.
144   When my family came to New England, they lived with Uncle
155 Charles for a few months. Uncle Charles had become a fisherman
166 in New England. Since it was so cold in the winter, it was hard
180 to have a farm. Many people there were fishermen because it
191 was more reliable for them to fish than to grow food. They could
204 trade the fish for other food. Trying to grow crops in the rocky
217 soil that was covered in snow for months at a time was difficult.

| APPROACHING | BEYOND | ELL |
| pp. 263–264 | pp. 263–264 | pp. 263–264 |

ENGLISH LANGUAGE LEARNERS SCAFFOLD

Beginning

Monitor Reread the second paragraph of page 421. Say: *The blizzard, or snowstorm, is the biggest one New York City ever had. People need to help each other in the face of this disaster.* In the face of *means "during" or "despite."* Have students ask one question they have about New York City or the blizzard.

Intermediate

Describe Have students reread page 421. Ask: *What is the mayor's message during the blizzard?* (people should help each other) Point out why this text is confusing. In the face of *can have different meanings. In this case, it means "during" or "against."*

Advanced/High

Discuss Have students reread page 421. Elicit from students why the text is confusing. Ask: *What does the author mean by saying that Mayor O'Dwyer's message to all New Yorkers is to help each other in the face of this disaster?* Have students discuss with partners. Elicit details to develop their responses.

→ Comprehension Skill

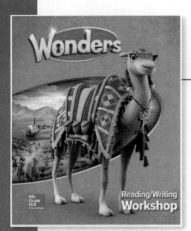

Reading/Writing Workshop

OBJECTIVES

 Recount stories, including fables, folktales, and myths from diverse cultures; determine the central message, lesson, or moral and explain how it is conveyed through key details in the text. **RL.3.2**

Identify the theme in historical fiction.

ACADEMIC LANGUAGE
theme, characters, inferences, summary

Theme

1 Explain

Explain to students that authors often have a message for the reader. This is the **theme** of a story. It tells what the author thinks about the main idea.

- To identify the theme, students should look for details in the actions and words of the characters.

- Students can recount the story to determine the central message, lesson, or moral and explain how it is conveyed through details in the text.

- Students can make inferences about theme based on the details found in the text.

2 Model Close Reading: Text Evidence

Identify the key details in the actions of the characters in "The Big Blizzard." Then model using the graphic organizer to figure out the theme supported by the details.

 Write About Reading: Summary Model for students how to use the notes from the graphic organizer to write a summary of the theme of "The Big Blizzard."

3 Guided Practice of Close Reading

 Have students work in pairs to find more important details and add them to the graphic organizer for "The Big Blizzard." Remind students to use the details to determine the theme of the story.

 Write About Reading: Summary Have pairs work together to write a summary about the theme of "The Big Blizzard." Encourage students to include key details in the text that support the theme.

Go Digital

Present the Lesson

SKILLS TRACE

THEME

Introduce Unit 2 Week 1

Review Unit 2 Weeks 2, 6; Unit 3 Week 6; Unit 4 Weeks 5, 6; Unit 6 Weeks 1, 2, 6

Assess Units 2, 4, 6

Comprehension Skill

Theme

The theme of a story is the author's message. Think about what the characters do and say. This will help you figure out the theme.

 Find Text Evidence

In "The Big Blizzard," Mayor O'Dwyer tells New Yorkers to help one another. I think this is an important detail about the theme. I will read to find more details about the characters' actions. Then I can figure out the story's theme.

> **Detail**
> Mayor O'Dwyer's message to all New Yorkers is, "Help one another in the face of this disaster."
>
> ↓
>
> **Detail**
> The Hernandez family helps Mr. Colón shovel snow.
>
> ↓
>
> **Detail**
>
> ↓
>
> **Detail**
>
> ↓
>
> **Theme**

Your Turn

Reread "The Big Blizzard." Find more important details and write them in your graphic organizer. Then use the details to figure out the theme.

Go Digital!
Use the interactive graphic organizer

425

READING/WRITING WORKSHOP, *p. 425*

ENGLISH LANGUAGE LEARNERS SCAFFOLD

Beginning

Recognize Reread the second paragraph on page 421. Point out important details and explain that the last sentence is an important detail that tells about the theme. Have students complete the frame: ____ *is an important detail that tells about the theme.* Correct students' responses for meaning and pronunciation as needed.

Intermediate

Describe Reread the second paragraph on page 421. Ask: *What is an important detail that tells about the theme? How do you know? Explain to a partner.* Then have partners describe the important detail that tells about the theme. ____ *is an important detail because ____.* Elicit details to develop students' responses.

Advanced/High

Discuss Have students review the details in "The Big Blizzard" that help them discover the theme of the story. Ask: *Based on these details, what might be the theme of "The Big Blizzard"?* Have partners discuss how these clues support the theme. Encourage them to use vocabulary words.

Monitor and *Differentiate*

 Quick Check

As students complete the graphic organizer for "The Big Blizzard," are they able to identify the theme of the story?

⬇

Small Group Instruction

If No → | Approaching Level | Reteach p. T111

| ELL | Develop p. T121

If Yes → | On Level | Review p. T115

| Beyond Level | Extend p. T119

ON-LEVEL PRACTICE BOOK pp. 263–265

A. Reread the passage and answer the questions.
Possible responses provided.

1. In paragraph 1, what does the narrator say helped the family decide where they would move?

   The weather helped the family decide where to move.

2. What are two reasons the family moved from New England to the Middle Colonies?

   The father was not good at fishing. Father and Mother both wanted a farm, and it was easier to have a farm in the Middle Colonies.

3. What is the theme of this story?

   The theme is that making good choices helps a person to be happy.

B. Work with a partner. Read the passage aloud. Pay attention to phrasing. Stop after one minute. Fill out the chart.

	Words Read	–	Number of Errors	=	Words Correct Score
First Read		–		=	
Second Read		–		=	

APPROACHING pp. 263–265	BEYOND pp. 263–265	ELL pp. 263–265

→ Genre: Literature

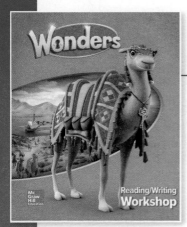

Reading/Writing Workshop

OBJECTIVES

CCSS Recount stories, including fables, folktales, and myths from diverse cultures; determine the central message, lesson, or moral and explain how it is conveyed through key details in the text. **RL.3.2**

CCSS Explain how specific aspects of a text's illustrations contribute to what is conveyed by the words in a story (e.g., create mood, emphasize aspects of a character or setting). **RL.3.7**

Recognize the characteristics and features of historical fiction.

ACADEMIC LANGUAGE

• *historical fiction, illustrations*

• Cognates: *ficción histórica, ilustraciones*

Historical Fiction

1 Explain

Share the following characteristics of **historical fiction**.

• It is a made-up story that takes place in the past.

• Characters and events may be made-up.

• Setting is a real place in the past.

• Some events may be real events from history. In "The Big Blizzard," the blizzard is a famous storm that occurred in 1947 in New York City.

Point out to students that illustrations can help them understand details from a time and place in history.

2 Model Close Reading: Text Evidence

Model identifying and using literary elements and illustrations on page 422 of "The Big Blizzard" to show it is historical fiction. Point out to students that although the story and characters are made up, the events could happen in real life. Discuss with students how the illustrations show details of the setting and of how people lived and performed tasks.

3 Guided Practice of Close Reading

Have students work with partners to find two details about the past in the story and in the illustrations. Partners should discuss why these things could happen in real life. Then have them talk about why "The Big Blizzard" is historical fiction, using details from the text and illustrations. Have students discuss how the author uses the genre *historical fiction* to explain or teach readers a lesson.

Go Digital

Present the Lesson

Genre › Literature

Historical Fiction

"The Big Blizzard" is historical fiction. **Historical fiction:**
- Is a made-up story that takes place in the past
- Has illustrations that show the setting and how people lived, and often helps create a mood

Find Text Evidence

I can tell that "The Big Blizzard" is historical fiction. The characters and events are made up. The story is based on real events that happened in 1947 in New York City.

The story and characters are made up, but the events could happen in real life. Events in historical fiction happened a long time ago.

Illustrations show details of the setting and how people lived.

Your Turn

Find two details about the past in the story and in the illustrations. Talk about why "The Big Blizzard" is historical fiction.

426

READING/WRITING WORKSHOP, *p. 426*

Monitor and *Differentiate*

✓ Quick Check

Are students able to identify two features of historical fiction in "The Big Blizzard"? Can they explain why the story is historical fiction?

Small Group Instruction

If No →	Approaching Level	Reteach p. T104
	ELL	Develop p. T120
If Yes →	On Level	Review p. T112
	Beyond Level	Extend p. T116

ENGLISH LANGUAGE LEARNERS SCAFFOLD

Beginning

Use Visuals Point to the picture on page 422. Read the last paragraph on page 422. Say: *Rosa asks Mr. Colón if she can borrow his shovels. Can this happen in real life?* (yes) *What does she want to do with them?* (help Mrs. Sanchez) Help students point to the date on page 421 that shows the story is historical fiction.

Intermediate

Describe Remind students that events in historical fiction could have happened in real life. Ask: *What is one thing on page 422 that could have happened in real life?* Have partners find one more element of historical fiction.

Advanced/High

Discuss Have partners find two elements of historical fiction on page 422. Have them discuss how the examples indicate the story is historical fiction. Monitor students' discussions and assist them as needed.

ON-LEVEL PRACTICE BOOK p. 266

Tigris River Valley Boy

The hot sun shone down over the dry valley. Ilulu had been digging for hours and was quite tired. He stopped to take a short rest and looked out over the canals stretching across the valley. Work was coming along well, but there was still much to do before the rainy season arrived. If canals were finished on time, the people of the valley could use the water to grow crops. But if the canals were not finished, the river would flood and wash away the crops.

Answer the questions about the text.

1. How do you know this text is historical fiction?
   It tells a made-up story about a real time period.

2. What text feature is included in the text?
   Illustration

3. How does the illustration help you understand the text?
   Possible answer: It shows you that the story is set in another time and place.

4. How does weather affect people in the Tigris River valley?
   Possible answer: The rainy season causes the river to flood, so people

APPROACHING p. 266	BEYOND p. 266	ELL p. 266

→ Vocabulary Strategy

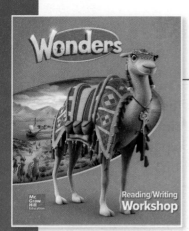

Reading/Writing Workshop

OBJECTIVES

 Distinguish the literal and nonliteral meanings of words and phrases in context (e.g., *take steps*). **L.3.5a**

ACADEMIC LANGUAGE

• *idiom, literal, nonliteral*

• Cognates: *idioma, literal, no literal*

 MINILESSON 10 Mins

Figurative Language

1 Explain

Tell students that authors use figurative language to help readers visualize what is happening in the story. An **idiom** is a special kind of nonliteral language that means something different from the meaning of each word in it.

• An idiom is a phrase, or group of words, that means something different from the literal meaning of each word in it.

• Students should look for phrases where the literal meaning seems out of place in the text to identify idioms.

• Students should use context clues in the surrounding text to help them distinguish the literal and nonliteral meanings of the idiom.

2 Model Close Reading: Text Evidence

Model identifying an idiom on page 422 of "The Big Blizzard." Point out that *stick* means to fasten or attach to help students draw inferences in order to unlock the meaning of the idiom "stick together."

3 Guided Practice of Close Reading

Have students work in pairs to find the nonliteral meanings of the idioms *bundle up, give Mrs. Sanchez a hand,* and *a piece of cake* in "The Big Blizzard." Encourage partners to use the surrounding text to distinguish and discuss the meanings of the phrases. Tell partners to use a dictionary to determine or clarify the meaning of any phrases they are uncertain about.

Go Digital

Present the Lesson

SKILLS TRACE

FIGURATIVE LANGUAGE: IDIOMS

Introduce Unit 3 Week 2

Review Unit 3 Weeks 2, 6; Unit 6 Weeks 2, 5, 6

Assess Units 3, 6

Vocabulary Strategy

Idioms

An idiom is a group of words that mean something different from the meaning of each word in it. The phrase *under the weather* is an idiom. It doesn't mean someone is outside in bad weather. It means that someone feels sick.

 Find Text Evidence

On page 422, the phrase stick together *is an idiom. I can use clues in the story to help me figure out that it means "to stay close together in a group."*

> Oh please, take us outside! We can all go to the store together!" said Eddie.
>
> "Okay," said mamá." But we have to <u>stick together</u> and stay close to each other."

Your Turn

Talk about these idioms from "The Big Blizzard."
bundle up, *page 422*
give Mrs. Sanchez a hand, *page 422*
a piece of cake, *page 423*

427

Stacey Schuett

READING/WRITING WORKSHOP, *p. 427*

Monitor and *Differentiate*

 Quick Check

Are students able to distinguish the literal and nonliteral meanings of the idioms *bundle up, give Mrs. Sanchez a hand,* and *a piece of cake*?

⬇

Small Group Instruction

If No →	Approaching Level	Reteach p. T109
	ELL	Develop p. T125
If Yes →	On Level	Review p. T114
	Beyond Level	Extend p. T118

A C T **A**ccess **C**omplex **T**ext

▶ Specific Vocabulary

Students may need help distinguishing literal from nonliteral language. Point out the idiom *a piece of cake* on page 423.

- *What is described as "a piece of cake" for Eddie and Rosa?* (shoveling the walk)

- *Was there really a piece of cake on the walk?* (no)

- *Which words help you know what "it was a piece of cake" means?* ("was easy")

- *What does the idiom mean?* (It was easy.)

ON-LEVEL PRACTICE BOOK p. 267

Read each passage below. Underline the context clues that help you understand each idiom in bold. Then write the meaning of the idiom on the line.   Possible responses provided.

1. My father likes adventure. Mother says that if he isn't exploring, Father is **at sixes and sevens** and he doesn't know what to do with himself!

   restless, confused

2. Father **tried his hand** at fishing, but he wasn't much of a success.

   to make an attempt

3. Father didn't succeed at fishing. He found that he didn't like being on the boat! He must not have **had sea legs.**

   to be used to being on a boat

4. After **sleeping on it** and giving it a lot of thought, my parents bought a farm in the Middle Colonies.

   thinking something over carefully

5. Our life is the best life I can think of—it **takes the cake!** I know my parents made the right choice.

   to be the best choice or option

APPROACHING p. 267	BEYOND p. 267	ELL p. 267

Nora's Ark

Literature Anthology

Text Complexity Range

Lexile

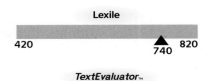

420   740   820

TextEvaluator™

2   35

What makes this text complex?

- ▶ **Specific Vocabulary**
- ▶ **Connection of Ideas**
- ▶ **Genre**
- ▶ **Sentence Structure**
- ▶ **Prior Knowledge**
- ▶ **Organization**

Close Reading Routine

| **Read** | DOK 1–2 |

- Identify key ideas and details about weather.
- Take notes and summarize.
- Use **A C T** prompts as needed.

| **Reread** | DOK 2–3 |

- Analyze the text, craft, and structure.
- Use *Close Reading Companion,* pp. 173–175.

| **Integrate** | DOK 4 |

- Integrate knowledge and ideas.
- Make text-to-text connections.
- Use the Integrate lesson.

Genre · Historical Fiction

NORA'S ARK

by Natalie Kinsey-Warnock
illustrated by Emily Arnold McCully

? Essential Question
How can weather affect us?
Read about a farm family that
survives a storm and terrible flood.

Go Digital!

482

A C T   Access Complex Text

▶ Specific Vocabulary

Review strategies for finding the meaning of
unfamiliar words, such as using context clues, word
parts, or dictionaries.

- *Reread the first paragraph. What clue does the
  author give to help you figure out what a* wren
  is? (Wren got her name because she looks like a
  small bird, so a *wren* must be a small bird.)

W hen I was born, Grandma said I was so small I looked like a little bird. That's why I was named Wren. Grandma may look small, too, but she's made of granite, and she says I'm tough, just like she is. Good thing, or we never would have survived the 1927 Flood.

Grandma and Grandpa lived on a little farm by a river in Vermont. They didn't have much money, but there was always plenty to eat—milk from Grandpa's cows, vegetables from Grandma's garden, apples and plums from the orchard, fish from the river, and maple syrup that Grandpa and Grandma made each spring.

Text Copyright © 2005 by Natalie Kinsey-Warnock. Used by permission of HarperCollins Publishers.

483

LITERATURE ANTHOLOGY, pp. 482–483

Read

Tell students they will be reading about a farm community that experiences a terrible storm and flood. Ask students to predict how the selection will help them answer the Essential Question.

Note Taking:
Use the Graphic Organizer

Remind students to take notes as they read. Have them fill in the graphic organizer on **Your Turn Practice Book** page 262. Ask them to record the theme. They can also note words they don't understand and questions they have.

Reread

Genre: Historical Fiction

What elements of historical fiction do you notice on these pages? (The story takes place in the past, in 1927. It is about a real historical event—the Flood of 1927. The illustration shows an old-fashioned farm and characters wearing old-fashioned clothes.)

- *With a partner, look up the word* granite. *What is granite?* (a hard, gray rock)
- *Why might the author compare Grandma to granite?* (to show that she is strong and steady, like a rock)

Read

1 Skill: Theme

What characters do and say can often help you determine the theme. What does Grandma say about the new house that Grandpa is building? (She says it "is just gravy." She doesn't need it because she has happily raised a family in her old house.) What does this detail tell you about what Grandma thinks is important? (She thinks family and happiness are more important than having a lot of things.) Add this detail to your graphic organizer.

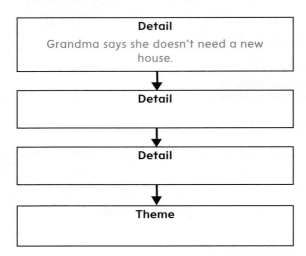

Detail
Grandma says she doesn't need a new house.

↓

Detail

↓

Detail

↓

Theme

Grandpa was building Grandma a new house. It sat on a hill and, when finished, it would have electricity, a wringer washing machine, and best of all, an indoor bathroom.

"I don't need a new house, Horace," Grandma said. "We've lived here forty years, raised eight children, and been as happy as a family could be. That new house is just gravy."

"What do you mean?" I asked her.

Grandma thought how she could explain it to me.

"You like potatoes, don't you, Wren?"

484

A C T Access Complex Text

▶ Organization

Explain that fiction often contains foreshadowing, or hints about what will happen later in the story.

- Review that on page 483, Wren says it's good that she and Grandma were tough, because otherwise they wouldn't have survived the 1927 Flood. Ask: *What does this tell you about what*

will happen in the story? (The flood will be dangerous, but Grandma and Wren will survive.)

- Reread paragraph 6 on page 485 with students. Ask: *What does this tell you about the effects that the flood will have?* (The effects must be extreme, because the story says, "Life in Vermont was about to change forever.")

"Yes, ma'am," I told her. Grandma made the best mashed potatoes in the world, with lots of milk, butter, and pepper in them. You could make a meal out of just her potatoes.

"You like gravy on them?"

"I reckon." Grandma did make good gravy. "But your potatoes taste good without gravy, too," I told her.

"Exactly," Grandma said. "Gravy tastes good, but you don't need it, and I don't need that new house. I like living here."

But Grandpa kept right on building.

When it began to rain on November 2, 1927, no one along the river had any idea nine inches of rain would fall in two days. Life in Vermont was about to change forever.

The rain came down in torrents. It drummed so loudly on the roof we couldn't talk. Grandma spent the morning baking bread. By noon, she'd made twenty-seven loaves.

"Grandma, why'd you make so much bread?" I shouted. Grandma watched the water stream down the windows.

"We might need it," she said, but I couldn't imagine how we'd eat twenty-seven loaves of bread.

When Grandpa came in for lunch, he poured a quart of water out of each boot.

"I've never seen the river rise so fast," he said. "I think we'd best get up to the new house." **2**

485

LITERATURE ANTHOLOGY, *pp. 484–485*

2 Strategy: Make, Confirm, and Revise Predictions

Teacher Think Aloud As I read, I make predictions and try to confirm them as I read more of the story. Right now, Grandma does not seem very excited about her new house. However, Grandpa keeps right on building it. I predict that the new house will be important and Grandma will come to appreciate it by the end of the story.

Build Vocabulary page 485

torrents: large amounts of water that move very quickly

Reread *Close Reading Companion*

Author's Craft: Literary Device

What words and phrases does the author use to hint that something is going to happen in the story? (Grandma bakes 27 loaves of bread. She says, "We might need it." This hints that Grandma might need to feed many people for many days because of the flood.)

• *What clue does Grandma's twenty-seven loaves of bread give you about the rain?* (Grandma thinks that the storm will be so bad that she will need to have extra food available for people.)

ELL Read aloud the description of the storm. Point out cognates *Noviembre* and *torrentes.* Demonstrate the sound of drumming rain by drumming your fingers on the desk. Check understanding by asking:

• *Is a flood a lot of rain or a little bit of rain?* (a lot)

• *When was the flood?* (November 1927)

• *How many inches of rain fell?* (nine)

Read

3 Vocabulary: Idioms

Grandpa says, "Guess I built this place just in time." What does he mean? (He means that he built the house at exactly the right moment, not too late to be useful.)

4 Strategy: Confirm or Revise Predictions

COLLABORATE

Teacher Think Aloud There is information on page 486 that we can use to confirm or revise our prediction about Grandma's feelings for the new house.

Prompt students to apply the strategy in a Think Aloud by paraphrasing the text that helps them confirm their prediction. Have them turn to a partner to confirm or revise their prediction.

Student Think Aloud Grandma jokes that she thinks Grandpa caused the flood so that she would have to move into the new house, but Wren says that Grandma seemed glad to be moving up to higher ground. This shows that Grandma has started to appreciate the new house.

Build Vocabulary page 486

oilcloth: cloth treated with oil or paint to keep it from getting soaked with water

---

For once, Grandma didn't **argue**. By the time she'd packed quilts, candles, her photo albums, and a sack of potatoes, the water was up to the porch.

Grandpa let all the cows and horses out of the barn.

"What will happen to them?" I asked.

"They'll get to higher ground and be all right," he said. "Don't worry, Wren." But I could tell he was the one who was worried.

I loaded all those loaves of bread into my old baby carriage, covered it with an oilcloth, and pushed it through the mud and rain to the new house.

3 "Guess I built this place just in time," Grandpa said.

4 "If I didn't know better, I'd think you caused this flood just so I'd have to move into the new house," Grandma said, but she seemed glad to be on higher ground, too.

486

A C T Access Complex Text

▶ Connection of Ideas

Tell students that to understand characters' actions, they need to use their prior knowledge and what they have already read.

- *Why do you think the idea of "higher ground" is so important in this story?* (The river is flooding. If the ground is higher, the water will be less likely to reach it and the people can stay dry.)

- *Why do you think the Guthrie boys bring their chickens to the house?* (because the house is built on higher ground and is the safest place to go)

We'd scarcely set foot inside when we heard pounding on the door.

The three Guthrie boys stood on the porch, burlap bags in each hand. The bags squirmed and squawked.

"Our barn's flooded. Can we keep the chickens here?"

They emptied the chickens onto the kitchen floor.

"Some of our heifers are **stranded** in the fields," one of the boys said. "We're gonna see if we can push them to higher ground."

"I'll go with you," Grandpa said.

"May I go, too?" I asked.

"No!" Grandpa and Grandma both said at once.

"Be careful," Grandma told him, and he and the boys disappeared through the rain.

Even with all those chickens, the house seemed empty with Grandpa gone.

487

5 Skill: Theme

Remember that a character's actions can help you determine the theme. What does Grandpa do when the Guthrie boys tell him their heifers are stranded? (He goes to help them, even though it is dangerous and raining hard.) What might this tell you about the theme? (Good neighbors help each other.) Add this detail to your organizer.

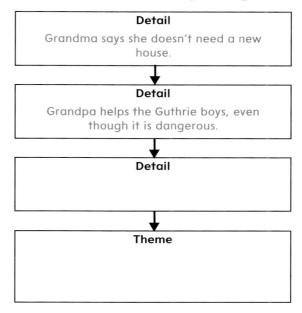

Detail
Grandma says she doesn't need a new house.

↓

Detail
Grandpa helps the Guthrie boys, even though it is dangerous.

↓

Detail

↓

Theme

Build Vocabulary page 487

scarcely: hardly

▶ Specific Vocabulary

Students may be unfamiliar with terms related to farming. Have them work with a partner and use a dictionary to look up the definition and pronunciation of *heifer*. (A *heifer* is a young female cow that has not had a calf.)

ELL Use the illustration to understand the concept of *higher ground*. Point to the illustration on page 486. Use your finger to trace Wren's path uphill. Say: *Wren is going up. She is going to higher ground.* Explain that when there is a flood, people are safer on higher ground. The water stays below them.

Read

6 Strategy: Ask and Answer Questions

COLLABORATE

Generate a question of your own about the text and share it with a partner. To find the answer, try rereading and paraphrasing the text. For example, you might ask, "Why does Grandma let a horse into the house?" To find the answer, try rereading the last paragraph. (Grandma lets the horse in because the horse needs shelter too and he will help keep them warm with his body heat.)

Build Vocabulary page 488

shiver: shake slightly because of the cold

shrieked: yelled

Grandma saw me shiver and wrapped a quilt around me.

"It's getting colder," she said. "I wish I had my cookstove here." She held me close as we stood watching the rain.

"I wish Grandpa would come back," I said.

"Me, too," said Grandma.

We both shrieked when a huge head appeared in the window. It was Major, one of the Fergusons' horses.

I was even more **astonished** when Grandma opened the door and led him in.

"You're bringing Major into the house?"

6 "We don't have a stove," Grandma said. "He's big. He'll add heat to the place."

488

A C T Access Complex Text

▶ Specific Vocabulary

Read aloud the last paragraph on page 489 with students. Explain that Mrs. Lafleur and her daughter are French, so Madeleine is speaking in French. Point out that the sentence following Madeleine's question can help them understand what she asked.

- *What does Madeleine want to know?* (She wants to know why there are chickens in the baby carriage.)

▶ Connection of Ideas

Review with students what they have read about the problem facing the characters in this story. Then ask:

- *Why are people and animals starting to show up at the house?* (The house is built on higher ground. The animals and Mrs. Lafleur and Madeleine need a place to stay that is dry.)

Major took up half the kitchen. The other half was taken up by loaves of bread and chickens.

We had chickens in the cupboards, chickens on the shelves and in the baby carriage, even chickens roosting on Major's back.

Our next visitors were Mrs. Lafleur and her daughter, Madeleine. Mrs. Lafleur didn't speak much English.

"Our house wash away," Mrs. Lafleur said. "We row boat here." **7**

Madeleine looked around the kitchen, and her eyes opened wide.

"Des poulets dans le chariot de bébé?" she said. I guess she'd never seen chickens in a baby carriage before.

489

LITERATURE ANTHOLOGY, *pp. 488–489*

Read

7 Skill: Make Inferences

What can you infer about Mrs. Lafleur and her daughter's plan to survive the flood, even though it is not directly stated? (I can infer that Mrs. Lafleur and her daughter plan to stay at the house with Wren and her grandmother. They no longer have a house and have nowhere else to go.) Based on what you know about them, do you think Wren and Grandma will let Mrs. Lafleur and Madeleine stay? (I'm sure they'll let them stay, they let a horse inside and have chickens roosting all over the house.)

Reread

Text Feature: Illustration

Reread the text on page 489 and examine the illustration. How do the illustration and the text work together to help you understand what Madeleine says in French? (The illustration shows Madeleine looking at the chickens in the baby carriage with a surprised look on her face. The text after her question says "I guess she'd never seen chickens in a baby carriage before." That helps me know she asked about the chickens in the baby carriage.)

ELL Invite any students who speak French to read aloud the last paragraph on page 483 and explain its meaning. Use the illustration to further clarify, pointing to the baby carriage full of chickens as you read. Ask:

• *What is the question Madeleine is asking?* Help students state Madeleine's question in English:

Why are there chickens in the baby carriage? Have students repeat the question in English.

Read

8 Skill: Theme

What has happened to Grandma's house by nightfall? (It is full of people and animals.) What does this tell you about the theme of the story? (It is important to help neighbors in times of need.) Add this detail to your graphic organizer.

Detail
Grandma says she doesn't need a new house.

↓

Detail
Grandpa helps the Guthrie boys, even though it is dangerous.

↓

Detail
By nightfall, the house was full to bursting.

↓

Theme

By nightfall, the house was full to bursting. Besides Mrs. Lafleur and Madeleine, Mr. and Mrs. Guthrie, the Fergusons, and the Craig family had moved in, twenty-three people in all. There were also three horses, a cow, five pigs, a duck, four cats, and one hundred chickens.

8

490

A C T Access Complex Text

▶ Connection of Ideas

Remind students that their prior knowledge can help them understand comparisons that an author makes and connect ideas. Ask:

- *What is an island?* (a body of land that is surrounded by water)

- *The author says "the river rose until the house became an island." What does that tell you about the house?* (It is surrounded by water on all sides.)

The river rose until the house became an island, and we watched our neighbors' houses wash down the river.

491

LITERATURE ANTHOLOGY, *pp. 490–491*

Reread   *Close Reading Companion*

Text Features: Illustrations

How does the author use illustrations to help you understand what is happening during the flood? (The illustration on page 490 shows how many people Grandma has allowed to come into her home during the storm. Even though they are all crowded into the room, they seem happy to be there. The illustration on page 491 shows how bad the storm and flood are. No wonder people are happy to be safe, warm, and dry.)

ELL Point out that *island* and *isla* are cognates. Clarify multiple-meaning words, such as *rose*. Ask:

- *What is Grandma's house like?* (an island)
- *What is all around it?* (water) Students can draw or describe Grandma's house.

Read

9 Skill: Theme

How do the neighbors help each other on pages 492–493? (The neighbors share their food and supplies. They entertain each other with stories and songs.) Add this detail to your graphic organizer.

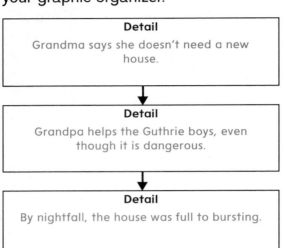

Detail
Grandma says she doesn't need a new house.

↓

Detail
Grandpa helps the Guthrie boys, even though it is dangerous.

↓

Detail
By nightfall, the house was full to bursting.

↓

Detail
The neighbors share their food and supplies. They entertain each other with stories and songs.

Build Vocabulary page 492

skillet: frying pan

Mr. and Mrs. Guthrie had brought a side of salt pork with them, though we had no way to cook it. The Fergusons had saved their radio, a skillet, a bag of dried apples, and a three-legged cat. They were delighted to find Major alive and well and in our kitchen.

The Craigs had lost everything but the clothes on their backs.

"We're just glad we all got out alive," Mrs. Craig said, which only reminded Grandma and me that Grandpa had still not returned.

We had bread and dried apples for supper, and rainwater Madeleine and I scooped out of the Lafleurs' rowboat. The water had a few fish scales in it, but no one **complained**.

9

492

A C T Access Complex Text

▶ Genre

Remind students what you previously discussed about foreshadowing.

- *How did Grandma's twenty-seven loaves of bread foreshadow the events on pages 492–493.* (It showed that she was preparing for an extraordinary event. It hinted at the number of people that would come to fill her house.)

▶ Connection of Ideas

The characters in the story are facing a difficult time, but the author says it is almost like a party. How is being in Grandma's house during the flood like a party? How is it different? (People are sharing food, music, and stories, just like they would at a party. They are enjoying each other's company. It is different because they are there due to an emergency.)

With no stove or beds, we all huddled together for warmth, sharing Grandma's quilts as best we could. We sang Scottish songs and "Row, Row, Row Your Boat" in a round, and Mrs. Lafleur taught us "À la Claire Fontaine," a tune that brought tears to our eyes even though we couldn't understand the words. Mrs. Guthrie told how her grandfather had fought at Gettysburg, and Mr. Craig kept us laughing with stories of his boyhood days in a logging camp in Maine. If it hadn't been for the thought of Grandpa out there somewhere, it would have almost seemed like a party. **10**

> **STOP AND CHECK**
>
> **Make Predictions** What do you think will happen to Grandpa?

LITERATURE ANTHOLOGY, *pp. 492–493*

10 **Skill: Make Inferences**

How do Grandma and Wren feel about Grandpa? Paraphrase the text that helps you make your inference. (Grandma and Wren are worried about Grandpa. Though they don't say it directly, I can tell because Wren says that the house almost would have felt like a party except for the thought of Grandpa out there somewhere.)

STOP AND CHECK

Make Predictions What do you think will happen to Grandpa? (He hasn't come back yet, so I predict he has been caught in the flood and will need to be rescued.)

ELL Reread page 493 with students, clarifying words such as *quilts, huddled,* and *tunes* through demonstration or restatement. Then say:

- *What are the neighbors doing? Are they eating?* (yes)

- *What else do they do?* Elicit that they sing and tell stories. *How is this like a party you have been to? How is it different?* Help students elaborate on their responses.

Read

11 Strategy: Make Predictions

Reread page 494. Turn to your partner and share a prediction you made as you read.

Student Think Aloud I read that Wren snuck out to go look for Grandpa alone, but ran into Grandma doing the same thing. I know Grandma thinks it is too dangerous for Wren to be out in the flood, but I predict that she'll let Wren come with her anyway and that together, they'll find Grandpa.

Build Vocabulary page 494

sprinted: ran very fast

I knew Grandma was worried about Grandpa. I was worried, too. He should have been home by now.

I wanted to ask Peter Ferguson if he would come with me to look for Grandpa, but I knew if Grandma overheard she'd **forbid** me to go, so when the sky was getting light, I sneaked out and sprinted for the rowboat.

Grandma was just getting into it.

"What are you doing here?" she wanted to know.

"Same as you, I reckon. Going to look for Grandpa."

494

A C T Access Complex Text

▶ Sentence Structure

Explain that when authors write dialogue, they may not always write complete sentences. Instead, they may write fragments or phrases to show the way people speak in casual conversation. Read aloud the last paragraph on page 494 and ask:

• *When Wren says, "Same as you, I reckon," what does she mean? What part of the sentence does*

she leave out? (She means that she is doing the same thing as Grandma. She leaves out the words "I am doing the...")

• *What words does Wren leave out when she says, "Going to look for Grandpa"?* (I am)

"It's too dangerous," Grandma said. "Go back to the house," but I shook my head.

Grandma looked at me hard.

"All right," she said. "We'll look for him together."

I pushed us off into water that was full of furniture and trees and dead animals. Grandma had to be careful where she rowed. It was raining so hard I had to keep bailing water out of the boat.

Nothing looked the same. Fields had become lakes. Just the roofs of houses stuck up above the water.

On one of those roofs we saw a dog.

"Why, I believe that's Sam Burroughs' collie," Grandma said, and she rowed toward the house. The collie barked when she saw us coming.

I held on to the roof to steady the boat.

"Come on, girl," I said, and the dog jumped into the boat beside me. She whined and licked my face.

495

LITERATURE ANTHOLOGY, *pp. 494–495*

Build Vocabulary page 495

bailing: scooping water out of a boat and throwing it over the side

Reread *Close Reading Companion*

Author's Craft: Characterization

What words and phrases help you visualize what Grandma is like? (The words that Grandma speaks to Wren show that she is very straightforward, and wants to protect Wren. After Wren insists on going with her to look for Grandpa, Grandma looks at Wren "hard." Then she agrees. This helps me picture Grandma as someone both caring but firm. The description of her saving the collie show that Grandma is kind and helpful to both people and animals.)

ELL Reread the last paragraph on page 494 with students. Restate *reckon* as *think*. Explain that the author wrote these sentences to sound like the way people speak when they talk to a friend. Model writing Wren's words as complete sentences. Read the complete sentences aloud with students to help them understand the meaning of the less formal language in the selection.

Read

12 Strategy: Ask and Answer Questions
COLLABORATE

Generate a question of your own about the story and share it with a partner. To find the answer, try rereading the text. For example, you might ask, "How does Grandpa get stuck in the tree?" To find the answer, you can reread and paraphrase paragraph 5 on page 497. (Grandpa was holding onto the cow after he got swept away and held on until the both of them got stuck in the tree.)

496

A C T Access Complex Text

▶ Specific Vocabulary

Reread paragraph 3 on page 497, pointing out the words *bawling* and *piteously*. Ask:

- *Can you find a synonym for* bawling *in the paragraph?* (Grandpa was hollering almost as loud as the cow, so *hollering* must be a synonym for *bawling*.)

- *What does* bawling *mean?* (crying out loudly)

- *Look at the word* piteously. *What is the root word?* (pity) *What does* pity *mean?* (sorrow or sympathy for the unhappiness of others)

- *Remember that the suffix* -ly *means "in a certain way." What do you think* bawling piteously *means?* (crying out in a way that causes others to feel sympathy)

The strangest sight was yet to come. We rounded a bend in the river and I squinted, sure that my eyes were fooling me. Then I heard Grandma's voice behind me.

"Wren, are these old eyes failing me, or is that a cow in a tree?" Grandma asked.

It was indeed. A red and white Ayrshire was wedged into the crook formed by two branches, and she was bawling piteously. Higher up in the branches was a man. He was hollering almost as loudly as the cow.

"I believe we've found your grandpa," Grandma said, **relief** flooding her face.

"I was on my way home when I got swept away by the water," Grandpa said. "I thought I was a goner, too, but when this cow floated by, I grabbed her tail and stayed afloat until she got hung up in this tree." **12**

We pushed and pulled on that cow, but she was stuck fast and we finally had to leave her. Grandpa promised he'd come back and try to cut her free, but he was crying as we rowed away. **13**

> **STOP AND CHECK**
>
> **Confirm Predictions** What happened to Grandpa? Was your prediction correct?

497

LITERATURE ANTHOLOGY, *pp. 496–497*

13 Skill: Theme

After being rescued, what does Grandpa, along with Wren and Grandma, do? (The three of them try to help the cow that is stuck.) What do their actions tell you about the theme, or author's message? (Their actions show that the author believes that it is important to help people and animals, especially during difficult times.)

STOP AND CHECK

Confirm Predictions What happened to Grandpa? Was your prediction correct? (Grandpa got washed away and then grabbed on to a cow to stay afloat. He ended up getting stuck in a tree. My prediction was correct. I thought going out in the flood put Grandpa in danger and he would need help, and he did.)

ELL Before reading, clarify expressions that may be unfamiliar to students, such as "are these old eyes failing me" and "I thought I was a goner." Restate them as "Am I really seeing that?" and "I thought I was going to die." Then reread paragraph 3:

- Using the illustration on page 496, point to the crook in the tree. *What is stuck in the crook?*

(a cow) *Is a crook straight or bent?* (bent) Use your arm to clarify straight and bent, if necessary.

- *What do you think* bawling *sounds like?* Have students demonstrate.

LITERATURE ANTHOLOGY **T89P**

Read

14 **Skill: Cause and Effect**

What causes Grandpa to cry? (All the cows and horses drowned. The barn and old house are gone. He's overwhelmed by the experience, and he thinks they've lost everything.)

15 **Skill: Theme**

Grandma says, "You're safe, and that's all that matters." What message is the author trying to give with Grandma's words? (The author is trying to say that as long as the family has each other, nothing else matters, not even losing all of their possessions.)

"Goodness," Grandma said. "All that fuss over a cow." But Grandpa wasn't crying over just one cow.

"All our cows drowned, Nora," he said. "The house, the barn, the horses, they're all gone." **14**

Grandma wiped the tears from his cheeks.

"You're safe, and that's all that matters," she said. **15**

"We'll have to start over," Grandpa said, and Grandma smiled.

"We can do that," she said.

Grandpa smiled back at her, and I knew then that, no matter what, everything would be all right.

498

A C T Access Complex Text

▶ Prior Knowledge

Have students recall the title of the story. Direct them to pages 482–483, if necessary. Then have them reread the last sentence on page 499. Ask:

- *Does the title of this story remind you of anything else you have heard before?* (The title *Nora's Ark* sounds similar to the story of Noah's ark.)

- *How are the two stories similar?* (Both tell about a devastating flood, where people and animals must take shelter in order to survive.)

The Craigs, Fergusons, Guthries, and Lafleurs were glad to see us. Madeleine even hugged me.

"She was afraid you'd drowned," Peter said. He blushed. "I was, too," he added.

When Grandpa saw all the animals in the kitchen, he burst out laughing.

"Nora, I thought I was building you a house, but I see it was really an ark." **16**

499

LITERATURE ANTHOLOGY, *pp. 498–499*

16 Skill: Make Inferences

Why do you think Grandpa calls the house an ark? (Grandpa calls the house an ark because he is shocked to see the house filled with people and animals taking shelter from a huge flood, much like in the story of Noah and his ark.)

ELL Reread the last sentence with students. Tell them that *ark* and *arca* are cognates. Use the illustration to help students connect Grandma's house with Noah's ark.

- *Did Noah's ark have people and animals on it?* (yes)

- *What does Grandma's house have inside of it? Point to the illustration or tell me.* (people and animals)

Help students complete this frame:

Grandma's house is like an ark because it has ____ inside.

Read

17 Skill: Theme

What is the theme of this selection?
(Family, friends, and neighbors helping each other is the most important thing.) Add the theme to your graphic organizer.

Detail
Grandma says she doesn't need a new house.

↓

Detail
Grandpa helps the Guthrie boys, even though it is dangerous.

↓

Detail
By nightfall, the house was full to bursting.

↓

Detail
The neighbors share their food and supplies. They entertain each other with stories and songs.

↓

Theme
Family, friends, and neighbors helping each other is the most important thing.

It took three days for the water to go down enough so our neighbors could go see what was left of their farms.

Grandpa put his arm around Grandma.

"I'll finish this house the way you want it, Nora," he said. But he shook his head when the Fergusons led Major out.

"I don't know as I'll ever be able to get those hoofprints out of this floor," he said.

500

A C T Access Complex Text

▶ Organization

Tell students that authors of fiction often tell story events in sequence. However, they may suddenly shift forward or backward in time to clarify events or wrap up the story. Readers must be able to recognize these shifts in sequence. Reread page 501 with students. Ask:

- *What words help you recognize that the story has shifted from events that happened in the past back to the present day?* ("I've now lived in my grandparents' house for more than forty years")

- *How does this shift forward in time help wrap up the story?* (It shows that the house, hoofprints and all, is still part of Wren's life, and she still values the lessons she learned during the flood of 1927.)

I've now lived in my grandparents' house for more than forty years, and those hoofprints are still in the floor. I never sanded them out because they remind me of what's important: family and friends and neighbors helping neighbors. **17**

Like Grandma said, everything else is just gravy.

STOP AND CHECK

Summarize What happened after Wren and Grandma rescued Grandpa? Tell the events in order.

501

LITERATURE ANTHOLOGY, *pp. 500–501*

Return to Purposes Review students' predictions and purposes for reading. Ask them to use text evidence to answer the Essential Question. (Weather can affect us in many ways, and it can be both helpful and harmful. Rain can help us grow plants and flowers, but too much rain can cause floods and destroy homes and farms.)

STOP AND CHECK

Summarize What happened after Wren and Grandma rescued Grandpa? (After Wren and Grandma rescued Grandpa, they returned to the new house. After three days, the neighbors left to go see what was left of their farms. Grandpa promised to finish the house just the way Grandma wanted it. The hoofprints from Major were always a part of the house.)

Read

About the Author and Illustrator

Natalie Kinsey-Warnock and Emily Arnold McCully

Have students read the biographies of the author and illustrator. Ask:

- What was Natalie Kinsey-Warnock's inspiration for writing this story?
- What role did family play in Emily Arnold McCully's decision to become an artist?

Author's Purpose

To Entertain

Remind students that authors who write fiction often tell an interesting story that entertains readers, but can also teach a lesson. Students may say that the author wrote this story to entertain while showing the theme of neighbors working together and figuring out what things are truly important in life.

Reread

Author's Craft

Explain that authors use dialect to show how people from certain parts of the country speak and to add realism to the dialogue. For example, from page 485: "You like gravy on them?" "I reckon." What affect does the dialect have on the story? (It is less formal and makes the characters sound more natural and real. It also reminds me that the story takes place in the past.)

ABOUT THE AUTHOR AND ILLUSTRATOR

NATALIE KINSEY-WARNOCK'S family has lived in Vermont for nearly two hundred years. Family stories like "Norah's Ark" inspire her writing. She says, "Every family has stories that are too good to be forgotten. These stories need to be passed on to the next generation." Natalie has written more than twenty books for young people. Most are about life in Vermont.

EMILY ARNOLD MCCULLY'S family inspired her to become an artist. She started drawing as a child. Her mother encouraged her to practice, so she drew everything she saw. She never stopped creating art. Emily has illustrated more than a hundred books for children. Emily hopes to inspire people's imaginations through her books.

AUTHOR'S PURPOSE
Why do you think the author wrote a story about a Vermont flood that happened long ago?

502

LITERATURE ANTHOLOGY, *pp. 502–503*

Respond to the Text

Summarize

How did the weather affect Wren and her grandparents? Use details from your Theme chart to help you summarize the events in the story.

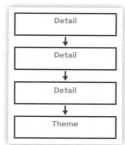

Detail
↓
Detail
↓
Detail
↓
Theme

Write

How does what the author says about Wren and her grandmother at the beginning of the story help you understand the message? Use these sentence frames to help organize your text evidence.

> At the beginning of the story, the author . . .
> She uses illustrations to . . .
> This helps me understand . . .

Make Connections

What did people in the community do to survive bad weather and a flood? **ESSENTIAL QUESTION**

Explain why people are always watching the weather report. **TEXT TO WORLD**

503

Integrate

Make Connections
COLLABORATE

Essential Question Answer: They found shelter at Grandma's house, where they waited until the weather got better.
Evidence: On page 486, Grandma, Grandpa, and Wren move to the new house on higher ground. On pages 487–490, they let in many people and animals. On page 500, the water has gone down enough for people to go back to their farms.

Text to World Responses may vary, but encourage students to cite text evidence from their sources.

Respond to the Text

Read

Summarize

Tell students they will use the information from their Theme charts to summarize. As I read *Nora's Ark*, I collected key details and figured out the theme of the text. To summarize, I will paraphrase, or reword, the most important details.

Reread

Analyze the Text

After students summarize the selection, have them reread to develop a deeper understanding of the text and answer the questions on **Close Reading Companion** pages 173–175. For students who need support in citing text evidence, use the Reread prompts on pages T89B–T89U.

Write About the Text

Review the writing prompt and sentence frames. Remind students to use their responses from the **Close Reading Companion** to support their answers. For a full lesson on writing a response using text evidence, see page T94.

Answer: The author describes Wren and Grandma as tough survivors, who are focused on important things, like family. **Evidence:** On page 483, Grandma is compared to granite, a very strong rock. On pages 494–495, Grandma and Wren go looking for Grandpa in the dangerous flood. They even rescue a dog.

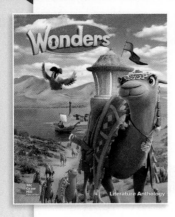

"The Wind and the Sun"

Text Complexity Range

Lexile

420   ▲   820
570

Literature Anthology
Unfamiliar genre elements place this selection above TextEvaluator range. Content is grade-level appropriate.

TextEvaluator™

2   35 ▲
*43

What makes this text complex?
 Genre

Compare Texts 🖉 *Analytical Writing*

As students read and reread "The Wind and the Sun" encourage them to take notes and think about the Essential Question: *How can weather affect us?* Tell students to think about how this text compares with Nora's Ark.

Read

Ask and Answer Questions

Why do the Sun and the Wind have a contest? (The Wind and the Sun have a contest to see who is stronger.)

Reread   *Close Reading Companion*

Author's Craft: Descriptive Words

How does the author use what the characters say and do to tell the theme or moral of the story? (For the Wind: *boasted, topple trees, flatten homes, spoil weather, blast away, howling.* For the Sun: *provide daylight, keep people warm, smiled, warmest rays*) How does this reinforce the story's theme? (The Sun wins by being warm and gentle.)

Genre • Fable

Compare Texts
Read about a contest between the Wind and the Sun to see who is stronger.

The Wind and the Sun
from the fable by Aesop

The Wind and the Sun both lived in the sky. Like most neighbors, they got along much of the time. However, sometimes they argued about who was strongest.

"I am stronger than you!" boasted the Wind one day. "I can topple trees and flatten homes. On a sunny day, I can spoil the weather **conditions** by blowing in clouds and rain."

The Sun smiled, "No! I am stronger. I provide daylight and the heat that keeps people warm."

"Let's have a contest to determine who is stronger," blustered the Wind. "See that farmer down there in his field? We'll each try to make him take off his coat. Whoever succeeds is **1** the winner."

Illustration: Rendra Gallo

504

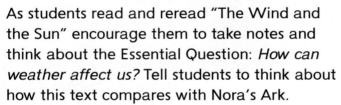

A C T   Access Complex Text

 **Genre**

Tell students that fables often contain nonhuman characters that behave like humans, in order to teach a lesson.

- *Describe how the Wind and the Sun are portrayed in this story?* (The Wind is boastful and mean-spirited. He thinks strength means destroying homes and ruining the weather. The Sun is quiet

"Okay, you go first," the Sun agreed.

The Wind took a big breath and blew and blew. He tried to blast away the farmer's coat with all his strength, but the farmer only pulled his coat tighter.

"*Brrr!* That's peculiar," said the farmer. "The weather **forecast** on the radio didn't predict a freezing wind for today."

Soon the Wind grew tired and stopped howling. "Your turn, Sun," he panted.

Sun nodded and smiled. He sent out his warmest rays.

The farmer began to sweat as he labored in the field. "Ah, it certainly has become a warm, sunny day," he sighed with relief as he removed his coat. And with that, the Sun won the contest.

Gentle persuasion works better than force.

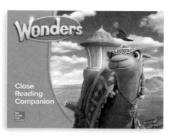

Make Connections

Why is the Sun stronger than the Wind? **ESSENTIAL QUESTION**

Compare this story to other stories about the weather. **TEXT TO TEXT**

505

LITERATURE ANTHOLOGY, *pp. 504–505*

Read

Summarize

Guide students to summarize the selection.

Reread

Analyze the Text

After students read and summarize, have them reread to develop a deeper understanding of the text by annotating and answering questions on pages 176–178 of the **Close Reading Companion**.

Integrate

Make Connections

Essential Question <u>Answer:</u> The Sun is stronger than the Wind because it got the farmer to take off his coat using gentle persuasion. <u>Evidence:</u> On page 505, the text tells me that, after the Wind grew tired and stopped blowing, the Sun nodded and smiled and sent out his warmest rays. The moral of the fable is "Gentle persuasion works better than force," which is the last line of the story.

Text to Text Responses may vary, but encourage students to cite text evidence from each source.

and confident. He thinks strength is providing light and warmth that people need.)

- *How does this show in the way each tries to win the contest?* (The Wind tries to blow the coat off the farmer using force, but fails. The Sun succeeds because he knows that by being gentle, he can get the farmer to take off the coat himself.)

ELL Have pairs of students take turns role-playing the Wind and the farmer and the Sun and the farmer. As students act out their roles, model using language to describe their actions. Have students repeat.

→ Phonics/Fluency

MINILESSON 20 Mins

Consonant + *le* Syllables

Go Digital

OBJECTIVES

CCSS Know and apply grade-level phonics and word analysis skills in decoding words. Decode words with common Latin suffixes. **RF.3.3b**

CCSS Know and apply grade-level phonics and word analysis skills in decoding words. Decode multisyllable words. **RF.3.3c**

CCSS Read on-level text with purpose and understanding. **RF.3.4a**

Rate: 97–117 WCPM

ACADEMIC LANGUAGE
• *phrasing*
• Cognate: *fraseo*

 ELL

Refer to the sound transfers chart in the **Language Transfers Handbook** to identify sounds that do not transfer in Spanish, Cantonese, Vietnamese, Hmong, and Korean.

1 Explain

Remind students when a word ends in *le*, the consonant before it plus the letters *le* usually form the last syllable. This is also true of consonant + *el*, consonant + *al*, and consonant + *il*. Tell students that breaking words into syllables helps identify open and closed syllables. Remind them that open syllables may have a long vowel sound and closed syllables may have a short vowel sound.

2 Model

Write the word *table* on the board. Underline the syllable *ble* and point out the open syllable *ta*. Model how to say the word, pronouncing each word part, and then sounding out the whole word.

3 Guided Practice

Write the following words on the board. Help students identify the final syllable and determine whether the first syllable is open or closed. Guide students as they pronounce each full word. Then write three sentences that each contain three of the words on the board. Have partners read the sentences to each other.

purple	bundle	middle
candle	tunnel	little
eagle	able	global

Consonant+*le* Syllables

Present the Lesson

The Big Blizzard

View "The Big Blizzard"

Read Multisyllabic Words

Transition to Longer Words Give students additional practice with reading words with final consonant + *le* (*al, el, il*) syllables. Draw a T-chart on the board. In the first column write *accident, rid, hand,* and *understand*. In the second column, write *accidental, riddle, handle,* and *understandable*. Point to the words in the first column and model how to read each word. Have students repeat the words.

Explain that the words in the second column contain a consonant + *le* (*al, el, il*) syllable. Have students underline the final syllable in each word. Point to each word in random order and have students read the words chorally.

Latin Suffixes

1 Explain

A suffix changes the meaning of the base word and the word's part of speech. It can also change the word's spelling.

- The suffix *-able* means "able to." When added to a base word that ends in consonant + *e*, the final *e* is often dropped.
- The suffix *-ous* means "full of." When added to a base word that ends in consonant + *y*, the final *y* is changed to an *i*.
- The suffix *-y* means "having the quality of." When added to a base word that ends in consonant + *e*, the final *e* is often dropped before adding *-y*.

2 Model

Write and say *lovable, furious*, and *shiny*. Have students say the words. Model using the suffixes to determine the meanings.

3 Guided Practice

Write the following words: *adorable, reusable, various, marvelous, dusty, lucky*. Have students identify each suffix and use the suffix to determine the meaning of each word.

Phrasing

Explain/Model When readers use appropriate phrasing, they break longer sentences into groups of phrases. This adds meaning and understanding to the text.

Model reading the first two paragraphs of "The Big Blizzard" on page 421. Emphasize phrasing when reading the news announcement in the second paragraph.

Practice/Apply Have one group read the passage a sentence at a time. A second group echo-reads, using the same phrasing. Then have groups switch roles. Help students use appropriate phrasing and offer feedback as needed.

Daily Fluency Practice FLUENCY

Students can practice fluency using **Your Turn Practice Book**.

Monitor and *Differentiate*

 Quick Check

Can students decode words with consonant + *le* syllables? Can students read words with Latin suffixes and determine the meanings of the words? Can students read fluently?

Small Group Instruction

If No →	Approaching Level	Reteach pp. T104, T106
	ELL	Develop p. T60
If Yes →	On Level	Review p. T112
	Beyond Level	Extend p. T116

ON-LEVEL PRACTICE BOOK p. 268

A. Read each pair of words. Underline the word that has a final consonant + *-le, -el,* or *-al* syllable. Then circle the final syllable. Write the word on the line.

1. able	below	able
2. glowing	eagle	eagle
3. purple	planning	purple
4. valley	squirrel	squirrel
5. metal	melted	metal

B. Add the suffix to each base word. Write the word on the line. Pay attention to spelling changes.

1. use + able =	usable
2. fury + ous =	furious
3. ice + y =	icy
4. wash + able =	washable
5. poison + ous =	poisonous

APPROACHING p. 268	BEYOND p. 268	ELL p. 268

Write to Sources

DAY 1

Writing Fluency

Write to a Prompt Provide students with the prompt: *Write about how the blizzard affected the Hernandez family.* Have students share their ideas about bad winter weather. *What did the family do during the blizzard?* When students finish sharing ideas, have them write continuously for fifteen minutes in their Writer's Notebook. If students stop writing, encourage them to keep going.

 When students finish writing have them work with a partner to compare ideas and make sure they both have a clear understanding of the story.

Genre Writing

Feature Article pp. T344–T349

Second Week Focus: Over the course of the week, focus on the following stages of the writing process:

Draft Distribute copies of the Student Model found online in Writer's Workspace. Teach the minilesson on choosing precise words. Have students review the Sequence Charts they prepared in Prewrite and write a draft.

Revise Analyze the Revised Student Model found online in Writer's Workspace. Teach the minilesson on strong conclusions. Have students review their partner's draft and revise their own. Distribute the Revise and Edit Checklist from Writer's Workspace to guide them.

DAY 2

Write to the Reading/Writing Workshop Text

Analyze the Prompt Read aloud the first paragraph on page 428 of the **Reading/Writing Workshop.** Ask: *What is the prompt asking?* (to write a letter describing a character's feelings) Say: *Let's reread to what Rosa said and did during the blizzard. We can note text evidence.*

Analyze Text Evidence Display Graphic Organizer 53 in Writer's Workspace. Say: *Let's see how one student, Harrison, took notes to answer the prompt. He notes that Rosa and Eddie jumped up and begged to go with mamá to Maria's Market.* Guide the class through the rest of Harrison's notes.

Analyze the Student Model Explain how Harrison used text evidence from his notes to write a response to the prompt.

- **Strong Opening** Harrison's opening sentence is strong and grabs the reader's attention. He used text evidence from his notes to write the opening. Trait: Ideas

- **Linking Words** Linking words and phrases connect ideas and help the reader understand how events and ideas are related. Harrison used linking words to connect and compare the ideas in the letter. Trait: Word Choice

- **Supporting Details** Harrison found supporting details from the text. He described how Rosa and Eddie had to shovel a lot of snow so that mamá could get to the market. Harrison's details supported his strong opening. Trait: Ideas

For additional practice with word choice and linking words and phrases, assign **Your Turn Practice Book** page 269.

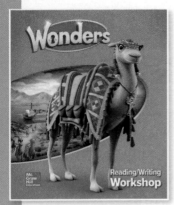

Reading/Writing Workshop

OBJECTIVES

CCSS Write narratives to develop real or imagined experiences or events using effective technique, descriptive details, and clear event sequences. Use dialogue and descriptions of actions, thoughts, and feelings to develop experiences and events or show the response of characters to situations. **W.3.3b**

ACADEMIC LANGUAGE

linking words and phrases, connect

Go Digital

U6W2 Word Choice: Linking Words and Phrases

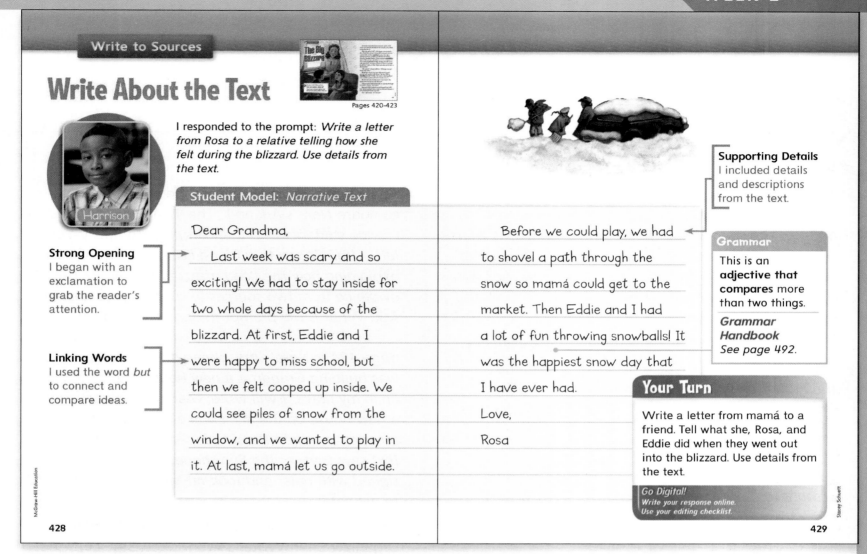

Write to Sources

Write About the Text

Pages 420-423

Harrison

I responded to the prompt: *Write a letter from Rosa to a relative telling how she felt during the blizzard. Use details from the text.*

Strong Opening
I began with an exclamation to grab the reader's attention.

Linking Words
I used the word *but* to connect and compare ideas.

Student Model: *Narrative Text*

Dear Grandma,

Last week was scary and so exciting! We had to stay inside for two whole days because of the blizzard. At first, Eddie and I were happy to miss school, but then we felt cooped up inside. We could see piles of snow from the window, and we wanted to play in it. At last, mamá let us go outside.

Before we could play, we had to shovel a path through the snow so mamá could get to the market. Then Eddie and I had a lot of fun throwing snowballs! It was the happiest snow day that I have ever had.

Love,

Rosa

Supporting Details
I included details and descriptions from the text.

Grammar
This is an **adjective that compares** more than two things.
Grammar Handbook See page 492.

Your Turn
Write a letter from mamá to a friend. Tell what she, Rosa, and Eddie did when they went out into the blizzard. Use details from the text.

Go Digital!
Write your response online.
Use your editing checklist.

428
429

McGraw-Hill Education

Stacey Schuett

READING/WRITING WORKSHOP, *pp. 428–429*

Your Turn Writing Read the Your Turn prompt on page 429 of the Reading/Writing Workshop aloud. Discuss the prompt with students. If necessary, review with students that authors use linking words and phrases to help readers connect ideas.

Have students take notes as they look for text evidence to answer the prompt. Remind them to include the following elements as they craft their response from their notes:

- Strong Opening
- Linking Words
- Supporting Details

Have students use **Grammar Handbook** page 492 in the Reading/Writing Workshop to edit for errors in adjectives that compare.

ELL **ENGLISH LANGUAGE LEARNERS SCAFFOLD**

Beginning
Write Help students complete the sentence frames.
During the blizzard, Rosa, Eddie, and mamá _____.
They helped _____.

Intermediate
Describe Ask students to complete the sentence frames. Encourage students to provide details.
Rosa and Eddie wanted to go with mamá because _____.
Outside they saw _____.

Advanced/High
Discuss Check for understanding. Ask: *What did Rosa, Eddie, and mamá do when they finally went outside? To whom did they talk?*

Write to Sources

DAY 3 For students who need support to complete the writing assignment for the Literature Anthology, provide the following instruction.

DAY 4

Write to the Literature Anthology Text

Analyze the Prompt Explain that students will write about *Nora's Ark* on **Literature Anthology** pages 482–501. Provide the following prompt: *How does what the author says about Wren and her grandmother at the beginning help you understand the message?* Ask: *What is the prompt asking you to do?* (to connect the author's character descriptions to the story's message)

Analyze Text Evidence Help students note evidence.

Page 483 Read the page aloud. Ask: *What does the author compare Grandma to?* (granite) *What is granite like?* (It is a very hard, strong rock.) *How does Grandma describe Wren?* (Grandma says Wren is tough, jus like she is.)

Page 484 Read the page aloud. Ask: *Is Grandma anxious to move into the new house? Why or why not?* (No; she doesn't think she needs it.) *Why is this important?*

Encourage students to look for more text evidence about characterization and theme in the story. Then have them craft a short response. Use the conference routine below.

Write to Two Sources

Analyze the Prompt Explain that students will compare *Nora's Ark* and "The Wind and the Sun." Provide students with the following prompt: *Write a letter from Wren to a friend living in another state, explaining how the flood affected her family. Use text evidence from two sources to support your answer.* Ask: *What is the prompt asking you to do?* (to write a letter describing the effects of the flood) Say: *On page 484 in* Nora's Ark, *the text says that Grandpa was building Grandma a new house that sat on a hill. So in my notes, I will write:* Grandpa builds the family a new house on the hill. *I will also note the page number and the title of the source. On page 505, the text says that, as the Sun shone warmly, the farmer sighed with relief and took off his coat. I will add this to my notes.*

Analyze Text Evidence Display online Graphic Organizer 54 in Writer's Workspace. Say: *Let's see how one student took notes to answer the prompt. Here are Harrison's notes.* Read through the text evidence for each selection and have students point out what effect the weather had on people.

Teacher Conferences

STEP 1

Talk about the strengths of the writing.

You included strong, concrete details in the opening. You used these details to organize the rest of your writing.

STEP 2

Focus on how the writer uses text evidence.

The details you include support your first point. It would help me understand better if you added more text evidence to support your additional points.

STEP 3

Make concrete suggestions.

This section is interesting. It would be stronger if you used linking words or phrases to connect your ideas.

DAY

5

Share the Prompt Provide the following prompt to students: *Write a letter to a friend or family member, describing each of the texts and explaining the lesson that you learned from each one. Use text evidence from* Nora's Ark *and "The Wind and the Sun" to support your answer.*

Find Text Evidence Have students take notes. Find text evidence and give guidance where needed. If necessary, review with students how to paraphrase. Remind them to write the page number and source of the information.

Analyze the Student Model Review the prompt and Harrison's notes from Day 4. Display the student model on page 270 of the **Your Turn Practice Book**. Explain to students that Harrison synthesized his notes to write a response to the prompt. Discuss the page together with students or have them do it independently.

Write the Response Review the prompt from Day 4 with students. Remind them that they took notes on this prompt on Day 4. Have students use their notes to craft a short response. Tell students to include the title of both sources and the following elements:

• Strong Opening

• Linking Words

• Supporting Details

COLLABORATE

Share and Reflect Have students share their responses with a partner. Use the Peer Conference routine below.

Suggested Revisions

Provide specific direction to help focus young writers.

Focus on a Sentence
Read the draft and target one sentence for revision. *Rewrite this sentence by adding a supporting detail that describes ____.*

Focus on a Section
Underline a section that needs to be revised. Provide specific suggestions. *I want to know more about how ____ connects to ____. Add a linking word or phrase to help me understand.*

Focus on a Revision Strategy
Underline a section. Have students use a specific revision strategy, such as adding. *All of your linking words appear in this section. Try to add linking words throughout your writing.*

Peer Conferences

Focus peer responses on using linking words to connect ideas. Provide these questions:

• Is the opening strong and interesting?

• Are there enough linking words and phrases to connect ideas and events?

• What supporting details can be added to improve the writing?

→ Grammar: Adjectives That Compare

Reading/Writing Workshop

OBJECTIVES

 Form and use comparative and superlative adjectives and adverbs, and choose between them depending on what is to be modified. **L.3.1g**

- Identify and use comparative and superlative adjectives
- Use adjectives correctly
- Proofread sentences for mechanics and usage errors

Write ____ -er than ____ on the board. Underneath write the words *heavy, big,* and *cute.* Have students construct sentences comparing an elephant and cat using the words. Example: *An elephant is heavier than a cat.*

DAY 1

DAILY LANGUAGE ACTIVITY

It is 500. That mean we have too ours to go.
(1: 5:00; 2: means; 3: two; 4: hours)

Introduce Adjectives That Compare

- An adjective that compares is a descriptive adjective:
  They are **good**.
- Use comparative adjectives to compare two nouns. Superlatives compare more than two nouns:
  My second draft is **better** than the first.
- Add -*er* to an adjective to compare two nouns:
  My computer is **faster** than yours.
- Add -*est* to compare more than two nouns:
  He is the **sweetest** boy!

Discuss adjectives using page 492 of the Grammar Handbook.

DAY 2

DAILY LANGUAGE ACTIVITY

One of our tree has a large broken branch. They has to be cut down.
(1: trees; 2: large,; 3: It)

Review Adjectives

Review comparative adjectives.

Introduce Adjectives that Compare with Spelling Changes

- When the **adjective** ends in a consonant and *y*, change the *y* to *i* and add -*er* or -*est*:
  My towel is finally **dry**.
  Your towel is **drier** than it was.
- When the adjective ends in *e*, drop the *e* and add -*er* or -*est*:
  That flower is **nice**.
  I think that is the **nicest** flower.
- When adjectives have a short vowel sound before a final consonant, double the final consonant and add -*er* or -*est*:
  That is a **big** fish.
  It's the **biggest** fish I have ever seen.

 TALK ABOUT IT

COLLABORATE

MAKE A SENTENCE

Have partners create a list of extreme weather events they have heard about or seen. Then, have each student create a sentence using a word from the list and either a comparative or superlative adjective to describe the weather.

PLAY QUESTION QUIZ

Partners should write five sentences using adjectives that compare. Each partner should take turns reading their sentences aloud, and the other should identify the adjective by using it in question form.

DAY 3

Were going to market now. Is there everything you need?

(1: We're; 2: the; 3: anything)

Mechanics and Usage: Correct Comparative and Superlative Forms

- Some adjectives that compare do not add *-er* or *-est*.
- The comparative form of *good* is *better*, and the superlative form is *best*.
- The comparative form of *bad* is *worse*, and the superlative form is *worst*.
- *Many* is an adjective that refers to more than one thing. The adjective *more* compares two things. *Most* compares more than two.

As students write, refer them to Grammar Handbook page 492.

DAY 4

Thats the most good lasagna I've ever had! This restaurant is best than the one we went to last week.

(1: That's; 2: best; 3: better)

Proofread

Have students correct errors in these sentences.

1. This is the most sad movie. I like the one we watched yesterday more better.
   (1: saddest; 2: better.)

2. That is the lighter box out of all of them. (lightest)

3. I'm more lucky than you because I didn't get caught in the rain. (luckier)

4. Sam told the most funny story. It was the most good one.
   (1: funniest; 2: best)

Have students check their work using Grammar Handbook page 492.

DAY 5

This is the colder winter that we had had in years!

(1: coldest; 2: have)

Assess

Use the Daily Language Activity and Grammar Practice Reproducibles page 135 for assessment.

Reteach

Use Grammar Practice Reproducibles pages 131–134 and selected pages from the Grammar Handbook for reteaching. Remind students that it is important to use comparative and superlative adjectives correctly as they write and speak.

Check students' writing for use of the skill and listen for it in their speaking. Assign Grammar Revision Assignments in their Writer's Notebooks as needed.

See Grammar Practice Reproducibles pages 131–135.

DESCRIBE AND COMPARE

Have students in small groups each write a way weather can affect our everyday lives. Students will take turns selecting a paper and forming a sentence about weather using a comparative or superlative adjective and read it aloud.

ROLE-PLAY A SCENE

Have students reenact a favorite scene from a story the class has read. As students role-play, be sure they use adjectives that compare. As other students watch, have them listen for the adjectives and identify them.

GUESS THE NOUN

Have students in small groups write ten nouns that name kinds of weather. Each student will pick a noun and describe the weather using comparative and superlative adjectives as the other students try to guess the word. The student who guesses the most nouns wins.

Spelling: Consonant + *le* Syllables

DAY 1

DAY 2

OBJECTIVES

CCSS Use spelling patterns and generalizations (e.g., *word families, position-based spellings, syllable patterns, ending rules, meaningful word parts*) in writing words. **L.3.2f**

CCSS Consult reference materials, including beginning dictionaries, as needed to check and correct spellings. **L.3.2g**

Spelling Words

able	purple	riddle
handle	eagle	puzzle
castle	little	pickle
towel	nickel	camel
travel	tunnel	squirrel

Review preschool, rebuild, unlucky
Challenge motel, couple

Differentiated Spelling

Approaching Level

able	purple	table
eagle	puzzle	middle
ankle	little	pickle
bottle	towel	camel
travel	tunnel	global

Beyond Level

able	terrible	riddle
handle	whistle	castle
pickle	icicle	single
motel	nickel	towel
camel	tunnel	squirrel

Assess Prior Knowledge

Display the spelling words. Read them aloud, drawing out and slowly enunciating the consonant + *le* syllables.

Model for students how to spell the word *able*. Draw a line between the syllables: *a/ble*. Point out that the consonant + *-le* or *-el* syllable is usually the final syllable.

Demonstrate sorting the spelling words by pattern under key words *able* and *towel*. (Write the words on index cards or the IWB.) Sort a few words by the spelling of the final consonant sound. Review the spellings of final syllables with the consonant + *-le* or *-el* pattern. Point out that they always follow a consonant.

Then use the Dictation Sentences from Day 5. Say the underlined word, read the sentence, and repeat the word. Have students write the words.

COLLABORATE WORD SORTS

OPEN SORT

Have students cut apart the **Spelling Word Cards BLM** in the Online Resource Book and initial the backs of each card. Have them read the words aloud with a partner. Then have partners do an **open sort**. Have them record the sort in their word study notebook.

Spiral Review

Review the prefixes in the words *preschool, rebuild,* and *unlucky*. Use the Dictation Sentences below for the review words. Read the sentence, say the word, and have students write the words.

1. Nadia's <u>preschool</u> teacher drew shapes on the board.
2. We had to <u>rebuild</u> the house after the tornado.
3. Kevin lost his homework, and felt very <u>unlucky</u>.

Have partners check the spellings.

Challenge Words Review this week's spelling words, pointing out the consonant + *-le* and *-el* syllables. Use these Dictation Sentences for challenge words. Read the sentence, say the word, have students write the word.

1. We stayed at a <u>motel</u> last night.
2. I forgot a <u>couple</u> of things.

Have students write the words in their word study notebook.

PATTERN SORT

Complete the **pattern sort** using the key words, pointing out the consonant + *-le* and *-el* syllables. Have students use Spelling Word Cards to do their own pattern sort. A partner can compare and check their sorts.

DAY 3

Word Meanings

Have students copy the words below into their Writer's Notebooks. Have them figure out the spelling word that goes with each definition.

1. a royal color (purple)
2. large bird with strong claws (eagle)
3. not big (little)
4. path under ground or water (tunnel)
5. animal with a big tail (squirrel)

Challenge students to come up with clues for other spelling, review, or challenge words.

See Phonics/Spelling Reproducibles pp. 157–162.

DAY 4

Proofread and Write

Write the sentences below on the board. Have students circle and correct each misspelled word. Remind students they can use print or electronic resources to check and correct spelling.

1. Paint the tunnle purpel. (tunnel, purple)
2. Were you abel to solve the riddel? (able, riddle)
3. We will travle to a castel. (travel, castle)

Error Correction Students will confuse *-el* words with *-le* words. They will need to memorize the correct spelling. Students may also substitute other vowels for *e*, especially *a*.

DAY 5

Assess

Use the Dictation Sentences for the Posttest. Have students list misspelled words in their word study notebooks. Look for students' use of these words in their writings.

Dictation Sentences

1. Andy was <u>able</u> to help with the work.
2. My favorite color is <u>purple</u>.
3. Can you answer this <u>riddle</u>?
4. Hold the basket by the <u>handle</u>.
5. An <u>eagle</u> is a large bird.
6. This <u>puzzle</u> is hard to solve.
7. There are walls around the <u>castle</u>.
8. There is a <u>little</u> bit of snow on the ground.
9. That <u>pickle</u> was sour!
10. Wipe your face with the <u>towel</u>.
11. I paid a <u>nickel</u> for this apple.
12. The <u>camel</u> has a long neck.
13. We will <u>travel</u> a long way.
14. The train went through a <u>tunnel</u>.
15. The <u>squirrel</u> stored nuts for winter.

Have students self-correct the tests.

SPEED SORT

Have partners do a **speed sort** to see who is faster. Then have partners write sentences for each spelling word, leaving blanks where the words should go. Have them trade papers and fill in the blanks.

BLIND SORT

Have partners do a **blind sort**: one reads a spelling word card; the other tells under which key word it belongs. Have them take turns until both have sorted all their words. Then have students explain how they sorted the words.

→ Build Vocabulary

DAY **1**

DAY 2

Connect to Words

Practice this week's vocabulary.

1. What might friends **argue** about?
2. Describe feeling **astonished**.
3. Have you ever **complained** to a family member?
4. What weather **conditions** are good for playing outdoors?
5. What might your teacher **forbid** you to do?
6. What is the weather **forecast**?
7. Describe feelings of **relief**.
8. What items would you need if you were **stranded** on an island?

Expand Vocabulary

Help students generate different forms of this week's words by adding, changing, or removing inflectional endings.

- Draw a four-column chart. Write *complain* in the left column. Then write *complains, complained,* and *complaining*. Read aloud the words and discuss the meanings.

- Have students share sentences with each form of *complain*.

- Students can fill in the chart for other words, such as *argue*.

- Have students copy the chart in their word study notebook.

Vocabulary Words

argue	forbidding
astonished	forecast
complained	relief
conditions	stranded

 ELL

Pair students of different language proficiency levels to practice vocabulary. Have partners discuss different shades of meaning in synonyms or other words with similar meanings, such as *astonished* and *amazed*.

 BUILD MORE VOCABULARY

COLLABORATE

ACADEMIC VOCABULARY

Discuss important academic words.

- Display *predict* and *affect* and discuss the meanings with students.

- Display *predict* and *prediction*. Have partners look up and define related words.

- Write the related words on the board. Have partners ask and answer questions using the words. Repeat with *affect*. Elicit examples from students.

ROOT WORDS

- Remind students that understanding a root word can help them figure out unfamiliar words. Display the words *astonish, astonished,* and *astonishment*. Identify and discuss the root word *astonish*.

- Have partners generate other examples and invite partners to share their words. Discuss the root words and their meanings.

DAY 3

Reinforce the Words

Review this week's vocabulary words. Have students orally complete each sentence stem.

1. Please don't <u>argue</u> with your ____.

2. We were <u>astonished</u> by the huge ____ in our yard.

3. She <u>complained</u> that the food was too ____.

4. I <u>forbid</u> my little brother to play with my ____.

5. What a <u>relief</u> that ____ is over!

6. I saw a movie about a ____ who was <u>stranded</u> on an island.

DAY 4

Connect to Writing

- Have students write sentences in their word study notebooks using this week's vocabulary.

- Tell them to write sentences that provide information about the words and their meanings.

- **ELL** Provide the Day 3 sentence stems for students needing extra support.

Write About Vocabulary Have students write something they learned from this week's words in their word study notebook. For example, they might write about being *stranded* on a fictional island. Who would they want along?

DAY 5

Word Squares

Ask students to create Word Squares for each vocabulary word.

- In the first square, students write the word. (example: *astonished*)

- In the second square, students write their own definition of the word and any related words. (examples: *amazed, surprised*)

- In the third square, students draw an illustration to help them remember the word. (example: someone looking surprised)

- In the fourth square, students write non-examples. (examples: *bored, tired*)

- Have students share their Word Squares with a partner.

IDIOMS

Remind students that an idiom is a type of figurative language that has a meaning other than the literal meaning.

- Display **Your Turn Practice Book** pages 263–264. Read the first page. Model figuring out the meanings of the idioms.

- For additional practice with idioms, have students complete page 267. Discuss the literal and nonliteral meanings of the idioms.

SHADES OF MEANING

Help students generate words related to *forecast*.

- Explain that you will write an idiom about weather. Write on the board: *The forecast says it will rain cats and dogs!* Ask: *Does this mean it will really rain cats and dogs? What does it mean?*

- Have partners work together to write words and idioms related to forecasting the weather.

- Ask students to copy the words and idioms in their word study notebook.

MORPHOLOGY

Use the word *forecast* as a springboard for students to learn more words.

- Write the prefix *fore*, explaining that it means "before" or "front." Model how to use the prefix to determine the meaning of *forecast*.

- Have students give examples of other words with the prefix *fore-*, such as *forehead, foreground,* and *foreman*.

- Tell students to use the prefix to determine the meanings of the words.

→ Integrate Ideas

Close Reading Routine

Read   DOK 1–2

- Identify key ideas and details about Weather.
- Take notes and summarize.
- Use prompts as needed.

Reread   DOK 2–3

- Analyze the text, craft, and structure.
- Use the **Close Reading Companion.**

Integrate   DOK 4

- Integrate knowledge and ideas.
- Make text-to-text connections.
- Use the Integrate lesson.
- Use *Close Reading Companion,* p. 179.

TEXT CONNECTIONS

Connect to the Essential Question

Write the essential question on the board: How can weather affect us? Divide the class into small groups. Tell students that each group will compare the information that they have learned about how weather can affect people. Model how to compare this information by using examples from this week's **Leveled Readers** and "The Big Blizzard," **Reading/Writing Workshop** pages 420–423.

Evaluate Text Evidence Have students review their class notes and completed graphic organizers before they begin their discussions. Encourage students to compare information from all the week's

Dinah Zike's
FOLDABLES
Study Organizer

Extreme Weather

Go Digital

Collaborate

Research Roadmap

Resources: Research and Inquiry

RESEARCH AND INQUIRY

Write a Summary

Explain that students will work with a partner to complete a short research project about the effects of extreme weather. They will then summarize and present their research to the class. Discuss the following steps:

❶ **Brainstorm** As they begin thinking about the effects of extreme weather, students should think about the selections they read this week and extreme weather they have experienced.

❷ **Find Resources** Have students select one extreme weather event to research and look for print and digital articles about its effects. Remind them to keep track of all of their sources by recording the author, title, and publication information.

reads. Have each group pick one student to take notes. Explain that each group will use an Accordion Foldable® to record their ideas. You may wish to model how to use an Accordion Foldable® to record comparisons.

Text to Media

Post Online Remind students to discuss their responses to the Blast along with information from all the week's reads. Tell students to include the painting on page 179 of the **Close Reading Companion** as a part of their discussion. Guide students to see the connections among media, the painting, and text. Ask: *How does the Blast connect to what you read this week? To the painting?*

Present Ideas and Synthesize Information

When students finish their discussions, ask for a volunteer from each group to read his or her notes aloud.

OBJECTIVE

CCSS Recount stories, including fables, folktales, and myths from diverse cultures; determine the central message, lesson, or moral and explain how it is conveyed through key details in the text. **RL.3.2**

③ **Guided Practice** Have students select one article and take notes on the information in the article. Remind students to paraphrase the information in the article and to take notes on only the most important facts and details.

④ **Create the Project: Summary** Have students use their notes to neatly write or type a summary of the information they learned from their article. Have students add appropriate visuals, such as illustrations, digital images, or videos, to their summaries to emphasize and enhance certain supporting details and the conclusion.

Present the Summary

Have students present their summaries to the class and then post on the Shared Research Board. Remind students to speak at an understandable pace and to make eye contact with the audience. Have students use the online Presentation Checklist 1 to evaluate their presentations.

OBJECTIVES

CCSS Conduct short research projects that build knowledge about a topic. **W.3.7**

CCSS Create engaging audio recordings of stories or poems that demonstrate fluid reading at an understandable pace; add visual displays when appropriate to emphasize or enhance certain facts or details. **SL.3.5**

• Use print and digital sources for research.

• Write a summary.

ACADEMIC LANGUAGE
extreme, weather, summarize

→ Approaching Level

Lexile 470
TextEvaluator™ 30

OBJECTIVES

CCSS Recount stories, including fables, folktales, and myths from diverse cultures; determine the central message, lesson, or moral and explain how it is conveyed through key details in the text. **RL.3.2**

CCSS Distinguish the literal and nonliteral meanings of words and phrases in context (e.g., *take steps*). **L.3.5a**

- Identify the theme of the story.
- Determine the meanings of idioms.
- Make and confirm or revise predictions.

ACADEMIC LANGUAGE

make, confirm, revise predictions, theme, historical fiction, idioms, fable

---

Leveled Reader:
The Big Storm

Before Reading

Preview and Predict

Have students read the Essential Question. Then have them read the title and table of contents of *The Big Storm*. Have students make a prediction about the plot of the story and share it with a partner.

Review Genre: Historical Fiction Review with students that historical fiction is fiction that is set in the past. It includes characters, events, and settings that could have occurred in real life. As they preview *The Big Storm*, have students identify features of historical fiction.

During Reading

Close Reading

Note Taking Have students use their graphic organizer as they read.

Pages 2–5 Point out the title of Chapter 1. Then point out the line *There were big, black clouds in the distance* on page 2. *Based on this information, what do you predict will happen in the story?* (There will be a big storm.) Point out the idiom *rain cats and dogs* in the next sentence. *Will cats and dogs literally come down from the sky like rain?* (no) *What is the nonliteral meaning of this phrase?* (Possible Response: It will rain hard.) *What phrase on page 5 tells the literal meaning about the rain?* (*Big fat raindrops began to fall.*)

Pages 6–7 *Was your first prediction correct?* (yes) *What helped you confirm or revise your prediction?* (On page 5, Henry says there is a storm coming.) *Now turn to a partner and make another prediction about what will happen to their house.* (Possible Response: The storm will tear up the house.)

Pages 8–11 Have students confirm or revise their predictions by pointing out that Pa says there is almost no damage. Point out the idiom *stood up to the storm* on page 8. *Which words help you understand what the phrase* stood up to the storm *means?* (*no damage* on page 9) *Why do Loretta and her family decide to check on the neighbors?* (They worry their neighbors were not as lucky during the tornado.) *Turn to a partner and describe how much damage the tornado did to the town.*

Go Digital

Leveled Readers

Fill in the Graphic Organizer

Pages 12–15 *What happened to Bonnie's brother?* (He got lost during the storm.) *What does the family decide to do?* (They help Bonnie find her brother.) *Turn to a partner and describe how this and other details from the story relate to the theme.* (Theme: Prepare for emergencies, and pay attention to signs of danger.)

After Reading

Respond to Reading Revisit the Essential Question, and ask students to complete the Text Evidence questions on page 16.

Write About Reading Make sure students include details from the story that support the theme. Have students refer to the graphic organizer they completed to help with their writing.

Fluency: Phrasing

Model Model reading page 2 with proper phrasing. Next, reread the page aloud, and have students read along with you.

Apply Have students practice reading with a partner.

PAIRED READ

Leveled Reader

"The Oak and the Reeds"

Make Connections: Write About It

Before reading, have students note that the genre of this text is a fable, which is a fictional story that teaches a lesson. Then discuss the Essential Question.

After reading, have students make connections between how the extreme weather affects the characters in "The Oak and the Reeds" and *The Big Storm*.

Analytical Writing

COMPARE TEXTS

• Have students use text evidence to compare a historical fiction story to a fable.

Literature Circles

Ask students to conduct a literature circle using the Thinkmark questions to guide the discussion. You may wish to have a whole-class discussion on other types of extreme weather and how they should prepare.

Level Up

Level-up lessons available online.

IF students read the Approaching Level fluently and answered the questions

THEN pair them with students who have proficiently read On Level and have approaching-level students

• echo-read the On Level main selection with their partner.

• use self-stick notes to mark a detail to discuss in each section.

A C T Access Complex Text

The On Level challenges students by including more **domain-specific words** and **complex sentence structures**.

Approaching Level

Phonics/Decoding

DECODE WORDS WITH CONSONANT + *le* SYLLABLE

TIER 2

OBJECTIVES

 Decode multisyllable words. **RF.3.3c**

Decode words with a consonant + *le* syllable.

 I Do Write the word *table* on the board, and underline the syllable *ble*. Remind students that when a word ends in a consonant + *le*, the consonant and *le* form the the word's last syllable. Model how to pronounce the final syllable in *table*. Then say the whole word, emphasizing each syllable. Point out how, because the first syllable is an open syllable, the vowel *a* is long.

 We Do Write the words *eagle, ankle, single, sample,* and *fable* on the board. Model how to decode the first word. Have students repeat. Point out the three letters that form the final syllable. Have students decode the rest of the words and identify the letters that form each word's final syllable.

 You Do Add these words to the board: *noodle, purple, chuckle, apple,* and *beagle.* Have students read them aloud, identifying the letters that form the final syllable. Point to all of the words randomly for students to read chorally.

BUILD WORDS WITH CONSONANT + *le* SYLLABLES

TIER 2

OBJECTIVES

 Decode multisyllable words. **RF.3.3c**

Build words with consonant + *le, el, al, il* syllables.

I Do Tell students that they will be building multisyllable words that are formed by adding a consonant + *le, el, al,* or *il.* Point out that, when a word ends in a consonant + *le,* the consonant + *le* form the word's last syllable. The same goes for consonant + *el, al,* and *il.* Display the **Word-Building Cards** one at a time: *un, nel, vel, ble, gle, cal, mal, ral;* write the syllables *tra, tun, an, ca, nor, lo, til,* and *plu* on the board. Model sounding out each syllable.

We Do Have students chorally read each syllable several times. Next, display all cards and syllables. Work with students to combine the cards and syllables to form two-syllable words ending in *le, el, il,* or *al.* Have students chorally read the words: *tunnel, travel, cable, angle, local, normal, until, plural.*

 You Do Write other syllables on the board, such as *an, fun, le, ta, bu, fo, mam, vil, spi.* Again, display the cards *ble, cal, gle, nel, mal, ral,* and *vel.* Have students work with partners to build words using these syllables.

PRACTICE WORDS WITH CONSONANT + *le* SYLLABLES

OBJECTIVES

 Decode multisyllable words. **RF.3.3c**

Decode multisyllable words with consonant + *le* syllables.

 I Do Remind students that, when a word ends in a consonant + *le, el, al,* or *il,* the consonant + *le, el, al,* or *il* form the word's last syllable. Write the words *handle, nickel, global, pupil,* and read them aloud. Have students repeat.

 We Do Write the words *miracle, terrible, comical, animal, caramel, unravel, peril* on the board. Model how to decode the first word. Then guide students as they decode the remaining words.

 You Do Afterward, point to the words in random order for students to chorally read. Repeat several times.

LATIN SUFFIXES *-y, -able, -ous*

OBJECTIVES

 Identify and know the meaning of the most common prefixes and derivational suffixes. **RF.3.3a**

 Decode words with common Latin suffixes. **RF.3.3b**

 Determine the meaning of the new word formed when a known affix is added to a known word. **L.3.4b**

Decode words with suffixes *-y, -able, -ous.*

I Do Review the Latin suffixes *-y, -able,* and *-ous.* When added to a root word, these suffixes turn the word into an adjective. Review that *-y* means "having the quality of," *-able* means "able to," and *-ous* means "full of." When *-y* or *-able* is added to a word ending in a consonant + *e,* the *e* is often dropped (*ice/icy; use/usable*). When *-ous* is added to a root word ending in a consonant + *y,* the *y* is changed to *i* (*fury/furious*).

We Do Write *windy, bendable, dangerous* on the board. Say each word aloud and have students repeat. Model identifying the suffix for *windy* and using the suffix to determine the word's meaning. Guide students in identifying the suffixes and determining the meanings of the remaining words.

 You Do Write *stony, believable, poisonous* on the board. Have students say each word. Have them identify each word's suffix and use it to determine the word's meaning. Point to the words in random order for students to read chorally. Occasionally ask for a word's suffix and definition.

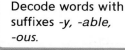 **ENGLISH LANGUAGE LEARNERS**

For the students who need **phonics**, **decoding**, and **fluency** practice, use scaffolding methods as necessary to ensure students understand the meaning of the words. Refer to the **Language Transfers Handbook** for phonics elements that may not transfer in students' native languages.

→ Approaching Level

Vocabulary

REVIEW HIGH-FREQUENCY WORDS

OBJECTIVES

 Use conventional spellings for high-frequency and other studied words and for adding suffixes to base words (e.g., *sitting, smiled, cries, happiness*). **L.3.2e**

Review high-frequency words.

 Use **Word Cards** 211–220. Display one word at a time, following the routine:

Display the word. Read the word. Then spell the word.

 Ask students to state the word and spell the word with you. Model using the word in a sentence and have students repeat after you.

 Display the word. Ask students to say the word and then spell it. When completed, quickly flip through the word card set as students chorally read the words. Provide opportunities for students to use the words in speaking and writing. For example, provide sentence starters such as *We took a _____ in the park after lunch.* Ask students to write each word in their **Writer's Notebook**.

REVIEW VOCABULARY WORDS

OBJECTIVES

 Acquire and use accurately grade-appropriate conversational, general academic, and domain-specific words and phrases, including those that signal spatial and temporal relationships. **L.3.6**

Review vocabulary words.

 Display each **Visual Vocabulary Card** and state the word. Explain how the photograph illustrates the word. State the example sentence and repeat the word.

 Point to the word on the card and read the word with students. Ask them to repeat the word. Engage students in structured partner talk about the image as prompted on the back of the vocabulary card.

 Display each visual in random order, hiding the word. Have students match the definitions and context sentences of the words to the visuals displayed. Then ask students to complete **Approaching Reproducibles** page 261.

IDENTIFY RELATED WORDS

OBJECTIVES

Demonstrate understanding of word relationships and nuances in word meanings. Identify real-life connections between words and their use (e.g., describe people who are *friendly* or *helpful*). **L.3.5b**

Identify words that are related in meanings.

 I Do Display the *argue* **Visual Vocabulary Card**. Say aloud the word set *argue, ignore, disagree*. Point out that *disagree* and *argue* have similar meanings.

 We Do Display the vocabulary card for the word *astonished*. Say aloud the word set *astonished, amazed, unhappy*. With students, identify the word that means close to the same thing as *astonished*, and discuss why.

 You Do Using the word sets below, display the remaining cards one at a time, saying aloud each word set. Ask students to identify the word in each set that has the closest meaning to the vocabulary word.

complained, grumbled, complimented   forecast, prediction, mistake

conditions, characteristics, centers   relief, comfort, problem

forbidding, inviting, prohibiting   stranded, helpless, thrilled

IDIOMS

OBJECTIVES

Determine the meaning of words and phrases as they are used in a text, distinguishing literal from nonliteral language. **RL.3.4**

Distinguish the literal and nonliteral meanings of words and phrases in context (e.g., *take steps*). **L.3.5a**

Use context clues to determine the meanings of idioms.

 I Do Display the Comprehension and Fluency passage on **Approaching Reproducibles** pages 263–264. Read aloud the first two paragraphs. Point to the phrase *at sixes and sevens*. Explain that this is an idiom, a phrase that means something different from the meaning of each word in it. Students can use clues in the story to figure out the meaning of an idiom.

Think Aloud I read in the sentence before that the father likes to try new things. After the idiom, it says he does not know what to do with himself if he is not trying something new. I think *at sixes and sevens* means "confused" or "in a panic."

Write the meaning of the idiom.

 We Do Have students point to the phrase *tried his hand*. With students, discuss how to use clues in the story to figure out the meaning of this idiom. Write the meaning of the idiom.

 You Do Have students find the meaning of the idioms *sea legs, sleeping on it,* and *it takes the cake* using clues in the story.

→ **Approaching Level**

Comprehension

FLUENCY

TIER 2

OBJECTIVES

CCSS Read on-level text with purpose and understanding. **RF.3.4a**

CCSS Read on-level prose and poetry orally with accuracy, appropriate rate, and expression on successive readings. **RF.3.4b**

Read fluently with appropriate phrasing.

 I Do Explain that, when reading aloud, good readers focus on reading with appropriate phrasing. Phrasing means breaking longer sentences into chunks of text. This helps listeners better understand the content. One way to read with appropriate phrasing is to pause briefly at commas and stop at periods. Read the first two paragraphs of the Comprehension and Fluency passage on **Approaching Reproducibles** pages 263–264. Tell students to listen for when you pause at commas and stop at periods.

 We Do Read the rest of the page aloud, and have students repeat each sentence after you using the same phrasing. Explain that you broke sentences into chunks of text, paused briefly at commas, and stopped at periods.

 You Do Have partners take turns reading sentences from the Approaching Reproducibles passage. Remind them to focus on their phrasing. Listen in and provide corrective feedback as needed by modeling proper fluency.

IDENTIFY KEY DETAILS

TIER 2

OBJECTIVES

CCSS Recount stories, including fables, folktales, and myths from diverse cultures; determine the central message, lesson, or moral and explain how it is conveyed through key details in the text. **RL.3.2**

Identify key details in a story.

 I Do Write the topic: *Moving to America.* Then write: *narrator's family leaves England for America; weather helps family decide where they will live; he doesn't know what to do with himself.* Read the statements aloud. Explain that the first two details are key because they tell us about the family moving to America. Help students understand that the last detail is not key because it is not connected to the topic or key details.

 We Do Read the first page of the Comprehension and Fluency passage in the **Approaching Reproducibles**. Ask: *What is this selection about so far?* Point out that this is the topic of the selection. Ask: *Which details give more information about the topic?* Point out that these are the key details.

 You Do Have students read the rest of the passage. After each paragraph, they should write down the details that seem most important to the topic. Review their lists with them, and help them identify the key details.

REVIEW THEME

OBJECTIVES

 Recount stories, including fables, folktales, and myths from diverse cultures; determine the central message, lesson, or moral and explain how it is conveyed through key details in the text. **RL.3.2**

Identify the theme of a selection.

 I Do Remind students that an author often includes a message in a story, which is the story's theme. Explain that when readers determine the theme, they will identify what the author thinks is important. Students can determine a story's theme by thinking about what characters do and say. Then they should look at what happens as a result of characters' actions. As they read, students should ask: *What is the author's message?*

 We Do Read the first paragraph of the Comprehension and Fluency passage in the **Approaching Reproducibles** together. Pause to point out details that show what the character or narrator says. Model how to decide which details in the paragraph are important to the author. Then work with students to identify key details in each paragraph of the passage.

You Do Have students use key details from each paragraph to come up with the theme for the whole passage.

SELF-SELECTED READING

OBJECTIVES

 Recount stories, including fables, folktales, and myths from diverse cultures; determine the central message, lesson, or moral and explain how it is conveyed through key details in the text. **RL.3.2**

• Determine the theme of a selection.

• Make and confirm or revise predictions.

Read Independently

Have students choose a book of historical fiction for sustained silent reading. Remind students that:

• to determine the theme of a selection, students should think about what the characters do and say.

• as they read, students should use details in the story to predict what they think will happen next. As they read on they should look for clues that will help them confirm or revise their predictions.

Read Purposefully

Have students record key details on **Graphic Organizer 148** as they read independently. After they finish, they can conduct a Book Talk, each telling about the book they read.

• Students should share their organizers and answer these questions: *What is the theme of the selection? Which details show information that is most important to the author?*

• Students can share any illustrations in their books that show the setting and give details about how people from past generations lived.

→ On Level

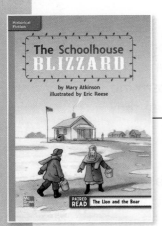

Lexile 610
TextEvaluator™ 31

OBJECTIVES

CCSS Recount stories, including fables, folktales, and myths from diverse cultures; determine the central message, lesson, or moral and explain how it is conveyed through key details in the text. **RL.3.2**

CCSS Distinguish the literal and nonliteral meanings of words and phrases in context (e.g., *take steps*). **L.3.5a**

• Identify the theme of the story.
• Determine the meanings of idioms.
• Make and confirm or revise predictions.

ACADEMIC LANGUAGE

make, confirm or revise predictions, theme, historical fiction, idioms, fable

Leveled Reader:
The Schoolhouse Blizzard

Before Reading

Preview and Predict

Have students read the Essential Question. Then have them read the title and table of contents of *The Schoolhouse Blizzard*. Have students make a prediction about the plot of the story.

Review Genre: Historical Fiction Review with students that historical fiction is fiction that is set in the past. It includes characters, events, and settings that could have occurred in real life. As they preview *The Schoolhouse Blizzard*, have students identify features of historical fiction.

During Reading

Close Reading

Note Taking Have students use their graphic organizer as they read.

Pages 2–4 *How does the author show that this story is set in the past? Name two details.* (On page 2, I read that Lily grabs her lunch pail. On page 4, I read that the children attend a one-room schoolhouse.)

Page 5 *What is the problem on page 5?* (There is a blizzard and the students are left alone.) *Make a prediction about how the children will deal with the blizzard on their own.* (Possible Response: They will try to stay warm by keeping the fire going.)

Pages 6–9 *How does Lily take charge to help in Chapter 2? Summarize to a partner.* (Lily thinks of using a jumping rope to safely find coal and warms her brother's feet to prevent frostbite.) *Confirm or revise your prediction from page 5.* (Possible Response: The students try to keep warm by getting coal; this confirms my prediction.) *Make a prediction about how the children might get by without light and water.* (Possible Response: I predict they use the light of the fire and melt snow or ice to drink for water.)

Pages 10–12 *Does the phrase warm as toast on page 10 have a literal meaning?* (no) *Define the idiom using context clues.* (When toast is first made, it is very warm. *Warm as toast* means "very warm and cozy.") *Why does Lily tell stories?* (to reassure the younger children and take their minds off the blizzard)

Go
Digital

Leveled Readers

Fill in the Graphic Organizer

Pages 13–15 Have students confirm or revise their last prediction and explain which clues from the story helped them. *Summarize the theme of the story to a partner. Think about Lily's actions.* (It is important to stay calm and make sensible decisions in an emergency.)

After Reading

Respond to Reading Revisit the Essential Question, and ask students to complete the Text Evidence questions on page 16.

Analytical Writing **Write About Reading** Make sure students include details from the story that support the story's theme. Encourage students to use the graphic organizer they completed as they write.

Fluency: Phrasing

Model Model reading page 2 with proper phrasing. Next, reread the page aloud, and have students read along with you.

Apply Have students practice reading with a partner.

PAIRED READ

"The Lion and the Boar"

Make Connections:
Write About It ✏️ *Analytical Writing*

Before reading, have students note that the genre of this text is a fable, which is a fictional story that teaches a lesson. Then discuss the Essential Question.

After reading, have students make connections between how the characters survive extreme weather in "The Lion and the Boar" and *The Schoolhouse Blizzard*.

Leveled Reader

✏️ *Analytical Writing*

COMPARE TEXTS

- Have students use text evidence to compare a historical fiction story to a fable.

Literature Circles

Ask students to conduct a literature circle using the Thinkmark questions to guide the discussion. You may wish to have a whole-class discussion on other types of extreme weather and how they should act if they are in those situations.

Level Up

Level-up lessons available online.

IF students read the On Level fluently and answered the questions

THEN pair them with students who have proficiently read Beyond Level and have on-level students

- partner-read the Beyond Level main selection.
- list vocabulary words they find difficult and look them up with their partner.

A C T Access Complex Text

The Beyond Level challenges students by including more **domain-specific words** and **complex sentence structures**.

On Level

Vocabulary

REVIEW VOCABULARY WORDS

 OBJECTIVES

Acquire and use accurately grade-appropriate conversational, general academic and domain-specific words and phrases, including those that signal spatial and temporal relationships (e.g., *After dinner that night we went looking for them*). **L.3.6**

Review vocabulary words.

 I Do

Use the **Visual Vocabulary Cards** to review key vocabulary words *argue, astonished, complained, forbidding, relief,* and *stranded.* Point to each word, read it aloud, and have students chorally repeat it.

 We Do

Ask these questions and help students respond and explain their answers.
- What is the last thing you saw, heard, or tasted that *astonished* you?
- Is it better to *argue* or talk about a problem with a friend? Why?
- What situation caused you to feel *relief* when it was over?

 You Do

Have students respond to these questions and explain their answers.
- What is something you or someone else has *complained* about?
- Why would you see a sign on a beach *forbidding* you to swim?
- Have you ever been *stranded* somewhere? What happened?

IDIOMS

 OBJECTIVES

Determine the meaning of words and phrases as they are used in a text, distinguishing literal from nonliteral language. **RL.3.4**

Distinguish the literal and nonliteral meanings of words and phrases in context (e.g., *take steps*). **L.3.5a**

Use context clues to determine the meanings of idioms.

 I Do

Remind students that they can figure out the meaning of an idiom using clues from the story. Use the Comprehension and Fluency passage on **Your Turn Practice Book** pages 263–264 to model.

Think Aloud I want to figure out the meaning of the idiom *at sixes and sevens.* I can look for clues to the meaning in the story. I read that the father likes adventures and does not know what to do with himself if he is not exploring. I think it means that he is confused or in a panic.

 We Do

Have students read the fourth paragraph, where they will encounter the phrase *tried his hand at.* Then, have students use clues from the story to figure out the meaning of the idiom.

 You Do

Have students work in pairs to determine the meanings of the idioms *sea legs, sleeping on it,* and *takes the cake* as they read the rest of the passage.

Comprehension

REVIEW THEME

OBJECTIVES

CCSS Recount stories, including fables, folktales, and myths from diverse cultures; determine the central message, lesson, or moral and explain how it is conveyed through key details in the text. **RL.3.2**

Identify the theme of a selection.

 I Do Remind students that authors often include a message in their stories. This message is the story's theme. When students are able to identify the theme of a story, they will identify what is important to the author. To identify a theme, students should look at what the characters do and say. Then they should look at what happens as a result of these actions. As they read, students should ask themselves: *What is the author's message?*

 We Do Have a volunteer read the first paragraph of the Comprehension and Fluency passage on **Your Turn Practice Book** pages 263–264. Have students orally list key details and explain why they are key. Then model using the details to determine the author's message. Work with students to identify key details and the author's message on the rest of the page.

You Do Have partners keep track of key details using **Graphic Organizer 148** for the rest of the passage. Then have partners identify the theme of the whole passage.

SELF-SELECTED READING

OBJECTIVES

CCSS Recount stories, including fables, folktales, and myths from diverse cultures; determine the central message, lesson, or moral and explain how it is conveyed through key details in the text. **RL.3.2**

• Determine the theme of a selection.

• Make and confirm or revise predictions.

Read Independently

Have students choose a historical fiction book for sustained silent reading.

• Before they read, have students preview the book, looking for illustrations that show the setting and how people of the era lived.

• As students read, remind them to make predictions about the story. As they read on, they should confirm or revise their predictions.

Read Purposefully

Encourage students to read different historical-fiction books in order to learn about a variety of eras.

• As students read, they can fill in **Graphic Organizer 148**. They can refer back to it to write a summary of the book.

• Students should share their organizers and answer these questions: *What is the theme of the story? Which details helped you determine the theme?*

• Have students share their predictions about the book with classmates and explain whether they confirmed or had to revise the predictions.

→ Beyond Level

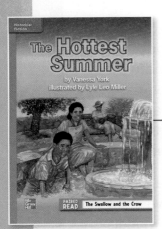

Lexile 630
TextEvaluator™ 35

CCSS **OBJECTIVES**

Recount stories, including fables, folktales, and myths from diverse cultures; determine the central message, lesson, or moral and explain how it is conveyed through key details in the text. **RL.3.2**

Distinguish the literal and nonliteral meanings of words and phrases in context (e.g., *take steps*). **L.3.5a**

- Identify the theme of the story.
- Determine the meanings of idioms.
- Make and confirm or revise predictions.

ACADEMIC LANGUAGE

make, confirm, revise predictions, theme, historical fiction, idioms, fable

Leveled Reader:
The Hottest Summer

Leveled Readers

Before Reading

Preview and Predict

Have students read the Essential Question. Then have them read the title and table of contents of *The Hottest Summer*. Have students make a prediction about the plot of the story.

Review Genre: Historical Fiction Review with students that historical fiction is fiction that is set in the past. It includes characters, events, and settings that could have occurred in real life. As they preview *The Hottest Summer,* have students identify features of historical fiction.

During Reading

Close Reading

Note Taking Have students use their graphic organizer as they read.

Fill in the Graphic Organizer

Pages 2–3 *How does the author show the impact of the heatwave?* (The descriptions *people were irritable in the high heat* and *heat hung more heavily than ever* show how much it affected people's lives.)

Pages 4–5 *Do you think there is something wrong with Grandma? Why?* (Yes, because it says she was struggling in the heat and that she seemed tired; she was also puffing and bright red in the face.) *Make a prediction about what Grandma's problem might be and how the other characters could help solve it.* (Possible Response: I predict she is sick from the heat; they should get her in a cool place and give her water.)

Pages 6–7 *Does the author intend the phrase "neverending pile of mending" on page 6 to be literal or nonliteral?* (nonliteral) *What is meant by the idiom?* (There is always something that needs to be mended.)

Pages 8–9 *Summarize Grandma's symptoms to a partner.* (She is dizzy, disoriented, and has a burning forehead.) *Confirm or revise your prediction about Grandma's health problem. Do you think Alberta and Frank will be able to help?* (Possible Response: The symptoms do sound serious; I need to read on to find out more.)

Pages 10–12 *How does Alberta help her grandmother?* (She finds an ice truck and uses the ice to cool her grandmother.)

Pages 13–15 *Can you confirm or revise your prediction about what is wrong with grandmother now?* (Possible Response: Yes; on page 13 the ice man says that many people have been suffering from heat stroke, and Alberta's grandmother might have heat stroke as well.) *What does the idiom* kept her cool *on page 15 mean?* (*Kept her cool* means "she stayed calm under pressure.") *Summarize the theme of the story to a partner.* (In an emergency, stay calm and make wise decisions.)

After Reading

Respond to Reading Revisit the Essential Question, and ask students to complete the Text Evidence questions on page 16.

Analytical Writing **Write About Reading** Make sure students clearly state the theme and include details from the text that support the story's theme.

Fluency: Phrasing

Model Model reading page 2 with proper phrasing. Next, reread the page aloud, and have students read along with you.

Apply Have students practice reading with a partner.

PAIRED READ

Leveled Reader

"The Swallow and the Crow"

Make Connections: Write About It *Analytical Writing*

Before reading, have students note that the genre of this text is a fable, which is a fictional story that teaches a lesson. Then discuss the Essential Question.

After reading, have students make connections between how the characters survive extreme weather in "The Swallow and the Crow" and *The Hottest Summer*.

Analytical Writing

COMPARE TEXTS

• Have students use text evidence to compare a historical fiction story to a fable.

Literature Circles

Ask students to conduct a literature circle using the Thinkmark questions to guide the discussion. You may wish to have a whole-class discussion on other types of extreme weather and how they should react in those situations.

Gifted and Talented

Synthesize Challenge students to write about the next day of the heat wave for Alberta and her family. Have Alberta think of additional ways to keep the family cool. Invite volunteers to share their stories with the class.

Beyond Level

Vocabulary

REVIEW DOMAIN-SPECIFIC WORDS

OBJECTIVES

 Produce simple, compound, and complex sentences. **L.3.1i**

Review and discuss domain-specific words.

 Model Use the **Visual Vocabulary Cards** to review the meanings of the words *conditions* and *forecast*. Write social studies related sentences on the board using the words.

On the board, write *pressure, temperate, climate,* and discuss the meanings with students. Then work with students to write sentences using these words.

 Apply Have students work in pairs to discuss the meanings of the words *extreme, thermometer,* and *heatwave*. Then challenge students to write sentences that relate to the topic of how weather affects us.

IDIOMS

OBJECTIVES

 Determine the meaning of words and phrases as they are used in a text, distinguishing literal from nonliteral language. **RL.3.4**

Distinguish the literal and nonliteral meanings of words and phrases in context (e.g., *take steps*). **L.3.5a**

Use context clues to determine the meanings of idioms.

 Model Read aloud the first two paragraphs of the Comprehension and Fluency passage on **Beyond Reproducibles** pages 263–264.

Think Aloud I want to figure out the meaning of the idiom *at sixes and sevens*. I can look for clues in the story. I read that the narrator's father craves adventure and cannot figure out what to do with himself if he is not exploring. I think that the idiom means he is confused and in a state of panic.

With students, read the third paragraph. Help them figure out the meaning of the idiom *tried his hand at* using clues from the story.

 Apply Have pairs of students read the rest of the passage. Ask them to use clues from the story to determine the meanings of the idioms *sea legs, sleeping on it,* and *takes the cake.*

 Plan of Action Have students write a short story about a character who takes idioms literally. For instance, he or she thinks that when someone bends over backwards for someone else, that person arches his or her back and looks up into the sky. Encourage them to add illustrations to accompany their stories. Have students read their stories and present their illustrations to the class.

Comprehension

REVIEW THEME

OBJECTIVES

 Recount stories, including fables, folktales, and myths from diverse cultures; determine the central message, lesson, or moral and explain how it is conveyed through key details in the text. **RL.3.2**

Determine the theme of a selection.

 Model Remind students that authors often include a theme, or message, in their stories. Explain that students can determine the theme by looking at what characters do and say and the resulting actions. Remind students that, as they read, they should ask themselves: *What is the author's message?*

Have students read the first paragraph of the Comprehension and Fluency passage of **Beyond Reproducibles** pages 263–264. Ask open-ended questions to facilitate discussion, such as *What does the author consider important in this paragraph? What do the characters say and do? What happens as a result of their actions?* Students should support their responses with details from the text.

 Apply Have students fill in **Graphic Organizer 148** as they read the rest of the passage. Then have partners determine the theme of the whole passage.

SELF-SELECTED READING

OBJECTIVES

 Recount stories, including fables, folktales, and myths from diverse cultures; determine the central message, lesson, or moral and explain how it is conveyed through key details in the text. **RL.3.2**

• Determine the theme of a selection.

• Make and confirm or revise predictions.

Read Independently

Have students choose a historical fiction book for sustained silent reading.

- As students read, have them fill in **Graphic Organizer 148**.
- Remind students to make predictions about the story. They should read on to confirm or revise their predictions.

Read Purposefully

Encourage students to keep a reading journal. Ask them to read different historical-fiction books to learn about a variety of eras.

- Students can write summaries of the books in their journals.
- Ask students to give their reactions to the books to the class. Have them give the stories' themes and the details they used to determine them.

 Gifted and Talented **Independent Study** Challenge students to discuss how their books relate to the weekly theme of weather and the effect weather has on us. Have students compare some of the stories and historical eras they read about. Then have them write a few paragraphs describing how weather affected some of the characters and settings they read about.

English Language Learners

Reading/Writing Workshop

 ## OBJECTIVES

Recount stories, including fables, folktales, and myths from diverse cultures; determine the central message, lesson, or moral and explain how it is conveyed through key details in the text. **RL.3.2**

• Determine the meanings of idioms.

• Make and confirm or revise predictions.

LANGUAGE OBJECTIVE

Identify the theme of a story.

ACADEMIC LANGUAGE

• *theme, confirm, revise predictions, historical fiction, idioms*

• Cognates: *tema, confirmar, revisar, predicciones, ficción histórica*

Shared Read
The Big Blizzard

Go Digital

View "The Big Blizzard"

Before Reading

Build Background

Read the Essential Question: How can weather affect us?

• Explain the meaning of the Essential Question. Describe a recent storm. Demonstrate how it affected students. For example, they wore raincoats to school, carried umbrellas, took a bus rather than walked somewhere.

• **Model an answer:** *Weather causes us to change how we act, what we do, and what we wear. In a blizzard, we may close the schools. We may have to wear warm clothing or stay inside.*

• Ask students a question that ties the Essential Question to their own background knowledge: *Turn to a partner and tell about a day you did something because of the weather outside. What was the weather like? How did it change your behavior?* Call on pairs to share their responses.

During Reading

Interactive-Question Response

• Ask questions that help students understand the meaning of the text after each paragraph.

• Reinforce the meanings of key vocabulary.

• Ask students questions that require them to use key vocabulary.

• Reinforce strategies and skills of the week by modeling.

Page 421

Paragraph 1
Have a student read the title of the story. (The Big Blizzard) Explain that a *blizzard* is a big snowstorm. *Now look at the images. What are we going to read about?* (a family that goes through a big blizzard) Demonstrate *huddled* and explain that it means "gathered close to something or someone."

Paragraph 2
Rosa and Eddie listening to the radio. Why? (for updates on the snowstorm)

Explain to a partner why the mayor's message might be important.

Paragraphs 3–4
Explain and Model Making a Prediction *I can make a guess about what will happen next. Why is Rosa worried?* (Her father is stuck at work.) *Does Rosa's mother think he will make it home?* (yes) *I predict that Rosa's father will make it home because her mother says the snow is slowing down. I will read on to find out.*

Paragraphs 5–8
Mamá needs to go to the store. Why might the blizzard make it hard to go? (It is too cold. It is snowing too hard.)

Page 422

Paragraph 4
Define the vocabulary word *astonished* and point out that *amazed* nearby is a context clue. *What problem does the family face in getting to the store?* (a wall of snow blocking them) *How can they solve this problem?* (by shoveling their way out)

Paragraph 7
Explain and Model Idioms Point out the idiom, *give a hand. Is Rosa really giving Mrs. Sanchez her hand?* Put your hand on a student's desk to demonstrate. (no) *Rosa wants to borrow Mr. Colón's shovels to help clear the snow. I think that "give a hand" means "to help with something."*

Page 423

Paragraph 1
Is shoveling the walk really a piece of cake *for Rosa and Eddie?* (no) *This idiom means that something is easy to do.* Have a student say the sentence, replacing the idiom with what it literally means.

Paragraphs 3–5
Have students choral read the remaining dialogue. *How do Rosa and Eddie feel when they see their father?* (excited) *What detail in the text tells you?* (they shouted and ran over to him)

Model Theme Ask students to turn back to page 421: *What is similar about what the mayor and papá say?* (It is important to help others.) *I see that the importance of helping others is repeated throughout the story. I also see the town benefited from people helping each other. I think the theme of the story is that it is important to help others, especially during hard times.*

Explain and Model Confirming or Revising Predictions *My prediction was correct. Rosa and Eddie's father was able to come home.* What clues allow me to confirm my prediction? (Papá says: *It is such a relief and a comfort to finally be home.*)

How do you predict the town will react during future blizzards? Have students use the sentence frame: *I predict _____ because _____.*

After Reading

Make Connections
- Review the Essential Question: How can weather affect us?
- Make text connections.
- Have students complete the **ELL Reproducibles** pages 263–265.

→ English Language Learners

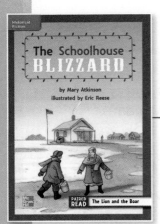

Lexile 490
TextEvaluator™ 5

 OBJECTIVES
Recount stories, including fables, folktales, and myths from diverse cultures; determine the central message, lesson, or moral and explain how it is conveyed through key details in the text. **RL.3.2**

• Determine the meanings of idioms.
• Make and confirm or revise predictions.

LANGUAGE OBJECTIVE
Identify the theme of the story.

ACADEMIC LANGUAGE
• make, confirm and revise predictions, theme, historical fiction, idioms, fable
• Cognates: *confirmar, revisar, predicciones, ficción histórica, tema*

Leveled Reader:
The Schoolhouse Blizzard

Before Reading

Preview

• Read the Essential Question: How can weather affect us?

• Refer to Weather Affects Us: *How can the weather affect the decisions we make?*

• Preview *The Schoolhouse Blizzard* and "The Lion and the Boar": *Let's read about how the weather affects us.*

Vocabulary

Use the **Visual Vocabulary Cards** to preteach the ELL vocabulary: *calm, panic, sensible.* Use the routine found on the cards. Point out the cognates: *calma, pánico.*

During Reading

Interactive Question-Response

Note Taking Have students use their graphic organizer in **ELL Reproducibles** page 262. Use the following questions after reading each section. Use visuals or pictures to define key vocabulary.

Pages 2–3 Point to the picture on page 2. *Do you think the story is in the past or in the present?* (past) Have students point out clues that help them know this is historical fiction. (the one-room schoolhouse in the picture; the children carry lunch pails)

Pages 4–5 Have one student complete the frame and another verify the answer: *Miss Adams leaves the school classroom while there is a ___* (blizzard). *How do you think the students will react to the blizzard?* Have students make a prediction based on what they have read so far. (I predict they will try to stay warm by keeping the fire going.)

Pages 6–9 Chorally read the first sentence on page 8 with students. *How did Lily help?* (She tied a rope to Harry's belt.) *Harry was able to get coal for the stove. Was your prediction correct? Why?* (Possible Response: Yes; the children were trying to stay warm.) *Talk to a partner about how you think the children will get through the storm without light.*

Go Digital

Leveled Readers

Fill in the Graphic Organizer

Pages 10–12 Point out the idiom *fighting back tears* on page 10. *Was Alice really fighting tears?* Gesture boxing with your fists. (no) *What was Alice doing?* Have students complete the sentence frame: *Alice was trying not to* _____ (cry).

Pages 13–15 *Was Lily calm during the blizzard?* (yes) *Did Lily make sensible decisions?* (yes) *These actions tell about the theme: stay calm and be sensible in an emergency. Turn to a partner and tell how you think this helped Lily help her class.*

After Reading

Respond to Reading Revisit the Essential Question, and ask students to complete the Text Evidence questions on page 16.

Write About Reading *Analytical Writing* Have students work with a partner to write a paragraph that tells details that support the story's theme.

Fluency: Phrasing

Model Model reading page 2 with proper phrasing. Next, reread the page aloud, and have students read along with you.

Apply Have students practice reading with a partner.

PAIRED READ

Leveled Reader

"The Lion and the Boar"

Make Connections: Write About It *Analytical Writing*

Before reading, have students note that the genre of this text is a fable, which is a fictional story that teaches a lesson. Then discuss the Essential Question.

After reading, have students make connections between how the characters survive extreme weather in "The Lion and the Boar" and *The Schoolhouse Blizzard*.

Analytical Writing

COMPARE TEXTS

• Have students use text evidence to compare a historical fiction story to a fable.

Literature Circles

Ask students to conduct a literature circle using the Thinkmark questions to guide the discussion. You may wish to have a whole-class discussion on other types of extreme weather and how they should react in those situations.

Level Up

Level-up lessons available online.

IF students read the **ELL Level** fluently and answered the questions

THEN pair them with students who have proficiently read **On Level** and have ELL students

• echo-read the **On Level** main selection with their partner.

• list difficult words and discuss them with their partner.

A C T Access Complex Text

The **On Level** challenges students by including more **domain-specific words** and **complex sentence structures**.

→ English Language Learners
Vocabulary

PRETEACH VOCABULARY

OBJECTIVES
Acquire and use accurately grade-appropriate conversational, general academic and domain-specific words and phrases, including those that signal spatial and temporal relationships (e.g., *After dinner that night we went looking for them*). **L.3.6**

LANGUAGE OBJECTIVE
Use vocabulary words.

 Preteach vocabulary from "The Big Blizzard" following the Vocabulary Routine found on the **Visual Vocabulary Cards** for *argue, astonished, complained, conditions, forbidding, forecast, relief* and *stranded*.

 After completing the Vocabulary Routine for each word, point to the word on the Visual Vocabulary Card and read the word with students. Ask students to repeat the word.

 Have students work with a partner to write sentence frames using three of the words. Then have each pair read their sentence frames aloud.

Beginning	Intermediate	Advanced/High
Help students write their sentence frames correctly and read them aloud.	Have students find a synonym for each word.	Have students write a synonym and antonym for each word.

REVIEW VOCABULARY

OBJECTIVES
Acquire and use accurately grade-appropriate conversational, general academic and domain-specific words and phrases, including those that signal spatial and temporal relationships. **L.3.6**

LANGUAGE OBJECTIVE
Review vocabulary words.

 Review the previous week's vocabulary words over a few days. Read each word aloud and point to the word on the **Visual Vocabulary Card**. Ask students to repeat after you. Then follow the Vocabulary Routine on the back of each card.

 Act out the vocabulary words for students. Ask students to guess each word you act out. Give clues by describing your actions (e.g., For *reward*, say: *I would like to give you a prize for finding my lost dog*).

 Have students write clues for two of the words. Then have partners use the clues to determine the word. Students can ask additional questions about each word if necessary.

Beginning	Intermediate	Advanced/High
Help students write clues and determine the words.	Have students write clues using complete sentences.	Have students write questions as their clues.

IDIOMS

OBJECTIVES

CCSS Distinguish between the literal and nonliteral meanings of words and phrases in context (e.g., *take steps*). **L.3.5a**

CCSS Determine the meaning of words and phrases as they are used in a text, distinguishing literal from nonliteral language. **RL.3.4**

LANGUAGE OBJECTIVE

Use context clues to determine the meanings of idioms.

I Do Read aloud the first three paragraphs of "The Big Blizzard" on page 422 while students follow along. After summarizing the paragraphs, point to the phrase *stick together*. Explain that this phrase is an idiom. Remind students that idioms are phrases that mean something different from the meaning of each word in them. Point out that students can use clues in the story to help figure out the meaning of an idiom.

Think Aloud I will look for clues in the story. I see that Rosie and Eddie want to go to the store with their mother. She thinks it is too cold for them, though. She also says that it will be okay if they *stay close to each other*. I think *stick together* means "to stay together in a group."

We Do Have students point to the idiom *bundle up* on page 422. Using story clues, help students determine its meaning. Write the meaning on the board.

You Do Have pairs write meanings for *give Mrs. Sanchez a hand* on page 422 and *a piece of cake* on page 423 by using story clues to help determine meaning.

Beginning	Intermediate	Advanced/High
Help students locate the idioms and determine the meanings.	Have students write definitions for the two idioms.	Have students write sentences for all the idioms in the passage.

ADDITIONAL VOCABULARY

OBJECTIVES

CCSS Produce simple, compound, and complex sentences. **L.3.1i**

Discuss concept and high-frequency words.

LANGUAGE OBJECTIVE

Use concept and high-frequency words.

I Do List concept and high-frequency words from "The Big Blizzard": *us, warm, snowstorm;* and *The Schoolhouse Blizzard: shelter, frostbite, drought.* Define each word for students: Shelter *is a place that is safe. Amina ran home to take* shelter *from the rain.*

We Do Model using the word *us* for students in a sentence: *The bus will take* us *home.* Then provide sentence frames and complete them with students: *She gave* us ____.

You Do Have pairs write a sentence using each word and share the completed sentences with the class.

Beginning	Intermediate	Advanced/High
Help students write the completed sentences.	Have students write their sentences on the board.	Have students write a question for each word.

→ English Language Learners
Writing/Spelling

WRITING TRAIT: WORD CHOICE

OBJECTIVES

 Use dialogue and descriptions of actions, thoughts, and feelings to develop experiences and events or show the response of characters to situations. **W.3.3b**

Identify linking words and understand how to use them to connect ideas.

LANGUAGE OBJECTIVE

Use linking words to connect ideas.

 I Do Explain that good writers use linking words to connect ideas and show how ideas are the same or different. Some examples of linking words are *and, another, also, but,* and *more.* Read the Student Model passage aloud as students follow along and listen for words that connect or compare ideas.

 We Do Read aloud page 421 from "The Big Blizzard" as students follow along. Point out examples of linking words. Model showing how linking words are used to connect ideas and show how ideas are alike or different.

 You Do Have pairs write a short paragraph that compares two of their favorite activities. They should use linking words to help show how the activities are alike and different. Edit each paragraph. Ask students to revise.

Beginning	Intermediate	Advanced/High
Have students copy the edited writing.	Have students revise to clarify how the activities are alike and different.	Have students revise to add more sensory details and edit for errors.

SPELL WORDS WITH CONSONANT + *le* SYLLABLES

OBJECTIVES

 Use spelling patterns and generalizations (e.g., word families, position-based spellings, syllable patterns, ending rules, meaningful word parts) in writing words. **L.3.2f**

LANGUAGE OBJECTIVE

Spell words with consonant + *le* syllables.

 I Do Read the Spelling Words on page T98 aloud. Point out that in spelling, *le, el,* and *al* usually follow a consonant.

 We Do Read the Dictation Sentences on page T99 aloud. With each sentence, read the underlined word slowly. Have students repeat after you and write the word.

 You Do Display the words. Have students exchange their lists with a partner to check the spelling and write the words correctly.

Beginning	Intermediate	Advanced/High
Have students copy the words correctly and say them aloud.	Have students circle the last syllable in each corrected word.	Have students correct their words and partners quiz each other.

Grammar

ADJECTIVES THAT COMPARE

OBJECTIVES

 Form and use comparative and superlative adjectives and adverbs, and choose between them depending on what is to be modified. **L.3.1g**

Identify adjectives that compare.

LANGUAGE OBJECTIVE

Use adjectives that compare.

Language Transfers Handbook

In Spanish, adjectives follow the nouns they modify rather than coming before them, as is common in English. This may make it more difficult for Spanish-speaking students to identify the adjective (*strongest*) before identifying the noun (*animal*). Provide additional practice for students.

 I Do

Remind students that comparative adjectives are used to compare two people or things. On the board, write *Tara is a faster runner than Jim.* Explain that -*er* is added to *fast* to compare Tara and Jim. Write *Jamie is the fastest runner in the class.* Explain that -*est* is added to an adjective to compare more than two people or things. Explain that some adjectives change their spelling when -*er* or -*est* is added. Write *lucky, luckier,* and *luckiest.* Explain that when the adjective ends in a consonant and *y*, the *y* changes to *i* before adding -*er* or -*est*. Write *blue, bluer, bluest.* Explain that when an adjective ends in *e,* the *e* is dropped before adding -*er* or -*est*.

 We Do

Write the sentences below on the board. For each sentence, have a volunteer fill in the blank with the correct adjective. Have each volunteer read his or her sentence aloud.

> Carrie is the ____ runner in our class. *(faster, fastest)*
>
> That is the ____ apple I have ever tasted. *(sweeter, sweetest)*
>
> I think this is the ____ zoo in the state. *(bigger, biggest)*
>
> This garden is ____ than the other garden. *(prettyer, prettier)*
>
> The weather now is ____ than it was this morning. *(nicer, niceer)*

 You Do

Have student pairs write three sentence frames comparing two things. Then have them swap their sentence frames with another pair to compare more than two things. Have students read their sentences aloud and draw pictures to accompany their sentences.

Beginning	Intermediate	Advanced/High
Help students write their sentence frames and complete them. Read the sentences aloud for students to repeat.	Have students write their sentences on the board. Have them list other adjectives that could complete the sentences.	Have students write sentence frames with two comparative adjectives and then read the completed sentences aloud.

For extra support, have students complete the activities in the **Grammar Practice Reproducibles** during the week, using the routine below:

- Explain the grammar skill.
- Model the first activity in the Grammar Practice Reproducibles.
- Have the whole group complete the next couple of activities and then have partners complete the rest.
- Review the activities with correct answers.

PROGRESS MONITORING

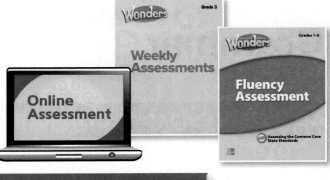

Unit 6 Week 2 Formal Assessment	Standards Covered	Component for Assessment
Text Evidence	RL.3.1	• *Selection Test* • *Weekly Assessment* • *Approaching-Level Weekly Assessment*
Theme	RL.3.2	• *Weekly Assessment* • *Approaching-Level Weekly Assessment*
Figurative Language: Idioms	RL.3.4, L.3.5a	• *Selection Test* • *Weekly Assessment* • *Approaching-Level Weekly Assessment*
Writing About Text	W.3.8	*Weekly Assessment*

Unit 6 Week 2 Informal Assessment	Standards Covered	Component for Assessment
Research/Listening/ Collaborating	SL.3.1d, SL.3.2, SL.3.3	• *RWW* • *Teacher's Edition*
Oral Reading Fluency (ORF) Fluency Goal: 97–117 words correct per minute (WCPM) Accuracy Rate Goal: 95% or higher	RF.3.4a, RF.3.4b, RF.3.4c	*Fluency Assessment*

Using Assessment Results

Weekly Assessments Skills and Fluency	If . . .	Then . . .
COMPREHENSION	Students score below 70% . . .	. . . assign Lessons 34–36 on Theme from the *Tier 2 Comprehension Intervention online PDFs.*
VOCABULARY	Students score below 70% . . .	. . . assign Lesson 166 on Idioms, Proverbs, and Adages from the *Tier 2 Vocabulary Intervention online PDFs.*
WRITING	Students score below "3" on constructed response . . .	. . . assign Lessons 34–36 and/or Write About Reading Lesson 194 from the *Tier 2 Comprehension Intervention online PDFs.*
FLUENCY	Students have a WCPM score of 89–96 . . .	. . . assign a lesson from Section 1, 7, 8, 9 or 10 of the *Tier 2 Fluency Intervention online PDFs.*
	Students have a WCPM score of 0–88 . . .	. . . assign a lesson from Sections 2–6 of the *Tier 2 Fluency Intervention online PDFs.*

Using Weekly Data

Check your data Dashboard to verify assessment results and guide grouping decisions.

Data-Driven Recommendations

Response to Intervention

Use the appropriate sections of the *Placement and Diagnostic Assessment* as well as students' assessment results to designate students requiring:

 Intervention Online PDFs

 WonderWorks Intervention Program

WEEKLY OVERVIEW

Build Knowledge
Success!

? Essential Question:
Why are goals important?

Teach and Model
Close Reading and Writing

**Reading/Writing
Workshop**

"Rocketing Into Space," 434–437
Genre Biography **Lexile** 790 ETS *TextEvaluator* 35

Practice and Apply
Close Reading and Writing

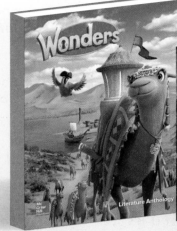

Literature Anthology

Out of This World! The Ellen Ochoa Story,
506–515
Genre Biography **Lexile** 780 ETS *TextEvaluator* 34

"A Flight to Lunar City," 518–519
Genre Adventure Story **Lexile** 600 ETS *TextEvaluator* 27

Differentiated Texts

APPROACHING
Lexile 600
ETS *TextEvaluator* 27

ON LEVEL
Lexile 750
ETS *TextEvaluator* 35

BEYOND
Lexile 850
ETS *TextEvaluator* 43

ELL
Lexile 680
ETS *TextEvaluator* 25

Leveled Readers

Extended Complex Texts

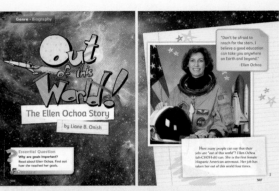 

Moonwalk: The First
Trip to the Moon
Genre Informational Text
Lexile 550

Moonshot: The Flight
of Apollo 11
Genre Informational Text
Lexile 990

Classroom Library

Student Outcomes

Close Reading of Complex Text
- Cite relevant evidence from text
- Describe Problem and Solution
- Reread

RI.3.1, RI.3.3, RI.3.10

Writing

Write to Sources
- Draw evidence from informational texts
- Write informative texts
- Conduct short research on how to set goals and achieve them

Writing Process
- Proofread/Edit and Publish a Feature Article

W.3.2a, W.3.8, W.3.10, W.4.9b

Speaking and Listening
- Engage in collaborative discussions about learning to succeed
- Paraphrase portions of "Mae Jamison, Astronaut" and presentations on learning to succeed
- Present information on learning to succeed

SL.3.1b, SL.3.1d, SL.3.2, SL.3.3

Content Knowledge
- Explain how work in school and effort can pay off.

Language Development

Conventions
- Identify and use adverbs

Vocabulary Acquisition
- Acquire and use academic vocabulary

communicated	essential	goal	motivated
professional	research	serious	specialist

- Use Greek and Latin roots as clues to the meaning of a word

L.3.1a, L.3.1g, L.3.4c, L.3.5b, RI.3.4

Foundational Skills

Phonics/Word Study
- Vowel-team syllables
- Greek and Latin roots

Spelling Words

explained	remain	reading	detail
presoak	monkey	brief	preteen
about	allowing	complain	enjoys
poison	repeats	unreal	

Fluency
- Accuracy

RF.3.3c, RF.3.4a, RF.3.4b, RF.3.4c

Professional Development
- See lessons in action in real classrooms.
- Get expert advice on instructional practices.
- Collaborate with other teachers.
- Access PLC Resources.

Ken Karp/McGraw-Hill Education

Go Digital! www.connected.mcgraw-hill.com.

Talk About Goals

Guide students in collaborative conversations.

Discuss the essential question: *Why are goals important?*

Develop academic language and domain specific vocabulary on goals.

Listen to "Mae Jamison, Astronaut" to summarize a passage about a woman who reached her goals.

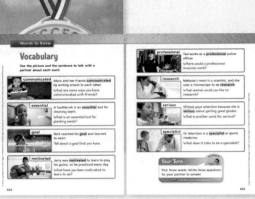

2

Read "Rocketing into Space"

Model close reading with a short complex text.

Read

"Rocketing into Space" to learn how one man used his education and experience to reach his goals, citing text evidence to answer text-dependent questions.

Reread

"Rocketing into Space" to analyze text, craft, and structure, citing text evidence.

Write About Goals

3

Model writing to a source.

Analyze a short response student model.

Use text evidence from close reading to write to a source.

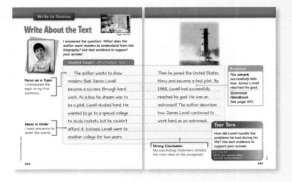

4 Read and Write About Goals

Practice and apply close reading of the anchor text.

> **Read**

Out of This World! The Ellen Ochoa Story to learn about Ellen Ochoa and how she reached her goals.

> **Reread**

Out of This World! The Ellen Ochoa Story and use text evidence to understand how the author presents information to show how Ellen Ochoa achieved her goal of becoming an astronaut.

Write a short response about *Out of This World! The Ellen Ochoa Story*.

> **Integrate**

Information about other people who reached their goals.

Write to Two Sources, citing text evidence from *Out of This World! The Ellen Ochoa Story* and "A Flight to Lunar City."

5 Independent Partner Work

Gradual release of support to independent work

- Text-Dependent Questions
- Scaffolded Partner Work
  Talk with a Partner
  Cite Text Evidence
  Complete a sentence frame.
- Guided Text Annotation

6 Integrate Knowledge and Ideas

Connect Texts

Text to Text Discuss how each of the texts answers the question: Why are goals important?

Text to Music Compare Ochoa's path to becoming an astronaut in the texts read with the message in, "Turn Me 'Round."

Conduct a Short Research Project

Interview a classmate about his or her goals.

DEVELOPING READERS AND WRITERS

Write to Sources

Day 1 and Day 2

Build Writing Fluency

- Quick write on "Rocketing Into Space," p. T156

Write to a Source

- Analyze a student model, p. T156
- Write about "Rocketing Into Space," p. T157
- Apply Writing Trait: Order Ideas, p. T156
- Apply Grammar Skill: Adverbs, p. T157

Day 3

Write to a Source

- Write about *Out of this World! The Ellen Ochoa Story*, independent practice, p. T153L
- Provide scaffolded instruction to meet student needs, p. T158

Day 4 and Day 5

Write to Two Sources

- Analyze a student model, pp. T158–T159
- Write to compare *Out of this World! The Ellen Ochoa Story* with "A Flight to Lunar City," p. T159

Writing Process

Go Digital

Writer's Workspace

Genre Writing: Informative Text

Feature Article
Proofread/Edit

- Discuss the edited student model
- Review adverbs

Publish

- Review options for publishing writing

Evaluate

- Use rubric and anchor papers to evaluate student writing.

Edited Student Model • Feature Article • 108

Making Newport Beautiful
by Devin P.

Edited Student Model

Proofreading Marks

Edit Checklist

Explanatory Essay: Rubric

Explanatory Essay: Anchor Papers

Grammar and Spelling Resources

Online PDFs

Reading/Writing Workshop Grammar Handbook
p. 493

Online Spelling and Grammar Games

Grammar Practice, pp. 136–140

Phonics/Spelling Practice, pp. 163–168

SUGGESTED LESSON PLAN

READING		DAY 1	DAY 2
Teach, Model and Apply	Core	**Introduce the Concept** T138–T139 **Vocabulary** T142–T143 **Close Reading** "Rocketing Into Space," T144–T145	**Close Reading** "Rocketing Into Space," T144–T145 **Strategy** Reread, T146–T147 **Skill** Problem and Solution, T148–T149 **Vocabulary Strategy** Greek and Latin Roots, T152–T153
	Options	**Listening Comprehension** T140–T141	**Genre** Biography, T150–T151

LANGUAGE ARTS			
Writing **Grammar** **Spelling** **Build Vocabulary**	Core	**Grammar** Adverbs, T160 **Spelling** Vowel Team Syllables, T162 **Build Vocabulary** T164	**Write About the Text** Model Note-Taking and Write to a Prompt, T156–T157 **Grammar** Adverbs, T160 **Build Vocabulary** T164
	Options	**Write About the Text** Writing Fluency, T156 **Genre Writing** Feature Article: Discuss the Edited Model, T348	**Genre Writing** Feature Article: Proofread/Edit, T348 **Spelling** Vowel Team Syllables, T162

Whole Group

Writing Process: Informative Text Feature Article, T344–T349   Use with Weeks 1–3

Differentiated Instruction Use your data dashboard to determine each student's needs. Then select instructional support options throughout the week.

Small Group

APPROACHING LEVEL

Leveled Reader
Reach for the Stars, T168–T169

"Melina Shows Her Mettle," T169

Literature Circles, T169

Phonics/Decoding
Decode Words with Vowel Teams *ea, ee, ie,* T170 ②
Build Words with Vowel Team Syllables, T170 ②
Practice Words with Vowel Team Syllables, T171

Greek and Latin Roots, T171

Vocabulary
• Review High-Frequency Words, T172 ②
• Answer Yes/No Questions, T173
Greek and Latin Roots, T173

Comprehension
• Identify Text Structure: Problem and Solution, T174 ②
• Review Problem and Solution, T175
Self-Selected Reading, T175

Fluency
Accuracy and Phrasing, T174 ②

ON LEVEL

Leveled Reader
Reach for the Stars, T176–T177

"Melina Shows Her Mettle," T177

Literature Circles, T177

Vocabulary
Review Vocabulary Words, T178
Greek and Latin Roots, T178

Comprehension
Review Text Structure: Problem and Solution, T179
Self-Selected Reading, T179

Go Digital

CUSTOMIZE YOUR OWN LESSON PLANS
www.connected.mcgraw-hill.com

WEEK 3

DAY 3	DAY 4	DAY 5
Close Reading *Out of this World! The Ellen Ochoa Story,* T153A–T153L Literature Anthology	**Fluency** T155 **Close Reading** "A Flight to Lunar City," T153M–T153N **Integrate Ideas** Research and Inquiry, T166–T167	**Integrate Ideas** T166–T167 • Text Connections • Research and Inquiry **Weekly Assessment**
Phonics/Decoding T154–T155 • Vowel-Team Syllables • Greek and Latin Roots	**Close Reading** *Out of this World! The Ellen Ochoa Story,* T153A–T153L	

Grammar Adverbs, T161	**Write About Two Texts** Model Note-Taking and Taking Notes, T158	**Write About Two Texts** Analyze Student Model and Write to the Prompt, T159 **Spelling** Vowel Team Syllables, T163
Write About the Text and Write to a Prompt T158 **Genre Writing** Feature Article: Publish, T348 **Spelling** Vowel Team Syllables, T163 **Build Vocabulary** T165	**Genre Writing** Feature Article: Evaluate, T349 **Grammar** Adverbs, T161 **Spelling** Vowel Team Syllables, T163 **Build Vocabulary** T165	**Genre Writing** Feature Article: Conference with Students, T349 **Grammar** Adverbs, T161 **Build Vocabulary** T165

Writing Process **Writing Process: Informative Text** Feature Article, T344–T349   Use with Weeks 1–3

BEYOND LEVEL

Leveled Reader
Reach for the Stars, T180–T181
"Melina Shows Her Mettle," T181
Literature Circles, T181

Vocabulary
Review Domain-Specific Words, T182
• Greek and Latin Roots, T182
• Independent Study, T182

 Gifted and Talented

Comprehension
Review Text Structure: Problem and Solution, T183
• Self-Selected Reading, T183
• Independent Study, T183

ENGLISH LANGUAGE LEARNERS

Shared Read
"Rocketing Into Space," T184–T185

Leveled Reader
Reach for the Stars, T186–T187
"Melina Shows Her Mettle," T187
Literature Circles, T187

Phonics/Decoding
Decode Words with Vowel Teams *ea, ee, ie,* T170
Build Words with Vowel Team Syllables, T170
Practice Words with Vowel Team Syllables, T171
Greek and Latin Roots, T171

Vocabulary
• Preteach Vocabulary, T188
• Review High-Frequency Words, T172
Review Vocabulary, T188
Greek and Latin Roots, T189
Additional Vocabulary, T189

Spelling
Words with Vowel Team Syllables, T190

Writing
Writing Trait: Organization, T190

Grammar
Adverbs, T191

DIFFERENTIATE TO ACCELERATE

  Scaffold to **A**ccess **C**omplex **T**ext

IF ➤ the text complexity of a particular selection is too difficult for students

THEN ➤ see the references noted in the chart below for scaffolded instruction to help students Access Complex Text.

Qualitative — Quantitative
Reader and Task
TEXT COMPLEXITY

	Reading/Writing Workshop	Literature Anthology	Leveled Readers		Classroom Library
Quantitative	 "Rocketing into Space" **Lexile** 790 *TextEvaluator* 35	 *Out of This World! The Ellen Ochoa Story* **Lexile** 780 *TextEvaluator* 34 *"A Flight to Lunar City"* **Lexile** 600 *TextEvaluator* 27	**Approaching Level** **Lexile** 600 *TextEvaluator* 27 **Beyond Level** **Lexile** 850 *TextEvaluator* 43	**On Level** **Lexile** 750 *TextEvaluator* 35 **ELL** **Lexile** 680 *TextEvaluator* 25	 *Moonwalk: The First Trip to the Moon* **Lexile** 550 *Moonshot: The Flight of Apollo 11* **Lexile** 990
Qualitative	**What Makes the Text Complex?** • **Genre** Text Features T145, T151 **A C T** *See Scaffolded Instruction in Teacher's Edition T145 and T151.*	**What Makes the Text Complex?** • **Specific Vocabulary** Figurative Language T153A–T153B; Unfamiliar Words T153E, T153G–T153H, T153M • **Connection of Ideas** Make Inferences T153C; Synthesize T153G, T153J • **Genre** Text Features T153E, T153I **A C T** *See Scaffolded Instruction in Teacher's Edition T153A–T153N.*	**What Makes the Text Complex?** • **Specific Vocabulary** • **Prior Knowledge** • **Sentence Structure** • **Connection of Ideas** • **Genre** **A C T** *See Level Up lessons online for Leveled Readers.*		**What Makes the Text Complex?** • **Genre** • **Specific Vocabulary** • **Prior Knowledge** • **Sentence Structure** • **Organization** • **Purpose** • **Connection of Ideas** **A C T** *See Scaffolded Instruction in Teacher's Edition T360–T361.*
Reader and Task	The Introduce the Concept lesson on pages T138–T139 will help determine the reader's knowledge and engagement in the weekly concept. See pages T144–T153 and T166–T167 for questions and tasks for this text.	The Introduce the Concept lesson on pages T138–T139 will help determine the reader's knowledge and engagement in the weekly concept. See pages T153A–T153N and T166–T167 for questions and tasks for this text.	The Introduce the Concept lesson on pages T138–T139 will help determine the reader's knowledge and engagement in the weekly concept. See pages T168–T169, T176–T177, T180–T181, T186–T187, and T166–T167 for questions and tasks for this text.		The Introduce the Concept lesson on pages T138–T139 will help determine the reader's knowledge and engagement in the weekly concept. See pages T360–T361 for questions and tasks for this text.

Monitor and *Differentiate*

✓ Quick Check

To differentiate instruction, use the Quick Checks to assess students' needs and select the appropriate small group instruction focus.

Comprehension Strategy Reread T147

Comprehension Skill Problem and Solution T149

Genre Biography T151

Vocabulary Strategy Greek and Latin Roots T153

Phonics/Fluency Vowel-Team Syllables, Accuracy T155

If No →	Approaching Level	**Reteach** T168–T175
	ELL	**Develop** T184–T191
If Yes →	On Level	**Review** T176–T179
	Beyond Level	**Extend** T180–T183

Using Weekly Data

Check your data Dashboard to verify assessment results and guide grouping decisions.

Level Up with Leveled Readers

IF → students can read their leveled text fluently and answer comprehension questions

THEN → work with the next level up to accelerate students' reading with more complex text.

Beyond

T177

On Level

Approaching

T169   T187

ELL

ENGLISH LANGUAGE LEARNERS

Small Group Instruction

Use the ELL small group lessons in the Wonders Teacher's Edition to provide focused instruction.

Language Development
Vocabulary preteaching and review, additional vocabulary building, and vocabulary strategy lessons, pp. T188–T189

Close Reading
Interactive Question-Response routines for scaffolded text-dependent questioning for reading and rereading the Shared Read and Leveled Reader, pp. T184–T187

Writing
Focus on the weekly writing trait, grammar skills, and spelling words, pp. T190–T191

Additional ELL Support

Use *Reading Wonders for English Learners* for ELD instruction that connects to the core.

Language Development
Ample opportunities for discussions, and scaffolded language support

Close Reading
Companion Worktexts for guided support in annotating text and citing text evidence. Differentiated Texts about the weekly concept.

Writing
Scaffolded instruction for writing to sources and revising student models

Reading Wonders for ELLs Teacher Edition and Companion Worktexts

→ Introduce the Concept

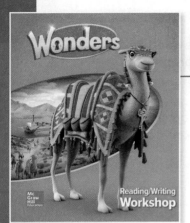

Reading/Writing Workshop

OBJECTIVES

CCSS Follow agreed-upon rules for discussions (e.g., gaining the floor in respectful ways, listening to others with care, speaking one at a time about the topics and texts under discussion). **SL.3.1b**

CCSS Determine the main ideas and supporting details of a text read aloud or information presented in diverse media and formats, including visually, quantitatively, and orally. **SL.3.2**

ACADEMIC LANGUAGE
• *goal, motivate*
• Cognate: *motivar*

Build Background

ESSENTIAL QUESTION
Why are goals important?

Have students read the Essential Question on page 430 of the **Reading/ Writing Workshop**.

Discuss the photo of the girl on the podium with students. Focus on the details in the photo that show that Kayla achieved her *goal*—the thing she wanted to do, or her aim or purpose—because she was *motivated*.

• When you set a *goal*, you decide that achieving your goal is more important than other things. Setting goals helps you pay less attention to things that are not important so you can focus your time and energy on the things that are.

• When you want something and work willingly toward it, you are *motivated* to achieve that goal. Ask: *Do you do better work when you are told to do something, or when you are motivated to do it yourself?*

Talk About It

Ask: *What do goals help us do? What are some ways to stay motivated when pursuing a goal?* Have students discuss in pairs or groups.

• Model using the Concept Web to generate words and phrases related to goals. Add students' contributions.

• Have partners continue the discussion by sharing what they have learned about goals. They can complete the Concept Webs, generating additional words and phrases.

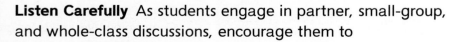

Collaborative Conversations

Listen Carefully As students engage in partner, small-group, and whole-class discussions, encourage them to

• always look at the person who is speaking.

• respect others by not interrupting them.

• ask questions about peers' ideas to check understanding.

Go Digital

Discuss the Concept

Watch Video

Use Graphic Organizer

Essential Question
Why are goals important?

Go Digital!

Kayla had a goal. She wanted to win her race in the Special Olympics. Her goal was important to her, so she worked hard. Kayla is so proud of herself today.

► Goals are important.
► They help us focus and learn new things.
► Achieving our goals makes us feel good about ourselves.

Talk About It

Write words you have learned about goals. Talk with a partner about why goals are important.

Goals

430 | 1 | 431

READING/WRITING WORKSHOP, *pp. 430–431*

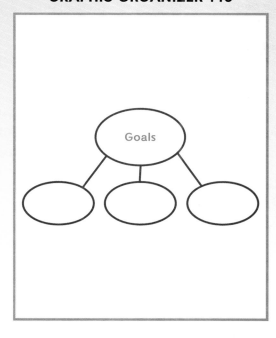

ENGLISH LANGUAGE LEARNERS
ELL SCAFFOLD

GRAPHIC ORGANIZER 140

Beginning	Intermediate	Advanced/High
Clarify Review the definition of a goal with students. *A goal is something we want to do.* Point to the picture of Kayla on page 430. *Kayla wanted to win the race. Winning the race was her goal. What is a goal that you have?* Guide students in completing using the sentence frame *My goal is to ____.*	**Demonstrate Comprehension** Have students describe the pictures. Ask: *What was Kayla's goal?* (She wanted to win the race.) *Did she meet her goal?* (Yes) *How did she meet it?* (She worked hard.) Help students think of how she might have worked hard to meet her goal. Encourage students to use the word *motivate* in their answers.	**Discuss** Ask students to work in pairs to discuss goals that they have. Ask: *What is a goal that you have already reached?* Elicit why goals are important to them and what will motivate them to pursue their goals. Have students work in pairs to come up with responses.

Goals

→ Listening Comprehension

Interactive Read Aloud
MINILESSON 10 Mins

OBJECTIVES

CCSS Ask and answer questions to demonstrate understanding of a text, referring explicitly to the text as the basis for the answers. **RI.3.1**

CCSS Determine the main ideas and supporting details of a text read aloud or information presented in diverse media and formats, including visually, quantitatively, and orally. **SL.3.2**

- Listen for a purpose.
- Identify characteristics of biography

ACADEMIC LANGUAGE
- *biography, reread*
- Cognate: *biografía*

Connect to Concept: Learning to Succeed

Tell students it is important for people to set goals for themselves. Let students know you will be reading aloud a passage about a woman who was successful in reaching her goals. As students listen, have them think about how the text answers the essential question.

Preview Genre: Biography

Explain that the story you will read aloud is a biography. Discuss features of a biography:

- gives information about the time period and place in which the subject lived
- includes character traits of the subject
- may focus on one or two key events in the subject's life

Preview Comprehension Strategy: Reread

Point out that when reading a biography, it can be helpful to reread a section of text to make sure you are clear on the facts and details given about a person's life. Rereading is also a good way to understand and remember details about the time and place in which the person lived.

Use the Think Alouds on page T141 to model the strategy.

Respond to Reading

Think Aloud Clouds Display Think Aloud Master 4: *When I read ____, I had to reread. . .* to reinforce how you used the Reread strategy to understand content.

Genre Features With students, discuss the elements of the Read Aloud that let them know it is a biography. Ask them to think about other texts you have read aloud or they have read independently that were biographies.

Summarize Have students determine the main ideas and details in "Mae Jemison, Astronaut." Then have them briefly restate the important information from the text in their own words.

Go Digital

View Photos

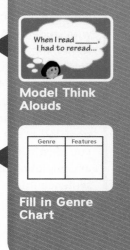
Model Think Alouds

Fill in Genre Chart

Mae Jemison, Astronaut

In Alabama in 1956, a baby was born. Her parents named her Mae. As they watched their new baby in the crib, they could not have imagined that one day she would fly through space. **1**

Dreaming of Space

At an early age, Mae Jemison became fascinated with space travel. She was thirteen when Apollo 11 made its moon mission. For the first time, astronauts walked on the moon. This historic event gave Mae dreams of traveling into space.

Mae graduated from high school with honors at the age of sixteen. She went to Stanford University and majored in chemical engineering and Afro-American studies. But Mae had many other interests as well. She enjoyed dance, theater, and football. And always, Mae held a deep love for science and space. **2**

Helping Others

Her thirst for knowledge led Mae to medical school. She traveled to Africa and Asia where she used her skills to help poor people get the medical treatment they needed. Back in the United States, she opened her own doctor's office in California.

Space at Last!

In 1985 she decided it was time to apply to the space program. She had never lost her interest in space travel. She knew it was a long shot as not many women had been accepted. She felt confident that the time was right for her. Only a few African American men had gone into space but no African American women. In 1987, she got the call she hoped for. Mae had made it into the space program.

In September of 1992, after years of training, Mae Jemison boarded the space shuttle, Endeavour. Mae, along with six other astronauts, blasted off into space. Realizing her dreams at last, Mae Jemison became the first African American woman in space. **3**

Image Source/Getty Images

1 **Think Aloud** An introduction gives important information about what I am about to read. I can **reread** it again to make sure I understand who this biography will be about.

2 **Think Aloud** I want to **reread** this section to help me understand and remember these details about Mae's life. I think this will help me better understand who she is.

3 **Think Aloud** This tells me about the space mission when Mae finally realized her dream. I want to **reread** this paragraph to make sure I understand and remember this important fact.

→ # Vocabulary

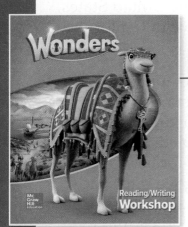

Reading/Writing Workshop

OBJECTIVES

CCSS Determine the meaning of general academic and domain-specific words and phrases in a text relevant to a grade 3 topic or subject area. **RI.3.4**

CCSS Identify real-life connections between words and their use (e.g., describe people who are *friendly* or *helpful*). **L.3.5b**

• Learn meanings of new vocabulary words.

• Write questions using new words.

ACADEMIC LANGUAGE
Cognate: *motivado*

 MINILESSON 10 Mins

Words in Context

Model the Routine

Introduce each vocabulary word using the Vocabulary Routine found on the **Visual Vocabulary Cards.**

Visual Vocabulary Cards

Vocabu
Define:
Example:
Ask:

> **Vocabulary Routine**
>
> **Define:** Something **essential** is very important or necessary.
>
> **Example:** A toothbrush is an essential tool for cleaning teeth.
>
> **Ask:** What is an *essential* tool for planting seeds?

Definitions

• **communicated**   A person who **communicated** with others passed along feelings, thoughts, or information to them.

• **goal**   A **goal** is something a person wants and tries to get or become.

• **motivated**   A person who is **motivated** has a reason for doing something.
  Cognate: *motivado*

• **professional**   A **professional** job requires special education.
  Cognate: *profesional*

• **research**   **Research** is careful study to find and learn facts.

• **serious**   When something is **serious**, it is important.
  Cognate: *serio*

• **specialist**   A **specialist** knows a great deal about something.

Talk About It

COLLABORATE

Have students work with a partner and look at each picture and discuss the definition of each word. Then ask students to choose three words and write questions for their partner to answer.

Go Digital

essential

Use Visual Glossary

Words to Know

Vocabulary

Use the picture and the sentence to talk with a partner about each word.

communicated

Mora and her friends **communicated** by writing emails to each other.

What are some ways you have communicated with friends?

essential

A toothbrush is an **essential** tool for cleaning teeth.

What is an *essential* tool for planting seeds?

goal

Nick reached his **goal** and learned to swim.

Tell about a goal that you have.

motivated

Jerry was **motivated** to learn to play his guitar, so he practiced every day.

What have you been motivated to learn to do?

professional

Ted works as a **professional** police officer.

Where would a professional musician work?

research

Melanie's mom is a scientist, and she uses a microscope to do **research**.

What animal would you like to research?

serious

Winnie pays attention because she is **serious** about getting good grades.

What is another word for *serious*?

specialist

Dr. Morrison is a **specialist** in sports medicine.

What does it take to be a specialist?

Your Turn

COLLABORATE

Pick three words. Write three questions for your partner to answer.

Go Digital! Use the online visual glossary

432

433

READING/WRITING WORKSHOP, *pp. 432–433*

ELL ENGLISH LANGUAGE LEARNERS SCAFFOLD

Beginning

Clarify Have students describe the picture for the word *essential*. Say: *The girl is brushing her teeth. Does she need a toothbrush?* (yes) Guide students in completing the sentence frame: *A toothbrush is ___ for brushing your teeth. Esencial* is Spanish for *essential*.

Intermediate

Demonstrate Comprehension Have students describe the picture. Ask: *Is a toothbrush essential for brushing your teeth?* (yes) Have partners think of other tasks that require essential tools. Ask each pair to write one sentence using the word *essential*.

Advanced/High

Write Have partners review the definition of *essential*. Have them make a list of five things that are essential to their lives. Then have students write one sentence for each item on their list that tells why it is essential. Invite students to share their sentences with the class.

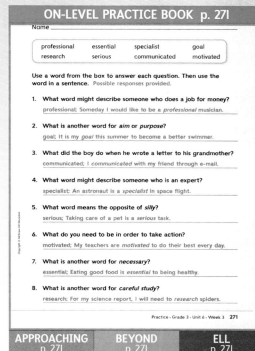

ON-LEVEL PRACTICE BOOK p. 271

Name _____

| professional | essential | specialist | goal |
| research | serious | communicated | motivated |

Use a word from the box to answer each question. Then use the word in a sentence. Possible responses provided.

1. **What word might describe someone who does a job for money?**
   professional; Someday I would like to be a *professional* musician.

2. **What is another word for *aim* or *purpose*?**
   goal; It is my *goal* this summer to become a better swimmer.

3. **What did the boy do when he wrote a letter to his grandmother?**
   communicated; I *communicated* with my friend through e-mail.

4. **What word might describe someone who is an expert?**
   specialist; An astronaut is a *specialist* in space flight.

5. **What word means the opposite of *silly*?**
   serious; Taking care of a pet is a *serious* task.

6. **What do you need to be in order to take action?**
   motivated; My teachers are *motivated* to do their best every day.

7. **What is another word for *necessary*?**
   essential; Eating good food is *essential* to being healthy.

8. **What is another word for *careful study*?**
   research; For my science report, I will need to *research* spiders.

Practice · Grade 3 · Unit 6 · Week 3 **271**

| APPROACHING p. 271 | BEYOND p. 271 | ELL p. 271 |

Shared Read › Genre · Biography

ROCKETING INTO SPACE

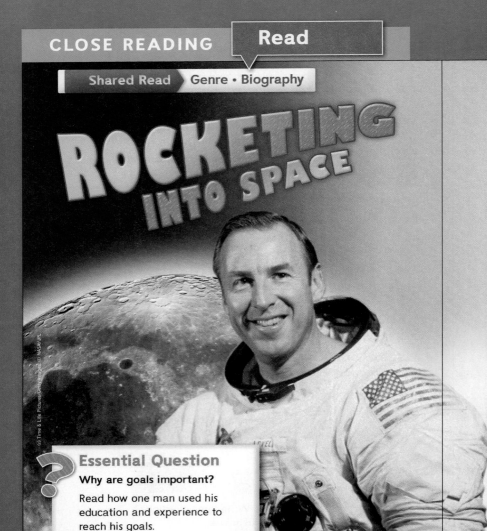

Essential Question

Why are goals important?

Read how one man used his education and experience to reach his goals.

434

When James A. Lovell, Jr. was a boy, he loved to build rockets and launch them into the sky. But his dreams went a lot farther than his rockets. Like many boys who grew up in the 1930s, Lovell dreamed of being a pilot. And as he watched his rockets soar, he knew someday he would, too.

HIGH FLYING DREAMS

Lovell was born in Cleveland, Ohio, in 1928. He worked hard in school and planned to go to a special college to study **astronomy** and rockets. Unfortunately, he didn't have enough money to attend. Lovell had to figure out another way to reach his **goal**.

Lovell was **motivated** to find a way to fly rockets. So, he went to college near his home for two years and then signed up for flight training at the United States Naval Academy. After four years at the academy, Lovell joined the United States Navy and became a **professional** naval test pilot. His job was to fly planes before anyone else was allowed to fly them.

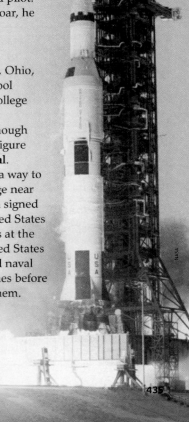

James A. Lovell, Jr. became an astronaut in 1962. He flew four space missions.

435

READING/WRITING WORKSHOP, *pp. 434–435*

Shared Read

Lexile 790   *TextEvaluator*™ 35

Close Reading Routine

Read   **DOK 1–2**

- Identify key ideas and details about Learning to Succeed.
- Take notes and summarize.
- Use Ⓐ Ⓒ Ⓣ prompts as needed.

Reread   **DOK 2–3**

- Analyze the text, craft, and structure.
- Use the Reread minilessons.

Integrate   **DOK 4**

- Integrate knowledge and ideas.
- Make text-to-text connections.
- Use the Integrate lesson.

ELL

See pages T184–T185 for Interactive Question-Response routine for the Shared Read.

Reading/Writing Workshop

Read

Connect to Concept: Learning to Succeed Tell students they will read about how Astronaut James Lovell reached his goals.

Note Taking Read page 435 together. As you read, model how to take notes. *I will think about the Essential Question as I read and note key ideas and details.* Encourage students to note words they don't understand and questions they have.

Paragraphs 2 and 3: Reread the second and third paragraphs together. Ask: *Why did James Lovell join the Navy?*

I see that James didn't have enough money to attend college. He created another route to his goal by becoming a test pilot.

PILOT TO ASTRONAUT

As a pilot, Lovell spent more than half of his flying time in jets. He taught other pilots how to fly. He also worked as a **specialist** in air flight safety. Soon, the National Aeronautics and Space Administration, or NASA, put out a call for astronauts. Lovell applied for the job because he had all the **essential** skills needed to fly into space. As a result, NASA chose him. By 1962, James Lovell was an astronaut! He had finally reached his goal.

BIG CHALLENGES

Lovell flew on three space missions, and then, in April 1970 he became commander of the Apollo 13 mission. This was a big responsibility and a great honor. This was also one of the biggest **challenges** of Lovell's life.

Apollo 13 was supposed to land on the Moon. Two days after leaving Earth, however, the spacecraft had a **serious** problem. One of its oxygen tanks exploded. The crew did not have enough power or air to breathe. They could not make it to the Moon.

Lovell **communicated** with the experts at NASA. No one knew what to do at first. Then the team on the ground did some **research** and came up with a solution. The astronauts followed the team's directions and built an invention using plastic bags, cardboard, and tape. It worked! It cleaned the air in the spacecraft. But the next problem was even bigger. How were the astronauts going to get back to Earth?

NASA's team works to solve Apollo 13's problem.

436

A JOB WELL DONE

The NASA team decided the astronauts would use the **lunar**, or moon, module as a lifeboat. James and the other two astronauts climbed into the smaller spacecraft and shut the hatch tight. They moved away from the main spaceship. With little power, water, food, or heat, the astronauts listened carefully to the team at NASA.

The trip back to Earth was dangerous and scary. For almost four days, the astronauts traveled in a cramped capsule. They were cold, thirsty, and hungry. Then, with millions of people watching on television, the module fell to Earth.

The Apollo 13 crew splashed down safely on April 17, 1970.

Years later, James Lovell said that Apollo 13 taught him how important it was for people to work together. His favorite memory was when the capsule splashed down in the Pacific Ocean and the diver knocked on the window to let them know they were safe.

A DREAM COME TRUE

DID YOU EVER DREAM OF GOING INTO SPACE? CHECK OUT SPACE CAMP!

Space camps have been around for more than 30 years. They make science, math, and technology exciting so kids will want to learn more. And like the NASA training programs, these camps teach the importance of teamwork and leadership.

Make Connections

How did James A. Lovell's goals as a child help him as an adult? ESSENTIAL QUESTION

Tell about one of your goals and how you might achieve it. TEXT TO SELF

437

READING/WRITING WORKSHOP, *pp. 436–437*

Paragraphs 6 and 7: Model how to find the problem and solution in a text. Ask: *What went wrong during the Apollo 13 mission? How did the astronauts fix it?*

I can look for signal words that will lead me to the information I need. I see that the *problem* was that an oxygen tank exploded. The *solution* was to build an invention that could clean the air.

Make Connections
COLLABORATE

Essential Question Have partners talk about how Lovell's childhood goals helped him as an adult. Use these sentence frames to focus discussion.

> *James Lovell wanted to . . .*
> *Lovell's experience as a naval test pilot . . .*

A C T Access Complex Text

▶ **Genre**

One reason people read biographies is for inspiration. People want to know how their heroes accomplished the things they did so they can achieve their own goals.

- *What text feature do you see on page 437?* (a sidebar or text box) *What does it tell the reader?* (It tells about space camps.)

- *Why do you think the author included it?* (The reader might be inspired by James's story and want to learn more about science, math, and technology.)

→ Comprehension Strategy

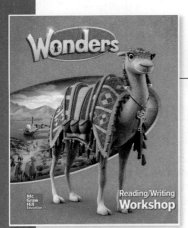

**Reading/Writing
Workshop**

OBJECTIVES

CCSS Ask and answer questions to demonstrate understanding of a text, referring explicitly to the text as the basis for the answers. **RI.3.1**

CCSS By the end of the year, read and comprehend informational texts, including history/social studies, science, and technical texts, at the high end of the grades 2–3 text complexity band independently and proficiently. **RI.3.10**

Reread text to improve understanding.

ACADEMIC LANGUAGE
reread

Reread

10 Mins MINILESSON

1 Explain

Remind students that when they read a biography, they may come across unfamiliar concepts and detailed explanations. Tell students that they can reread difficult sections of text to increase their understanding.

- Good readers reread something they do not understand.

- When students encounter unclear or difficult text, they can stop and reread that section. They may need to reread it more than once before they understand it.

- Often, students may find that rereading will improve their understanding of new facts and ideas in informational text.

2 Model Close Reading: Text Evidence

Model how rereading can help students understand what James A. Lovell did to become a pilot. Reread "High Flying Dreams" on page 435 of "Rocketing into Space."

3 Guided Practice of Close Reading

Have students work in pairs to explain how James Lovell helped get his Apollo 13 space ship back home. Direct them to "Big Challenges" and "A Job Well Done" on pages 436–437. Have partners discuss other sections of "Rocketing into Space" they might want to reread.

Go Digital

View "Rocketing into Space"

Comprehension Strategy

Reread

Stop and think about the text as you read. Are there new facts and ideas? Do they make sense? Reread to make sure you understand.

 Find Text Evidence

Do you understand what James A. Lovell, Jr. did to become a pilot? Reread "High Flying Dreams" on page 435.

> **page 435**
>
> in 1928. He worked hard in school and planned to go to a special college to study **astronomy** and rockets. Unfortunately, he didn't have enough money to attend. Lovell had to figure out another way to reach his **goal**.
>
> Lovell was **motivated** to find a way to fly rockets. So, he went to college near his home for two years and then signed up for flight training at the United States Naval Academy. After four years at the academy, Lovell joined the United States Navy and became a **professional** naval test pilot. His job was to fly planes before

I read that James Lovell <u>went to college and then to the United States Naval Academy. He signed up for flight training and became a professional naval test pilot.</u> James Lovell became a pilot by going to school. He never gave up.

Your Turn

How did James Lovell help get his Apollo 13 space ship back home? Reread pages 436 and 437.

NASA

438

READING/WRITING WORKSHOP, *p. 438*

ELL ENGLISH LANGUAGE LEARNERS SCAFFOLD

Beginning	**Intermediate**	**Advanced/High**
Understand Have students reread the second and third paragraphs of page 435. Point out and define difficult words or phrases such as *college, astronomy, attend, motivated,* and *the United States Naval Academy.* Invite students to ask one question they have about James Lovell after reading this section.	**Comprehend** Have students reread the second and third paragraphs on page 435. After each paragraph, ask: *What is the most important part of this paragraph? What are two important steps James Lovell took toward working with rockets?* Help expand and elaborate on students' answers.	**Recognize** Have students reread "High Flying Dreams" on page 435. Elicit from students why the text is confusing or difficult to understand. Ask: *What are the most important events in the paragraphs you just read?* Have students work with partners to discuss.

Monitor and *Differentiate*

 Quick Check

Do students reread portions of a text to increase understanding?

Small Group Instruction

If No →	Approaching Level	Reteach p. T168
	ELL	Develop p. T184
If Yes →	On Level	Review p. T176
	Beyond Level	Extend p. T180

ON-LEVEL PRACTICE BOOK pp. 273–274

Read the passage. Use the reread strategy to help you understand the biography.

John Glenn

Many people admire John Glenn as an American hero. He was
11 a pilot, an astronaut, and a U.S. senator. When he was 77 years
24 old, he became the oldest person ever to fly in space.

35 **Serving His Country**
38 John Glenn was born in Ohio in 1921. When he was 20 years
51 old, World War II broke out. Glenn signed up for the army. Yet he
65 was not called to serve. This was a problem for Glenn. He wanted
78 to serve his country. So Glenn joined the navy. There, he became
90 a pilot. As a pilot, Glenn fought in World War II and the Korean
104 War. Later, he joined the marines.

110 **First Place**
112 John Glenn kept flying after the war. He flew a plane faster
124 than the speed of sound. That's more than 768 miles per hour!
136 He flew the plane all the way across the country. Glenn was the
149 first person to do this. That's why he was picked to be in the U.S.
164 space program. The program is called NASA. At the time, there
175 were only six other astronauts in NASA.
182 Glenn trained for months. On February 20, 1962, Glenn flew
192 in a ship all the way around Earth. He was the first American to
206 orbit Earth.

Practice · Grade 3 · Unit 6 · Week 3 **273**

APPROACHING pp. 273–274	**BEYOND** pp. 273–274	**ELL** pp. 273–274

→ Comprehension Skill

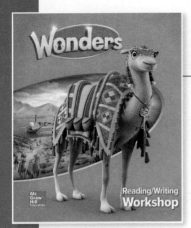

Reading/Writing Workshop

OBJECTIVES

CCSS Describe the relationship between a series of historical events, scientific ideas or concepts, or steps in technical procedures in a text, using language that pertains to time, sequence, and cause/effect. **RI.3.3**

Identify a text's problem and solution.

ACADEMIC LANGUAGE
problem, solution

SKILLS TRACE

TEXT STRUCTURE

Introduce Unit 1 Week 3

Review Unit 1 Weeks 4, 6; Unit 2 Week 6; Unit 3 Weeks 5, 6; Unit 4 Weeks 3, 4; Unit 5 Weeks 5, 6; Unit 6 Weeks 3, 4, 6

Assess Units 1, 3, 4, 5, 6

MINILESSON 10 Mins
Text Structure: Problem and Solution

1 Explain

Explain that text structure is a way authors organize a text. The relationship between the **problem** faced by the main characters and its **solution** is one kind of text structure. It shows how and why things happen in time order.

- A cause is why something happens. An effect is what happens.
- When showing how characters solve their problems, an author shows each step in the problem-solving sequence. This helps readers see the effects of each of the characters' actions.
- Students can look for words and phrases that indicate problem and solution, such as *problem, solution, solve,* and *as a result.*

2 Model Close Reading: Text Evidence

Identify the steps that James Lovell took to solve his problem in "High Flying Dreams" on page 435. Explain how the cause-and-effect events are sequentially related.

 Write About Reading: Problem and Solution Model how to use the notes from the graphic organizer to write how events lead from the problem to the solution in "High Flying Dreams" on page 435.

3 Guided Practice of Close Reading

COLLABORATE Have students work in pairs to complete the graphic organizer and demonstrate the steps taken to solve the problem in "Big Challenges," going back into the text to find these steps.

 Write About Reading: Problem and Solution Ask pairs to work together to write in sequence about the cause-and-effect relationships in the last part of "Big Challenges." They should make sure they are using words and phrases explaining cause and effect as well as sequence.

Go Digital

Present the Lesson

Comprehension Skill

Problem and Solution

Some informational texts describe a problem, tell the steps taken to solve the problem, and give the solution. Signal words, such as *problem, solution, solve,* and *as a result,* show there is a problem and the steps to a solution.

Find Text Evidence

James Lovell wanted to fly rockets but didn't have enough money to go to a special college. That was his problem. What steps did he take to solve his problem? What was the solution?

Problem
James wanted to fly rockets, but he didn't have enough money to go to a special college.

↓

James went to college near his home.

↓

He became a test pilot.

↓

He joined NASA and became an astronaut.

↓

Solution
As an astronaut, James Lovell was able to fly in rocket ships.

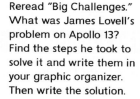

Your Turn COLLABORATE

Reread "Big Challenges." What was James Lovell's problem on Apollo 13? Find the steps he took to solve it and write them in your graphic organizer. Then write the solution.

Go Digital!
Use the interactive graphic organizer

439

READING/WRITING WORKSHOP, *p. 439*

ELL ENGLISH LANGUAGE LEARNERS SCAFFOLD

Beginning

Use Visuals Reread paragraphs 2–3 on page 435. Say: *James didn't have enough money for college. This is the problem. Point to the word so. This shows this is a step toward the solution.* Reread the sentence and have students chorally say: *This is a step toward the solution.*

Intermediate

Describe Have students reread the second, third, and fourth paragraphs on pages 435–436. Ask: *What are the most important events in these paragraphs?* Have students work in pairs to explain how the events relate to James's goal of flying rockets. Help students expand upon their thoughts.

Advanced/High

Describe Have students review and summarize the events of "High Flying Dreams" and "Pilot to Astronaut." Encourage them to elaborate upon the ways each step leads to the next and brings about the end solution.

Monitor and *Differentiate*

 Quick Check

As students complete the graphic organizer, do they determine the steps the astronauts took to solve their problem?

↓

Small Group Instruction

If No → | **Approaching Level** | Reteach p. T175
| **ELL** | Develop p. T184

If Yes→ | **On Level** | Review p. T179
| **Beyond Level** | Extend p. T183

ON-LEVEL PRACTICE BOOK pp. 273–275

A. Reread the passage and answer the questions.
Possible responses provided.

1. Reread paragraph 2 on the first page of the passage. What problem did John Glenn face?

He signed up for the army, but was not called to serve.

2. How did signing up for the navy solve Glenn's problem?

He became a pilot in the navy. He was able to serve his country.

3. Reread paragraph 1 on the second page of the passage. What problem did John Glenn face? What was the solution?

He injured himself and could not run for the senate. Glenn kept trying, ran again, and won the senate seat.

B. Work with a partner. Read the passage aloud. Pay attention to accuracy and phrasing. Stop after one minute. Fill out the chart.

	Words Read	–	Number of Errors	=	Words Correct Score
First Read		–		=	
Second Read		–		=	

Practice · Grade 3 · Unit 6 · Week 3   **275**

| **APPROACHING** pp. 273–275 | **BEYOND** pp. 273–275 | **ELL** pp. 273–275 |

→ # Genre: Informational Text

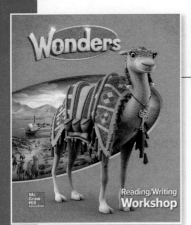

Reading/Writing Workshop

OBJECTIVES

CCSS Use text features and search tools (e.g., key words, sidebars, hyperlinks) to locate information relevant to a given topic efficiently. **RI.3.5**

CCSS By the end of the year, read and comprehend informational texts, including history/social studies, science, and technical texts, at the high end of the grades 2–3 text complexity band independently and proficiently. **RI.3.10**

Recognize the characteristics and features of biography.

ACADEMIC LANGUAGE

• *biography*

• Cognate: *biografía*

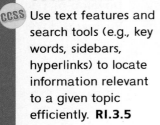

Biography

1 Explain

Share with students the following key characteristics of a **biography**:

- A biography tells the true story of a real person's life.
- A biography is written by another person.
- A biography often includes text features, such as keywords, photographs, and captions.

2 Model Close Reading: Text Evidence

Model for students how to identify the characteristics and text features of a biography on page 436 of "Rocketing into Space."

Keywords Keywords name concepts that are important to the understanding of the text. They are usually printed in special type to let the reader know they are important.

Photographs Photographs give the reader more information about a biographical subject by showing the person's appearance or an important event in the person's life. Ask: *What event does this picture show?*

3 Guided Practice of Close Reading

Have students work in pairs to reread the rest of "Rocketing into Space." Ask: *What other keyword can you find in James Lovell's biography?* Have students explain why the keyword is an important word in James A. Lovell's biography. You may want to have partners find other keywords and describe why knowing the meaning of each is important for understanding the text. Have partners share their responses with the rest of the class.

Go Digital

Present the Lesson

Genre **Informational Text**

Biography

"Rocketing Into Space" is a biography. A **biography**:
- Tells the true story of a real person's life
- Is written by another person
- Includes text features such as keywords, photographs and captions

 Find Text Evidence

I can tell that "Rocketing Into Space" is a biography. It is the true story of James Lovell's life. It has photographs with captions and key words that are important to the biography.

page 436

PILOT TO ASTRONAUT
As a pilot, Lovell spent more than half of his flying time in jets. He taught other pilots how to fly. He also worked as a specialist in air flight safety. Soon, the National Aeronautics and Space Administration, or NASA, put out a call for astronauts because he had all the essential skills needed to fly into space. As a result, NASA chose him. By 1962, James Lovell was an astronaut! He had finally reached his goal.

BIG CHALLENGES
Lovell flew on three space missions, and then, in April 1970 he became commander of the Apollo 13 mission. This was a big responsibility and a great honor. This was also one of the biggest challenges of Lovell's life.

Apollo 13 was supposed to land on the Moon. Two days after leaving Earth, however, the spacecraft had a serious problem. One of its oxygen tanks exploded. The crew did not have enough power or air to breathe. They could not make it to the Moon.

Lovell communicated with the experts at NASA. No one knew what to do at first. Then the team on the ground did some research and came up with a solution. The astronauts followed the team's directions and built an invention using plastic bags, cardboard, and tape. It worked! It cleaned the air in the spacecraft. But the next problem was even bigger. How were the astronauts going to get back to Earth?

Text Features

Keywords Keywords are important words. They are in dark type.

Photographs Photographs and their captions show more about the events in the person's life.

Your Turn COLLABORATE

Find another keyword. Why is this an important word in James Lovell's biography?

440

READING/WRITING WORKSHOP, *p. 440*

A C T Access Complex Text

▶ **Genre**

Some students may need help in order to understand why particular keywords are important in a given informational text.

- *Look under the heading "Big Challenges." What keyword do you see?* (challenges)

- *If you call a task a* challenge, *what does that mean?* (The task requires great effort.)

- *How does the word* challenges *help you understand this section?* (The section describes how Lovell and the team responded to a big problem, or challenge, the exploded oxygen tank.)

✓ **Quick Check**

Are students able to identify an additional keyword in "Rocketing into Space"? Can they explain why it is important to the text?

⬇

Small Group Instruction

If No → | Approaching Level | Reteach p. T168
| ELL | Develop p. T184
If Yes → | On Level | Review p. T176
| Beyond Level | Extend p. T180

ON-LEVEL PRACTICE BOOK p. 276

Bessie Coleman

In Chicago, Bessie worked with her brother Walter in a barbershop but still wanted more in life. When her brother John came home after World War I, he teased her, telling her how much better French women were. They had real careers; some even flew airplanes! After hearing this, Bessie decided to become a pilot. As an African American woman, though, she was unable to get a pilot's license in America. With friends' support, she was finally able to enroll in a pilot course in France.

Bessie Coleman received her pilot's license in France.

Answer the questions about the text.

1. How do you know this text is biography?
   It tells a true story about a real person's life.

2. What text feature is included in the text?
   Photograph and caption

3. How does the text feature help you understand the text?
   It shows what Bessie Coleman looked like in real life.

4. What made Bessie Coleman want to become a pilot?
   Her brother told her that women in France had better careers.

| APPROACHING p. 276 | BEYOND p. 276 | ELL p. 276 |

→ Vocabulary Strategy

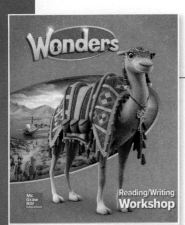

Reading/Writing Workshop

OBJECTIVES

CCSS Use a known root word as a clue to the meaning of an unknown word with the same root (e.g., *company, companion*). **L.3.4c**

ACADEMIC LANGUAGE
Greek and Latin roots, root word

Go Digital

Present the Lesson

⏱ MINILESSON 10 Mins — Greek and Latin Roots

1 Explain

Explain to students that knowing the meanings of common Latin and Greek roots can help them figure out the meanings of unfamiliar words that contain them. Remind students that the root of a word is the simplest part of a word, to which no prefixes or suffixes have been added.

- Two common Greek roots are *astro*, meaning "star," and *naut*, meaning "ship." Example words are *asteroid*, meaning "resembling a star," and *nautical*, meaning "relating to ships."

- A common Latin root is *luna*, meaning "moon." For example, something *sublunary* is anything under the moon that is located on Earth. *Spect* is a Latin root meaning "look at." A common word containing *spect* is *inspect*, meaning "to look at closely."

- As students read, they should look for Latin and Greek roots in unfamiliar words. The roots provide clues to the meanings of the words.

2 Model Close Reading: Text Evidence

Model using the meanings of the Greek word *astro* to determine the meaning of *astronomy* ("the study of the stars") in the second sentence of the second paragraph on page 435.

3 Guided Practice of Close Reading

Have students work in pairs to determine the meanings of *astronauts* on page 436 and *lunar* on page 437 in "Rocketing into Space." Encourage partners to look for other words with Greek and Latin roots in the selection and to determine their meanings.

SKILLS TRACE

GREEK AND LATIN ROOTS

Introduce Unit 6 Week 3

Review Unit 6 Weeks 3, 6

Assess Unit 6

Vocabulary Strategy

Greek and Latin Roots

Many words have word parts, such as Greek or Latin roots, in them. The Greek root *astro* means "star," and *naut* means "ship." The Latin root *luna* means "moon."

 Find Text Evidence

On page 435, I see the word astronomy. *I remember that* astro *comes from a Greek root that means "star." I think* astronomy *must have something to do with the stars. It may mean "the study of the stars."*

He worked hard in school and planned to go to a special college to study astronomy and rockets.

Your Turn COLLABORATE

Use the Greek or Latin roots to figure out the meaning of each word.
astronauts, *page 436*
lunar, *page 437*

441

READING/WRITING WORKSHOP, *p. 441*

 **ENGLISH LANGUAGE LEARNERS**
SCAFFOLD

Beginning	Intermediate	Advanced/High
Use Visuals Remind students that some words in English come from Greek and Latin words. Write *astro* and *luna* on the board. Say: Astro *is a Greek word. It means "star."* Luna *is a Latin word. It means "moon."* Point to the word *astronomy* on page 435, and discuss how the meaning of *astro* relates to the meaning of *astrology.* Provide the sentence frame: ___ *is the study of the stars.*	**Recognize** Look at page 435 with students and point to the word *astronomy.* Write the word on the board and ask: *What Greek root do you see in the word* astronomy? Have a volunteer underline *astro.* Then ask: *What is* astro *the Greek word for?* ("star") Provide the sentence frames: ___ *means "star."* ___ *is the study of stars.*	**Expand** Ask students to list out all the meanings they can think of for these three words. Tell them astronomy means the study of the stars. Then ask: *If astronomy means "study of the stars" and astro means "star," what do you think* -nomy *means?* Help students to write a sentence that defines *astronomy* based on their answers.

 Monitor and *Differentiate*

 Quick Check

Can students identify and use Greek and Latin roots to determine the meanings of *astronauts* and *lunar*?

Small Group Instruction

If No →	Approaching Level	Reteach p. T173
	ELL	Develop p. T189
If Yes →	On Level	Review p. T178
	Beyond Level	Extend p. T182

ON-LEVEL PRACTICE BOOK p. 277

Greek and Latin root meanings:
mir = wonder or amazement   *or* = mouth   *fin* = end
orb = circle   *cid* = fall

Use the Greek and Latin roots from the box above to find the meaning of each word in bold below. Write the meaning of the word on the line. Then use each word in a sentence of your own. Possible responses provided.

1. **orbit** circle around something

   The moon *orbits* Earth.

2. **accident** when you fall or do something you did not mean to do

   I once had an *accident* where I fell and skinned my knee.

3. **orator** a person who makes speeches

   I would like to be a great *orator* and make a great speech.

4. **admire** to have wonder or amazement about something

   I *admire* my brother because he is so nice to me.

APPROACHING p. 277	BEYOND p. 277	ELL p. 277

Out of This World!

Literature Anthology

Text Complexity Range

Lexile

420   ▲ 820
                 780

TextEvaluator™

2   ▲ 35
                 34

What makes this text complex?
▶ **Specific Vocabulary**
▶ **Connection of Ideas**
▶ **Genre**

Close Reading Routine

Read   DOK 1–2

- Identify key ideas and details about Learning to Succeed.
- Take notes and summarize.
- Use 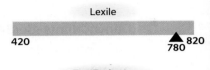 prompts as needed.

Reread   DOK 2–3

- Analyze the text, craft, and structure.
- Use *Close Reading Companion,* pp. 180–182.

Integrate   DOK 4

- Integrate knowledge and ideas.
- Make text-to-text connections.
- Use the Integrate lesson.

Genre · Biography

Out of this World!

The Ellen Ochoa Story

by Liane B. Onish

Essential Question
Why are goals important?
Read about Ellen Ochoa. Find out how she reached her goals.

Go Digital!

506

A C T   Access Complex Text

▶ Specific Vocabulary

Point out the figurative expressions "reach for the stars" and "out of this world" on page 507. Guide students to recognize that these expressions apply to Ellen Ochoa, both figuratively and literally.

- *What does Ellen Ochoa mean when she says "reach for the stars"?* (She means you should set high goals for yourself and try to achieve them.)

"Don't be afraid to reach for the stars. I believe a good education can take you anywhere on Earth and beyond."

-Ellen Ochoa

How many people can say that their jobs are "out of this world"? Ellen Ochoa (uh-CHOH-ah) can. She is the first female Hispanic American astronaut. Her job has taken her out of this world four times.

507

LITERATURE ANTHOLOGY, pp. 506–507

Read

Tell students they will be reading about how Ellen Ochoa achieved her goal to become an astronaut. Ask students to predict how the selection will help them answer the Essential Question.

Note Taking: Use the Graphic Organizer

Remind students to take notes as they read. Have them fill in the graphic organizer on **Your Turn Practice Book** page 272. Ask them to record the problem and solution of each section. They can also note words they don't understand and questions they have.

Reread   *Close Reading Companion*

Genre: Biography

How can you tell this selection is a biography? (It is about the life of a real person, astronaut Ellen Ochoa.) How does the author use text features to help you understand the information about Ellen Ochoa? (The quote tells me Ellen Ochoa values a good education. The text in the box under the photograph summarizes who she is and what she has done. The photograph shows me what Ellen looks like.)

- *What does the expression "out of this world" mean?* (It means something that's extraordinary.)
- *How do these expressions both apply to Ochoa's job as an astronaut?* (Ochoa leaves Earth and travels into space.)

Read

1 Skill: Problem and Solution

What problem did Ellen Ochoa have?
(Ochoa was not chosen for the astronaut
program.) What actions did she take to solve
her problem? (She studied subjects related to
space. She researched inventions that solve
problems in space. She invented a guide for
robotic arms.) Add the problem, actions,
and solution to the organizer.

Problem
Ochoa was not chosen for the space program.

↓

Action
She studied subjects related to space.

↓

Action
She researched space inventions.

↓

Action
She invented a guide for robotic arms.

↓

Solution
Ochoa gets into the astronaut program.

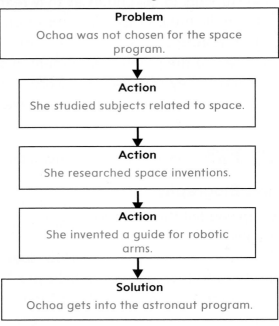

Ellen Ochoa trained hard to become an astronaut.

Young Ellen was a good math and science student.

(clockwise from top) NASA-JSC (2) A. Nulla (ESA/STScI) et al-ESA-NASA (3) NASA-MSFC (4) Dr. Ellen Ochoa (5) NASA-JSC (6) NASA-JSC

508

Reaching for the Stars

Ellen Ochoa was born in California in 1958,
the same year the space program began. Back then,
only men became astronauts. This was a problem
for women who wanted to go into space. Women
were not allowed to even apply for the job. Luckily,
the space program began accepting women in 1978.
Sally Ride, the first female astronaut, went into space
in 1983. In fact, it was Sally Ride's mission that gave
Ellen Ochoa the idea of becoming an astronaut.

When Ellen Ochoa began college, she thought
she would be a **professional** musician. Then she
changed her mind. When she went to Stanford
University, she heard about the skills an astronaut
required. She decided to try to join the astronaut
program. Unfortunately, Ochoa was not chosen.
She did not have the right skills. Most astronauts
were men. She wasn't a military pilot like many
astronauts. She wasn't athletic and strong. But
Ellen wanted to go into space. She knew this was
a problem she could solve.

"I can't imagine not wanting to go into space,"
Ochoa says. She did not give up her dream.

STOP AND CHECK

Reread What inspired Ellen
Ochoa to become an astronaut?
Reread to find out.

A C T Access Complex Text

▶ Connection of Ideas

Help students make inferences to understand Ellen
Ochoa's actions.

- *Why was Ellen not accepted into the astronaut
  program at first?* (She didn't have the right skills.)

- *Why do you think Ellen studied subjects related
  to space and worked on space inventions?* (She
  wanted to gain the skills she didn't have and show
  she could be a good astronaut.)

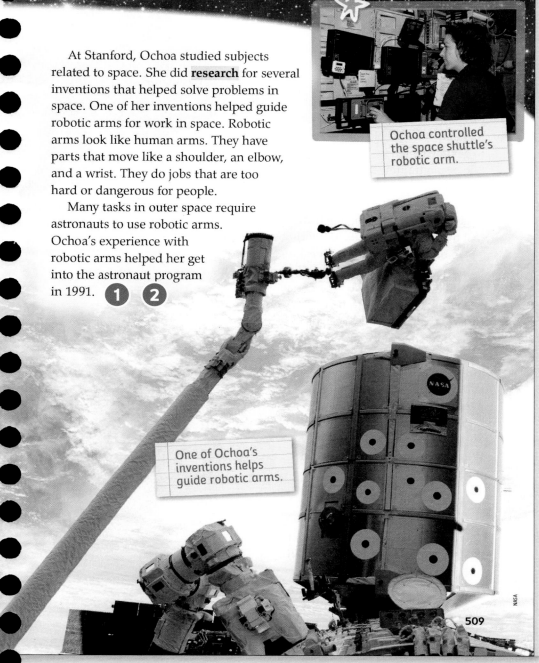

Ochoa controlled the space shuttle's robotic arm.

At Stanford, Ochoa studied subjects related to space. She did **research** for several inventions that helped solve problems in space. One of her inventions helped guide robotic arms for work in space. Robotic arms look like human arms. They have parts that move like a shoulder, an elbow, and a wrist. They do jobs that are too hard or dangerous for people.

Many tasks in outer space require astronauts to use robotic arms. Ochoa's experience with robotic arms helped her get into the astronaut program in 1991. **1** **2**

One of Ochoa's inventions helps guide robotic arms.

509

LITERATURE ANTHOLOGY, *pp. 508–509*

STOP AND CHECK

Reread What inspired Ellen Ochoa to become an astronaut? (Sally Ride's mission)

2 Strategy: Reread

Teacher Think Aloud I'm not sure why Ellen's work with robotic arms was so important, so I can reread the last paragraph on page 509 and paraphrase to make sure I understand. Ochoa's work with robotic arms was very important because astronauts have to use robotic arms for many jobs in space. Her work helped her get into the astronaut program.

Reread   *Close Reading Companion*

Text Features: Photographs and Captions

How does the author use photographs and captions to help you understand that goals are important? (The text explains how the invention of the robotic arm was a step in the achievement of Ochoa's goal, and the photographs and captions help me understand the importance of Ochoa's achievement.)

CONNECT TO CONTENT
SCIENCE AND COMMUNICATION

Ellen Ochoa worked on inventions that helped solve problems in space. By communicating with others and focusing on astronauts' needs, Ochoa created new technologies that helped her achieve her goal of becoming an astronaut.

STEM

ELL Explain that Ellen was not chosen for the astronaut program the first time. Tell students that *She did not give up her dream* means that Ellen kept trying to be an astronaut.

* *When did Ellen get into the astronaut program?* (in 1991)

* *Did learning about space help her?* (yes)

Read

③ Vocabulary: Greek Roots

Find *mission* on page 510. How can Greek roots help you figure out the word's meaning? (The root *miss* means "send." This helps me figure out that a *mission* is a trip where you are sent to do something.)

STOP AND CHECK

Reread How did Ellen Ochoa train to be an astronaut?

Teacher Think Aloud How can we remember the most important details about Ellen Ochoa's astronaut training?

Prompt students to apply the strategy in a Think Aloud by rereading "Training in Space." Have them turn to a partner and paraphrase the important details.

Student Think Aloud I can reread "Training in Space." Ellen Ochoa took new classes, practiced using machines that astronauts use during space flights, and trained on machines that prepared her for space conditions, such as weightlessness.

Training in Space

Before she could join the space program and be an astronaut, Ochoa had one more problem to solve. She had to get herself ready. It was not an easy task. She began training in 1990. Her strong background in math and science helped her do well in these new classes. She also had to pass a physical exam to get into the program. She learned to work on the real machines astronauts use during space flights.

Astronauts are trained to get used to feeling weightless.

"In training, things keep breaking, and problems have to be solved," Ochoa says. "I was in training ③ for three years before my first mission."

During training, astronauts work on machines that get them used to working in space. One machine creates "weightlessness" conditions that astronauts feel in space.

"Weightlessness is the fun part of the mission," Ochoa says. "I guess the closest thing would be swimming or scuba diving. What is odd is that weightlessness seems more natural."

STOP AND CHECK

Reread How did Ellen Ochoa train to be an astronaut? Reread to find out.

510

A C T Access Complex Text

▶ Specific Vocabulary

Model finding the meaning of unfamiliar words.

- *What word parts are in* weightlessness? (The root *weight* and suffixes *-less* and *-ness.*) *What does -less mean?* (without) Tell students *-ness* means "the condition of."

- Help put the parts together for the definition. (The condition of being without weight.)

▶ Genre

Discuss the interview on page 511. Be sure students understand the blue text gives the questions asked by student interviewers. The answers are the exact words of Ellen Ochoa. The ellipses (...) show where sentences were edited out of the answers.

- *How is the interview related to the rest of the text?* (It gives information about astronauts.)

AN INTERVIEW WITH
ELLEN OCHOA

Student reporters interviewed Ellen Ochoa. Here are some of their questions and her answers.

What is NASA training like?

In training, we prepare for anything that could happen on a space mission—anything that could go wrong. . . . Nothing has ever gone wrong on any of my missions, and our training helps us make sure that nothing will. . . . For my last mission, we trained for nine months before the actual flight.

Astronauts are able to sleep even in weightless conditions.

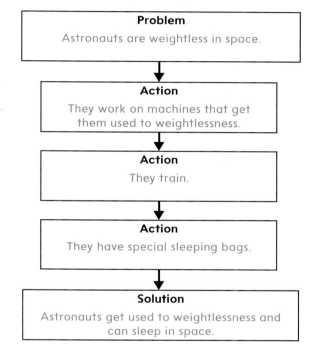

How do you sleep on the space shuttle?

On my last mission . . . we slept in what can best be described as a sleeping bag with hooks. You would find a place to hook on to, and float in. **4**

What do you look for in a potential astronaut, and what is their average age?

Most of the people who are selected are between the ages of 30 to 40. We look for a college education in science or technology. . . . We look for people who can do many things well, because people with multiple skills can usually learn things quickly. This is a very important skill for an astronaut.

511

LITERATURE ANTHOLOGY, *pp. 510–511*

Read

4 Skill: Problem and Solution

What are some ways that astronauts solve the problem of weightlessness and sleeping in space? (They work together on machines that get them used to weightlessness. They train. They have special sleeping bags.) How does this help? (Astronauts get used to weightlessness and can sleep in space.) Add the information to your organizer.

Problem
Astronauts are weightless in space.

↓

Action
They work on machines that get them used to weightlessness.

↓

Action
They train.

↓

Action
They have special sleeping bags.

↓

Solution
Astronauts get used to weightlessness and can sleep in space.

Build Vocabulary page 511

potential: having the ability to do something in the future

ELL Use the photographs and restatement to clarify *weightlessness.* Say: *When you are weightless, you weigh nothing.* Compare being weightless to a floating balloon.

- *Point to the astronauts that are weightless. Are they floating?* (yes)

- *Does Ellen Ochoa like being weightless?* Choral read Ellen Ochoa's quote about being weightless on page 510 with students. Invite volunteers to show or tell what they would feel like if they were weightless.

Read

5 Make Inferences

Why does Ochoa tell students who want to become astronauts to learn to work closely with others? (These activities prepare you for being a team player.) Why is this important? (Astronauts work in teams.) What text evidence supports your answer? (Paragraph 2 and the caption say astronauts work as a team, and Mission Control works with the astronauts.)

6 Strategy: Reread

COLLABORATE

What does a Mission Control worker do? Reread paragraph 2. Then turn to a partner and paraphrase.

Student Think Aloud Mission Control workers communicate with the astronauts and talk them through each second of the mission and explain the procedures. They need to know if all the equipment is working and if the astronauts are okay. They communicate with the astronauts to make sure the space mission is a success.

Build Vocabulary page 512

debrief: ask questions about a subject

procedures: the set ways of doing things

Space Work Is Teamwork

"An astronaut must be both a team player and a leader as well," Ochoa says. She tells students, "You should get involved in activities where you work closely with other people. Working closely with others is an **essential** part of being an astronaut and solving problems in space."

5 First, there is the ground crew. They inspect and repair the shuttle before each mission. Next, Mission Control workers guide the astronauts through each moment of a mission and debrief them on procedures. They are responsible for knowing how equipment is working and how the astronauts are feeling. 6

The crew on a space shuttle must work together to get their jobs done.

(l) NASA (b) NASA (br) NASA

512

A C T Access Complex Text

▶ Connection of Ideas

Ellen Ochoa says that astronauts must be team players and leaders. Help connect this with what students learned about an astronaut's job.

- *When are astronauts team players?* (When they work with Mission Control and other astronauts.)

- *When are they leaders?* (When they make decisions or do special jobs.)

▶ Specific Vocabulary

Explain that when authors use domain-specific words, they often follow them with a brief definition. Help students locate context clues for *mission specialist, payload,* and *climate.* Ask:

- *What does a mission specialist do?* (He or she does experiments.)

Each person in Mission Control works together to make the mission a success.

During a space flight, the teamwork continues. Ochoa and the other astronauts work together to meet the goals of their mission. A space flight crew is like a sports team. The commander of the shuttle is the team captain. He or she makes the crucial decisions that have **serious** effects on a mission. **7**

On her first mission in 1993, Ellen Ochoa was a mission **specialist.** Mission specialists are scientists who do experiments. Ochoa used a robotic arm to send and get back a satellite that collected information about the Sun.

Then in 1994, Ochoa was the payload commander on her second mission. The payload might be supplies or equipment, such as the robotic arm. She did satellite studies of the Sun's effect on Earth's climate, or weather.

513

NASA-JSC

LITERATURE ANTHOLOGY, *pp. 512–513*

Read

7 Skill: Problem and Solution

Space missions are complicated. What steps are taken to make a mission a success? (The ground crew inspects and repairs the shuttle. Mission Control guides the astronauts. Teamwork and communication continues during the space flight.) What is the resolution? (The mission is successful.) Add this information to your organizer.

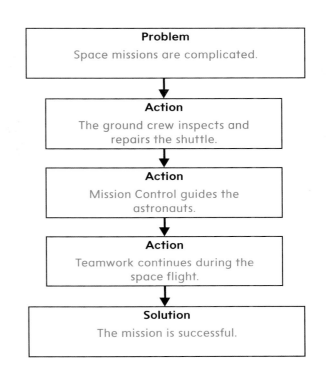

| **Problem** |
| Space missions are complicated. |

↓

| **Action** |
| The ground crew inspects and repairs the shuttle. |

↓

| **Action** |
| Mission Control guides the astronauts. |

↓

| **Action** |
| Teamwork continues during the space flight. |

↓

| **Solution** |
| The mission is successful. |

- *What is* payload? (supplies or equipment)
- *What is* climate? (weather)

ELL Before reading, encourage students to notice cognates on page 513: *capitán; experimento; clima.* Help them identify and understand context clues for domain-specific words.

Then simplify the main idea of pages 512 and 513 by saying: *Astronauts are a team. Do they work alone or together?* (together)

Read

8 Ask and Answer Questions

COLLABORATE

Generate a question of your own about the text and share it with a partner. To find the answer, try rereading the text. For example, you might ask, "What did Ellen Ochoa do between space missions?" To find the answer, you can reread the third paragraph on page 514. (She continued working with other scientists, ground crew, and astronauts to prepare for future space missions.)

9 Make Inferences

Based on what you read about Ellen Ochoa's different responsibilities, what is an inference you can make about an astronaut's job? (Astronauts need to be well trained and educated because they do many different kinds of jobs. They do experiments, deliver supplies, build things, and prepare and plan for new missions. They need to have good communication skills so they can work together effectively as a team.)

Space Jobs

In 1999, Ochoa was a mission specialist again on a space flight. During this flight, she and the crew delivered supplies to the International Space Station. She also "walked" in space for the first time during this mission.

Finally, in 2002, Ochoa took her last space flight. Again, she worked on the International Space Station. She used the robotic arm to deliver supplies and help build new parts of the space station.

8 Between missions, Ochoa continued working. She worked with astronauts and ground crew to prepare for 9 other space missions.

Astronauts have to work closely together in tight spaces.

(t) NASA-MSFC (b) NASA Human Spaceflight Collection/NASA

514

A C T Access Complex Text

▶ Genre

Point to the sidebar on page 515. Explain that nonfiction texts, such as biographies, may have text features that give additional information about topics in the text. Guide students to read the sidebar.

- *How many times did Ellen go into space?* (four)
- *On which trip was she in space the longest?* (Her 1994 trip on Atlantis.)
- *On which trip did she travel the shortest distance in space?* (Her 1999 trip on Discovery.)

Ellen Ochoa's Life Today

Today, Ochoa likes to travel to tell students and teachers about her experiences as an astronaut. She finds it exciting to **communicate** with students. She tells them how she solved the problem of becoming an astronaut. She likes to describe life aboard the space shuttle.

"I'm not trying to make every kid an astronaut, but I want kids to think about a career and the preparation they'll need," Ochoa says. "I tell students that the opportunities I had were a result of having a good educational background. Education is what allows you to stand out."

Ellen Ochoa has realized her dream. She became an astronaut and she has traveled into space four times. Altogether, Ochoa has spent nearly 980 hours in space! Her space missions have taken her more than 16 million miles around Earth. That is more than 640 trips around Earth at the equator. Ellen Ochoa's job has truly taken her "out of this world!"

> **STOP AND CHECK**
>
> Summarize What do astronauts do? Tell the details you learned in this story.

BLAST OFF!
Some facts about Ellen's trips

STS-56 ATLAS-2 Discovery
Date: April 4–17, 1993
Time in Space: 9 days
Miles Traveled: 3.9 million

STS-66 Atlantis
Date: November 3–14, 1994
Time in Space: 11 days
Miles Traveled: 4.5 million

STS-96 Discovery
Date: May 27–June 6, 1999
Time in Space: 10 days
Miles Traveled: 3.8 million

STS-110 Atlantis
Date: April 8–19, 2002
Time in Space: 10 days
Miles Traveled: 4.5 million

515

STOP AND CHECK

Summarize What do astronauts do? Tell the details you learned in this story. (Astronauts travel into space. They work together to conduct experiments and build and repair space equipment. On land, they work together to prepare for missions and plan for future space projects.)

Return to Purposes Review students' predictions and purposes for reading. Ask them to use text evidence to answer the Essential Question. (Goals help you decide what skills and preparation you will need to achieve your dreams.)

Reread *Close Reading Companion*

Text Feature: Sidebar

How does the sidebar help you understand Ochoa's career? (The sidebar gives facts and details about Ochoa's accomplishments. This helps me understand how much she was able to achieve in her career. I read that she went on four space missions, each lasting an average of 10 days and covering about 4 million miles.)

LITERATURE ANTHOLOGY, *pp. 514–515*

▶ Connection of Ideas

Ellen Ochoa tells students about the importance of education. Have students connect Ellen's quotes about education on page 515 with what they learned about the role of education in Ellen's career.

• *How did Ellen become an astronaut after she was told she didn't have the skills?* (She took space-related classes.)

• *How did Ellen's background in math and science prepare her?* (It helped her in her new classes.)

• *Is education only important for children who want to become astronauts? Why or why not?* (No. Education helps you stand out, no matter what career you choose.)

About the Author

Liane B. Onish

Have students read the biography of the author. Ask:

- What is Liane B. Onish's goal as a writer?
- How do photographs help you visualize what Liane B. Onish is describing?

Author's Purpose

To Inform

Review with students that when authors write to inform, they also want to keep their readers' interest. Students may say that the author included the interview with Ellen Ochoa because the questions are about things that interest students. By including them, the author makes the article more interesting and meaningful for students.

Reread

Author's Craft

Explain that authors of biographies often use transitional words to guide readers through the events in the subject's life. How are transitional words useful in a biography? (Transitional words help show the time order sequence of events.) What are some examples? (On page 508, the author uses the word *when* in the sentence: "When Ellen Ochoa began college, she thought she would become a professional musician." The author uses the transitional word *before* on page 510: "*Before she could join the space program and be an astronaut, Ochoa had one more problem to solve.*")

About the Author

Liane B. Onish is a writer and teacher with a goal. She wants to help kids learn in fun and exciting ways. She has taught students in preschool through fifth grade. She has worked as a writer and editor for children's television programs and educational publishing companies. She now writes children's books, magazines, games, and classroom materials.

Author's Purpose
Why do you think that the author included the interview with Ellen Ochoa?

516

LITERATURE ANTHOLOGY, *pp. 516–517*

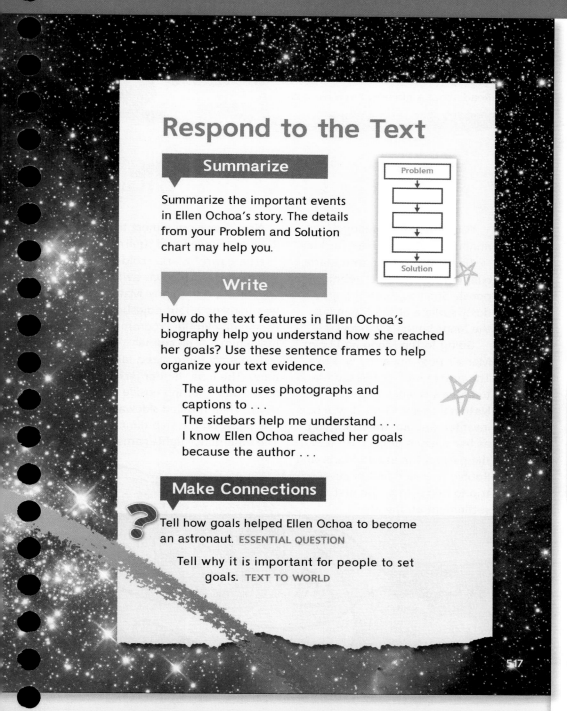

Respond to the Text

Summarize

Summarize the important events in Ellen Ochoa's story. The details from your Problem and Solution chart may help you.

Write

How do the text features in Ellen Ochoa's biography help you understand how she reached her goals? Use these sentence frames to help organize your text evidence.

The author uses photographs and captions to . . .
The sidebars help me understand . . .
I know Ellen Ochoa reached her goals because the author . . .

Make Connections

Tell how goals helped Ellen Ochoa to become an astronaut. ESSENTIAL QUESTION

Tell why it is important for people to set goals. TEXT TO WORLD

517

Integrate

Make Connections COLLABORATE

Essential Question <u>Answer:</u> Ochoa set about to accomplish certain goals to get her into the NASA space program. Once in, she had much more to learn to become an astronaut. <u>Evidence:</u> Ochoa studied subjects related to space and researched several inventions such as a robotic arm (page 509). Ochoa had to train to become an astronaut after she was accepted to the program (page 510).

Text to World Responses may vary, but encourage students to do research online and cite text evidence from sources.

Respond to the Text

Read

Summarize

Tell students they will use the information from their Problem-Solution charts to summarize. As I read, I collected key details and figured out how problems were solved for each section. To summarize, I will retell key details in a logical way.

Reread

Analyze the Text

After students summarize the selection, have them reread to develop a deeper understanding of the text and answer the questions on **Close Reading Companion** pages 180–182. For students who need support in citing text evidence, use the Reread prompts on pages T153B–T153J.

Write About the Text

Review the writing prompt and sentence frames. Remind students to use their responses from the **Close Reading Companion** to support their answers. For a full lesson on writing a response using text evidence, see page T158.
<u>Answer:</u> Text features fill in details by showing how hard Ochoa worked and the depth of her success. <u>Evidence:</u> Ochoa's quote on page 507 shows she thinks a good education is key. Captions on page 508 tell that she excelled in math and science. Photos on pages 508–509 show her training and using the robotic arm and other equipment. The subheads and time line sequence events in her career.

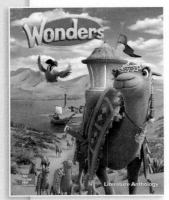

Literature Anthology

"A Flight to Lunar City"

Text Complexity Range

Lexile

420   600   820

TextEvaluator™

2   27   35

What makes this text complex?
▶ **Specific Vocabulary**

Compare Texts ✏ *Analytical Writing*

As students read and reread "A Flight to Lunar City," encourage them to take notes and think about the Essential Question: *Why are goals important?* Tell students to think about how this text compares with *Out of This World!*.

Read

1 Skill: Problem and Solution

What is the main problem Maria and Commander Buckley face? (The lunar lander is not operating correctly.) How did they solve the problem? (The robot dog fixed the control stick and solved the problem.)

Reread   *Close Reading Companion*

Genre: Science Fiction

How does the author use details to help you visualize how Robbie fixed the problem? (The author uses strong, descriptive verbs, such as *leaped, jumped,* and *growled,* to describe Robbie's actions in detail.)

Genre • Adventure Story

Compare Texts
Read about a girl who has a big goal.

A Flight to Lunar City

"Get ready for landing," announced Commander Buckley.

"Fantastic!" whispered Maria, clinging tightly to her robot pooch. She could see the grey dusty surface of the Moon out the lunar lander's window.

Going to the Moon had been Maria's **goal** since she was five. The dream had **motivated** Maria to enter a science project in the National Space Contest. She had invented Robbie, the robot dog, as her science project. He was the perfect Moon pet. Maria and Robbie had won first prize—a trip to Lunar City, the first settlement on the Moon.

Now they were almost there! Robbie wriggled and squirmed. "Settle down!" Maria scolded. Sometimes Robbie was awfully wild, like a real puppy. Maria was thinking about adjusting his Personality Profile Program to make him a little calmer.

Suddenly there was a large bang. The lunar lander jerked forward and turned upside down. Then it rolled sideways. The lights on the ship dimmed. The emergency lights came on.

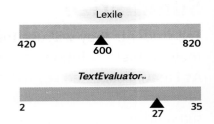

518

 **Access Complex Text**

▶ Specific Vocabulary

Point out the word *lunar* on page 518.

- *What context clue helps you figure out what lunar means?* (the Moon) Help students state a definition for *lunar.* (Related to the Moon.)

"The power is off!" gasped 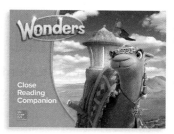 Commander Buckley. "We're stuck."

"Oh, no!" cried Maria.

"Woof!" yapped Robbie, as he squirmed and wiggled in Maria's arms.

"Hold on!" said Commander Buckley. She pushed buttons and touched the control screen. She tried to contact the landing station. Nothing worked. "This control stick is broken!" said Commander Buckley in a panic. "We can't move ahead." She tried to push the control stick into the right position for landing, but it would not budge.

Just then Robbie jumped out of Maria's arms and leaped across the landing ship. He jumped onto the stick with all four paws and growled fiercely. He tugged and chewed on it. "Stop!" cried Maria.

All at once, the control stick shifted into position. The lights came back on. The landing ship whooshed forward.

"Robbie, you did it!" laughed Commander Buckley. "Good dog!" She handed Robbie back to Maria. "Now we can land on the Moon."

Maria smiled proudly. Robbie was the best robot dog ever!

Make Connections

What was Maria's goal? What did she do to reach it? ESSENTIAL QUESTION

What other people with goals have you read about? How are they like Maria? How are they different? TEXT TO TEXT

519

LITERATURE ANTHOLOGY, pp. 518–519

Read

Summarize

Guide students to summarize the selection.

Reread

Analyze the Text

After students read and summarize, have them reread to develop a deeper understanding of the text by annotating and answering questions on pages 183–185 of the **Close Reading Companion**.

Integrate

Make Connections

COLLABORATE

Essential Question Answer: Maria's goal is to go to the Moon, so she enters a contest where the prize is to fly the Moon. She invents a robot dog, wins the contest, and goes to the Moon. Evidence: Page 518 states that it had been Maria's goal to go the Moon "since she was five" and this dream motivated her to enter a National Space Contest. She invented Robbie and won first prize, a trip to the Moon.

Text to Text Responses may vary, but encourage students to cite text evidence from other texts they have read.

ELL Point out that the Spanish word for moon is *luna.* Ask:

• *Where does a lunar lander land?* (on the Moon)

Use demonstration to help students understand the action words in the story, such as *wriggled,* *squirmed, push,* and *tugged.* Invite volunteers to demonstrate an action while other students tell what they are doing.

Phonics/Fluency

 Vowel-Team Syllables
MINILESSON 20 Mins

OBJECTIVES

CCSS Know and apply grade-level phonics and word analysis skills in decoding words. Decode multisyllable words. **RF.3.3c**

CCSS Read on-level prose and poetry orally with accuracy, appropriate rate, and expression on successive readings. **RF.3.4.b**

CCSS Use context to confirm or self-correct word recognition and understanding, rereading as necessary. **RF.3.4c**

CCSS Use a known root word as a clue to the meaning of an unknown word with the same root (e.g., *company, companion*). **L.3.4c**

Rate: 97–117 WCPM

Refer to the sound transfers chart in the **Language Transfers Handbook** to identify sounds that do not transfer in Spanish, Cantonese, Vietnamese, Hmong, and Korean.

1 Explain

Remind students that every syllable in a word has one vowel sound. Explain that a vowel team is two or more letters working together in a word to form one vowel sound.

2 Model

Write the word *remain* on the board. Underline the syllable *main*. Model identifying the letters *ai* in the second syllable. Point out that this vowel team stands for one vowel sound, the long *a* sound. Model how to say the word, pronouncing each syllable. Run your finger under each syllable as you sound out the whole word.

3 Guided Practice

Write the following list of words on the board. Help students identify the vowel teams and then pronounce each full word. Remind students that the letters *y* and *w* can be part of vowel teams such as *ay* and *ow*.

complain	oatmeal	indeed
afraid	mailbox	reading
coatrack	today	pillow

Read Multisyllabic Words

Transition to Longer Words Provide extra practice with multisyllabic words with vowel teams. Draw a T-chart. In column one write *rain, heat, point, joy*. In column two, write *rainbow, preheated, viewpoint,* and *enjoyment*. Point to the words in the first column and explain that each word contains a vowel team. Model how to read each word. Have students repeat.

Explain that the words in the second column contain a vowel team syllable from the first column. Have students underline the vowel team in each word. Point to each word and have students read the words chorally. Write simple sentences using column-one words and have students read them.

 **Go Digital**

Vowel-Team Syllables

Present the Lesson

View "Rocketing Into Space"

Greek and Latin Roots

1 Explain

Knowing the meanings of Greek and Latin roots can help readers figure out the meanings of unfamiliar words.

- The word part *astro* means "star" or "outer space." The word *astronaut* refers to someone who travels to outer space.
- The word part *graph* means "something written." The word part *photo* means "light." A *photograph* is a picture that has been "written with light."
- The word part *tele* means "far." A *telephone* is used to speak with someone who is far away.

2 Model

Write and say the words *astronomy, autograph, telephoto*. Underline the root in each one. Model using the definition of each root to figure out the meanings of the words.

3 Guided Practice

Write the words *astronomer, telescope*, and *telegraph* on the board. Have students identify the roots and use the roots to determine the meaning of each word.

Accuracy

Explain/Model Explain that good readers know that an important part of reading is accuracy, or saying every word and pronouncing them correctly. Tell students that paying attention to the context can help them confirm their accuracy.

Model reading the first two paragraphs of "Rocketing Into Space" on page 435, using the context to confirm or self-correct your accuracy.

Practice/Apply Have partners take turns reading each sentence aloud. Remind students to confirm or self-correct their accuracy using the context.

Daily Fluency Practice FLUENCY

Students can practice fluency using **Your Turn Practice Book**.

Monitor and *Differentiate*

✓ Quick Check

Can students decode words with vowel teams? Can students read words with Greek and Latin roots? Can students read fluently?

Small Group Instruction

If No →	Approaching Level	Reteach pp. T168, T170
	ELL	Develop p. T186
If Yes→	On Level	Review p. T176
	Beyond Level	Extend p. T180

ON-LEVEL PRACTICE BOOK p. 278

A. Read each sentence. Underline the word with a vowel-team syllable. Then circle the vowel-team syllable.

1. He explained how to get to the lake from his home.

2. She is reading the novel that you gave me.

3. He repeats the sentence so we can write it correctly.

4. Mom had to presoak the shirt to remove all the dirt.

5. I think we forgot to tell him that important detail.

B. Read each sentence. Underline the word with the root *astro, graph, photo,* or *tele*. Write the word on the line and circle the root(s).

1. The astronaut told us about his space mission. astronaut

2. I checked out a biography on Thomas Edison at the library. biography

3. When I go to college, I want to take a photography class. photography

4. I hope to get a telescope for my birthday. telescope

5. We really enjoyed the pictures in this graphic novel. graphic

APPROACHING p. 278	BEYOND p. 278	ELL p. 278

Write to Sources

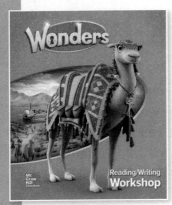

Reading/Writing Workshop

OBJECTIVES

CCSS Write informative/explanatory texts to examine a topic and convey ideas and information clearly. Introduce a topic and group related information together; include illustrations when useful to aiding comprehension. **W.3.2a**

ACADEMIC LANGUAGE

purpose, organize, order

Go Digital

U6W3 Organization: Order Ideas

DAY 1

Writing Fluency

Write to a Prompt Provide students with the prompt: *Who was James A. Lovell Jr.?* Have students share their ideas about what they learned about James A. Lovell Jr. *What did he achieve during his career? What lessons did he learn from his achievements?* When students finish sharing ideas, have them write continuously for fifteen minutes in their Writer's Notebook. If students stop writing, encourage them to keep going.

 COLLABORATE When students finish writing, have them work with a partner to compare ideas and make sure that they both have a clear understanding of the topic.

Genre Writing

Feature Article pp. T344–T349

Third Week Focus Over the course of the week, focus on the following stages of the writing process:

Edit Analyze the Revised Student Model found online in Writer's Workspace. Have students use the Edit questions on the Revise and Edit Checklist to guide them as they review and edit their drafts.

Publish For the final presentation of their feature articles, have students choose a format for publishing.

Evaluate Distribute the Student Rubric found online at Writer's Workspace to students. Have students set writing goals to prepare for a Teacher conference.

DAY 2

Write to the Reading/Writing Workshop Text

Analyze the Prompt Read aloud the first paragraph on page 442 of the **Reading/Writing Workshop**. Ask: *What is the prompt asking?* (to explain the author's purpose) Say: *Let's reread to find the main points of the biography. We can note text evidence.*

Analyze Text Evidence Display Graphic Organizer 55 in Writer's Workspace. *Say: Let's see how one student, Yusuf, took notes to answer the prompt. He notes that when Lovell couldn't afford a special college to study astronomy, he went to another school for two years.* Guide the class through the rest of Yusuf's notes.

Analyze the Student Model Explain how Yusuf used text evidence from his notes to write a response to the prompt.

- **Focus on a Topic** A topic sentence lets readers know what the writing will be about. Yusef used his notes and the evidence he wanted to include in his writing to write the topic sentence. Trait: Ideas

- **Ideas in Order** Yusuf organizes the ideas in order in his response and signals this to the reader by using words and phrases that show time order. Trait: Organization

- **Strong Conclusion** The conclusion sums up the text. Yusuf sums up the main points that support his topic sentence and provides a conclusion about ideas he presented in his response. Trait: Organization

For additional practice with organization and putting ideas in order, assign **Your Turn Practice Book** page 279.

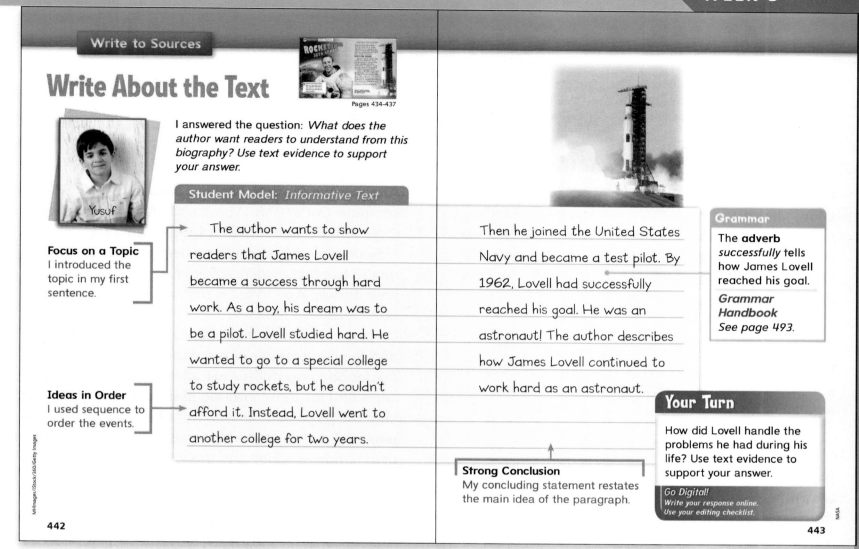

Write to Sources

Write About the Text

Pages 434-437

Yusuf

I answered the question: *What does the author want readers to understand from this biography? Use text evidence to support your answer.*

Student Model: *Informative Text*

Focus on a Topic
I introduced the topic in my first sentence.

The author wants to show readers that James Lovell became a success through hard work. As a boy, his dream was to be a pilot. Lovell studied hard. He wanted to go to a special college to study rockets, but he couldn't afford it. Instead, Lovell went to another college for two years.

Ideas in Order
I used sequence to order the events.

Then he joined the United States Navy and became a test pilot. By 1962, Lovell had successfully reached his goal. He was an astronaut! The author describes how James Lovell continued to work hard as an astronaut.

Grammar

The **adverb** *successfully* tells how James Lovell reached his goal.

Grammar Handbook
See page 493.

Your Turn

How did Lovell handle the problems he had during his life? Use text evidence to support your answer.

Go Digital!
Write your response online.
Use your editing checklist.

Strong Conclusion
My concluding statement restates the main idea of the paragraph.

442

443

READING/WRITING WORKSHOP, *pp. 442-443*

Your Turn Writing Read the Your Turn prompt on p. 443 of the Reading/Writing Workshop aloud. Discuss the prompt with students. If necessary, review with students that authors present ideas in a logical order and use time-order words to guide their readers.

Have students take notes as they look for the text evidence to answer the prompt. Remind them to include the following elements as they craft their response from their notes:

- Focus on a Topic
- Ideas in Order
- Strong Conclusion

Have students use the **Grammar Handbook** on page 493 in the Reading/Writing Workshop to edit and correct improper use of adverbs.

ENGLISH LANGUAGE LEARNERS SCAFFOLD

ELL

Beginning

Write Help students complete the sentence frames.
On problem Lovell faced was ____.
He handled this problem by ____.

Intermediate

Describe Ask students to complete the sentence frames. Encourage students to provide details.
To reach his goal, Lovell had to ____, but he faced this problem by ____.

Advanced/High

Discuss Check for understanding. Ask: *How did Lovell solve the problems he faced on his path toward becoming an astronaut? How did he continue to solve problems during his career?*

Write to Sources

DAY 3

For students who need support to complete the writing assignment for the Literature Anthology, provide the following instruction.

DAY 4

Write to the Literature Anthology Text

Analyze the Prompt Explain that students will write about *Out of This World!* in the **Literature Anthology,** pages 506–515. Provide the following prompt: *How do the text features in Ellen Ochoa's biography help you understand how she reached her goals?* Ask: *What is the prompt asking you to do?* (to analyze the author's use of text features)

Analyze Text Evidence Help students note evidence.

Page 511 Read the page. Ask: *How do the photograph and caption help you better understand the interview with Ellen Ochoa?* (The photograph and caption show what the sleeping bag with hooks look like. That helps me visualize the challenges of being an astronaut.)

Page 515 Read the text on this page, and study the time line. Ask: *How do the text and time line work together to explain how Ellen Ochoa reached her goals?* (The time line tells me when Ochoa met some of her goals as stated in the text.) *What does this help you understand about meeting goals?*

Encourage students to look for more text evidence within the text features. Then have them craft a short response. Use the conference routine below.

Write to Two Sources

Analyze the Prompt Explain to students they will compare *Out of This World!* and "A Flight to Lunar City." Provide students with the following prompt: *How does working as a team help people meet their goals? Use text evidence from two texts to support your answer.* Ask: *What is the prompt asking you to do?* (to explain how teamwork helps meet goals) Say: *On page 513 I read that astronauts work together, and the commander of the shuttle is the team leader. So in my notes I will write:* Teamwork is very important for those involved in space flight. *I will also note the page number and the title of the source. On page 519, I read that Maria relied on the teamwork of Commander Buckley and the robot dog, Robbie. I will add this to my notes.*

Analyze Text Evidence Display online Graphic Organizer 56 in Writer's Workspace. Say: *Let's see how one student took notes to answer the prompt. Here are Yusuf's notes.* Read through the text evidence for each selection and have students point out examples of teamwork and goals met.

Teacher Conferences

STEP 1

Talk about the strengths of the writing.

The opening paragraph has a clearly stated topic that identifies the main idea of the paragraph. It tells me what the passage will be about.

STEP 2

Focus on how the writer organizes text evidence.

This text evidence you cited provides interesting details. It would help if you used more time-order words to help make the order of events and ideas clearer.

STEP 3

Make concrete suggestions.

You restate your main idea in your conclusion, but you do not sum up any of the details that you used to support it. Be sure to mention key details to strengthen your conclusion.

DAY
5

Share the Prompt Provide the following prompt to students: *How is Maria similar to Ellen Ochoa? Use evidence from both texts to respond. Use text evidence from* Out of This World! *and "A Flight to Lunar City" to support your answer.*

Find Text Evidence Have students take notes. Find text evidence and give guidance where needed. If necessary, review with students how to paraphrase. Remind them to write the page number and source of the information.

Analyze the Student Model Review the prompt and Yusuf's notes from Day 4. Display the student model on page 280 of the **Your Turn Practice Book**. Explain to students that Yusuf synthesized his notes to write a response to the prompt. Discuss the page together with students or have them do it independently.

Write the Response Review the prompt from Day 4 with students. Have students use their notes to craft a short response. Tell students to include the titles of both sources and the following elements:

- Focus on a Topic
- Ideas in Order
- Strong Conclusion

COLLABORATE

Share and Reflect Have students share their responses with a partner. Use the Peer Conference routine below.

Suggested Revisions

Provide specific direction to help focus young writers.

Focus on a Sentence
Read the draft and target one sentence for revision. *Rewrite this sentence using a transitional word to connect ____.*

Focus on a Section
Underline a section that needs to be revised. *Rearrange the details in this section to strengthen your claim that ____.*

Focus on a Revision Strategy
Underline a section. Have students use a specific revision strategy, such as restating. *You have presented solid text evidence throughout the passage. Be sure to restate your topic in your conclusion to tie your ideas together.*

Peer Conferences

Focus peer response on writing a strong conclusion that sums up the writer's response to the prompt. Ask these questions:

- Does the topic sentence clearly state the writer's main idea?
- Are ideas in order and did the writer connect them with time-order words?
- Does the conclusion sum up the main idea and details?

→ Grammar: Adverbs

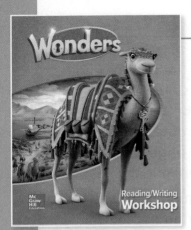

Reading/Writing Workshop

OBJECTIVES

CCSS Explain the function of nouns, pronouns, verbs, adjectives, and adverbs in general and their functions in particular sentences. **L.3.1a**

CCSS Form and use comparative and superlative adjectives and adverbs, and choose between them depending on what is to be modified. **L.3.1g**

• Identify and use adverbs

• Use adverbs and adjectives correctly

Have small groups of students complete the sentence, [She/He] talked _____. Have them use the adverbs *slowly, quickly, quietly, angrily,* and *sadly.* Have students take turns choosing an adverb and acting out the sentence.

DAY 1

DAILY LANGUAGE ACTIVITY

keith is going to have a party he wants to plan it by themselves.

(1: Keith; 2: party.; 3: He; 4: himself)

Introduce Adverbs That Tell How

• An **adverb** describes an action verb. Most adverbs that tell **how** an action takes place end in *-ly*:
   He paints **beautifully**.

• Adverbs can tell the place, time, or the manner an action takes place. Some adverbs answer the question *how?*
   We are going **slowly**.

Discuss adverbs using page 493 of the Grammar Handbook in **Reading/Writing Workshop**.

DAY 2

DAILY LANGUAGE ACTIVITY

Dan willn't share with myself. I'm go to find everyone else to play with.

(1: won't; 2: me.; 3: going; 4: someone)

Review Adverbs

Review adverbs that tell how, such as *slowly.* Have students give examples of adverbs that tell *how.*

Introduce Place Adverbs That Tell Where and When

• Some adverbs that tell where are: *there, ahead, outside, around, up, far, here, away, nearby, everywhere*:
   We are going to play **outside**.

• Some adverbs tell the time, or when, an action happens. Some adverbs that tell when are *first, soon, always, early, next, today, later, tomorrow,* and *then*:
   I wake up **early** every morning.

 TALK ABOUT IT

COLLABORATE

ADVERB QUESTION QUIZ

Partners should select a paragraph from a book with sentences containing adverbs. Taking turns, one partner should read the paragraph one sentence at a time. At the end of each sentence, the other partner identifies the adverbs using a question form. (Example: What is *quickly*?).

FIND THE ADVERB

Have partners write a list of goals they would like to achieve. Then have each student write a sentence describing their goal, using adverbs. Have students read their sentences aloud. The other students should name the adverbs in the sentences and explain their function in each sentence.

DAY

We look all over franklin square to find the right batterie for the toy.
(1: looked; 2: Franklin Square; 3: battery)

Mechanics and Usage: Adverbs and Adjectives

- Use an adjective to describe a noun.
- Use an adverb to describe a verb.
- Don't mix up adjectives with adverbs that tell *how*.

As students write, refer them to Grammar Handbook pages 491, 493, and 494.

See Grammar Practice Reproducibles pages 136–140.

DAY

DAILY LANGUAGE ACTIVITY

My notebook was right away. Where have it go.
(1: here; 2: has; 3: gone?)

Proofread

Have students correct errors in these sentences.

1. Mary is waiting patient. She will be near when we're ready. (1: patiently; 2: nearby)

2. Larry quiet left the house. He didn't want to wake no one up. (1: quietly; 2: anyone)

3. Max doesn't feel good. He will go home short. (1: well; 2: shortly)

4. I accident cut my hand. Now I needs a bandage. (1: accidentally; 2: need)

Check work using Grammar Handbook pp. 491, 493–494.

DAY

DAILY LANGUAGE ACTIVITY

I usual walks home this way. I loves the tree-line streets.
(1: usually; 2: walk; 3: love; 4: tree-lined)

Assess

Use the Daily Language Activity and Grammar Practice Reproducibles page 140 for assessment.

Reteach

Use Grammar Practice Reproducibles pages 136–139 and selected pages from the Grammar Handbook for reteaching. Remind students that it is important to use adverbs of time, place, and manner that tell how, when, and where correctly as they write and speak.

Check students' writing for use of the skill and listen for it in their speaking. Assign Grammar Revision Assignments in their Writer's Notebooks as needed.

CHOOSE A MODIFIER

Have small groups write nouns that are related to having goals. Have them place the cards in a pile. Then have each student take a card and say an adjective that would modify the word on their card. Have them make up a sentence with the two words.

ADD AN ADVERB

Have partners write five sentences each about why they think it is important to have goals. Then, have partners switch sentences and write a companion sentence for each, using adverbs that tell how. For example, students may write *Goals help me focus. Goals help me focus* clearly *on my future.*

ANSWER THE QUESTION

Have students in small groups each write down five questions that relate to why people set goals. Students will take turns selecting a card and answering the question using a sentence with adverbs that tell how, where, when, or adverbs that compare two or more actions.

Spelling: Vowel Team Syllables

DAY 1

DAY 2

OBJECTIVES

CCSS Use spelling patterns and generalizations (e.g., *word families, position-based spellings, syllable patterns, ending rules, meaningful word parts*) in writing words. **L.3.2f**

CCSS Consult reference materials, including beginning dictionaries, as needed to check and correct spellings. **L.3.2g**

Spelling Words

explained	monkey	complain
remain	brief	enjoys
reading	preteen	poison
detail	about	repeats
presoak	allowing	unreal

Review able, castle, towel
Challenge repaid, approached

Differentiated Spelling

Approaching Level

away	unreal	chief
complain	reading	key
explained	detail	allow
remain	soaked	enjoys
repeats	streets	poison

Beyond Level

explained	preheated	textbook
remain	brief	allowing
repeatedly	replay	viewpoint
detail	preteen	complain
monkey	approached	enjoyment

Assess Prior Knowledge

Display the spelling words. Read them aloud, drawing out and slowly enunciating the vowel team syllables.

Model for students how to spell the word *explained*. Draw a line between the syllables: *ex/plained* and identify the vowel team syllable *ai*. Point out that the vowel team sounds like one of the vowel's sounds.

Demonstrate sorting the spelling words by pattern under key words *detail, monkey,* and *unreal*. (Write the words on index cards or the IWB.) Sort a few words with vowel team syllables by the vowel sound they produce. Point out that a vowel team stays in the same syllable.

Then use the Dictation Sentences from Day 5. Say the underlined word, read the sentence, and repeat the word. Have students write the words.

Spiral Review

Review the consonant + *-le* or *-el* syllable in the words *able, castle,* and *towel*. Use the Dictation Sentences below for the review words. Read the sentence, say the word, and have students write the words.

1. The athlete was <u>able</u> to run faster.
2. She liked the <u>castle</u> painting.
3. The old <u>towel</u> was used only to clean the floor.

Have partners trade papers and check the spellings.

Challenge Words Review this week's spelling words, pointing out the vowel team syllables. Use these Dictation Sentences for challenge words. Read the sentence, say the word, have students write the word.

1. I <u>repaid</u> the favor to Ingrid.
2. Tony <u>approached</u> the sleeping kitten quietly.

Have students write the words in their word study notebook.

WORD SORTS

COLLABORATE

OPEN SORT

Have students cut apart the **Spelling Word Cards BLM** in the Online Resource Book and initial the backs of each card. Have them read the words aloud with a partner. Then have partners do an **open sort**. Have them record the sort in their word study notebook.

PATTERN SORT

Complete the **pattern sort** using the key words, pointing out the vowel team syllables. Have students use Spelling Word Cards to do their own pattern sort.

A partner can compare and check their sorts.

DAY 3

Alphabetizing

Display *repeats, reading, remain.* Model how to alphabetize to the third letter.

Say: *Look at the first two letters. Decide which ones come first in the alphabet. If the first and second letters are the same, go to the third letter.* Put the words in ABC order: *reading, remain, repeats.* Explain that since the letters *re* are the same, it is necessary to go to the third letter to alphabetize the words: the letter *a* comes before *m*, and *m* comes before *p*.

Have students alphabetize the words *allowing, about, approached, able,* and *away* to the third letter. (able, about, allowing, approached, away)

See Phonics/Spelling Reproducibles pp. 163–168.

SPEED SORT

Have partners do a **speed sort** to see who is faster. Then have partners write sentences for each spelling word, leaving blanks where the words should go. Have them trade papers and fill in the blanks.

DAY 4

Proofread and Write

Write these sentences on the board. Have students circle and correct each misspelled word. Remind students they can use print or electronic resources to check and correct spelling.

1. She will complayn about the breef and unhelpful instructions. (complain, brief)

2. The teacher put preeteen books on the reeding table. (preteen, reading)

3. The travel agent explayned every detale of the vacation plan. (explained, detail)

4. He enjoiys the book's unreel fantasy story. (enjoys, unreal)

Error Correction Remind students to pay attention to vowels teams that have the same vowel sound, such as *ai* and *ay* or *ee* and *ea*.

BLIND SORT

Have partners do a **blind sort**: one reads a spelling word card; the other tells under which key word it belongs. Have them take turns until both have sorted all their words. Then have students explain how they sorted the words.

DAY 5

Assess

Use the Dictation Sentences for the Posttest. Have students list misspelled words in their word study notebooks. Look for students' use of these words in their writings.

> ### Dictation Sentences
>
> 1. She <u>explained</u> why the window was broken.
> 2. <u>Remain</u> there until I return.
> 3. Joan was <u>reading</u> a book for class.
> 4. She painted each <u>detail</u> carefully.
> 5. You must <u>presoak</u> the dirty shirts.
> 6. The zoo had only one baby <u>monkey</u>.
> 7. Denis read the <u>brief</u> news story.
> 8. The <u>preteen</u> still liked the children's book.
> 9. She talked <u>about</u> his test score.
> 10. My mother is <u>allowing</u> me to invite a friend over.
> 11. Do not <u>complain</u> about the food!
> 12. My class <u>enjoys</u> recess.
> 13. There was <u>poison</u> in the king's cup.
> 14. She often <u>repeats</u> what she said before.
> 15. Winning the lottery seemed <u>unreal</u>.
>
> Have students self-correct the tests.

→ Build Vocabulary

OBJECTIVES

CCSS Determine the meaning of words and phrases as they are used in a text, distinguishing literal from nonliteral language. **RL.3.4**

CCSS Use a known root word as a clue to the meaning of an unknown word with the same root (e.g., *company, companion*). **L.3.4c**

CCSS Distinguish the literal and nonliteral meanings of words and phrases in context (e.g., *take steps*). **L.3.5a**

Expand vocabulary by adding inflectional endings and suffixes.

Vocabulary Words

communicate	professional
essential	research
goal	serious
motivated	specialist

Have partners practice using other academic vocabulary terms from the week, such as **communicate** and **contact,** precisely while speaking and writing. They should discuss any synonyms or antonyms they know for these words and shades of meaning differences.

DAY 1

Connect to Words

Practice this week's vocabulary.

1. How do you **communicate** with friends?
2. What is an **essential** part of any school?
3. Name one **goal** you have.
4. How can you **motivate** yourself to do well in school?
5. Do you like watching **professional** sports?
6. How can **research** into illnesses help people?
7. How do you make **serious** decisions?
8. What does a computer **specialist** do?

DAY 2

Expand Vocabulary

Help students generate different forms of this week's words by adding, changing, or removing inflectional endings.

- Draw a four-column chart. Write *motivate* in the left column. Then write *motivates, motivated,* and *motivation* in the other columns. Read aloud the words and discuss the meanings.
- Have students share sentences with each form of *motivate*.
- Students can fill in the chart for other words, such as *communicate*.
- Have students copy the chart in their word study notebook.

 BUILD MORE VOCABULARY

COLLABORATE

ACADEMIC VOCABULARY

Discuss important academic words.

- Display *achieve* and *evaluate* and discuss the meanings with students.
- Display *achieve* and *achievement*. Have partners look up and define related words.
- Write the related words on the board. Have partners ask and answer questions using the words. Repeat with *evaluate*. Elicit examples from students.

IDIOMS

- Remind students that idioms are a type of figurative language that have a meaning other than the literal meaning.
- Write an idiom and discuss it as a class, such as *Reach for the stars!* Discuss that the idiom means to dream big dreams, but not literally to reach out for the stars.
- Have partners generate other examples. Invite partners to share their work. Discuss the literal and nonliteral meanings of the idioms.

DAY

3

Reinforce the Words

Review this week's vocabulary words. Have students orally complete each sentence stem.

  1. We use _____ to <u>communicate</u> with each other.
  2. His dad is a _____ <u>specialist</u>.
  3. That _____ was a little too <u>serious</u> for me.
  4. Studying is <u>essential</u> if you want to _____.
  5. I think scientific <u>research</u> is _____.
  6. _____ is a <u>professional</u> sports team.

DAY

4

Connect to Writing

• Have students write sentences in their word study notebooks using this week's vocabulary.

• Tell them to write sentences that provide information about the words and their meanings.

• **ELL** Provide the Day 3 sentence stems for students needing extra support.

Write About Vocabulary Have students write something they learned from this week's words in their word study notebook. For example, they might write about a dream or *goal* they have. How can they get *motivated* to achieve it?

DAY

5

Word Squares

Ask students to create Word Squares for each vocabulary word.

• In the first square, students write the word. (example: *communicate*)

• In the second square, students write their own definition of the word and any related words. (examples: *talk, speak*)

• In the third square, students draw an illustration to help them remember the word. (example: someone talking on a phone)

• In the fourth square, students write non-examples. (example: *silence*)

• Have students share their Word Squares with a partner.

GREEK AND LATIN ROOTS

Remind students that many words have Greek or Latin roots, such as *astronaut,* which comes from the Greek *astron,* meaning "star."

• Display **Your Turn Practice Book** pages 273–274. Read the first paragraph. Model figuring out the meaning of *admire.*

• For additional practice with Greek and Latin roots, have students complete page 277. Discuss with students how the root words helped them figure out the meanings of the words.

SHADES OF MEANING

Help students generate words related to *serious.* Draw a synonym/antonym scale.

• Discuss synonyms, such as *important* and *crucial,* and antonyms, such as *humorous* and *amusing.* Add the words to the scale.

• Have partners list other synonyms and antonyms for *serious.*

• Discuss the meanings of the words and add them to the scale.

• Ask students to copy the words in their word study notebook.

MORPHOLOGY

Use the word *communicate* as a springboard for students to learn more words.

• Write *communicate* and discuss its meaning. Then write the suffix *–ion,* noting that it means "the action of." Use the base word and suffix to discuss the meaning of *communication.*

• Have partners list other words with the suffix *–ion,* such as *connection* and *deletion.*

• Tell students to use the base words and suffix to determine the meanings of the words.

→Integrate Ideas

Close Reading Routine

Read   DOK 1–2

- Identify key ideas and details about Learning to Succeed.
- Take notes and summarize.
- Use prompts as needed.

Reread   DOK 2–3

- Analyze the text, craft, and structure.
- Use the **Close Reading Companion.**

Integrate   DOK 4

- Integrate knowledge and ideas.
- Make text-to-text connections.
- Use the Integrate lesson.
- Use *Close Reading Companion,* p. 186.

 TEXT CONNECTIONS

Connect to the Essential Question

Write the essential question on the board: Why is having goals important? Divide the class into small groups. Tell students that each group will compare the information that they have learned about why having goals is important. Model how to compare this information by using examples from this week's **Leveled Readers** and "Rocketing into Space," **Reading/Writing Workshop** pages 434–437.

Evaluate Text Evidence Have students review their class notes and completed graphic organizers before they begin their discussions. Encourage students to compare information from all the week's reads. Have each group pick one student to take notes. Explain that

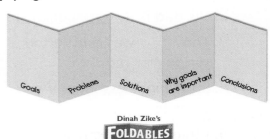

Dinah Zike's
FOLDABLES
Study Organizer

Setting Goals

Go Digital

Collaborate

Research Roadmap

Resources: Research and Inquiry

 RESEARCH AND INQUIRY

Interview a Classmate

Explain that students will work in small groups to brainstorm why it is important to have goals. Students will then interview each other about their goals, where they came from, and how they plan to achieve them. Discuss the following steps:

❶ **Brainstorm** As they begin thinking about the goals they would like to achieve, have students think about their own experiences and the selections they read this week.

❷ **Discuss Goals** Have groups discuss the kinds of things they would like to do by the time they finish high school. Encourage them to consider why they have these goals and how they intend to achieve them.

OBJECTIVE

CCSS Compare and contrast the most important points and key details presented in two texts on the same topic. **RI.3.9**

each group will use an Accordion Foldable® to record their ideas. You may wish to model how to use an Accordion Foldable® to record comparisons.

Text to Music

As students discuss the information from all the week's reads, have them include the American spiritual "Turn Me Round" on page 186 of the **Close Reading Companion** as a part of their discussion. Guide students to see the connections between the song and text. Ask: *How does the song connect to what you read this week?*

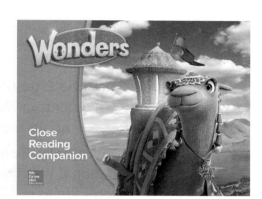

Present Ideas and Synthesize Information

When students finish their discussions, ask for a volunteer from each group to read his or her notes aloud.

OBJECTIVES

CCSS Conduct short research projects that build knowledge about a topic. **W.3.7**

CCSS Recognize and observe differences between the conventions of spoken and written standard English. **L.3.3b**

• Write interview questions.
• Interview a classmate.

❸ **Guided Practice** Discuss effective interviewing skills with students. Have them take notes about their groups' discussion and begin writing interview questions. Have them use the Interview Form for help. Remind students that informal English is usually used in brainstorming sessions, but they should use more formal English as they write their interview questions.

❹ **Create the Project: Interview a Classmate** Have students interview the other members of their group about their goals. Remind students to take notes on their answers.

Present the Interview

Have students present the results of their interviews to the rest of the class. Conduct a class discussion on steps students can take to achieve their goals. Remind students to be respectful listeners. Have students use the online Listening Checklist to evaluate their listening skills.

ACADEMIC LANGUAGE

goals, achieve, interview

→ Approaching Level

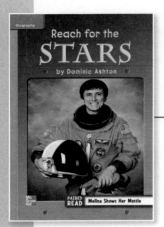

Lexile 600
TextEvaluator™ 27

OBJECTIVES

(CCSS) Describe the overall structure (e.g., chronology, comparison, cause/effect, problem/solution) of events, ideas, concepts, or information in a text or part of a text. **RI.4.5**

(CCSS) Use common, grade-appropriate Greek and Latin affixes and roots as clues to the meaning of a word (e.g., *telegraph*, *photograph*, *autograph*). **L.4.4b**

• Reread text to check understanding.
• Identify the problem and solution in a text.

ACADEMIC LANGUAGE
reread, problem, solution, biography, Greek, Latin, roots

Leveled Reader:
Reach for the Stars

Go Digital

Leveled Readers

Before Reading

Preview and Predict

Have students read the Essential Question. Then have them read the title and table of contents of *Reach for the Stars*. Have students predict what this selection is about and share their predictions with a partner.

Review Genre: Biography Review with students that a biography is a type of informational text that tells about a person's life. It tells the events of a person's life in order and includes text features like headings and timelines. As they preview *Reach for the Stars*, have students identify features of a biography.

During Reading

Close Reading

Note Taking Have students use their graphic organizer as they read.

Pages 2–3 *Why do you think the author includes the detail about Franklin Chang Díaz watching for the satellite on page 2?* (It shows the start of his desire to become an astronaut.) *Remind students that the Greek root* astro *means* star *and* naut *means* ship. Help students define *astronaut.* (An *astronaut* is someone who travels through space on a ship.)

Pages 4–5 *What problems did Chang Díaz have to overcome in order to achieve his dream?* (His parents did not have the money to send him to college; he did not know English.) *What was his solution to these problems?* (He studied hard and won a scholarship.)

Page 6 *Explain to a partner what you learn from the sidebar on page 6. Reread the sidebar to help you answer the question.* (Astronauts need to learn many subjects and learn to survive in harsh environments.)

Pages 7–10 *What happened after Franklin Chang Díaz was chosen for the space shuttle program?* (He spent six years at NASA training to go into space.) *How many times did Franklin Chang Díaz go into space? What was important about that? Reread the information about Franklin Chang Diaz's missions to answer the questions.* (He flew seven space missions, as many as anyone in the world at the time.)

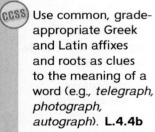
Fill in the Graphic Organizer

Page 11 *What information do you get from the sidebar on page 11?* (I learn the date, length, number of orbits, miles, and the name of the ship of each of Franklin's missions.) *Between what years did Chang Díaz fly?* (1986–2002)

Pages 12–14 *What has Chang Díaz focused on since he left NASA?* Point students to the first paragraphs on each page to answer the question. (He is developing a special rocket; he is studying tropical diseases; he helps young Costa Ricans pursue their own dreams.)

After Reading

Respond to Reading Revisit the Essential Question, and ask students to complete the Text Evidence questions on page 15.

Analytical Writing **Write About Reading** Make sure students provide details from the story that tell the problems Chang Díaz faced and how he solved them.

Fluency: Accuracy and Phrasing

Model Model reading page 13 with proper accuracy and phrasing. Next, reread the page aloud, and have students read along with you.

Apply Have students practice reading with a partner.

PAIRED READ

"Melina Shows Her Mettle"

Make Connections: Write About It **Analytical Writing**

Before reading, have students note that the genre of this text is science fiction, which is a type of fiction based on scientific ideas. Then discuss the Essential Question.

After reading, have students make connections between how Melina and Franklin Chang Díaz reach their goals in "Melina Shows Her Mettle" and *Reach for the Stars*.

Leveled Reader

🧪 FOCUS ON SCIENCE

Students can extend their knowledge of space flight by completing the science activity on page 20. **STEM**

Literature Circles

Ask students to conduct a literature circle using the Thinkmark questions to guide the discussion. You may wish to have a whole-class discussion on how they could take lessons from the way Franklin Chang Díaz followed his goals.

Level Up

Level-up lessons available online.

IF students read the **Approaching Level** fluently and answered the questions

THEN pair them with students who have proficiently read the **On Level** and have approaching-level students

• echo-read the **On Level** main selection with their partner.

• use self-stick notes to mark a detail to discuss in each section.

A C T Access Complex Text

The **On Level** challenges students by including more **domain-specific words** and **complex sentence structures**.

→ Approaching Level

Phonics/Decoding

DECODE WORDS WITH VOWEL TEAMS *ea, ee, ie*

TIER 2

OBJECTIVES

 Decode multisyllable words. **RF.3.3c**

Decode words with long-*e* vowel team syllables.

 I Do Write *grief* on the board and underline *ie*. Point out that, when two letters work together to form one vowel sound, this is called a vowel team. Point out the letters *ie*. Explain that this vowel team stands for the long-*e* vowel sound. Model how to say the word one syllable at a time. Tell students that other vowel teams that form the long-*e* sound are *ea* and *ee*.

 We Do On the board, write *meat, teen, brief*. Model how to decode the first word. Have students repeat. Point out the vowel team that forms the long-*e* sound. Have students decode the rest of the words and identify vowel teams that form each long-*e* sound.

 You Do Add these words to the board: *peach, week, chief, seat, meet*. Have students read them aloud, identifying the letters that form the vowel teams. Point to all of the words randomly for students to read chorally.

BUILD WORDS WITH VOWEL TEAM SYLLABLES

TIER 2

OBJECTIVES

 Decode multisyllable words. **RF.3.3c**

Build words with vowel team syllables.

 I Do Tell students that they will be building multisyllable words with vowel team syllables. On the board, write: *ee, ea, ie, ey* as in *beaver; ai, ay* as in *raining; oe, oa, ow* as in *floating*. Read the words and underline the vowel team syllables. Then display these **Word-Building Cards**, one at a time: *row, main, mon, ing, tain, day, bor, read, a, up;* write the syllables *ey, light, gree, load, roes, he* on the board. Model sounding out each syllable.

 We Do Have students chorally read each syllable. Repeat in random order. Next, display all the Word-Building Cards and syllables. Work with students to combine the Word-Building Cards and syllables to form two-syllable words with the vowel teams. Have students chorally read the words: *money, reading, agree, maintain, daylight, borrow, upload, heroes.*

 You Do Write other syllables on the board, such as *feed, soap, ow,* and *ing,* and display the Word-Building Cards *ner, ern, east, y, re,* and *play*. Have students work with partners to build words using these syllables.

PRACTICE WORDS WITH VOWEL TEAM SYLLABLES

OBJECTIVES

 Decode multisyllable words. **RF.3.3c**

Decode multisyllable words with vowel team syllables.

 I Do Remind students that a vowel team syllable is when a syllable has two letters working together to form one vowel sound. Write the words *teaching, unknown,* and *playful* and read them aloud. Have students repeat.

 We Do Write the words *foamiest, buffaloes, tomorrow, beekeeper, eagerly, honeydew, anyway, brainstorming,* and *replaying* on the board. Model how to decode the first word. Then guide students as they decode the remaining words.

 You Do Afterward, point to the words in random order for students to chorally read. Repeat several times.

GREEK AND LATIN ROOTS

OBJECTIVES

 Use a known root word as a clue to the meaning of an unknown word with the same root (e.g., *company, companion*). **L.3.4c**

Decode words with Greek and Latin roots.

I Do Review Greek root words. Explain that the root word *astro* comes from the Greek word for *star.* The word *astronomer* means "someone who studies the stars." Review: *tele,* meaning "far" (*telescope:* "a device used to see things that are far away"); *photo,* meaning "light" (*photosynthesis:* "the process by which plants use light and other materials to make their own food"); *graph,* meaning "written" (*autograph:* "a self-written name").

 We Do Write *photograph, astronaut,* and *television* on the board. Say each word aloud, and have students repeat. Guide students in identifying the words' Greek roots then using the root words to determine the words' meanings.

 You Do Next, write *telegraph, astronomical,* and *photographer* on the board. Have students say each word. Then, have students identify each word's Greek root. Ask them to use the root word to determine the word's meaning. Point to the words in random order for students to read and define.

ENGLISH LANGUAGE LEARNERS

For the students who need **phonics**, **decoding**, and **fluency** practice, use scaffolding methods as necessary to ensure students understand the meaning of the words. Refer to the **Language Transfers Handbook** for phonics elements that may not transfer in students' native languages.

Approaching Level

Vocabulary

REVIEW HIGH-FREQUENCY WORDS

 TIER 2

OBJECTIVES

CCSS Use conventional spelling for high-frequency and other studied words and for adding suffixes to base words (e.g., *sitting, smiled, cries, happiness*). **L.3.2e**

Review high-frequency words.

 I Do Use **Word Cards** 221–230. Display one word at a time, following the routine:

Display the word. Read the word. Then spell the word.

 We Do Ask students to state the word and spell the word with you. Model using the word in a sentence and have students repeat after you.

 You Do Display the word. Have students say the word and then spell it. When completed, quickly flip through the word card set as students chorally read the words. Provide opportunities for students to use the words in speaking and writing. For example, provide sentence starters such as *She will call us _ she gets home*. Have students write each word in their **Writer's Notebook**.

REVIEW VOCABULARY WORDS

TIER 2

OBJECTIVES

 CCSS Acquire and use accurately grade-appropriate conversational, general academic, and domain-specific words and phrases, including those that signal spatial and temporal relationships. **L.3.6**

Review vocabulary words.

 I Do Display each **Visual Vocabulary Card** and state the word. Explain how the photograph illustrates the word. State the example sentence and repeat the word.

 We Do Point to the word on the card and read the word with students. Ask them to repeat the word. Engage students in structured partner talk about the image as prompted on the back of the vocabulary card.

 You Do Display each visual in random order, hiding the word. Have students match the definitions and context sentences of the words to the visuals displayed. Then ask students to complete **Approaching Reproducibles** page 271.

ANSWER YES/NO QUESTIONS

OBJECTIVES

CCSS Demonstrate understanding of word relationships and nuances in word meanings. Identify real-life connections between words and their use (e.g., describe people who are *friendly* or *helpful*). **L.3.5b**

Answer questions to demonstrate understanding of meanings of words.

 I Do Display the *communicated* **Visual Vocabulary Card** and ask: *If you communicated your ideas, did you tell them to someone?* Point out that *communicated* means "shared information with another person."

 We Do Display the card for *essential* and ask: *Is a television essential for camping?* Discuss why a television would not be *essential,* or necessary, for camping.

 You Do Using the questions below, display the remaining cards one at a time, and read each question aloud. Have students answer *yes* or *no*.

Could wanting to learn how to swim be considered a goal?

If you are motivated *to learn how to play the guitar, do you stop practicing?*

Do professional *athletes play sports for free?*

If you research *a topic, do you use only the information you already know?*

If you are serious *about learning, is learning important to you?*

If someone is a specialist, *is that person also an expert?*

GREEK AND LATIN ROOTS

OBJECTIVES

CCSS Use a known root word as a clue to the meaning of an unknown word with the same root (e.g., *company, companion*). **L.3.4c**

Use knowledge of Greek and Latin roots to determine the meanings of words.

 I Do Display the Comprehension and Fluency passage on **Approaching Reproducibles** pages 273–274. Read aloud the first paragraph. Point to the word *admire*. Tell students that knowing the meaning of Greek and Latin roots can help them figure out the meaning of an unknown word.

Think Aloud I know that the Latin root *ad* of *admire* means "to" or "toward." The Latin root *mir* means "wonder" or "amazement." I think *admire* means "to look to someone with wonder or amazement."

Write the meaning of *admire*.

 We Do Have students point to the word *senator*. With students, discuss how to use their knowledge of Greek and Latin roots to figure out the meaning of this word. Write the meaning of the word.

 You Do Have students find the meanings of the words *orbit, accident, orator,* and *final* using their knowledge of Greek and Latin roots.

→ Approaching Level

Comprehension

FLUENCY

OBJECTIVES

 Read on-level text with purpose and understanding. **RF.3.4a**

 Read on-level prose and poetry orally with accuracy, appropriate rate, and expression on successive readings. **RF.3.4b**

Read fluently with accuracy and appropriate phrasing.

 I Do Explain that when reading aloud, good readers focus on reading with accuracy and appropriate phrasing. Point out that reading with accuracy means pronouncing words correctly and not leaving out any words. Phrasing means breaking longer sentences into chunks of text, pausing at commas and stopping at periods. Read the first two paragraphs of the Comprehension and Fluency passage on **Approaching Reproducibles** pages 273–274. Tell students to listen for how you pronounce each word and pause or stop at punctuation marks.

 We Do Read the rest of the page aloud, and have students repeat each sentence after you using the same phrasing and accuracy. Explain that you correctly pronounced each word and broke longer sentences into chunks of text.

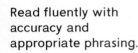 **You Do** Have partners take turns reading sentences from the Approaching Reproducibles passage. Remind them to focus on accuracy and phrasing. Listen in and provide feedback as needed by modeling proper fluency.

IDENTIFY TEXT STRUCTURE

OBJECTIVES

 Describe the logical connection between particular sentences and paragraphs in a text (e.g., comparison, cause/effect, first/second/third in a sequence). **RI.3.8**

Identify a sequence of events in a text.

 I Do Write the topic: *John Glenn.* Then write: *First: John Glenn was born in 1921; Second: Glenn signed up for the army at age 20; Third: He was not called to serve.* Read the statements aloud. Point out that these details show the sequence of events. Explain that authors often structure a text to show that one event took place after another. They often use key words such as *first, next, then,* and *finally* to show the order of events.

 We Do Read the first page of the Comprehension and Fluency passage in the **Approaching Reproducibles**. Ask: *How did Glenn feel about not being called to serve in the army? What happened next?* Point out that the author gives details in the order they occurred. This is the sequence of events.

 You Do Have students read the rest of the passage. After each paragraph, they should write down the events in the order they occurred. Then review the events with them, and make sure they are in the correct order.

REVIEW TEXT STRUCTURE: PROBLEM AND SOLUTION

OBJECTIVES

CCSS Describe the overall structure (e.g., chronology, comparison, cause/effect, problem/solution) of events, ideas, concepts, or information in a text or part of a text. **RI.4.5**

Identify problem and solution in a text.

 I Do Remind students that some informational texts describe a problem, tell the steps to solve the problem, and give the solution. Words and phrases such as *problem, solution, solve,* and *as a result* can help signal to readers that an author is discussing a problem and the steps to its solution. Point out that, as students read, they should ask themselves: *What is the problem? Which details show the solution to the problem?*

 We Do Read the first two paragraphs of the Comprehension and Fluency passage in the **Approaching Reproducibles** together. Pause to point out the first problem John Glenn faced. Model how to decide which details show the solution to this problem. Then work with students to identify other examples of problem and solution in the first page of the passage.

 You Do Have students work in pairs using **Graphic Organizer 78**. They should fill in the organizer with one problem, provide details from the text that show the steps taken to solve the problem, and give the solution.

SELF-SELECTED READING

OBJECTIVES

CCSS Describe the overall structure (e.g., chronology, comparison, cause/effect, problem/solution) of events, ideas, concepts, or information in a text or part of a text. **RI.4.5**

• Identify problem and solution in a text.

• Reread text to increase understanding.

Read Independently

Have students choose a biography for sustained silent reading. Remind students that:

• sometimes authors use words or phrases such as *problem, solution, solve,* and *as a result* to signal there is a problem and the steps to a solution.

• if they have trouble understanding any new facts or ideas presented in the text, they can reread to make sure all of the information makes sense.

Read Purposefully

Have students fill in **Graphic Organizer 78** as they read independently. After they finish, they can conduct a Book Talk, each telling about the biography they read.

• Students should share their organizers and answer these questions: *What was one problem identified in the book? Which details tell how the problem was solved and give the solution?*

• Students should also share any keywords, photographs, and captions that give more information about the person in their biography.

On Level

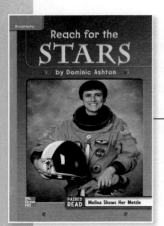

Lexile 750
TextEvaluator™ 35

OBJECTIVES

CCSS Describe the overall structure (e.g., chronology, comparison, cause/ effect, problem/ solution) of events, ideas, concepts, or information in a text or part of a text. **RI.4.5**

CCSS Use common, grade-appropriate Greek and Latin affixes and roots as clues to the meaning of a word (e.g., *telegraph, photograph, autograph*). **L.4.4b**

- Reread text to check understanding.
- Identify the problem and solution in a text.

ACADEMIC LANGUAGE
reread, problem, solution, biography, Greek, Latin, roots

Leveled Reader:
Reach for the Stars

Before Reading

Preview and Predict

Have students read the Essential Question. Then have them read the title and table of contents of *Reach for the Stars*. Have students predict what this selection is about and share their predictions with a partner.

Review Genre: Biography

Review with students that a biography is a type of informational text that tells about a person's life. It tells the events of a person's life in order and includes text features like headings and timelines. As they preview *Reach for the Stars*, have students identify features of a biography.

During Reading

Close Reading

Note Taking Have students use their graphic organizer as they read.

Pages 2–3 *Why did the author choose this title for Chapter 1? Reread the text to answer the question.* (A spark of desire ignited in Franklin Chang Díaz when he looked for the light from the satellite as it went by. As a result, he decided to become an astronaut.)

Pages 4–6 *How does the author use a problem-and-solution text structure to show how Franklin reached his goals?* (Franklin had problems that made it hard for him to become an astronaut, such as not knowing English and having no money for college. The author shows that Franklin was able to overcome these problems by studying hard to reach his goals.)

Pages 7–10 *Did Franklin Chang Díaz believe astronauts should be pilots or scientists? Reread the sidebar on page 8.* (Franklin Chang Díaz believed astronauts should be scientists.) *The Latin root* sci *means "to know." Use this information and context clues to define* scientist. (*Scientist* means "someone who seeks to know by studying facts and through experimentation.")

Leveled Readers

Fill in the Graphic Organizer

Page 11 *On which mission did Dr. Chang Díaz orbit Earth the most times? Explain what you reread to find the answer.* (his 1996 mission on the *Columbia*; the column for the largest number in the Orbits of Earth)

Pages 12–14 *How did Dr. Chang Díaz's goals change after he left NASA?* (He decided to focus on building better and faster rockets instead of flying. He also counsels young people to follow their dreams.)

After Reading

Respond to Reading Revisit the Essential Question, and ask students to complete the Text Evidence questions on page 15.

Analytical Writing **Write About Reading** Make sure students provide details from the text that tell the problems Franklin Chang Díaz faced in becoming an astronaut and how he solved those problems.

Fluency: Accuracy and Phrasing

Model Model reading page 13 with proper accuracy and phrasing. Next, reread the page aloud, and have students read along with you.

Apply Have students practice reading with a partner.

PAIRED READ

"Melina Shows Her Mettle"

Make Connections:
Write About It **Analytical Writing**

Before reading, have students note that the genre of this text is science fiction, which is a type of fiction based on scientific ideas. Then have them discuss the Essential Question.

After reading, have students make connections between how Melina and Franklin Chang Díaz reach their goals in "Melina Shows Her Mettle" and *Reach for the Stars*.

Leveled Reader

🧪 **FOCUS ON SCIENCE**

Students can extend their knowledge of space flight by completing the science activity on page 20. **STEM**

Literature Circles

Ask students to conduct a literature circle using the Thinkmark questions to guide the discussion. You may wish to have a whole-class discussion on how they could take lessons from how Franklin Chang Díaz followed his goals.

Level Up

Level-up lessons available online.

IF students read the **On Level** fluently and answered the questions

THEN pair them with students who have proficiently read the **Beyond Level** and have on-level students.

• partner-read the **Beyond Level** main selection.

• name two details in the text that they want to learn more about.

A C T Access Complex Text

The **Beyond Level** challenges students by including more **domain-specific words** and **complex sentence structures**.

On Level

Vocabulary

REVIEW VOCABULARY WORDS

OBJECTIVES

 Acquire and use accurately grade-appropriate conversational general academic, and domain-specific words and phrases, including those that signal spatial and temporal relationships (e.g., *After dinner that night we went looking for them*). **L.3.6**

Review vocabulary words.

 I Do

Use the **Visual Vocabulary Cards** to review key vocabulary words *communicated, essential, professional, research, serious,* and *specialist*. Point to each word, read it aloud, and have students chorally repeat it.

 We Do

Ask these questions and help students respond and explain their answers.

- How are ideas most quickly *communicated*: by letter or e-mail?
- Which is *essential* for making a car work: gas or a radio?
- Which is more likely a *professional* activity: being a nurse or reading?

 You Do

Have students respond to these questions and explain their answers.

- Who usually does more *research*: a firefighter or a scientist?
- When you are *serious* about something, are you more likely to make fun of it or pay close attention to it?
- Who is more likely to be a *specialist*: a surgeon or a taxi driver?

GREEK AND LATIN ROOTS

OBJECTIVES

 Use a known root word as a clue to the meaning of an unknown word with the same root (e.g., *company, companion*). **L.3.4c**

Use Greek and Latin roots to determine the meanings of words.

 I Do

Remind students that many unfamiliar words have Greek or Latin roots that can help to determine the words' meanings. Use the Comprehension and Fluency passage on **Your Turn Practice Book** pages 273–274 to model.

Think Aloud I want to know what *admire* means. I can use what I know of Latin roots to help me. I know that the Latin root *ad* means "to" or "toward." The Latin root *mir* means "wonder" or "amazement." I think to *admire* someone means "to look at someone with wonder or amazement."

 We Do

Have students reread the first paragraph, where they will encounter the word *senator*. Have students figure out the meaning of the word by identifying Greek or Latin roots. Write the meaning of the word.

 You Do

Have students work in pairs to determine the meanings of the words *orbit, accident, orator,* and *final* as they read the rest of the passage.

Comprehension

REVIEW TEXT STRUCTURE: PROBLEM AND SOLUTION

OBJECTIVES

Describe the overall structure (e.g., chronology, comparison, cause/effect, problem/solution) of events, ideas, concepts, or information in a text or part of a text. **RI.4.5**

Identify problem and solution in a text.

 Remind students that some informational texts describe a problem, tell the steps to solve the problem, and give the solution. Explain that words and phrases such as *problem, solution, solve,* and *as a result* can help signal to readers that an author is discussing a problem and the steps to its solution. As students read, they should try to identify a problem in the text. Then they should look for details that show the solution to the problem. As they read, students should ask: *What is the problem? What steps are taken to solve this problem? What is the solution?*

 Have a volunteer read the first page of the Comprehension and Fluency passage on **Your Turn Practice Book** pages 273–274. Have students orally list details that show a problem. Then model how to identify possible steps to its solution. Work with students to identify examples of problem and solution on the next page.

 Have partners read the rest of the passage and write details about a problem and its solution in the section titled "One More Flight." Remind students to use text evidence when writing their notes.

SELF-SELECTED READING

OBJECTIVES

Describe the overall structure (e.g., chronology, comparison, cause/effect, problem/solution) of events, ideas, concepts, or information in a text or part of a text. **RI.4.5**

• Reread to increase understanding.

• Identify problem and solution in a text.

Read Independently

Have students choose a biography for sustained silent reading.

- Before they read, have students preview the book, looking for any text features such as charts or photographs that tell more about the book.

- As students read, ask them to reread difficult sections of the text and confirm that all of the information makes sense.

Read Purposefully

Encourage students to read different biographies in order to learn about a variety of people.

- As students read, they can fill in **Graphic Organizer 78**.

- Students can use their organizers to write a summary of the book.

- Ask students to share their reactions to the book with classmates. Ask them to tell if there were any sections of the text they reread in order to check their understanding.

Beyond Level

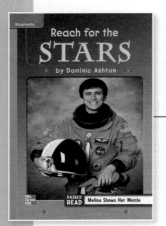

Lexile 850
TextEvaluator™ 43

OBJECTIVES

(CCSS) Describe the overall structure (e.g., chronology, comparison, cause/ effect, problem/ solution) of events, ideas, concepts, or information in a text or part of a text. **RI.4.5**

(CCSS) Use common, grade-appropriate Greek and Latin affixes and roots as clues to the meaning of a word (e.g., *telegraph, photograph, autograph*). **L.4.4b**

• Reread text to check understanding.
• Identify the problem and solution in a text.

ACADEMIC LANGUAGE

reread, problem, solution, biography, Greek, Latin, roots

Leveled Reader:
Reach for the Stars

Before Reading

Preview and Predict

Have students read the Essential Question. Then have them read the title and table of contents of *Reach for the Stars*. Have students predict what this selection is about and share their predictions with a partner.

Review Genre: Biography

Review with students that a biography is a type of informational text that tells about a person's life. It tells the events of a person's life in order and includes text features like headings and timelines. As they preview *Reach for the Stars*, have students identify features of a biography.

During Reading

Close Reading

Note Taking Have students use their graphic organizer as they read.

Pages 2–3 *How does the author use the launch of Sputnik 1 as a symbol?* (It stands for the moment Dr. Chang Díaz realized he wanted to be an astronaut. It also represents a new era of space exploration.)

Pages 4–6 *How does the author use a problem-and-solution text structure in Chapter 1? Give examples.* (The author uses a problem-and-solution text structure to show how Dr. Chang Díaz achieves goals despite hardships. He did not know English and had no money for college, but was able to overcome these problems by studying hard.)

Pages 7–11 *Use your knowledge of Greek and Latin roots to define* International *on page 7.* (Possible Response: I know that the root *inter* means "between" or "among," and *national* means "belonging to nations, or countries," so *International* means "between or among different countries.") *What other word meanings can you determine using Greek and Latin roots?* (Possible Response: I know the Greek root *astro* means "star" and *naut* has to do with sailing or ships, so an *astronaut* is a person who travels by ship through space.)

Go Digital

Leveled Readers

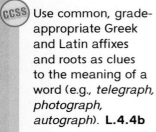
Fill in the Graphic Organizer

Page 12 *Reread page 12 and then summarize to a partner how a plasma rocket could be superior to current spacecraft.* (A plasma rocket would allow a spacecraft to travel farther and much faster. It could also be refueled.)

Pages 13–14 *Why is Franklin Chang Díaz a good person to advise others how to achieve their goals?* (Possible Response: He overcame a lot to achieve his goals. He has helped people in many ways.)

After Reading

Respond to Reading Revisit the Essential Question, and ask students to complete the Text Evidence questions on page 15.

Write About Reading Have students work with a partner to write a short paragraph about the problems Franklin Chang Díaz faced and how he solved them.

Fluency: Accuracy and Phrasing

Model Model reading page 13 with proper accuracy and phrasing. Next, reread the page aloud, and have students read along with you.

Apply Have students practice reading with a partner.

PAIRED READ

"Melina Shows Her Mettle"

Make Connections: Write About It

Before reading, have students note that the genre of this text is science fiction, which is a type of fiction based on scientific ideas. Then discuss the Essential Question.

After reading, have students make connections between how Melina and Franklin Chang Díaz reach their goals in "Melina Shows Her Mettle" and *Reach for the Stars*.

Leveled Reader

🧪 FOCUS ON SCIENCE

Students can extend their knowledge of space flight by completing the science activity on page 20. **STEM**

Literature Circles

Ask students to conduct a literature circle using the Thinkmark questions to guide the discussion. You may wish to have a whole-class discussion on how they could take lessons from how Franklin Chang Díaz followed his goals.

Gifted and Talented

Synthesize Challenge students to write a paragraph about one of their goals and why they want to achieve it. Have them write a future timeline listing the steps they could take to achieve the goal. Invite students to share their goals with the class.

Beyond Level

Vocabulary

REVIEW DOMAIN-SPECIFIC WORDS

OBJECTIVES

 Produce simple, compound, and complex sentences. **L.3.1i**

Review and discuss domain-specific words.

 Model Use the **Visual Vocabulary Cards** to review the meaning of the words *research* and *specialist*. Write science related sentences on the board using the words.

Write the words *satellite, scientist,* and *exploration* on the board and discuss the meanings with students. Then help students write sentences using these words.

 Apply Have students work in pairs to discuss the meanings of the words *physics, designing,* and *technology.* Then have students write sentences using the words.

GREEK AND LATIN ROOTS

OBJECTIVES

 Use a known root word as a clue to the meaning of an unknown word with the same root (e.g., *company, companion*). **L.3.4c**

Use Greek and Latin roots to determine the meanings of unknown words.

 Model Read aloud the first paragraph of the Comprehension and Fluency passage on **Beyond Reproducibles** pages 273–274.

Think Aloud I want to know what the word *admire* means. I can use what I know of Latin roots to help me. I know that the Latin root *ad* means "to" or "toward." The Latin root *mir* means "wonder" or "amazement." I think to *admire* someone means "to look at someone, such as an astronaut, with wonder or amazement."

With students, reread the same paragraph. Help them figure out the meaning of the word *senator* by identifying its Latin root.

 Apply Have pairs of students read the rest of the passage. Ask them to use Greek or Latin roots to determine the meanings of the words *orbit, accident, orator,* and *final.*

 Independent Study Have students use classroom materials to study the origins of a word they choose. Encourage them to use a word from this week's vocabulary. Ask them to write a paragraph on the word, including its meaning and the language it comes from. Have them present their reports to the class and include artwork if appropriate.

Comprehension

REVIEW TEXT STRUCTURE: PROBLEM AND SOLUTION

OBJECTIVES

CCSS Describe the overall structure (e.g., chronology, comparison, cause/effect, problem/solution) of events, ideas, concepts, or information in a text or part of a text). **RI.4.5**

Identify problem and solution in a text.

 Model Remind students that some informational texts describe a problem, tell the steps to solve the problem, and give the solution. Explain that words and phrases such as *problem, solution, solve,* and *as a result* can help signal to readers that an author is discussing a problem and the steps to its solution. As students read, they should try to identify a problem in the text then look for details that show the solution to the problem.

Have students read the second paragraph of the Comprehension and Fluency passage on **Beyond Reproducibles** pages 273–274. Ask open-ended questions to facilitate discussion, such as *What was Glenn's problem? How did he solve his problem?* Students should provide text evidence to support their answers.

 Apply Have students take notes about problems, the steps to solve the problems, and the solutions as they read the rest of the passage. Then have them write a summary about one of the problems, steps, and solutions.

SELF-SELECTED READING

OBJECTIVES

CCSS Describe the overall structure (e.g., chronology, comparison, cause/effect, problem/solution) of events, ideas, concepts, or information in a text or part of a text). **RI.4.5**

• Reread to increase understanding.

• Identify problem and solution in a text.

Read Independently

Have students choose a biography for sustained silent reading.

• As students read, have them fill in **Graphic Organizer 78**.

• Remind students to reread any difficult sections or paragraphs to make sure the information is clear.

Read Purposefully

Encourage students to keep a reading journal. Ask them to read different biographies to learn about a variety of people.

• Students can write summaries of the books in their journals.

• Have students give their reactions to the books to the class. Have them explain a problem and solution they read about in one of the books.

 Independent Study Challenge students to discuss how their books relate to the weekly theme of Learning to Succeed. Have students identify the problems faced by some of the people they read about. What steps did they take to solve their problems? What were their solutions?

English Language Learners

Reading/Writing Workshop

OBJECTIVES

(CCSS) Describe the overall structure (e.g., chronology, comparison, cause/ effect, problem/ solution) of events, ideas, concepts, or information in a text or part of a text. **RI.4.5**

• Reread to increase understanding.

• Use Greek and Latin roots to determine word meanings.

LANGUAGE OBJECTIVE

Identify problems and their solutions in a text.

ACADEMIC LANGUAGE

• *reread, problem, solution, biography, Greek, Latin, roots*

• Cognates: *problema, solución, biografía*

Shared Read
Rocketing Into Space

View "Rocketing Into Space"

Before Reading

Build Background

Read the Essential Question: Why are goals important?

• Explain the meaning of the Essential Question. Point out that *important* has a cognate: *importante. One of my goals might be learning a new language. Why is this goal important?*

• **Model an answer:** *I want to learn to speak Chinese so that I can go to China and speak with the people there. It is important to learn about new places.*

• Ask students a question that ties the Essential Question to their own background knowledge: *Think about a goal that you have about learning. What would you like to learn? What would it allow you to do? Why do you want to learn it? Share your goal with a partner. Write down steps that you need to take to reach your goal.* Call on several pairs to share their goals.

During Reading

Interactive-Question Response

• Ask questions that help students understand the meaning of the text after each paragraph.

• Reinforce the meanings of key vocabulary.

• Ask students questions that require them to use key vocabulary.

• Reinforce strategies and skills of the week by modeling.

Page 435

Paragraph 1
Have students choral read the first sentence. *Who is this biography about?* (James A. Lovell, Jr.) *What did Lovell dream of as a boy?* Have one student answer and another verify the answer. (He dreamed of becoming a pilot)

Paragraph 2
Model Problem and Solution *I read that Lovell had a problem. What did he not have enough of to go to a special college?* (money) *Then I read that Lovell had to find another way to reach his goal. I will read on to find the solution that Lovell found for his problem.*

Paragraph 3
How did Lovell solve the problem of not being able to afford a special college? Complete the sentence frame: He solved his problem by ____ (going to college near his home) *and* ____ (joining the navy).

Explain and Model Greek and Latin Roots Point out the word *astronaut* in the caption. Astronaut has two Greek roots. Astro *means "star,"* and naut *means "ship."* Demonstrate the meaning of the word by pointing to the picture of Lovell on page 434. *Use this information to figure out what* astronaut *means. An* astronaut *is someone who* ____ (travels to the stars in a ship).

Have a student read the caption at the bottom of the page. *How many space missions did Lovell fly?* (four)

Page 436

Paragraph 1
Read the heading. What do you think this section will be about? (Lovell becoming an astronaut) *When did Lovell apply for a job at NASA?* Have one student answer and another verify the answer. (after they put out a call for astronauts)

Explain that *essential* means "that is needed." *What do you think are some of the essential skills for being an astronaut?*

Paragraphs 2–4
What was the problem on the Apollo 13 mission? (One of the oxygen tanks exploded.)

Find the word solution *in paragraph 4. What solution did the astronauts come up with?* (They built an invention to clean the air.) *What problem was "even bigger"?* (how to get back to Earth)

Page 437

Paragraphs 1–2
Explain and Model Rereading *Sometimes I may not understand all of the information when I read the first time, so I reread to understand better. When I read the first paragraph under "A Job Well Done," I did not understand how the astronauts used the lunar module. What did the astronauts do in the module?* (They moved away from their spacecraft.) *What did the module help them do?* (get back to Earth)

Paragraph 3
What did Lovell learn from the Apollo 13 mission? Complete the sentence frame: It is important for people to ____ (work together).

Tell a partner what you think the astronauts felt when they landed in the ocean.

After Reading

Make Connections
- Review the Essential Question: Why are goals important?
- Make text connections.
- Have students complete the **ELL Reproducibles** pages 273–275.

→ English Language Learners

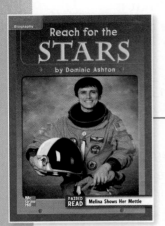

Lexile 680
TextEvaluator™ 25

OBJECTIVES

(CCSS) Describe the overall structure (e.g., chronology, comparison, cause/effect, problem/solution) of events, ideas, concepts, or information in a text or part of a text. **RI.4.5**

- Reread text to check understanding.
- Use Greek and Latin roots to determine word meanings.

LANGUAGE OBJECTIVE
Identify the problem and solution.

ACADEMIC LANGUAGE
reread, problem, solution, biography, Greek, Latin, roots

Leveled Reader:
Reach for the Stars

Leveled Readers

Before Reading

Preview

- Read the Essential Question: Why are goals important?
- Refer to Success!: *What is one goal that is important to you?*
- Preview *Reach for the Stars* and "Melina Shows Her Mettle": *Let's read about how people solve problems to achieve their goals.*

Vocabulary

Use the **Visual Vocabulary Cards** to preteach the ELL vocabulary: *developed, exploration, mission.* Use the routine found on the cards. Point out the cognates: *exploración, misión.*

During Reading

Interactive Question-Response

Note Taking Have students use their graphic organizer on **ELL Reproducibles** page 272. Use the following questions after reading each section. As you read, use visuals or pictures to define key vocabulary.

Pages 2–3 *Who is this biography about?* (Franklin Chang Díaz) *What did Franklin Chang Díaz learn about that made him want to become an astronaut?* (a satellite) Have students point to the picture of Sputnik 1.

Pages 4–6 *What problem did Franklin have that could prevent him from going to college?* Have one student answer and then another verify the answer. (His parents could not afford to pay for college.) *How did he solve this problem?* Have students complete the sentence frame: *He solved this problem by ____* (studying hard and getting a scholarship).

Pages 7–10 *The Greek root* sci *in* scientist *means "to know." Use this information to help you define* scientist *on page 8. Complete the sentence frame: A* scientist *is a person who seeks ____* (to know) *about the world through experimenting, or doing different tests.*

Page 11 *Point to the title of the chart on page 11. It shows information about Chang Díaz's missions. How long was his flight in 1992?* (7 days)

Fill in the Graphic Organizer

Pages 12–14 *After Chang Díaz stopped flying, what did he do next?* (He worked on a new rocket.) *What do you think is Chang Díaz's biggest achievement?* Have students reread parts of the text.

After Reading

Respond to Reading Help students complete the graphic organizer. Revisit the Essential Question. Have student pairs summarize and answer the Text Evidence questions. Review all responses as a group.

Analytical Writing **Write About Reading** Have students work with a partner to write a short paragraph about what happened when Franklin Chang Díaz first applied to work for NASA. Have them tell what he did after.

Fluency: Accuracy and Phrasing

Model Model reading page 13 with proper accuracy and phrasing. Next, reread the page aloud, and have students read along with you.

Apply Have students practice reading with a partner.

PAIRED READ

Leveled Reader

"Melina Shows Her Mettle"

Make Connections: Write About It • *Analytical Writing*

Before reading, have students note that the genre of this text is science fiction, which is a type of fiction based on scientific ideas. Then discuss the Essential Question.

After reading, have students make connections between how Melina and Franklin Chang Díaz reach their goals in "Melina Shows Her Mettle" and *Reach for the Stars*.

FOCUS ON SCIENCE

Students can extend their knowledge of space flight by completing the science activity on page 20. **STEM**

Literature Circles

Ask students to conduct a literature circle using the Thinkmark questions to guide the discussion. You may wish to have a whole-class discussion on how they could take lessons from how Franklin Chang Díaz followed his goals.

Level Up

Level-up lessons available online.

IF students read the **ELL Level** fluently and answered the questions

THEN pair them with students who have proficiently read **On Level** and have ELL students

• echo-read the **On Level** main selection with their partner.

• list difficult words and discuss them with their partner.

A C T Access Complex Text

The **On Level** challenges students by including more **domain-specific words** and **complex sentence structures**.

English Language Learners
Vocabulary

PRETEACH VOCABULARY

OBJECTIVES

 Acquire and use accurately grade-appropriate conversational, general academic, and domain-specific words and phrases, including those that signal spatial and temporal relationships (e.g., *After dinner that night we went looking for them*). **L.3.6**

LANGUAGE OBJECTIVE

Use vocabulary words.

 I Do Preteach vocabulary from "Rocketing Into Space" following the Vocabulary Routine found on the **Visual Vocabulary Cards** for *communicated, essential, goal, motivated, professional, research, serious,* and *specialist*.

 We Do Complete the Vocabulary Routine for each word, and point to the word on the Visual Vocabulary Card. Next, read the word with students. Ask students to repeat the word.

 You Do Have students work with a partner to write a sentence describing a photo in "Rocketing Into Space." Have students read the sentence aloud.

Beginning	Intermediate	Advanced/High
Help students write a sentence describing a photo from the selection.	Have students use the word *goal* to describe one of the photographs.	Ask students to use the words *professional* and *motivated* in sentences.

REVIEW VOCABULARY

OBJECTIVES

 Acquire and use accurately grade-appropriate conversational, general academic, and domain-specific words and phrases, including those that signal spatial and temporal relationships (e.g., *After dinner that night we went looking for them*). **L.3.6**

LANGUAGE OBJECTIVE

Review vocabulary words.

 I Do Review the previous week's vocabulary words over a few days. Read each word aloud and point to the word on the **Visual Vocabulary Card**. Ask students to repeat after you. Then follow the Vocabulary Routine on the back of each card.

 We Do Provide a sentence frame for the word *argue* and complete it with students: *I do not like to _____ with my friends.* Have students suggest possible clues, such as synonyms, antonyms, or actions, for the sentence frame.

 You Do Have students work with a partner to use three words in sentence frames. Then have each pair read the sentence frames aloud to the class.

Beginning	Intermediate	Advanced/High
Help students write the sentence frames correctly.	Have students write three sentence frames and one clue for each sentence.	Challenge students to write five sentence frames and one clue per sentence.

GREEK AND LATIN ROOTS

OBJECTIVES

CCSS Use a known root word as a clue to the meaning of an unknown word with the same root (e.g., *company, companion*). **L.3.4c**

LANGUAGE OBJECTIVE

Use Greek or Latin root words to figure out the meanings of unknown words.

 I Do Read aloud page 435 of "Rocketing Into Space" as students follow along. Point to the word *astronomy*. Remind students that they can use Greek and Latin roots to figure out the meanings of words with those roots. Tell students that the Greek root *astro* means "star." The Greek root *naut* means "ship." The Latin root *luna* means "moon."

Think Aloud I see the word *astronomy* on page 435. I know that the word *astro* is a Greek root word. It means "star." I think *astronomy* has something to do with the stars or studying the stars.

 We Do Have students read page 436. Ask them to find the meaning of the word *astronauts* using *astro* and *naut*. Write the meaning on the board.

 You Do In pairs, have students reread page 437 and find the word *lunar*. Ask them to determine the meaning of *lunar* by using the Latin root *luna*.

Beginning	Intermediate	Advanced/High
Help students find the word and write its meaning using the Latin root *luna*.	Have students find another word with the Latin root *luna*. Ask students to define it.	Ask students to find a new word with the Latin root *luna*. Have them write a sentence using the word.

ADDITIONAL VOCABULARY

OBJECTIVES

CCSS Use conventional spelling for high-frequency and other studied words and for adding suffixes to base words (e.g., *sitting, smiled, cries, happiness*). **L.3.2e**

Discuss concept and high-frequency words.

LANGUAGE OBJECTIVE

Use concept and high-frequency words.

 I Do List concept and high-frequency words from "Rocketing Into Space": *module, what, when;* and *Reach for the Stars: developed, docked, of.* Define each word for students and use each word in a sentence.

 We Do Model using the word *what* for students in a sentence: What *do you think of my new glasses?* Then, provide sentence frames and complete them with students: *The campers _____ what they were going to bring on their trip.*

 You Do Have pairs describe an aspect of a spacecraft's module using the words *module* and *of*. Have students present the sentence to the class.

Beginning	Intermediate	Advanced/High
Help students copy the description correctly.	Have students write another sentence using the words *what* or *when*.	Have students write another sentence using the word *developed*.

→ English Language Learners
Writing/Spelling

WRITING TRAIT: ORGANIZATION

OBJECTIVES

 Introduce a topic and group related information together; include illustrations when useful to aiding comprehension. **W.3.2a**

Put ideas in order.

LANGUAGE OBJECTIVE

Use complete sentences to describe events.

 I Do Remind students that good writers organize their ideas when they write. Putting ideas in order makes the text easier for readers to understand. Read the Student Model passage as students follow along.

 We Do Read aloud page 435 from "Rocketing Into Space" as students follow along. Model identifying the sequence of events in the text. Point out that the author talks about events in the order in which they happened.

 You Do Have pairs make a timeline of the events described in the first paragraph of page 436. Students should use complete sentences to describe the events.

Beginning	Intermediate	Advanced/High
Help students copy the edited timeline.	Have students revise the timeline, describing three events in the paragraph.	Challenge students to combine three events in one paragraph.

SPELL WORDS WITH VOWEL TEAM SYLLABLES

OBJECTIVES

 Use spelling patterns and generalizations (e.g., word families, position-based spellings, syllable patterns, ending rules, meaningful word parts) in writing words. **L.3.2f**

LANGUAGE OBJECTIVE

Spell words with vowel team syllables.

 I Do Read the Spelling Words on page T162 aloud, modeling how to pronounce the vowel team syllables. Remind students that two vowels work together as a team to form one vowel sound. Model how to say the word *grain*.

 We Do Read the Dictation Sentences on page T163 aloud. With each sentence, read the underlined word. Model drawing a line between the vowel team syllables and the rest of the word. Have students repeat after you and write the word.

 You Do Display the words. Have students exchange their lists with a partner to check the spelling and write the words correctly.

Beginning	Intermediate	Advanced/High
Help students copy the words with correct spelling and say the words aloud.	Have students circle the vowel team syllables in each word.	After students correct their words, have pairs write sentences for five words.

Grammar

ADVERBS

OBJECTIVES

Explain the function of nouns, pronouns, verbs, adjectives, and adverbs in general and their functions in particular sentences. **L.3.1a**

Identify adverbs.

LANGUAGE OBJECTIVE

Use adverbs.

Language Transfers Handbook

In Hmong, adverbs are not used. Instead, two repeated verbs take the place of a verb and an adverb. Rather than saying, *I laughed loudly at the funny story,* Hmong-speaking students might want to say, *I laughed laughed at the funny story.* Give these students additional practice with adverbs, taking opportunities to model correct usage.

I Do Remind students that an adverb describes an action verb. It can be put in different places in a sentence. An adverb can describe the place, time, or way an action takes place. For instance: *The girl ran quickly.* Tell students that adverbs answer the questions *how, when,* or *where* an action is done. Most adverbs that tell how an action takes place end in *-ly,* such as *quietly.* Some adverbs tell when an action happens. These adverbs include: *first, soon, always, early, next, today, later, tomorrow,* and *then. Matthew will play tennis soon.* Other adverbs tell where an action happens, such as *here, away, far, ahead, there, outside, up,* and *around,* as in *Gabrielle walked away.*

We Do Write the sentences below on the board. Have volunteers choose the correct adverb and identify the kind of adverb needed for each sentence.

> *The hikers reached the top of the mountain (tomorrow, early).*
>
> *Phoebe (carefully, careful) signed the card.*
>
> *William's story ended (happily, nervously).*
>
> *David and Cara waited (soon, up) for their friends.*
>
> *The audience laughed (loudly, slowly).*

You Do Have students act out three actions for each other, such as jumping in place, organizing their desks, reading a book, or writing a note. Have each student answer the questions *how, when,* and *where* using adverbs in three separate sentences. Have students read the sentences to the class.

Beginning	Intermediate	Advanced/High
Help students write another sentence answering the questions *how, when,* and *where.*	Ask students to write two more sentences answering the questions *how, when,* and *where.*	Challenge students to write four more sentences answering the questions *how, when,* and *where.*

For extra support, have students complete the activities in the **Grammar Practice Reproducibles** during the week, using the routine below:

- Explain the grammar skill.
- Model the first activity in the Grammar Practice Reproducibles.
- Have the whole group complete the next couple of activities, then the rest with a partner.
- Review the activities with correct answers.

PROGRESS MONITORING

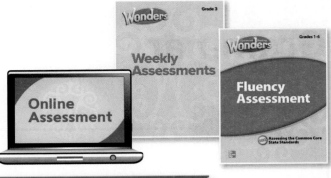

Unit 6 Week 3 Formal Assessment	Standards Covered	Component for Assessment
Text Evidence	RI.3.1	• *Selection Test* • *Weekly Assessment* • *Approaching-Level Weekly Assessment*
Text Structure: Problem and Solution	RI.3.3	• *Weekly Assessment* • *Approaching-Level Weekly Assessment*
Greek and Latin Roots	L.3.4c	• *Selection Test* • *Weekly Assessment* • *Approaching-Level Weekly Assessment*
Writing About Text	W.3.8	*Weekly Assessment*
Unit 6 Week 3 Informal Assessment	**Standards Covered**	**Component for Assessment**
Research/Listening/ Collaborating	SL.3.1d, SL.3.2, SL.3.3	• *RWW* • *Teacher's Edition*
Oral Reading Fluency (ORF) **Fluency Goal:** 97–117 words correct per minute (WCPM) **Accuracy Rate Goal:** 95% or higher	RF.3.4a, RF.3.4b, RF.3.4c	*Fluency Assessment*

Using Assessment Results

Weekly Assessments Skills and Fluency	If . . .	Then . . .
COMPREHENSION	Students score below 70% . . .	. . . assign Lessons 83–84 on Problem and Solution from the *Tier 2 Comprehension Intervention online PDFs.*
VOCABULARY	Students score below 70% . . .	. . . assign Lesson 157 on Greek, Latin, and Other Roots from the *Tier 2 Vocabulary Intervention online PDFs.*
WRITING	Students score below "3" on constructed response . . .	. . . assign Lessons 82–84 and/or Write About Reading Lesson 200 from the *Tier 2 Comprehension Intervention online PDFs.*
FLUENCY	Students have a WCPM score of 89–96 . . .	. . . assign a lesson from Section 1, 7, 8, 9 or 10 of the *Tier 2 Fluency Intervention online PDFs.*
	Students have a WCPM score of 0–88 . . .	. . . assign a lesson from Sections 2–6 of the *Tier 2 Fluency Intervention online PDFs.*

Using Weekly Data

Check your data Dashboard to verify assessment results and guide grouping decisions.

Data-Driven Recommendations

Response to Intervention

Use the appropriate sections of the *Placement and Diagnostic Assessment* as well as students' assessment results to designate students requiring:

 Intervention Online PDFs

 WonderWorks Intervention Program

Build Knowledge
Animals and You

? Essential Question:
How can learning about animals help you respect them?

Teach and Model
Close Reading and Writing

Reading/Writing Workshop

"Butterflies Big and Small," 448–451
Genre Expository Text **Lexile** 870 ETS *TextEvaluator* 32

Practice and Apply
Close Reading and Writing

Literature Anthology

Alligators and Crocodiles, 520–541
Genre Expository Text **Lexile** 870 ETS *TextEvaluator* 29

"The Monkey and the Crocodile" 544–545
Genre Folktale **Lexile** 730 ETS *TextEvaluator* 40

Differentiated Texts

APPROACHING
Lexile 580
ETS *TextEvaluator* 25

ON LEVEL
Lexile 720
ETS *TextEvaluator* 32

BEYOND
Lexile 840
ETS *TextEvaluator* 37

ELL
Lexile 660
ETS *TextEvaluator* 26

Leveled Readers

Extended Complex Texts

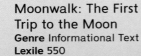

Moonwalk: The First Trip to the Moon
Genre Informational Text
Lexile 550

Moonshot: The Flight of Apollo 11
Genre Informational Text
Lexile 990

Classroom Library

Student Outcomes

Close Reading of Complex Text
- Cite relevant evidence from text
- Describe compare and contrast
- Reread

RI.3.1, RI.3.8

Writing

Write to Sources
- Draw evidence from informational text
- Write informative text
- Conduct short research on animal's unique abilities

Writing Process
- Prewrite a Research Report

W.3.2d, W.3.8, W.3.10, W.4.9b

Speaking and Listening
- Engage in collaborative discussions about animals and you
- Paraphrase portions of "Respect for the Florida Panther" and presentations on animals and you
- Present information on animals and you

SL.3.1c, SL.3.2

Content Knowledge
- Identify how in an environment organisms survive well, some less well, and some cannot survive.

Language Development

Conventions
- Identify and use adverbs that compare

Vocabulary Acquisition
- Acquire and use academic vocabulary

endangered	fascinating	illegal	inhabit
requirements	respected	unaware	wildlife

- Use context clues to understand the meaning of a word

L.3.1a, L.3.1g, L.3.4a, L.3.5b, RI.3.4

Foundational Skills

Phonics/Word Study
- *r*-Controlled vowel syllables
- Latin suffixes

Spelling Words

severe	prepared	declare	later
writer	cellar	trailer	author
person	circus	garlic	partner
restore	sister	actor	

Fluency
- Phrasing

RF.3.3b, RF.3.4a, RF.3.4b, RF.3.4c

Ken Karp/McGraw-Hill Education

Professional Development
- See lessons in action in real classrooms.
- Get expert advice on instructional practices.
- Collaborate with other teachers.
- Access PLC Resources.

Go Digital! www.connected.mcgraw-hill.com.

1 Talk About Respecting Animals

Guide students in collaborative conversations.

Discuss the essential question: *How can learning about animals help you respect them?*

Develop academic language and domain specific vocabulary on respecting animals.

Listen to "Respect for the Florida Panther" to summarize a passage about Florida's panthers.

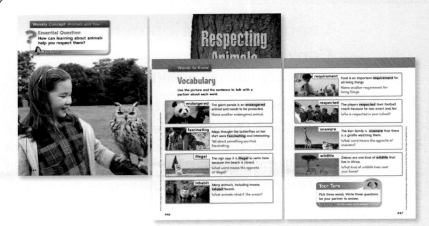

2

Read "Butterflies Big and Small"

Model close reading with a short complex text.

Read

"Butterflies Big and Small" to learn how respecting butterflies can help them survive, citing text evidence to answer text-dependent questions.

Reread

"Butterflies Big and Small" to analyze text, craft, and structure, citing text evidence.

3 Write About Respecting Animals

Model writing to a source.

Analyze a short response student model.

Use text evidence from close reading to write to a source.

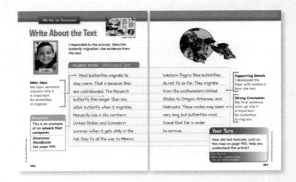

4 Read and Write About Respecting Animals

Practice and apply close reading of the anchor text.

 Read

Alligators and Crocodiles to learn about two amazing reptiles and why we should respect them.

Reread

Alligators and Crocodiles and use text evidence to understand how the author presents information to show how alligators and crocodiles are alike and how they are different.

Write a short response about *Alligators and Crocodiles.*

Integrate

Information about how this folktale is similar to other selectionsyou have read involving animals.

Write to Two Sources, citing text evidence from *Alligators and Crocodiles* and "The Monkey and the Crocodile."

5 Independent Partner Work

Gradual release of support to independent work

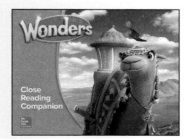

- Text-Dependent Questions
- Scaffolded Partner Work
  Talk with a Partner
  Cite Text Evidence
  Complete a sentence frame.
- Guided Text Annotation

6 Integrate Knowledge and Ideas

Connect Texts

Text to Text Discuss how each of the texts answers the question: How can learning about animals help you respect them?

Text to Photo Compare the similarities between the author's work in the texts read and the work of the photographer.

Conduct a Short Research Project

Create illustrations of an animal's interesting ability.

DEVELOPING READERS AND WRITERS

Write to Sources

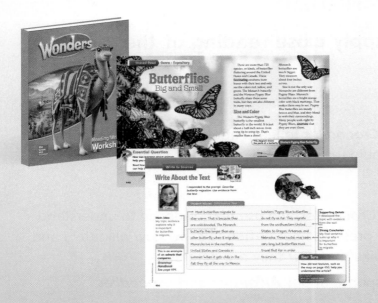

Day 1 and Day 2

Build Writing Fluency

• Quick write on "Butterflies Big and Small," p. T220

Write to a Source

• Analyze a student model, p. T220

• Write about "Butterflies Big and Small," p. T221

• Apply Writing Trait: Strong Conclusions, p. T220

• Apply Grammar Skill: Adverbs That Compare, p. T221

Day 3

Write to a Source

• Write about *Alligators and Crocodiles*, independent practice, p. T217X

• Provide scaffolded instruction to meet student needs, p. T222

Day 4 and Day 5

Write to Two Sources

• Analyze a student model, pp. T222–T223

• Write to compare *Alligators and Crocodiles* with "The Monkey and the Crocodile," p. T223

Writing Process

Go Digital

Writer's Workspace

Genre Writing: Informative Text

Research Report
Expert Model

- Discuss features of informational writing
- Discuss the expert model

Prewrite

- Discuss purpose and audience
- Plan the topic

Expert Model

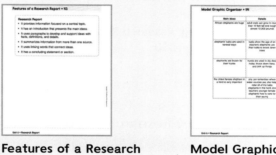  

Features of a Research Report

Model Graphic Organizer

Graphic Organizer

Grammar and Spelling Resources

Online PDFs

Reading/Writing Workshop Grammar Handbook p. 494

Online Spelling and Grammar Games

Grammar Practice, pp. 141–145

Phonics/Spelling blms pp. 169–174

SUGGESTED LESSON PLAN

READING		DAY 1	DAY 2
Teach, Model and Apply	**Core**	**Introduce the Concept** T202–T203 **Vocabulary** T206–T207 **Close Reading** "Butterflies Big and Small," T208–T209	**Close Reading** "Butterflies Big and Small," T208–T209 **Strategy** Reread, T210–T211 **Skill** Compare and Contrast, T212–T213 **Vocabulary Strategy** Context Clues, T216–T217
Reading/Writing Workshop	**Options**	**Listening Comprehension** T204–T205	**Genre** Expository Text, T214–T215

LANGUAGE ARTS			
Writing **Grammar** **Spelling** **Build Vocabulary**	**Core**	**Grammar** Adverbs That Compare, T224 **Spelling** *r*-Controlled Vowel Syllables, T226 **Build Vocabulary** T228	**Write About the Text** Model Note-Taking and Write to a Prompt, T220–T221 **Grammar** Adverbs That Compare, T224 **Build Vocabulary** T228
	Options	**Write About the Text** Writing Fluency, T220 **Genre Writing** Research Report: Read Like a Writer, T350	**Genre Writing** Research Report: Discuss the Expert Model, T350 **Spelling** *r*-Controlled Vowel Syllables, T226

Writing Process: Informative Text Research Report, T350–T355   Use with Weeks 4–6

Differentiated Instruction Use your data dashboard to determine each student's needs. Then select instructional support options throughout the week.

APPROACHING LEVEL

Leveled Reader
 African Cats, T232–T233
 "How Leopard Got His Spots," T233
 Literature Circles, T233

Phonics/Decoding
 Decode Words with *r*-Controlled Vowel Syllables, T234 TIER 2
 Build Words with *r*-Controlled Vowel Syllables, T234 TIER 2
 Practice Words with *r*-Controlled Vowel Syllables, T235
 Latin Suffixes, T235

Vocabulary
 • Review High-Frequency Words, T236 TIER 2
 • Identify Related Words, T237
 Context Clues: Paragraph Clues, T237

Comprehension
 • Text Structure, T238 TIER 2
 • Review Text Structure: Compare and Contrast, T239
 Self-Selected Reading, T239

Fluency TIER 2
 Phrasing, T238

ON LEVEL

Leveled Reader
 African Cats, T240–T241
 "How Leopard Got His Spots," T241
 Literature Circles, T241

Vocabulary
 Review Vocabulary Words, T242
 Context Clues: Paragraph Clues, T242

Comprehension
 Review Text Strucure:Compare and Contrast, T243
 Self-Selected Reading, T243

DAY 3	DAY 4	DAY 5
Close Reading *Alligators and Crocodiles,* T217A–T217X	**Fluency** T219 **Close Reading** "The Monkey and the Crocodile," T217Y–T217Z **Integrate Ideas** Research and Inquiry, T230–T231	**Integrate Ideas** T230–T231 • Text Connections • Research and Inquiry **Weekly Assessment**
Phonics/Decoding T218–T219 • *r*-Controlled Vowel Syllables, T218 • Latin Suffixes, T219	**Close Reading** *Alligators and Crocodiles,* 520–543	

Grammar Adverbs That Compare, T225	**Write About Two Texts** Model Note-Taking and Taking Notes, T222	**Write About Two Texts** Analyze Student Model and Write to the Prompt, T223 **Spelling** *r*-Controlled Vowel Syllables, T229
Write About the Text and Write to a Prompt T222 **Genre Writing** Research Report: Discuss the Expert Model, T351 **Spelling** *r*-Controlled Vowel Syllables, T227 **Build Vocabulary** T229	**Genre Writing** Research Report: Teach the Prewrite Minilesson, T351 **Grammar** Adverbs That Compare, T225 **Spelling** *r*-Controlled Vowel Syllables, T227 **Build Vocabulary** T229	**Genre Writing** Research Report: Choose Your Topic, T351 **Grammar** Adverbs That Compare, T225 **Build Vocabulary** T229

Writing Process: Informative Text Research Report, T350–T355   Use with Weeks 4–6

DIFFERENTIATE TO ACCELERATE

  Scaffold to Access Complex Text

IF the text complexity of a particular selection is too difficult for students

THEN see the references noted in the chart below for scaffolded instruction to help students Access Complex Text.

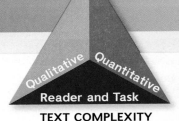

Qualitative Quantitative
Reader and Task
TEXT COMPLEXITY

	Reading/Writing Workshop	Literature Anthology	Leveled Readers	Classroom Library

Quantitative	**"Butterflies Big and Small"** **Lexile** 870 *TextEvaluator*™ 32	***Alligators and Crocodiles*** **Lexile** 870 *TextEvaluator*™ 29 **"The Monkey and the Crocodile"** **Lexile** 730 *TextEvaluator*™ 40	**Approaching Level** **Lexile** 580 *TextEvaluator*™ 25 **Beyond Level** **Lexile** 840 *TextEvaluator*™ 37 **On Level** **Lexile** 720 *TextEvaluator*™ 32 **ELL** **Lexile** 660 *TextEvaluator*™ 26	***Moonwalk: The First Trip to the Moon*** **Lexile** 550 ***Moonshot: The Flight of the Apollo 11*** **Lexile** 990
Qualitative	**What Makes the Text Complex?** • **Prior Knowledge** Classifying Animals T209 • **Connection of Ideas** Synthesize T211 **ACT** *See Scaffolded Instruction in Teacher's Edition T209 and T211.*	**What Makes the Text Complex?** • **Purpose** Author's Purpose T217B, T217U • **Genre** Text Features T217C, T217G, T217M, T217Q, T217S • **Specific Vocabulary** Unfamiliar Words T217I, T217Y–T217Z • **Sentence Structure** T217E, T217K • **Connection of Ideas** Diagrams T217O **ACT** *See Scaffolded Instruction in Teacher's Edition T217A–T217Z.*	**What Makes the Text Complex?** • **Specific Vocabulary** • **Prior Knowledge** • **Sentence Structure** • **Connection of Ideas** • **Genre** **ACT** *See Level Up lessons online for Leveled Readers.*	**What Makes the Text Complex?** • **Genre** • **Specific Vocabulary** • **Prior Knowledge** • **Sentence Structure** • **Organization** • **Purpose** • **Connection of Ideas** **ACT** *See Scaffolded Instruction in Teacher's Edition T360–T361.*
Reader and Task	The Introduce the Concept lesson on pages T202–T203 will help determine the reader's knowledge and engagement in the weekly concept. See pages T208–T217 and T230–T231 for questions and tasks for this text.	The Introduce the Concept lesson on pages T202–T203 will help determine the reader's knowledge and engagement in the weekly concept. See pages T217A–T217Z and T230–T231 for questions and tasks for this text.	The Introduce the Concept lesson on pages T202–T203 will help determine the reader's knowledge and engagement in the weekly concept. See pages T232–T233, T240–T241, T244–T245, T250–T251, and T230–T231 for questions and tasks for this text.	The Introduce the Concept lesson on pages T202–T203 will help determine the reader's knowledge and engagement in the weekly concept. See pages T360–T361 for questions and tasks for this text.

Monitor and *Differentiate*

✓ Quick Check

To differentiate instruction, use the Quick Checks to assess students' needs and select the appropriate small group instruction focus.

Comprehension Strategy Reread T211

Comprehension Skill Compare and Contrast T213

Genre Expository Text T215

Vocabulary Strategy Context Clues T217

Phonics/Fluency *r*-Controlled Vowel Syllables, Phrasing T219

If No → | Approaching Level | **Reteach** T232–T239
| ELL | **Develop** T248–T255

If Yes → | On Level | **Review** T240–T243
| Beyond Level | **Extend** T244–T247

Using Weekly Data

Check your data Dashboard to verify assessment results and guide grouping decisions.

Level Up with Leveled Readers

IF ▶ students can read their leveled text fluently and answer comprehension questions

THEN ▶ work with the next level up to accelerate students' reading with more complex text.

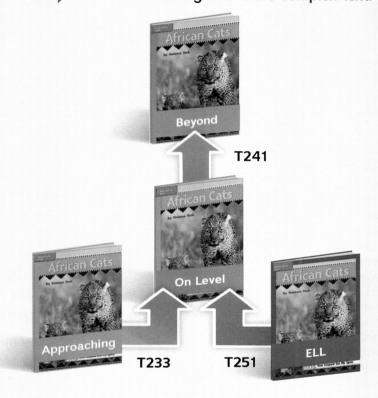

Beyond

T241

On Level

Approaching   T233   T251   ELL

ELL ENGLISH LANGUAGE LEARNERS

Small Group Instruction

Use the ELL small group lessons in the Wonders Teacher's Edition to provide focused instruction.

Language Development
Vocabulary preteaching and review, additional vocabulary building, and vocabulary strategy lessons, pp. T252–T253

Close Reading
Interactive Question-Response routines for scaffolded text-dependent questioning for reading and rereading the Shared Read and Leveled Reader, pp. T248–T251

Writing
Focus on the weekly writing trait, grammar skills, and spelling words, pp. T254–T255

Additional ELL Support

Use *Reading Wonders for English Learners* for ELD instruction that connects to the core.

Language Development
Ample opportunities for discussions, and scaffolded language support

Close Reading
Companion Worktexts for guided support in annotating text and citing text evidence. Differentiated Texts about the weekly concept.

Writing
Scaffolded instruction for writing to sources and revising student models

Reading Wonders for ELLs Teacher Edition and Companion Worktexts

Introduce the Concept

Reading/Writing Workshop

OBJECTIVES

CCSS Engage effectively in a range of collaborative discussions (one-on-one, in groups, and teacher-led) with diverse partners on grade 3 topics and texts, building on others' ideas and expressing their own clearly. Ask questions to check understanding of information presented, stay on topic, and link their comments to the remarks of others. **SL.3.1c**

ACADEMIC LANGUAGE
• *wildlife, requirements*
• Cognate: *requisitos*

MINILESSON 10 Mins

Build Background

ESSENTIAL QUESTION
How can learning about animals help you respect them?

Have students read the Essential Question on page 444 of the **Reading/Writing Workshop**. Tell them that *wildlife* refers to wild animals that live naturally in an area.

Discuss the photo with students. Focus on how learning about animals can help you respect them.

• Max the Great Horned Owl's job is to teach kids like Nora all about owls. Learning about owls helps Nora respect them.

• The more you know about animals, the more you can do to help them. You can help keep them safe and provide other **requirements**, or things they need to survive.

Talk About It

Ask: *Why is it important to respect animals? What can you provide by knowing more about them?* Have students discuss in pairs or groups.

• Model using the Concept Web to generate words and phrases related to respecting animals. Add students' contributions.

• Have partners continue the discussion by talking about ways they can help protect animals. They can complete the Concept Webs, generating additional words and phrases.

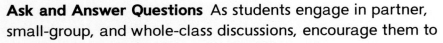

Collaborative Conversations

Ask and Answer Questions As students engage in partner, small-group, and whole-class discussions, encourage them to

• ask questions to clarify ideas they do not understand.

• wait a few seconds after asking a question, to give others a chance to think before responding.

• answer questions thoughtfully, using complete sentences, not one-word answers, that are on topic and related to the comments of others.

Go Digital

Discuss the Concept

Watch Video

View Photos

Use Graphic Organizer

BLAST BACK!

studysync

Assign Blast

Weekly Concept Animals and You

Essential Question
How can learning about animals help you respect them?

Go Digital!

Respecting Animals

My name is Max and I'm a Great Horned Owl. My job here at the wildlife preserve is to help kids like Nora learn all about owls. All animals deserve respect.

▶ Learning about animals helps you respect them.

▶ The more you know about animals, the more you can do to help them.

Talk About It

Write words you have learned about respecting animals. Talk with a partner about ways you can help protect animals.

READING/WRITING WORKSHOP, *pp. 444–445*

 BLAST BACK! studysync

Share the Blast assignment. Point out that you will discuss students' responses during the **Integrate Ideas** lesson at the end of the week.

GRAPHIC ORGANIZER 62

ELL ENGLISH LANGUAGE LEARNERS SCAFFOLD

Beginning	Intermediate	Advanced/High
Use Visuals Point to the picture. Say: *Look at the picture of Max the owl. Learning about Max helps us to respect wildlife.* Have students ask one question they have about wildlife. Correct students' pronunciation as needed.	**Describe** Have students describe the picture. Ask: *Who is Nora holding?* (Max the owl) *Why is she holding Max?* (To learn about him.) *Why should we learn about wildlife?* (to respect it) Elicit details to further develop students' responses.	**Discuss** Have partners discuss what the picture shows. Ask: *Why is Nora holding Max the owl?* Encourage students to use Academic Language in their discussions. Correct their responses for meaning as needed.

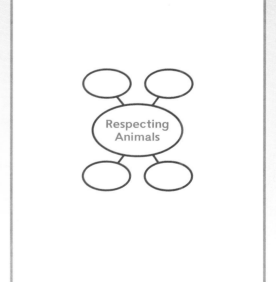

Respecting Animals

→ Listening Comprehension

MINILESSON 10 Mins

Interactive Read Aloud

OBJECTIVES

CCSS Ask and answer questions to determine understanding of a text, referring explicitly to the text as the basis for the answers. **RI.3.1**

CCSS Determine the main ideas and supporting details of a text read aloud or information presented in diverse media and formats, including visually, quantitatively, and orally. **SL.3.2**

• Listen for a purpose.
• Identify characteristics of expository text.

ACADEMIC LANGUAGE
expository text, reread

Connect to Concept: Animals and You

Tell students that when people know more about animals, they learn to respect them. Let students know that they will be listening to a passage that will help them get to know Florida's panthers. As students listen, have them think about how the passage answers the Essential Question.

Preview Genre: Expository Text

Explain that the story you will read aloud is expository text. Discuss features of expository text:

- presents facts and information about a topic
- may include headings and subheadings that summarize main ideas
- may include photographs, maps, charts, or other graphic aids

Preview Comprehension Strategy: Reread

Explain that when reading expository text, it can be helpful to reread a section of text if an idea or concept does not make sense. If a text contains complex or unfamiliar content, students can use the Reread strategy to help them monitor what they read.

Use the Think Alouds on page T205 to model the strategy.

Respond to Reading

Think Aloud Clouds Display Think Aloud Master 4: *When I read ____, I had to reread. . .* to reinforce how you used the Reread strategy to understand content.

Genre Features With students, discuss the elements of the Read Aloud that let them know it is expository text. Ask them to think about other texts that you have read or they have read independently that were expository texts.

Summarize Have students briefly restate the main idea and supporting details from "Respect for the Florida Panther" in their own words.

Go Digital

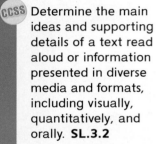

View Photos

When I read _____, I had to reread...

Model Think Alouds

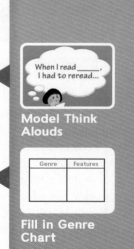

Genre	Features

Fill in Genre Chart

Respect for the Florida Panther

In 1982, the panther was named Florida's state animal. This large cat, like many other mammals, is on the endangered species list. Why is the Florida panther in trouble? What do people need to know in order to respect and protect the Florida panther? **1**

Florida Panther Facts

The Florida panther is a member of the cougar family. It has a sharp sense of smell and good vision. The panther is known for its speed. It can run up to 35 miles per hour when hunting prey. In the wild, the panther can live about twelve years. It lives on a diet of small mammals, deer, and wild pigs. The panther finds its prey in the forests, swamps, and marshes of southern Florida. **2**

Threats to the Florida Panther

For several years, the panther's habitat has been disappearing. Humans have taken over areas where the panthers once lived. People are building homes, businesses, highways, and malls in the panther's habitat.

With fewer places to hunt, the panther must look elsewhere for food. Many panthers have been killed trying to cross highways. Hunters and farmers who are afraid of the big cats have shot many panthers.

Air and water pollution is a huge threat to panthers. Some swamps and marshes have been ruined by run-off from factories. This bad water destroys the clean water supply. Dirty air and water has also hurt the panther's immune system. This means that the panther is more likely to get sick. **3**

Saving Florida's Panther

The Florida Panther Refuge is a group that works to inform people about the Florida panther. They have created a wildlife refuge that is a safe area for panthers to hunt and roam. They teach school children to have respect for the panther. They hope the Florida panther will be around for many generations to come.

Stockbroker/SuperStock

1 Think Aloud I've read about other endangered animals before but I don't know much about the panther. I think I'll **reread** this paragraph again because the questions will help me focus on what this article is about.

2 Think Aloud This paragraph includes interesting facts about the panther. I want to **reread** this section to help me understand and remember these details.

3 Think Aloud This is an important section because it tells about the threats to the Florida panther. I want to **reread** this paragraph to make sure I understand and remember these causes.

→ # Vocabulary

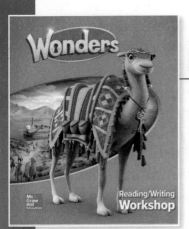

Reading/Writing Workshop

OBJECTIVES

ⒸⒸⓈⓈ Determine the meaning of general academic and domain-specific words and phrases in a text relevant to a grade 3 topic or subject area. **RI.3.4**

ⒸⒸⓈⓈ Demonstrate understanding of word relationships and nuances in word meanings. Identify real-life connections between words and their use (e.g., describe people who are *friendly* or *helpful*). **L.3.5b**

- Learn meanings of new vocabulary words.
- Write questions using new words.

ACADEMIC LANGUAGE
- *wildlife, requirement*
- Cognate: *requisito*

MINILESSON **10** Mins

Words in Context

Model the Routine

Introduce each vocabulary word using the **Vocabulary Routine** found on the **Visual Vocabulary Cards**.

Visual Vocabulary Cards

Vocabulary Routine

<u>Define:</u> **Wildlife** includes wild animals that live naturally in an area.

<u>Example:</u> Zebras are one kind of wildlife that live in Africa.

<u>Ask:</u> What kind of wildlife lives near your home?

Definitions

- **endangered**   Something that is **endangered** is in danger of becoming extinct.

- **fascinating**   Something that is **fascinating** attracts people's interest.
  Cognate: *fascinante*

- **illegal**   Something that is **illegal** is against the law.
  Cognate: *ilegal*

- **inhabit**   To **inhabit** something means to live in or on something.

- **requirement**   A **requirement** is something that is necessary.
  Cognate: *requisito*

- **respected**   To be **respected** means to be shown honor or consideration.
  Cognate: *respetado*

- **unaware**   When people are **unaware** of something, they do not know or realize something.

Talk About It

Have students work with a partner to look at each picture and discuss the definition of each word. Then ask students to choose three words and write questions for their partner to answer.

Go Digital

wildlife

Use Visual Glossary

Words to Know

Vocabulary

Use the picture and the sentence to talk with a partner about each word.

endangered

The giant panda is an **endangered** animal and needs to be protected.

Name another endangered animal.

fascinating

Maya thought the butterflies on her shirt were **fascinating** and interesting.

Tell about something you find fascinating.

illegal

The sign says it is **illegal** to swim here because the beach is closed.

What word means the opposite of illegal?

inhabit

Many animals, including moose, **inhabit** forests.

What animals inhabit the ocean?

requirement

Food is an important **requirement** for all living things.

Name another requirement for living things.

respected

The players **respected** their football coach because he was smart and fair.

Who is respected in your school?

unaware

The Karr family is **unaware** that there is a giraffe watching them.

What word means the opposite of unaware?

wildlife

Zebras are one kind of **wildlife** that live in Africa.

What kind of wildlife lives near your home?

Your Turn

COLLABORATE

Pick three words. Write three questions for your partner to answer.

Go Digital! *Use the online visual glossary*

446

447

READING/WRITING WORKSHOP, *pp. 446–447*

ELL ENGLISH LANGUAGE LEARNERS SCAFFOLD

Beginning

Use Visuals Say: *Let's look at the picture for* wildlife. *Zebras are one kind of wildlife. Zebras live in Africa.* Point out the window. Ask: *What is part of the wildlife here?* Have students repeat after you: *Birds are one kind of ____ that live near school.* Correct students' pronunciation as necessary.

Intermediate

Describe Point to the picture for *wildlife* and read the sentence. Ask: *What kind of wildlife lives near your home?* Have students complete the frame: *____ lives near my home.* Ask students to use the word *wildlife* in a sentence that tells about animals near their home. Elicit details to develop students' responses.

Advanced/High

Discuss Ask students to talk about the picture for *wildlife* with a partner and write a definition. Then have them share the definition with the class. Challenge pairs to use each vocabulary word in a sentence and share one sentence with the class. Correct the meaning of students' responses as needed.

ON-LEVEL PRACTICE BOOK p. 281

illegal	unaware	wildlife	requirement
respected	endangered	fascinating	inhabit

Finish each sentence using the vocabulary word provided.
Possible responses provided.

1. **(inhabit)** There are many types of small animals that *inhabit* our backyard.

2. **(wildlife)** We took a long hike through the woods and we saw a variety of *wildlife*.

3. **(endangered)** I learned that a certain type of owl *is endangered* and it needs our help.

4. **(illegal)** Driving over the speed limit *is illegal and can get you a ticket*.

5. **(unaware)** When I left class, *I was unaware that I had left my book behind*.

6. **(requirement)** If I want to get a library card, *it is a requirement that I give my identification and address*.

7. **(respected)** My mother had been a teacher for ten years *and everyone respected her*.

8. **(fascinating)** Helping my brother fix his car *was a fascinating learning experience*.

APPROACHING p. 281	BEYOND p. 281	ELL p. 281

Read

Shared Read | Genre • Expository

Butterflies
Big and Small

Essential Question

How can learning about animals help you respect them?

Read how respecting butterflies can help them survive.

Monarch butterflies like to land in the same trees when they migrate.

There are more than 725 species, or kinds, of butterflies fluttering around the United States and Canada. These **fascinating** creatures taste leaves with their feet and only see the colors red, yellow, and green. The Monarch butterfly and the Western Pygmy Blue butterfly share these same traits, but they are also different in many ways.

Size and Color

The Western Pygmy Blue butterfly is the smallest butterfly in the world. It is just about a half-inch across from wing tip to wing tip. That's smaller than a dime!

Monarch butterflies are much bigger. They measure about four inches across.

Size is not the only way Monarchs are different from Pygmy Blues. Monarch butterflies are a bright orange color with black markings. That makes them easy to see. Pygmy Blue butterflies are mostly brown and blue, and they blend in with their surroundings. Many people walk right by Pygmy Blues, **unaware** that they are even there.

This diagram shows the parts of a butterfly. **Western Pygmy Blue Butterfly**

wing
antennae
head
thorax
leg
abdomen

448

449

READING/WRITING WORKSHOP, *pp. 448–449*

Shared Read

Lexile 870   *TextEvaluator*™ 32

Close Reading Routine

Reading/Writing Workshop

ELL

See pages T248–T249 for Interactive Question-Response routine for the Shared Read.

Read | DOK 1–2

• Identify key ideas and details about Animals and You.
• Take notes and summarize.
• Use **A C T** prompts as needed.

Reread | DOK 2–3

• Analyze the text, craft, and structure.
• Use the Reread minilessons.

Integrate | DOK 4

• Integrate knowledge and ideas.
• Make text-to-text connections.
• Use the Integrate lesson.

T208 UNIT 6 WEEK 4

Read

Connect to Concept: Animals and You Tell students they will read about how Monarch butterflies and Western Pygmy Blue butterflies are different and alike.

Note Taking Read page 449 together. As you read, model how to take notes. *I will think about the Essential Question as I read and note key ideas and details.* Encourage students to note words they don't understand and questions they have.

Paragraph 1: Reread the first paragraph together. Model how to paraphrase the opening paragraph.

There are more than 725 species of butterflies in North America. They all taste leaves with their feet and see only red, yellow, and green. Despite these similarities, the Monarch butterfly and the Western Pygmy Blue butterfly have many differences.

Moving Around

Almost all butterflies migrate, or move to different areas. The Monarch's journey is the longest migration of any butterfly in the world. It spends summers in the northern United States and Canada. Then it migrates south to Mexico in early fall. Many Monarchs travel more than 3,000 miles.

Western Pygmy Blue butterflies **inhabit** southwestern deserts and marshes from California to Texas. They migrate short distances north to Oregon, and also to Arkansas, and Nebraska.

Both Monarchs and Blue Pygmies migrate when the weather gets chilly. Butterflies are cold-blooded insects. They are hot when the weather is hot and cold when the weather is cold. As a result, both butterflies migrate to stay warm. They also journey north or south to find food.

Finding Food

The Western Pygmy Blue drinks the nectar of many kinds of flowers. It finds the sweet, thick liquid easily, so its population has steadily grown. However, Monarch butterflies are not so lucky.

Just like the Pygmy Blue, Monarch butterflies sip nectar from flowers. But the Monarch butterfly has one main food **requirement** — the milkweed. Monarch butterflies must find this plant along their migration route. But what happens if there are no milkweed leaves?

When people build houses and roads, there are fewer places for Monarchs to find milkweed. If the Monarch cannot find food, its population will decrease. The Western Pygmy Blue and Monarch butterflies are not **endangered**, or at risk for becoming extinct now, but biologists are worried. Many other butterflies are endangered because people destroy their habitats.

Help Butterflies

Like all **wildlife**, Monarch and Pygmy Blue butterflies should be **respected**. People need to preserve butterfly habitats. To help, they can work to change laws, plant milkweed, and make it **illegal** to destroy animal habitats.

Learning about butterflies and what they need to survive is important. That way there will be plenty of Western Pygmy Blue and Monarch butterflies for future generations to enjoy.

Monarch butterflies feed on milkweed.

This Western Pygmy Blue butterfly stops to eat.

Butterfly Migration

CANADA

Great Lakes

Pacific Ocean

UNITED STATES

Map Key
← Monarch butterfly migration route
← Western Pygmy Blue butterfly migration route

MEXICO

450

451

Make Connections

? How can people learn to respect butterflies? ESSENTIAL QUESTION

Talk about some butterflies you've seen. How are they alike and different? TEXT TO SELF

READING/WRITING WORKSHOP, pp. 450–451

Paragraph 3: Reread the paragraph together. Ask: *What is one way that the butterflies are different?* Model how to cite evidence to answer.

Monarch butterflies are bright orange with black markings. Western Pygmy Blues, on the other hand, are mostly brown and blue. They blend with their surroundings, while Monarchs are easy to see.

Make Connections

COLLABORATE

Essential Question Encourage partners to discuss the needs of butterflies, and things people can do to help them. Ask them to cite text evidence. Use these sentence frames to focus discussion:

> *Monarch butterflies require . . .*
> *People can help butterflies by . . .*

A C T   Access Complex Text

▶ **Prior Knowledge**

Students may lack background knowledge about the difference between warm-blooded and cold-blooded animals.

- The body temperatures of warm-blooded animals always stays the same, regardless of the temperature around them. Birds, dogs, and humans are warm-blooded.

- Cold-blooded animals' body temperatures do not stay the same. They are hot when the weather is hot and cold when the weather is cold. This is why butterflies migrate when the weather gets cold.

→ Comprehension Strategy

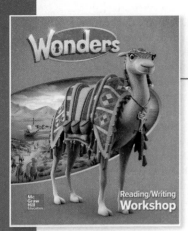

Reading/Writing Workshop

OBJECTIVES

CCSS Ask and answer questions to demonstrate understanding of a text, referring explicitly to the text as the basis for the answers. **RI.3.1**

ACADEMIC LANGUAGE
reread, expository text

MINILESSON 10 Mins — Reread

1 Explain

Review with students that when they read an expository text, they may come across information they do not understand. Students should stop and think about the text as they read. Remind students that rereading can help them remember important information and clarify confusing ideas.

- Good readers reread something they do not understand.
- When they encounter unclear or difficult text, they can stop and reread that section.
- Students may need to reread a text more than once before they understand it.

Point out that rereading parts or all of a text will help them understand it better.

2 Model Close Reading: Text Evidence

Model how rereading can help readers understand some ways the Monarch butterfly is different from the Western Pygmy Blue butterfly. Reread "Size and Color" on page 449 of "Butterflies Big and Small."

3 Guided Practice of Close Reading

Have students reread the section "Moving Around" on page 450. Direct them to work with partners to find out how Monarch butterflies and Western Pygmy Blue butterflies are alike. Have students refer directly to the text to reread and answer any questions they may still have about "Butterflies Big and Small."

Go Digital

View "Butterflies Big and Small"

Comprehension Strategy

Reread

Stop and think about the text as you read. Are there new facts and ideas? Do they make sense? Reread to make sure you understand.

Find Text Evidence

Do you understand some ways the Monarch butterfly is different from the Western Pygmy Blue butterfly? Reread "Size and Color" on page 449.

There are more than 725 species, or kinds, of butterflies fluttering around the United States and Canada. These **fascinating** creatures taste leaves with their feet and only see the colors red, yellow, and green. The Monarch butterfly and the Western Pygmy Blue butterfly share these same traits, but they are also different in many ways.

Size and Color

The Western Pygmy Blue butterfly is the smallest butterfly in the world. It is just about a half-inch across from wing tip to wing tip. That's smaller than a dime!

Monarch butterflies are much bigger. They measure about four inches across.

Size is not the only way Monarchs are different from Pygmy Blues. Monarch butterflies are a bright orange color with black markings. That makes them easy to see. Pygmy Blue butterflies are mostly brown and blue, and they blend in with their surroundings. Many people walk right by Pygmy Blues, **unaware** that they are even there.

I read that the Western Pygmy Blue butterfly is smaller than a dime and is mostly brown and blue in color. The Monarch butterfly is about four inches wide and is orange and black. Now I understand some of the ways these two butterflies are different.

Your Turn

How are Monarch butterflies and Western Pygmy Blue butterflies alike? Reread "Moving Around" on page 450 to find out.

452

READING/WRITING WORKSHOP, p. 452

A C T Access Complex Text

▶ Connection of Ideas

Students may need help to understand why the Pygmy Blue population has grown steadily, while the Monarch population has not.

- Have students review "Finding Food." *Why has the number of Pygmy Blues grown?* (They drink nectar, which is easy to find.)

- *What food do Monarchs need that Blue Pygmies do not?* (milkweed) *What is happening to the milkweed supply?* (Construction is making it harder to find.)

- *What will happen if the Monarch can't find milkweed?* (Its population will decrease.)

Monitor and *Differentiate*

✓ Quick Check

Do students reread to find out how Monarch butterflies and Western Pygmy Blue butterflies are alike?

⬇

Small Group Instruction

If No → | Approaching Level | Reteach p. T232
| ELL | Develop p. T248
If Yes → | On Level | Review p. T240
| Beyond Level | Extend p. T244

ON-LEVEL PRACTICE BOOK pp. 283–284

Read the passage. Use the reread strategy to help you understand new facts or difficult explanations.

The Disappearance of Bees

Take a walk outside in nature. It may not be long before you
13 see bees buzzing around a flower. This is a sight that most people
26 are used to seeing. But now there is concern for bees. People are
39 worried because the number of honey bees has been going down.
49 And no one is sure why.

55 **What Is Happening and Why**
60 Studies show that bee colonies in the United States are
70 vanishing. This is a problem that is being called Colony Collapse
81 Disorder. It was first noticed in 2006 by beekeepers. Large groups
92 of bees living together had fewer bees. Since then, nearly
102 one-third of the colonies have gone away.
109 So, what is the cause? The answer is still not clear. Plant sprays
122 may have a role in making the bees sick. Chemicals are often
134 sprayed on plants to keep certain bugs from harming the plants.
145 Newer sprays may be bothering the bees.
152 There are other possible causes. New unknown germs, or tiny
162 living things that can cause disease, may also play a part in
174 getting bees sick. A lack of food and water is also a problem for
188 bees. Too many bees in the hive also adds to the bees' stress.

| APPROACHING | BEYOND | ELL |
| pp. 283–284 | pp. 283–284 | pp. 283–284 |

→ Comprehension Skill

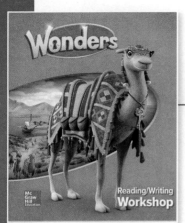

Reading/Writing Workshop

OBJECTIVES

CCSS Describe the logical connection between particular sentences and paragraphs in a text (e.g., comparison, cause/effect, first/second/third in a sequence). **RI.3.8**

Identify the similarities and differences between animals.

ACADEMIC LANGUAGE

compare and contrast, expository text, signal words

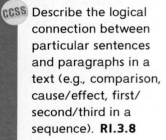

SKILLS TRACE

TEXT STRUCTURE

Introduce Unit 1 Week 3

Review Unit 1 Weeks 4, 6; Unit 2 Week 6; Unit 3 Weeks 5, 6; Unit 4 Weeks 3, 4; Unit 5 Weeks 5, 6; Unit 6 Weeks 3, 4, 6

Assess Units 1, 3, 4, 5, 6

Text Structure: Compare and Contrast

1 Explain

Explain to students that they can compare and contrast two things in expository texts to understand how they are alike and different.

- To compare, students should look for ways that two things are alike. To contrast, students should look for ways two things are different.

- Students can look for signal words like *both, alike, same,* or *different* to help them compare and contrast.

2 Model Close Reading: Text Evidence

Model identifying signal words that show the similarities and differences between the Monarch butterfly and the Western Pygmy Blue butterfly in "Butterflies Big and Small." Then model using the details written on the graphic organizer to compare and contrast the two species.

 Write About Reading: Compare and Contrast Model for students how to use the notes from the graphic organizer to write a summary of how the Monarch butterfly and the Western Pygmy Blue butterfly are alike and different.

3 Guided Practice of Close Reading

 Have students work in pairs to find more details that tell how Monarch butterflies and Western Pygmy Blue butterflies are alike and different and list them in the graphic organizer. Remind them to look for signal words. Discuss each sentence and paragraph and the signal words students find as they complete the graphic organizer.

 Write About Reading: Compare and Contrast Ask pairs to work together to identify the sentences and paragraphs that compare and contrast Monarch butterflies and Western Pygmy Blue butterflies. Then have them write a summary of how they are alike and different. Select pairs of students to share their summaries with the class.

Go Digital

Present the Lesson

Comprehension Skill

Compare and Contrast

When authors compare, they show how two things are alike. When authors contrast, they tell how the things are different. Authors use signal words, such as *both, alike, same,* or *different,* to compare and contrast.

 Find Text Evidence

How are the Monarch butterfly and Western Pygmy Blue butterfly alike and different? I will reread "Butterflies Big and Small" and look for signal words.

Monarch Butterflies — Colorful and big

Both — Taste leaves with their feet

Western Pygmy Blue Butterflies — Blend in with their surroundings, very small

Your Turn
COLLABORATE

Reread "Butterflies Big and Small." Find details that tell how Monarch butterflies and Western Pygmy Blue butterflies are alike and different. Write them in the graphic organizer. What signal words helped you?

Go Digital!
Use the interactive graphic organizer

453

READING/WRITING WORKSHOP, *p. 453*

Monitor and *Differentiate*

 Quick Check

As students complete the graphic organizer, do they compare and contrast two things? Can they identify signal words?

Small Group Instruction

If No →	Approaching Level	Reteach p. T239
	ELL	Develop p. T248
If Yes →	On Level	Review p. T243
	Beyond Level	Extend p. T247

ENGLISH LANGUAGE LEARNERS
ELL SCAFFOLD

Beginning	Intermediate	Advanced/High
Respond Orally Reread page 449. After each sentence, ask: *What did you learn about the butterflies in this sentence?* Have students list the details describing the butterflies using a sentence frame. *Monarch butterflies are ____, ____, and ____. Western Pygmy Blue butterflies are ____, ____, and ____.*	**Comprehend** Have students reread page 449. Ask questions to help students compare and contrast. *How big is the Monarch butterfly?* (It is four inches across.) *How big is the Western Pygmy Blue butterfly?* (It is smaller than a dime.) *How are they the same?* (They both taste leaves with their feet.) Expand upon answers.	**Explain** Have students reread page 449 of "Butterflies Big and Small." Have students describe how Monarch butterflies and Western Pygmy Blue butterflies are alike and different. Then have them explain how they used signal words to compare and contrast.

ON-LEVEL PRACTICE BOOK pp. 283–285

A. Reread the passage and answer the questions.
Possible responses provided.

1. **What do the things mentioned in paragraphs 3–4 have in common?**

   They are all possible reasons the bees are disappearing.

2. **How are the things mentioned in paragraphs 3–4 different from one another?**

   They are different because they harm bees in different ways.

3. **Compare and contrast pollen and nectar in paragraphs 5 and 8. How are they similar and different?**

   Pollen and nectar are both substances carried by bees that benefit people. Pollen helps the plants make seeds. Bees make nectar into honey.

B. Work with a partner. Read the passage aloud. Pay attention to phrasing. Stop after one minute. Fill out the chart.

	Words Read	–	Number of Errors	=	Words Correct Score
First Read		–		=	
Second Read		–		=	

APPROACHING pp. 283–285	BEYOND pp. 283–285	ELL pp. 283–285

Genre: Informational Text

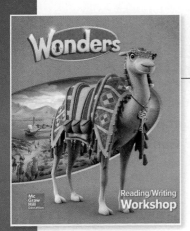

Reading/Writing Workshop

OBJECTIVES

CCSS Use information gained from illustrations (e.g., maps, photographs) and the words in a text to demonstrate understanding of the text (e.g., where, when, why, and how key events occur). **RI.3.7**

CCSS By the end of the year, read and comprehend informational texts, including history/ social studies, science, and technical texts, at the high end of the grades 2–3 text complexity band independently and proficiently. **RI.3.10**

Recognize the characteristics and features of expository text.

ACADEMIC LANGUAGE

• expository text, headings, diagram

• Cognate: diagrama

 MINILESSON 10 Mins

Expository Text

1 Explain

Share with students the following key characteristics of **expository text**.

• Expository text gives important facts and information about a topic. The topic may be about science.

• Expository text may include text features such as maps, headings, diagrams, photographs, and captions. However, even if a text has none of these features, it may still be an expository text.

2 Model Close Reading: Text Evidence

Model identifying and using the text features on page 449 of "Butterflies Big and Small."

Headings Point out the heading "Size and Color." Remind students that a heading tells what a section of text is mostly about. Ask: *What do you think this section is about?*

Diagram Point out the diagram. Explain that a diagram is a simple picture or illustration with labels. Ask: *What does the diagram tell you about the parts of a butterfly?*

3 Guided Practice of Close Reading

 Have students work with partners to find more text features in "Butterflies Big and Small." Partners should discuss something they learned from each feature.

Go Digital

Present the Lesson

Genre | Informational Text

Expository Text

"Butterflies Big and Small" is an expository text.
Expository text:
- May give information about a science topic
- Has headings that tell what a section is about
- Includes text features such as diagrams and maps

Find Text Evidence

I can tell that "Butterflies Big and Small" is expository text. It give facts about Monarch and Western Pygmy Blue butterflies. This science article also has headings, a diagram, and a map.

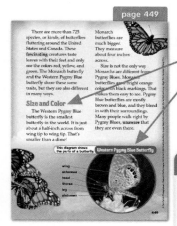

page 449

There are more than 725 species, or kinds, of butterflies fluttering around the United States and Canada. These **fascinating** creatures taste leaves with their feet and only see the colors red, yellow, and green. The Monarch butterfly and the Western Pygmy Blue butterfly share these same traits, but they are also different in many ways.

Size and Color
The Western Pygmy Blue butterfly is the smallest butterfly in the world. It is just about a half-inch across from wing tip to wing tip. That's smaller than a dime!

Monarch butterflies are much bigger. They measure about four inches across.

Size is not the only way Monarchs are different from Pygmy Blues. Monarch butterflies are bright orange color with black markings. That makes them easy to see. Pygmy Blue butterflies are mostly brown and blue, and they blend in with their surroundings. Many people walk right by Pygmy Blues, **unaware** that they are even there.

Text Features

Headings Headings tell what a section of text is mostly about.

Diagram A diagram is a simple picture with labels.

Your Turn

COLLABORATE

Look at the text features in "Butterflies Big and Small." Tell your partner about something you learned.

454

READING/WRITING WORKSHOP, *p. 454*

ENGLISH LANGUAGE LEARNERS SCAFFOLD

Beginning

Use Visuals Point to the diagram on page 449. Explain that this diagram tells about the parts of a butterfly. Read the labels and have students chorally read each label and run their fingers to the part being named. Guide pairs of students in writing one sentence that describes the butterfly diagram. You might offer a sentence frame: *The butterfly diagram helps ___.*

Intermediate

Describe Point to the diagram. Explain that diagrams usually give us interesting information related to the main topic. Ask: *What do we learn about in this diagram?* (the parts of a butterfly) Have students name the part. Correct answers as needed.

Advanced/High

Discuss Explain that diagrams give us interesting information related to the main topic. Have students talk to a partner about what they learn in this diagram and how it gives them a better understanding of the parts of a butterfly.

Monitor and *Differentiate*

✓ Quick Check

Are students able to identify features of expository text in "Butterflies Big and Small"? Can they tell what they learned from each feature?

⬇

Small Group Instruction

If No →	Approaching Level	Reteach p. T232
	ELL	Develop p. T248
If Yes →	On Level	Review p. T240
	Beyond Level	Extend p. T244

ON-LEVEL PRACTICE BOOK p. 286

What Good Are Mosquitoes?

Some people think mosquitoes are not very helpful animals. After all, most of us know mosquitoes because of their itching bite. But mosquitoes are an important part of the food chain. For example, dragonflies rely on mosquitoes to eat. Without a large mosquito population, dragonflies could not survive. If the number of dragonflies drops enough, animals that depend on dragonflies might not survive.

Wetland Food Chain
Large birds
Frogs
Dragonflies
Mosquitoes

Dragonflies need mosquitoes, frogs need dragonflies, and birds need frogs.

Answer the questions about the text.

1. How do you know this text is expository text?
   It gives information about a science topic.

2. What text feature is included in the text?
   Diagram

3. How does the text feature help you understand the topic?
   Possible response: It shows how the food chain connects animals.

4. Why are mosquitoes important?
   Possible response: They provide food for other animals.

APPROACHING p. 286	BEYOND p. 286	ELL p. 286

→ Vocabulary Strategy

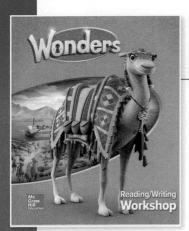

Reading/Writing Workshop

OBJECTIVES

 Determine or clarify the meaning of unknown and multiple-meaning words and phrases based on grade 3 reading and content, choosing flexibly from a range of strategies. Use sentence-level context as a clue to the meaning of a word or phrase. **L.3.4a**

ACADEMIC LANGUAGE

- *context clues, paragraph clues*
- Cognate: *contexto*

 MINILESSON **10 Mins**

Context Clues

1 Explain

Remind students that they can often figure out the meaning of an unknown word by using context clues found within the paragraph they are reading.

- To find **paragraph clues**, students can look for words and phrases in the same paragraph as the unknown word that provide context.

- Paragraph clues may define the unknown word, restate what it means, or provide a further description of the word.

2 Model Close Reading: Text Evidence

Model using paragraph clues on page 450 to find the meaning of *migrate*.

3 Guided Practice of Close Reading

 Have students work in pairs to figure out the meanings of *cold-blooded* and *nectar* from page 450 of "Butterflies Big and Small." Encourage partners to go back into the text and use context clues within each paragraph to develop each word's definition.

Use Reference Sources

Dictionaries Have students use either a print or digital dictionary to look up the precise meanings of *cold-blooded insects* and *nectar*. Have them confirm the definitions they developed using paragraph clues, and revise their definitions if necessary. If the dictionary gives more than one meaning, have students use context to determine the proper one.

Go Digital

Present the Lesson

SKILLS TRACE

CONTEXT CLUES: PARAGRAPH CLUES

Introduce Unit 6 Week 4

Assess Unit 6

Vocabulary Strategy

Context Clues

Context clues are words or phrases that help you figure out the meaning of an unfamiliar word. In many science texts, context clues appear in the same paragraph as an unfamiliar word.

 Find Text Evidence

On page 450, I'm not sure what the word migrate *means. I will look for clues in the paragraph. I read that butterflies "move to different areas" and "travel more than 3,000 miles." I also see the word "journey." I think* migrate *means to move or travel to different places.*

> Almost all butterflies migrate, or move to different areas. The Monarch's journey is the longest migration of any butterfly in the world. It spends summers in the northern United States and Canada. Then it migrates south to Mexico in early fall. Many Monarchs travel more than 3,000 miles.

Your Turn COLLABORATE

Find context clues. Use them to figure out the meanings of the following words.
   cold-blooded, *page 450*
   nectar, *page 451*

Don Farrall/Photographer's Choice RF/Getty Images

455

READING/WRITING WORKSHOP, *p. 455*

ENGLISH LANGUAGE LEARNERS SCAFFOLD

Beginning

Explain Point out the words *cold-blooded* and *nectar* and define them for students. Use the words in sentences, and help students replace them with words they know. Point out that *nectar* has the cognate *néctar.*

Intermediate

Describe Point out the words *cold-blooded* and *nectar*. Help students define the words by finding context clues. Then, have pairs write a sentence for each word. Elicit from students how cognates helped them understand the text.

Advanced/High

Discuss Point out the words *cold-blooded* and *nectar* and ask students to define the use them in sentences. Have them find paragraph clues and replace the words with words they know. Ask students to find cognates with a partner.

Monitor and *Differentiate*

✓ Quick Check

Can students identify and use paragraph clues to determine the meanings of *cold-blooded* and *nectar*?

⬇

Small Group Instruction

If No → | Approaching Level | Reteach p. T237
| ELL | Develop p. T253
If Yes → | On Level | Review p. T242
| Beyond Level | Extend p. T246

ON-LEVEL PRACTICE BOOK p. 287

Read the sentences below. Underline the context clues that help you understand the meaning of each word in bold. Then write the meaning of the word in bold on the line.
Possible responses provided.

1. Now there is **concern** for bees. People are worried because the number of honeybees has been going down. And no one is sure why.

   worry

2. Studies show that bee **colonies** in the United States are vanishing. This is a problem that is being called Colony Collapse Disorder. It was first noticed in 2006 by beekeepers. Large groups of bees living together had fewer bees.

   large groups of bees living together

3. New unknown **germs**, or tiny living things that can cause disease, may also play a part in getting bees sick. A lack of food and water is also a problem for bees.

   tiny living things that can cause disease

4. Bees carry out the same **process**, or series of actions, for many plants that farmers grow.

   string of actions

5. Honeybees take sweet **fluid** called nectar from plants. They use this liquid to make honey in their hives.

   a liquid

| APPROACHING p. 287 | BEYOND p. 287 | ELL p. 287 |

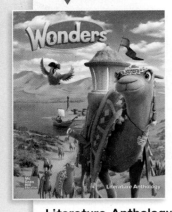

Read

Alligators and Crocodiles

Literature Anthology

Text Complexity Range

Lexile

420   820   870

Literature Anthology
Complex vocabulary and sentence structure place this selection above Lexile range. Content is grade-level appropriate.

TextEvaluator™

2   29   35

What makes this text complex?

- ▸ **Purpose**
- ▸ **Organization**
- ▸ **Prior Knowledge**
- ▸ **Genre**
- ▸ **Specific Vocabulary**
- ▸ **Sentence Structure**
- ▸ **Connection of Ideas**

This selection is suggested for use as an Extended Complex Text. See pages T356–359.

Close Reading Routine

Read   DOK 1–2

- Identify key ideas and details about Animals and You.
- Take notes and summarize.
- Use **ACT** prompts as needed.

Reread   DOK 2–3

- Analyze the text, craft and structure.
- Use *Close Reading Companion,* pp. 187–189.

Integrate   DOK 4

- Integrate knowledge and ideas.
- Make text-to-text connections.
- Use the Integrate lesson.

Genre • Expository Text

Alligators and Crocodiles

? Essential Question
How can learning about animals help you respect them?
Read about two amazing reptiles. Find out why we should respect them.

Go Digital!

520

A C T — Access Complex Text

▸ Purpose

Remind students that the purpose of a text is what the writer wants to tell the reader. Look at the title of the selection *Alligators and Crocodiles* and the illustrations.

- *What do you think the author wants to tell the reader?* (The author wants to inform the reader about alligators and crocodiles, including how they are alike and different.)

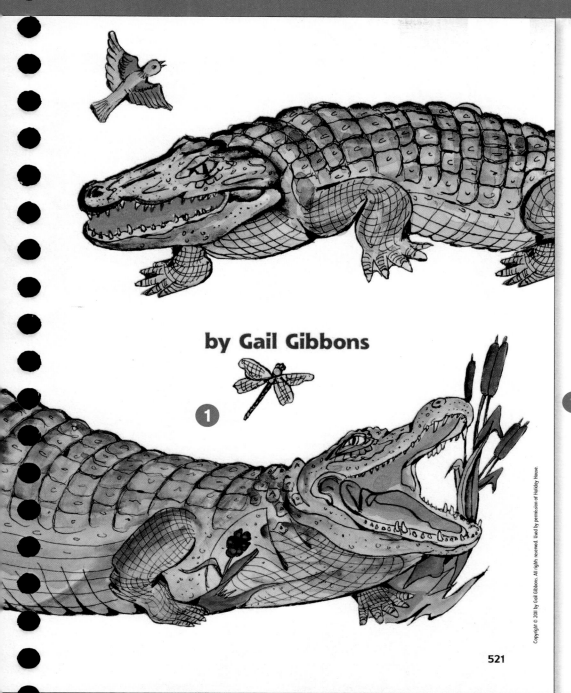

by Gail Gibbons

521

LITERATURE ANTHOLOGY, pp. 520-521

Read

Tell students they will be reading about alligators and crocodiles, including how they are alike and how they are different. Ask students to predict how the selection will help them answer the Essential Question.

Note Taking: Use the Graphic Organizer

Remind students to take notes as they read. Have them fill in the graphic organizer on **Your Turn Practice Book** page 282 to compare and contrast alligators and crocodiles. They can also note words they don't understand and questions they have.

1 Text Features: Illustrations

Look at the illustrations on pages 520–521 with a partner. What living things are shown? (dragonflies, a bird, an alligator, a crocodile) Can you tell the alligator apart from the crocodile? What is coming out of the egg? (a baby alligator or crocodile)

• *What other clues tell us about the purpose of this selection before we begin reading?* (The egg hatching tells us that we will learn about the animals from when they are born to when they grow up. The other animals in the picture show us that we learn where alligators and crocodiles live and what other animals live with them.)

Read

2 Skill: Compare and Contrast

What similarities do alligators and crocodiles have? (They glide through water, are bumpy, and have two eyes and a snout.)

A C T Access Complex Text

▶ Genre

Remind students to use the illustrations to help them visualize the descriptions in the text.

- *Reread the second sentence on page 523. What hides most of the alligator or crocodile?* (Most of the animal is underwater.)

- *Why does the alligator or crocodile look like a bumpy log?* (The part of its body above the water is dark and bumpy, like the bark of a log.)

- *What does it look like the alligator or crocodile is doing?* (chasing a fish)

Something glides slowly through the water, barely making a ripple. It is well hidden and looks like a bumpy drifting log. Two eyes and a snout appear above the water. It is an alligator or a crocodile. **2**

LITERATURE ANTHOLOGY, *pp. 522–523*

Read

Build Vocabulary page 523

drifting: floating slowly on a current of water

Reread

Author's Craft: Figurative Language

How does the author describe what is in the water? (glides, barely making a ripple, is well hidden, has two eyes, a snout) What is it being compared to? (a bumpy drifting log) What animal can it be? (an alligator or a crocodile) Why does the author not say which of these animals it is? (to emphasize that these reptiles look very similar when they are seen just below the surface of the water.)

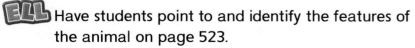 Have students point to and identify the features of the animal on page 523.

- Ask: *Who can tell me or point to something about alligators and crocodiles?* (I see two eyes, a snout, five toes in front, four toes in back, a big mouth, sharp teeth, and it is in water.)

- Point out that alligator and crocodile are cognates. (*aligador, cocodrilo*)

Read

3 Skill: Compare and Contrast

When authors compare two things, they tell how they are alike. When they contrast, they tell how they are different. How are alligators and crocodiles alike? (Both are reptiles and members of a group of reptiles called crocodilians.) What is the author comparing alligators and crocodiles to? (dinosaurs) How are they all alike? (They all lived on Earth about 230 million years ago.) How are they different? (Dinosaurs are now extinct. Alligators and crocodiles are still alive.) What signal words tells us this? (but) Add this information to your chart.

Dinosaurs
extinct

Both
reptiles, crocodilians, lived on Earth 230 million years ago

Alligators and Crocodiles
alive

ALLIGATOR

CROCODILE

All reptiles are cold-blooded animals. In order to survive, they must keep their body temperature from getting too hot or too cold. They do this by moving to a cooler or warmer place.

3 Alligators and crocodiles are members of a group of reptiles called crocodilians (krok-uh-DILL-ee-ans). They are the closest living relatives of dinosaurs and the world's largest reptiles.

524

A C T Access Complex Text

▶ Sentence Structure

Some students may need help with long sentences. Lead them to break sentences into parts. Have them read the first part of the sentence about paleontologists on page 525, stopping at the comma.

- *What do paleontologists study? What does this tell paleontologists about?* (They study fossils, which give information about ancient life.)

- Have students read the rest of the sentence. *What does this part of the sentence have to do with the part that comes before the comma?* (It explains the meaning of the word *fossil*.)

PALEONTOLOGISTS are scientists who learn about ancient life by studying fossils, the remains of a plant or animal that lived at least ten thousand years ago.

EXTINCT means no longer in existence. **④**

According to paleontologists (pay-lee-on-TOL-o-jists), alligators, crocodiles, and dinosaurs lived on Earth about 230 million years ago. About 65 million years ago dinosaurs became extinct, but alligators and crocodiles continued to live.

525

LITERATURE ANTHOLOGY, *pp. 524–525*

Read

④ Text Features: Captions

What information do you learn about reptiles in the caption on page 524 that is not in the main text? (All reptiles, such as alligators and crocodiles, are cold-blooded. They must move to cooler or warmer places to control the temperature of their bodies.) What terms are defined in the captions on page 525? (*extinct* and *paleontologists*) How do paleontologists learn about ancient life? (They study fossils, which are the remains of plant and animal life that lived long ago.)

ELL Have students use the images on pages 524 and 525 to better understand the history of alligators and crocodiles.

- Have students use the labels to identify the alligator and the crocodile on page 524. *Do these animals look alike?* (yes)

- *What animal was related to alligators and crocodiles?* (dinosaurs) *Are any dinosaurs alive?* (no) Point out that *dinosaur* is a cognate. (dinosaurio)

- Point to and read aloud the definition of *extinct*. Have students list ideas about what animal the fossils on page 525 resemble.

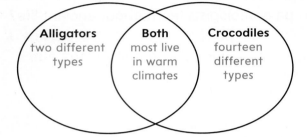

Read

5 Skill: Compare and Contrast

How are alligators and crocodiles alike? (They can be found on the southern tip of Florida and the Florida Keys.) What signal word tells us this? (*both*) What is a way they are different? (There are two different kinds of alligators and fourteen different types of crocodiles.) Use the maps and add this information to your chart.

Alligators	Both	Crocodiles
two different types	most live in warm climates	fourteen different types

Build Vocabulary page 526

keys: low islands or reefs

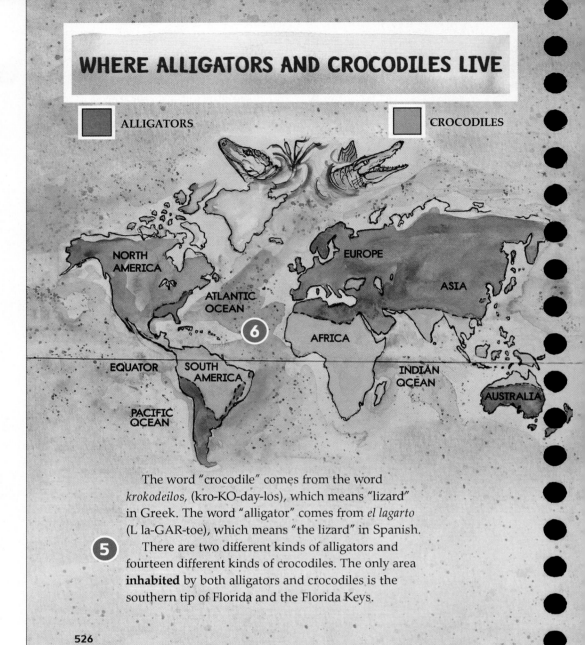

WHERE ALLIGATORS AND CROCODILES LIVE

■ ALLIGATORS   ■ CROCODILES

NORTH AMERICA
EUROPE
ASIA
ATLANTIC OCEAN
6
AFRICA
EQUATOR   SOUTH AMERICA
INDIAN OCEAN
AUSTRALIA
PACIFIC OCEAN

The word "crocodile" comes from the word *krokodeilos*, (kro-KO-day-los), which means "lizard" in Greek. The word "alligator" comes from *el lagarto* (L la-GAR-toe), which means "the lizard" in Spanish.

5   There are two different kinds of alligators and fourteen different kinds of crocodiles. The only area **inhabited** by both alligators and crocodiles is the southern tip of Florida and the Florida Keys.

526

A C T Access Complex Text

▶ Genre

Students may misinterpret or ignore important text features, such as maps. Direct students' attention to the maps and keys on pages 526–527. Then ask:

- *How are the maps on pages 526 and 527 connected?* (The map on page 527 provides details of an area shown on the map on page 526.)

- *What details can you see on the U.S. map on page 527 that you cannot see on the world map on page 526?* (You can see the names of the states that have alligators. The U.S. map also makes it easier to see where crocodiles and alligators live together.)

- *How does the U.S. map show where crocodiles and alligators live together?* (The area is blue.)

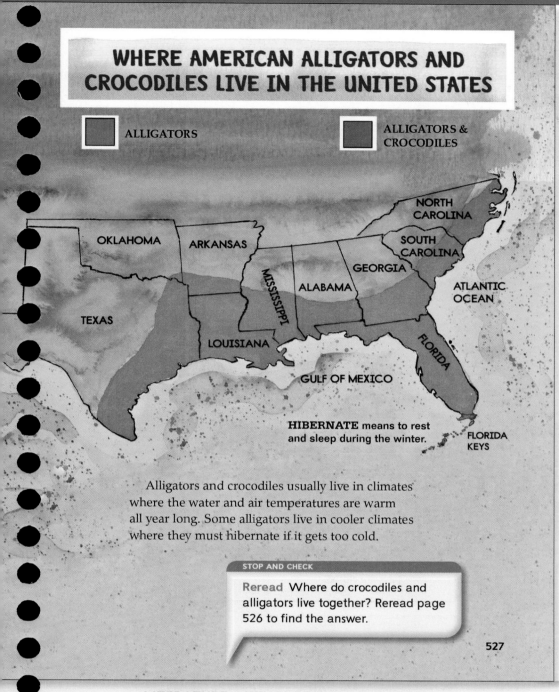

WHERE AMERICAN ALLIGATORS AND CROCODILES LIVE IN THE UNITED STATES

☐ ALLIGATORS

☐ ALLIGATORS & CROCODILES

NORTH CAROLINA

OKLAHOMA   ARKANSAS

SOUTH CAROLINA

GEORGIA

MISSISSIPPI

ALABAMA

ATLANTIC OCEAN

TEXAS

LOUISIANA

FLORIDA

GULF OF MEXICO

HIBERNATE means to rest and sleep during the winter.

FLORIDA KEYS

Alligators and crocodiles usually live in climates where the water and air temperatures are warm all year long. Some alligators live in cooler climates where they must hibernate if it gets too cold.

STOP AND CHECK

Reread Where do crocodiles and alligators live together? Reread page 526 to find the answer.

527

LITERATURE ANTHOLOGY, *pp. 526–527*

STOP AND CHECK

Reread Where do crocodiles and alligators live together?

Teacher Think Aloud To make sure I can identify the places where crocodiles and alligators live, I can reread. I can learn exactly where both crocodiles and alligators live by looking at the maps and rereading the headings. I can also reread the second paragraph on page 526 and retell the information in my own words. Alligators and crocodiles live in a warm climate and near the water. The only place both these animals live together is the southern tip of Florida and the Florida Keys.

Reread   *Close Reading Companion*

Text Features: Maps

How does the author use the maps to help you compare and contrast alligators and crocodiles? (The maps show areas where alligators live in red, and where crocodiles live in orange.) The color orange does not appear on the United States map or the map key on page 527. What can you infer from this? (There are no areas in the United States where crocodiles live but alligators do not live.)

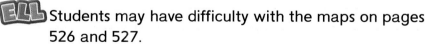 Students may have difficulty with the maps on pages 526 and 527.

- Have students identify the world map. Then have them point to and identify the places that have alligators and crocodiles. *Do more places in the world have alligators or crocodiles?* (There are

more places with crocodiles.) *Have you ever seen an alligator or crocodile?*

- Point to the water on both maps. *Do alligators and crocodiles need to live near water?* (yes) *Is it warm or cold?* (warm)

Read

6 Skill: Compare and Contrast

What is the author contrasting? (an American alligator and an American crocodile) What does the crocodile have that the alligator does not? (sensory pits all over the body, upper and lower teeth that can be seen when the jaws are closed, narrow head) Add this information and the additional details from the diagram to your chart.

American Alligator	Both	American Crocodile
wide head, wide and rounded snout	thick skin, long and strong tail, strong jaws	narrow head, narrow, long snout

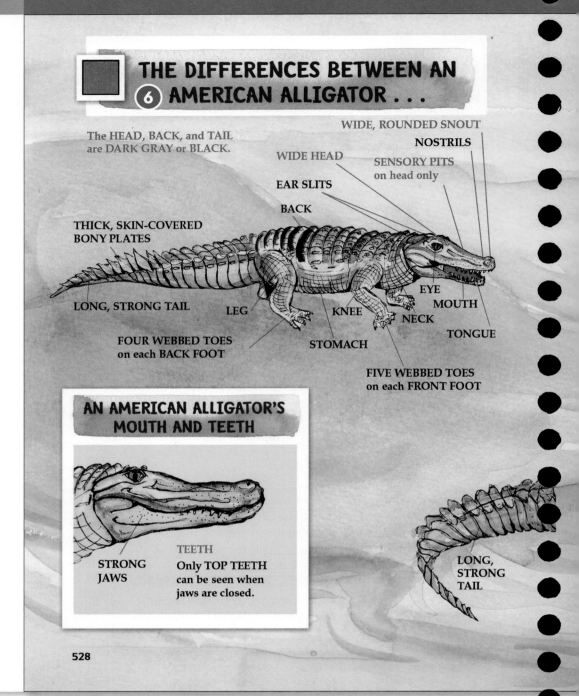

6 THE DIFFERENCES BETWEEN AN AMERICAN ALLIGATOR . . .

The HEAD, BACK, and TAIL are DARK GRAY or BLACK.

WIDE, ROUNDED SNOUT

NOSTRILS

WIDE HEAD

SENSORY PITS on head only

EAR SLITS

BACK

THICK, SKIN-COVERED BONY PLATES

EYE

MOUTH

LONG, STRONG TAIL

LEG

KNEE

NECK

TONGUE

FOUR WEBBED TOES on each BACK FOOT

STOMACH

FIVE WEBBED TOES on each FRONT FOOT

AN AMERICAN ALLIGATOR'S MOUTH AND TEETH

STRONG JAWS

TEETH Only TOP TEETH can be seen when jaws are closed.

LONG, STRONG TAIL

528

A C T Access Complex Text

▶ Specific Vocabulary

Review strategies for finding the meaning of an unfamiliar word, such as using context clues, word parts, or a dictionary. Point out specific words and where they appear in the diagram.

• Help students work together to define *sensory, webbed,* and *plates.*

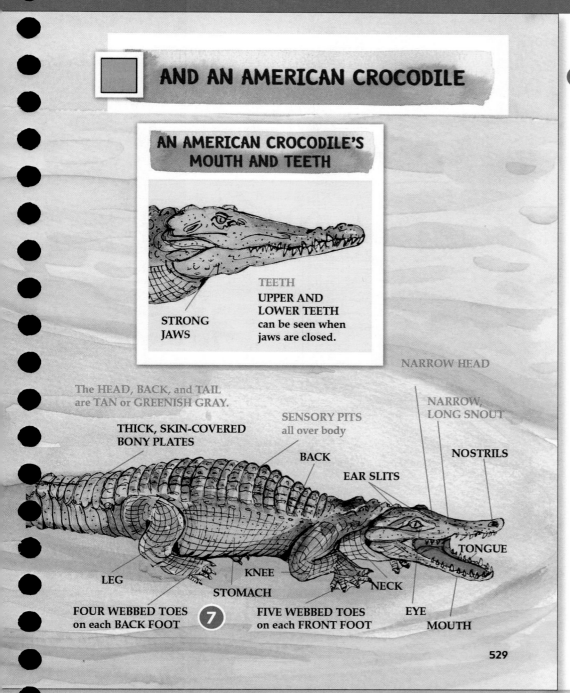

AND AN AMERICAN CROCODILE

AN AMERICAN CROCODILE'S MOUTH AND TEETH

STRONG JAWS

TEETH
UPPER AND LOWER TEETH can be seen when jaws are closed.

NARROW HEAD

The HEAD, BACK, and TAIL are TAN or GREENISH GRAY.

THICK, SKIN-COVERED BONY PLATES

SENSORY PITS all over body

NARROW, LONG SNOUT

BACK

NOSTRILS

EAR SLITS

LEG

KNEE

STOMACH

FOUR WEBBED TOES on each BACK FOOT ⑦

FIVE WEBBED TOES on each FRONT FOOT

NECK

EYE

MOUTH

TONGUE

529

LITERATURE ANTHOLOGY, pp. 528–529

Read

⑦ **Ask and Answer Questions**

Ask a question of your own about the text and share it with a partner. To find the answer, try rereading. For example, you might ask, *Why do both the alligator and crocodile have webbed feet and a strong tail?* (Both live by water and swim.)

Reread   *Close Reading Companion*

Text Features: Diagrams

What do you notice about the labels in the diagrams? (Some have black type and some have red type.) How does the author use the diagrams to help you compare and contrast alligators and crocodiles? (Similarities between American alligators and American crocodiles are labeled in black, and differences are labeled in red. The colors help me understand how these two reptiles are alike and how they are different.)

ELL Students may have difficulty understanding the names of certain parts of alligators and crocodiles. Have students point to and identify the bony plates. Explain the multiple meanings of *plate*.

Read

8 Skill: Compare and Contrast

Compare how alligators and crocodiles eat. How does the way younger alligators and crocodiles catch their prey differ from older alligators and crocodiles? (They prey on different types of animals and catch them in different ways.) Add this information to your chart.

Young
small prey (fish, frogs, birds), use jaws, and sharp teeth

Both
carnivores, sneak up and attack

Old
big animals (raccoons, deer) grab, leap on, drown prey

CARNIVORES are animals that eat meat.

Alligators and crocodiles each have about sixty pointed teeth. When they lose a tooth, a new tooth takes its place. They can grow about three thousand new teeth during their lives.

Alligators and crocodiles are carnivores. To catch their prey, they may stay perfectly still. When an animal comes near . . . SNAP! The animal is grabbed in a split second. Alligators and crocodiles may also swim slowly and quietly to their **unaware** prey and attack.

530

ACT Access Complex Text

Sentence Structure

Explain that the author uses punctuation and capitalization to add emphasis or excitement to the text.

- Point out the use of the ellipsis. *What do these three dots show?* (the passing of time) *What do the words before the ellipsis describe?* (The crocodile coming near its prey.)

- *What happens after the ellipsis?* (The animal is eaten.)

- *How does the author show the effect of what happens?* (Snap!)

Cold-blooded animals do not eat as often as warm-blooded animals.

Young alligators and crocodiles usually feed on small prey such as fish, frogs, and birds, using their powerful jaws and sharp teeth. Larger, older alligators and crocodiles may eat big animals such as raccoons and deer. Often they grab their prey and hold its nose underwater until the animal drowns. Also, they may leap to catch their prey. They eat by ripping the animal apart and swallowing the pieces whole.

STOP AND CHECK

Reread What do alligators and crocodiles eat? Reread to find the answer.

531

LITERATURE ANTHOLOGY, *pp. 530–531*

STOP AND CHECK

Reread What do alligators and crocodiles eat?

Teacher Think Aloud There is information about what alligators and crocodiles eat on pages 530 and 531. How can we recall facts and details about these animals?

Prompt students to apply the strategy in a Think Aloud by rereading. Have them turn to a partner to state what they have read in their own words.

Student Think Aloud I can reread the first sentence on page 530. Alligators and crocodiles are carnivores. By rereading the caption and looking at the illustrations, I know that they eat meat, or other animals. I can reread page 531 for examples of their prey. Young alligators and crocodiles eat smaller animals, such as fish, frogs and birds. Larger alligators and crocodiles eat bigger animals, such as raccoon and deer.

Reread

Author's Craft: Word Choice

What does *Snap!* tell you about the way alligators and crocodiles catch other animals? (They catch their prey by surprise and eat them very quickly. *Snap!* is the sound their mouths make when they close them.)

ELL Point out the caption about carnivores, and have students identify the different animals the alligators and crocodiles are eating in the pictures on pages 530 and 531.

• Then have pairs of students discuss different ways that alligators and crocodiles catch their prey.

• Point out that carnivore is a cognate. (carnívoro/a)

Read

9 Skill: Compare and Contrast

Compare how alligators and crocodiles move in water. How do they move around differently on land? (They are both good swimmers, use their tails and back legs to move and steer, tuck in legs to move faster. On land, they can crawl, walk, run, and "high walk.")

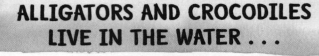

ALLIGATORS AND CROCODILES LIVE IN THE WATER . . .

They can swim up to 6 miles (9.6 kilometers) an hour.

They can stay underwater for as long as two hours.

9 Alligators and crocodiles are good swimmers and spend most of their time in the water. They use their powerful, swishing tails to move forward.

They are able to steer using their tails and back legs. By tucking in all four legs they are able to swim faster.

532

A C T Access Complex Text

▶ Genre

Remind students that the heading, illustrations, and captions add to and support the information presented in the text.

- Reread the sentence: *By tucking in all four legs they are able to swim faster.* Point out the alligators and crocodiles are swimming underwater.

... AND ON THE LAND.

CRAWL

WALK

RUN

HIGH WALK

They can crawl, walk, and run.
Sometimes they walk with their bodies high **10**
off the ground. This is called the "high walk."

533

LITERATURE ANTHOLOGY, *pp. 532–533*

Read

10 Vocabulary: Context Clues

What context clues in the surrounding paragraph can help you figure out or clarify the meaning of *high walk*? (Alligators and crocodiles can crawl, walk, and run. I can use the clues in the paragraph to learn that high walking is different from walking or crawling. The sentence on this page tells the reader that they can stretch their legs to be higher off the ground when they walk. This is known as "high walk.")

ELL Have students discuss the different ways alligators and crocodiles move.

Read

11 Ask and Answer Questions

COLLABORATE

Generate a question of your own about the text and share it with a partner. To find the answer, try rereading the text. For example, you might ask, "Why is it important that alligators and crocodiles have nerves on their bodies?" To find the answer, you can reread the captions and the text on page 534. (The nerves help them to pick up vibrations in the water. The vibrations tell them that there might be prey nearby. This is helpful when they are underwater and can't see well.)

Build Vocabulary page 534

detect: feel

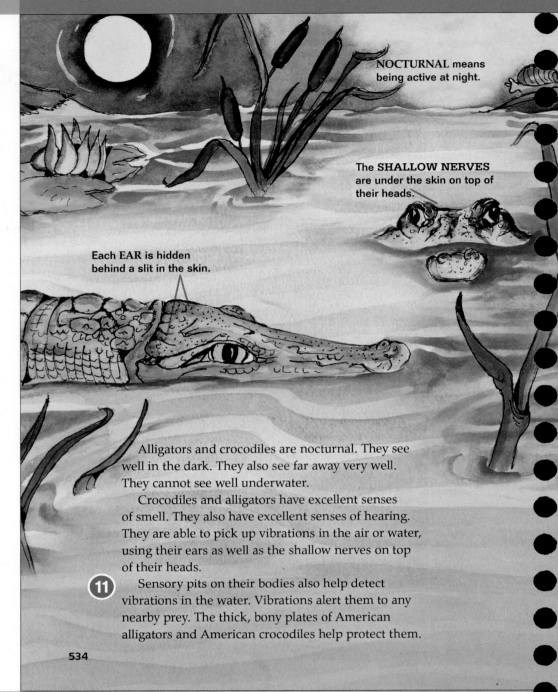

NOCTURNAL means being active at night.

The **SHALLOW NERVES** are under the skin on top of their heads.

Each **EAR** is hidden behind a slit in the skin.

Alligators and crocodiles are nocturnal. They see well in the dark. They also see far away very well. They cannot see well underwater.

Crocodiles and alligators have excellent senses of smell. They also have excellent senses of hearing. They are able to pick up vibrations in the air or water, using their ears as well as the shallow nerves on top of their heads.

11 Sensory pits on their bodies also help detect vibrations in the water. Vibrations alert them to any nearby prey. The thick, bony plates of American alligators and American crocodiles help protect them.

534

A C T Access Complex Text

▶ Connection of Ideas

Remind students to refer to the diagrams on pages 528–529. Connect the body parts of the alligators and crocodiles with how they are used on pages 534–535.

Alligators and crocodiles can make roaring, grumbling, and hissing sounds when they are protecting their territory. They will puff out their necks to show that they are ready to fight. **12**

During mating season, males and females communicate by making grunts, barks, and low, rumbling sounds. Often they rub snouts, blow bubbles on the water's surface, and swim together in circles. Sometimes they will make sounds by slapping the surface of the water to attract a mate. **13**

535

LITERATURE ANTHOLOGY, *pp. 534–535*

Read

12 Skill: Compare and Contrast

Compare and contrast the sounds alligators and crocodiles make for protection and the sounds they make for mating. (For protection, they make roaring, grumbling, and hissing sounds. They puff their necks to show they are ready to fight. When mating they make different sounds: grunts, barks, low rumbling sounds, slapping.)

13 Strategy: Reread
COLLABORATE

Reread pages 534 and 535. Turn to a partner and tell in your own words how alligators and crocodiles rely on their senses.

Student Think Aloud Alligators and crocodiles have an excellent sense of sight, smell, hearing, and touch. I can reread to remember that they must be able to see well if they are active at night. They use their ears and nerves to feel vibrations in the air or water. They can listen to the sounds of their mates to communicate during mating season.

Build Vocabulary page 535

   territory: area under control

ELL Read aloud the first paragraph on page 534. *Alligators and crocodiles are nocturnal. They see well in the dark.*

- Turn off the lights. Ask: *Can you see well in the dark?* (no) *Are we awake during the day or at night?* (day) *Are we nocturnal?* (no) *Are alligators and crocodiles nocturnal?* (yes)

- Have students list their strongest senses. Then have them list the strongest senses of an alligator and crocodile.

Read

⑭ Skill: Compare and Contrast

Compare and contrast an American alligator's nest with an American crocodile's nest. (Both keep eggs warm and protected on land. A female alligator lays about forty-five eggs on a mound of leaves and grasses. A female crocodile lays about fifty eggs in a hole and covers it with sand.)

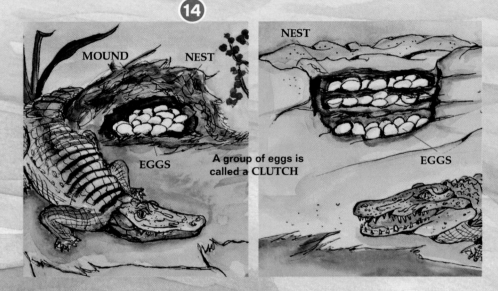

AN AMERICAN ALLIGATOR'S NEST

The female lays about forty-five eggs on a bed of leaves and grasses. She then completely covers them with a mound made of leaves, grasses, and mud. The mound is about 6 feet (1.8 meters) wide.

⑭

MOUND   NEST

EGGS

A group of eggs is called a CLUTCH

AN AMERICAN CROCODILE'S NEST

The female digs a hole in the ground and lays about fifty eggs. She covers each layer and the top with sand.

NEST

EGGS

A few weeks later the females lay their eggs in nests, where the eggs will be kept warm and protected. Mother alligators and crocodiles are always on the alert, guarding their nests to protect their young from any egg-eating animals, such as skunks and raccoons.

536

A C T Access Complex Text

▶ Genre

Remind students that the illustrations and captions are used with the text to give the reader a detailed understanding of the selection.

- *What do we learn from the captions and pictures that is not included in the main text?* (What alligator and crocodile nests look like, how many eggs the female lays, the temperature.)

- *What is a hatchling?* (A hatchling is a newborn alligator or crocodile) *How do they hatch?* (A baby may use its egg tooth to crack an egg open or the mother rolls the egg in her mouth to crack the shell.) *What do they look like?* (They look like smaller alligators and crocodiles, about 10 inches long.)

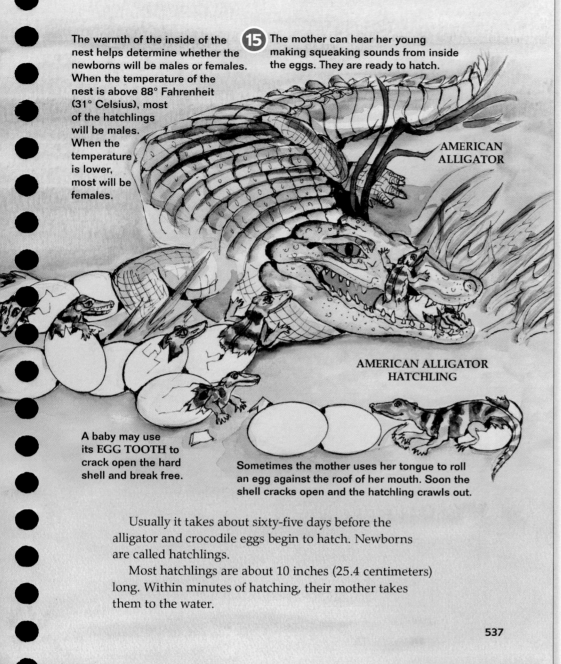

The warmth of the inside of the nest helps determine whether the newborns will be males or females. When the temperature of the nest is above 88° Fahrenheit (31° Celsius), most of the hatchlings will be males. When the temperature is lower, most will be females.

15 The mother can hear her young making squeaking sounds from inside the eggs. They are ready to hatch.

AMERICAN ALLIGATOR

AMERICAN ALLIGATOR HATCHLING

A baby may use its EGG TOOTH to crack open the hard shell and break free.

Sometimes the mother uses her tongue to roll an egg against the roof of her mouth. Soon the shell cracks open and the hatchling crawls out.

Usually it takes about sixty-five days before the alligator and crocodile eggs begin to hatch. Newborns are called hatchlings.

Most hatchlings are about 10 inches (25.4 centimeters) long. Within minutes of hatching, their mother takes them to the water.

537

LITERATURE ANTHOLOGY, *pp. 536–537*

15 **Skill: Make Inferences**

What would happen if most alligators brought their eggs to a cooler place? (There would be more female alligators.) What can alligators do to keep their nests warm? (dig a hole and cover with a mound made of leaves, grasses, and mud)

Reread   *Close Reading Companion*

Text Features: Illustrations and Captions

How does the author organize the information to help you understand the animals' nests? (The text explains that female alligators and crocodiles lay their eggs in nests. The illustrations show what the nests look like, and the captions explain how they are made and how many eggs they hold.) Why did the author put the nest illustrations side by side? (to make it easy to understand how the nests are similar and how they are different.)

ELL Read aloud the labels, and have students identify how alligators and crocodiles are hatched. Then have students make a list or illustrate other examples of animals that hatch from eggs.

Read

16 **Skill: Compare and Contrast**

Contrast the size of an American crocodile with the size of an American alligator. (An American alligator can grow to be about 12 feet long, while an American crocodile can grow to be about 20 feet long.)

Build Vocabulary page 538

marshlands: areas where the land is wet and mostly covered by grasses

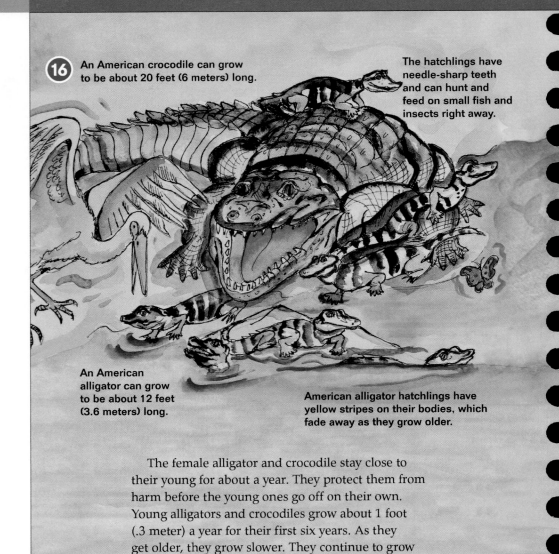

16 An American crocodile can grow to be about 20 feet (6 meters) long.

The hatchlings have needle-sharp teeth and can hunt and feed on small fish and insects right away.

An American alligator can grow to be about 12 feet (3.6 meters) long.

American alligator hatchlings have yellow stripes on their bodies, which fade away as they grow older.

The female alligator and crocodile stay close to their young for about a year. They protect them from harm before the young ones go off on their own. Young alligators and crocodiles grow about 1 foot (.3 meter) a year for their first six years. As they get older, they grow slower. They continue to grow throughout their lives.

Alligators and crocodiles use their strong legs, feet, and tails to dig holes in muddy marshlands. The holes fill with water. Other wildlife living nearby will also make use of these water holes.

538

A C T Access Complex Text

▶ Genre

Remind students that expository text uses features like captions to provide the reader with more information. Discuss with students the illustration and captions about hatchlings on page 538.

- *Can hatchlings hunt right away?* (yes) *What do they eat?* (small fish and insects)

- *What do hatchlings of American alligators look like?* (They have yellow stripes that fade away as they grow.)

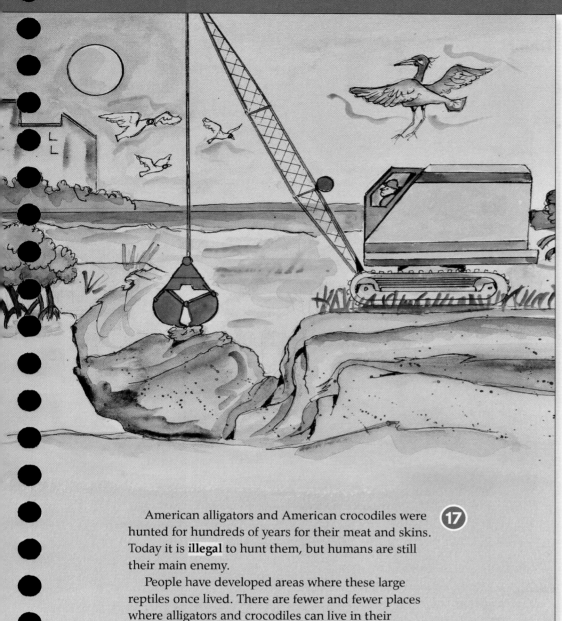

American alligators and American crocodiles were hunted for hundreds of years for their meat and skins. Today it is **illegal** to hunt them, but humans are still their main enemy.

People have developed areas where these large reptiles once lived. There are fewer and fewer places where alligators and crocodiles can live in their natural environment.

539

LITERATURE ANTHOLOGY, *pp. 538–539*

Read

17 Skill: Make Inferences

Why do you think laws were passed to make hunting alligators and crocodiles illegal? (Laws against hunting animals usually are meant to protect the animals from extinction.) What evidence from the text supports the inference that alligators and crocodiles need to be protected from humans? (The end of the first paragraph says "humans are still their main enemy.") What would happen if there were more laws against developing areas where alligators and crocodiles live? (There would be more natural environments in which these reptiles could live. The number of alligators and crocodiles would grow.)

CONNECT TO CONTENT
SCIENCE
LIVING THINGS NEED ENERGY

All living things have many different needs. All around us are examples of living things using their environment to get what they need. Almost all living things need food, water, sunlight, space to live, air, and the right temperature to grow and reproduce. Living things grow when cells divide and become other cells. The process continues until the person, plant, or animal has grown.

STEM

STOP AND CHECK

Ask and Answer Questions Why are alligators and crocodiles endangered? (They have been hunted for hundreds of years and their natural environment has been taken and used by people.)

STOP AND CHECK

Ask and Answer Questions Why are alligators and crocodiles endangered? Reread page 539 to find the answer.

540

A C T Access Complex Text

▶ Purpose

Remind students that a purpose of *Alligators and Crocodiles* is to provide the reader with information about how these two animals are fascinating but are now in danger of extinction.

- *Why does the author choose to tell us how long alligators and crocodiles have been around?* (They survived millions of years and are now in danger because people harm them and their environment.)

- *What is the purpose of the author telling us that these animals need to be respected?* (To tell the reader that it is up to the people to keep these animals safe because it is people who have left them in danger of extinction.)

ENDANGERED means
threatened with extinction.

Wildlife preserves have been created to
protect them.
   Alligators and crocodiles have been around
for millions of years. Now they are **endangered**.
The lives of these **fascinating** creatures should
be **respected**.

541

LITERATURE ANTHOLOGY, *pp. 540–541*

Read

Return to Purposes Review students'
predictions and purposes for reading. Ask
them to use text evidence to answer the
Essential Question. (Learning about animals
helps us to realize how they are special and
important. Alligators and crocodiles can
be found in many parts of the world. Their
features and abilities make them fascinating
creatures that we need to keep safe.)

ELL Students may have difficulty with the terms
endangered and *respected.*

- Have students point to the word danger within
  endangered.

- Then have students make a list of people and
  animals they *respect.*

About the Author and Illustrator

Read

Gail Gibbons

Have students read the biography of the author. Ask:

- What do many of Gail Gibbons's books have in common? How does she get her ideas for writing?

- How do her illustrations help readers better understand the topic?

Author's Purpose

To Inform

Remind students that authors who write to inform present the reader with information and examples. Students may say that the author includes illustrations and captions to add additional information. It is presented in a way to make the information easier for readers to understand.

Reread

Author's Point of View

Authors use points of view for different purposes. Point of view is the perspective of the narrator, or the person telling the story. The information in the selection is presented in the third person. The author includes facts to show the fascinating features and the importance of these animals. Which idea or statement from the text best indicates the author's point of view about the value and protection of these reptiles? (On page 541, the author states, "The lives of these fascinating creatures should be respected.")

About the Author and Illustrator

Gail Gibbons created her first picture book when she was four. She used yarn to hold the pages together. She studied art and went on to become an award-winning author and illustrator. Gail has written more than 170 nonfiction books about topics, such as dogs, dinosaurs, penguins, apples, knights, kites, and giant pandas. She lives mostly in Vermont, where she makes maple syrup in the spring. When she is not at home, you might find her in a tropical rain forest or at the top of a skyscraper! Gail travels around the world doing research for her books.

Author's Purpose
Why do you think the author wrote about alligators and crocodiles?

542

LITERATURE ANTHOLOGY, pp. 542–543

Respond to the Text

Summarize

Tell what you learned about alligators and crocodiles. The details from your Venn Diagram may help you summarize.

Write

Does Gail Gibbons do a good job organizing the information so that you understand how alligators and crocodiles are alike and different? Use these sentence frames to help organize text evidence.

> Gail Gibbons uses text features to . . .
> The illustrations and captions tell me . .
> This helps me understand . . .

Make Connections

Why did learning about alligators and crocodiles teach you to respect them? ESSENTIAL QUESTION

In what ways are people helping alligators and other endangered animals? TEXT TO WORLD

543

Integrate

Make Connections

COLLABORATE

Essential Question <u>Answer:</u> I learned that alligators and crocodiles are fascinating animals that deserve to be respected for many reasons. <u>Evidence:</u> On pages 524–525, I read that alligators and crocodiles have been around for 230 million years. On page 539, I read that humans are the biggest threat to alligators and crocodiles.

Text to World Responses will vary, but encourage students to do Internet research and cite text evidence.

Respond to the Text

Read

Summarize

Tell students they will use the information from their Compare and Contrast Venn diagrams to summarize. *As I read Alligators and Crocodiles, I collected information comparing and contrasting these two reptiles. To summarize, I will paraphrase, or reword, the most important details.*

Reread

Analyze the Text

After students summarize the selection, have them reread to develop a deeper understanding of the text and answer the questions on **Close Reading Companion** pages 187–189. For students who need support in citing text evidence, use the Reread prompts on pages T217D–T217W.

Write About the Text

Review the writing prompt and sentence frames. Remind students to use their responses from the **Close Reading Companion** to support their answers. For a full lesson on writing a response using text evidence, see page T222.

Answer: Yes. The author of "Alligators and Crocodiles" uses text, illustrations, diagrams, and maps to compare and contrast these two reptiles. <u>Evidence:</u> On page 532, both alligators and crocodiles are good swimmers. They move forward by swishing their tails.

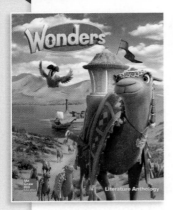

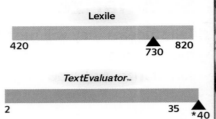

"The Monkey and the Crocodile"

Literature Anthology
Complex vocabulary places this selection above TextEvaluator range. Content is grade-level appropriate.

Text Complexity Range

Lexile

420   730   820

TextEvaluator™

2   35   *40

What makes this text complex?
▶ **Specific Vocabulary**

Compare Texts *Analytical Writing*

As students read and reread *The Monkey and the Crocodile*, encourage them to take notes and think about the Essential Question: *How can learning about animals help you respect them?* Tell students to think about how this text compares with *Alligators and Crocodiles*.

Read

1 **Skill: Character, Setting, Plot: Character**

What skills and qualities do Old Croc and Monkey have? (Old Croc is a great hunter. Monkey is clever, nimble, and fast.) How do they show these qualities? (Old Croc catches Monkey by hiding in the river and making his back look like a rock. Monkey tricks Old Croc into letting him go.)

Reread   *Close Reading Companion*

Author's Craft

How does the author help you visualize what Old Croc and Monkey are like? (The author uses words like "said the Old Croc with a toothy grin." This helps me picture that Old Croc is tricking Monkey.)

Genre • Folktale

Compare Texts

Read this folk tale about how Old Croc learns to respect Monkey.

The Monkey and the Crocodile
an African folktale

Old Croc was the greatest hunter on the Congo River. All the **wildlife** that lived there feared him. The only animal he couldn't catch was Monkey. Each day he watched Monkey scamper *fast, fast,* across the rocks in the river to play with his friends on the other side.

One day, Old Croc came up with a plan. He would catch Monkey and have him for lunch. Old Croc hid in the river so his back stuck out of the water like a rock, and he waited for Monkey to cross. When Monkey stepped on his back, Old Croc grabbed his tail. "You're caught, Monkey! Now I will eat you," he growled.

544

A C T   **A**ccess **C**omplex **T**ext

▶ **Specific Vocabulary**

Review strategies for finding the meaning of an unfamiliar word by using clues on the page, such as context clues and illustrations. Point out the words the author uses to describe Monkey's speed.

• *What clues helps us find the meaning of the word scamper?* (fast, fast across, couldn't catch)

Monkey, who was clever as well as nimble, said, "Oh, then it is too bad you can't climb the tamarind tree. It is a **requirement** that you must have a monkey with tamarind fruit. Otherwise, I am poisonous to eat."

Old Croc frowned. He was very hungry but he didn't want to eat a poisonous monkey. Then he had an idea.

"Oh, but *you* can climb, Monkey," said Old Croc with a toothy grin. "Go pick a fruit and bring it back to me."

"No problem!" said Monkey, and with a *hop, hop* **(1)** he jumped to the shore and climbed to the top of the tamarind tree. Then he laughed, "Old Croc, you have been tricked! You should know that a monkey is always too clever and fast to get caught by a crocodile."

With a grumble, Old Croc swam away and never tried to catch a monkey again.

Make Connections

Explain why Old Croc learns to respect monkeys. ESSENTIAL QUESTION

Discuss how this folktale is like other folktales. How is it different? TEXT TO TEXT

545

LITERATURE ANTHOLOGY, *pp. 544–545*

Read

Summarize

Guide students to summarize the selection.

Reread

Analyze the Text

After students read and summarize, have them reread to develop a deeper understanding of the text by annotating and answering questions on pages 190–192 of the **Close Reading Companion.**

Integrate

Make Connections

Essential Question <u>Answer:</u> Old Croc learns to respect monkeys because Monkey outsmarts him. <u>Evidence:</u> In paragraph 1 on page 545, Monkey makes up a story to trick Old Croc into letting him go. In paragraph 3 on that page, Old Croc falls for the trick and lets Monkey go.

Text to Text Responses may vary, but encourage students to cite text evidence from other folktales they have read.

- *How can we tell that Monkey is nimble?* (He is able to climb to the top of trees.)

- *Does clever mean the same as smart?* (Clever means to not only know a lot about something, but to be quick and alert.)

ELL Guide students to identify the features that helped Monkey, by looking at the image of Monkey. Have them point out and list what Monkey used to escape. *How does Old Croc feel at the end?* (sad, surprised) *Does he learn a lesson?* (yes)

→ Phonics/Fluency

MINILESSON 20 Mins

r-Controlled Vowel Syllables

Go Digital

r-Controlled Vowel Syllables

Present the Lesson

OBJECTIVES

CCSS Know and apply grade-level phonics and word analysis skills in decoding words. Decode words with common Latin suffixes. **RF.3.3b**

CCSS Read on-level text with purpose and understanding. **RF.3.4a**

CCSS Determine the meaning of the new word formed when a known affix is added to a known word (e.g., *agreeable/ disagreeable, comfortable/ uncomfortable, care/careless, heat/ preheat*). **L.3.4b**

Rate: 97–117 WCPM

ACADEMIC LANGUAGE

• phrasing
• Cognate: *fraseo*

Refer to the sound transfers chart in the **Language Transfers Handbook** to identify sounds that do not transfer in Spanish, Cantonese, Vietnamese, Hmong, and Korean.

1 Explain

Remind students that every syllable in a word has one vowel sound. Point out that when a vowel is followed by the letter *r*, both letters remain in the same syllable and act as a team to form a special vowel sound called an *r*-controlled vowel syllable.

2 Model

Write the word *person* on the board. Model identifying the letters *er* in the first syllable. Underline the syllable *per*. Model how to say the word, pronouncing each syllable. Run your finger under each syllable as you sound out the whole word.

3 Guided Practice

Write the following list of words on the board. Guide students as they identify the *r*-controlled vowel syllable and then pronounce each full word.

sister	winter	circus
artist	partner	cellar
purple	later	garlic

View "Butterflies Big and Small"

Read Multisyllabic Words

Transition to Longer Words Help students transition to reading longer words with *r*-controlled vowel syllables. Draw a T-chart. In the first column write *author, director, store*, and *remark*. In the second column, write *authority, directory, restore*, and *remarkable*. Point to the words in the first column and explain that each word contains an *r*-controlled vowel syllable. Model how to read each word. Have students repeat.

Explain that the words in the second column contain a word with an *r*-controlled vowel syllable from the first column. Have students identify and underline the *r*-controlled vowel in each word. Point to each word in random order and have students read the words chorally.

Latin Suffixes

1 Explain

Suffixes are added to the ends of words and change the meaning of the words. The Latin suffixes *-able* and *-ment* change the part of speech and sometimes change the spelling of the root word.

- The suffix *-able* means "able to." When added to a word that ends in a consonant + *e*, the final *e* is often dropped (*excite + able = excitable*).

- The suffix *-ment* means "an act of doing something." When added to a base word that ends in a consonant + *e*, the final *e* may be dropped (*argue + ment = argument*).

2 Model

Write and say the words *agreeable* and *movement*. Have students repeat the words. Underline the suffixes in each one. Model using the definition of each suffix to figure out the meaning of the words.

3 Guided Practice

Write the words *bendable, enjoyable, payment,* and *enjoyment* on the board. Have students say each word and identify the suffix. Then have students determine the meaning of each word.

Phrasing

Explain/Model Remind students that appropriate phrasing means grouping words to convey meaning and understanding to the text. Point out that paying attention to punctuation marks is a good way to know how to group words.

Model reading the first paragraph on page 451 of "Butterflies Big and Small" Emphasize paying attention to the dash used in the second sentence. Point out how the dash and other punctuation marks help you use appropriate phrasing.

Practice/Apply Divide the class into two groups and have the groups alternate reading the sentences. Remind students to use appropriate phrasing. Offer feedback as needed.

Daily Fluency Practice FLUENCY

Students can practice fluency using **Your Turn Practice Book.**

Monitor and *Differentiate*

 Quick Check

Can students decode words with *r*-controlled vowel syllables? Can students read words with Latin suffixes and use the suffixes to determine the meanings of the words? Can students read fluently?

Small Group Instruction

If No →	Approaching Level	Reteach pp. T232, T234
	ELL	Develop p. T250
If Yes →	On Level	Review p. T240
	Beyond Level	Extend p. T244

ON-LEVEL PRACTICE BOOK p. 288

A. Read each sentence. Underline the word with an *r*-controlled vowel syllable. Write the word on the line. Then circle the *r*-controlled vowel syllable.

1. She put the canned fruit in the cool cellar.   cellar
2. The author read from his new book.   author
3. I hope to go to the skating rink later.   later
4. My dad is helping his friend restore an old truck.   restore
5. The circus was in town last week.   circus

B. Read the words with the Latin suffixes *-able* and *-ment* in the box. Match a word from the box to each meaning below. Write the word on the line. Not all words will be used.

movement	usable	excitement	argument
adorable	enjoyable	agreeable	encouragement

1. an act of arguing   argument
2. able to be used   usable
3. an act of moving   movement
4. able to be adored   adorable
5. an act of encouraging   encouragement
6. able to be enjoyed   enjoyable

APPROACHING p. 288	BEYOND p. 288	ELL p. 288

→ Write to Sources

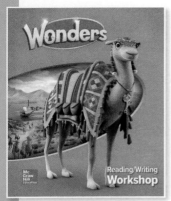

Reading/Writing Workshop

OBJECTIVES

CCSS Write informative/explanatory texts to examine a topic and convey ideas and information clearly. Provide a concluding statement or section. **W.3.2d**

CCSS Write routinely over extended time frames (time for research, reflection, and revision) and shorter time frames (a single sitting or a day or two) for a range of discipline-specific tasks, purposes, and audiences. **W.3.10**

ACADEMIC LANGUAGE

conclusion

Go Digital

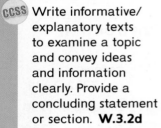

U6W4 Organization: Strong Conclusions

DAY 1

Writing Fluency

Write to a Prompt Provide students with the prompt: *Describe butterflies.* Have students share their ideas about butterflies. *How are Monarch and Western Pygmy Blue butterflies similar and different?* When students finish sharing ideas, have them write continuously for fifteen minutes in their Writer's Notebook. If students stop writing, encourage them to keep going.

 When students finish writing, have them work with a partner to compare ideas and make sure that they both have a clear understanding of the topic.

Writing Process — Genre Writing

Research Report pp. T350–T355

Fourth Week Focus: Over the course of the week, focus on the following stages of the writing process:

Expert Model Discuss the Expert Model found online at Writer's Workspace. Work with students to identify the features of a research report.

Prewrite Teach the minilesson on organization. Analyze the Model Main Idea and Details Chart found online at Writer's Workspace. Provide blank Main Idea and Details Chart found online at Writer's Workspace, and have students use the chart to brainstorm topics that are important to them.

DAY 2

Write to the Reading/Writing Workshop Text

Analyze the Prompt Read aloud the first paragraph on page 456 of the **Reading/Writing Workshop**. Ask: *What is the prompt asking?* (to describe butterfly migration) Say: *Let's reread to see find details about migration. We can note text evidence.*

Analyze Text Evidence Display Graphic Organizer 57 in Writer's Workspace. Say: *Let's see how one student, Collin, took notes to answer the prompt. He notes that Monarch butterflies migrate from the northern United States and Canada to Mexico.* Guide the class through the rest of Collin's notes.

Analyze the Student Model Explain how Collin used text evidence from his notes to write a response to the prompt.

- **Main Idea** The main idea is the most important point that the author wants to communicate to the reader. Collin clearly states his main idea in his short, simple first sentence. Trait: Ideas

- **Supporting Details** Collin used his notes and text evidence to provide details about butterflies and their migrations. These details support his main idea. Trait: Ideas

- **Strong Conclusion** The conclusion of an informative text sums up the main ideas and details of the writing. Collin concludes strongly by restating his main idea. Trait: Organization

For additional practice with organization and strong conclusions, assign **Your Turn Practice Book** page 289.

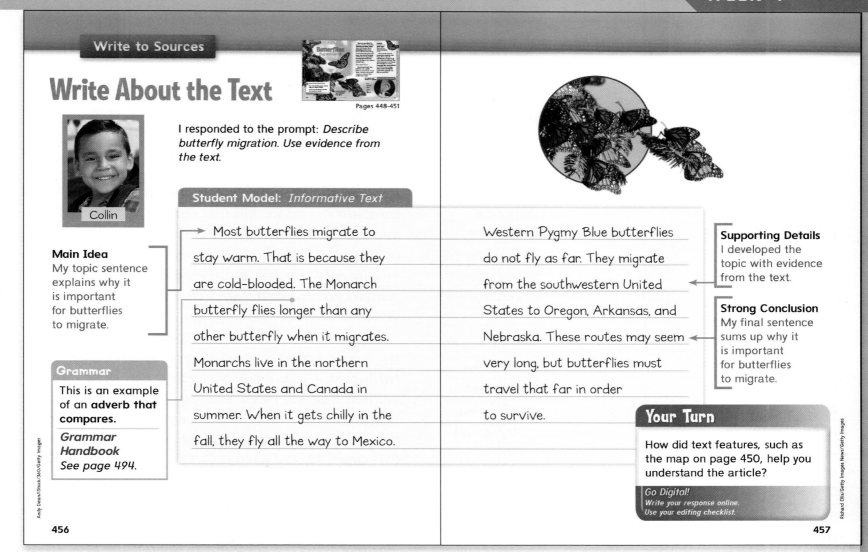

Write to Sources

Write About the Text

Pages 448-451

I responded to the prompt: *Describe butterfly migration. Use evidence from the text.*

Collin

Main Idea
My topic sentence explains why it is important for butterflies to migrate.

Grammar

This is an example of an **adverb that compares.**

Grammar Handbook
See page 494.

Student Model: *Informative Text*

Most butterflies migrate to stay warm. That is because they are cold-blooded. The Monarch butterfly flies longer than any other butterfly when it migrates. Monarchs live in the northern United States and Canada in summer. When it gets chilly in the fall, they fly all the way to Mexico.

Western Pygmy Blue butterflies do not fly as far. They migrate from the southwestern United States to Oregon, Arkansas, and Nebraska. These routes may seem very long, but butterflies must travel that far in order to survive.

Supporting Details
I developed the topic with evidence from the text.

Strong Conclusion
My final sentence sums up why it is important for butterflies to migrate.

Your Turn

How did text features, such as the map on page 450, help you understand the article?

Go Digital!
Write your response online.
Use your editing checklist.

456

457

READING/WRITING WORKSHOP, *pp. 456–457*

Your Turn Writing Read the Your Turn prompt on page 457 of the Reading/Writing Workshop aloud. Discuss the prompt with students. If necessary, remind students that "compare and contrast" means to tell how two or more things are similar and different.

Have students take notes as they look for text evidence to answer the prompt. Remind them to include the following elements as they craft their response from their notes:

- Main Idea
- Supporting Details
- Strong Conclusion

Have students use **Grammar Handbook** page 494 in the Reading/Writing Workshop to edit and correct improper use of adverbs that compare.

ELL ENGLISH LANGUAGE LEARNERS SCAFFOLD

Beginning

Write Help students complete the sentence frames.
The Monarch butterfly's route is ____.
The Western Pygmy Blue butterfly's route is ____.

Intermediate

Describe Ask students to complete the sentence frames. Encourage students to provide details.
The Western Pygmy Blue butterflies migrates ____. The Monarch also migrates, but ____.

Advanced/High

Discuss Check for understanding. Ask: *How are the migrations of the Monarch and Western Pygmy Blue butterflies alike? How are they different?*

Write to Sources

DAY 3 For students who need support to complete the writing assignment for the Literature Anthology, provide the following instruction.

DAY 4

Write to the Literature Anthology Text

Analyze the Prompt Explain that students will write about *Alligators and Crocodiles* on **Literature Anthology** pages 520–541. Provide the following prompt: *Does Gail Gibbons do a good job organizing the information so that you understand how alligators and crocodiles are alike and different?* Ask: *What is the prompt asking you to do?* (to analyze how the author compares and contrasts two reptiles)

Analyze Text Evidence Help students note evidence.

Page 526 Examine the map. Ask: *How does this map help you understand how alligators and crocodiles are alike and different?* (The map shows that both reptiles are found in areas near the Equator. It also shows that crocodiles inhabit many areas of the world, but alligators inhabit only part of North America.)

Pages 528–529 Examine the diagrams. Ask: *Why are the alligator and crocodile shown in the same pose and facing in the same direction?* (So they can be easily compared.) *Why is this important to the reader?*

Encourage students to look for more text features that compare and contrast. Then have them craft a short response. Use the conference routine below.

Write to Two Sources

Analyze the Prompt Explain that students will compare *Alligators and Crocodiles* and "The Monkey and the Crocodile." Provide students with the following prompt: *Was Old Croc like a real crocodile? Why or why not? Use text evidence from two sources to support your answer.* Ask: *What is the prompt asking you to do?* (to describe the ways Old Croc was the same as and different from a real crocodile) Say: *On page 530, I read that alligators and crocodiles are carnivores. A caption explains that carnivores are animals that eat meat. So in my notes, I will write:* Alligators and crocodiles both eat meat. *I will also note the page number and the title of the source. On page 544, I read that Old Croc was the greatest hunter on the Congo River. I will add this to my notes.*

Analyze Text Evidence Display online Graphic Organizer 58 in Writer's Workspace. Say: *Let's see how one student took notes to answer the prompt. Here are Collin's notes.* Read through the text evidence for each selection and have students point out details and discuss ways in which Old Croc is similar to and different from a real crocodile.

Teacher Conferences

STEP 1

Talk about the strengths of the writing.

The opening is strong. It clearly states the main idea and tells me what the response will be about.

STEP 2

Focus on how the writer uses text evidence.

You cite text evidence well in your first paragraph, but you need to add some details from the text to support your ideas in your second paragraph.

STEP 3

Make concrete suggestions.

The conclusion could be stronger. Try rewriting it to more clearly summarize your ideas.

DAY

5

Share the Prompt Provide the following prompt to students: *Compare and contrast how crocodiles and alligators move. Use evidence from* Alligators and Crocodiles *and "The Monkey and the Crocodile" to support your answer.*

Find Text Evidence Have students take notes. Find text evidence and give guidance where needed. If necessary, review with students how to paraphrase. Remind them to write the page number and source of the information.

Analyze the Student Model Review the prompt and Collin's notes from Day 4. Display the student model on page 290 of the **Your Turn Practice Book**. Explain to students that Collin synthesized his notes to write a response to the prompt. Discuss the page together with students or have them do it independently.

Write the Response Review the prompt from Day 4 with students. Have students use their notes to craft a short response. Remind them that they took notes on this prompt on Day 4. Tell students to include the title of both sources and the following elements:

- Main Idea
- Supporting Details
- Strong Conclusion

COLLABORATE

Share and Reflect Have students share their responses with a partner. Use the Peer Conference routine below.

Suggested Revisions

Provide specific direction to help focus young writers.

Focus on a Sentence
Read the draft and target one sentence for revision. *Rewrite this sentence by adding an adverb that compares to explain ___.*

Focus on a Section
Underline a section that needs to be revised. *I want to know more about ___. Provide more supporting details.*

Focus on a Revision Strategy
Underline a section. Have students use a specific revision strategy, such as using transitions. *There are good ideas and details in your writing, but they are not connected to each other. Add transitions to make your writing clearer.*

Peer Conferences

Focus peer responses on adding details to support the topic. Provide these questions:

- Does the opening sentence clearly state the main idea?
- Does the writing include details that support the main idea?
- Is the writing clear and well organized, and does it have a strong conclusion?

Grammar: Adverbs That Compare

Reading/Writing Workshop

OBJECTIVES

CCSS Explain the function of nouns, pronouns, verbs, adjectives, and adverbs in general and their functions in particular sentences. **L.3.1a**

CCSS Form and use comparative and superlative adjectives and adverbs, and choose between them depending on what is to be modified. **L.3.1g**

Identify and use adverbs that compare

Write on the board slow and fast. Then write: *[She/He] jogs _____ than Robin. Maureen jogs _____ of all.* Choose an adverb and ask a student to complete both of the sentences. Ask other students to complete the sentences with a word they choose.

DAY 1

DAILY LANGUAGE ACTIVITY

Tomorrow I was having my friend and her mother over. We are all going to bake cookies by themselves.
(1: Tomorrow,; 2: am; 3: ourselves.)

Introduce Adverbs That Compare

- Adverbs can be used to compare two or more actions. To compare using most one-syllable adverbs, add *-er* or *-est*:
    Jay runs **faster** than me.
    Mara runs **fastest** of all.

- *More* and *most* are used with adverbs with two or more syllables. When using *more* or *most,* do not change adverbs' endings to make comparisons:
    We opened the jar **more carefully** the second time.

Discuss adverbs that compare using page 494 of the Grammar Handbook.

DAY 2

DAILY LANGUAGE ACTIVITY

dina have two watchs. Sometime she wears both.
(1: Dina; 2: has; 3: watches.;
4: Sometimes,)

Review Adverbs That Compare

Have students share rules for deciding whether to add *-er* or *-est* or to use *more* and *most.*

Introduce More Adverbs That Compare

- To make comparisons using the adverb *well,* use *better* and *best:*
    I did **well** at the science fair.
    Lauren did **best** of all. She won the grand prize.

- To make comparisons using *badly,* use *worse* and *worst*:
    My plant did **badly** when it got lots of sun.
    It did even **worse** when I gave it more water.

 # TALK ABOUT IT

COLLABORATE

ADD COMPARATIVE ADVERBS

Have pairs write five sentences each about why it is important to protect animals' habitats. Have them trade and write a companion sentence for each, using adverbs that compare. (For example: Animals in a protected habitat will live long lives. Animals in a protected habitat will live *longer.*)

DESCRIBE USING ADVERBS

Have partners each write five reasons why learning about animals will help people respect them. Students will take turns reading a sentence and then rewrite the sentence by adding a form of *well* or *bad* to it.

DAY 3

I think I will where my pink green and white sweater. It is the most pretty sweater I own.

(1: wear; 2: pink, green,; 3: prettiest)

Mechanics and Usage: Using More and Most

- Add -er or -est to the end of short adverbs to compare.

- Use *more* and *most* with adverbs that have two or more syllables.

- Adverbs that are used with *more* or *most* do not change their endings to make comparisons.

- Use comparative adverbs to compare two actions. The superlative form of an adverb is used to compare three or more actions.

As students write, refer them to Grammar Handbook page 494.

DAY 4

Third grade is more hard than second grade. I has the more difficultest class this year.

(1: harder; 2: have; 3: most difficult)

Proofread

1. I tried to ran more fast, but I still missed the bus. (1: run; 2: faster)

2. The sun reflects more bright here. I need a more good coat of sunscreen. (1: brighter; 2: better)

3. Sam did the most good on the test. Mr. Simms said the rest of us should study more hard. (1: best; 2: harder)

4. Ham sandwiches taste the most bad. I like turkey the most good. (1: worst; 2: best)

Have students check work using Grammar Handbook page 494.

DAY 5

I want to goes to new york but I have to convince my sister. She wants to go to florida

(1: go; 2: New York,; 3: Florida.)

Assess

Use the Daily Language Activity and Grammar Practice Reproducibles page 145 for assessment.

Reteach

Use Grammar Practice Reproducibles pages 141–144 and selected pages from the Grammar Handbook for reteaching. Remind students that it is important to use comparative and superlative adverbs correctly as they read, write, and speak.

Check students' writing for use of the skill and listen for it in their speaking. Assign Grammar Revision Assignments in their Writer's Notebooks as needed.

See Grammar Practice Reproducibles pages 141–145.

FIND THE ADVERBS

Ask pairs to find paragraphs that contain sentences with comparative and superlative adverbs. Taking turns, have one partner read a sentence to the other partner, who will identify the adverbs. Have them discuss each adverb and its function in the sentence.

ADVERB QUESTION QUIZ

Students can write five sentences using comparative adverbs. Sentences should relate to what can be done to protect endangered animals. Taking turns, each student reads a sentence. The other students will identify the adverb using a question form.

QUESTION AND ANSWER

Have each group member think of an endangered animal and write the name, keeping it secret. The others will take turns asking questions to guess the animal. Questions and answers should include comparative and superlative adverbs.

Spelling: *r*-Controlled Vowel Syllables

OBJECTIVES

CCSS Use spelling patterns and generalizations (e.g., *word families, position-based spellings, syllable patterns, ending rules, meaningful word parts*) in writing words. **L.3.2f**

CCSS Consult reference materials, including beginning dictionaries, as needed to check and correct spellings. **L.3.2g**

Spelling Words

severe	cellar	garlic
prepared	trailer	partner
declare	author	restore
later	person	sister
writer	circus	actor

Review explained, brief, enjoys
Challenge circular, editor

Differentiated Spelling

Approaching Level

sister	better	artists
remark	silver	report
winter	cellar	dirty
doctor	actor	severe
later	author	circus

Beyond Level

circular	cellar	circus
restore	trailer	border
feather	partner	market
dancer	author	further
later	expert	desert

DAY 1

Assess Prior Knowledge

Display the spelling words. Read them aloud, drawing out the *r*-controlled vowel syllables.

Model for students how to spell the word *sister*. Draw a line between the syllables: *sis/ter*. Point out that students should note the *r*-controlled vowel syllable, *ter*, isolating it from the rest of the word before spelling the entire word.

Demonstrate sorting the spelling words by pattern under key words *later, cellar, actor,* and *restore.* (Write the words on index cards or the IWB.) Sort a few words, pointing out the *r*-controlled vowel syllables. Have them say each word and identify the *r*-controlled vowels in each word.

Then use the Dictation Sentences from Day 5. Say the underlined word, read the sentence, and repeat the word. Have students write the words.

DAY 2

Spiral Review

Review the vowel team syllables in the words *explained, brief,* and *enjoys.* Have students find words in this week's readings with the same sounds. Use the Dictation Sentences below for the review words. Read the sentence, say the word, and have students write the words.

1. Tabitha <u>explained</u> her idea.
2. The meeting was <u>brief</u>.
3. Brock <u>enjoys</u> his family.

Have partners check the spellings.

Challenge Words Review this week's spelling words, pointing out the *r*-controlled vowel syllables. Use these Dictation Sentences for challenge words. Read the sentence, say the word, have students write the word.

1. They have a <u>circular</u> driveway.
2. The magazine <u>editor</u> quit last week.

Have students write the words in their word study notebook.

 WORD SORTS

COLLABORATE

OPEN SORT

Have students cut apart the **Spelling Word Cards BLM** in the Online Resource Book and initial the backs of each card. Have them read the words aloud with a partner. Then have partners do an **open sort**. Have them record the sort in their word study notebook.

PATTERN SORT

Complete the **pattern** sort using the key words, pointing out the *r*-controlled vowel syllables. Have students use Spelling Word Cards to do their own pattern sort. A partner can compare and check their sorts.

DAY 3

Word Meanings

Write the groups of words below on the board. Have students copy them into their Writer's Notebooks and complete each group by adding a spelling word.

1. created, made, organized, ____ (prepared)
2. hard, strict, serious ____ (severe)
3. carnival, sideshow, ____ (circus)
4. in the future, not now, ____ (later)
5. attic, garage, ____ (cellar)

Challenge students to think of other word groups that use spelling, review, or challenge words.

DAY 4

Proofread and Write

Write these sentences on the board. Have students circle and correct each misspelled word. Remind students they can use print or electronic resources to check and correct spelling.

1. The acter appeared lator in the show. (actor, later)
2. The writor spoke to my sistor. (writer, sister)
3. The cercus clowns kept their costumes in a special trailor. (circus, trailer)

Error Correction Remind students to separate each word into syllables, paying particular attention to the *r*-controlled vowel syllable. They should sound out each syllable before attempting to spell or write the word.

DAY 5

Assess

Use the Dictation Sentences for the Posttest. Have students list misspelled words in their word study notebooks. Look for students' use of these words in their writings.

Dictation Sentences

1. The cramp from swimming was <u>severe</u>.
2. The campers came <u>prepared</u>.
3. <u>Declare</u> your thoughts about the story.
4. We will write the songs <u>later</u>.
5. She is a talented <u>writer</u>.
6. My house doesn't have a <u>cellar</u>.
7. The horse traveled in a <u>trailer</u>.
8. I met my favorite <u>author</u> at the bookstore!
9. Her mom was a nice <u>person</u>.
10. Will someone take us to the <u>circus</u>?
11. I like the taste of <u>garlic</u>.
12. The teacher asked us to pick a <u>partner</u>.
13. We want to <u>restore</u> the historic site.
14. This girl is my <u>sister</u>.
15. That <u>actor</u> could play anyone.

Have students self-correct the tests.

See Phonics/Spelling Reproducibles pp. 169–174.

SPEED SORT

Have partners do a **speed sort** to see who is faster. Then have partners write sentences for each spelling word, leaving blanks where the words should go. Have them trade sentences and fill in the blanks.

BLIND SORT

Have partners do a **blind sort**: one reads a spelling word card; the other tells under which key word it belongs. Have them take turns until both have sorted all their words. Then have students explain how they sorted the words.

→ Build Vocabulary

DAY 1

Connect to Words

Practice this week's vocabulary.

1. Name an **endangered** animal.
2. What animals do you find **fascinating**?
3. Why is it usually **illegal** to pollute?
4. What animals have **inhabited** your local area?
5. Describe two **requirements** people need to live.
6. Tell about a person who is **respected**.
7. Why are some people **unaware** of the dangers animals face?
8. Give an example of **wildlife** you have seen.

DAY 2

Expand Vocabulary

Help students generate different forms of this week's words by adding, changing, or removing inflectional endings.

- Draw a four-column chart. Write *endanger* in the left column. Then write *endangered, endangers,* and *endangering* in the other columns. Read aloud the words and discuss the meanings.

- Have students share sentences with each form of *endanger*.

- Students can fill in the chart for other words, such as *inhabited*.

- Have students copy the chart in their word study notebook.

 BUILD MORE VOCABULARY

COLLABORATE

ACADEMIC VOCABULARY

Discuss important academic words.

- Display *conservation* and *protection* and discuss the meanings with students.

- Display *conserve* and *conservation*. Have partners look up and define related words.

- Write the related words on the board. Have partners ask and answer questions using the words. Repeat with *protection*. Elicit examples from students.

GREEK AND LATIN ROOTS

- Review Greek and Latin roots. Write the word *inhabited* on the board. Identify the root *habit* and explain that it comes from the Latin *habitare,* meaning "to live in."

- Have partners generate other examples with the root *habit,* such as *habitat,* or other Greek or Latin roots. They may check roots and meanings in an online or print dictionary.

- Invite partners to share their words and discuss the meanings of the words as a class.

OBJECTIVES

CCSS Use sentence-level context as a clue to the meaning of a word or phrase. **L.3.4a**

CCSS Use a known root word as a clue to the meaning of an unknown word with the same root (e.g., *company, companion*). **L.3.4c**

CCSS Identify real-life connections between words and their use (e.g., describe people who are *friendly* or *helpful*). **L.3.5b**

Expand vocabulary by adding inflectional endings and suffixes.

Vocabulary Words

endangered	requirement
fascinating	respected
illegal	unaware
inhabited	wildlife

 ELL

Have partners practice using this week's words in an oral presentation, such as a brief retelling of a selection or a description of a character, event, or scientific process. Help them plan their presentations.

DAY

3

Reinforce the Words

Review this week's vocabulary words. Have students orally complete each sentence stem.

1. The ____ inhabited the rainforest.

2. Why do you think ____ are endangered?

3. It is illegal to dump ____ here.

4. My ____ is a respected person in our area.

5. That book was fascinating because ____.

6. My friends were unaware that I had a new ____.

DAY

4

Connect to Writing

- Have students write sentences in their word study notebooks using this week's vocabulary.

- Tell them to write sentences that provide information about the words and their meanings.

- Provide the Day 3 sentence stems for students needing extra support.

Write About Vocabulary Have students write something they learned from this week's words in their word study notebook. For example, they might write about an *endangered* animal. What is *fascinating* or unique about the animal?

DAY

5

Word Squares

Ask students to create Word Squares for each vocabulary word.

- In the first square, students write the word. (example: *illegal*)

- In the second square, students write their own definition of the word and any related words. (example: *against the law*)

- In the third square, students draw a simple illustration that will help them remember the word. (example: a no parking sign)

- In the fourth square, students write non-examples. (examples: *legal, allowed*)

- Have students share their Word Squares with a partner.

PARAGRAPH CLUES

Remind students that they should look for clues within a paragraph to help them determine the meanings of unfamiliar words.

- Display **Your Turn Practice Book** pages 283–284. Read the first paragraph. Model figuring out the meaning of *concern*.

- For additional practice with paragraph clues, have students complete page 287.

- Discuss the clues students identified for unfamiliar words.

SHADES OF MEANING

Help students generate words related to *fascinating*.

- Discuss the meaning of *fascinating*. As a class, identify a few synonyms, such as *intriguing* and *charming*. Write the words on a word web.

- Have partner work together to list other synonyms.

- Discuss the synonyms that the students identified and write the words on the word web.

- Ask students to copy the words in their word study notebook.

MORPHOLOGY

Use the word *endanger* as a springboard for students to learn more words.

- Write *danger* and discuss its meaning. Then write the prefix *en-*, noting that it means "to make, to put in, or to be in." Use the prefix and base word to discuss the meaning of *endanger*.

- Elicit or suggest other words with the prefix *en-*, such as *enable, enact, enliven, enjoy*.

- Tell students to use the prefix and base words to determine the meanings of the words.

VOCABULARY **T229**

Integrate Ideas

Close Reading Routine

Read   DOK 1–2

- Identify key ideas and details about respecting animals.
- Take notes and summarize.
- Use **A C T** prompts as needed.

Reread   DOK 2–3

- Analyze the text, craft, and structure.
- Use the **Close Reading Companion.**

Integrate   DOK 4

- Integrate knowledge and ideas.
- Make text-to-text connections.
- Use the Integrate lesson.
- Use *Close Reading Companion,* p. 193.

TEXT CONNECTIONS

Connect to the Essential Question

Write the essential question on the board: How can learning about animals help you respect them? Divide the class into small groups. Tell students that each group will compare the information that they have learned about how learning about animals can help people protect them. Model how to compare this information by using examples from this week's **Leveled Readers** and "Butterflies Big and Small," **Reading/Writing Workshop** pages 448–451.

Evaluate Text Evidence Have students review their class notes and completed graphic organizers before they begin their discussions. Encourage students to compare information from all the week's reads. Have each group pick one student to take notes. Explain that each group

Animals

Abilities

How can learning about animals help us respect them?

Dinah Zike's
FOLDABLES
Study Organizer

Animals

 RESEARCH AND INQUIRY

Create Illustrations

Explain that students will work with a partner to complete a short research project about an interesting animal. Then students will create three illustrations of the animal with captions explaining its abilities. Discuss the following steps:

1. **Brainstorm Animals** As students begin thinking about which animal they might choose, discuss the online Fact Sheet. Encourage them to also think of the selections they read this week.

2. **Find Resources** Students should explore appropriate print or digital sources to raise and answer questions about their animal. They should list their source information.

OBJECTIVE

CCSS Compare and contrast the most important points and key details presented in two texts on the same topic. **RI.3.9**

will use a Three-Tab Foldable® to record their ideas. You may wish to model how to use a Three-Tab Foldable® to record comparisons.

Text to Media

Post Online Remind students to discuss their responses to the Blast along with information from all the week's reads. Tell students to include the photograph on page 193 of the **Close Reading Companion** as a part of their discussion. Guide students to see the connections among media, the photograph, and text. Ask: *How does the Blast connect to what you read this week? To the photograph?*

Present Ideas and Synthesize Information

When students finish their discussions, ask for a volunteer from each group to read his or her notes aloud.

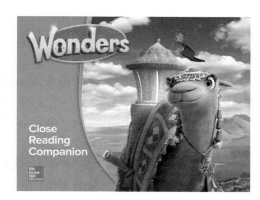

❸ **Guided Practice** Have students take notes about the abilities of the animal they have chosen. They should begin thinking about the captions they will write for their illustrations.

❹ **Create the Project: Create Illustrations** Have students use their research and the photographs they found to create illustrations and captions exploring the animal's interesting ability. Tell students to use descriptive words in their captions.

Present the Illustrations

Have students present their illustrations and captions to the class. Remind students to speak clearly at an understandable pace and in complete sentences as they present their illustrations. Conduct a class discussion about what they learned from each illustration. Have students use the online Research Process Checklist 3 to evaluate their research. Encourage students to post their illustrations on the Shared Research Board.

OBJECTIVES

CCSS Conduct short research projects that build knowledge about a topic. **W.3.7**

CCSS Determine the main ideas and supporting details of a text read aloud or information presented in diverse media and formats, including visually, quantitatively, and orally. **SL.3.2**

CCSS Speak in complete sentences when appropriate to task and situation in order to provide requested detail or clarification. **SL.3.6**

ACADEMIC LANGUAGE

abilities, illustration, caption

→ Approaching Level

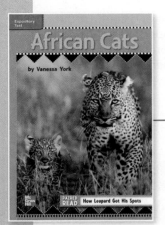

Lexile 580
TextEvaluator 25

OBJECTIVES

Use information gained from illustrations (e.g., maps, photographs) and the words in a text to demonstrate understanding of the text (e.g., where, when, why, and how key events occur). **RI.3.7**

• Compare and contrast at least two things in a text.

• Reread text to check understanding.

• Use paragraph clues to determine the meanings of words.

ACADEMIC LANGUAGE

reread, compare, contrast, paragraph clues, map, diagram

Leveled Reader:
African Cats

Go
Digital

Leveled Readers

Before Reading

Preview and Predict

Have students read the Essential Question. Then have them read the title and table of contents of *African Cats*. Have students make two predictions about the text and share them with partners.

Review Genre: Expository Text

Review with students that an expository text can tell information about a science topic. It often contains text features such as headings, photographs and captions, labels, and diagrams. As they preview *African Cats*, have students identify features of expository text.

During Reading

Fill in the Graphic Organizer

Close Reading

Note Taking Have students use their graphic organizer as they read.

Pages 2–4 *What does the map on page 3 show?* (where cats live in Africa) Point out the word *pride* on page 4. *Which words in the paragraph help you know the meaning of the word* pride? (*family groups*)

Pages 5–7 *Turn to a partner and describe how a male lion's job is different from a female lion's job.* (The male lion's job is to defend its territory. The female's job is to hunt and provide food for the pride.) *How are leopards different from lions? Use the conjunction* but *to contrast the two.* (Leopards prefer to live alone, but lions live in a pride.)

Pages 8–9 *What is the conservation status of cheetahs, according to the sidebar on page 8?* (near threatened) *How are cheetahs different from lions and leopards?* (Cheetahs are fast.)

Pages 10–12 Point out the chapter title "Little Big Cats" on page 10. Then read the first paragraph with students. *Why do you think the author compares little big cats with the cats we keep at home?* (The author wants the reader to visualize how big "little big cats" actually are. Little big cats are really not little at all.) *How are servals and caracals alike? Use the word* both *to compare the two.* (Both servals and caracals are good at hunting birds.)

Pages 13–14 Reread pages 13–14. *What are three things you have learned about African cats?* (Possible Response: They are losing their habitats. They may soon be endangered. People are trying to help.)

After Reading

Respond to Reading Revisit the Essential Question, and ask students to complete the Text Evidence questions on page 15.

Analytical Writing **Write About Reading** Have students write a paragraph that compares servals to leopards. Students should cite details from the text that tell how they are alike and different.

Fluency: Phrasing

Model Model reading page 4 with proper phrasing. Next, reread the page aloud, and have students read along with you.

Apply Have students practice reading with a partner.

PAIRED READ

"How Leopard Got His Spots"

Leveled Reader

Make Connections: Write About It **Analytical Writing**

Before reading, have students note that the genre of this text is a folktale, which means that it tells a story that tries to explain why things are the way they are. Then discuss the Essential Question.

After reading, have students make connections between how leopards' spots help the cats in *African Cats* and "How Leopard Got His Spots."

FOCUS ON SCIENCE

Students can extend their knowledge of what living things need to thrive by completing the science activity on page 20. **STEM**

Literature Circles

Ask students to conduct a literature circle using the Thinkmark questions to guide the discussion. You may wish to have a whole-class discussion on how learning about animals can help people respect them.

Level Up

Level-up lessons available online.

IF students read the Approaching Level fluently and answered the questions

THEN pair them with students who have proficiently read On Level and have approaching-level students

• echo-read the On Level main selection with their partner.

• use self-stick notes to mark a detail to discuss in each section.

A C T Access Complex Text

The On Level challenges students by including more **domain-specific words** and **complex sentence structures**.

→ Approaching Level

Phonics/Decoding

DECODE WORDS WITH *r*-CONTROLLED VOWEL SYLLABLES

OBJECTIVES

 Know and apply grade-level phonics and word analysis skills in decoding words. Decode multisyllable words. **RF.3.3c**

Decode words with *r*-controlled vowel *ar*.

 I Do Remind students that when a vowel is followed by the letter *r*, both letters act as a team to form a special vowel sound called an *r*-controlled vowel sound. Write the word *far* on the board. Underline the *r*-controlled vowel *ar*. Model how to say the word, emphasizing the *r*-controlled vowel sound.

 We Do Write *yard, car, smart*, and *bargain* on the board. Model how to decode each word. Underline the letters making the *r*-controlled vowel sound in each word, and say the vowel sound. Then read the whole word. Have students read along with you.

 You Do Add these words to the board: *starve, barking, margin, start*. Have students read each word aloud and identify the *r*-controlled vowel sound. Point to the words in random order for students to read chorally. Repeat several times as needed.

BUILD WORDS WITH *r*-CONTROLLED VOWEL SYLLABLES

OBJECTIVES

 Know and apply grade-level phonics and word analysis skills in decoding words. Decode multisyllable words. **RF.3.3c**

Build words with *r*-controlled vowel syllables.

 I Do Tell students that they will be building multisyllable words with *r*-controlled vowel syllables. Remind students that when a vowel is followed by *r*, both letters remain in the same syllable and act as a team. Display these **Word-Building Cards** one at a time: *lar, ter, cir, mer*, and *tle*. Write these syllables on the board: *cel, hot, cus, for, tur*. Read each syllable.

 We Do Have students chorally read each syllable. Repeat at varying speeds and in random order. Next, display all the cards and syllables. Work with students to combine the Word-Building Cards and the syllables to form multisyllable words with *r*-controlled vowel syllables. Have students chorally read the words: *cellar, hotter, circus, former, turtle*.

 You Do Write other syllables on the board, such as *dol, lat, thir, re, cur, lar, er, sty, store*, and *sor*. Have students work with partners to build words using these syllables. Then have partners share the words they built.

PRACTICE WORDS WITH *r*-CONTROLLED VOWEL SYLLABLES

OBJECTIVES

 Know and apply grade-level phonics and word analysis skills in decoding words. Decode multisyllable words. **RF.3.3c**

Decode words with *r*-controlled vowel syllables.

 I Do Remind students that when a vowel is followed by *r*, both letters remain in the same syllable and act as a team. Write *doctor* on the board. Underline *tor*. Model how to say the word, emphasizing *or*. Write *remark, better, dirty, stormy*, and *surface* on the board. Model how to read each word.

 We Do Write *artist, silver, circle, report, turkey* on the board. Model how to decode the first word, then guide students as they decode the remaining words. Underline the letters making the *r*-controlled vowel sound in each word.

 You Do Point to the words in random order for students to chorally read.

LATIN SUFFIXES

OBJECTIVES

 Identify and know the meaning of the most common prefixes and derivational suffixes. **RF.3.3a**

 Decode words with common Latin suffixes. **RF.3.3b**

Decode words with Latin suffixes.

I Do Review that Latin suffixes *-able* and *-ment* change the meaning and part of speech of the root word to which they are added. Note that when *-able* or *-ment* are added to base words that end in consonant + *e*, the final *e* is often dropped. The suffix *-able* means "able to" and changes the root word's part of speech to an adjective, so *argue* + *able* becomes *arguable*. The suffix *-ment* means "an act of doing something" and changes the root word's part of speech to a noun, so *judge* + *ment* becomes *judgment*.

 We Do Write the words *breakable, likable*, and *agreement* on the board. Say each word, and have students repeat. Underline the suffix in each word. Help students figure out the meaning of each word based on its root word and suffix. Read the list out loud again while students read with you.

 You Do Write the words *fixable, amusement*, and *punishment* on the board. Have students determine the meaning of each word. Then point to the words in random order for students to chorally read.

ELL ENGLISH LANGUAGE LEARNERS

For the students who need **phonics**, **decoding**, and **fluency** practice, use scaffolding methods as necessary to ensure students understand the meaning of the words. Refer to the **Language Transfers Handbook** for phonics elements that may not transfer in students' native languages.

→ Approaching Level

Vocabulary

REVIEW HIGH-FREQUENCY WORDS

OBJECTIVES

 Use conventional spelling for high-frequency and other studied words and for adding suffixes to base words (e.g., *sitting, smiled, cries, happiness*). **L.3.2e**

Review high-frequency words.

 Use **Word Cards** 231–240. Display one word at a time, following the routine:

Display the word. Read the word. Then spell the word.

 Ask students to state the word and spell the word with you. Model using the word in a sentence, and have students repeat after you.

 Display the word. Ask students to say the word then spell it. When completed, quickly flip through the word card set as students chorally read the words. Provide opportunities for students to use the words in speaking and writing. For example, provide sentence starters such as *Do you know ____ owns this book?* Ask students to write each word in their **Writer's Notebook**.

REVIEW VOCABULARY WORDS

OBJECTIVES

 Acquire and use accurately grade-appropriate conversational, general academic, and domain-specific words and phrases, including those that signal spatial and temporal relationships. **L.3.6**

Review vocabulary words.

 Display each **Visual Vocabulary Card** and state the word. Explain how the photograph illustrates the word. State the example sentence and repeat the word.

 Point to the word on the card and read the word with students. Ask them to repeat the word. Engage students in structured partner talk about the image as prompted on the back of the vocabulary card.

 Display each visual in random order, hiding the word. Have students match the definitions and context sentences of the words to the visuals displayed. Then ask students to complete **Approaching Reproducibles** page 281.

IDENTIFY RELATED WORDS

OBJECTIVES

 Demonstrate understanding of word relationships and nuances in word meanings. Identify real-life connections between words and their use (e.g., describe people who are *friendly* or *helpful*). **L.3.5b**

Identify words that have similar meanings.

 I Do Display the *endangered* **Visual Vocabulary Card** and read the word set *endangered, threatened, protected*. Explain why *protected* does not belong.

 We Do Display the vocabulary card for the word *fascinating*. Say aloud the word set *fascinating, boring, exciting*. With students, identify the word that does not belong, and discuss why.

You Do Using the word sets below, display the remaining cards one at a time, saying aloud each set. Have students identify the word in each set that does not belong.

illegal, criminal, lawful   inhabit, abandon, occupy

requirement, luxury, necessity   respected, honored, ignored

unaware, clueless, focused   wildlife, environment, animals

CONTEXT CLUES: PARAGRAPH CLUES

OBJECTIVES

 Use sentence level context as a clue to the meaning of a word or phrase. **L.3.4a**

Use paragraph clues to determine the meanings of words.

I Do Display the Comprehension and Fluency passage on **Approaching Reproducibles** pages 283–284. Read aloud the first paragraph. Point to the sentence *But now there is concern for bees.* Explain that in many science texts, context clues appear in the same paragraph as an unfamiliar word. Use paragraph clues to find the meaning of the word *concern*.

Think Aloud I do not know the meaning of the word *concern*, but I can use context clues in the same paragraph to figure it out. I see that the next sentence says *People are worried.* When I worry about something, I care about it, so I think that *concern* means "care."

Write the meaning of the word *concern*.

 We Do Ask students to point to the sentence *Studies show that bee colonies in the United States are vanishing.* With students, discuss how to determine the meaning of *colonies* using paragraph clues. Write the meaning of the word.

 You Do Have students use paragraph clues to find the meanings of *role, germs, substance, process, fluid,* and *scarce* as they read the rest of the passage.

Approaching Level

Comprehension

FLUENCY

TIER 2

OBJECTIVES

 Read on-level prose and poetry orally with accuracy, appropriate rate, and expression on successive readings. **RF.3.4b**

Read fluently with appropriate phrasing.

I Do Explain that paying attention to punctuation marks, such as commas, dashes, and periods, is a good way to read with appropriate phrasing. Read paragraph 1 of the Comprehension and Fluency passage on **Approaching Reproducibles** pages 283–284. Point out how you grouped words depending on the punctuation surrounding the words.

We Do Read the rest of the page aloud, and have students repeat each sentence after you using the same phrasing. Explain that you grouped certain words and phrases to express meaning, paying attention to punctuation.

You Do Have partners take turns reading sentences from the Approaching Reproducibles passage. Remind them to focus on their phrasing. Listen in and provide corrective feedback as needed by modeling proper fluency.

TEXT STRUCTURE

TIER 2

OBJECTIVES

 Describe the logical connection between particular sentences and paragraphs in a text (e.g., comparison, cause/effect, first/second/third in a sequence). **RI.3.8**

Examine similarities and differences.

I Do Write the topic: *Possible Causes of Colony Collapse Disorder* on the board. Beneath, write: *Same* and *Different.* Explain that the text is structured to show how these possible causes of Colony Collapse Disorder are the same and how they are different. Write two columns on the board labeled *Same* and *Different.* Explain the two words. Tell students that they will help find information to put in these columns as they read.

We Do Read the first page of the Comprehension and Fluency passage in the **Approaching Reproducibles**. Ask, *How are the plant sprays and germs the same?* Note how they are the same in the column on the board. Discuss why the author would choose to note the ways that these things are alike.

You Do Have students reread the first page. After they finish, they should work to fill in the *Different* column on the board. Review how the possible causes of Colony Collapse Disorder are the same and how they are different.

REVIEW TEXT STRUCTURE: COMPARE AND CONTRAST

OBJECTIVES

(CCSS) Describe the logical connection between particular sentences and paragraphs in a text (e.g., comparison, cause/effect, first/ second/third in a sequence). **RI.3.8**

Compare and contrast two things in a text.

 I Do Remind students that they can compare and contrast two things in a text to understand how they are alike and different. To *compare*, students should look for ways that two things are alike. To *contrast*, they should look for ways two things are different. Students can look for signal words like *both, alike, same,* or *different* to help them compare and contrast.

 We Do Read the first page of the Comprehension and Fluency passage in **Approaching Reproducibles** together. Pause to point out similarities that may be comparisons in the text. Model how to decide what three things are being compared and how. Then, work with students to determine how the three things are being contrasted by referring to the text.

 You Do Have students work in small groups to come up with a list of comparisons and contrasts on the next page in the Approaching Reproducibles. Make sure they are comparing and contrasting life with and without bees using text evidence.

SELF-SELECTED READING

OBJECTIVES

(CCSS) Describe the logical connection between particular sentences and paragraphs in a text (e.g., comparison, cause/effect, first/ second/third in a sequence). **RI.3.8**

• Compare and contrast two things in a text.

• Reread difficult sections in a text to increase understanding.

Read Independently

Have students choose an expository text comparing and contrasting something for sustained silent reading. Remind students that:

• they should look for ways two or more things are alike or different.

• if they have trouble finding comparisons and contrasts, they should reread a paragraph or section to look for more information.

Read Purposefully

Have students fill out **Graphic Organizer 66** as they read independently. After they finish, they can conduct a Book Talk, each telling about the text they read.

• Students should share their organizers and answer this question: *What was one comparison and one contrast you read about?*

• They should also tell the group if there were any sections they reread in order to find more ways to compare and contrast two or more things.

On Level

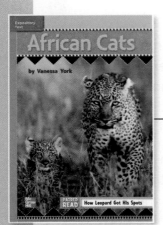

Lexile 720
TextEvaluator™ 32

OBJECTIVES

 Use information gained from illustrations (e.g., maps, photographs) and the words in a text to demonstrate understanding of the text (e.g., where, when, why, and how key events occur). **RI.3.7**

• Compare and contrast at least two things in a text.

• Reread text to check understanding.

• Use paragraph clues to determine the meanings of words.

ACADEMIC LANGUAGE

reread, compare, contrast, paragraph clues, expository, map, diagram

Leveled Reader:
African Cats

Before Reading

Preview and Predict

Have students read the Essential Question. Then have them read the title and table of contents of *African Cats*. Have students make two predictions about the text and share them with partners.

Review Genre: Expository Text

Review with students that an expository text can tell information about a science topic. It often contains text features such as headings, photographs and captions, labels, and diagrams. As they preview *African Cats*, have students identify features of expository text.

During Reading

Close Reading

Note Taking Have students use their graphic organizer as they read.

Pages 2–3 *Look at the map. What does the shaded area of the map show?* (The shaded area of the map shows where the cats live in Africa.)

Pages 4–5 *What does the word* pride *mean on page 4? Use paragraph clues to find the meaning.* (A *pride* is a family group of lions.) *What is the purpose of a lion's mane? Reread the sidebar on page 5 to find the answer.* (A lion's mane attracts females.)

Pages 6–7 *Turn to a partner and explain what makes leopards successful at catching birds, reptiles, and mammals.* (Leopards' markings help them blend in with their surroundings.)

Pages 8–9 *How are cheetahs different from lions and leopards?* (Cheetahs do not roar.) *What word signals a contrast?* (*unlike*)

Pages 10–12 *Turn to a partner and describe how little big cats and big cats are alike or different.* (Little big cats are much smaller than lions and leopards. Servals purr, growl, and chirp just like cheetahs.) **Reread the first paragraph on page 10.** *Why do you think the author contrasts little big cats with the cats we keep at home?* (The author wants the reader to visualize the size of little big cats by comparing them with pet cats.)

Go Digital

Leveled Readers

Fill in the Graphic Organizer

Pages 13–14 *What is one danger these cats face?* (People are building and leaving less space for wildlife.) *How do conservation organizations work with farmers?* (They remove big cats that live close to people and relocate them to a safe reserve.)

After Reading

Respond to Reading Revisit the Essential Question, and ask students to complete the Text Evidence questions on page 15.

Analytical Writing **Write About Reading** Have students write a paragraph that compares servals to leopards. Students should cite details from the text that tell how they are alike and different.

Fluency: Phrasing

Model Model reading page 8 with proper phrasing. Next, reread the page aloud, and have students read along with you.

Apply Have students practice reading with a partner.

PAIRED READ

"How Leopard Got His Spots"

Make Connections: Write About It *Analytical Writing*

Before reading, have students note that the genre of this text is a folktale, which means that it tells a story that tries to explain why things are the way they are. Then discuss the Essential Question.

After reading, have students make connections between how leopards' spots help them in *African Cats* and "How Leopard Got His Spots."

Leveled Reader

 FOCUS ON SCIENCE

Students can extend their knowledge of what living things need to thrive by completing the science activity on page 20. **STEM**

Literature Circles

Ask students to conduct a literature circle using the Thinkmark questions to guide the discussion. You may wish to have a whole-class discussion on how learning about animals can help people respect them.

Level Up

Level-up lessons available online.

IF students read the On Level fluently and answered the questions

THEN pair them with students who have proficiently read Beyond Level and have on-level students

• partner-read the Beyond Level main selection.

• name two details in the text that they want to learn more about.

A C T Access Complex Text

The Beyond Level challenges students by including more **domain-specific words** and **complex sentence structures**.

On Level

Vocabulary

REVIEW VOCABULARY WORDS

OBJECTIVES
 Acquire and use accurately grade-appropriate conversational, general academic, and domain-specific words and phrases, including those that signal spatial and temporal relationships. **L.3.6**

Review vocabulary words.

 I Do Use the **Visual Vocabulary Cards** to review key vocabulary words *endangered, fascinating, illegal, inhabit, respected*, and *unaware*. Point to each word, read it aloud, and have students chorally repeat it.

 We Do Ask these questions and help students respond and explain their answers.
- What is one kind of *endangered* animal?
- Which subject at school is the most *fascinating* to you?
- What can happen to someone who does something *illegal*?

 You Do Have students respond to these questions and explain their answers.
- What kind of animals *inhabit* the area where you live?
- How do you know if someone is *respected* by his or her peers?
- What can happen if someone is *unaware* of his or her surroundings?

CONTEXT CLUES: PARAGRAPH CLUES

OBJECTIVES
 Use sentence level context as a clue to the meaning of a word or phrase. **L.3.4a**

Use paragraph clues to determine the meanings of words.

 I Do Remind students that they can use context clues in the same paragraph as an unfamiliar word to help them determine its meaning. Use the Comprehension and Fluency passage on **Your Turn Practice Book** pages 283–284 to model.

Think Aloud I want to know what *concern* means. I can look for clues in the paragraph. I read in the next sentence that *People are worried.* When I worry about something, I care about it, so *concern* must mean "care."

 We Do Have students read the next paragraph, where they will encounter the word *colonies*. Have students figure out the meaning of the word by using context clues in the same paragraph.

 You Do Have students work in pairs to determine the meanings of the words *role, germs, substance, process, fluid*, and *scarce* as they read the rest of the passage.

Comprehension

REVIEW TEXT STRUCTURE: COMPARE AND CONTRAST

OBJECTIVES

CCSS Describe the logical connection between particular sentences and paragraphs in a text (e.g., comparison, cause/effect, first/second/third in a sequence). **RI.3.8**

Compare and contrast two things in expository text.

 I Do

Remind students that they can compare and contrast two things in an expository text to understand how they are alike and different. Point out that to compare, students should look for ways two things are alike. To contrast, students should figure out ways they are different. Signal words such as *both, alike, same,* or *different* can help them compare and contrast.

 We Do

Have a volunteer read the first page of the Comprehension and Fluency passage on **Your Turn Practice Book** pages 283–284. Have students orally list details that show how two possible causes of Colony Collapse Disorder are alike and different. Then model how to compare and contrast the two possible causes. Work with students to identify another example to compare and contrast in the last paragraph on the page.

 You Do

Have partners read the rest of the passage and write a list of ways in which life without bees would be similar to and different from life now. Remind students to use text evidence when they compile their lists.

SELF-SELECTED READING

OBJECTIVES

CCSS Describe the logical connection between particular sentences and paragraphs in a text (e.g., comparison, cause/effect, first/second/third in a sequence). **RI.3.8**

• Compare and contrast two things in an expository text.
• Reread difficult sections to increase comprehension.

Read Independently

Have students choose an expository text comparing and contrasting two things for sustained silent reading.

• Before they read, have students preview the text, looking for any text features such as maps or photographs that tell more about the text.

• Encourage students to reread sections of the text that are unclear.

Read Purposefully

Encourage students to read different expository texts in order to learn about a variety of subjects.

• As students read, they can fill in **Graphic Organizer 66**.

• Students can refer back to their organizers to write a summary of the text.

• Ask students to share their reactions to the text with classmates. Ask them to tell if there were any sections of the text they reread in order to increase their understanding.

Beyond Level

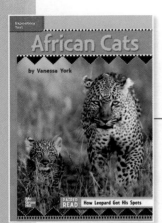

Lexile 840
TextEvaluator 37

OBJECTIVES

CCSS Use information gained from illustrations (e.g., maps, photographs) and the words in a text to demonstrate understanding of the text (e.g., where, when, why, and how key events occur). **RI.3.7**

- Compare and contrast at least two things in a text.
- Reread text to check understanding.
- Use paragraph clues to determine the meanings of words.

ACADEMIC LANGUAGE
reread, compare, contrast, paragraph clues, map, diagram

Leveled Reader: *African Cats*

Before Reading

Preview and Predict

Have students read the Essential Question. Then have them read the title and table of contents of *African Cats*. Have students make two predictions about the text and share them with a partner.

Review Genre: Expository Text

Review with students that an expository text can tell information about a science topic. It often contains text features such as headings, photographs and captions, labels, and diagrams. As they preview *African Cats,* have students identify features of expository text.

During Reading

Close Reading

Note Taking Have students use their graphic organizer as they read.

Pages 2–3 *Look at the map on page 3. Where do the big cats live?* (most of Africa) *How are all species of cats alike?* (They are good predators.)

Pages 4–5 *Based on paragraph clues, what is a* pride? (A *pride* is a family group.) *What does a pride include?* (A pride can include up to three males and a dozen females.) *Reread page 5. Then, turn to a partner, and describe the jobs of the male and female lions in a pride.* (The males defend their territory. The females work together to hunt.)

Pages 6–9 *How do leopards' markings help them become successful hunters?* (Their markings help them blend in with their surroundings. This helps them be hidden while they hunt.) *How are leopards' markings different from the markings of a cheetah?* (Leopards' markings help them hunt. Cheetahs' markings help keep the sun out of their eyes.)

Pages 10–12 *Why does the author say that little big cats are still a lot bigger than house cats?* (Despite the name "little big cats," they are actually quite big.) *How are servals and caracals alike and different? Use words signaling that you are comparing and contrasting.* (Servals prefer to live on the savannah, while caracals prefer to live in the semidesert. Both cats are great hunters.)

Go Digital

Leveled Readers

Fill in the Graphic Organizer

Pages 13–14 *How are people a threat to African cats?* (Human activities leave less space for the cats to live on. Some people kill the cats for their pelts. Others kill them for use in traditional medicines.) *How do some people help?* (They protect the cats' habitats and relocate big cats away from people.)

After Reading

Respond to Reading Revisit the Essential Question, and ask students to complete the Text Evidence questions on page 15.

Analytical Writing **Write About Reading** Have students write a paragraph that compares servals to leopards. Students should cite details from the text that tell how they are alike and different.

Fluency: Phrasing

Model Model reading page 4 with proper phrasing. Next, reread the page aloud, and have students read along with you.

Apply Have students practice reading with a partner.

PAIRED READ

Leveled Reader

"How Leopard Got His Spots"

Make Connections:
Write About It **Analytical Writing**

Before reading, have students note that the genre of this text is a folktale, which means it tells a story that tries to explain why things are the way they are. Then discuss the Essential Question.

After reading, have students make connections between how leopards' spots help the cats in *African Cats* and "How Leopard Got His Spots."

FOCUS ON SCIENCE

Students can extend their knowledge of what living things need to thrive by completing the science activity on page 20. **STEM**

Literature Circles

Ask students to conduct a literature circle using the Thinkmark questions to guide the discussion. You may wish to have a whole-class discussion on how learning about animals can help people respect them.

Gifted and Talented

Synthesize Challenge students to write about an animal that they respect. Have them write a three-paragraph essay explaining why they respect it, and what they know about it that made them respect it. Invite volunteers to share their animals with the class.

Beyond Level

Vocabulary

REVIEW DOMAIN-SPECIFIC WORDS

OBJECTIVES

 Produce simple, compound, and complex sentences. **L.3.1i**

Review and discuss the meanings of domain-specific words.

Model Use the **Visual Vocabulary Cards** to review the meanings of the words *endangered* and *illegal*. Write science related sentences on the board using the words.

Write *species, native,* and *territory* on the board and discuss the meanings with students. Then help students write sentences using these words.

Apply Have students work in pairs to discuss the meanings of the words *adaptability, surroundings,* and *vulnerable*. Challenge students to write science related sentences that use two of these words in each sentence.

CONTEXT CLUES: PARAGRAPH CLUES

OBJECTIVES

 Use sentence level context as a clue to the meaning of a word or phrase. **L.3.4a**

Use paragraph clues to determine the meanings of words.

Model Read aloud the first paragraph of the Comprehension and Fluency passage on **Beyond Reproducibles** pages 283–284.

Think Aloud I want to know what *concern* means. I can look for clues in the paragraph. I read in the next sentence that *People are worried.* When I worry about something, I care about it, so *concern* must mean "care."

With students, read the next paragraph. Help them figure out the meaning of the word *colonies* using context clues in the same paragraph.

Apply Have pairs of students read the rest of the passage. Ask them to use paragraph clues to determine the meanings of the words *role, germs, substance, process, fluid,* and *scarce*.

 Compare and Contrast Have students use classroom resources to learn about the similarities and differences between butterflies and moths. Ask them to write a short report that compares and contrasts the two. Encourage them to use words from this week's vocabulary and language that signals how the two animals are alike and different, and include artwork. Have them present their reports to the class.

Comprehension

REVIEW TEXT STRUCTURE: COMPARE AND CONTRAST

OBJECTIVES

CCSS Describe the logical connection between particular sentences and paragraphs in a text (e.g., comparison, cause/effect, first/second/third in a sequence). **RI.3.8**

Compare and contrast two things in an expository text.

Model Remind students that they can compare and contrast two things in an expository text to understand how they are alike and different. Review the meanings of *compare* and *contrast*. Point out that students can look for signal words such as *alike, both, same* or *different* to help them compare and contrast.

Have students read the first page of the Comprehension and Fluency passage of **Beyond Reproducibles** pages 283–284. Ask open-ended questions to facilitate discussion, such as *How are the three possible causes of Colony Collapse Disorder alike? Which details show how they are different?* Students should provide text evidence to support their answers.

Apply As they read the rest of the passage, have students identify details that compare and contrast what life with bees is like with what life would be like without bees. Remind students to use evidence from the text when they compare and contrast the two.

SELF-SELECTED READING

OBJECTIVES

CCSS Describe the logical connection between particular sentences and paragraphs in a text (e.g., comparison, cause/effect, first/second/third in a sequence). **RI.3.8**

• Compare and contrast two things in an expository text.

• Reread to increase comprehension of a text.

Read Independently

Have students choose an expository text that compares and contrasts at least two things for sustained silent reading.

- As students read, have them fill in **Graphic Organizer 66**.
- Remind students that they should reread any difficult sections.

Read Purposefully

Encourage students to keep a reading journal. Ask them to read different expository texts to learn about a variety of subjects.

- Students can write summaries of the texts in their journals.
- Ask students to give their reactions to the texts to their classmates. Have them tell about what was compared and contrasted and how.

Independent Study Challenge students to discuss how their texts relate to the weekly theme of Animals and You. Have students compare some of the ways people rely on animals. How do animals and people interact? How can we show respect to animals?

English Language Learners

Reading/Writing Workshop

Go Digital

View "Butterflies Big and Small"

OBJECTIVES

CCSS Use information gained from illustrations (e.g., maps, photographs) and the words in a text to demonstrate understanding of the text (e.g., where, when, why, and how key events occur). **RI.3.7**

• Reread to increase understanding.

• Use paragraph clues to determine word meanings.

LANGUAGE OBJECTIVE

Compare and contrast at least two things in a text.

ACADEMIC LANGUAGE

• *compare, contrast, reread, expository, headings, diagrams, paragraph clues*

• Cognates: *comparar, contrastar, expositivo, diagramas*

Shared Read
Butterflies Big and Small

Before Reading

Build Background

Read the Essential Question: How can learning about animals help you respect them?

• Explain the meaning of the Essential Question. Point out that *animals* and *respect* have cognates: *animales* and *respeto*. Show students a photograph of a dolphin. *How can learning about a dolphin help us respect it?*

• **Model an answer:** *I learn that a dolphin can "see" things underwater by listening for echoes. This makes me respect dolphins for their unique abilities and want to learn more about them.*

• Ask students a question that ties the Essential Question to their own background knowledge: *Think about an animal you have learned about. How did what you learned help you respect the animal? Discuss your answers with a partner.* Call on several pairs to share their answers with the class.

During Reading

Interactive-Question Response

• Ask questions that help students understand the meaning of the text after each paragraph.

• Reinforce the meanings of key vocabulary.

• Ask students questions that require them to use key vocabulary.

• Reinforce strategies and skills of the week by modeling.

Page 449

What is this text about? (butterflies) *Look at the caption for the photograph on page 448 and the heading for the diagram on page 449. Which two butterflies will you learn about?* (the Monarch butterfly and the Western Pygmy Blue butterfly)

Size and Color

Paragraph 1
Read the heading. *What will this section be about?* (the size and color of butterflies) *Which type of butterfly is the smallest?* (the Western Pygmy Blue)

Paragraph 3
Model Compare and Contrast *In paragraph 3, I see the word* different. *This tells me that the author is contrasting the two butterflies. What kind of markings do Monarch butterflies have?* (bright orange with black markings) *What color are Pygmy Blue butterflies?* (mostly blue and brown) *So I can contrast the two butterflies by their color: Monarch butterflies are easy to see because of their bright colors, while Pygmy Blue butterflies blend in.*

Look at the diagram. Which butterfly is shown? (the Western Pygmy Blue)

Work with a partner to name and point out the different parts of a butterfly in the diagram.

Page 450

Moving Around

Explain and Model Paragraph Clues *The first sentence of the first paragraph says that almost all butterflies migrate. I see words in the paragraph that help me figure out what* migrate *means. It is the phrase "move to different areas."*

What is the same about how they migrate? What is different? Use signal words both *and* but. Have one student answer and another elaborate on the answer. (They both migrate when it gets cold. The Monarch travels the longest distance, but the Western Pygmy blue travels a short distance.)

Point out the word cold-blooded *in paragraph 3. The next sentence helps define* cold-blooded. *Are butterflies hot or cold when the weather is cold?* (cold) *What about when the weather is hot?* (hot) *So an animal is* cold-blooded *when it is the same temperature as its surroundings.*

Map
Look at the map. What does it show? (butterfly migration) *Which butterfly's route does the orange arrow show?* (the Monarch butterfly's)

Page 451

Paragraphs 1–2
What do Monarch butterflies eat? (milkweed)

Explain and Model Rereading *Sometimes I reread to understand better. When I read paragraph 2 the first time, I did not understand why Monarch butterflies have trouble finding milkweed. What do people do that affects milkweed?* (They build houses and roads.) *What happens to the Monarch butterfly population when the Monarch cannot find milkweed?* (It decreases.)

Help Butterflies

Paragraph 2
What are two ways that people can help these butterflies? Complete the sentence frame: People can help them by ____ (changing laws; planting milkweed; making it illegal to destroy animal habitats).

Tell a partner what you have learned about butterflies that makes you respect them more.

After Reading

Make Connections

- Review the Essential Question: How can learning about animals help you respect them?

- Make text connections.

- Have students complete the **ELL Reproducibles** pages 283–285.

English Language Learners

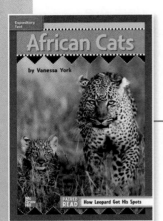

Lexile 660
TextEvaluator 26

OBJECTIVES
Use information gained from illustrations (e.g., maps, photographs) and the words in a text to demonstrate understanding of the text (e.g., where, when, why, and how key events occur). **RI.3.7**

• Use paragraph clues to determine word meanings.
• Reread text to check understanding

LANGUAGE OBJECTIVE

Compare and contrast things in a text.

ACADEMIC LANGUAGE
• compare, contrast, paragraph clues, map, diagram
• Cognates: *comparar, contrastar, mapa, diagrama*

Leveled Reader:
African Cats

Before Reading

Preview

• Read the Essential Question: How can learning about animals help you respect them?

• Refer to Animals and You: *What is one way you can show respect for animals?*

• Preview *African Cats* and "How Leopard Got His Spots": *Let's read about how the different cats of Africa all hunt and survive.*

Vocabulary

Use the **Visual Vocabulary Cards** to preteach the ELL vocabulary: *adaptations, stalk*. Use the routine found on the cards. Point out the cognate: *adaptaciones*.

During Reading

Interactive Question-Response

Note Taking Have students use their graphic organizer on **ELL Reproducibles** page 282. Use the following questions after reading each section. Use visuals or pictures to define key vocabulary.

Pages 2–3 Have students point to the map on page 3. *What does the shaded area show?* Provide the sentence frame: *The shaded area shows ____* (where the cats live).

Pages 4–5 Point out *prides* on page 4. *What is a pride? Reread to look for clues in the paragraph. A pride is a ____* (family group). Point to and chorally read the sidebar on page 5. Have students show you the lion's mane. Ask: *What does a lion's mane do?* (It attracts females.)

Pages 6–7 Chorally read pages 6 and 7. Point out that *blend in* means the same as *hide* or *camouflage*. Then point out the cognate *camuflar*. *What makes a leopard good at catching animals?* (leopard markings) *What do leopard markings help them do?* (hide in leaves and long grass)

Pages 8–9 Remind students that *unlike* is a clue word for *different. How is a cheetah unlike lions and leopards?* (Cheetahs do not roar.)

Go Digital

Leveled Readers

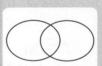

Fill in the Graphic Organizer

Pages 10–12 *How are servals like caracals?* (They are both little big cats.) *How are they different? Servals usually live on a* ____ (savannah), *but caracals usually live in* ____ (semidesert) *habitats.*

Pages 13–14 *Reread page 13. What is one way people try to protect African cats?* (Possible Response: They help protect habitats.) **Help students with vocabulary.**

After Reading

Respond to Reading Help students complete the graphic organizer. Revisit the Essential Question. Have student pairs summarize and answer the Text Evidence questions. Support students as necessary, and review all responses as a group.

Analytical Writing **Write About Reading** Have students work with a partner to write a paragraph that compares servals with leopards using text evidence.

Fluency: Phrasing

Model Model reading page 4 with proper phrasing. Next, reread the page aloud, and have students read along with you.

Apply Have students practice reading with a partner.

PAIRED READ

Leveled Reader

"How Leopard Got His Spots"

Make Connections: Write About It *Analytical Writing*

Before reading, have students note that the genre of this text is a folktale, which means it tells a story that tries to explain why things are the way they are. Then discuss the Essential Question.

After reading, have students make connections between how leopards' spots help them in *African Cats* and "How Leopard Got His Spots."

🧪 **FOCUS ON SCIENCE**

Students can extend their knowledge of what living things need to thrive by completing the science activity on page 20. **STEM**

Literature Circles

Ask students to conduct a literature circle using the Thinkmark questions to guide the discussion. You may wish to have a whole-class discussion on how learning about animals can help people respect them.

Level Up

Level-up lessons available online.

IF students read the ELL Level fluently and answered the questions

THEN pair them with students who have proficiently read On Level and have ELL students

• echo-read the On Level main selection with their partner.

• list difficult words and discuss them with their partner.

A C T Access Complex Text

The On Level challenges students by including more **domain-specific words** and **complex sentence structures**.

English Language Learners
Vocabulary

PRETEACH VOCABULARY

 OBJECTIVES
Acquire and use accurately grade-appropriate conversational, general academic, and domain-specific words and phrases, including those that signal spatial and temporal relationships (e.g., *After dinner that night we went looking for them*). **L.3.6**

LANGUAGE OBJECTIVE
Use vocabulary words.

I Do Preteach vocabulary from "Butterflies Big and Small" following the Vocabulary Routine on the **Visual Vocabulary Cards** for words *fascinating, unaware, inhabit, requirement, endangered, wildlife, respected,* and *illegal.*

We Do After completing the Vocabulary Routine for each word, point to the word on the Visual Vocabulary Card and read the word with students. Ask students to repeat the word.

You Do Have students work with a partner to write sentence frames for three words. Ask pairs to exchange each other's sentences to complete.

Beginning	Intermediate	Advanced/High
Help students write their sentence frames correctly and read them aloud.	Have students write three sentence frames and provide a synonym for one word.	Challenge students to write four sentence frames and provide a synonym for each word.

REVIEW VOCABULARY

 OBJECTIVES
Acquire and use accurately grade-appropriate conversational, general academic, and domain-specific words and phrases, including those that signal spatial and temporal relationships. **L.3.6**

LANGUAGE OBJECTIVE
Use vocabulary words.

I Do Review vocabulary words from the previous week. The words can be reviewed over a few days. Read each word aloud pointing to the word on the **Visual Vocabulary Card**. Have students repeat after you. Act out three of the words using gestures or actions.

We Do Ask students to guess the definitions of the words you have acted out. Give students additional clues, including synonyms or antonyms.

You Do Have pairs of students think of ways to act out three words. Help students with the definitions, and suggest appropriate gestures or actions. Then have them act out the meanings of the words for the class.

Beginning	Intermediate	Advanced/High
Help students come up with ways to act out at least two words.	Have students think of ways to act out at least three of the words.	Ask students to come up with ways to act out each word.

CONTEXT CLUES: PARAGRAPH CLUES

OBJECTIVES

 Use sentence-level context as a clue to the meaning of a word or phrase. **L.3.4a**

LANGUAGE OBJECTIVE

Use paragraph clues to determine word meanings.

 I Do Read aloud page 449 of "Butterflies Big and Small" while students follow along. Point to *species* in paragraph 1. Remind students that they can look for the meanings of words using context clues. Point out that the sentence or paragraph might even define or restate the word.

Think Aloud After the word *species* is the phrase *or kinds*. Later in the paragraph, it says that two kinds of butterfly share the same traits. These clues tell me that *species* is another word for "kind" or "type."

 We Do Have students point to the word *nectar* on page 450. Guide them as they figure out the meaning of the word using paragraph clues. Write the definition of the word on the board.

You Do Have pairs of students define the word *milkweed* on page 451 using paragraph clues. Ask students to write a sentence using the word to describe a type of butterfly from "Butterflies Big and Small."

Beginning	Intermediate	Advanced/High
Help students write their definition and sentence using *milkweed*.	Have students also write their own definition and sentence for *species* or *nectar*.	Have students also write their own definitions and sentences for *species* and *nectar*.

ADDITIONAL VOCABULARY

OBJECTIVES

 Produce simple, compound, and complex sentences. **L.3.1i**

Discuss concept and high-frequency words.

LANGUAGE OBJECTIVE

Use concept and high-frequency words.

 I Do List concept and high-frequency words from "Butterflies Big and Small": *destroy, preserve;* and *African Cats: pride, where, which.* Define each word for students: *A pride of lions is a group of lions.*

 We Do Model using the words for students in sentences: Where *are you going this summer?* Next, write short-answer questions and answer them with students: Where *could you swim?*

 You Do Have pairs make up their own question using the word *which*. Ask students to answer the questions.

Beginning	Intermediate	Advanced/High
Help students write their question correctly.	Have students use *destroy* and *preserve* in complete sentences.	Have students use all of the words in questions.

English Language Learners

Writing/Spelling

WRITING TRAIT: ORGANIZATION

OBJECTIVES
Provide a concluding statement or section. **W.3.2d**

LANGUAGE OBJECTIVE
Add a strong conclusion to writing.

 I Do Remind students that a strong conclusion retells the main idea in different words. For expository text, writers restate their topic and remind readers why they are writing the text. Read the Student Model passage aloud as students follow along. Point out the strong concluding statement.

 We Do Read aloud the section titled "Help Butterflies" on page 451 as students follow along. Help students fill out a word web identifying the topic and information about the topic.

You Do Have students write a short paragraph about their favorite animal. Remind them to clearly restate their topic in a concluding statement. Edit each student's writing, and ask students to revise.

Beginning	Intermediate	Advanced/High
Help students write their paragraphs, focusing on a strong closing statement.	Have students revise their paragraphs, clearly restating their main idea.	Have students revise to ensure a strong conclusion and edit for errors.

SPELL WORDS WITH *r*-CONTROLLED VOWEL SYLLABLES

OBJECTIVES
Use spelling patterns and generalizations in writing words. **L.3.2f**

LANGUAGE OBJECTIVE
Spell words with *r*-controlled vowel syllables.

 I Do Read aloud the Spelling Words on page T226. Point out that when *r* follows a vowel, the sound of the vowel changes. Have students repeat the words.

 We Do Read the Dictation Sentences on page T227 aloud for students. With each sentence, read the underlined word slowly, modeling proper pronunciation. Have students repeat after you and write the word.

 You Do Display the words. Have students exchange their lists with partners to check the spelling and write the words correctly.

Beginning	Intermediate	Advanced/High
Help students copy the corrected words and say the words aloud.	Have students underline the r-controlled vowel syllables.	After students have corrected their words, have pairs quiz each other.

Grammar

ADVERBS THAT COMPARE

OBJECTIVES

 Form and use comparative and superlative adjectives and adverbs, and choose between them depending on what is to be modified. **L.3.1g**

LANGUAGE OBJECTIVE

Write sentences using adverbs that compare.

Language Transfers Handbook

Speakers of Haitian Creole and Hmong may use an adjective where an adverb is needed, as in *Talk quiet*. In their native languages, adjectives and adverb forms are interchangeable. Reinforce the use of adjectives to modify nouns and adverbs to modify verbs by using contrastive analysis to show the differences in sentences between the student's primary language and English.

 I Do

Remind students that adverbs are used to describe how actions happen. Some adverbs compare two or more actions. Write on the board: *I jump high, but Hannah jumps higher*. Underline *high* and *higher*, and explain that *-er* or *-est* can be added to most one-syllable adverbs to compare. Tell students that *more* and *most* are used with adverbs that have two or more syllables to make comparisons. Write: *The teacher asked that we study more quietly*. Underline *more quietly*. Point out that in such cases adverbs do not change their endings to make comparisons. Explain that to make comparisons using the adverb *well*, use *better* and *best*, and to make comparisons using *badly*, use *worse* and *worst*.

We Do

Write the sentences below on the board. Have volunteers choose one of the adverbs in parentheses to complete each sentence.

We did _____ on the test than we thought we would. (better, best)

Karina finished her project the _____ quickly out of the whole class. (more, most)

Finn spoke _____ after he practiced his lines. (more easily, more easier)

It rained _____ today than it has all week. (worse, worst)

 You Do

Brainstorm a list of adverbs with students. Then have student pairs write sentences using those adverbs. Remind them to use *more* and *most* with adverbs that have two or more syllables when making comparisons.

Beginning	Intermediate	Advanced/High
Help students write at least one sentence using an adverb that compares from the class list.	Have students write at least three complete sentences using adverbs from the class list.	Have students write at least three sentences and act out at least one comparison.

For extra support, have students complete the activities in the **Grammar Practice Reproducibles** during the week, using the routine below:

- Explain the grammar skill.
- Model the first activity in the Grammar Practice Reproducibles.
- Have the whole group complete the next couple of activities and then have partners complete the rest.
- Review the activities with correct answers.

PROGRESS MONITORING

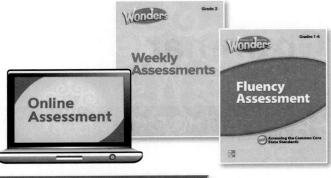

Unit 6 Week 4 Formal Assessment	Standards Covered	Component for Assessment
Text Evidence	RI.3.1	• *Selection Test* • *Weekly Assessment* • *Approaching-Level Weekly Assessment*
Compare and Contrast	RI.3.8	• *Weekly Assessment* • *Approaching-Level Weekly Assessment*
Context Clues: Paragraph Clues	L.3.4a	• *Selection Test* • *Weekly Assessment* • *Approaching-Level Weekly Assessment*
Writing About Text	W.3.8	*Weekly Assessment*

Unit 6 Week 4 Informal Assessment	Standards Covered	Component for Assessment
Research/Listening/ Collaborating	SL.3.1d, SL.3.2, SL.3.3	• *RWW* • *Teacher's Edition*
Oral Reading Fluency (ORF) **Fluency Goal:** 97–117 words correct per minute (WCPM) **Accuracy Rate Goal:** 95% or higher	RF.3.4a, RF.3.4b, RF.3.4c	*Fluency Assessment*

Using Assessment Results

Weekly Assessments Skills and Fluency	If . . .	Then . . .
COMPREHENSION	Students score below 70% . . .	. . . assign Lessons 79–81 on Compare and Contrast from the *Tier 2 Comprehension Intervention online PDFs.*
VOCABULARY	Students score below 70% . . .	. . . assign Lesson 142 on Paragraph Context Clues from the *Tier 2 Vocabulary Intervention online PDFs.*
WRITING	Students score below "3" on constructed response . . .	. . . assign Lessons 79–81 and/or Write About Reading Lesson 200 from the *Tier 2 Comprehension Intervention online PDFs.*
FLUENCY	Students have a WCPM score of 89–96 . . .	. . . assign a lesson from Section 1, 7, 8, 9 or 10 of the *Tier 2 Fluency Intervention online PDFs.*
	Students have a WCPM score of 0–88 . . .	. . . assign a lesson from Sections 2–6 of the *Tier 2 Fluency Intervention online PDFs.*

Using Weekly Data

Check your data Dashboard to verify assessment results and guide grouping decisions.

Data-Driven Recommendations

Response to Intervention

Use the appropriate sections of the *Placement and Diagnostic Assessment* as well as students' assessment results to designate students requiring:

 Intervention Online PDFs   **WonderWorks Intervention Program**

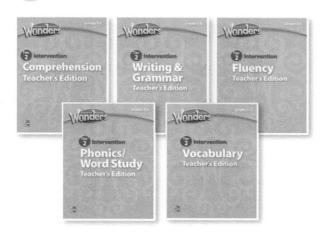

Build Knowledge
Funny Times

? Essential Question:
What makes you laugh?

Teach and Model
Close Reading and Writing

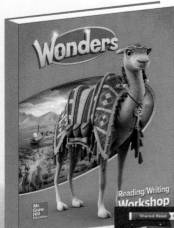

Reading/Writing Workshop

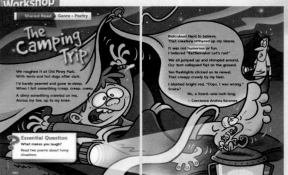

"The Camping Trip" and "Bubble Gum" 462–465
Genre Narrative Poem **Lexile** N/A **ETS** *TextEvaluator* N/A

Practice and Apply
Close Reading and Writing

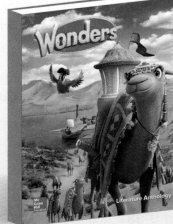

Literature Anthology

"Ollie's Escape," 546–548
Genre Poetry **Lexile** N/A **ETS** *TextEvaluator* N/A

"The Gentleman Bookworm," 550–551
Genre Poetry **Lexile** N/A **ETS** *TextEvaluator* N/A

Differentiated Texts

APPROACHING
Lexile 450
ETS *TextEvaluator* 24

ON LEVEL
Lexile 670
ETS *TextEvaluator* 35

BEYOND
Lexile 780
ETS *TextEvaluator* 49

ELL
Lexile 600
ETS *TextEvaluator* 16

Leveled Readers

Extended Complex Texts

The Hurricane Mystery
(Boxcar Children)
Genre Fiction
Lexile 580

Amos and Boris
Genre Fiction
Lexile 810

Classroom Library

Student Outcomes

Close Reading of Complex Text
- Cite relevant evidence from text
- Identify point of view
- Identify rhythm and rhyme

RL.3.6

Writing
Write to Sources
- Draw evidence from literature
- Write narrative texts
- Conduct short research on how to use language to create humor in writing

Writing Process
- Draft and Revise a Research Report

W.3.3b, W.3.8, W.3.10, W.3.9a

Speaking and Listening
- Engage in collaborative discussions about funny times
- Paraphrase portions of "Show and Tell" and presentations on funny times.
- Present information on funny times

SL.3.1b, SL.3.1d, SL.3.2, SL.3.3

Language Development
Conventions
- Distinguish prepositions and prepositional phrases

Vocabulary Acquisition
- Acquire and use academic vocabulary
  entertainment   humorous   ridiculous   slithered
- Demonstrate understanding of idioms

L.3.1i, L.3.5a, L.3.5b, RL.3.4

Foundational Skills
Phonics/Word Study
- Suffixes *-ful, -less, -ly*
- Frequently misspelled words

Spelling Words

careful	cheerful	helpful	colorful
harmful	pitiful	painless	priceless
helpless	sleepless	rainless	helplessly
peacefully	carefully	wisely	

Fluency
- Phrasing and expression

RF.3.3a, RF.3.3d, RF.3.4a, RF.3.4b, RF.3.4c

Ken Karp/McGraw-Hill Education

Professional Development
- See lessons in action in real classrooms.
- Get expert advice on instructional practices.
- Collaborate with other teachers.
- Access PLC Resources.

Go Digital! www.connected.mcgraw-hill.com.

1 Talk About Thinking It Over

Guide students in collaborative conversations.

Discuss the essential question: *What makes you laugh?*

Develop academic language.

Listen to "Show and Tell" and discuss the poem.

2 Read Poetry

Model close reading with a short complex text.

Read

"The Camping Trip" and **"Bubble Gum"** to learn about funny situations, citing text evidence to answer text-dependent questions.

Reread

"The Camping Trip" and **"Bubble Gum"** to analyze text, craft, and structure, citing text evidence.

Write About Poetry

3 Model writing to a source.

Analyze a short response student model.

Use text evidence from close reading to write to a source.

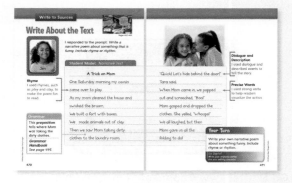

4 Read and Write About Poetry

Practice and apply close reading of the anchor text.

Read

"Ollie's Escape" to learn about a lively classroom pet.

Reread

"Ollie's Escape" and use text evidence to understand how the poet uses text, craft, and structure to develop a deeper understanding of the poem.

Write a short response about **"Ollie's Escape."**

Integrate

Information about other narrative poems you've read.

Write to Two Sources, citing text evidence from **"Ollie's Escape,"** and "The Gentleman Bookworm."

5 Independent Partner Work

Gradual release of support to independent work

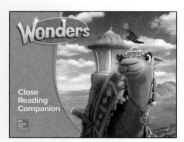

- Text-Dependent Questions
- Scaffolded Partner Work
  Talk with a Partner
  Cite Text Evidence
  Complete a sentence frame.
- Guided Text Annotation

6 Integrate Knowledge and Ideas

Connect Texts

Text to Text Discuss how each of the texts answers the question: What makes you laugh?

Text to Poetry Compare the tone in the poem read and the poem, "The Twins," by Henry Leigh.

Conduct a Short Research Project

Write a short humorous piece of writing..

Write to Sources

Day 1 and Day 2

Build Writing Fluency

- Quick write on "The Camping Trip," p. T284

Write to a Source

- Analyze a student model, p. T284

- Write about "The Camping Trip," p. T285

- Apply Writing Trait: Word Choice, p. T284

- Apply Grammar Skill: Prepositions, p. T285

Day 3

Write to a Source

- Write about "Ollie's Escape," independent practice, p. T281D

- Provide scaffolded instruction to meet student needs, p. T286

Day 4 and Day 5

Write to Two Sources

- Analyze a student model, pp. T286–T287

- Write to compare "Ollie's Escape," with "The Gentleman Bookworm," p. T287

WEEK 4: PREWRITE | WEEK 5: DRAFT AND REVISE | WEEK 6: PROOFREAD/EDIT, PUBLISH, EVALUATE

Writer's Workspace

Genre Writing: Informative Text

Research Report
Draft

- Discuss the student draft model
- Students write their drafts

Revise

- Discuss the revised student model
- Students revise their drafts

Revised Student Model

Student Draft Research Report

Revised Checklist Research Report

Grammar and Spelling Resources

Online PDFs

Reading/Writing Workshop Grammar Handbook p. 495

Online Spelling and Grammar Games

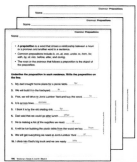

Grammar Practice, pp. 146–150

Phonics/Spelling Practice, pp. 175–180

SUGGESTED LESSON PLAN

Whole Group

READING

READING		DAY 1	DAY 2
Teach, Model and Apply	Core	**Introduce the Concept** T266–T267 **Vocabulary** T270–T271 **Close Reading** "The Camping Trip" and "Bubble Gum," T272–T273	**Close Reading** "The Camping Trip" and "Bubble Gum," T272–T273 **Skill** Point of View, T276–T277 **Literary Element** Rhythm and Rhyme, T278–T279 **Vocabulary Strategy** Idioms, T280–T281
Wonders Reading/Writing Workshop	Options	**Listening Comprehension** T268–T269	**Genre** Narrative Poem, T274–T275

LANGUAGE ARTS

LANGUAGE ARTS			
Writing **Grammar** **Spelling** **Build Vocabulary**	Core	**Grammar** Prepositions, T288 **Spelling** Suffixes *-ful, -less,* and *-ly,* T289 **Build Vocabulary** T292	**Write About the Text** Model Note-Taking and Write to a Prompt, T284–T285 **Grammar** Prepositions, T288 **Build Vocabulary** T292
	Options	**Write About the Text** Writing Fluency, T285 **Genre Writing** Research Report: Draft, T352	**Genre Writing** Research Report: Teach the Draft Minilesson, T352 **Spelling** Suffixes *-ful, -less,* and *-ly,* T290

Writing Process **Writing Process: Informative Text** Research Report, T350–T355   Use with Weeks 4–6

Small Group

Differentiated Instruction Use your data dashboard to determine each student's needs. Then select instructional support options throughout the week.

APPROACHING LEVEL

Leveled Reader
Funny Faces,
T296–T297

"My Cheeky Puppy,"
T297

Literature Circles, T297

Phonics/Decoding
Decode Words with
Suffix *-ful,* T298 **TIER 2**
Build Words with Suffixes
-ful, -less, -ly, T298 **TIER 2**
Practice Words with Suffixes
-ful, -less, -ly, T299
Frequently Misspelled Words, T299

Vocabulary
• Review High-
  Frequency Words, T300 **TIER 2**
• Answer Choice Questions, T301
Idioms, T301

Comprehension
• Identify a Narrator's
  Thoughts and Feelings, T302 **TIER 2**
• Review Point of View, T303
Self-Selected Reading, T303

Fluency
Phrasing and Expression, T302 **TIER 2**

ON LEVEL

Leveled Reader
Too Many Frogs,
T304–T305

"Pet Day," T305
Literature Circles, T305

Vocabulary
Review Vocabulary Words, T306
  T315

Idioms, T306

Comprehension
Review Point of View, T307

Self-Selected Reading, T307

DAY 3

Close Reading "Ollie's Escape," T281A–T281D

Literature Anthology

Phonics/Decoding T282–T283
• Suffixes -ful, -less, -ly
• Frequently Misspelled Words

Grammar Prepositions, T289

Write About the Text and Write to a Prompt T286
Genre Writing Research Report: Revise, T353
Spelling Suffixes -ful, -less, and -ly, T291
Build Vocabulary T293

DAY 4

Fluency T283
Close Reading "The Gentleman Bookworm," T281E–T281F
Integrate Ideas Research and Inquiry, T294–T295

Close Reading "Ollie's Escape," T281A–T281D

Write About Two Texts Model Note-Taking and Taking Notes, T286

Genre Writing Research Report: Prewrite the Minilesson, T353
Grammar Prepositions, T289
Spelling Suffixes -ful, -less, and -ly, T291
Build Vocabulary T293

DAY 5

Integrate Ideas T294–T295
• Text Connections
• Research and Inquiry
Weekly Assessment

Write About Two Texts
Analyze Student Model and Write to the Prompt, T287
Spelling Suffixes -ful, -less, and -ly, T291

Genre Writing Research Report: Choose Your Topic and Plan, T354
Grammar Prepositions, T289
Build Vocabulary T293

Writing Process · **Writing Process: Informative Text** Research Report, T350–T355   Use with Weeks 4–6 ➔

BEYOND LEVEL

Leveled Reader
The Joke's On You, T308–T309
"The Homework Blues," T309
Literature Circles, T309

Vocabulary
Review Domain-Specific Words, T310
• Idioms, T310
• Independent Study, T310

 Gifted and Talented

Comprehension
Review Point of View, T311
• Self-Selected Reading, T311
• Independent Study, T311

ENGLISH LANGUAGE LEARNERS

Shared Read
"The Camping Trip" and "Bubble Gum," T312–T313

Leveled Reader
Too Many Frogs, T314–T315
"Cat and Dog," T315
Literature Circles, T315

Phonics/Decoding
Decode Words with Suffix -ful, T298
Build Words with Suffixes -ful, -less, -ly, T298
Practice Words with Suffixes -ful, -less, -ly, T299
Frequently Misspelled Words, T299

Vocabulary
• Preteach Vocabulary, T316
• Review High-Frequency Words, T300
Review Vocabulary, T316
Idioms, T317
Additional Vocabulary, T317

Spelling
Spell Words with Suffixes -ful, -less, -ly, T318

Writing
Writing Trait: Word Choice, T318

Grammar
Prepositions, T319

DIFFERENTIATE TO ACCELERATE

 Scaffold to **A**ccess **C**omplex **T**ext

IF the text complexity of a particular selection is too difficult for students

THEN see the references noted in the chart below for scaffolded instruction to help students Access Complex Text.

Qualitative | Quantitative
Reader and Task
TEXT COMPLEXITY

	Reading/Writing Workshop	Literature Anthology	Leveled Readers	Classroom Library

			Approach · On Level · Beyond · ELL	
Quantitative	**"The Camping Trip"** Lexile N/A *TextEvaluator*™ N/A	**Ollie's Escape** Lexile N/A *TextEvaluator*™ N/A **"The Gentleman Bookworm"** Lexile N/A *TextEvaluator*™ N/A	**Approaching Level** Lexile 450 *TextEvaluator*™ 24 **Beyond Level** Lexile 780 *TextEvaluator*™ 49	**On Level** Lexile 670 *TextEvaluator*™ 35 **ELL** Lexile 600 *TextEvaluator*™ 16	**The Hurricane Mystery** Lexile 580 **Amos and Boris** Lexile 810
Qualitative	**What Makes the Text Complex?** • **Specific Vocabulary** Repetition T273; Figurative Language T281 **A C T** *See Scaffolded Instruction in Teacher's Edition T273 and T281.*	**What Makes the Text Complex?** • **Genre** Narrative Poems T281A • **Sentence Structure** T281C • **Specific Vocabulary** Wordplay T281E–T281F **A C T** *See Scaffolded Instruction in Teacher's Edition T281A–T281F.*	**What Makes the Text Complex?** • **Specific Vocabulary** • **Sentence Structure** • **Connection of Ideas** • **Genre** **A C T** *See Level Up lessons online for Leveled Readers.*		**What Makes the Text Complex?** • **Genre** • **Specific Vocabulary** • **Prior Knowledge** • **Sentence Structure** • **Organization** • **Purpose** • **Connection of Ideas** **A C T** *See Scaffolded Instruction in Teacher's Edition T360–T361.*
Reader and Task	The Introduce the Concept lesson on pages T266–T267 will help determine the reader's knowledge and engagement in the weekly concept. See pages T272–T281 and T294–T295 for questions and tasks for this text.	The Introduce the Concept lesson on pages T266–T267 will help determine the reader's knowledge and engagement in the weekly concept. See pages T281A–T281F and T294–T295 for questions and tasks for this text.	The Introduce the Concept lesson on pages T266–T267 will help determine the reader's knowledge and engagement in the weekly concept. See pages T296–T297, T304–T305, T308–T309, T314–T315, and T294–T295 for questions and tasks for this text.		The Introduce the Concept lesson on pages T266–T267 will help determine the reader's knowledge and engagement in the weekly concept. See pages T360–T361 for questions and tasks for this text.

Monitor and *Differentiate*

✓ Quick Check

To differentiate instruction, use the Quick Checks to assess students' needs and select the appropriate small group instruction focus.

Genre Narrative Poem T275

Comprehension Skill Point of View T277

Literary Elements Rhythm and Rhyme T279

Vocabulary Strategy Idioms T281

Phonics/Fluency Suffixes *-ful, -less, -ly,* Phrasing and Expression T283

If No → | **Approaching Level** | **Reteach** T296–T303
| **ELL** | **Develop** T312–T319
If Yes → | **On Level** | **Review** T304–T307
| **Beyond Level** | **Extend** T308–T311

Using Weekly Data

Check your data Dashboard to verify assessment results and guide grouping decisions.

Level Up with Leveled Readers

IF ➤ students can read their leveled text fluently and answer comprehension questions

THEN ➤ work with the next level up to accelerate students' reading with more complex text.

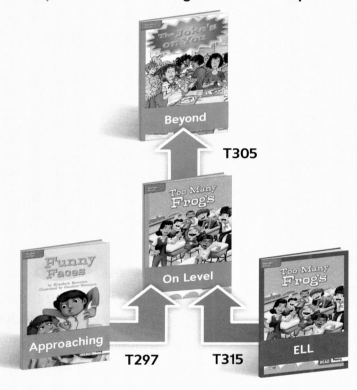

Beyond

T305

On Level

Approaching   T297   T315   ELL

ELL ENGLISH LANGUAGE LEARNERS

Small Group Instruction

Use the ELL small group lessons in the Wonders Teacher's Edition to provide focused instruction.

Language Development
Vocabulary preteaching and review, additional vocabulary building, and vocabulary strategy lessons, pp. T316–T317

Close Reading
Interactive Question-Response routines for scaffolded text-dependent questioning for reading and rereading the Shared Read and Leveled Reader, pp. T312–T315

Writing
Focus on the weekly writing trait, grammar skills, and spelling words, pp. T318–T319

Additional ELL Support

Use *Reading Wonders for English Learners* for ELD instruction that connects to the core.

Language Development
Ample opportunities for discussions, and scaffolded language support

Close Reading
Companion Worktexts for guided support in annotating text and citing text evidence. Differentiated Texts about the weekly concept.

Writing
Scaffolded instruction for writing to sources and revising student models

Reading Wonders for ELLs Teacher Edition and Companion Worktexts

→ Introduce the Concept

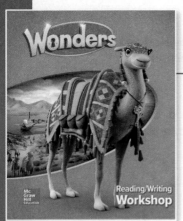

Reading/Writing Workshop

OBJECTIVES

ccss Follow agreed-upon rules for discussions (e.g., gaining the floor in respectful ways, listening to others with care, speaking one at a time about the topics and texts under discussion). **SL.3.1b**

Build background knowledge on humor.

ACADEMIC LANGUAGE

- *entertainment, humorous*
- Cognates: *entretenimiento, humorístico*

Build Background

ESSENTIAL QUESTION
What makes you laugh?

Have students read the Essential Question on page 458 of the **Reading/ Writing Workshop**. Tell them something that is *humorous* makes people laugh.

Discuss the photograph of the pigs. Focus on how lots of things can make people laugh.

- Your sense of humor is how much you understand or appreciate humor.

- Laughing can make you feel good. Lots of *entertainment* is made to make people laugh.

- Laughing helps you share feelings with friends.

Talk About It

Ask: *What do you think is humorous? What is something that made you laugh today?* Have students discuss in pairs or groups.

- Model using the Concept Web to generate words and phrases related to humor. Add students' contributions.

- Have partners continue the discussion by talking about what they think is humorous.

Collaborative Conversations

Be Open to All Ideas As students engage in partner, small-group, and whole-class discussions, encourage them to share and listen openly in their conversations. Remind students

- that all ideas, questions, or comments are important and should be heard.

- not to be afraid to ask a question if something is unclear.

- to respect the opinions of others.

- not to be afraid to offer opinions, even if they are different from others' viewpoints.

Go Digital

Discuss Funny Times

Watch Video

Use Graphic Organizer

Essential Question
What makes you laugh?

Go Digital!

LET'S LAUGH   *Poetry*

Lots of things make you laugh - jokes, funny stories, silly pictures. Just look at these pink pigs. Aren't they funny?

▶ Having a good sense of humor is important.

▶ Laughing makes you feel good.

▶ Laughing helps you share feelings with friends.

Talk About It

Talk with a partner about what you think is humorous. Write words about things that make you laugh.

Humorous

Bob Elsdale/Photonica/Getty Images

458

459

READING/WRITING WORKSHOP, *pp. 458–459*

ENGLISH LANGUAGE LEARNERS
ELL SCAFFOLD

GRAPHIC ORGANIZER 62

Beginning	Intermediate	Advanced/High
Use Visuals Point to the picture on pages 458–459. Say: *One pig looks like it is laughing. The picture is humorous, or funny.* Have students laugh for you. Ask: *What do you think is humorous? What makes you laugh?* Then have students complete the frame: *The picture is ____ (humorous). It makes me laugh.* Correct responses for pronunciation if necessary.	**Describe** Have students describe why the photograph is humorous. Then ask: *What do you think is humorous? What makes you laugh?* Have students complete the frame: *____ makes me laugh.* Elicit details to develop their responses. Encourage students to use the concept words in their responses.	**Discuss** Have students work in pairs. Ask: *What do you think is humorous? What makes you laugh?* Encourage them to use the concept words in their responses. Correct their answers for meaning as needed.

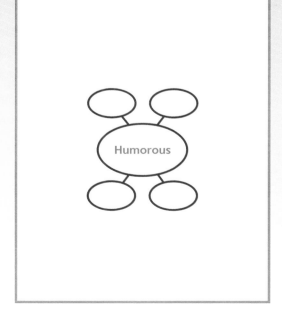

Humorous

→ Listening Comprehension

MINILESSON
10 Mins

Interactive Read Aloud

OBJECTIVES

CCSS Ask and answer questions to demonstrate understanding of a text, referring explicitly to the text as the basis for the answers. **RL.3.1**

- Listen for a purpose.
- Identify characteristics of poetry.

ACADEMIC LANGUAGE

- *poetry, reread*
- Cognate: *poesía*

Concept to Concept: Funny Times

Tell students that lots of things make people laugh. Let students know that you will be reading aloud a funny poem about something unusual that happens to a boy when he walks to school one day.

Preview Genre: Poetry

Explain that the selection you will read aloud is a narrative poem. Discuss features of poetry.

- may have a rhyme scheme or set rhythm
- may use personification in which animals or objects are given human feelings, thoughts, and attitudes
- uses imaginative writing combining images, language, and sound to create a special emotional effect

Preview Comprehension Strategy: Reread

Explain that when reading poetry, it is helpful to reread certain stanzas or parts of the poem to better hear the rhythm or to make sure you understand the imagery and figurative language of the poem. Use the Think Alouds on page T269 to model the strategy.

Respond to Reading

Think Aloud Clouds Display Think Aloud Master 4: *When I read _____, I had to reread...* to reinforce how you used the reread strategy to understand content.

Genre Features With students, discuss the elements of the Read Aloud that let them know it is poetry. Ask them to think about other texts that you have read or they have read independently that were poems.

Summarize Have students briefly retell the poem "Show and Tell" in their own words.

Go Digital

View Illustrations

Model Think Alouds

Fill in Genre Chart

Show and Tell

I walked to school
but like a fool,
I broke a rule
on my way there. **1**

I went by the lake
and met a snake
who hissed, "Please take
me with you!"

After a while we saw
two squirrels in some straw
and eight furry paws
came running.

Then just past the trees,
three busy bees,
buzzing, "Please, please, please,
take us, too!" **2**

We kept walking and met
a smelly quartet
of stinky striped pets,
four skunks!

When we got to Room 8
Mrs. Lee said, "Not great!
I can't educate
with these pets here!"

I said, "They're alright.
They're very polite.
There won't be one fight.
I promise."

So the animals stayed
and I got a good grade
when I happily displayed
my show and tell! **3**

1 **Think Aloud** I think I'll **reread** this part of the poem again to hear the rhythm that the poet has created.

2 **Think Aloud** When I read this section, I hear similar sounds in "busy," "bees," "buzzing," so I think this is alliteration. I want to **reread** this section again and listen for the sounds.

3 **Think Aloud** Now that I've finished the poem, I think I'll **reread** and listen for the rhyming pattern, the rhythm of the language, and any other examples of alliteration.

Yellow Dog Productions/Digital Vision/Getty Images

→ Vocabulary

Words in Context

MINILESSON
10 Mins

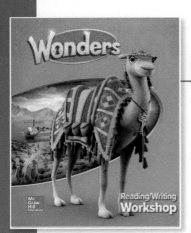

Wonders
Reading/Writing Workshop

Reading/Writing Workshop

OBJECTIVES

CCSS Identify real-life connections between words and their use (e.g., describe people who are *friendly* or *helpful*). **L.3.5b**

CCSS Determine the meaning of words and phrases as they are used in a text, distinguishing literal from nonliteral language. **RL.3.4**

ACADEMIC LANGUAGE

• *entertainment, narrative poem, rhyme, rhythm*

• Cognates: *entretenimiento, poema narrativo, rima, ritmo*

Model the Routine

Introduce each vocabulary word using the Vocabulary Routine found on the Visual Vocabulary Cards.

Visual Vocabulary Cards

Vocabu...
Define:
Example:
Ask:

Vocabulary Routine

<u>Define:</u> Something that is **humorous** is funny and makes people laugh.

<u>Example:</u> Evan couldn't stop laughing at Nick's humorous story.

<u>Ask:</u> Tell a *humorous* story to a partner.

Definitions

• **entertainment** — **Entertainment** is something that interests and amuses.

• **ridiculous** — Something that is **ridiculous** is very silly or foolish.
Cognate: *ridículo*

• **slithered** — Something that **slithered** slid or glided like a snake.

• **narrative poem** — My favorite **narrative poem** tells about Paul Revere's ride.

• **rhyme** — The words *moon* and *spoon* **rhyme** because they end in the same sound.

• **rhythm** — Ben's poem has a **rhythm** that sounds like a drumbeat.

• **stanza** — Each **stanza** in Maggie's poem has five lines.

Talk About It

COLLABORATE

Have partners look at each picture and definition. Have students choose three words and write questions for their partner to answer. Introduce each poetry word on page 165, and explain that students will find examples of these elements in the poems they read this week.

Go Digital

humorous

Use Visual Glossary

Words to Know

Vocabulary

Use the picture and the sentence to talk with a partner about each word.

entertainment Grandpa and Devon think playing chess is great **entertainment**.

What do you like to do for entertainment?

humorous Evan couldn't stop laughing at Nick's **humorous** story.

Tell a humorous story to a partner.

ridiculous Jess wore a **ridiculous** clown nose and made his friends giggle.

What is another word for *ridiculous*?

slithered The long, thin snake **slithered** across the floor.

Move your hands to show what slithered looks like.

460

Poetry Words

narrative poem

My favorite **narrative poem** tells about Paul Revere's ride.

What story would you tell in a narrative poem?

rhyme

The words *moon* and *spoon* **rhyme** because they end in the same sound.

Name another word that rhymes with *moon* and *spoon*.

rhythm

Ben's poem has a **rhythm** that sounds like a drumbeat.

Why might a poet include rhythm in a poem?

stanza

Each **stanza** in Maggie's poem has five lines.

Write a poem with two stanzas.

Your Turn COLLABORATE

Pick three words. Then write three questions for your partner to answer.

Go Digital! Use the online visual glossary

461

READING/WRITING WORKSHOP, *pp. 460–461*

ELL ENGLISH LANGUAGE LEARNERS SCAFFOLD

Beginning

Use Visuals Say: *Let's look at the picture for* ridiculous. *The clown nose is* ridiculous. *It is funny and silly.* Make a silly face. Say: *I am making a* ridiculous *face. What other* ridiculous *things make you laugh?* Have students complete the sentence frame: ____ *is* ridiculous. (a joke, funny movie) Give students ample time to respond.

Intermediate

Describe Have students describe the picture for *ridiculous.* Say: *The red nose is silly and funny. It is ridiculous. Turn to a partner and discuss things that you think are ridiculous.* Ask students to use the word *ridiculous* in a sentence that tells about something that they find silly. Correct responses for meaning as needed.

Advanced/High

Discuss Say: *The word* ridiculous *means very funny or silly. It is stronger than the word* funny. *What is something that you think is ridiculous, or very silly?* Have students write a sentence that tells why something is ridiculous. Invite volunteers to share their sentence with the class. Correct responses for meaning as needed.

ON-LEVEL PRACTICE BOOK p. 291

| entertainment | ridiculous | humorous | slithered |

Use a word from the box to answer each question. Then use the word in a sentence. Possible responses provided.

1. What does a performer provide? __entertainment__
   The clown provided *entertainment* to the guests.

2. What is another word for *funny*? __humorous__
   I like to tell *humorous* stories to make people laugh.

3. What did the snake do as it moved through the grass? __slithered__
   The small newt *slithered* across the front porch.

4. What word might describe someone who is acting very silly? __ridiculous__
   The dizzy boy looked *ridiculous* trying to walk a straight line.

| APPROACHING p. 291 | BEYOND p. 291 | ELL p. 291 |

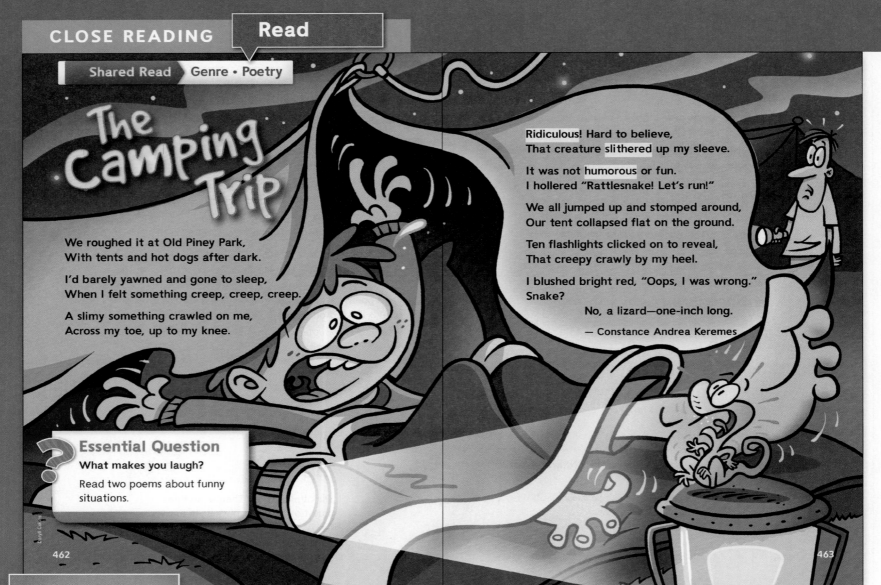

Shared Read ▸ Genre • Poetry

The Camping Trip

We roughed it at Old Piney Park,
With tents and hot dogs after dark.

I'd barely yawned and gone to sleep,
When I felt something creep, creep, creep.

A slimy something crawled on me,
Across my toe, up to my knee.

Ridiculous! Hard to believe,
That creature slithered up my sleeve.

It was not humorous or fun.
I hollered "Rattlesnake! Let's run!"

We all jumped up and stomped around,
Our tent collapsed flat on the ground.

Ten flashlights clicked on to reveal,
That creepy crawly by my heel.

I blushed bright red, "Oops, I was wrong."
Snake?

No, a lizard—one-inch long.

— Constance Andrea Keremes

Essential Question
What makes you laugh?
Read two poems about funny situations.

462
463

READING/WRITING WORKSHOP, *pp. 462–463*

Reading/Writing Workshop

See pages T312–T313 for Interactive Question-Response routine for the Shared Read.

Shared Read

Close Reading Routine

Read DOK 1–2

• Identify key ideas and details about Funny Times.
• Take notes and summarize.
• Use **ACT** prompts as needed.

Reread DOK 2–3

• Analyze the text, craft, and structure.
• Use the Reread minilessons.

Integrate DOK 4

• Integrate knowledge and ideas.
• Make text-to-text connections.
• Use the Integrate lesson.

Read

Connect to Concept: Funny Times Tell students they will read two poems that were written to make the reader laugh.

Note Taking Read page 462 together. As you read, model how to take notes. *I will think about the Essential Question as I read and note key ideas and details.* Encourage students to note words they don't understand and questions they have.

Tell students that narrative poems tell a story. Sometimes the narrator is a character in the poem. Tell students to look for elements of narrative poetry as they read.

Bubble Gum

I bought a pack of bubble gum,
    As I do every week,
Unwrapping 10 or 20 sticks,
    I popped them in my cheek.

I started masticating,
    That's a fancy word for chew,
The gum became a juicy gob,
    I took a breath and blew.

I suddenly inflated,
    Puffing up like a balloon,
I was a giant bubble,
    Big and round as a full moon.

My father hit the ceiling,
    He was really in a stew,
He hollered, "Stop! Don't go!"
    As out the door I flew.

The neighbors' eyes were popping.
    They dropped everything to see.
I was the entertainment of the day.
    Forget about TV.

If you like bubble gum, beware—
    Chew just one stick a day,
Or you'll become a bubble, too
    And float up   Up   AWAY!

I saw my friends below me,
    And let loose a mighty roar.
WHOOSH!
All my air blew out,
    And I was just a kid once more.

— Diana Kent

Make Connections

Which poem made you laugh? Talk about what funny thing happens in each of the poems. ESSENTIAL QUESTION

Which poem has the funniest events or characters? TEXT TO SELF

464

465

READING/WRITING WORKSHOP, pp. 464–465

Stanzas 1–3: Model how to summarize the first three stanzas of "The Camping Trip."

The narrator is camping at Old Piney Park, and the poem is set at night. The narrator had just gone to sleep when he felt something crawling on him. Ask: *What details tell you "The Camping Trip" is a narrative poem?* Model how to cite text evidence.

I know this is a narrative poem because it tells a story. The narrator is a character in the poem.

Make Connections COLLABORATE

Essential Question Have partners discuss the funny things that happened in each poem. Use these sentence frames to focus discussion:

> *In the first poem, the narrator thought . . .*
> *In the second poem, the narrator chewed . . .*

A C T Access Complex Text

▶ Specific Vocabulary

Students may be unfamiliar with the poet's use of repetition in "The Camping Trip."

- Point out the words *creep, creep, creep* in the second stanza on page 462.

- Explain to students that poets use repetition to emphasize a point and help readers visualize what is happening.

- Ask: *What do you picture in your mind in the second stanza?* (a tiny creature slowly creeping up the narrator's leg)

→ # Genre: Poetry

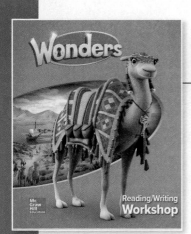

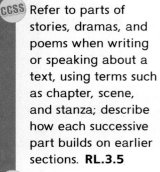

Reading/Writing Workshop

OBJECTIVES

CCSS Refer to parts of stories, dramas, and poems when writing or speaking about a text, using terms such as chapter, scene, and stanza; describe how each successive part builds on earlier sections. **RL.3.5**

CCSS By the end of the year, read and comprehend literature, including stories, dramas, and poetry, at the high end of the grades 2–3 text complexity band independently and proficiently. **RL.3.10**

Identify characteristics of narrative poetry.

ACADEMIC LANGUAGE

• *narrative poetry*

• Cognate: *poesía narrativa*

Narrative Poem

1 Explain

Share with students the following key characteristics of **narrative poetry**:

- Narrative poetry tells a story. Narrative poems can read like a story.

- Narrative poetry may be written in stanzas, or groups of lines.

2 Model Close Reading: Text Evidence

Model identifying features of narrative poetry in "Bubble Gum" on pages 464 and 465.

Stanza Point out that the first four lines of "Bubble Gum" make a stanza. A stanza is a group of lines. Ask: *Which lines rhyme in this stanza?*

3 Guided Practice of Close Reading

Have students work with partners to reread "The Camping Trip" and explain why it is a narrative poem. Then ask how many stanzas are in it. Ask volunteers to share their answers with the class.

Go Digital

Present the Lesson

Genre › Poetry

Narrative Poem

Narrative poetry: • Tells a story. • Can have any number of lines and stanzas.

A **stanza**: • Is a group of lines that form part of a poem.
• Often has rhyme and rhythm.

 Find Text Evidence

I can tell that "Bubble Gum" is a narrative poem. It tells a story. It also has stanzas. Each stanza has four lines. The second and fourth lines rhyme.

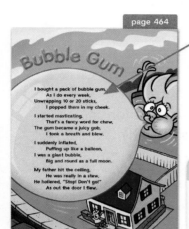

page 464

Bubble Gum

I bought a pack of bubble gum,
    As I do every week,
Unwrapping 10 or 20 sticks,
    I popped them in my cheek.

I started masticating,
    That's a fancy word for chew,
The gum became a juicy gob,
    I took a breath and blew.

I suddenly inflated,
    Puffing up like a balloon,
I was a giant bubble,
    Big and round as a full moon.

My father hit the ceiling,
    He was really in a stew,
He hollered, "Stop! Don't go!"
    As out the door I flew.

This is a stanza. It is a group of lines. There are four stanzas on this page.

Your Turn

 COLLABORATE

Reread the poem "The Camping Trip." Explain why it is a narrative poem. Tell how many stanzas are in it.

466

READING/WRITING WORKSHOP, *p. 466*

Monitor and *Differentiate*

✓ Quick Check

Do students identify the elements of narrative poetry in "The Camping Trip"? Can they tell how many stanzas are included in the poem?

⬇

Small Group Instruction

If No →	**Approaching Level**	**Reteach p. T296**
	ELL	**Develop p. T312**
If Yes→	**On Level**	**Review p. T304**
	Beyond Level	**Extend p. T308**

ELL ENGLISH LANGUAGE LEARNERS SCAFFOLD

Beginning	**Intermediate**	**Advanced/High**
Clarify Point out that the poem tells a funny story. Reread each stanza chorally with students. Have students raise their hands each time they begin a new stanza with you. Explain any difficult words or phrases to students. Ask: *What is the poem about?* Guide students in understanding the humor in the story about bubble gum.	**Describe** Have students reread "Bubble Gum." Ask: *What is the poem about?* Point out why the text is difficult. The narrator is a girl who chewed on too many pieces of bubble gum. She describes how she floated away when she blew a giant bubble. Point out that the second and fourth lines of each stanza rhyme.	**Discuss** Have partners reread "Bubble Gum." Elicit why the text is difficult. Ask: *What is the story in this poem? Turn to a partner and explain.* If necessary, ask additional questions to develop students' responses.

ON-LEVEL PRACTICE BOOK p295

The Snowman

We made his eyes out of pudding cups,
    his mouth from pizza crust.
His mustache was tortilla chips
    we'd pounded into dust.

In his right hand we stuck a broken stick
    topped by a tuna tin.
His left hand held the head that wore
    a grim leftover grin.

Answer the questions about the poem.

1. How many stanzas does this poem have? How many lines does each stanza have?
   two; four

2. Which lines in the first stanza rhyme?
   the second and fourth line

3. What does the poem tell a story about?
   The speaker tells about making a snowman.

4. What does the speaker think of the snowman?
   The speaker thinks the snowman is strange or creepy.

APPROACHING p. 295	BEYOND p. 295	ELL p. 295

→ Comprehension Skill

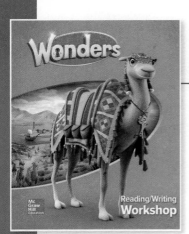

Reading/Writing Workshop

OBJECTIVES

 CCSS Distinguish their own point of view from that of the narrator or those of the characters. **RL.3.6**

Identify the narrator's point of view in a poem.

ACADEMIC LANGUAGE

• narrator, point of view, details

• Cognates: narrador, detalles

 MINILESSON 10 Mins ## Point of View

1 Explain

Explain to students that narrators in a story often have opinions, thoughts, or feelings about a story's events or characters. This opinion is the narrator's point of view.

• To identify the narrator's point of view, students should look for details that show what the narrator thinks or feels.

• Students should use the actions and reactions of the narrator or characters to infer their point of view when it is not directly stated.

2 Model Close Reading: Text Evidence

Model identifying details that help identify the narrator's point of view. Then model listing the details in the graphic organizer.

 Analytical Writing **Write About Reading: Point of View** Model for students how to use the notes in their graphic organizer to write a summary of the details that describe the narrator's point of view in "The Camping Trip."

3 Guided Practice of Close Reading

 COLLABORATE Have students work in pairs to complete a graphic organizer for the narrator's point of view in "The Camping Trip," going back into the text to find more clues that show how the narrator feels about the creepy creature. Remind them to use these clues to determine the narrator's point of view. Discuss each detail as students complete the graphic organizer.

 Analytical Writing **Write About Reading: Point of View** Ask pairs to work together to write a summary of their points of view about the creepy creature in "The Camping Trip." Students' summaries should distinguish their own points of view from that of the poem's narrator.

  **Go Digital**

Present the Lesson

SKILLS TRACE

POINT OF VIEW

Introduce Unit 2 Week 5

Review Unit 4 Weeks 1, 2, 6; Unit 5 Weeks 1, 2; Unit 6 Week 5

Assess Units 2, 4, 5, 6

Comprehension Skill

Point of View

Point of view in a poem is what the narrator thinks about an event, a thing, or a person. Look for details that show the narrator's point of view.

 Find Text Evidence

In "The Camping Trip" I read that the narrator feels something creeping on him. He calls it slimy. He says it slithered. The details tell me he is either afraid of or dislikes small, creepy crawly things. This is the narrator's point of view.

Details

"A slimy something crawled on me,"

↓

Point of View

Your Turn COLLABORATE

Reread "The Camping Trip." Find more details about how the narrator feels about the creepy creature. Write them in the graphic organizer. Then write the narrator's point of view. Do you agree with the narrator's point of view? Why or why not?

Go Digital!
Use the interactive graphic organizer

467

READING/WRITING WORKSHOP, *p. 467*

ENGLISH LANGUAGE LEARNERS SCAFFOLD

ELL

Beginning

Actively Engage Say: *To find what the narrator thinks, I look at the words used.* Read the third stanza on page 462 of "The Camping Trip" chorally with students. Point out the word *slimy*. Ask: *Do you think the narrator likes slimy things?* Elicit from students how they might react if a slimy lizard crawled on them. Students may respond nonverbally.

Intermediate

Describe Reread the third stanza of "The Camping Trip" on page 462. Ask: *Which word is a clue that shows what the narrator thinks of the creature?* (slimy) Explain that this is the narrator's point of view. Have students complete the frame: *The narrator thinks ____.* Elicit details to develop students' responses.

Advanced/High

Explain Have students reread "The Camping Trip." Ask: *What is the narrator's point of view in the poem?* Have students work in pairs to describe the narrator's point of view about the creepy creature. Then ask volunteers to share what they think of the creature. Elicit details to develop their responses.

Monitor and *Differentiate*

 Quick Check

Can students find and list details that show how the narrator feels about the creepy creature? Do they compare their point of view with the narrator's?

↓

Small Group Instruction

If No → **Approaching Level** Reteach p. T303
ELL Develop p. T312
If Yes→ **On Level** Review p. T307
Beyond Level Extend p. T311

ON-LEVEL PRACTICE BOOK pp. 293-294

A. Reread the passage and answer the questions.
Possible responses provided.

1. **What is this poem about?**

   A boy is telling the story of how he found out he was an alien.

2. **What is the narrator's point of view in the poem?**

   The narrator is shocked, but interested and fascinated by the things
   that his dad tells him.

3. **What clues in the poem tell you the narrator's point of view?**

   He says that he was shocked as they flew into the sky. He also says his
   dad sounded profound when he spoke.

B. Work with a partner. Read the passage aloud. Pay attention to phrasing and expression. Stop after one minute. Fill out the chart.

	Words Read	–	Number of Errors	=	Words Correct Score
First Read		–		=	
Second Read		–		=	

APPROACHING pp. 293-294	BEYOND pp. 293-294	ELL pp. 293-294

→ Literary Elements

**Reading/Writing
Workshop**

MINILESSON 10 Mins — Rhythm and Rhyme

1 Explain

Explain that poets use rhythm and rhyme to make a poem
interesting to listen to and fun to read.

- A poem's **rhythm** is the pattern of stressed and unstressed
  syllables in each line. Students can clap their hands as they read
  to follow the poem's rhythm.

- Words **rhyme** when their endings sound the same, such as
  pouring and *roaring*.

2 Model Close Reading: Text Evidence

Model identifying rhythm and rhyme in "Bubble Gum" on page
464–465. Remind students to listen for words that rhyme and to clap
their hands as they read to follow the rhythm.

3 Guided Practice of Close Reading

Have students work with partners to reread "The Camping Trip" on
pages 462–463. Have partners identify more examples of rhythm
and rhyme in the poem. Ask volunteers to share their answers with
the class.

**Go
Digital**

Present the
Lesson

Literary Elements

Rhythm and Rhyme

Poets use rhythm and rhyme make a poem interesting to listen to and fun to read.

 Find Text Evidence

Reread the poem "Bubble Gum" on pages 464–465 aloud. Listen for words that rhyme. Clap your hands as you read the poem to follow the poem's rhythm.

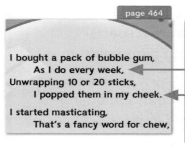

page 464

I bought a pack of bubble gum,
   As I do every week,
Unwrapping 10 or 20 sticks,
   I popped them in my cheek.

I started masticating,
   That's a fancy word for chew,

In the second and fourth lines of the poem, the words week *and* cheek *rhyme. I clapped my hands to find the rhythm. I like the way the poem has a pattern of sounds that repeat themselves.*

Your Turn

Find more examples of rhythm and rhyme in "The Camping Trip" on pages 462–463.

Daryl Collins

468

READING/WRITING WORKSHOP, *p. 468*

 **Monitor and** *Differentiate*

 Quick Check

Can students identify examples of rhythm and rhyme in "The Camping Trip"?

⬇

Small Group Instruction

If No → Approaching Level Reteach p. T297

ELL Develop p. T313

If Yes → On Level Review p. T305

Beyond Level Extend p. T309

ELL ENGLISH LANGUAGE LEARNERS SCAFFOLD

Beginning

Clarify Chorally read the first stanza of "Bubble Gum" on page 464, and then discuss the poem's main elements. Explain that rhyming words have the same ending sound. Point to and say the words *gum* and *sticks*. Have students repeat. Ask: *Do these words rhyme?* Repeat with *week* and *cheek*. Ask: *What sounds are repeated?* Correct students responses for meaning as necessary.

Intermediate

Describe Reread the first stanza of "Bubble Gum." Ask: *Which words rhyme?* Provide the frame: ____ *and* ____ *rhyme.* Then have students chorally reread the stanza. Clap out the rhythm, and have students repeat.

Advanced/High

Discuss Have partners read the first stanza of "Bubble Gum" together. Ask: *Which words rhyme?* Elicit details to develop students' responses. Then have partners clap out the rhythm of the first stanza together.

ON-LEVEL PRACTICE BOOK p. 296

Read the lines of the narrative poem below. Then answer the questions. Possible responses provided.

Aliens!

While waiting in the car for Mom,
Dad says, sounding very profound,
"I'm afraid I have to drop a bomb:
there are aliens around.

We didn't want to tell you boys,
we thought it might just freak you out.
I need you to stay calm and keep your poise
while I tell you what this is about.

1. Find two examples of rhyme in the poem. Write them on the line.
   mom and bomb; boys and poise

2. How can you pick out the rhythm in the poem?
   I can clap my hands to hear the pattern of beats in the lines.

3. Write another stanza for this poem that includes rhythm and rhyme.
   Answers will vary, but should include the use of rhythm and rhyme.

| APPROACHING p. 296 | BEYOND p. 296 | ELL p. 296 |

→ Vocabulary Strategy

 Figurative Language

MINILESSON
10 Mins

Go Digital

Present the Lesson

1 Explain

Tell students that authors use figurative language to help readers visualize what is happening in the poem. An **idiom** is a special kind of nonliteral word or phrase that means something different from the literal meaning of the words in it.

- An idiom is a phrase, or group of words, that mean something different from the literal meaning of each word in it.

- Students should look for phrases where the literal meaning seems out of place in the text to identify idioms.

- Students should use context clues in the surrounding text to help them distinguish the literal and nonliteral meanings of the idiom.

2 Model Close Reading: Text Evidence

Model identifying idioms in "The Camping Trip" on page 462. Show students how to determine the meaning of the phrase *roughed it*.

3 Guided Practice of Close Reading

Have students work in pairs to find the nonliteral meanings of the idioms *hit the ceiling* and *eyes were popping* on pages 464 and 465 of "Bubble Gum." Encourage partners to use the surrounding text to determine the meanings of the idioms.

Reading/Writing Workshop

OBJECTIVES

 Distinguish the literal and nonliteral meanings of words and phrases in context (e.g., *take steps*). **L.3.5a**

Determine the meaning of words and phrases as they are used in a text, distinguishing literal from nonliteral language. **RL.3.4**

ACADEMIC LANGUAGE
- *idiom*
- Cognate: *idioma*

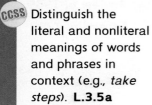

SKILLS TRACE

FIGURATIVE LANGUAGE: IDIOM

Introduce Unit 3 Week 2

Review Unit 3 Week 3; Unit 6 Weeks 2, 3, 5

Assess Units 3, 6

Vocabulary Strategy

Idioms

An idiom is a group of words that means something different from the usual meaning of each word in it. The phrase *lend a hand* is an idiom. It doesn't mean "to give someone your hand." It means "to help someone do something."

 **Find Text Evidence**

On page 462 in "The Camping Trip," the phrase *roughed it is* an idiom. I can use clues in the poem to help me figure out that it means "to live without the usual comforts of home."

page 462

We *roughed it* at Old Piney Park,
With tents and hot dogs after dark.

Your Turn COLLABORATE

Talk about these idioms from "Bubble Gum."
hit the ceiling, *page 464*
eyes were popping, *page 465*

469

Daryll Collins

READING/WRITING WORKSHOP, *p. 469*

 **Access Complex Text**

▶ **Specific Vocabulary**

Students may have difficulty distinguishing the literal meaning from the nonliteral meaning of an idiom.

- Read the idiom: *My father hit the ceiling.*
- Ask: *Does he really hit the ceiling?* (no)
- *Which words help you understand the literal meaning?* ("He was really in a stew"; "He hollered")
- *What is the literal meaning of the idiom?* (he was really upset)

 **Monitor and *Differentiate***

 Quick Check

Are students able to determine the literal meanings of the idioms *hit the ceiling* and *eyes were popping*?

Small Group Instruction

If No →	Approaching Level	Reteach p. T301
	ELL	Develop p. T317
If Yes →	On Level	Review p. T306
	Beyond Level	Extend p. T310

ON-LEVEL PRACTICE BOOK p. 297

Read each passage. Write the idiom in the passage on the line. Then write the meaning of the idiom.

1. I'm afraid I have to drop a bomb: there are *aliens* around.

   drop a bomb; meaning: say or do something shocking or surprising

2. We didn't want to tell you boys, we thought it might just freak you out.

   freak you out; meaning: make you scared or upset

3. But Mom was clever enough to say, "Did something go down while I was away?"

   go down; meaning: happen

| APPROACHING p. 297 | BEYOND p. 297 | ELL p. 297 |

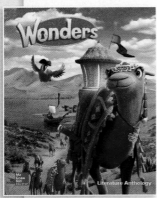

"Ollie's Escape"

Literature Anthology

Lexile and TextEvaluator scores are not provided for non-prose selections, such as poetry and drama.

Text Complexity Range

Lexile

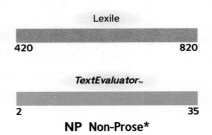

420   820

TextEvaluator™

2   35

NP Non-Prose*

What makes this text complex?

▶ **Genre**

▶ **Sentence Structure**

Close Reading Routine

Read   DOK 1–2

- Identify key ideas and details about funny times.
- Take notes and summarize.
- Use **A C T** prompts as needed.

Reread   DOK 2–3

- Analyze the text, craft, and structure.
- Use *Close Reading Companion,* pp. 194–195.

Integrate   DOK 4

- Integrate knowledge and ideas.
- Make text-to-text connections.
- Use the Integrate lesson.

Genre · Poetry

From Reading, Rhyming, and 'Rithmatic by Dave Crawley, illustrated by Liz Callen. Copyright © 2010 by Dave Crawley and Liz Callen. Published by Wordsong, an imprint of Boyds Mills Press. Reprinted by permission.

? Essential Question

What makes you laugh?

Read this **humorous** poem about a lively classroom pet.

Go Digital!

546

A C T Access Complex Text

▶ **Genre**

Explain that narrative poems tell a story and often have a problem and solution text structure, just as stories do.

- *What is the problem in this poem?* (Ollie the snake escapes.)

Tell students that as they continue reading, they should look for the way the problem is resolved.

Ollie's Escape

Ollie escaped in the classroom,
and that was an awful mistake.
It would have been folly
to try and catch Ollie,
since Ollie's a seven-foot snake.

He wiggled his way toward the teacher,
who jumped on her desk with a scream.
Faster and faster,
he squiggled right past her.
Old Ollie was picking up steam!

The rest of us ran for the closet
as Ollie slid right out the door.
We heard a loud squall **1**
as he entered the hall.
He's a difficult snake to ignore.

He slithered his way to the office
as teachers jumped out of his way.
But Principal Poole
is the boss of the school.
We wondered just what he would say.

547

Illustration: Shaffo Walker

LITERATURE ANTHOLOGY, pp. 546–547

Read

Essential Question Ask a student to read aloud the Essential Question. Have students discuss how the poem will help them answer the question.

Note Taking:
Use the Graphic Organizer

Remind students to take notes as they read. Have them fill in the graphic organizer on **Your Turn Practice Book** page 292 to record the point of view.

1 Skill: Point of View

How do the characters in the poem feel when Ollie escapes? (The characters are afraid.) How do you know? (The teacher jumps on her desk and screams. The children in the classroom run for the closet. The people in the hallway scream.)

Reread *Close Reading Companion*

Author's Craft: Descriptive Language

Reread page 547. How does the poet use words and phrases to make the poem funny? (The poet uses words, such as *wiggled, squiggled, slid,* and *slithered* to describe how Ollie moved and to help me visualize the action in the poem.)

ELL Chorally read each stanza with students, emphasizing the rhythm and rhyme of the words. Restate each stanza in a prose sentence. Ask:

- *Is Ollie a boy or a snake?* (a snake) *Read the line that tells you.*

- *What happens to Ollie?* (He escapes.)

- *Show me or tell me what the characters do when they see Ollie.*

Read

2 Skill: Point of View

What is Principal Poole's point of view about Ollie's escape? (Principal Poole is afraid of the snake.) What details support this point of view? (He decided to scoot. He burst through the door with a terrified roar. Principal Poole was on the run.)

Reread   *Close Reading Companion*

Author's Craft: Idiom

Reread the sixth stanza of the poem. How does the poet use an idiom to help you visualize the character's actions? (The idiom "on the run" means "trying to avoid being caught" or "running away." Principal Poole doesn't want to be near the snake. The idiom fits the rhythm and rhyme of the poem. The idiom is funnier than a literal phrase.)

It didn't take long for an answer.
In fact, he decided to scoot.
He burst through the door with a terrified roar
and a seven-foot snake in pursuit!

Ollie the snake was excited,
and we, of course, thought it was fun
to see teachers hiding
while Ollie was sliding
2 and Principal Poole on the run.

They ordered us out of the building,
and somebody called the police.
There were doctors and vets
and men with big nets
to make sure the problem would cease.

But Ollie, at last, was exhausted.
He snaked his way back to his den.
When they searched all around,
he was finally found—
curled up, asleep, in his pen.

—Dave Crawley

548

LITERATURE ANTHOLOGY, *pp. 548–549*

A C T Access Complex Text

▶ Sentence Structure

Read aloud the third line of the last stanza. The pronoun *they* is far from its antecedent. Help students determine who *they* refers to.

- *Reread stanza 3. Who is searching for Ollie?* (police, doctors, vets, men with big nets)

- *So who does* they *refer to?* (The police, doctors, vets, and men with big nets who are looking for Ollie.)

ELL Use illustrations and restatements to clarify the words *pursuit* ("chase after") and *exhausted* ("very tired"). Have students demonstrate or state a simple meaning for both words. Restate the multiple-meaning word *pen* as *cage*. Have students name animals that sleep in pens.

Respond to the Text

Summarize

Use important details from "Ollie's Escape" to summarize the poem. Information in your Point of View chart may help you.

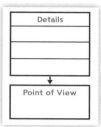

Details

↓

Point of View

Write

How does the poet use words and phrases to help you understand how the characters in the poem feel about Ollie? Use these sentence frames to organize text evidence.

The poet uses sensory language to . . .
His words and phrases help me visualize . . .
This is important because it helps me understand . . .

Make Connections

? What did the poet do to make you laugh?
ESSENTIAL QUESTION

What other kinds of things make people laugh?
TEXT TO WORLD

549

Integrate

Make Connections

COLLABORATE

Essential Question <u>Answer:</u> The poet used rhyme and rhythm to give the poem a humorous tone. He described how Ollie's escape was both scary and fun at the same time for the children. <u>Evidence:</u> Every stanza has the same rhyming pattern. In the sixth stanza, the children think its fun to see the adults scared of Ollie.

Text to World Answers may vary, but encourage students to cite text evidence from their sources and from their own experiences.

Respond to the Text

Read

Summarize

Tell students they will use details from their Point of View notes to summarize "Ollie's Escape." As I read the poem, I wrote down details. I can use these details to summarize the poem and explain the poet's point of view.

Reread

Analyze the Text

After students summarize, have them reread to develop a deeper understanding of the poem and answer the questions on **Close Reading Companion** pages 194–195. For students who need support in citing text evidence, use the Reread prompts on pages T281B–T281C.

Write About the Text

Review the writing prompt and sentence frames. Remind students to use their responses from the Close Reading Companion to support their answers. For a full lesson on writing a response using text evidence, see page T286.

<u>Answer:</u> The poet uses vivid descriptions and funny words and idioms to tell what happens. The language helps me visualize how scary it was to be around Ollie. <u>Evidence:</u> Ollie "wiggled" and "squiggled" and "slithered." One teacher jumped on her desk and others jumped out of the way and hid, and the children "ran for the closet." The principal ran away with Ollie chasing after him.

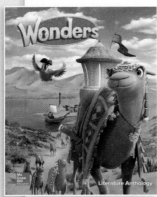

Literature Anthology
Lexile and TextEvaluator scores are not provided for non-prose selections, such as poetry and drama.

"The Gentleman Bookworm"

Text Complexity Range

Lexile

420   820

TextEvaluator™

2   35

NP Non-Prose*

What makes this text complex?
▶ **Specific Vocabulary**

Compare Texts *Analytical Writing*

As students read and reread "The Gentleman Bookworm," encourage them to take notes and think about the Essential Question: *What makes you laugh?* Tell students to compare this poem with "Ollie's Escape."

Read

1 **Strategy: Reread**

What did the guest worm do after the host worm gave his toast? (waved her napkin, curled up in a ball, and swallowed poems)

Reread   *Close Reading Companion*

Author's Craft: Illustration

How does the poet use the illustration to support the details in the poem? (It shows the worms eating books, in a formal setting.)

Reread   *Close Reading Companion*

Author's Craft: Personification

How does the author use personification to show what the bookworms are doing? (The worms eat with a fork and spoon, and speak French. They give toasts and use napkins.)

Genre · Poetry

Compare Texts
Read this **humorous** poem about hungry bookworms.

The Gentleman Bookworm

There once was a Gentleman Bookworm
Ate his words with a fork and a spoon.
When friends crawled down
From Book End Town,
He offered them *Goodnight, Moon.*

He fed them *The Wind in the Willows*
And a page out of *Charlotte's Web.*
They were eating bizarre
Where the Wild Things Are,
When one of the guestworms said,

550

A C T Access Complex Text

▶ Specific Vocabulary

- Students may need help understanding the wordplay in the poem.
- *Bookworms are worms that eat books. Who else do we call bookworms?* (People who enjoy books.)

"How sinfully rich and delicious!
Why should anyone bother to cook?
    You've done it, dear boy!
    Now sit down and enjoy
A bite of this poetry book!"

Having dined on the Table of Contents,
A worm, wiggling up to the host,
    Said, "When do we eat?"
    "Ah, *bon appétit!*"
Cried the Gentleman Bookworm. "A toast!

"Here's a bowl of my favorite verses
And a dish of ridiculous rhyme!
    But might I suggest . . . ?"
    Said the host to the guest,
"Chew them slowly. One line at a time!"

So the worm waved her postage-stamp napkin.
Curled up in a little round ball,
    She proceeded to swallow
    The poems that follow
Until she had swallowed them all. **1**

—J. Patrick Lewis

Make Connections

Why is a poem like "The Gentleman
Bookworm" good **entertainment?**
ESSENTIAL QUESTION

What other narrative poems have you
read? How are the poems similar?
How are they different? TEXT TO TEXT

551

LITERATURE ANTHOLOGY, *pp. 550–551*

Summarize

Guide students to summarize the poem.

Analyze the Text

After students read and summarize, have them reread to develop a deeper understanding of the text by annotating and answering questions on pages 196–197 of the **Close Reading Companion.**

Make Connections
COLLABORATE

Essential Question Answer: It is fun to compare how the bookworms in the poem like books with how people like books. It is also funny that the poet chose poems as the main course for their dinner. Evidence: The host "ate his words with a fork and a spoon." Before the guest ate her poems, the host suggested she "chew them slowly. One line at a time!"

Text to Text Answers will vary, but encourage students to cite text evidence from sources.

• *The bookworm tells his guests to chew the poems slowly, one line at a time. What might this mean about how poems should be read?* (They should be read slowly, line by line.)

• Make sure students understand that the titles in italics are well-known children's books.

ELL Before reading, clarify terms such as *bookworms, toast,* and the titles of the children's books.

• Tell students that a bookworm is also a person who likes books.

• Ask: *How are people who are bookworms and the bookworms in the poem the same?* Provide this frame: *They both like ____* (books).

→ Phonics/Fluency

MINILESSON 20 Mins

Suffixes -ful, -less, -ly

OBJECTIVES

CCSS Identify and know the meaning of the most common prefixes and derivational suffixes. **RF.3.3a**

CCSS Read grade-appropriate irregularly spelled words. **RF.3.3d**

CCSS Read on-level prose and poetry orally with accuracy, appropriate rate, and expression on successive readings. **RF.3.4b**

Rate: 97–117 WCPM

ACADEMIC LANGUAGE
• phrasing, expression
• Cognates: fraseo, expresión

ELL

Refer to the sound transfers chart in the **Language Transfers Handbook** to identify sounds that do not transfer in Spanish, Cantonese, Vietnamese, Hmong, and Korean.

1 Explain

Remind students that a suffix is a word part added to the end of a word. Point out that a suffix changes the meaning of the root word and can also change the word's part of speech. Explain that the suffixes -ful, -less, and -ly are three common suffixes.

2 Model

Write the words *pity* and *pitiful* on the board. Model changing the *y* to an *i* and then adding the suffix -*ful* to the word *pity*. Tell students that adding the suffix changes *pity* to an adjective. Repeat with *help/helpless* and *wise/wisely*. Point out that adding the suffix -*less* changes *help* to an adjective and adding the suffix -*ly* changes *wise* to an adverb. Model pronouncing each syllable as you sound out the whole word.

3 Guided Practice

Write the following list of words on the board. Help students identify the suffix and then pronounce each full word.

helpful	harmless	weekly
peaceful	useless	angrily

> **Read Multisyllabic Words**
>
> **Transition to Longer Words** Draw a T-chart on the board. In the first column write *careless, careful, helpless,* and *helpful*. In the second column, write *carelessly, carefully, helplessly,* and *helpfully*. Point to the words in the first column and explain that each word contains a suffix. Model how to read each word. Have students repeat. Write simple sentences using the words from column one and have students read them.
>
> Explain that the words in the second column contain a word with a suffix from the first column along with another suffix. Have students underline the suffixes in each word. Point to each word in random order and have students read the words chorally.

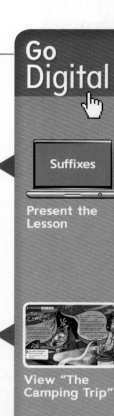

Go Digital

Suffixes

Present the Lesson

View "The Camping Trip"

Frequently Misspelled Words

1 Explain

Irregularly spelled words do not follow common spelling patterns and may have silent letters, such as *kn* in *know* or unusual vowel-sound spellings, such as *u* in *busy*.

• Preteach irregularly spelled words before students begin weekly reading. Have them say the word and write it. Place these words on the word wall.

• During independent reading, students can ask an adult or classmate for help if they can't decode an irregularly spelled word, or they can look it up in a dictionary.

2 Model

Display *weather, receive,* and *women*. Say each word. Have students repeat and then write it. Point out the irregular spellings.

3 Guided Practice

Display *busy, gnawing, Wednesday, roughly, scissors, mission, dough,* and *wonder*. Help students to decode each word.

Phrasing and Expression

Explain/Model Remind students that appropriate phrasing means grouping words and phrases to convey meaning. Explain that using appropriate expression also helps to convey meaning. Dialogue should be read the way a character would speak it. Point out that punctuation marks, such as an exclamation mark, can be used as guides to help readers use the appropriate expression.

Model reading page 463 of "The Camping Trip". Emphasize phrasing and expression when reading the second stanza.

Practice/Apply Have students take turns reading aloud with appropriate phrasing and expression. Offer feedback as needed.

Daily Fluency Practice FLUENCY

Students can practice fluency using **Your Turn Practice Book**.

Monitor and *Differentiate*

 Quick Check

Can students decode words with suffixes? Can students read frequently misspelled words? Can students read fluently?

Small Group Instruction

If No →	Approaching Level	Reteach pp. T296, T298
	ELL	Develop p. T314
If Yes →	On Level	Review p. T304
	Beyond Level	Extend p. T308

ON-LEVEL PRACTICE BOOK p. 298

A. Read the words with the suffixes *-less, -ful,* and *-ly* in the word box. Match each word to the correct meaning below. Write the word on the line. Not all words will be used.

wisely	hopeful	finally	careless
endless	adorable	argument	pitiful

1. full of pity ____pitiful____   4. in a wise way ____wisely____

2. in a final way ____finally____   5. without end ____endless____

3. without care ____careless____   6. full of hope ____hopeful____

B. Read each sentence below. Choose the correct word from the word box to complete each sentence. Write the word on the line. Not all the words will be used. Use a dictionary to check your answers.

thorough	your	scissors	through
sissors	journey	you're	weather
gourney	perswade	persuade	minute

1. Mom found ____your____ coat under the bed.

2. We will need ____scissors____ for this art project.

3. We did a ____thorough____ job cleaning the kitchen.

4. The speaker told us about her exciting ____journey____ to India.

5. An advertisement tries to ____persuade____ you to buy something.

6. The clock ticked down to the final ____minute____ of the game.

APPROACHING p. 298	BEYOND p. 298	ELL p. 298

→ Write to Sources

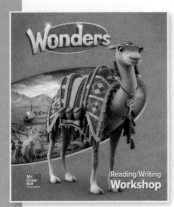

Reading/Writing Workshop

OBJECTIVES

CCSS Write narratives to develop real or imagined experiences or events using effective technique, descriptive details, and clear event sequences. Use dialogue and descriptions of actions, thoughts, and feelings to develop experiences and events or show the response of characters to situations. **W.3.3b**

ACADEMIC LANGUAGE

precise language

Go Digital

U6W5 Word Choice: Precise Language

DAY 1

Writing Fluency

Write to a Prompt Provide students with the prompt: *Describe what made one of the poems funny.* Have students share their ideas about what they think is funny. *What did the narrator say and do that was funny?* When students finish sharing ideas, have them write continuously for fifteen minutes in their Writer's Notebook. If students stop writing, encourage them to keep going.

 When students finish writing have them work with a partner to compare ideas and make sure that they both have a clear understanding of the poem.

Genre Writing

Research Report pp. T350–T355

Fifth Week Focus: Over the course of the week, focus on the following stages of the writing process:

Draft Distribute copies of the Student Model found online in Writer's Workspace. Teach the minilesson on developing a topic. Have students review the Main Idea and Details Charts they prepared in Prewrite, and write a draft.

Revise Analyze the Revised Student Model found online in Writer's Workspace. Teach the minilesson on tone. Have students review their partner's draft and revise their own. Distribute the Revise and Edit Checklist from Writer's Workspace to guide them.

DAY 2

Write to the Reading/Writing Workshop Text

Analyze the Prompt Read aloud the first paragraph on page 470 of the **Reading/ Writing Workshop**. Ask: *What is the prompt asking?* (to write a funny narrative poem using rhyme or rhythm) Say: *Let's reread to find examples of rhyme and rhythm. We can note literary elements.*

Analyze Text Evidence Display Graphic Organizer 59 in Writer's Workspace. Say: *Let's see how one student, Jen, took notes to answer the prompt. She notes the strong verb used in the line "That creature slithered up my sleeve."* Guide the class through the rest of Jen's notes.

Analyze the Student Model Explain how Jen used literary elements from her notes to write a response to the prompt.

- **Rhyme** Words rhyme when their endings sound the same. For example, Jen used *broom* and *room* in the first stanza. Jen used examples of rhyme from her notes to write rhymes in her poem. Trait: Word Choice

- **Dialogue and Description** Jen's poem is a narrative poem, which means it is a poem that tells a story. Jen used dialogue and descriptions to tell what's happening in the story. Trait: Ideas

- **Strong Verbs** Precise language helps create a clearer picture of the action and setting in the reader's mind. Jen used strong, precise verbs that show rather than tell. Trait: Word Choice

For additional practice with word choice and precise language, assign **Your Turn Practice Book** page 299.

Write to Sources

Write About the Text

Pages 462–465

Jen

I responded to the prompt: *Write a narrative poem about something that is funny. Include rhyme or rhythm.*

Rhyme
I used rhymes, such as *play* and *clay*, to make the poem fun to read.

Grammar

This **preposition** tells where Mom was taking the dirty clothes.

Grammar Handbook See page 495.

Student Model: *Narrative Text*

A Trick on Mom

One Saturday morning my cousin
came over to play.
As my mom cleaned the house and
swished the broom,
We built a fort with boxes.
We   made animals out of clay.
Then we saw Mom taking dirty
clothes to the laundry room.

"Quick! Let's hide behind the door!"
Tara said.
When Mom came in, we popped
out and screeched, "Boo!"
Mom gasped and dropped the
clothes. She yelled, "Whoops!"
We all laughed, but then
Mom gave us all the
folding to do!

Dialogue and Description
I used dialogue and described events to tell the story.

Precise Words
I used strong verbs to help readers visualize the action.

Your Turn

Write your own narrative poem about something funny. Include rhyme or rhythm.

Go Digital!
Write your response online.
Use your editing checklist.

470

471

READING/WRITING WORKSHOP, *pp. 470–471*

Your Turn Writing Read the Your Turn prompt on page 471 of the Reading/Writing Workshop aloud. Discuss the prompt with students. If necessary, review with students that poets use precise language to paint pictures with words so their readers can visualize actions and ideas.

Have students take notes as they look for literary elements to answer the prompt. Remind them to include the following elements as they craft their response from their notes:

- Rhyme
- Dialogue and Description
- Strong Verbs

Have students use **Grammar Handbook** page 495 in the Reading/Writing Workshop to edit for errors in prepositions.

ELL ENGLISH LANGUAGE LEARNERS SCAFFOLD

Beginning

Write Help students complete the sentence frames.
____ is/are funny.
I can use the rhyming words ____ and ____.

Intermediate

Describe Ask students to complete the sentence frame. Encourage students to provide details.
Something funny happened when I was with ____. They said, "____."

Advanced/High

Discuss Check for understanding. Ask: *What recent event did you find funny? How can describe so that others think it's funny?*

→ Write to Sources

DAY 3 For students who need support to complete the writing assignment for the Literature Anthology, provide the following instruction.

DAY 4

Write to the Literature Anthology Text

Analyze the Prompt Explain that students will write about "Ollie's Escape" on **Literature Anthology** pages 546–548. Provide the following prompt: *How does the poet use words and phrases to help you understand how the characters in the poem feel about Ollie?* Ask: *What is the prompt asking you to do?* (to analyze the poet's use of figurative language)

Analyze Text Evidence Help students note evidence.

Page 547 Read the second stanza aloud. Ask: *What verbs describe how Ollie moves?* (*wiggled, squiggled*) *What effect does this have on the reader?*

Page 548 Read the sixth stanza aloud. Ask: *What does Principal Poole do, and how does the poet describe his actions?* (He ran from the snake; the poet says he was "on the run.")

Encourage students to look for more text evidence of figurative language. Then have them craft a short response. Use the conference routine below.

Write to Two Sources

Analyze the Prompt Explain that students will write a poem inspired by the poems "Ollie's Escape" and "The Gentleman Bookworm." Provide students with the following prompt: *Write a funny narrative poem about something at school. Include rhyme or rhythm. Use examples of literary elements from two sources to help craft your poem.* Ask: *What is the prompt asking you to do?* (to write a narrative poem using rhyme or rhythm) Say: *On page 547 of the Literature Anthology, the poem describes the teachers jumping out of the way of the snake. So in my notes, I will write:* The poet puts the teachers in funny situations, which makes this poem humorous to me. *I will also note the page number and the title of the source. On page 550, in the first stanza,* spoon *rhymes with* Moon *and* down *rhymes with* Town. *I will add this to my notes.*

Analyze Text Evidence Display online Graphic Organizer 60 in Writer's Workspace. Say: *Let's see how one student took notes to answer the prompt. Here are Jen's notes.* Read through each poem and have students point out examples of literary elements such as humor, rhyme, and rhythm.

Teacher Conferences

STEP 1

Talk about the strength of the writing.

You use strong, precise verbs in your writing. I can understand your point clearly.

STEP 2

Focus on how the writer uses text evidence.

Your writing would be strengthened if you included more text evidence, including descriptions from the poem.

STEP 3

Make concrete suggestions.

This section is interesting. It would help me if you used more transitional words to link your ideas and show how they are related.

DAY
5

Share the Prompt Provide the following prompt to students: *Write a narrative poem about your favorite hobby. Include rhyme or rhythm. Use examples of literary elements from "Ollie's Escape" and "The Gentleman Bookworm" to craft your poem.*

Find Text Evidence Have students take notes. Find literary elements and give guidance where needed. If necessary, review with students how to paraphrase. Remind them to write the page number and source of the information.

Analyze the Student Model Review the prompt and Jen's notes from Day 4. Display the student model on page 300 of the **Your Turn Practice Book**. Explain to students that Jen synthesized her notes to write a response to the prompt. Discuss the page together with students or have them do it independently.

Write the Response Review the prompt from Day 4 with students. Remind them that they took notes on this prompt on Day 4. Have students use their notes to craft a short response. Tell students to include the title of all sources and the following elements:

- Rhyme
- Dialogue and Description
- Strong Verbs

 COLLABORATE

Share and Reflect Have students share their responses with a partner. Use the Peer Conference routine below.

Suggested Revisions

Provide specific direction to help focus young writers.

Focus on a Sentence
Read the draft and target one sentence for revision. *Rewrite this sentence to replace these verbs with strong, precise verbs.*

Focus on a Section
Underline a section that needs to be revised. Provide specific suggestions. *I want to know more about ____. Add an interesting description to help me visualize your idea.*

Focus on a Revision Strategy
Underline a section. Have students use a specific revision strategy, such as adding. *There are not enough details in this section. Try to add more details to show ____.*

Peer Conferences

Focus peer responses on using precise language. Provide these questions:

- Is the pattern of rhyme or rhythm clear?
- Can more dialogue or descriptions be added to improve the writing?
- What commonplace verbs can be replaced by more precise verbs?

→ Grammar: Prepositions

Reading/Writing Workshop

OBJECTIVES

CCSS Produce simple, compound, and complex sentences. **L.3.1i**

- Distinguish prepositions and prepositional phrases
- Use prepositions and prepositional phrases
- Use introductory words correctly
- Proofread sentences for mechanics and usage errors

Ask pairs of students to construct sentences with prepositional phrases. Use a pencil. Each student takes a turn giving placement directions for moving a pencil. The other student completes the action. Example: *Put the pencil under the chair.*

DAY 1

DAILY LANGUAGE ACTIVITY

My little sister is jelous. My bike is more fast than her.
(1: jealous; 2: faster; 3: hers)

Introduce Prepositions

- A **preposition** is a word that shows the relationship between a noun or a pronoun and another word in a sentence:
    The dog is **under** the couch.
- Common prepositions include *in, on, at, over, under, to, from, for, with, by, of, into, before, after,* and *during:*
    We went **to** the store.
- The noun or the pronoun that follows a preposition is the object of the preposition:
    We went to the **store**.

Have partners discuss prepositions, using page 495 of the Grammar Handbook.

DAY 2

DAILY LANGUAGE ACTIVITY

I cann't go today and I can go tomorrow. Can you goes, after school tomorrow. (1: can't; 2: today, but; 3: go; 4: tomorrow?)

Review Prepositions

Review with students how to recognize prepositions and what they do in a sentence.

Introduce Prepositional Phrases

- A **prepositional phrase** is a group of words containing a preposition, the object of the preposition, and any words in between, such as *at the beach:*
    We will have dessert **after dinner**.
- When a pronoun follows a preposition, it should be an object pronoun such as *me, you, him, her, it, us,* and *them*.
    This was a problem **for him**.

 TALK ABOUT IT

COLLABORATE

ADD A PREPOSITION

Pair students together and have them write simple, compound, and complex sentences about how people decide what's important. Have students read their sentences aloud. Their partner will add a preposition and an object of the preposition to each sentence.

MAKE A SENTENCE

Have partners create a list of what is important to them. Then have each student form a simple, compound, or complex sentence with a prepositional phrase about each item on the list.

DAY

Mechanics and Usage: Commas after Introductory Words

- A comma is used to separate an introductory word from the rest of a sentence.

- An introductory word could be a name, an adverb, or another word that should be separated from the rest of the ideas in the sentence.

As students write, refer them to Grammar Handbook pages 495 and 503.

DAY

Proofread

Have students correct errors in these sentences.

1. Until now Stephanie have been getting good grades.
(1: now,; 2: has)

2. Jack let's go to the store for she. (1: Jack,; 2: her.)

3. I'ld love to jump at the leaves. (1: I'd; 2: in)

4. Is Bridget on the backyard. (1: in; 2: backyard?)

Have students check their work using Grammar Handbook pages 495 and 503 on prepositions and commas in sentences.

See Grammar Practice Reproducibles pages 146–150.

DAY 5

Assess

Use the Daily Language Activity and Grammar Practice Reproducibles page 150 for assessment.

Reteach

Use Grammar Practice Reproducibles pages 146–149 and selected pages from the Grammar Handbook for reteaching. Remind students that it is important to use prepositions and prepositional phrases correctly as they read, write, and speak.

Check students' writing for use of the skill and listen for it in their speaking. Assign Grammar Revision Assignments in their Writer's Notebooks as needed.

WRITE THE PHRASE

Pair students. Have one partner look in a book to find a sentence that includes an introductory word or phrase. The first student will read the sentence, and the partner will write the sentence with appropriate commas. Have students take turns.

ROLE PLAY

Have several students reenact a scene from a story with dialogue that they have read recently. The other students will listen and identify any prepositions or prepositional phrases.

PLACE THE COMMA

Have pairs write five sentences about poems they have read that relate to what is important, using introductory words and commas. Sentences should include prepositions. Partners will take turns reading their sentences and the other partner will repeat the prepositions and state where the commas should appear.

Spelling: Suffixes *-ful*, *-less*, and *-ly*

OBJECTIVES

CCSS Use conventional spelling for high-frequency and other studied words and for adding suffixes to base words (e.g., *sitting, smiled, cries, happiness*). **L.3.2e**

CCSS Consult reference materials, including beginning dictionaries, as needed to check and correct spellings. **L.3.2g**

Spelling Words

careful	cheerful	helpful
colorful	harmful	pitiful
painless	priceless	helpless
sleepless	rainless	helplessly
peacefully	carefully	wisely

Review later, declare, partner
Challenge wonderful, cloudless

Differentiated Spelling

Approaching Level

careful	cheerful	helpful
harmful	careless	handful
painless	priceless	helpless
sleepless	rainless	weekly
hopeful	restless	wisely

Beyond Level

careful	graceful	ungrateful
colorful	harmful	wonderful
pitiful	priceless	rainless
cloudless	helplessly	carefully
peacefully	wisely	angrily

Assess Prior Knowledge

Display the spelling words. Read them aloud, drawing out the suffixes *-ful*, *-less*, and *-ly*, and reviewing their meanings.

Point out the spelling pattern in *careful*. Draw a line between the syllables: *care/ful*. Point out that the last syllable is the suffix.

Sort the spelling words by suffixes. Write the headings *-ful*, *-less*, and *-ly* on index cards or the IWB. (Write the words beneath these headings.) Sort a few words by identifying the suffix. Point out that, in some cases, spelling changes occur when adding suffixes. For example, *pity* becomes *pitiful*.

Then use the Dictation Sentences from Day 5. Say the underlined word, read the sentence, and repeat the word. Have students write the words.

Spiral Review

Review *r*-controlled vowel syllables. Use these Dictation Sentences for review words. Read the sentence, say the word, and have students write the words.

1. Class will cover division <u>later</u>.
2. The race was a tie, so there was no winner to <u>declare</u>.
3. Ellin was my <u>partner</u> in the science lab this week.

Have partners check the spellings.

Challenge Words Review the spelling words, pointing out the suffixes. Use these Dictation Sentences for challenge words. Read the sentence, say the word, have students write the word.

1. It was <u>wonderful</u> at the zoo.
2. The sky is blue and <u>cloudless</u>.

Have students write the words in their word study notebook.

 ## WORD SORTS

COLLABORATE

OPEN SORT

Have students cut apart the **Spelling Word Cards BLM** in the Online Resource Book and initial the backs of each card. Have them read the words aloud with a partner. Then have partners do an **open sort**. Have them record the sort in their word study notebook.

PATTERN SORT

Complete the **pattern sort** using the key words, pointing out the suffixes *-ful*, *-less*, and *-ly*. Have students use Spelling Word Cards to do their own pattern sort.
A partner can compare and check their sorts.

DAY 3

Word Meanings

Have students copy the words below into their Writer's Notebooks. Have them figure out the spelling word that goes with each definition.

1. full of caution (careful)
2. full of happiness (cheerful)
3. without hurt (painless)
4. without rest (sleepless)
5. in a calm manner (peacefully)

Challenge students to come up with clues for other spelling, review, or challenge words.

See Phonics/Spelling Reproducibles pp. 175–180.

DAY 4

Proofread and Write

Write the sentences below on the board. Have students circle and correct each misspelled word. Remind students they can use print or electronic resources to check and correct spelling.

1. Be carefl with priceles gems. (careful, priceless)
2. The pitifull cats seem helplss. (pitiful, helpless)
3. Put chemicals away carfully or they could be harmfull. (carefully, harmful)
4. The cherful girl walked peacefolly. (cheerful, peacefully)

Error Correction Students may make unnecessary spelling changes when adding suffixes. Students may drop the final *e*, spelling *careful* as *carful* or *priceless* as *pricless*.

DAY 5

Assess

Use the Dictation Sentences for the Posttest. Have students list misspelled words in their word study notebooks. Look for students' use of these words in their writings.

Dictation Sentences
1. Be <u>careful</u> not to break the glass.
2. The boy has a <u>cheerful</u> smile.
3. The museum workers were very <u>helpful</u>.
4. Flamingos are <u>colorful</u>.
5. Cold is <u>harmful</u> to tropical birds.
6. One cub was a <u>pitiful</u> sight.
7. Will the shot be <u>painless</u>?
8. The help she gave was <u>priceless</u>.
9. The baby tiger was <u>helpless</u>.
10. She had a <u>sleepless</u> night.
11. The <u>rainless</u> days caused a drought.
12. We had to look on <u>helplessly</u>.
13. The lions slept <u>peacefully</u>.
14. Helen picked up the vase <u>carefully</u>.
15. You must dress <u>wisely</u> for the weather.

Have students self-correct the tests.

SPEED SORT

Have partners do a **speed sort** to see who is faster. Then have partners write sentences, leaving blanks where spelling words should go. Have them trade papers and write the missing words. Have them record the words in their Day 2 pattern sort in the word study notebook.

BLIND SORT

Have partners do a **blind sort**: one reads a spelling word card; the other tells under which key word it belongs. Have them take turns until both have sorted all their words. Then have students explain how they sorted the words.

Build Vocabulary

OBJECTIVES

CCSS Determine the meaning of words and phrases as they are used in a text, distinguishing literal from nonliteral language. **RL.3.4**

CCSS Distinguish the literal and nonliteral meanings of words and phrases in context (e.g., *take steps*). **L.3.5a**

Expand vocabulary by adding inflectional endings and suffixes.

Vocabulary Words

entertainment	ridiculous
humorous	slithered

Have students of different language proficiency levels work together on the Build More Vocabulary activities. Partners should help each other choose language appropriate to the setting and task. For example, they should identify words that are better for talking on the playground than writing.

DAY 1

Connect to Words

Practice this week's vocabulary words.

1. What do you do for **entertainment** on weekends?
2. Tell about something **humorous**.
3. Why do clowns act in a **ridiculous** way?
4. What kind of animal could have **slithered** across the pavement?

DAY 2

Expand Vocabulary

Help students generate different forms of this week's words by adding, changing, or removing inflectional endings.

- Draw a four-column chart. Write *slithered* in the left column. Then write *slither, slithers,* and *slithering*. Discuss the meanings.
- Have students share sentences with each form of *slither*.
- Students can fill in the chart for other words, such as *entertainment*.
- Have students copy the chart in their word study notebook.

 # BUILD MORE VOCABULARY

COLLABORATE

ACADEMIC VOCABULARY

Discuss important academic words.

- Display the terms *interpret* and *evaluate* and discuss the meanings.
- Display *interpret* and *interpretation*. Have partners look up and define related words.
- Write the related words on the board. Have partners ask and answer questions using the words. Repeat with *evaluate*. Elicit examples from students.

SIMILE

- Review similes with students. Write an example on the board, such as: *I feel as free as a bird.* Point out that this doesn't mean that a person really feels like a bird.
- Have partners find or write other similes. Encourage them to use the pattern: ____ *as a* ____.
- Show several student examples on the board and discuss the literal and nonliteral meanings as a class.

DAY 3

Reinforce the Words

Review this week's vocabulary words. Have students orally complete each sentence frame.

1. This _____ is pretty <u>ridiculous</u>!
2. The snake <u>slithered</u> across the _____.
3. I like to watch _____ for <u>entertainment</u>.
4. My brother told me a <u>humorous</u> _____.

DAY 4

Connect to Writing

- Have students write sentences in their word study notebooks using this week's vocabulary.
- Tell them to write sentences that provide information about the words and their meanings.
- **ELL** Provide the Day 3 sentence frames for students needing extra support.

Write About Vocabulary Have students write something they learned from this week's words in their word study notebook. For example, they might write about something *humorous* or *ridiculous* that has happened.

DAY 5

Word Squares

Ask students to create Word Squares for each vocabulary word.

- In the first square, students write the word. (example: *ridiculous*)
- In the second square, students write their own definition of the word and any related words. (examples: *silly, funny*)
- In the third square, students draw a simple illustration that will help them remember the word. (example: an elephant wearing a dress)
- In the fourth square, students write non-examples. (examples: *realistic, serious*)

IDIOMS

Review idioms with students, giving examples if necessary.

- Display **Your Turn Practice Book** page 293. Read the first two stanzas. Model figuring out the meanings of the idioms.
- For additional practice with idioms, have students complete page 297.
- Discuss the literal and nonliteral meanings of the idioms.

SHADES OF MEANING

Help students generate words related to *humorous*. Draw a synonym/antonym scale on the board.

- Begin a discussion about the word *humorous*. Discuss synonyms, such as *funny, amusing,* and *hilarious* and write them on the scale.
- Ask follow-up questions such as: *What is the opposite of humorous? (sad, not funny, serious)* Write them on the scale.
- Ask students to copy the words in their word study notebook.

MORPHOLOGY

Use the word *entertainment* as a springboard for students to learn more words. Draw a T-chart.

- Write the word *entertain* in the first column. Discuss the meaning with students.
- In the second column, write the suffix -*ment* and tell students it means "the state or condition of." Discuss the meaning of *entertainment*.
- Have partners list other words with the suffix -*ment*, such as *encouragement* and *advertisement*.
- Ask partners to use the base words and suffix to determine the meanings of the words.

→ Integrate Ideas

Close Reading Routine

 Read   DOK 1–2

- Identify key ideas and details about Funny Times.
- Take notes and summarize.
- Use prompts as needed.

Reread   DOK 2–3

- Analyze the text, craft, and structure.
- Use the **Close Reading Companion.**

Integrate   DOK 4

- Integrate knowledge and ideas.
- Make text-to-text connections.
- Use the Integrate lesson.
- Use *Close Reading Companion,* p. 198.

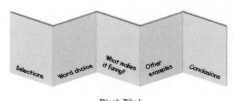

TEXT CONNECTIONS

Connect to the Essential Question

Write the essential question on the board: What makes you laugh? Divide the class into small groups. Tell students that each group will compare the information that they have learned about how learning about what makes them laugh. Model how to compare this information by using examples from this week's **Leveled Readers** and "The Camping Trip" and "Bubble Gum," **Reading/Writing Workshop** pages 462–465.

Evaluate Text Evidence Have students review their class notes and completed graphic organizers before they begin their discussions. Encourage students to compare information from all the week's reads. Have each group pick one student to take notes. Explain that each group

Dinah Zike's
FOLDABLES
Study Organizer

Humorous Poems

Go Digital

Collaborate

Research Roadmap

Resources: Research and Inquiry

RESEARCH AND INQUIRY

Write a Humorous Poem

Explain that students will work with a partner to write a humorous poem, such as a limerick, about a funny event Discuss the following steps:

❶ **What Makes You Laugh?** As they begin thinking about creating their poems, students should think of the selections that they read this week. Encourage students to also think about funny events in their own lives that made them laugh.

❷ **Find Resources** Students should refer to the online Fact Sheet about how to craft a limerick. Encourage them to research other examples of humorous poems to mimic. Have them list their source information.

will use an Accordion Foldable® to record their ideas. You may wish to model how to use an Accordion Foldable® to record comparisons.

Text to Poetry

As students discuss the information from all the week's reads, have them include the excerpt of Henry Leigh's poem "The Twins" on page 198 of the **Close Reading Companion** as a part of their discussion. Guide students to see the connections between Leigh's poem and text. Ask: *How does Leigh's poem connect to what you read this week?*

Present Ideas and Synthesize Information

When students finish their discussions, ask for a volunteer from each group to read his or her notes aloud.

OBJECTIVE

CCSS Refer to parts of stories, dramas, and poems when writing or speaking about a text, using terms such as chapter, scene, and stanza; describe how each successive part builds on earlier sections. **RL.3.5**

❸ **Guided Practice** Have students use their research as a guide to writing their own humorous poems. Remind students that effective word choices will make their poems funnier. Tell them to choose details carefully.

❹ **Create the Project: Write a Humorous Poem** Have students use their research and their own experiences to write their poems. Encourage students to think about word choice since humorous poems should be short and funny.

Present the Poems

Have students present their poems to other sets of partners. Afterward, conduct a class discussion about humorous poems and other forms of writing that make them laugh. Remind students to be attentive listeners and to share their own ideas during the discussion. Have students use the online Listening Checklist to evaluate their listening skills.

OBJECTIVES

CCSS Conduct short research projects that build knowledge about a topic. **W.3.7**

CCSS Use knowledge of language and its conventions when writing, speaking, reading, or listening. Choose words and phrases for effect. **L.3.3a**

ACADEMIC LANGUAGE
word choice

Approaching Level

Lexile 450
TextEvaluator™ 24

OBJECTIVES

(CCSS) Distinguish their own point of view from that of the narrator or those of the characters. **RL.3.6**

(CCSS) Demonstrate understanding of word relationships and nuances in word meanings. Distinguish the literal and nonliteral meanings of words and phrases in context (e.g., *take steps*). **L.3.5a**

• Reread text to check understanding.
• Identify a character's point of view.
• Determine the meanings of idioms.

ACADEMIC LANGUAGE

reread, point of view, realistic fiction, idioms, narrative poem

---

Leveled Reader:
Funny Faces

Before Reading

Preview and Predict

Have students read the Essential Question. Then have them read the title and table of contents of *Funny Faces*. Have students predict what the story will be about and share the prediction with a partner.

Review Genre: Realistic Fiction

Review with students that realistic fiction is a form of fiction that includes characters, settings, and events that could exist or happen in real life. As they preview *Funny Faces*, have students identify features of realistic fiction.

During Reading

Close Reading

Note Taking Have students use their graphic organizer as they read.

Pages 2–3 *From whose point of view is the story being told?* (Max's) *Find two examples that help you know the story is being told from Max's point of view.* (The story follows Max; Max hears Ella sniff and realizes she is crying.) *Why is Ella home from school?* (She has a bad cold.) *Turn to a partner and tell a clue that this story is realistic fiction.* (Max is doing everyday things. He comes home from school, eats a snack, and goes to talk to his sister.)

Pages 4–5 *Why is Ella crying?* (She missed the trip to the zoo.) *What does Max think when Ella explains why she is crying? Explain your answer using details from the story.* (Max knows that Ella has been really looking forward to the trip because for weeks now she has been talking about all the animals she would see.) *Why does Max offer to act out the animals for Ella?* (to make her laugh) *Tell a partner what you would do for a friend or sibling if he or she were upset.*

Pages 6–8 *Reread page 6. How does Ella feel about Max's lion impression?* (It scares her.) *What did Max mean to do?* (make her laugh) *What other impressions does Max do?* (parrot, snake) *Do they make Ella laugh?* (no)

Go Digital

Leveled Readers

Fill in the Graphic Organizer

Pages 9–10 *How does Max finally succeed in making Ella laugh?* (He acts like a monkey.) *Why does the author include monkey noises in the dialogue?* (to better portray Max's impression) *Find two other details that describe how Max imitates a monkey.* (He scratches his armpits and pretends to scratch his mom's back.)

Pages 11–15 Read the idiom on page 14. *Can a person really smile from ear to ear?* (no) *Look at the picture of Ella. What does it mean to smile from ear to ear?* ("to have a big smile on your face") *With a partner, list two details from the story that you found funny.*

After Reading

Respond to Reading Revisit the Essential Question, and ask students to complete the Text Evidence questions on page 16.

Analytical Writing **Write About Reading** Have partners write a short paragraph about whether Max does a good or bad job of trying to understand how Ella is feeling using details from the story to support their answer.

Fluency: Phrasing and Expression

Model Model reading page 11 with proper phrasing and expression. Next, reread the page aloud, and have students read along with you.

Apply Have students practice reading with a partner.

PAIRED READ

"My Cheeky Puppy"

Make Connections: Write About It **Analytical Writing**

Before reading, have students note that the genre is narrative poetry. A narrative poem tells a story. Then discuss the Essential Question.

Leveled Reader

After reading, have students use the information from "My Cheeky Puppy" to expand their discussion of what makes people laugh in *Funny Faces*.

FOCUS ON LITERARY ELEMENTS

Students can extend their knowledge of narrative poetry by completing the literary elements activity on page 20.

Literature Circles

Ask students to conduct a literature circle using the Thinkmark questions to guide the discussion. You may wish to have a whole-class discussion on how success can mean different things.

Level Up

Level-up lessons available online.

IF students read the Approaching Level fluently and answered the questions

THEN pair them with students who have proficiently read On Level and have approaching-level students

- echo-read the On Level main selection with their partner.

- use self-stick notes to mark a detail they want to discuss in each section.

A C T Access Complex Text

The On Level challenges students by including more **domain-specific words** and **complex sentence structures**.

Approaching Level

Phonics/Decoding

DECODE WORDS WITH SUFFIX -ful

 TIER 2

OBJECTIVES

 Identify and know the meaning of the most common prefixes and derivational suffixes. **RF.3.3a**

Decode words with suffix -ful.

I Do Remind students that a suffix is a letter or group of letters added to the end of a word. A suffix changes the meaning of the base or root word to which it is added, and it can also change the base word's part of speech. Write the words *care* and *careful* on the board. Tell students that *careful* means "full of care," or "attentive." Point out that adding the suffix -*ful* usually changes a noun to an adjective.

We Do Write *cheerful, helpful, harmful, handful* on the board. Model how to decode *cheerful*. Model splitting the word into syllables. Model how to decode the other words. Have students sound out the words with you.

You Do Add to the board: *hopeful, mouthful, peaceful, painful*. Have students read each word aloud. Point to the words randomly for them to read chorally.

BUILD WORDS WITH SUFFIXES -ful, -less, -ly

TIER 2

OBJECTIVES

 Know and apply grade-level phonics and word analysis skills in decoding words. Decode multisyllable words. **RF.3.3c**

Build words with suffixes -ful, -less, -ly.

I Do Tell students that they will be building multisyllable words with suffixes. Review suffixes -*ful*, -*less*, and -*ly* with students. Display the **Word-Building Cards** one at a time: *ly, ful, less*. Then write these syllables on the board: *dear, bare, joy, fear, use, end*. Sound out each syllable several times.

We Do Have students chorally read each syllable. Repeat at varying speeds and in random order. Next, display all the cards and syllables. Work with students to combine the Word-Building Cards and the syllables to form two-syllable words with suffixes. Have students chorally read the words: *dearly, barely, joyful, fearful, useless, endless*.

You Do Write other syllables on the board, such as *ly, ful, less, deep, gent, glee, doubt, mind, clue*. Have students work with partners to build words using these syllables. Then have partners share the words they built and make a class list.

PRACTICE WORDS WITH SUFFIXES *-ful, -less, -ly*

OBJECTIVES

(CCSS) Identify and know the meaning of the most common prefixes and derivational suffixes. **RF.3.3a**

Decode words with suffixes *-ful, -less,* and *-ly.*

 I Do Review that a suffix is a word part added to the end of a word which can change the meaning of the base word to which it is added. It can also change the base word's part of speech. Point out that when a base word ends in *y*, the *y* changes to *i* before adding a suffix, such as *happy/happily.*

 We Do Write *pitiful, beautiful, colorful, careless, priceless, helpless, weekly, wisely, carefully* on the board. Model how to decode *pitiful,* then guide students as they decode the remaining words. Help them divide each word into syllables using the syllable-scoop technique. Model changing the *y* to *i* before adding a suffix to a base word where appropriate.

 You Do Point to the words in random order for students to chorally read.

FREQUENTLY MISSPELLED WORDS

OBJECTIVES

(CCSS) Read grade-appropriate irregularly spelled words. **RF.3.3d**

Identify frequently misspelled words.

 I Do Review that many words in the English language do not have common spelling patterns and can be confusing in reading and writing. Some words are difficult to spell because of unusual spelling patterns or silent letters. Tell students to check a dictionary if they are unsure of a word's spelling, pronunciation, and meaning. Write *women, receive, people, company, pumpkin, minute, journey* on the board. Point out that these are frequently misspelled words.

 We Do Write *difference, thorough, library, persuade* on the board. Say each word as students repeat. Repeat several times. Tell students that it is helpful to keep a list of difficult words in a notebook and refer to it when writing.

 You Do Write *muscle, scissors, rhythm,* and *strength* on the board. Have volunteers define the words. Then point to the words for students to chorally read.

ELL ENGLISH LANGUAGE LEARNERS

For the **ELLs** who need **phonics**, **decoding**, and **fluency** practice, use scaffolding methods as necessary to ensure students understand the meaning of the words. Refer to the **Language Transfers Handbook** for phonics elements that may not transfer in students' native languages.

→ Approaching Level

Vocabulary

REVIEW HIGH-FREQUENCY WORDS

TIER 2

CCSS **OBJECTIVES**
Use conventional spelling for high-frequency and other studied words and for adding suffixes to base words (e.g., *sitting, smiled, cries, happiness*). **L.3.2e**

Review high-frequency words.

I Do Use **Word Cards** 201–240. Display one word at a time, following the routine:

Display the word. Read the word. Then spell the word.

We Do Ask students to state the word and spell the word with you. Model using the word in a sentence and have students repeat after you.

You Do Display the word. Ask students to say the word then spell it. When completed, quickly flip through the word card set as students chorally read the words. Provide opportunities for students to use the words in speaking and writing. For example, provide sentence starters such as *At what _____ do you have to be at school in the morning?* Ask students to write each word in their **Writer's Notebook**.

REVIEW VOCABULARY WORDS

TIER 2

CCSS **OBJECTIVES**
Acquire and use accurately grade-appropriate conversational, general academic, and domain-specific words and phrases, including those that signal spatial and temporal relationships. **L.3.6**

Review vocabulary words.

I Do Display each **Visual Vocabulary Card** and state the word. Explain how the photograph illustrates the word. State the example sentence and repeat the word.

We Do Point to the word on the card and read the word with students. Ask them to repeat the word. Engage students in structured partner talk about the image as prompted on the back of the vocabulary card.

You Do Display each visual in random order, hiding the word. Have students match the definitions and context sentences of the words to the visuals displayed. Then ask students to complete **Approaching Reproducibles** page 291.

ANSWER CHOICE QUESTIONS

OBJECTIVES

 Demonstrate understanding of word relationships and nuances in word meanings. Identify real-life connections between words and their use (e.g., describe people who are *friendly* or *helpful*). **L.3.5b**

Answer questions to demonstrate understanding of the meanings of words.

I Do Display the *entertainment* **Visual Vocabulary Card** and ask students: *Which is more likely a form of* entertainment: *homework or a TV show?* Point out that a TV show is a form of *entertainment*.

We Do Display the card for the word *humorous*. Read aloud the question: *When you hear something* humorous, *do you laugh or scream?* With students, explain that *humorous* things are funny, so people usually laugh.

You Do Using the questions below, display the remaining cards one at a time, saying each question aloud. Have students answer the choice questions.

When something slithers, *is it walking upright or moving on the ground?*

Does a narrative *poem tell a story or tell about a topic?*

Which words rhyme: thought/through or thought/bought?

Can rhythm *be found in music or in an expository text?*

Is a stanza *one line or several lines in a poem?*

IDIOMS

OBJECTIVES

 Distinguish the literal and nonliteral meanings of words and phrases in context (e.g., *take steps*). **L.3.5a**

Determine the meanings of idioms.

I Do Display the Comprehension and Fluency passage on **Approaching Reproducibles** page 293. Read aloud the first stanza. Point to the phrase *drop a bomb*. Explain to students that an idiom is a group of words that means something different from the meaning of each word in it.

Think Aloud I know that the father in the poem does not drop a real bomb, but he does tell his boys something very important and surprising. I think the idiom *drop a bomb* means "to tell someone something very surprising or important."

Write the meaning of the simile *drop a bomb*.

We Do Ask students to point to *freak you out* in the next stanza. Discuss how to determine the meaning of the idiom.

You Do Have students find the meanings of the idioms *make a fuss* and *did something go down* in the poem.

Approaching Level

Comprehension

FLUENCY

TIER 2

OBJECTIVES

 Read on-level prose and poetry orally with accuracy, appropriate rate, and expression on successive readings. **RF.3.4b**

Read fluently with appropriate phrasing and expression.

 I Do
Review with students that appropriate phrasing means grouping words and phrases to convey meaning. Reading with expression means emphasizing certain words and phrases to show emotion and understanding. Read the first stanza of the Comprehension and Fluency passage on **Approaching Reproducibles** page 293. Emphasize phrasing chunks of text, paying attention to punctuation, and grouping certain words together with expression.

 We Do
Read the rest of the page aloud, and have students repeat each line after you using the same phrasing and expression. Explain that you grouped certain words and phrases together to show meaning and emotion.

 You Do
Have partners take turns reading stanzas from the Approaching Reproducibles poem. Remind them to focus on their phrasing. Listen in and provide corrective feedback as needed by modeling proper fluency.

IDENTIFY A NARRATOR'S THOUGHTS AND FEELINGS

TIER 2

OBJECTIVES

Distinguish their own point of view from that of the narrator or those of the characters. **RL.3.6**

Identify the thoughts and feelings of a narrator in a poem.

 I Do
On the board, write: *In Maine, winter is the coldest season; Winter is the best season.* Explain that the average temperature of a season in a particular place is a fact because it can be proved. Saying that winter is the best season is what someone thinks about winter and is not necessarily what everyone thinks about winter. It is not a fact.

 We Do
Read the Comprehension and Fluency passage in the **Approaching Reproducibles**. Ask: *How does the narrator feel about learning what his Dad tells him?* Point out that students should look for words indicating emotion. Then ask: *Which lines show what the narrator is thinking or feeling?* Help students find words showing the narrator's thoughts or feelings.

 You Do
Have students reread the poem. After each stanza, they should write down any thoughts or feelings they found, including those of the parents. Then help students explain how they determined thoughts or feelings.

REVIEW POINT OF VIEW

OBJECTIVES

 Distinguish their own point of view from that of the narrator or those of the characters. **RL.3.6**

Identify the narrator's point of view.

 I Do Remind students that narrators often have a point of view on a topic. To identify the narrator's point of view, students should look for details that show what the narrator thinks about a topic. Students can then decide what these details have in common. This will help them figure out the narrator's point of view.

We Do Read the poem from the Comprehension and Fluency passage in **Approaching Reproducibles** together. Pause to point out details showing the narrator's point of view in the text. Then work with students to determine the narrator's point of view about the topic by referring to details in the poem.

You Do Have partners come up with the narrator's point of view in "Aliens!" in the Approaching Reproducibles. Then have them compare their point of view to that of the narrator.

SELF-SELECTED READING

OBJECTIVES

 Distinguish their own point of view from that of the narrator or those of the characters. **RL.3.6**

• Reread difficult sections in a text to increase understanding.

• Identify the narrator's point of view.

Read Independently

Have students choose a poem for sustained silent reading. Remind students that:

• the poem may include the narrator's thoughts on the topic. These show the narrator's point of view.

• if they have trouble finding the narrator's point of view, they should reread to look for details showing the narrator's thoughts or feelings.

Read Purposefully

Have students fill in **Graphic Organizer 146** as they read independently. After they finish, they can conduct a Book Talk, each telling about the poem they read.

• Students should share their organizers and answer these questions: *What was the narrator's point of view in the poem you read? Do you agree or disagree with this point of view? Explain why.*

• They should also tell the group if they reread any difficult parts of the poem to increase their understanding.

On Level

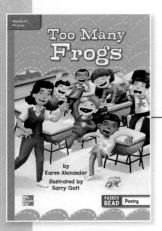

Lexile 670
TextEvaluator™ 35

OBJECTIVES

CCSS Distinguish their own point of view from that of the narrator or those of the characters. **RL.3.6**

CCSS Demonstrate understanding of word relationships and nuances in word meanings. Distinguish the literal and nonliteral meanings of words and phrases in context (e.g., *take steps*). **L.3.5a**

- Reread text to check understanding.
- Identify a character's point of view.
- Determine the meanings of idioms.

ACADEMIC LANGUAGE
reread, point of view, realistic fiction, idioms, narrative poem

Leveled Reader:
Too Many Frogs

Before Reading

Preview and Predict

Have students read the Essential Question. Then have them read the title and table of contents of *Too Many Frogs*. Have students predict what this story will be about and share their prediction with a partner.

Review Genre: Realistic Fiction

Review with students that realistic fiction has characters, settings, and events that could exist or happen in real life. As students preview *Too Many Frogs*, have them identify features of realistic fiction.

During Reading

Close Reading

Note Taking Have students use their graphic organizer as they read.

Pages 2–3 *Who is the main character in the story?* (Nat) *How do you know?* (The story begins with telling about Nat, and so far the story is following his actions.) *What does Nat love to do?* (play practical jokes on others) *What does Nat's mother think about his jokes?* (She does not like them.) *How do you know?* (It says: *she didn't think finding a furry toy mouse in the cereal was humorous at all,* and she bans Nat's tricks for two weeks.) *What do you think of practical jokes? Tell a partner.*

Pages 4–7 *What is Nat's point of view about April Fools' Day?* (He feels that he needs to come up with something really good to entertain his classmates.) *What does Nat do to play a trick on his classmates?* (He puts fake frogs out.)

Pages 8–9 *Reread page 8. What does Nat's principal think of April Fools' Day pranks? Explain your answer.* (He warns students not to do anything dangerous, so he must think they are okay as long as they are safe.) *Why does the author include the warning from Nat's principal?* (to give the reader a hint about what will happen in the story) *What does Mrs. Lopez do with the frogs?* (She puts them in her pockets.)

Leveled Readers

Fill in the Graphic Organizer

Go Digital

Pages 10–11 *Why are Nat's classmates screaming?* (Real frogs are hopping around.) *Summarize to a partner how Nat's prank has gone wrong.* (Nat left the top too far off the terrarium, and the frogs escape.)

Pages 12–15 *Why does Nat jump with fright?* (One of the frogs he set free is hiding under his desk.) Read the idiom on page 14. *What does Mrs. Lopez mean when she says that Nat has had a taste of his own medicine? Think about how medicine tastes.* (Now he knows what being tricked feels like, and it is not a good feeling.)

After Reading

Respond to Reading Revisit the Essential Question, and ask students to complete the Text Evidence questions on page 16.

Analytical Writing **Write About Reading** Have students work with a partner to write a short paragraph about what Mrs. Lopez thinks About Nat's prank using details from the text to support their answer.

Fluency: Phrasing and Expression

Model Model reading page 11 with proper phrasing and expression. Next, reread the page aloud, and have students read along with you.

Apply Have students practice reading with a partner.

PAIRED READ

"Pet Day"

Make Connections: Write About It *Analytical Writing*

Before reading, have students note that the genre is narrative poetry. A narrative poem tells a story. Then discuss the Essential Question.

After reading, have students make connections between how point of view helps you understand the characters in *Too Many Frogs* and "Pet Day."

Leveled Reader

FOCUS ON LITERARY ELEMENTS

Students can extend their knowledge of narrative poetry by completing the literary elements activity on page 20.

Literature Circles

Ask students to conduct a literature circle using the Thinkmark questions to guide the discussion. You may wish to have a whole-class discussion on things that make students laugh.

Level Up

Level-up lessons available online.

IF students read the On Level fluently and answered the questions

THEN pair them with students who have proficiently read Beyond Level and have on-level students

- partner-read the Beyond Level main selection.
- list difficult vocabulary words and look them up with their partner.

A C T Access Complex Text

The Beyond Level challenges students by including more **domain-specific words** and **complex sentence structures**.

On Level

Vocabulary

REVIEW VOCABULARY WORDS

 OBJECTIVES
Acquire and use accurately grade-appropriate conversational, general academic, and domain-specific words and phrases, including those that signal spatial and temporal relationships (e.g., *After dinner that night we went looking for them*). **L.3.6**

Review vocabulary words.

 I Do Use the **Visual Vocabulary Cards** to review key vocabulary words *ridiculous, slithered.* Also review poetry words *stanza, rhyme, rhythm, narrative poem.* Point to each word, read it aloud, and have students chorally repeat it.

 We Do Ask these questions and help students respond and explain their answers.

- What is something you think is *ridiculous*?
- What kinds of animals get around by *slithering*?
- What must a poem have to be called a *narrative poem*?

 You Do Have partners respond to these questions and explain their answers.

- What words can you think of that *rhyme*?
- What instruments are used to make *rhythm*?
- How are *stanzas* used in poetry?

IDIOMS

 OBJECTIVES
Distinguish the literal and nonliteral meanings of words and phrases in context (e.g., *take steps*). **L.3.5a**

Determine the meanings of idioms.

 I Do Remind students that an idiom is a group of words that means something different from the meaning of each word in it. Use the Comprehension and Fluency passage on **Your Turn Practice Book** page 293 to model.

Think Aloud I want to know the meaning of the idiom *drop a bomb*. I know that the father in the poem does not drop an actual bomb, but he does tell his boys something very important and surprising, which is that they are aliens. I think the idiom *drop a bomb* means to tell someone something very surprising or important.

 We Do Have students read the next stanza, where they will encounter the idiom *freak you out.* Then have students determine the meaning of the idiom.

 You Do Have partners work to determine the meanings of the idioms *make a fuss* and *did something go down* as they read the rest of the selection.

Comprehension

REVIEW POINT OF VIEW

OBJECTIVES

(CCSS) Distinguish their own point of view from that of the narrator or those of the characters. **RL.3.6**

Identify the narrator's point of view.

 I Do Remind students that a narrator often has a point of view on a topic. Explain that, to identify a narrator's point of view, students should look for details that show what the narrator thinks. Once they have determined the narrator's point of view, they can decide if they agree with it or not.

 We Do Have a volunteer read the first stanza of the Comprehension and Fluency passage on **Your Turn Practice Book** page 293. Have students give examples of the narrator's point of view. Model how to decide what the point of view is. Work with students to look for details that show the narrator's point of view in the next stanza.

 You Do Have partners identify the narrator's point of view in the remaining stanzas of the poem. Then have them identify the narrator's point of view for the entire poem. Have them tell whether or not they agree with this point of view and explain why.

SELF-SELECTED READING

OBJECTIVES

(CCSS) Distinguish their own point of view from that of the narrator or those of the characters. **RL.3.6**

• Reread difficult sections in a text to increase understanding.
• Identify the narrator's point of view.

Read Independently

Have students choose a poem for sustained silent reading.

• Before they read, have students preview the poem, reading the title and looking for text features such as stanza breaks and rhyme scheme.

• As students read, ask them to identify the narrator's point of view. Remind them to stop and reread difficult parts to help increase their understanding.

Read Purposefully

Encourage students to read different types of poems.

• As students read, they can fill in **Graphic Organizer 146**. They can refer back to it to write a summary of the poem.

• Students should share their organizers and answer these questions: *What is the narrator's point of view about the topic? Which details help show this point of view? Do you agree with the narrator's point of view? Why or why not?*

• Ask students to share their reactions to the poem with classmates.

Beyond Level

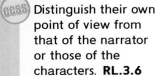

Lexile 780
TextEvaluator™ 49

OBJECTIVES

Distinguish their own point of view from that of the narrator or those of the characters. **RL.3.6**

Demonstrate understanding of word relationships and nuances in word meanings. Distinguish the literal and nonliteral meanings of words and phrases in context (e.g., *take steps*). **L.3.5a**

• Reread text to check understanding.
• Identify a character's point of view.
• Determine the meanings of idioms.

ACADEMIC LANGUAGE

reread, point of view, realistic fiction, idioms, narrative poem

---

Leveled Reader:
The Joke's on You

Go Digital

Before Reading

Preview and Predict

Have students read the Essential Question. Then have them read the title and table of contents of *The Joke's on You*. Have students predict the plot of the story and share their predictions with a partner.

Leveled Readers

Review Genre: Realistic Fiction

Review with students that realistic fiction has characters, settings, and events that could exist or happen in real life. As they preview *The Joke's On You*, have students identify features of realistic fiction.

During Reading

Close Reading

Note Taking Have students use their graphic organizers as they read.

Pages 2–3 *Who are the main characters in the story?* (Brad and Robbie) *What are two examples that tell from whose point of view of the story is?* (Brad likes playing practical jokes; Brad's best friend, Robbie, likes pulling pranks, too.) *Why does Robbie say the idiom* great minds think alike*?* (Because the boys have a similar idea at the same time.) *Tell a partner what you think of playing practical jokes on others.*

Pages 4–7 *What are two examples from the text that tell you this story is realistic fiction?* (Students should describe any of the dialogue and/or events.) *What practical joke do Brad and Robbie play in the lunchroom?* (They leave fake bugs in the food.) *How do their classmates react? Do they find the joke funny?* (They get frightened at first, but when they realize the bugs are fake, they do not think it is funny.) *Reread pages 6 and 7. What practical joke do the boys decide not to play, and why?* (They decide not to put glue on desks because it might hurt others or their belongings.) *What are Brad and Robbie planning to do instead?* (Make people confused about what time of day it is.)

Fill in the Graphic Organizer

Pages 8–10 *Why are Brad and Robbie's classmates arguing? Summarize to a partner how Brad and Robbie are able to trick their classmates and teachers.* (Brad and Robbie leave notes on the blackboards that make everyone think the clocks are wrong.)

Pages 11–15 *How does the author use suspense on page 12?* (Brad and Robbie are not sure if the messages are real or a prank.) *Think about the title of the story. How does it relate to what Brad and Robbie's classmates do?* (Brad and Robbie are usually the ones tricking people, but this time their classmates trick them instead.)

After Reading

Respond to Reading Revisit the Essential Question, and ask students to complete the Text Evidence questions on page 16.

Analytical Writing **Write About Reading** Have students work with a partner to write a short paragraph about what Brad and Robbie learn about other people's points of view. They should include details from the story to support their answers.

Fluency: Phrasing and Expression

Model Model reading page 3 with proper phrasing and expression. Next, reread the page aloud, and have students read along with you.

Apply Have students practice reading with a partner.

PAIRED READ

Leveled Reader

"The Homework Blues"

Make Connections:
Write About It *Analytical Writing*

Before reading, have students note that the genre is narrative poetry. A narrative poem tells a story. Then discuss the Essential Question.

After reading, have students make connections about the things that make people laugh in *The Joke's on You* and "The Homework Blues."

FOCUS ON LITERARY ELEMENTS

Students can extend their knowledge of narrative poetry by completing the literary elements activity on page 20.

Literature Circles

Ask students to conduct a literature circle using the Thinkmark questions to guide the discussion. You may wish to have a whole-class discussion on what makes students laugh.

Gifted and Talented

Synthesize Have students write a funny story of their own. Make sure the genre is realistic fiction and that students use at least one idiom. Have partners exchange stories and identify the point of view and idioms.

→ Beyond Level

Vocabulary

REVIEW DOMAIN-SPECIFIC WORDS

 OBJECTIVES

Produce simple, compound, and complex sentences. **L.3.1i**

Review and discuss domain-specific vocabulary words.

 Model
Use the **Visual Vocabulary Cards** to review the meanings of the words *slithered* and *ridiculous*. Write sentences on the board using the words.

Write the words *amused, inaccuracy,* and *spirited* on the board, and discuss the meanings with students. Then help students write sentences using these words.

 Apply
Have students work in pairs to discuss the meanings of the words *focused, scattered,* and *switcheroo.* Then have students write sentences using the words.

IDIOMS

 OBJECTIVES

Distinguish the literal and nonliteral meanings of words and phrases in context (e.g., *take steps*). **L.3.5a**

Determine the meanings of idioms.

 Model
Read aloud the first stanza of the Comprehension and Fluency passage on **Beyond Reproducibles** page 293.

Think Aloud I want to know the meaning of the idiom *drop a bomb.* I know that the father in the poem does not drop an actual bomb, but he does tell his boys something very important and surprising. I think *drop a bomb* means to tell someone something very surprising or important.

With students, read the next stanza. Help them figure out the meaning of the idiom *freak you out.*

 Apply
Have pairs of students read the rest of the poem. Ask them to determine the meanings of the similes *make a fuss* and *did something go down.*

 Gifted and Talented
Independent Study Have students use classroom resources to find other idioms. Ask pairs to write short poems using at least two idioms. Encourage them to use rhyme and rhythm in their poems where appropriate. Have students share their poems with the class.

Comprehension

REVIEW POINT OF VIEW

OBJECTIVES

CCSS Distinguish their own point of view from that of the narrator or those of the characters. **RL.3.6**

Identify the narrator's point of view.

Model Remind students that the narrator of a poem often has a point of view about the topic. Once students have identified the narrator's point of view, they should distinguish their own point of view from that of the narrator.

Have students read the first stanza of the Comprehension and Fluency poem on **Beyond Reproducibles** page 293. Ask open-ended questions to facilitate discussion, such as *What is the narrator's point of view in this stanza? Which details show this point of view?* Students should provide text evidence to support their answers.

Apply Have students identify details that show the parents' point of view as they read the rest of the poem. Then have them identify the narrator's point of view about what he learns from his father. Ask students to tell whether they agree with the narrator's point of view and explain why.

SELF-SELECTED READING

OBJECTIVES

CCSS Distinguish their own point of view from that of the narrator or those of the characters. **RL.3.6**

• Identify the narrator's point of view.

• Reread difficult sections in a text to increase understanding.

Read Independently

Have students choose a poem for sustained silent reading.

• As students read, have them fill in **Graphic Organizer 146**.

• Remind students to reread any sections they have difficulty with to help increase their understanding.

Read Purposefully

Encourage students to keep a reading journal. Ask them to read different types of poems.

• Students can write summaries of the poems in their journals.

• Ask students to give their reactions to the poems to their classmates. Have them tell the narrators' points of view, tell whether or not they agreed with these points of view, and explain why.

 Independent Study Challenge students to discuss how their poems relate to the weekly theme of funny times. Have students compare some of the things that make them laugh. Then have them write a few paragraphs describing something funny they saw or heard recently.

→ English Language Learners

Reading/Writing Workshop

OBJECTIVES

Refer to parts of stories, dramas, and poems when writing or speaking about a text, using terms such as chapter, scene, and stanza; describe how each successive part builds on earlier sections. **RL.3.5**

- Identify literary elements.
- Identify the meanings of idioms.

LANGUAGE OBJECTIVE
Determine the narrator's point of view.

ACADEMIC LANGUAGE
narrative poem, point of view, rhythm, rhyme, idioms

Shared Read
The Camping Trip, Bubble Gum

View "The Camping Trip," "Bubble Gum"

Before Reading

Build Background

Read the Essential Question: What makes you laugh?

- Explain the meaning of the Essential Question. *Some stories are funny. They make people laugh. Laughing makes you feel good. Laughing helps you share feelings with friends.*

- **Model an answer:** *Many things make me laugh. Jokes, funny stories, and silly pictures make me laugh.*

- Ask students a question that ties the Essential Question to their own background knowledge: *Work with a partner to think of stories and jokes that make you laugh. Discuss why you think they are funny.* Call on several pairs.

During Reading

Interactive-Question Response

- Ask questions that help students understand the meaning of the text after each paragraph.
- Reinforce the meanings of key vocabulary.
- Ask students questions that require them to use key vocabulary.
- Reinforce strategies and skills of the week by modeling.

Page 462

"The Camping Trip"

Stanzas 1–3

Explain and Model Idioms *It says* we roughed it at Old Piney Park. Roughed it *is an idiom, which means that the phrase has a different meaning than the individual words. It means* camped. Point to the title and illustration, and explain that camping is an outdoor activity. Provide the sentence frame for students to complete: *The boys _____ (camped) at Old Piney Park.*

Explain and Model Rhyme Point to the words *Park* and *dark,* and read them chorally with students. *These words have endings that sound the same.* Remind students that words that rhyme have the same ending sounds. *What other words rhyme?* (*sleep/creep, me/knee*)

Page 463

Stanzas 4–5

Model Point of View *Let's figure out the narrator's point of view. In the fourth stanza, the narrator states that having a creature crawl up his sleeve is not humorous or fun. That is his point of view. Why does he think it is not fun?* (It might be a rattlesnake.)

Do you agree with the narrator's point of view? Explain your answer.

Page 464

"Bubble Gum"

Stanza 1

Have students point to the first and second stanza. Remind them that a stanza is a group of lines that is part of a poem. *Which words rhyme in the first stanza?* (*week/cheek*)

Stanza 2

Explain and model Rhythm Have student pairs clap along with the rhythm of the second stanza. Monitor their progress as you move around the room, and assist them as necessary. Chorally read the stanza with the group and clap along with the rhythm.

Stanza 3

Chorally read the stanza with students and point out the word *inflated.* Demonstrate inflating a balloon, or use gestures to show how the poet inflates like a balloon. *What does* inflated *mean?* ("blew up")

What do you think the poet means when she says her father hit the ceiling? (He was upset.)

Page 465

Stanza 5

Read the first line chorally with students. *Were the neighbors' eyes really popping?* (no) Have students show you what it looks like when their eyes are popping. Show them a wide-eyed expression. *What do you think the neighbors were feeling if their eyes were popping?* (surprised; shocked)

After Reading

Make Connections

- Review the Essential Question: What makes you laugh?
- Make text connections.
- Have students complete the **ELL Reproducibles** page 293–295.

→ English Language Learners

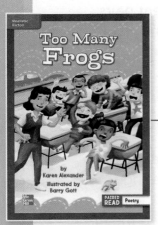

Lexile 600
TextEvaluator™ 16

OBJECTIVES
Distinguish their own point of view from that of the narrator or those of the characters. **RL.3.6**

• Reread text to check understanding.
• Determine the meanings of idioms.

LANGUAGE OBJECTIVE
Identify a character's point of view.

ACADEMIC LANGUAGE
• reread, point of view, realistic fiction, idioms, narrative poem
• Cognate: *ficción realista*

Leveled Reader:
Too Many Frogs

Go Digital

Before Reading

Preview

• Read the Essential Question with students: What makes you laugh?
• Refer to Let's Laugh: *Why is being able to laugh important?*
• Preview *Too Many Frogs* and "Cat and Dog": *Let's read about how the events in these stories can make people laugh.*

Vocabulary

Use the **Visual Vocabulary Cards** to preteach the ELL vocabulary: *convincing, practical, slinks.* Use the routine found on the cards.

Leveled Readers

During Reading

Interactive Question-Response

Note Taking Have students use their graphic organizer on **ELL Reproducibles** page 292. Use the following prompts after reading each section. As you read, use visuals or pictures to define key vocabulary.

Pages 2–3 *Which character is the first sentence about?* (Nat) *The story is being told from his point of view. What does Nat love to do? Complete the sentence frame: He loves to ____ (play practical jokes).*

Page 4 Have pairs read the first paragraph on page 4. *What is an example of Nat's thoughts and feelings on page 4?* Have one student answer and another elaborate on the answer. (Nat likes to make other kids laugh; Nat wants to provide everyone with good entertainment.) Have students talk about whether or not they like to entertain others.

Pages 5–6 *What is Nat planning to do?* (pretend that the frogs have escaped from the terrarium) *Why does Nat put the frog on Stacey's desk? Reread the first paragraph on page 6 to answer the question.* (She played a trick on him last April Fools' Day.)

Pages 8–9 *What does the principal warn students about on page 8?* (April Fools' practical jokes should not be dangerous.) *How does Stacey react to the frog on her desk?* (She screams.) *Think about how you might react if you found a fake frog on your desk.*

Fill in the Graphic Organizer

Pages 10–11 Use the illustrations to point out that Nat's practical joke has gone wrong. *Where do the real frogs live in the classroom?* (the terrarium) Then point out and explain the alliteration on page 10. *What slimy thing slithers past Nat's hand?* (a real frog)

Pages 12–15 Point out the idiom on page 14. Hold your nose and demonstrate eating something that tastes bad. *Sometimes medicine tastes bad. What does Mrs. Lopez mean when she says that Nat had a taste of his own medicine?* (Now he knows what getting tricked feels like.)

After Reading

Respond to Reading Help students complete the graphic organizer. Revisit the Essential Question. Have students pairs summarize and answer the Text Evidence questions. Support students as necessary, and review all responses as a group.

Write About Reading *Analytical Writing* Check that students have correctly used the point of view of the frog and included details from the story.

Fluency: Phrasing and Expression

Model Model reading page 11 with proper phrasing and expression. Next, reread the page aloud, and have students read along with you.

Apply Have students practice reading with a partner.

PAIRED READ

"Cat and Dog"

Make Connections: Write About It *Analytical Writing*

Before reading, have students note that the genre is narrative poetry. A narrative poem tells a story. Then discuss the Essential Question.

After reading, have students make connections between *Too Many Frogs* and "Cat and Dog." *What did you find funny in the story and poem?*

Leveled Reader

FOCUS ON LITERARY ELEMENTS

Students can extend their knowledge of narrative poetry by completing the literary elements activity on page 20.

Literature Circles

Ask students to conduct a literature circle using the Thinkmark questions to guide the discussion. You may wish to have a whole-class discussion on things that make students laugh.

Level Up

Level-up lessons available online.

IF students read the ELL Level fluently and answered the questions

THEN pair them with students who have proficiently read On Level and have ELL students

• echo-read the On Level main selection with their partner.

• list difficult words and discuss them with their partner.

A C T Access Complex Text

The On Level challenges students by including more **domain-specific words** and **complex sentence structures**.

English Language Learners
Vocabulary

PRETEACH VOCABULARY

OBJECTIVES

 Acquire and use accurately grade-appropriate conversational, general academic, and domain-specific words and phrases, including those that signal spatial and temporal relationships. **L.3.6**

LANGUAGE OBJECTIVE

Use vocabulary words.

 I Do Preteach vocabulary from the Shared Read poems following the routine on the **Visual Vocabulary Cards** for *entertainment, humorous, ridiculous,* and *slithered.* Also review the words *narrative poem, rhyme, rhythm,* and *stanza.*

 We Do Complete the Vocabulary Routine for each word, and point to the word on the card. Next, read the word. Ask students to repeat the word. Act out the word using gestures and actions.

 You Do Have partners define four of the words using complete sentences. Then have each pair read the sentences aloud.

Beginning	Intermediate	Advanced/High
Help students write the sentences and read them aloud.	Have students give an example of one of the poetry terms.	Have students identify each of the terms using the poems.

REVIEW VOCABULARY

OBJECTIVES

 Acquire and use accurately grade-appropriate conversational, general academic, and domain-specific words and phrases, including those that signal spatial and temporal relationships. **L.3.6**

LANGUAGE OBJECTIVE

Use vocabulary words.

 I Do Review the previous week's vocabulary words over a few days. Read each word aloud and point to the word on the **Visual Vocabulary Card**. Ask students to repeat after you. Then follow the Vocabulary Routine on the back of each card.

 We Do Tell students to ask questions about a vocabulary word. If they are not able to guess the vocabulary word at first, give them a synonym as a clue. Have students use the word in a sentence.

 You Do Have students individually choose three words and write a clue about each word. Partners should then guess each other's words.

Beginning	Intermediate	Advanced/High
Help students write their clues.	Have students include a synonym in at least one of their clues.	Challenge students to write a question about each word.

IDIOMS

OBJECTIVES

 Distinguish the literal and nonliteral meanings of words and phrases in context (e.g., *take steps*). **L.3.5a**

LANGUAGE OBJECTIVE

Determine the meanings of idioms.

 I Do Read aloud the first page of "Bubble Gum" on page 464 as students follow along. Point to *hit the ceiling*. Remind students that an idiom is a phrase that means something different from the meaning of each word in it.

Think Aloud I know that the narrator's father does not actually hit the ceiling, but he does seem to react strongly about what happens. I think that *hit the ceiling* means "became excited or angry about something."

 We Do Have students reread page 464. Ask them to determine the meaning of the idiom *in a stew*. Write the meaning on the board.

 You Do Have pairs of students read page 465 and find the idiom *the neighbor's eyes were popping*. Have them figure out the meaning of the idiom.

Beginning	Intermediate	Advanced/High
Help students find the idiom and determine the nonliteral meaning of the phrase.	Have students discuss the idiom and write its meaning using a complete sentence.	Challenge students to find an idiom in "The Camping Trip" on page 462 and determine its meaning.

ADDITIONAL VOCABULARY

OBJECTIVES

 Use conventional spelling for high-frequency and other studied words and for adding suffixes to base words (e.g., *sitting, smiled, cries, happiness*). **L.3.2e**

Discuss concept and high-frequency words.

LANGUAGE OBJECTIVE

Use concept and high-frequency words.

 I Do List concept and high-frequency words from the Shared Read poems: *we, up, creep, hollered, collapsed;* and *Too Many Frogs: notices, pretends, annoyed, giggling.* Define each word for students: We *is a plural subject pronoun that refers to more than one person including the person speaking.*

 We Do Model using the words in sentences: *She* pretends *she is a pirate when she plays.* Then have students answer questions using the words: *What do you like to* pretend *to be when you play?*

 You Do Have pairs write questions using the concept and high-frequency words. Ask students to present their questions to the class.

Beginning	Intermediate	Advanced/High
Help students write the questions correctly.	Have students ask and answer their questions for the class.	Have students write definitions for the words they used.

→ English Language Learners
Writing/Spelling

WRITING TRAIT: WORD CHOICE

OBJECTIVES
Use dialogue and description of actions, thoughts, and feelings to develop experiences and events or show the response of characters to situations. **W.3.3b**

Recognize precise words.

LANGUAGE OBJECTIVE
Use precise words in writing.

 I Do Remind students that good writers use descriptive words to make their writing clear. Strong or precise words show rather than tell the reader something. Read the Student Model poem as students follow along, and identify the precise words that help the reader visualize.

 We Do Read aloud the poem "The Camping Trip" on pages 462–463 as students follow along. List the strong nouns and verbs that help the reader to visualize the event that the narrator describes.

 You Do Have partners write a paragraph about something that made them laugh. Students should use precise words and phrases. Edit each pair's writing.

Beginning	Intermediate	Advanced/High
Help students copy the paragraph, and demonstrate how to add precise words.	Have students revise, adding precise words.	Have students revise, adding precise words, and edit for errors.

SPELL WORDS WITH SUFFIXES -ful, -less, -ly

OBJECTIVES
Use spelling patterns and generalizations (e.g., word families, position-based spellings, syllable patterns, ending rules, meaningful word parts) in writing words. **L.3.2f**

LANGUAGE OBJECTIVE
Spell words with suffixes -*ful*, -*less*, and -*ly*.

 I Do Read the Spelling Words on T290 aloud, modeling how to pronounce words with suffixes -*ful*, -*less*, and -*ly*. Display the word *careful*, dividing the syllables: *care/ful*. Point out that suffixes are their own syllable.

 We Do Read the Dictation Sentences on page T291 aloud for students. With each sentence, slowly read the underlined word. Model drawing a line between the syllables. Have students repeat after you and write the word.

 You Do Display the words. Have students exchange their lists with a partner to check the spelling and write the words correctly.

Beginning	Intermediate	Advanced/High
Help students copy the corrected words and say the words aloud.	Have students draw a line between the syllables in each word.	After students correct their words, have pairs write sentences for five words.

Grammar

PREPOSITIONS

OBJECTIVES

 Produce simple, compound, and complex sentences. **L.3.1i**

Identify prepositions.

LANGUAGE OBJECTIVE

Write sentences using prepositions.

Language Transfers Handbook

Speakers of Cantonese may have difficulty using prepositions as Cantonese does not use prepositions the way that English does. Students may omit prepositions, as in *I like go school.* Use contrastive analysis and additional activities to reinforce the correct use of prepositions and prepositional phrases in English.

 Review that a preposition is a word that shows the relationship between a noun or a pronoun and another word in a sentence. On the board, write: *The cat is on the porch.* Underline *on.* Tell students that the noun or pronoun that follows a preposition is the object of the preposition, so the object in the example is *porch.* Some of the most common prepositions are *in, on, at, over, under, to, from, for, with, by, of, into, before, after, during.* Tell students that a prepositional phrase includes a preposition, its object, and any words in between. For example, in the sentence *We ate lunch under the tree,* the prepositional phrase is *under the tree.*

 Write the sentences below on the board. Ask volunteers to identify the preposition, object of the preposition, and prepositional phrase in each. Have them read the sentences aloud, and ask other volunteers to repeat them.

> *We found the kitten hiding under the sofa.*
>
> *Mickey and Mallory finished their homework after the movie.*
>
> *Before school, we play tag on the playground.*
>
> *Jorge was late to Britney's birthday party.*

 Brainstorm a list of prepositions with students. Then ask pairs of students to write sentences that use those prepositions. Remind students to use object pronouns where appropriate. Have students read their completed sentences aloud for the class.

Beginning	Intermediate	Advanced/High
Help students write at least one sentence using a preposition from the class list.	Ask students to write at least three complete sentences using prepositions from the class list.	Challenge students to write at least five sentences using prepositions. Have them write at least one sentence using more than one preposition.

For extra support, have students complete the activities in the **Grammar Practice Reproducibles** during the week, using the routine below:

- Explain the grammar skill.
- Model the first activity in the Grammar Practice Reproducibles.
- Have the whole group complete the next couple of activities and then have partners complete the rest.
- Review the activities with correct answers.

PROGRESS MONITORING

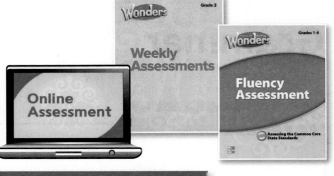

Unit 6 Week 5 Formal Assessment	Standards Covered	Component for Assessment
Text Evidence	RL.3.1	• *Selection Test* • *Weekly Assessment* • *Approaching-Level Weekly Assessment*
Point of View	RL.3.6	• *Weekly Assessment* • *Approaching-Level Weekly Assessment*
Figurative Language: Idioms	RL.3.4, L.3.5a	• *Selection Test* • *Weekly Assessment* • *Approaching-Level Weekly Assessment*
Writing About Text	W.3.8	*Weekly Assessment*

Unit 6 Week 5 Informal Assessment	Standards Covered	Component for Assessment
Research/Listening/ Collaborating	SL.3.1d, SL.3.2, SL.3.3	• *RWW* • *Teacher's Edition*
Oral Reading Fluency (ORF) **Fluency Goal:** 97–117 words correct per minute (WCPM) **Accuracy Rate Goal:** 95% or higher	RF.3.4a, RF.3.4b, RF.3.4c	*Fluency Assessment*

Using Assessment Results

Weekly Assessments Skills and Fluency	If . . .	Then . . .
COMPREHENSION	Students score below 70% . . .	. . . assign Lessons 37–39 on Point of View from the *Tier 2 Comprehension Intervention online PDFs.*
VOCABULARY	Students score below 70% . . .	. . . assign Lesson 166 on Idioms, Proverbs, and Adages from the *Tier 2 Vocabulary Intervention online PDFs.*
WRITING	Students score below "3" on constructed response . . .	. . . assign Lessons 37–39 and/or Write About Reading Lesson 194 from the *Tier 2 Comprehension Intervention online PDFs.*
FLUENCY	Students have a WCPM score of 89–96 . . .	. . . assign a lesson from Section 1, 7, 8, 9 or 10 of the *Tier 2 Fluency Intervention online PDFs.*
	Students have a WCPM score of 0–88 . . .	. . . assign a lesson from Sections 2–6 of the *Tier 2 Fluency Intervention online PDFs.*

Using Weekly Data

Check your data Dashboard to verify assessment results and guide grouping decisions.

Data-Driven Recommendations

Response to Intervention

Use the appropriate sections of the *Placement and Diagnostic Assessment* as well as students' assessment results to designate students requiring:

 Intervention Online PDFs

 WonderWorks Intervention Program

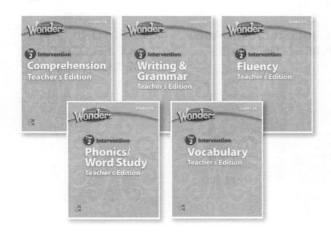

The Big Idea: *How do we decide what's important?*

Student Outcomes

Close Reading of Complex Text
- Cite relevant evidence from text
- Summarize the text
- Interpret information presented visually
- Gather relevant information from digital sources
- Navigate links

RI.3.2, RI.3.5, RI.3.7

Writing
Write to Sources
- Write an opinion
- Conduct research
- Select reliable sources

Writing Process
- Edit/proofread and publish an informative text
- **Celebrate** Share Your Writing

W.3.6, W.3.7, W.3.8

Speaking and Listening
- Paraphrase information presented digitally
- Report on a topic

SL.3.2

Foundational Skills
Fluency
- Read orally with prosody
- Read orally with accuracy
- Read orally with expression

RF.3.4a, RF.3.4b. RF.3.4c

Review and Extend

Reader's Theater

The Lion and the Ostrich Chicks

Genre Play

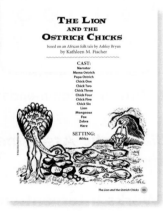

Reading Digitally

TIME FOR KIDS. "Life Boats"

Go Digital!

Level Up Accelerating Progress

FROM **APPROACHING** TO **ON LEVEL**

FROM **ON LEVEL** TO **BEYOND LEVEL**

FROM **ENGLISH LANGUAGE LEARNERS** TO **ON LEVEL**

FROM **BEYOND LEVEL** TO **SELF-SELECTED TRADE BOOK**

Advanced Level Trade Book

ASSESS

Presentations

Research and Inquiry
Project Presentations
Project Rubric

Writing
Informative Writing Presentations
Writing Rubric

Unit Assessments

UNIT 6 TEST

FLUENCY

Evaluate Student Progress

Use the Wonders online assessment reports to evaluate student progress and help you make decisions about small group instruction and assignments.

Stuart Pearce/age fotostock

SUGGESTED LESSON PLAN

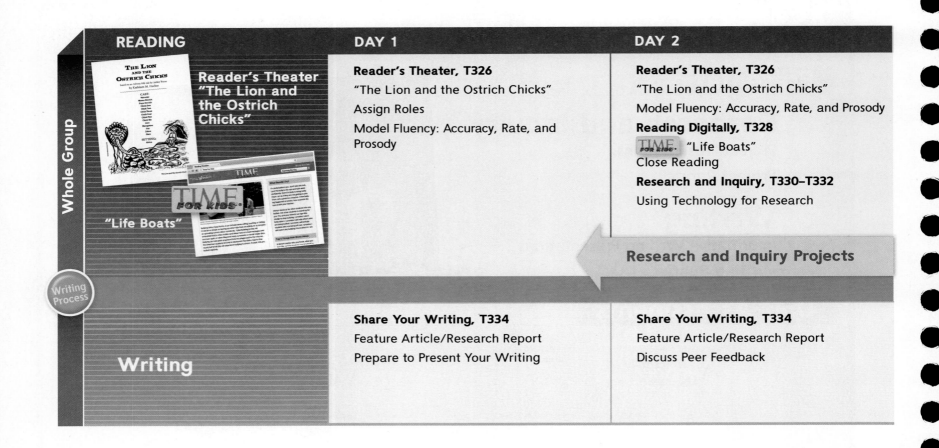

READING	DAY 1	DAY 2

Whole Group

Reader's Theater "The Lion and the Ostrich Chicks"

"Life Boats"

DAY 1

Reader's Theater, T326
"The Lion and the Ostrich Chicks"
Assign Roles
Model Fluency: Accuracy, Rate, and Prosody

DAY 2

Reader's Theater, T326
"The Lion and the Ostrich Chicks"
Model Fluency: Accuracy, Rate, and Prosody
Reading Digitally, T328
TIME FOR KIDS "Life Boats"
Close Reading
Research and Inquiry, T330–T332
Using Technology for Research

Research and Inquiry Projects

Writing Process

Writing

Share Your Writing, T334
Feature Article/Research Report
Prepare to Present Your Writing

Share Your Writing, T334
Feature Article/Research Report
Discuss Peer Feedback

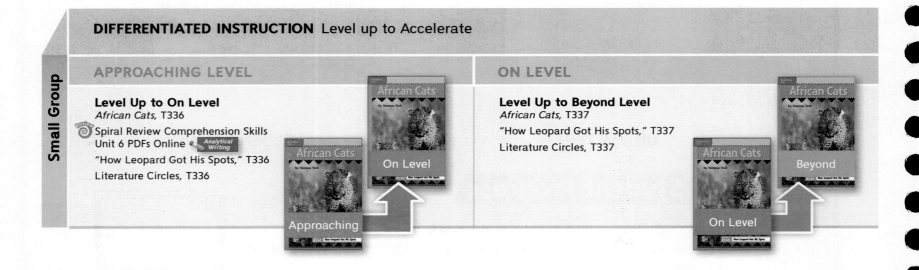

DIFFERENTIATED INSTRUCTION Level up to Accelerate

Small Group

APPROACHING LEVEL

Level Up to On Level
African Cats, T336
Spiral Review Comprehension Skills
Unit 6 PDFs Online ● *Analytical Writing*
"How Leopard Got His Spots," T336
Literature Circles, T336

ON LEVEL

Level Up to Beyond Level
African Cats, T337
"How Leopard Got His Spots," T337
Literature Circles, T337

DAY 3	DAY 4	DAY 5
Reading Digitally, T329 TIME FOR KIDS. "Life Boats" Write About Reading *Analytical Writing*	**Reader's Theater, T326** Performance	**Research and Inquiry, T330–T332** Presentations Wrap Up the Unit, T333 ✓ **Unit Assessment, T340–T341**

Research and Inquiry Projects → **Research and Inquiry Projects** *Analytical Writing* →

Share Your Writing, T334 Feature Article/Research Report Rehearse Your Presentation	**Share Your Writing, T334** Present Your Feature Article/Research Report Evaluate Your Presentation	**Share Your Writing, T335** Feature Article/Research Report Portfolio Choice

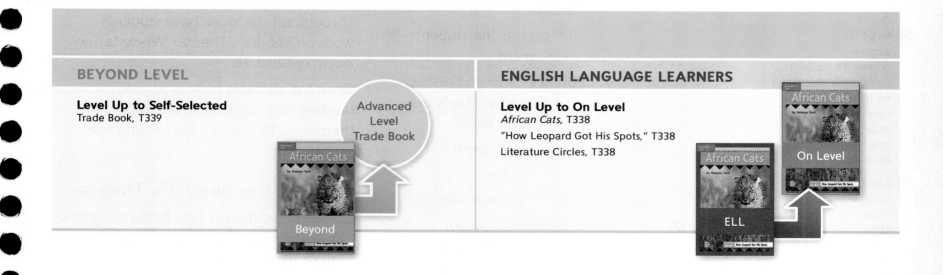

BEYOND LEVEL	ENGLISH LANGUAGE LEARNERS
Level Up to Self-Selected Trade Book, T339	**Level Up to On Level** *African Cats,* T338 "How Leopard Got His Spots," T338 Literature Circles, T338

Advanced Level Trade Book

Beyond

On Level

ELL

Reader's Theater

THE LION AND THE OSTRICH CHICKS

based on an African folk tale by Ashley Bryan
by Kathleen M. Fischer

CAST:
Narrator
Mama Ostrich
Papa Ostrich
Chick One
Chick Two
Chick Three
Chick Four
Chick Five
Chick Six
Lion
Mongoose
Fox
Zebra
Hare

SETTING:
Africa

The Lion and the Ostrich Chicks

Go Digital!

Teacher's Resource
PDF Online
pp. 71–82

OBJECTIVES

CCSS Read with sufficient accuracy and fluency to support comprehension. Read on-level prose and poetry orally with accuracy, appropriate rate, and expression. **RF.3.4b**

CCSS Read with sufficient accuracy and fluency to support comprehension. Use context to confirm or self-correct word recognition and understanding, rereading as necessary. **RF.3.4c**

The Lion and the Ostrich Chicks

Introduce the Play

Explain that *The Lion and the Ostrich Chicks* is a play set in Africa and based on a folktale. A lion captures six ostrich chicks, and intimidates the other animals into agreeing they are his children. In the end, a clever mongoose tricks the lion and saves the chicks. Distribute scripts and the Elements of Drama handout from the **Teacher's Resource PDF Online** pages 71–82.

- Review the features of a play.

- Review the list of characters. Build background on the setting, defining the roles of the animal characters in a folktale set in Africa.

- Discuss what students know about the folktale genre. Remind them that folktales usually end with a moral.

Shared Reading

Model reading the play as the students follow along in their scripts.

Focus on Vocabulary Stop and discuss any vocabulary words that students may not know. You may wish to teach:

- relays
- exception
- familiar
- proverb
- beget
- counselor

Model Fluency As you read each part, state the name of each character, and read the part emphasizing the appropriate phrasing and expression.

Discuss Each Role

- After reading the part of the Narrator, ask students to identify what information the Narrator is providing.

- After reading each part, ask partners to note the characters' traits. Model how to find text evidence that tells about the characters. Have students identify the good and bad characters.

Assign Roles

Depending on the number of students, you may wish to divide the play into two or more sections. Have different students play the 14 different roles.

Practice the Play

Each day, allow students time to practice their parts in the play. Pair fluent readers with less fluent readers. Pairs can echo-read or chorally read their parts. As needed, work with less fluent readers to mark pauses in their script using one slash for a short pause and two slashes for longer pauses.

Throughout the week have students work on Reader's Theater **Workstation Activity Card 26**.

Once the students have practiced reading their parts several times, allow them time to practice performing the script.

Perform the Reader's Theater

- As a class, discuss how performing the play's singing parts aloud is different from reading them aloud.

- Discuss what it is like to be an exotic animal character. How would you perform the animal sounds, such as an ostrich's hissing roar?

- Discuss how the animals' movements can be made during the performance.

ACTIVITIES

WHO'S AFRAID OF THE BIG, BAD LION?

The play *The Lion and the Ostrich Chicks* has characters that are victims, rescuers, and villains.

Reread *The Lion and the Ostrich Chicks* and pay attention to the good and bad roles. Then discuss the following questions with students:

1. Who are the helpless victims in the play? How can you show their helplessness?

2. Whom does Mama Ostrich choose as her ally against Lion? Why?

3. What role does Mongoose have in the play? What are his feelings toward Lion?

4. How does Lion feel about the other animals? How can you show Lion is mean?

THIS PLAY IS ABOUT...

To summarize, students must tell a story's main events in order. Use *The Lion and the Ostrich Chicks* to help students practice summarizing.

Review the steps of summarization, including telling what happens in the beginning, middle, and end of the play. Then, have students reread the play to note the main events.

Have students orally retell the main events in order to a partner, using some vocabulary from the play. Students can then write and illustrate their summaries.

ELL ENGLISH LANGUAGE LEARNERS

- Review the definitions of difficult words including: *scuffing, boomed, outrun, mound, confused, crafty, crouch, mistreat, bared,* and *resemblance.*

- Team a non-native speaker with a fluent reader who is also reading the part of Mama Ostrich. Have each reader take turns reading the lines.

- During practice sessions, shadow behind a non-native speaker. Read each line and then have them echo-read the line.

Reading Digitally

Go Digital!

Life Boats

Before Reading

Preview Scroll through the online article "Life Boats" at <u>www.connected.mcgraw-hill.com</u> and have students identify text features. Review how to navigate through the article. Point out the interactive features, such as **hyperlinks**, **maps**, and **bar graphs**. Explain that you will read the article together first and then access these features.

Close Reading Online

Take Notes Read the article aloud and ask questions to focus students on the problems the people of Bangladesh face and how Mohammed Rezwan is trying to solve them. Have students take notes using **Graphic Organizer 26**. After each section, have students turn to partners and paraphrase the main ideas, giving text evidence. Help students use context to understand multiple-meaning words, such as *land* and *faces*.

Access Interactive Elements Help students access the interactive elements by clicking or rolling over each text feature. Discuss what information these elements add to the text.

Tell students they will reread parts of the article to help them answer a specific question: *How is Rezwan's program helping people in Bangladesh?* Have students skim the article to find text detailing how Rezwan's program is helping people. Have partners share what they find.

Navigate Links to Information Use a **hyperlink** to access a new Web page for information related to the question *How is Rezwan's program helping people in Bangladesh?* Remind students that bookmarking a page makes it easy to return to the page later.

Tell students they should try to verify any facts they find in at least one other source. For example, to confirm information about Mohammed Rezwan or Bangladesh, they should visit another reliable Web site. Point out that if the information does not agree, they will need to consult a third reliable source. Have partners choose a fact from the article to confirm in another source. Have them share their findings.

WRITE ABOUT READING *Analytical Writing*

Summarize Review students' graphic organizers. Model using the information to summarize "Life Boats."

Ask students to write a summary of the article, stating the problem and how Rezwan is trying to solve it. Partners should discuss their summaries.

Make Connections Have students compare what they learned about deciding what's important with what they have learned about other ways that people decide what's important in the texts in this unit.

TAKE A STAND

Getting an Education

Have students state their opinion about why getting an education is important. Tell them they should

- clearly state their opinion and organize their ideas logically.
- support their position with precise, accurate information from the article or linked site.
- end with a concluding statement that restates their opinion.

Have students share their opinions and discuss why Rezwan's program is helpful.

RESEARCH ONLINE

Navigating the Internet

Tell students that when they conduct Internet research, they will need to return to their Results page to find other Web pages. Explain that students can also add sites to their "Favorites" if they want to visit the page again. Demonstrate adding a Web site to "Favorites" by using the "Favorites" drop down menu on the toolbar. Click on the link you added to demonstrate navigating back to that page. Point out that the "back" button may be useful in an individual browsing session, but they will not be able to use it to return to a site once they end the session.

INDEPENDENT STUDY

Investigate

Choose a Topic Students should brainstorm questions related to the article. For example, they might ask: *What can I do to help the people of Bangladesh?* Then have students choose a question to research. Help them narrow it.

Conduct Internet Research Encourage students to add useful Web sites to their "Favorites" and remind them that they can use the "back" arrow to navigate back to a previously visited Web page. Remind students to use precise key words in their searches.

Present Have groups give an informational or persuasive presentation about Mohammed Rezwan's work or Bangladesh.

→ Integrate Ideas

Collabororate

Research Roadmap

Resources: Research and Inquiry

RESEARCH AND INQUIRY

Research and Inquiry

Assign the Projects Break students into five groups. Assign each one of the five projects below. Before students begin present this minilesson.

Using Technology to Research and Present Information

Students can use computers to collect information for a research project. The Internet can be used to find information about any topic.

Tell students to enter key words into a search engine. The search engine will show a list of Web sites that contain the key words.

Tell students they can use visual displays, including graphs and charts, from Web sites for the purposes of gathering information for research, making a presentation, being informed, or taking a test.

OBJECTIVES

CCSS Conduct short research projects that build knowledge about a topic. **W.3.7**

Research Roadmap

Resources: Research and Inquiry

CHOOSE A PROJECT!

The Big Idea: *How do we decide what's important?*

Write an Essay
Write an essay about a person from history who embodies a quality that you value and admire. WEEK 1

Create a News Story
Create a news story about a real-life weather disaster, such as a tornado or hurricane, using information that you have gathered. WEEK 2

Write a Plan
Write a plan to help your school or town achieve an goal. Include the materials and skills necessary to accomplish the goal. WEEK 3

Fantasy Story
Learn facts about an animal and then use the information in a fantasy story featuring the animal as a character WEEK 4

Create a Slide Show
Create a slide show about the health benefits of laughter. Try to include a humorous poem. WEEK 5

Organizing Oral Presentations

Good oral presentations have an objective and are organized using an outline to help meet that objective, whether it's to inform, persuade, or entertain an audience. Outlining points helps a presenter to remember key words better and to add notes at the last minute. It also allows speech to flow more naturally.

Presentations can be organized according to their objective. Some common ways to organize information in presentations are by sequence, categories, problem and solution, and cause and effect. Remind students that good presentation skills include standing up straight, maintaining eye contact with the audience, and speaking clearly in complete sentences.

Remind students that presentations should be given using formal language and proper conventions of standard English, and not informal language that they would use to speak with their friends in casual situations.

OBJECTIVES

CCSS Recall information from experiences or gather information from print and digital sources; take brief notes on sources and sort evidence into provided categories. **W.3.8**

CONDUCT THE RESEARCH

Distribute the online Research Roadmap to students. Have them use it to complete the project.

STEP 1 **Set Research Goals** Discuss with students the Essential Question and the research project. Each group should make sure they are clear on their research focus and end product. Decide on each member's role.

STEP 2 **Identify Sources** Have the group brainstorm where they can find the information. Remind students that reliable online sources usually end in .edu, .org, or .gov.

STEP 3 **Find and Record Information** Have students review the research strategies on page T330. Then have them research their topic.

STEP 4 **Organize** After team members have completed the research, they can review and analyze all the information they collected. First they should categorize their notes in order of most reliable sources. Then they can create a web or chart as a way to clarify categories of information.

STEP 5 **Synthesize and Present** Have team members synthesize their research and decide on their final message. They should check that the key ideas are included in their presentations and that their findings relate to the Big Idea.

OBJECTIVES

CCSS Report on a topic or text, tell a story, or recount an experience with appropriate facts and relevant, descriptive details, speaking clearly at an understandable pace. **SL.3.4**

CCSS Plan and deliver an informative/explanatory presentation on a topic that: organizes ideas around major points of information, follows a logical sequence, includes supporting details, uses clear and specific vocabulary, and provides a strong conclusion.

Go Digital

Collaborate: Manage and Assign projects online. Students can work with their team online.

→ Integrate Ideas

Review and Evaluate

Distribute the online PDF of the checklists and rubrics. Use the following Teacher Checklist and rubric to evaluate students' research and presentations.

Student Checklist

Research Process
- ☑ Did you narrow your focus and create a research plan?
- ☑ Did you use print and digital sources?
- ☑ Did you use technology to gather research?

Presenting
- ☑ Did you practice your presentation?
- ☑ Did you express your ideas clearly?
- ☑ Did you use appropriate facts and details?
- ☑ Did you make eye contact?
- ☑ Did you use formal language?
- ☑ Did you address the Essential Question and the Big Idea?
- ☑ Did you use appropriate visual displays?

Teacher Checklist

Assess the Research Process
- ☑ Selected a focus and used multiple sources.
- ☑ Cited sources for information.
- ☑ Collaborated well with others.

Assess the Presentation
- ☑ Spoke clearly and at an appropriate pace.
- ☑ Used formal language and proper conventions of standard English.
- ☑ Addressed the Essential Question and Big Idea.
- ☑ Used appropriate visuals and technology.

Assess the Listener
- ☑ Listened quietly and politely.
- ☑ Asked clarifying questions.
- ☑ Made appropriate comments.

Project Rubric

④ Excellent	③ Good	② Fair	① Unsatisfactory
• presents the information clearly • includes many details • may include sophisticated observations	• presents the information adequately • provides adequate details • includes relevant observations	• attempts to present information • may offer few or vague details • may include few or irrelevant personal observations	• may show little grasp of the task • may present irrelevant information • may reflect extreme difficulty with research or presentation

Wrap Up the Unit

The Big Idea:
How do we decide what's important?

TEXT CONNECTIONS

Connect to the Big Idea

Text to Text Write the Unit Big Idea on the board: *How do you decide what is important?* Divide the class into small groups. Tell students that each group will compare the information that they have learned during the course of the unit in order to answer the Big Idea question. Model how to compare this information by using examples from the **Leveled Readers** and what they have read in this unit's selections.

Collaborative Conversations Have students review their class notes and completed graphic organizers before they begin their discussions. Encourage students to compare information from all the unit's selections and the Research and Inquiry presentations. Have each group pick one student to take notes.

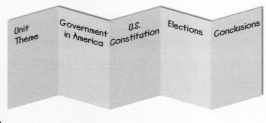

Dinah Zike's
FOLDABLES
Study Organizer

Explain that each group will use an Accordion Foldable® to record their ideas. You may wish to model how to use an Accordion Foldable® to record comparisons of texts.

Present Ideas and Synthesize Information When students finish their discussions, ask for a volunteer from each group to read their notes aloud. After each group has presented their ideas, ask: *What are the five most important things we have learned about how we decide what's important?* Lead a class discussion and list students' ideas on the board. If there are more than five things, have students vote to narrow down the list to the top five most important things.

Building Knowledge Encourage students to continue building knowledge about the Unit Big Idea. Display the online Unit Bibliography and have students search online for articles and other resources related to the Big Idea. After each group has presented their ideas, ask: *Why is it important to think carefully before making decisions?* Lead a class discussion asking students to use the information from their charts to answer the question.

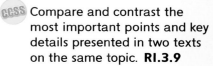

OBJECTIVES

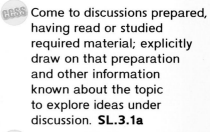

CCSS Compare and contrast the most important points and key details presented in two texts on the same topic. **RI.3.9**

CCSS Come to discussions prepared, having read or studied required material; explicitly draw on that preparation and other information known about the topic to explore ideas under discussion. **SL.3.1a**

CCSS Explain their own ideas and understanding in light of the discussion. **SL.3.1d**

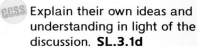

Celebrate Share Your Writing

Publishing Celebrations

Giving Presentations

Now is the time for students to share one of their pieces of informative text that they have worked on through the unit.

You may wish to invite parents or students from other classes to the Publishing Celebrations.

Preparing for Presentations

Tell students that they will present their writing. In order to provide the best representation of their hard work, they will need to prepare.

Allow students time to rehearse their presentations. Tell them to become very familiar with the piece they will be presenting by rereading it a few times. They should plan not to simply read straight from their paper, but rather to look at the audience and make eye contact. Tell them that the way they speak and present is as important as what they are presenting.

Students should consider any visuals or digital elements that they want to use during their presentation. Discuss a few possible options with students.

- Do they have photos about their topic they want to share? Can they include a diagram or illustration of a part that is difficult to explain?

- Do they include digital reference visuals that should be included in the presentation?

- Is there a video or animation that they can include to show about the topic?

Students can practice presenting to a partner in the classroom. They can also practice with family members at home or in front of a mirror. Share the following checklist with students to help them focus on important parts of their presentation as they rehearse. Discuss each point on the checklist.

Speaking Checklist

Review the Speaker's Checklist with students as they practice.

- ☑ Have all your notes and visual aids ready.
- ☑ Take a few deep breaths and stand up straight.
- ☑ Look at the audience.
- ☑ Speak clearly using an understandable pace.
- ☑ Speak loudly enough so everyone can hear.
- ☑ Speak with a tone appropriate to the topic.
- ☑ Use appropriate gestures.
- ☑ Display your visual aids at appropriate times to emphasize facts and details.

Stuart Pearce/age fotostock

Listening to Presentations

Remind students that they will be part of the audience for other students' presentations. Review with students the following Listening Checklist.

Listening Checklist

During the Presentation

- ☑ Pay attention to how the speaker uses his or her visuals in the presentation.
- ☑ Take notes on one or two things you liked about the presentation.
- ☑ Write one question or comment you have to check for understanding.
- ☑ Listen to the speaker carefully to determine the main idea and details.
- ☑ Do not talk during the presentation.

After the Presentation

- ☑ Only comment on the presentation when it is your turn.
- ☑ Tell why you liked the presentation.
- ☑ If someone else makes a similar comment, link your comment to his or hers.
- ☑ Ask an appropriate and detailed question about the topic.
- ☑ Ask the speaker to elaborate on any details you did not fully understand.

Portfolio Choice

Ask students to select one finished piece of writing, as well as two revisions to include in their writing portfolio. As students consider their choices, have them use the questions below.

Published Writing

Does your writing

- have an interesting introduction?
- focus primarily on one topic using good fluency and appropriate tone?
- have a concluding statement?
- have few or no errors in comma use, adjectives, spelling, or verb tense?
- appear neatly written in cursive or joined italics with proper margins and spacing?

Writing Entry Revisions

Did you choose a revised entry that shows

- a variety of sentence lengths to make the writing more interesting to read?
- precise language and linking words and phrases to connect ideas?
- a strong conclusion?

Go Digital

PORTFOLIO
Students can submit their writing to be considered for inclusion in their Digital Portfolio. Students' portfolios can be shared with parents.

Level Up Accelerating Progress

Leveled Reader

OBJECTIVES

CCSS By the end of the year, read and comprehend informational texts, including history/social studies, science, and technical texts, at the high end of the grades 2–3 text complexity band independently and proficiently. **RI.3.10**

Approaching Level to On Level

African Cats

Level Up Lessons also available online

Before Reading

Preview Discuss what students remember about the different types of African cats. Tell them they will be reading a more challenging version of *African Cats*.

Vocabulary Use the **Visual Vocabulary Cards** and routine.

A C T During Reading

▶ **Specific Vocabulary** Review with students the following words that are new to this title: *solitary, nocturnal, pounce, prefer, promote*. Model using context clues for students. Read page 4 aloud. Ask: *Do lions and lionesses live together?* (yes) *Is this different from other cats?* (yes) *What new word do you see that describes cats that live alone?* (solitary)

▶ **Connection of Ideas** Students may need help connecting and synthesizing new ideas and information. Have students chorally read the sidebar on page 5. Ask: *What did scientists used to think about a lion's mane?* (It was used for protection.) *What do scientists now know about a lion's mane?* (A full mane attracts lionesses.)

▶ **Sentence Structure** Students may need help understanding complex sentences that compare and contrast information. Read the first paragraph on page 10 with students, and then ask them what cats are being compared. (little big cats, lions, leopards, cats) Ask: *What is different about little big cats?* (They are smaller than lions and leopards but bigger and heavier than cats.) Point out other sentences that compare and contrast information, such as the last sentence on page 11.

After Reading

Ask students to complete the Respond to Reading on page 15. Then have them finish the Paired Read and hold Literature Circles.

Leveled Reader

OBJECTIVES

CCSS By the end of the year, read and comprehend informational texts, including history/social studies, science, and technical texts, at the high end of the grades 2–3 text complexity band independently and proficiently. **RI.3.10**

On Level
to Beyond Level

African Cats

Level Up Lessons also available online

Before Reading

Preview Discuss what students remember about the different types of African cats. Tell them they will be reading a more challenging version of *African Cats*.

Vocabulary Use the **Visual Vocabulary Cards** to review the vocabulary.

A C T During Reading

▶ **Specific Vocabulary** Review with students the following words that are new to this title: *scavengers, aerodynamic, coalitions.* Model how to use a glossary or context clues to find the meanings.

▶ **Sentence Structure** Students may need help understanding more complex sentence structures. Reread sentences 5 and 6 on page 4. Write the word *however* on the board. Say: *This word helps connect ideas in a sentence. What two ideas do you see in the first sentence?* (female cubs usually stay with their families for their whole lives; young males leave the family group) See pages 5 and 10 for more examples. Repeat the activity for *although* on page 13.

▶ **Connection of Ideas** Students might need help connecting and synthesizing ideas from page to page and paragraph to paragraph. Read page 12 with students. Ask: *What cats are considered big cats?* (lions, leopards, cheetahs) *Little big cats?* (servals, African golden cats, caracals) *What do caracals have in common with servals?* (Both are excellent at catching birds in midair.)

After Reading

Ask students to complete the Respond to Reading on page 15. Then have them finish the Paired Read and hold Literature Circles.

Level Up Accelerating Progress

Leveled Reader

OBJECTIVES

CCSS By the end of the year, read and comprehend informational texts, including history/ social studies, science, and technical texts, at the high end of the grades 2–3 text complexity band independently and proficiently. **RI.3.10**

English Language Learners to On Level

African Cats

Level Up Lessons also available online

Before Reading

Preview Remind students that expository text gives facts about a topic. Discuss what students remember about African cats. Tell them they will be reading a more challenging version of *African Cats.*

Vocabulary Use the **Visual Vocabulary Cards** to review the vocabulary. Use the routine found on the cards. Point out the cognates: *habitat, nocturno, solitario, territorio.*

A C T During Reading

▶ **Specific Vocabulary** Review with students the following words that are new to this title: *nocturnal, predators, retractable, sprint.* Model how to use a glossary to find the meaning of *nocturnal.* Define *retractable* for students. Say: *Cheetahs' claws can go into their paws and come back out. They are* retractable.

▶ **Sentence Structure** Students may need help understanding complex sentences that compare and contrast information. Read the first paragraph on page 10 with students, and then ask them what cats are being compared. (little big cats, lions, leopards, cats) Ask: *What is different about little big cats?* (They are smaller than lions and leopards but bigger and heavier than cats.) Point out other sentences that compare and contrast information, such as the last sentence on page 11.

▶ **Connection of Ideas** Point out the new information in the section "Leopards" on page 6. Point out how *hunt at night* after *nocturnal* explains the word's meaning. Ask: *Why do leopards hunt at night?* (because they are nocturnal)

After Reading

Ask students to complete the Respond to Reading on page 15. Then have them finish the Paired Read and hold Literature Circles.

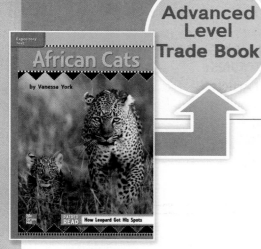

Leveled Reader

OBJECTIVES

(CCSS) By the end of the year, read and comprehend literature/informational text in the grades 2–3 text complexity band independently and proficiently.
RL/RI.3.10

Beyond Level
to Self-Selected Trade Book

Independent Reading

Level Up Lessons **also available online**

Before Reading

Together with students identify the particular focus of their reading based on the text they choose. Students who have chosen the same title will work in groups to closely read the selection.

Close Reading

Taking Notes Assign a graphic organizer for students to use to take notes as they read. Reinforce a specific comprehension focus from the unit by choosing one of the graphic organizers that best fits the book.

Examples:

Fiction	Informational Texts
Theme	Compare and Contrast
Graphic Organizer 148	Graphic Organizer 50

Ask and Answer Questions Remind students to ask questions as they read. Tell them it is helpful to keep notes in one place, such as in a notebook or on note cards, as it can be useful when studying. As students meet, have them discuss the section that they have read. They can share the questions that they noted and work together to find text evidence to support their answers. You may wish to have students write their responses to their questions.

After Reading

Write About Text

Have students work together to respond to the text using text evidence to support their writing.

Examples:

Fiction	Informational Text
How do the characters' actions tell about the theme?	Which details from the text can you compare? Which details can you contrast?

SUMMATIVE ASSESSMENT

TESTED SKILLS

✓ COMPREHENSION:
- Theme **RL.3.2**
- Text Structure: Problem and Solution **RI.3.8**
- Text Structure: Compare and Contrast **RI.3.8**
- Point of View **RL.3.6**
- Message/Lesson **RL.3.2**
- Illustrations **RL.3.7**
- Headings **RI.3.5**
- Stanza **RL.3.5**

✓ VOCABULARY:
- Root Words **L.3.4c**
- Idioms **RL.3.4**
- Greek and Latin Roots **L.3.4c**
- Paragraph Clues **L.3.4a**

✓ ENGLISH LANGUAGE CONVENTIONS:
- Adjectives and Articles **L.3.1a**
- Adjectives That Compare **L3.1g**
- Adverbs **L.3.1a**
- Adverbs That Compare **L.3.1a**
- Prepositions **L.3.2**

✓ WRITING:
- Writing About Text **W.3.8**
- Opinion Performance Task **W.3.1a-d**

Elements of Summative Assessment

✓ Variety of Item Types
- Selected Response
- Multiple Selected Response
- Evidence-Based Selected Response
- Constructed Response
- Tech-Enhanced Items

✓ Performance-Based Task

Additional Assessment Options

Conduct assessments individually using the differentiated passages in *Fluency Assessment*. Students' expected fluency goal for this Unit is **97–117 WCPM** with an accuracy rate of 95% or higher.

RUNNING RECORDS ⬅

Use the instructional reading level determined by the Running Record calculations for regrouping decisions. Students at Level 34 or below should be provided reteaching on specific Comprehension skills.

Using Assessment Results

Unit Assessment Skills and Fluency	If . . .	Then . . .
COMPREHENSION	Students score below 70% . . .	. . . reteach tested skills using the *Tier 2 Comprehension Intervention* online PDFs.
VOCABULARY	Students score below 70% . . .	. . . reteach tested skills using the *Tier 2 Vocabulary Intervention* online PDFs.
ENGLISH LANGUAGE CONVENTIONS	Students score below 70% . . .	. . . reteach tested skills using the *Tier 2 Writing and Grammar Intervention* online PDFs.
WRITING	Students score less than "2" on short-response items and "3" on extended constructed response items . . .	. . . reteach tested skills using appropriate lessons from the Strategies and Skills and/or Write About Reading sections in the *Tier 2 Comprehension Intervention* online PDFs.
	Students score less than "12" on the performance task . . .	. . . reteach skills using the *Tier 2 Writing and Grammar Intervention* online PDFs.
FLUENCY	Students have a WCPM score of 0–96 . . .	. . . reteach tested skills using the *Tier 2 Fluency Intervention* online PDFs.

Using Summative Data

Check online reports for this Unit Assessment as well as your data Dashboard. Use the data to assign small group instruction for students who are below the overall proficiency level for the tested skills.

Data-Driven Recommendations

Response to Intervention

Use the appropriate sections of the *Placement and Diagnostic Assessment* as well as students' assessment results to designate students requiring:

 **Intervention Online PDFs**   **WonderWorks Intervention Program**

Writing
Process
Genre Writing

Model
Lesson

Extended Complex Text

Genre Writing

Reading Extended Complex Text

Program Information

Writing Process

Genre Writing: Informative Text

Model Lesson

Reading Extended Complex Text

Program Information

Go Digital

For Additional Resources

Review Comprehension Lessons
Unit Bibliography
Word Lists
Literature and Informational Text Charts
Web Sites
Resources

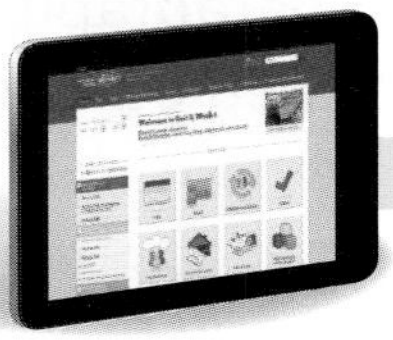

www.connected.mcgraw-hill.com

INFORMATIVE TEXT Feature Article

EXPERT MODEL

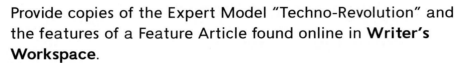

Techno-Revolution
by Sam G.

Computers are everywhere. Some people carry them around in their pockets. Some use them on a plane. You might have used one at home, at school, or at the library. Today smart phones have more processing power than computers from only a few years ago. But who built the first computers? And how did these machines become such a big part of our daily lives?

One of the very first techno-pioneers was Kenneth H. Olsen. He started out fixing radios in his basement. Later Olsen went to college to learn about building machines. Olsen was very good at his work. Soon he showed people how to build a computer. This machine was not meant for entertainment. It was a tool for gathering information. Olsen started his own company to make computers.

Who knew computers would become so important? Bill Gates did! He made some smart predictions. He and his friend Paul Allen worked together to create a computer program that many people could use. They formed their own company, which became and still is a great success. Bill Gates has even held the record as the world's richest man. Most computers today use this company's programs. If you have used a computer, you can bet you've used these programs.

Steve Jobs also loved computers. In order to get more people using and buying computers, Jobs wanted to find a way to make them cost less. He and his friend Steve Wozniak started a computer company. It made computers that were easy to use. The company also made a computer mouse that people liked. Today Jobs's and Wozniak's machines are sold all over and their innovations in technology have been astounding.

**Expert Model
PDF Online**

OBJECTIVES

CCSS Write informative/ explanatory texts to examine a topic and convey ideas and information clearly. Introduce a topic and group related information together; include illustrations when useful to aiding comprehension.
W.3.2a

ACADEMIC LANGUAGE
feature article, current event

Read Like a Writer

Explain to students that they might write a feature article for a school newspaper, a school assignment, or even as part of an application for a job or school. Tell students that feature articles give information about a notable event or an interesting topic. Explain that feature articles could be written about many different things, from the history of amusement parks to the story of a famous weather event. Have students share an article they've read in a newspaper or on a website. Read and discuss the features of a feature article.

Provide copies of the Expert Model "Techno-Revolution" and the features of a Feature Article found online in **Writer's Workspace**.

Go Digital

Writer's Workspace

Features of a Feature Article

- It tells about a current event or topic of interest.
- It has a lead that grabs readers' attention.
- It uses paragraphs to give facts, definitions, and details that explain the topic.
- It has a concluding statement or section that gives readers something to think about.

Discuss the Expert Model

COLLABORATE Use the questions below to prompt discussion of feature articles.

- **What does the writer tell about in the article?** (He tells about famous computer developers over the years.)

- **What different types of sentences does the writer use in the first paragraph?** (declarative sentences and questions) **Does this make you want to read more? Why or why not?** (Yes, because the first paragraph is interesting.)

- **What does each paragraph tell about?** (how computers became popular) **How is each paragraph different?** (Each tells about different people who made computers or programs.)

- **How does the writer end his article?** (talks about what will happen with computers in future) **How did you feel after you read the article?** (excited about what computers might do in the future)

PREWRITE

Discuss and Plan

Purpose Discuss with students the purpose for writing a feature article. Explain that feature articles are usually written to inform. The specific purpose for a feature article depends on the subject.

Audience Have students think about who will read their feature articles, such as fellow classmates, other students in the school, and community members. Ask: *What is an interesting topic or a current event that you want to tell people about? How can you make others interested in your topic?*

Teach the Minilesson

Organization Tell students that feature articles are usually organized in a specific way. Once the topic has been introduced, the ideas that develop it are presented in a logical order. This order can vary depending on the topic, but examples include telling events in the sequence in which they occurred or using cause and effect to examine a topic. Explain that a good organizational structure helps readers make sense of the text.

Distribute copies of the Model Sequence Chart found online in **Writer's Workspace**. Point out how the sequence of events matches the order in the Expert Model. Discuss how the writer organized his events in a logical way.

ENGLISH LANGUAGE LEARNERS

Beginning

Demonstrate Understanding Read aloud each box from the Model Sequence Chart in random order. Have students raise their hands when they hear the event that happens first in the article.

Intermediate

Summarize Have students orally summarize the main points from the Expert Model.

Advanced/High

Expand Have partners form responses to the questions about the Expert Model.

Your Turn

Choose Your Topic Have pairs or small groups brainstorm topics for their articles. Encourage them to think of a topic or event that is important, that they care about, or that they want to learn more about. They can also write about something they feel other people should learn about. Then ask students questions to prompt thinking. Have students record ideas in their Writer's Notebooks.

- Is there an important event that interests you? Is there something you want to tell others about?

- What do you already know about this topic? Are you an expert or do you need to research and find out more information?

- Why is the topic important? What do you want people to take away?

Plan Provide copies of the blank Sequence Chart found online in **Writer's Workspace**. Have students choose a topic that is important to them. Have them list important information in their charts.

MODEL SEQUENCE CHART

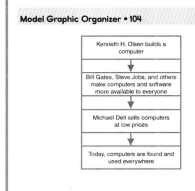

Model Graphic Organizer • 104

Kenneth H. Olsen builds a computer

↓

Bill Gates, Steve Jobs, and others make computers and software more available to everyone

↓

Michael Dell sells computers at low prices

↓

Today, computers are found and used everywhere

INFORMATIVE TEXT Feature Article

DRAFT

OBJECTIVES

CCSS Write informative/explanatory texts to examine a topic and convey ideas and information clearly. Provide a concluding statement or section. **W.3.2d**

ACADEMIC LANGUAGE

draft, linking word, peer review

Discuss the Student Model

Review the features of feature articles. Provide copies of the Student Model found online in **Writer's Workspace** and read it aloud.

Teach the Minilesson

Word Choice: Precise Words Remind students that good writers choose strong verbs and nouns to clearly communicate their ideas. Write on the board *helpers*. Say: *The helpers worked to clean up the beach.* Then write *volunteers*. Say: *The volunteers worked to clean up the beach.* Discuss with students how *volunteers* has a more precise meaning than *helpers*.

Look at Devin's draft and discuss with students how his use of strong nouns and verbs helps to strengthen his writing and make his writing more interesting. Encourage volunteers to point out areas in the draft where more precise words could be used.

Your Turn

Write a Draft Have students review their Sequence Charts that they prepared in Prewrite to begin their drafts. Encourage students to review the sequence and, if needed, to adjust their charts to show the most logical order for their writing.

Go Digital

Writer's Workspace

Conferencing Routines

Teacher Conferences

STEP 1

Talk about the strengths of the writing.

Your opening paragraph clearly introduces the topic in an interesting way and makes me want to read more.

STEP 2

Focus on how the writer uses a writing trait.

You did a good job of using precise words, but there are some areas in your article where you might want to make the words stronger.

STEP 3

Make concrete suggestions for revision.

Your writing could use a stronger concluding statement. You should add a paragraph that sums up your article and leaves your readers with something to think about.

REVISE

Discuss the Revised Model

Distribute copies of the Revised Student Model found online in **Writer's Workspace**. Read the model aloud and have students note the revisions that Devin made. Use the specific revisions to demonstrate how Devin revised his article to add time-order words and a concluding statement. Discuss with students how these revisions improved the article.

Teach the Minilesson

Strong Conclusions Explain to students that an effective feature article should end with a strong concluding section that sums up the article and leaves its readers with something to think about.

Direct students' attention to revisions made in the Revised Student Model. Discuss with students how Devin's revision to his draft gave his article a strong ending. It clearly sums up the article concisely. Discuss the difference made by Devin's revision.

Your Turn

COLLABORATE

Revise Have students use the **Peer Review Routine** and questions to review their partner's draft. Then have them select suggestions from the peer review to incorporate into their revisions. Provide the Revise and Edit Checklist from **Writer's Workspace** to guide them as they revise. Encourage them to see where improvements can be made to their conclusions. Circulate among students as they work and confer as needed.

REVISED STUDENT MODEL

Revised Student Model • Feature Article • 107

Making Newport Beautiful
by Devin P.

Things are looking up around Newport.

On a beach just outside of town, volunteers pick up trash. They sort bottles cans and plastic into seperate bags. They leave the beach much cleaner than they found it. This volunteers feel great about this work. They are making Newport beach gorgeous again.

There is a park across town where other volunteers gather. They are planting flowers and pulling up weeds. They have made up a slogan, "Newport make things grow!" If you take a tour of the park, you will see children of all ages gardening. They are learning a useful skill that also helps keep the park green. The children make new friends. The adults get to know new neighbors.

The people who live here in Newport all agree. This area was not always such a great place to live. Few people went to the park or the beach because these places did not look very inviting.

A concerned parent said, "Our families deserve a better place to live. Let's work to make things better." Volunteer groups were formed, and many people began to help. Things were looking up, and people started using the park and the beach again.

The people of Newport have really come together to make their community a better place.

Peer Conferences

Review with students the routine for peer review of writing. They should listen carefully as the writer reads his or her work aloud. Begin by telling what they liked about the writing. Then ask a question that will help the writer think more about the writing. Finally, make a suggestion that will make the writing stronger.

Use these questions for peer review.

- ☑ Does the introduction tell about current event or an interesting topic?
- ☑ Are precise words used? Is there a variety of sentence lengths?
- ☑ Are there linking words and phrases?
- ☑ Does the article contain a strong conclusion to sum up the main idea?

INFORMATIVE TEXT Feature Article

PROOFREAD/EDIT AND PUBLISH

OBJECTIVES

CCSS Plan and deliver an informative/explanatory presentation on a topic that: organizes ideas around major points of information, follows a logical sequence, includes supporting details, uses clear and specific vocabulary, and provides a strong conclusion. **SL.3.4a**

CCSS With guidance and support from peers and adults, develop and strengthen writing as needed by planning, revising, and editing. **W.3.5**

CCSS With guidance and support from adults, use technology to produce and publish writing (using keyboarding skills) as well as to interact and collaborate with others. **W.3.6**

EDITED STUDENT MODEL

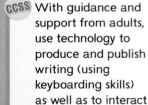

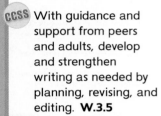

Discuss the Edited Model

Provide copies of the Edited Student Model found online in **Writer's Workspace**. Read the model aloud and have students note the editing changes that Devin made. Use the specific edits to show how Devin improved his article, including correcting the use of commas in a series, correcting the use of commas after introductory words, correcting the use of adjectives that limit, and correcting spelling mistakes.

Go Digital

Writer's Workspace

Your Turn

Edit Have students use the Edit questions on the Revise and Edit Checklist to guide them as they review and edit their drafts on their own. Remind them to read for one type of error at a time.

Publish

For the final presentation of their feature articles, have students choose a format for publishing. Students may want to consider:

Print Publishing	Digital Publishing
Magazine/Newspaper Article	Writer's Workspace
Collaborative Class Book	Class Blog
Classroom News Bulletin Board	Video News Report

Have students handwrite, use a typewriter, or use a word-processing program to produce their writing. They should be sure to use standard margins and format their final drafts so readers can easily follow the flow of the text.

Explain to students that adding visual and multimedia elements can strengthen their writing and presentation, making them more engaging for their readers and audience. Allow time for students to design and include illustrations, photos, maps, videos, audio, and other visual or multimedia elements that will enhance their articles.

Then have students plan and deliver a presentation of their informative feature articles with the added visual and multimedia elements. Remind students to make sure that their presentation has ideas organized around major points of information, flows in a logical sequence, features supporting details, includes clear and specific vocabulary, and provides a strong conclusion.

EVALUATE

Discuss Rubrics

Guide students as they use the Student Rubric found online in **Writer's Workspace**. Discuss how using a rubric helps them identify and focus on areas that might need further work. Work with the class to review the bulleted points on the rubric.

- **Focus and Coherence** Is there a strong introduction that grabs the reader's attention and states the topic?

- **Organization** Is information presented in a logical order?

- **Ideas and Support** Does the article include details, definitions, and/or facts?

- **Word Choice** Are precise words and linking words and phrases used?

- **Voice/Sentence Fluency** Does the writer's voice sound natural? Does it include a variety of sentence lengths?

- **Conventions** Are errors in grammar, spelling, punctuation, and capitalization corrected?

STUDENT RUBRIC

Writing Rubric • 110

	Feature Article Rubric
4 Excellent	• clearly introduces an event or topic • ideas are developed with facts, definitions, and/or details • all related information about the topic is grouped together and in logical order • effectively uses linking words and phrases • is free or almost free of errors • is easy to read, neat, and consistently formatted
3 Good	• discusses an event or topic • ideas generally supported with facts, definitions, and/or details mostly directly related to topic • most related information about the topic is grouped together in logical order • uses some linking words and phrases • has minor errors that do not confuse the reader • is mostly easy to read and mostly consistent
2 Fair	• discusses an event or topic, but strays from it at times • weak ideas that are not clearly developed • some related information grouped together, but lack of logical order • uses few linking words and phrases • makes errors that confuse the reader • is not always easy to read
1 Unsatisfactory	• does not clearly discuss one topic or event • ideas are not developed • organization is poor and confusing • uses no linking words and phrases • makes many serious errors • is difficult to read because of poor format or handwriting

Your Turn

Reflect and Set Goals After students have evaluated their own feature articles, tell them to reflect on their progress as writers. Encourage them to consider areas where they feel they have shown improvement, and to think about what areas need further improvement. Have them set writing goals to prepare for their conference with the teacher.

Conference with Students

Use the rubric and the Anchor Papers provided online in **Writer's Workspace** as you evaluate student writing. The Anchor Papers provide samples of papers that score from 1 to 4. These papers reflect the criteria described in the rubric. Anchor Papers offer a standard against which to judge writing.

Review with individual students the writing goals they have set. Discuss ways to achieve these goals and suggest any further areas of improvement students may need to target.

INFORMATIVE TEXT Research Report

The African Elephant
by Alicia P.

Africa is almost twice the size of the United States. It has deserts, grasslands, and rainforests. The continent of Africa is also home to the largest land mammal in the world—the elephant. Most African elephants live in the grasslands where there is enough rain and plenty of space for these enormous creatures to move around.

African elephants are huge! An adult male can grow to be more than 10 feet tall and weigh almost 12,000 pounds. What's more, these creatures never stop growing! You can always spot the oldest elephant in a herd because it will be the biggest one.

The tusks of an elephant are used in several ways. An elephant can survive for up to 60 years, and one way to determine an elephant's age is by its tusks. Male and female African elephants have long, curved tusks growing on either side of their faces. Elephants also use their tusks to knock down trees. Sometimes you will see an elephant with one very long tusk and one very short tusk. The short one has been worn down or broken during the elephant's many years of tree toppling. And why do they tear down trees? To eat them! Elephants eat the trunks of trees as well as the leaves, branches, and bark. Elephants have another tool to topple trees, too. Their trunks!

Elephants are known for their very long noses, or trunks. An adult elephant can use its trunk to snap a tree or to pick up something as small as a peanut. When it has not rained in a long time, elephants can use their trunks to dig deep holes in the ground in search of water.

How else do elephants find water when it has not rained? They live in family groups called herds. The oldest female elephant in the group leads the herd. She is called the

Expert Model PDF Online

OBJECTIVES

CCSS Write informative/ explanatory texts to examine a topic and convey ideas and information clearly. Introduce a topic and group related information together; include illustrations when useful to aiding comprehension. **W.3.2a**

ACADEMIC LANGUAGE
research, central topic, main idea, introduction, definition, facts, details

EXPERT MODEL

Read Like a Writer

Explain to students that when they research a topic, they learn as much as they can about that topic. Point out that research papers are written to share information found when researching a specific topic. Have students brainstorm topics they have previously researched. Invite volunteers to share a fact about a familiar topic. Then read and discuss the features of a research report.

Provide copies of the Expert Model "The African Elephant" and the features of Research Report found online in **Writer's Workspace**.

Go Digital

Writer's Workspace

Features of a Research Report

- It provides information focused on a central topic.
- It has an introduction that presents the main ideas.
- It uses paragraphs to develop and support ideas with facts, definitions, and details.
- It summarizes information from more than one source.
- It uses linking words that connect ideas.
- It has a concluding statement or section.

Discuss the Expert Model

Use the questions below to prompt discussion of research reports.

- **What does the writer tell about?** (African elephants)
- **When does the writer first mention elephants?** (She mentions them in the first paragraph.)
- **How is each paragraph similar?** (Each paragraph tells about African elephants.) **How is each paragraph different?** (Each paragraph tells about a different aspect of African elephants.)
- **In the second paragraph, which linking phrase does the writer use to connect ideas?** (She uses *What's more* to connect ideas.)
- **How does the writer end her report?** (She sums up her main idea in a concluding statement.)

PREWRITE

Discuss and Plan

Purpose Discuss with students the purpose for writing a research report. Remind them that research reports are written to share information, or to inform. Research reports can be about many different things, from dinosaurs to rock stars. Explain to students that strong research reports are supported by facts and carefully researched information.

Audience Have students think about who will read their research reports, such as fellow students. Ask: *What subject would you be most interested in learning more about? What subject do you think your classmates would find interesting?*

Teach the Minilesson

Organization Remind students that the topic of a research report is what the report is about. Each paragraph in the report should have a main idea related to the topic. The main idea of each paragraph is what that paragraph is mostly about. Explain that the paragraphs should be organized in a way that makes sense for the topic.

Distribute copies of the Model Main Idea and Details Chart found online in **Writer's Workspace**. Point out the main idea of the second paragraph. Then discuss with students how the individual details within the paragraph tell more about the main idea.

Your Turn

Choose Your Topic Have students work in pairs or small groups to brainstorm topics for their reports. Have them think about a subject that is important to them. Remind them that their reports must be on a subject that can be researched. Then ask students questions to prompt thinking. Have students record their ideas in their Writer's Notebooks.

- What is a subject that is important or interesting to you?
- Where will you look to get facts and information about your topic?
- Why do you want to learn more about the topic? What specifically would you like to find out?

Plan Provide copies of the blank Main Idea and Details Chart found online in **Writer's Workspace**. Have students list topics they would like to learn more about or that are important to them. Then have them research their topics, recording their findings on a separate sheet of paper. Once they have completed their research, have them organize it by using their charts.

ENGLISH LANGUAGE LEARNERS

Beginning

Demonstrate Understanding Have students cut their charts into individual cards and shuffle them into two piles. Then have them match up the details with the main idea they tell about and summarize the information.

Intermediate

Summarize Have students tell the main idea of each paragraph in the expert model.

Advanced/High

Expand Have partners discuss ideas they have for their research reports and summarize some of the ideas about each topic.

MODEL MAIN IDEA AND DETAILS CHART

Model Graphic Organizer • 114

Main ideas	Details
African elephants are huge	adult male can grow to more than 10 feet tall and weigh almost 12,000 pounds
elephants' tusks are used in several ways	tusks show the age of an elephant; elephants use their tusks to knock down trees
elephants are known for their trunks	trunks are used to dig deep holes, knock down trees, and pick up things
the oldest female elephant in a herd is very important	she can remember where water sources are; she helps raise all of the baby elephants in the herd; she teaches younger female elephants how to care for their young

INFORMATIVE TEXT Research Report

DRAFT

OBJECTIVES

CCSS Write informative/explanatory texts to examine a topic and convey ideas and information clearly. Develop the topic with facts, definitions, and details. **W.3.2b**

ACADEMIC LANGUAGE
draft, peer review

Discuss the Student Model

Review the features of research reports. Provide copies of the Student Model found online in **Writer's Workspace** and read it aloud.

Teach the Minilesson

Develop the Topic Remind students that good writers develop the topic of their research report by using facts, definitions, and details. In effective research reports, facts are used to provide provable information that is also interesting. These facts are found through the writer's research, using trusted reference sources that contain accurate information.

Discuss with students how the writer does not give her opinions about the Gobi Desert, instead she uses facts, definitions, and details to provide interesting information about it. Review ways to record information about a topic, including taking notes and making observations.

Your Turn

Write a Draft Have students review their Main Idea and Details Chart that they prepared in Prewrite to begin their drafts. Encourage students to do further research if needed to gain more information.

Go Digital

Writer's Workspace

Conferencing Routines

Teacher Conferences

STEP 1

Talk about the strengths of the writing.

The first paragraph clearly introduces your topic and tells something interesting about it.

STEP 2

Focus on how the writer uses a writing trait.

You did a good job of developing the topic of your report using interesting facts.

STEP 3

Make concrete suggestions for revision.

There are some details in this paragraph that do not relate to the main idea of the paragraph. Delete information that might be distracting for your readers.

REVISE

Discuss the Revised Model

Distribute copies of the Revised Student Model found online in **Writer's Workspace**. Read the model aloud and have students note the revisions that Jaime made. Use the specific changes to demonstrate how Jaime revised her report to clarify ideas and strengthen her conclusion. Discuss how these revisions helped to improve the report and connect the ideas.

Teach the Minilesson

Tone Explain that good writers stay aware of the appropriate tone for their writing. The tone of a research report should reflect the seriousness of the subject. Have students compare topics that would have a serious tone and light-hearted ones.

Have students find examples in the Revised Student Model where Jaime adjusted the tone of her writing. Discuss how these revisions help improve the consistency of her tone.

Your Turn

COLLABORATE

Revise Have students use the **Peer Review Routine** and questions to review their partner's draft. Have students select suggestions from the peer review to incorporate into their revisions. Provide the Revise and Edit Checklist from **Writer's Workspace** to guide them. Have them check that every detail tells more about the main idea. Circulate among students as they work and confer as needed.

REVISED STUDENT MODEL

Revised Student Model • Research Report • 117

The Gobi Desert
by Jaime P.

The Gobi Desert is a really really big desert. It is in China and southern Mongolia. When we think of deserts, we imagin sand, but large areas of the Gobi are rock.

The climate of this area is unusual and there are more different types of animals. While many deserts are very hot, the Gobi can have freezing temperatures. It can be very cold in winter and hot and rainy in summer. Snow even forms on the sand dunes of the Gobi.

The Gobi Desert is home to different types of plant and animal life. There are gazelles in the Gobi Desert. There are polecats. There are also lots of bears, wolves, and snow leopards are there, too. The Gobi has a longer, interesting history. Long ago, traders crossed it on camels. It was part of the Mongol Empire. For centuries, herders lived on the Gobi with their caddle. These people move from place to place and are called nomads. They live very much like people of old did.

The Gobi can seem like a place outside of time.

Peer Conferences

Review with students the routine for peer review of writing. They should listen carefully as the writer reads his or her work aloud. Begin by telling what they liked about the writing. Then ask a question that will help the writer think more about the writing. Finally, make a suggestion that will make the writing stronger.

Use these questions for peer review.

- ☑ Does the report have an introduction that tells about an interesting topic?
- ☑ Does each paragraph have a main idea that is developed with facts, definitions, and details?
- ☑ Are there a variety of sentences and linking words and phrases?

INFORMATIVE TEXT Research Report

PROOFREAD/EDIT AND PUBLISH

OBJECTIVES

CCSS With guidance and support from peers and adults, develop and strengthen writing as needed by planning, revising, and editing. **W.3.5**

CCSS With guidance and support from adults, use technology to produce and publish writing (using keyboarding skills) as well as to interact and collaborate with others. **W.3.6**

CCSS Write legibly in cursive or joined italics, allowing margins and correct spacing between letters in a word and words in a sentence. **L.3.1k**

ACADEMIC LANGUAGE

proofread, edit, publish, present, evaluate, multimedia, self-evaluation, rubric

EDITED STUDENT MODEL

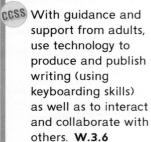

Discuss the Edited Model

Provide copies of the Edited Student Model found online in **Writer's Workspace**. Read the model aloud and have students note the editing changes that Jaime made. Use the specific edits to show how editing for spelling, verb tense, and correct usage of comparative and superlative forms improved the research report.

Your Turn

Edit Have students use the Edit questions on the Revise and Edit Checklist to guide them as they review and edit their drafts on their own. Remind them to read for one type of error at a time.

Publish

For the final presentation of their research reports, have students choose a format for publishing. Students may want to consider:

Print Publishing	Digital Publishing
Magazine/Newspaper Article	Writer's Workspace
Poster Board Presentation	Social Networking Page Devoted to Topic
A Coffee Table Book Summarizing Their Report with Pictures and Captions	Video Presentation

Have students write their research report in cursive or joined italics or use a word-processing program to produce their writing. They should be sure to use standard margins and format their final drafts so readers can easily follow the flow of the text.

- You may wish to have students practice their handwriting to make sure they can write legibly in cursive or joined italics. Review correct margins and proper letter and word spacing. Online resources for handwriting can be found at **www.connected.mcgraw-hill.com.**

Explain to students that adding visual and multimedia elements can strengthen their writing and presentation, making them more engaging for their readers and audience. Allow time for students to design and include illustrations, photos, maps, videos, audio, and other visual or multimedia elements that will enhance their research reports.

Go Digital

Writer's Workspace

EVALUATE

Discuss Rubrics

Guide students as they use the Student Rubric found online in **Writer's Workspace**. Discuss how using a rubric helps them identify and focus on areas that might need further work. Work with the class to review the bulleted points on the rubric.

- **Focus and Coherence** Does the report introduce a topic and focus on that topic throughout the writing?
- **Organization** Is related information about the topic grouped together?
- **Ideas and Support** Is the report supported with facts about the topic?
- **Word Choice** Are linking words used to connect ideas within a grouping of information?
- **Voice/Sentence Fluency** Is the tone appropriate for the subject? Is there a variety of sentence lengths?
- **Conventions** Are errors in grammar, spelling, punctuation, and capitalization corrected?

Your Turn

Reflect and Set Goals After students have evaluated their own research reports, tell them to reflect on their progress as writers. Encourage them to consider areas where they feel they have shown improvement, and to think about what areas need further improvement. Have them set writing goals to prepare for their conference with the teacher.

Conference with Students

Use the rubric and the Anchor Papers provided online in **Writer's Workspace** as you evaluate student writing. The Anchor Papers provide samples of papers that score from 1 to 4. These papers reflect the criteria described in the rubric. Anchor Papers offer a standard against which to judge writing.

Review with individual students the writing goals they have set. Discuss ways to achieve these goals and suggest any further areas of improvement students may need to target.

STUDENT RUBRIC

Writing Rubric • 120

Research Report Rubric

4 Excellent	• clearly introduces a topic • topic is well-researched and developed with facts, definitions, and/or details • all related information about the topic is grouped together • effectively uses linking words to connect related ideas • is free or almost free of errors • is easy to read, neat, and consistently formatted
3 Good	• discusses a topic • topic is supported with facts, definitions, and/or details mostly directly related to topic • most related information about the topic is grouped together • uses some linking words to connect related ideas • has minor errors that do not confuse the reader • is mostly easy to read and mostly consistent
2 Fair	• discusses a topic, but strays from it at times • topic is weak and does not seem well-researched • some related information about the topic is grouped together, but some is out of order • uses few linking words to connect related ideas • makes errors that confuse the reader • is not always easy to read
1 Unsatisfactory	• does not clearly discuss one topic • no facts presented about the topic • lack of organizational structure • uses no linking words to connect related ideas • makes many serious errors • is difficult to read because of poor format or handwriting

Close Reading Routine

Read — *What does the text say?*

Assign the Reading

Depending on the needs of your students, you can

- ask students to read the text silently
- read the text together with students
- read the text aloud

Take Notes

Students generate questions and take notes about aspects of the text that might be confusing for them. Encourage students to note

- key ideas and details
- difficult vocabulary words or phrases
- details that are not clear
- information that they do not understand

Students complete a graphic organizer to take notes on important information from the text.

Reread — *How does the author say it?*

Ask Text-Dependent Questions

Students reread shorter passages from the text and cite text evidence to answer deeper questions about craft and structure. Students should

- work with partners or small groups to talk about and identify evidence
- generate questions about the text

Integrate — *What does the text mean?*

Students reread to integrate knowledge and ideas and make text-to-text connections. Students should

- work with partners or small groups to identify and discuss connections
- use text evidence to write a response

Use the Literature Anthology

Getting Ready

CLOSE READING OF *ALLIGATORS AND CROCODILES,*
pages 520–541

Use the suggestions in the chart to assign reading of the text and to chunk the text into shorter passages for rereading.

ESSENTIAL QUESTION *How can learning about animals help you respect them?*

Ask students to discuss the different animals they have learned about and how it has helped them respect them.

Suggested Pacing

Days 1–4	**Read**
	pp. 520–525
	pp. 526–531
	pp. 532–535
	pp. 536–541
Days 5–12	**Reread**
	pp. 520–523
	pp. 524–525
	pp. 526–527
	pp. 528–529
	pp. 530–531
	pp. 532–533
	pp. 534–538
	pp. 539–541
Days 13–15	**Integrate**

Read | *What does the author tell us?*

Assign the Reading

Ask students to read the text independently. You may want to read pages 526–529 with students to help them use and interpret maps and diagrams.

Take Notes

As students read, remind them to take notes. They can record the main idea and key details of each section. They can also note words they do not understand and questions they have.

Think Aloud Page 523 says that the animal drifting through the water might be an alligator or a crocodile. I wonder how you can tell the difference.

p. 523

Is it an alligator or crocodile?

How can you tell the difference?

Assign **Graphic Organizer 66** to help students take notes on how the author compares and contrasts information.

As students share their questions and notes, use the Access Complex Text suggestions on pages T217A–T217V to help address features about the text that students found difficult.

> **Reread**   *How does the author say it?*

Analyze the Text

After students summarize the selection, have them reread to develop a deeper understanding of the text and answer the questions on **Close Reading Companion** pages 166–168. For students who need support in citing text evidence, model using the following Reread prompt:

• **Author's Craft: Figurative Language** Reread page 253. How does the author describe what is in the water? What is it being compared to? What animal can it be? Why does the author not say which of these animals it is?

Think Aloud The author describes something well hidden that looks like a bumpy log. I read that "It is an alligator or a crocodile." Because of this description, I can visualize that alligators and crocodiles are a lot alike. Both of them hide and look like logs in the water.

Continue using the following Reread prompts:

• **Author's Purpose: Text Features** How does the author use maps to help you compare and contrast alligators and crocodiles?

• **Author's Purpose: Text Features** How does the author use the diagrams to help you compare and contrast alligators and crocodiles?

• **Author's Purpose: Text Features** How does the author organize the information to help you understand the animals' nests on page 536?

• **Author's Craft: Word Choice** How does the author's use of strong verbs help you visualize the way alligators and crocodiles catch other animals?

• **Author's Point of View** Which idea or statement from the text best shows the author's point of view about the value and protection of these reptiles?

Turn to a partner and use this sentence frame to guide your conversation.

> *The statement you chose...*

Use text evidence to support your opinion.

Write About the Text

Review the following writing prompt and sentence frames. Remind students to use their responses from the **Close Reading Companion** to support their answers. For a full lesson on writing a response using text evidence, see page T222.

Does Gail Gibbons do a good job organizing the information so that you understand how alligators and crocodiles are alike and different? Use these sentence frames to help organize text evidence.

> *Gail Gibbons uses text features to ...*
>
> *The illustrations and captions tell me...*
>
> *This helps me understand...*

<u>Answer</u>: In my opinion, the author does a good job of helping me understand how alligators and crocodiles are alike and different. The author of "Alligators and Crocodiles" uses text, illustrations, diagrams, and maps to compare and contrast these reptiles. <u>Evidence</u>: On page 528 and 529, a diagram and illustrations show how these animals are alike and different from tails to teeth. On page 532, I read how both reptiles swim and move in the same way.

Integrate *What does the text mean?*

Essential Question

Have students respond in writing to the Essential Question using evidence from the text.

> *How can learning about animals help you respect them?*

Students should use their notes and graphic organizers to cite evidence from the text to support their answer.

Model how to use notes to respond to the Essential Question:

Think Aloud I can reread through all the notes I took while I read to find text evidence that helps me to answer the question. My notes on page 541 say that alligators and crocodiles have been around for millions of years but now they are endangered. I can use this information as text evidence. Then I will look through the rest of my notes to find additional text evidence that I can use to support my answer.

Students can work with a partner and use their notes and graphic organizer to locate evidence that can be used to answer the question. Encourage students to discuss the strength of the evidence cited and give arguments about what may be strong or weak about a particular citation.

Classroom Library

  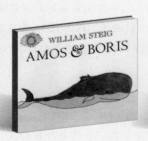 

Classroom Library lessons available online.

or Choose from your own Trade Books

The Hurricane Mystery
Genre Realistic Fiction

Lexile 580

Moonwalk: The First Trip to the Moon
Genre Informational Text

Lexile 550

Amos and Boris
Genre Fantasy

Lexile 810

Moonshot: The Flight of Apollo 13
Genre Informational Text

Lexile 990

- Use this model with a text of your choice. Go online for title-specific Classroom Library book lessons.
- Assign reading of the text. You may wish to do this by section or chapters.
- Chunk the text into shorter important passages for rereading.
- Present an Essential Question. You may want to use the Unit Big Idea.

 **sync** tv
Video Preview
studysync

Read · *What does the text say?*

Assign the Reading

Ask students to read the assigned sections of text independently. For more difficult sections, read the text aloud or ask partners to read. Model how to take notes. Encourage students to jot down difficult words and questions.

Ask Text-Dependent Questions

Ask students to reread a section of the text and focus on the following questions. Students should use text evidence in their answers:

Literature

- What are the plot and setting of the story?
- How would you describe the main character(s)?
- What is the theme or message of the story?

Informational Text

- What is the main idea? What are the supporting details?
- What kinds of text features does the author use?
- What is the author's point of view about the topic?

Have students write a brief summary of the section of text they read. When students finish writing, have partners compare ideas and make sure that they both have a clear understanding of the story events or the topic.

Help students access the complex features of the text. Scaffold instruction on the following features as necessary:

- Purpose
- Organization
- Prior Knowledge
- Genre

- Specific Vocabulary
- Sentence Structure
- Connection of Ideas

Reread *How does the author say it?*

Ask Text-Dependent Questions/Generate Questions

Have students reread the same section of text as above. Then focus on the following questions. Remind students to use text evidence in their answers:

Literature

- How does the main character change from the beginning of the story to the end of the story?
- What literary elements (figurative language, flashback, symbolism) did the author use, and how effective were they?
- What other story have you read with a similar theme? How are the two stories similar? Different?

Informational Text

- How does the author organize the information in this text?
- What was the author's purpose for writing this text?
- Was the author's use of visuals (photos, graphs, diagrams, maps) effective? Why or why not?

Integrate *What does the text mean?*

Essential Question

Have students respond in writing to the Essential Question, considering the complete text. Students can work with a partner and use their notes and graphic organizer to locate evidence that can be used to answer the question.

 SCOPE & SEQUENCE

	K	1	2	3	4	5	6
FOUNDATIONAL SKILLS							
Concepts About Print/Print Awareness							
Recognize own name							
Understand directionality (top to bottom; tracking print from left to right; return sweep, page by page)	✓						
Locate printed word on page	✓						
Develop print awareness (concept of letter, word, sentence)	✓						
Identify separate sounds in a spoken sentence	✓						
Understand that written words are represented in written language by a specific sequence of letters	✓						
Distinguish between letters, words, and sentences	✓						
Distinguish features of a sentence (first word, capitalization, ending punctuation)							
Identify and distinguish paragraphs							
Match print to speech (one-to-one correspondence)	✓						
Name uppercase and lowercase letters	✓						
Understand book handling (holding a book right-side-up, turning its pages)	✓						
Identify parts of a book (front cover, back cover, title page, table of contents); recognize that parts of a book contain information	✓						
Phonological Awareness							
Recognize and understand alliteration							
Segment sentences into correct number of words							
Identify, blend, segment syllables in words		✓					
Recognize and generate rhyming words	✓	✓					
Identify, blend, segment onset and rime	✓	✓					
Phonemic Awareness							
Count phonemes	✓	✓					
Isolate initial, medial, and final sounds	✓	✓					
Blend spoken phonemes to form words	✓	✓					
Segment spoken words into phonemes	✓	✓					
Distinguish between long- and short-vowel sounds	✓	✓					
Manipulate phonemes (addition, deletion, substitution)	✓	✓					
Phonics and Decoding/Word Recognition							
Understand the alphabetic principle	✓	✓					
Sound/letter correspondence	✓	✓	✓	✓			
Blend sounds into words, including VC, CVC, CVCe, CVVC words	✓	✓	✓	✓			
Blend common word families	✓	✓	✓	✓			

KEY	✓ = Assessed Skill
	Tinted panels show skills, strategies, and other teaching opportunities.

	K	1	2	3	4	5	6
Initial consonant blends		✓	✓	✓			
Final consonant blends		✓	✓	✓			
Initial and medial short vowels	✓	✓	✓	✓	✓	✓	✓
Decode one-syllable words in isolation and in context	✓	✓	✓	✓			
Decode multisyllabic words in isolation and in context using common syllabication patterns		✓	✓	✓	✓	✓	✓
Distinguish between similarly spelled words	✓	✓	✓	✓	✓	✓	✓
Monitor accuracy of decoding							
Identify and read common high-frequency words, irregularly spelled words	✓	✓	✓	✓			
Identify and read compound words, contractions		✓	✓	✓	✓	✓	✓
Use knowledge of spelling patterns to identify syllables		✓	✓	✓	✓	✓	✓
Regular and irregular plurals	✓	✓	✓	✓	✓	✓	✓
Distinguish long and short vowels		✓	✓				
Long vowels (silent *e*, vowel teams)	✓	✓	✓	✓	✓	✓	✓
Vowel digraphs (variant vowels)		✓	✓	✓	✓	✓	✓
r-Controlled vowels			✓	✓	✓	✓	✓
Hard/soft consonants		✓	✓	✓	✓	✓	✓
Initial consonant digraphs		✓	✓	✓	✓	✓	
Medial and final consonant digraphs		✓	✓	✓	✓	✓	
Vowel diphthongs		✓	✓	✓	✓	✓	✓
Identify and distinguish letter-sounds (initial, medial, final)	✓	✓	✓				
Silent letters		✓	✓	✓	✓	✓	✓
Schwa words				✓	✓	✓	✓
Inflectional endings		✓	✓	✓	✓	✓	✓
Triple-consonant clusters		✓	✓	✓	✓	✓	
Unfamiliar and complex word families				✓	✓	✓	✓
Structural Analysis/Word Analysis							
Common spelling patterns (word families)		✓	✓	✓	✓	✓	✓
Common syllable patterns		✓	✓	✓	✓	✓	✓
Inflectional endings		✓	✓	✓	✓	✓	✓
Contractions		✓	✓	✓	✓	✓	
Compound words		✓	✓	✓	✓	✓	✓
Prefixes and suffixes		✓	✓	✓	✓	✓	✓
Root or base words			✓	✓	✓	✓	✓
Comparatives and superlatives			✓	✓	✓	✓	✓
Greek and Latin roots			✓	✓	✓	✓	✓
Fluency							
Apply letter/sound knowledge to decode phonetically regular words accurately	✓	✓	✓	✓	✓	✓	✓
Recognize high-frequency and familiar words	✓	✓	✓	✓	✓	✓	✓
Read regularly on independent and instructional levels							
Read orally with fluency from familiar texts (choral, echo, partner, Reader's Theater)							
Use appropriate rate, expression, intonation, and phrasing		✓	✓	✓	✓	✓	✓
Read with automaticity (accurately and effortlessly)		✓	✓	✓	✓	✓	✓

	K	1	2	3	4	5	6
Use punctuation cues in reading		✓	✓	✓	✓	✓	✓
Adjust reading rate to purpose, text difficulty, form, and style							
Repeated readings							
Timed readings		✓	✓	✓	✓	✓	✓
Read with purpose and understanding		✓	✓	✓	✓	✓	✓
Read orally with accuracy		✓	✓	✓	✓	✓	✓
Use context to confirm or self-correct word recognition		✓	✓	✓	✓	✓	✓

READING LITERATURE

Comprehension Strategies and Skills

	K	1	2	3	4	5	6
Read literature from a broad range of genres, cultures, and periods		✓	✓	✓	✓	✓	✓
Access complex text		✓	✓	✓	✓	✓	✓
Build background/Activate prior knowledge							
Preview and predict							
Establish and adjust purpose for reading							
Evaluate citing evidence from the text							
Ask and answer questions	✓	✓	✓	✓	✓	✓	✓
Inferences and conclusions, citing evidence from the text	✓	✓	✓	✓	✓	✓	✓
Monitor/adjust comprehension including reread, reading rate, paraphrase							
Recount/Retell	✓	✓					
Summarize			✓	✓	✓	✓	✓
Story structure (beginning, middle, end)	✓	✓	✓	✓	✓	✓	✓
Visualize							
Make connections between and across texts		✓	✓	✓	✓	✓	✓
Point of view		✓	✓	✓	✓	✓	✓
Author's purpose							
Cause and effect	✓	✓	✓	✓	✓	✓	✓
Compare and contrast (including character, setting, plot, topics)	✓	✓	✓	✓	✓	✓	✓
Classify and categorize		✓	✓				
Literature vs informational text	✓	✓	✓				
Illustrations, using	✓	✓	✓	✓			
Theme, central message, moral, lesson		✓	✓	✓	✓	✓	✓
Predictions, making/confirming	✓	✓	✓				
Problem and solution (problem/resolution)		✓	✓	✓	✓	✓	✓
Sequence of events	✓	✓	✓	✓	✓	✓	✓

Literary Elements

	K	1	2	3	4	5	6
Character	✓	✓	✓	✓	✓	✓	✓
Plot development/Events	✓	✓	✓	✓	✓	✓	✓
Setting	✓	✓	✓	✓	✓	✓	✓
Stanza				✓	✓	✓	✓
Alliteration						✓	✓
Assonance						✓	✓
Dialogue							

KEY ✓ = Assessed Skill
Tinted panels show skills, strategies, and other teaching opportunities.

	K	1	2	3	4	5	6
Foreshadowing						✓	✓
Flashback						✓	✓
Descriptive and figurative language		✓	✓	✓	✓	✓	✓
Imagery					✓	✓	✓
Meter					✓	✓	✓
Onomatopoeia							
Repetition		✓	✓	✓	✓	✓	✓
Rhyme/rhyme schemes		✓	✓	✓	✓	✓	✓
Rhythm		✓	✓				
Sensory language							
Symbolism							
Write About Text/Literary Response Discussions							
Reflect and respond to text citing text evidence		✓	✓	✓	✓	✓	✓
Connect and compare text characters, events, ideas to self, to other texts, to world							
Connect literary texts to other curriculum areas							
Identify cultural and historical elements of text							
Evaluate author's techniques, craft							
Analytical writing							
Interpret text ideas through writing, discussion, media, research							
Book report or review							
Locate, use, explain information from text features		✓	✓	✓	✓	✓	✓
Organize information to show understanding of main idea through charts, mapping							
Cite text evidence	✓	✓	✓	✓	✓	✓	✓
Author's purpose/Illustrator's purpose							
READING INFORMATIONAL TEXT							
Comprehension Strategies and Skills							
Read informational text from a broad range of topics and cultures	✓	✓	✓	✓	✓	✓	✓
Access complex text		✓	✓	✓	✓	✓	✓
Build background/Activate prior knowledge							
Preview and predict	✓	✓	✓				
Establish and adjust purpose for reading							
Evaluate citing evidence from the text							
Ask and answer questions	✓	✓	✓	✓	✓	✓	✓
Inferences and conclusions, citing evidence from the text	✓	✓	✓	✓	✓	✓	✓
Monitor and adjust comprehension including reread, adjust reading rate, paraphrase							
Recount/Retell	✓	✓					
Summarize			✓	✓	✓	✓	✓
Text structure	✓	✓	✓	✓	✓	✓	✓
Identify text features		✓	✓	✓	✓	✓	✓
Make connections between and across texts	✓	✓	✓	✓	✓	✓	✓
Author's point of view					✓	✓	✓
Author's purpose		✓	✓				

	K	1	2	3	4	5	6
Cause and effect	✔	✔	✔	✔	✔	✔	✔
Compare and contrast	✔	✔	✔	✔	✔	✔	✔
Classify and categorize		✔	✔				
Illustrations and photographs, using	✔	✔	✔	✔			
Instructions/directions (written and oral)		✔	✔	✔	✔	✔	✔
Main idea and key details	✔	✔	✔	✔	✔	✔	✔
Persuasion, reasons and evidence to support points/persuasive techniques						✔	✔
Predictions, making/confirming	✔	✔					
Problem and solution		✔	✔	✔	✔	✔	✔
Sequence, chronological order of events, time order, steps in a process	✔	✔	✔	✔	✔	✔	✔

Write About Text/Write to Sources

	K	1	2	3	4	5	6
Reflect and respond to text citing text evidence		✔	✔	✔	✔	✔	✔
Connect and compare text characters, events, ideas to self, to other texts, to world							
Connect texts to other curriculum areas							
Identify cultural and historical elements of text							
Evaluate author's techniques, craft							
Analytical writing							
Read to understand and perform tasks and activities							
Interpret text ideas through writing, discussion, media, research							
Locate, use, explain information from text features		✔	✔	✔	✔	✔	✔
Organize information to show understanding of main idea through charts, mapping							
Cite text evidence		✔	✔	✔	✔	✔	✔
Author's purpose/Illustrator's purpose							

Text Features

	K	1	2	3	4	5	6
Recognize and identify text and organizational features of nonfiction texts		✔	✔	✔	✔	✔	✔
Captions and labels, headings, subheadings, endnotes, key words, bold print	✔	✔	✔	✔	✔	✔	✔
Graphics, including photographs, illustrations, maps, charts, diagrams, graphs, time lines	✔	✔	✔	✔	✔	✔	✔

Self-Selected Reading/Independent Reading

	K	1	2	3	4	5	6
Use personal criteria to choose own reading including favorite authors, genres, recommendations from others; set up a reading log							
Read a range of literature and informational text for tasks as well as for enjoyment; participate in literature circles							
Produce evidence of reading by retelling, summarizing, or paraphrasing							

Media Literacy

	K	1	2	3	4	5	6
Summarize the message or content from media message, citing text evidence							
Use graphics, illustrations to analyze and interpret information	✔	✔	✔	✔	✔	✔	✔
Identify structural features of popular media and use the features to obtain information, including digital sources				✔	✔	✔	✔
Identify reasons and evidence in visuals and media message							
Analyze media source: recognize effects of media in one's mood and emotion							
Make informed judgments about print and digital media							
Critique persuasive techniques							

KEY — ✔ = Assessed Skill
Tinted panels show skills, strategies, and other teaching opportunities.

WRITING	K	1	2	3	4	5	6
Writing Process							
Plan/prewrite/identify purpose and audience							
Draft							
Revise							
Edit/proofread							
Publish and present including using technology							
Teacher and peer feedback							
Writing Traits							
Conventions		✓	✓	✓	✓	✓	✓
Ideas		✓	✓	✓	✓	✓	✓
Organization		✓	✓	✓	✓	✓	✓
Sentence fluency		✓	✓	✓	✓	✓	✓
Voice		✓	✓	✓	✓	✓	✓
Word choice		✓	✓	✓	✓	✓	✓
Writer's Craft							
Good topic, focus on and develop topic, topic sentence			✓	✓	✓	✓	✓
Paragraph(s); sentence structure			✓	✓	✓	✓	✓
Main idea and supporting key details			✓	✓	✓	✓	✓
Unimportant details							
Relevant supporting evidence			✓	✓	✓	✓	✓
Strong opening, strong conclusion			✓	✓	✓	✓	✓
Beginning, middle, end; sequence		✓	✓	✓	✓	✓	✓
Precise words, strong words, vary words			✓	✓	✓	✓	✓
Figurative and sensory language, descriptive details							
Informal/formal language							
Mood/style/tone							
Dialogue				✓	✓	✓	✓
Transition words, transitions to multiple paragraphs				✓	✓	✓	✓
Select focus and organization			✓	✓	✓	✓	✓
Points and counterpoints/Opposing claims and counterarguments							
Use reference materials (online and print dictionary, thesaurus, encyclopedia)							
Writing Applications							
Write to sources	✓	✓	✓	✓	✓	✓	✓
Personal and fictional narrative (also biographical and autobiographical)	✓	✓	✓	✓	✓	✓	✓
Variety of expressive forms including poetry	✓	✓	✓	✓	✓	✓	✓
Informative/explanatory texts	✓	✓	✓	✓	✓	✓	✓
Description	✓	✓	✓	✓			
Procedural texts		✓	✓	✓	✓	✓	✓
Opinion pieces or arguments	✓	✓	✓	✓	✓	✓	✓
Communications including technical documents		✓	✓	✓	✓	✓	✓
Research report	✓	✓	✓	✓	✓	✓	✓

	K	1	2	3	4	5	6
Responses to literature/reflection				✓	✓	✓	✓
Analytical writing							
Letters		✓	✓	✓	✓	✓	✓
Write daily and over short and extended time frames; set up writer's notebooks							
Penmanship/Handwriting							
Write legibly in manuscript using correct formation, directionality, and spacing							
Write legibly in cursive using correct formation, directionality, and spacing							
SPEAKING AND LISTENING							
Speaking							
Use repetition, rhyme, and rhythm in oral texts							
Participate in classroom activities and discussions							
Collaborative conversation with peers and adults in small and large groups using formal English when appropriate							
Differentiate between formal and informal English							
Follow agreed upon rules for discussion							
Build on others' talk in conversation, adding new ideas							
Come to discussions prepared							
Describe familiar people, places, and things and add drawings as desired							
Paraphrase portions of text read alone or information presented							
Apply comprehension strategies and skills in speaking activities							
Use literal and nonliteral meanings							
Ask and answer questions about text read aloud and about media							
Stay on topic when speaking							
Use language appropriate to situation, purpose, and audience							
Use nonverbal communications such as eye contact, gestures, and props							
Use verbal communication in effective ways and improve expression in conventional language							
Retell a story, presentation, or spoken message by summarizing							
Oral presentations: focus, organizational structure, audience, purpose							
Give and follow oral directions							
Consider audience when speaking or preparing a presentation							
Recite poems, rhymes, songs							
Use complete, coherent sentences							
Organize presentations							
Deliver presentations (narrative, summaries, informative, research, opinion); add visuals							
Speak audibly (accuracy, expression, volume, pitch, rate, phrasing, modulation, enunciation)							
Create audio recordings of poems, stories, presentations							
Listening							
Identify musical elements in language							
Determine the purpose for listening							
Understand, follow, restate, and give oral directions							
Develop oral language and concepts							

KEY ✓ = Assessed Skill
Tinted panels show skills, strategies, and other teaching opportunities.

	K	1	2	3	4	5	6
Listen openly, responsively, attentively, and critically							
Listen to identify the points a speaker or media source makes							
Listen responsively to oral presentations (determine main idea and key details)							
Ask and answer relevant questions (for clarification to follow-up on ideas)							
Identify reasons and evidence presented by speaker							
Recall and interpret speakers' verbal/nonverbal messages, purposes, perspectives							

LANGUAGE

Vocabulary Acquisition and Use

	K	1	2	3	4	5	6
Develop oral vocabulary and choose words for effect							
Use academic language		✓	✓	✓	✓	✓	✓
Identify persons, places, things, actions		✓	✓	✓			
Classify, sort, and categorize words	✓	✓	✓	✓	✓	✓	✓
Determine or clarify the meaning of unknown words; use word walls		✓	✓	✓	✓	✓	✓
Synonyms, antonyms, and opposites		✓	✓	✓	✓	✓	✓
Use context clues such as word, sentence, paragraph, definition, example, restatement, description, comparison, cause and effect		✓	✓	✓	✓	✓	✓
Use word identification strategies		✓	✓	✓	✓	✓	✓
Unfamiliar words		✓	✓	✓	✓	✓	✓
Multiple-meaning words		✓	✓	✓	✓	✓	✓
Use print and online dictionary to locate meanings, pronunciation, derivatives, parts of speech		✓	✓	✓	✓	✓	✓
Compound words		✓	✓	✓	✓	✓	
Words ending in -er and -est		✓	✓	✓	✓	✓	
Root words (base words)		✓	✓	✓	✓	✓	✓
Prefixes and suffixes		✓	✓	✓	✓	✓	✓
Greek and Latin affixes and roots			✓	✓	✓	✓	✓
Denotation and connotation					✓	✓	✓
Word families		✓	✓	✓	✓	✓	✓
Inflectional endings		✓	✓	✓	✓	✓	✓
Use a print and online thesaurus			✓	✓	✓	✓	✓
Use print and online reference sources for word meaning (dictionary, glossaries)		✓	✓	✓	✓	✓	✓
Homographs				✓	✓	✓	✓
Homophones			✓	✓	✓	✓	✓
Contractions		✓	✓	✓			
Figurative language such as metaphors, similes, personification			✓	✓	✓	✓	✓
Idioms, adages, proverbs, literal and nonliteral language			✓	✓	✓	✓	✓
Analogies							
Listen to, read, discuss familiar and unfamiliar challenging text							
Identify real-life connections between words and their use							
Use acquired words and phrases to convey precise ideas							
Use vocabulary to express spatial and temporal relationships							
Identify shades of meaning in related words	✓	✓	✓	✓	✓	✓	✓
Word origins				✓	✓	✓	✓
Morphology				✓	✓	✓	✓

	K	1	2	3	4	5	6
Knowledge of Language							
Choose words, phrases, and sentences for effect							
Choose punctuation effectively							
Formal and informal language for style and tone including dialects							
Conventions of Standard English/Grammar, Mechanics, and Usage							
Sentence concepts: statements, questions, exclamations, commands		✓	✓	✓	✓	✓	✓
Complete and incomplete sentences; sentence fragments; word order		✓	✓	✓	✓	✓	✓
Compound sentences, complex sentences				✓	✓	✓	✓
Combining sentences		✓	✓	✓	✓	✓	✓
Nouns including common, proper, singular, plural, irregular plurals, possessives, abstract, concrete, collective		✓	✓	✓	✓	✓	✓
Verbs including action, helping, linking, irregular		✓	✓	✓	✓	✓	✓
Verb tenses including past, present, future, perfect, and progressive		✓	✓	✓	✓	✓	✓
Pronouns including possessive, subject and object, pronoun-verb agreement, indefinite, intensive, reciprocal, interrogative, relative; correct unclear pronouns		✓	✓	✓	✓	✓	✓
Adjectives including articles, demonstrative, proper, adjectives that compare		✓	✓	✓	✓	✓	✓
Adverbs including telling how, when, where, comparative, superlative, irregular		✓	✓	✓	✓	✓	✓
Subject, predicate; subject-verb agreement		✓	✓	✓	✓	✓	✓
Contractions		✓	✓	✓	✓	✓	✓
Conjunctions				✓	✓	✓	✓
Commas			✓	✓	✓	✓	✓
Colons, semicolons, dashes, hyphens						✓	✓
Question words							
Quotation marks			✓	✓	✓	✓	✓
Prepositions and prepositional phrases, appositives		✓	✓	✓	✓	✓	✓
Independent and dependent clauses						✓	✓
Italics/underlining for emphasis and titles							
Negatives, correcting double negatives					✓	✓	✓
Abbreviations			✓	✓	✓	✓	✓
Use correct capitalization in sentences, proper nouns, titles, abbreviations		✓	✓	✓	✓	✓	✓
Use correct punctuation		✓	✓	✓	✓	✓	✓
Antecedents				✓	✓	✓	✓
Homophones and words often confused			✓	✓	✓	✓	✓
Apostrophes				✓	✓	✓	✓
Spelling							
Write irregular, high-frequency words	✓	✓	✓				
ABC order	✓	✓					
Write letters	✓	✓					
Words with short vowels	✓	✓	✓	✓	✓	✓	✓
Words with long vowels	✓	✓	✓	✓	✓	✓	✓
Words with digraphs, blends, consonant clusters, double consonants		✓	✓	✓	✓	✓	✓
Words with vowel digraphs and ambiguous vowels		✓	✓	✓	✓	✓	✓
Words with diphthongs		✓	✓	✓	✓	✓	✓

KEY
✓ = Assessed Skill
Tinted panels show skills, strategies, and other teaching opportunities.

	K	1	2	3	4	5	6
Words with *r*-controlled vowels		✓	✓	✓	✓	✓	✓
Use conventional spelling		✓	✓	✓	✓	✓	✓
Schwa words				✓	✓	✓	✓
Words with silent letters			✓	✓	✓	✓	✓
Words with hard and soft letters			✓	✓	✓	✓	✓
Inflectional endings including plural, past tense, drop final *e* and double consonant when adding -*ed* and -*ing*, changing *y* to *i*		✓	✓	✓	✓	✓	✓
Compound words		✓	✓	✓	✓	✓	✓
Homonyms/homophones			✓	✓	✓	✓	✓
Prefixes and suffixes		✓	✓	✓	✓	✓	✓
Root and base words (also spell derivatives)				✓	✓	✓	✓
Syllables: patterns, rules, accented, stressed, closed, open				✓	✓	✓	✓
Words with Greek and Latin roots						✓	✓
Words from mythology						✓	✓
Words with spelling patterns, word families		✓	✓	✓	✓	✓	✓

RESEARCH AND INQUIRY

Study Skills

	K	1	2	3	4	5	6
Directions: read, write, give, follow (includes technical directions)			✓	✓	✓	✓	✓
Evaluate directions for sequence and completeness				✓	✓	✓	✓
Use library/media center							
Use parts of a book to locate information							
Interpret information from graphic aids		✓	✓	✓	✓	✓	✓
Use graphic organizers to organize information and comprehend text		✓	✓	✓	✓	✓	✓
Use functional, everyday documents				✓	✓	✓	✓
Apply study strategies: skimming and scanning, note-taking, outlining							

Research Process

	K	1	2	3	4	5	6
Generate and revise topics and questions for research				✓	✓	✓	✓
Narrow focus of research, set research goals				✓	✓	✓	✓
Find and locate information using print and digital resources		✓	✓	✓	✓	✓	✓
Record information systematically (note-taking, outlining, using technology)				✓	✓	✓	✓
Develop a systematic research plan				✓	✓	✓	✓
Evaluate reliability, credibility, usefulness of sources and information						✓	✓
Use primary sources to obtain information					✓	✓	✓
Organize, synthesize, evaluate, and draw conclusions from information							
Cite and list sources of information (record basic bibliographic data)					✓	✓	✓
Demonstrate basic keyboarding skills							
Participate in and present shared research							

Technology

	K	1	2	3	4	5	6
Use computer, Internet, and other technology resources to access information							
Use text and organizational features of electronic resources such as search engines, keywords, e-mail, hyperlinks, URLs, Web pages, databases, graphics							
Use digital tools to present and publish in a variety of media formats							

INDEX

A

B

C

F

H

I

M

N

O

S

T

W

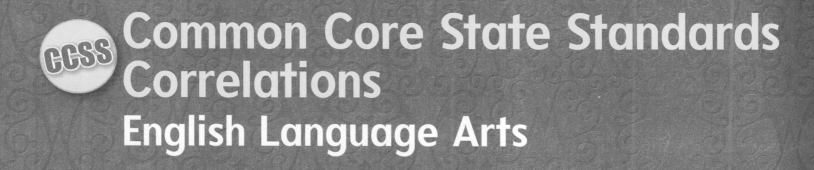

Common Core State Standards Correlations

English Language Arts

College and Career Readiness Anchor Standards for READING

The K-5 standards on the following pages define what students should understand and be able to do by the end of each grade. They correspond to the College and Career Readiness (CCR) anchor standards below by number. The CCR and grade-specific standards are necessary complements—the former providing broad standards, the latter providing additional specificity—that together define the skills and understandings that all students must demonstrate.

Key Ideas and Details

1. Read closely to determine what the text says explicitly and to make logical inferences from it; cite specific textual evidence when writing or speaking to support conclusions drawn from the text.

2. Determine central ideas or themes of a text and analyze their development; summarize the key supporting details and ideas.

3. Analyze how and why individuals, events, and ideas develop and interact over the course of a text.

Craft and Structure

4. Interpret words and phrases as they are used in a text, including determining technical, connotative, and figurative meanings, and analyze how specific word choices shape meaning or tone.

5. Analyze the structure of texts, including how specific sentences, paragraphs, and larger portions of the text (e.g., a section, chapter, scene, or stanza) relate to each other and the whole.

6. Assess how point of view or purpose shapes the content and style of a text.

Integration of Knowledge and Ideas

7. Integrate and evaluate content presented in diverse media and formats, including visually and quantitatively, as well as in words.

8. Delineate and evaluate the argument and specific claims in a text, including the validity of the reasoning as well as the relevance and sufficiency of the evidence.

9. Analyze how two or more texts address similar themes or topics in order to build knowledge or to compare the approaches the authors take.

Range of Reading and Level of Text Complexity

10. Read and comprehend complex literary and informational texts independently and proficiently.

CCSS Common Core State Standards
English Language Arts
Grade 3

Each standard is coded in the following manner:

Strand	Grade Level	Standard
RL	3	1

Reading Standards for Literature

Key Ideas and Details	*McGraw-Hill Wonders*
RL.3.1 Ask and answer questions to demonstrate understanding of a text, referring explicitly to the text as the basis for the answers.	**READING/WRITING WORKSHOP: Unit I:** 28, 29, 44, 45 **Unit 2:** 108, 109, 124 **Unit 3:** 188, 204, 205 **Unit 4:** 266, 267, 280, 281 **Unit 5:** 338, 339, 352, 353 **Unit 6:** 410, 411, 424 **LITERATURE ANTHOLOGY: Unit I:** 29, 31, 44 **Unit 2:** 119, 141, 191 **Unit 3:** 215, 237 **Unit 4:** 297, 302, 311, 319, 363 **Unit 5:** 385, 409, 411 **Unit 6:** 477, 503 **LEVELED READERS: Unit 4, Week I:** *The Weaver of Rugs: A Navajo Folktale* (A), *Why the Sea is Salty: A Scandinavian Folktale* (O, EL), *Finn MacCool and the Salmon of Knowledge: An Irish Folktale* (B) **Unit 4, Week 2:** *Every Picture Tells a Story* (A), *A Chef in the Family* (O, EL), *Stepping Forward* (B) **CLOSE READING COMPANION:** 1-6, 128-131, 194-197 **YOUR TURN PRACTICE BOOK:** 23-25, 163-165 **READING WORKSTATION ACTIVITY CARDS:** 19 **TEACHER'S EDITION: Unit I:** T27H, T27X, T93F, T159G, T159I **Unit 2:** T27Q, T93I, **Unit 3:** T27V, T93J, T93R **Unit 4:** T12, T16-T19, T25D, T25F, T25H, T25N, T25T, T76, T82-T83, T89D, T89G, T89J, T89K, T89O, T89T, T89X, T89Y, T89Z, T217R, T217R **Unit 5:** T12, T16-T17, T25K, T25T, T89K, T89V **Unit 6:** T25G, T25P, T25R, T25S, T89G, T89O www.connected.mcgraw-hill.com: RESOURCES **Student Resources:** Comprehension Interactive Games and Activities
RL.3.2 Recount stories, including fables, folktales, and myths from diverse cultures; determine the central message, lesson, or moral and explain how it is conveyed through key details in the text.	**READING/WRITING WORKSHOP: Unit I:** 22-27 **Unit 2:** 102-107, 118-123, 125 **Unit 4:** 318-321, 323 **Unit 5:** 338, 352 **Unit 6:** 406-409, 411, 420-423, 425 **LITERATURE ANTHOLOGY: Unit I:** 31, 33 **Unit 2:** 119, 141, 191 **Unit 3:** 215, 237 **Unit 4:** 319, 363 **Unit 5:** 385, 411 **Unit 6:** 475, 476, 477, 481, 502, 503 **LEVELED READERS: Unit 2, Week I:** *The Quarreling Quails* (A), *Jungle Treasures* (O, EL), *The Bear Who Stole the Chinook* (B) **Unit 2, Week 2:** *The Promise of Gold Mountain* (A), *Moving from Mexico* (O, EL), *Gustaf Goes to America* (B) **Unit 4, Week 5:** *In the Running* (A), *Melanie's Mission* (O, EL), *A Speech to Remember* (B) **Unit 6, Week I:** *Midas and the Donkey Ears* (A), *The Naming of Athens* (O, EL), *Odysseus and King Aeolus* (B) **Unit 6, Week 2:** *The Big Storm* (A), *The Schoolhouse Blizzard* (O, EL), *The Hottest Summer* (B) **YOUR TURN PRACTICE BOOK:** 53-55, 63-65, 193-194, 253-255 **READING WORKSTATION ACTIVITY CARDS:** 6 **TEACHER'S EDITION: Unit I:** T16-19, T24-T25, T27V-T27X, T40-T41, **Unit 2:** T12, T16-T19, T22, T24, T27C-T27E, T27K, T27L, T27M, T27Q, T27T, T78, T88, T90, T93O **Unit 3:** T12-T13, T16-T19, T24-T25, T27V, T225M-T225N **Unit 4:** T22-T23, T25R, T25T, T89T, T89Y, T217Q, T217R **Unit 5:** T22-T23, T25Q, **Unit 6:** T22-T23, T25B, T25H, T25M, T25P, T25T, T46-T47, T51, T55, T89W-T89X, T217Y-T217Z www.connected.mcgraw-hill.com: RESOURCES **Student Resources:** Comprehension Interactive Games and Activities **Teacher Resources:** Graphic Organizers, Interactive Read Aloud Images, Skills Review

Reading Standards for Literature

Key Ideas and Details		McGraw-Hill Wonders
RL.3.3	Describe characters in a story (e.g., their traits, motivations, or feelings) and explain how their actions contribute to the sequence of events.	**READING/WRITING WORKSHOP:** Unit I: 27, 29, 43, 45 Unit 3: 187, 189, 203, 205 **LITERATURE ANTHOLOGY:** Unit I: 31, 53 Unit 2: 119, 141 Unit 3: 215, 237 Unit 4: 297 Unit 5: 411 Unit 6: 477, 503, 549 **LEVELED READERS:** Unit I, Week I: *Berries, Berries, Berries* (A), *Duck's Discovery* (O, EL), *Robot Race* (B) **Unit I, Week 2:** *The Special Meal* (A), *A Row of Lamps* (O, EL), *Dragons on the Water* (B) **Unit 3, Week I:** *The Ballgame Between the Birds and the Animals: A Cherokee Folktale* (A), *King of the Birds* (O, EL), *Sheep and Pig Set Up Housekeeping* (B) **Unit 3, Week 2:** *On the Ball* (A), *Harry's Great Idea* (O, EL), *Best Friends in Business* (B) **CLOSE READING COMPANION:** 1-7, 8, 10, 74-76,91, 92, 100-103, 107-112, 117-119, 130-131, 133-135,140-142,166-171, 173-178 **YOUR TURN PRACTICE BOOK:** 13-15, 103-105, 113-115 **READING WORKSTATION ACTIVITY CARDS:** I, 2, 3, 4 **TEACHER'S EDITION: Unit I:** T22, T27C, T27E-T27G, T27I, T27K, T27M, T27O, T27Q, T27S, T27V, T27X, T41, T82, T86, T93C, T93E, T93G, T93J-T93L, T93N, T93P, T93R, T93T, T107 **Unit 2:** T93C, T93K, T93M **Unit 3:** T12, T16-T18, T22, T27E-T27I, T27K-T27S, T27V, T41, T82-T89, T93C-T93P, T93R, T159Q, T159R, T225N **Unit 4:** T16-T17, T20-T21, T25C, T25G, T25K, T25T, T89E, T89T, T89X **Unit 5:** T25C, T25E, T25M, T89D, T89J **Unit 6:** T25C, T25D, T25F, T25T **www.connected.mcgraw-hill.com: RESOURCES** **Student Resources:** Comprehension Interactive Games and Activities **Teacher Resources:** Graphic Organizers, Skills Review

Craft and Structure		McGraw-Hill Wonders
RL.3.4	Determine the meaning of words and phrases as they are used in a text, distinguishing literal from nonliteral language.	**READING/WRITING WORKSHOP: Unit I:** 79 **Unit 2:** 127, 173 **Unit 3:** 207 **Unit 4:** 325 **Unit 6:** 427, 469 **YOUR TURN PRACTICE BOOK:** 37, 67, 97, 117, 197, 267, 297 **PHONICS/WORD STUDY ACTIVITY CARDS:** 4, 6, 8 **CLOSE READING COMPANION:** 151, 177, 195 **TEACHER'S EDITION: Unit I:** T16, T27N, T80, T93D, T93K, T93M, T93O, T224-T225, T237, T240, T245, T248 **Unit 2:** T14, T27O, T92, T93, T93C, T93E-T93F, T93K, T93L, T113, T118, T122, T125, T129, T289C, T301 **Unit 3:** T14-T16, T27Q, T80-T82, T92-T93, T93E, T93G, T104-T105 **Unit 4:** T14-T15, T25L, T36-T37, T100-T101 **Unit 5:** T14, T24-T25, T25S, T78-T79 **Unit 6:** T78, T101, T109, T114, T118, T125, T166, T281C **www.connected.mcgraw-hill.com: RESOURCES** **Student Resources:** Vocabulary Interactive Games and Activities **Teacher Resources:** Graphic Organizers
RL.3.5	Refer to parts of stories, dramas, and poems when writing or speaking about a text, using terms such as chapter, scene, and stanza; describe how each successive part builds on earlier sections.	**READING/WRITING WORKSHOP: Unit 2:** 170 **Unit 4:** 322 **Unit 6:** 412, 466 **READING WORKSTATION ACTIVITY CARDS:** 23, 24 **CLOSE READING COMPANION:** 7, I, 130, 131, 139, 198 **TEACHER'S EDITION: Unit I:** T27Q, T27S, T93R, T93T **Unit 2:** T27M, T27O, T27T, T93R, T289C, T289F **Unit 3:** T93E, T93R **Unit 4:** T89Q, T89T, T281D, T289F **Unit 6:** T25E, T25G, T25P, T29, T46, T270, T274, T278, T281D, T281F **www.connected.mcgraw-hill.com: Resources** **Student Resources:** Comprehension Interactive Games and Activities

Reading Standards for Literature

Craft and Structure	McGraw-Hill Wonders
RL.3.6 Distinguish their own point of view from that of the narrator or those of the characters.	**READING/WRITING WORKSHOP:** Unit 2: 171 Unit 4: 267, 281 Unit 5: 339, 353 Unit 6: 467 **LITERATURE ANTHOLOGY:** Unit 1: 188–191 Unit 4: 278–297, 300–319, 360–363 Unit 5: 366–385, 390–411 Unit 6: 546–549 **LEVELED READERS:** Unit 2, Week 5: *Problem Solved* (A), *The Long Walk* (O, EL), *Two Up, One Down* (B) Unit 4, Week 1: *The Weaver of Rugs: A Navajo Folktale* (A), *Why the Sea is Salty: A Scandinavian Folktale* (O, EL), *Finn MacCool and the Salmon of Knowledge: An Irish Folktale* (B) **YOUR TURN PRACTICE BOOK:** 93–94, 153–155, 163–165, 203–205, 213–215, 293–294 **READING WORKSTATION ACTIVITY CARDS:** 5 **CLOSE READING COMPANION:** 101, 128, 198 **TEACHER'S EDITION:** Unit 4: T20–T21, T25D, T25E,T25G, T25J, T25K, T25Q, T25T, T29, T46, T47, T51, T55, T84, T89I, T89Q, T89T, T109–T111, T115, T117, T119 Unit 5: T20, T25T, T39, T46–T47, T51, T55, T84, T85, T89C, T89F, T89I, T89N, T89Q, T89V, T103, T111, T115, T119 www.connected.mcgraw-hill.com: **RESOURCES** **Student Resources:** Comprehension Interactive Games and Activities

Integration of Knowledge and Ideas	McGraw-Hill Wonders
RL.3.7 Explain how specific aspects of a text's illustrations contribute to what is conveyed by the words in a story (e.g., create mood, emphasize aspects of a character or setting).	**READING/WRITING WORKSHOP:** Unit 1: 30, 46 Unit 3: 206 Unit 4: 282 Unit 5: 354 Unit 6: 426 **LITERATURE ANTHOLOGY:** Unit 4: 281, 287, 296 **READING WORKSTATION ACTIVITY CARDS:** 7 **CLOSE READING COMPANION:** 5, 43,64, 135, 174, 179 **TEACHER'S EDITION:** Unit 1: T16, T27B, T27D, T27L, T27S, T93H Unit 2: T27B, T27F, T27J, T93G Unit 3: T28B, T27G, T27O, T93H, T108, T116 Unit 4: T25C, T25I, T25S, T86, T89B, T89E, T94 Unit 5: T25J, T25P, T86, T89L Unit 6: T86 www.connected.mcgraw-hill.com: **RESOURCES** **Student Resources:** Comprehension Interactive Games and Activities **Teacher Resources:** Interactive Read Aloud Images
RL.3.8 (Not applicable to literature)	(Not applicable to literature)
RL.3.9 Compare and contrast the themes, settings, and plots of stories written by the same author about the same or similar characters (e.g., in books from a series).	**LITERATURE ANTHOLOGY:** Unit 4: 300–325 **LEVELED READERS:** Unit 1, Week 2: *The Special Meal* (A), *A Row of Lamps* (O, EL), *Dragons on the Water* (B) Unit 4, Week 2: *Every Picture Tells a Story* (A), *A Chef in the Family* (O, EL), *Stepping Forward* (B) **READING WORKSTATION ACTIVITY CARDS:** 8 **TEACHER'S EDITION:** Unit 1: S14 Unit 4: T86, T89U, T89X, T89Y, T89Z, T102–T103, T105, T113, T117, T123 www.connected.mcgraw-hill.com: **RESOURCES** **Student Resources:** Comprehension Interactive Games and Activities

Range of Reading and Level of Text Complexity	McGraw-Hill Wonders
RL.3.10 By the end of the year, read and comprehend literature, including stories, dramas, and poetry, at the high end of the grades 2–3 text complexity band independently and proficiently.	**READING/WRITING WORKSHOP:** These units reflect the range of text complexity found throughout the book. Unit 2: 166–169 Unit 4: 318–321 Unit 6: 406–409 **LITERATURE ANTHOLOGY:** These units reflect the range of text complexity found throughout the book. Unit 2: 188–191 Unit 3: 194–215 Unit 4: 300–319 Unit 5: 366–385 Unit 6: 462–477, 546–549 **LEVELED READERS:** Unit 1, Week 2: *The Special Meal* (A), *A Row of Lamps* (O, EL), *Dragons on the Water* (B) Unit 6, Week 5: *Funny Faces* (A), *Too Many Frogs* (O, EL), *The Joke's on You* (B) **READING WORKSTATION ACTIVITY CARDS:** 27 **TEACHER'S EDITION:** Unit 1: T24, T27A, T90, T93A Unit 3: T24, T27A, T90, T93A, T159Q Unit 6: T22, T25A, T25Q, T86, T89A, T274, T281A

Reading Standards for Informational Text

Key Ideas and Details		*McGraw-Hill Wonders*
RI.3.1	Ask and answer questions to demonstrate understanding of a text, referring explicitly to the text as the basis for the answers.	**READING/WRITING WORKSHOP:** Unit 1: 60, 61, 76, 77, 90, 91 **Unit 2:** 140, 141, 156, 157 **Unit 3:** 220, 221, 236, 237, 250, 251 **Unit 4:** 294, 295, 308, 309 **Unit 5:** 366, 367, 380, 381, 394, 395 **Unit 6:** 438, 439, 452, 453 **LITERATURE ANTHOLOGY:** Unit 1: 58–71 **Unit 2:** 146–167, 172–185 **Unit 3:** 240–255, 258–269 **Unit 4:** 326–339 **Unit 5:** 416–429, 432–451, 456–459 **LEVELED READERS: Unit 1, Week 3:** *Judy Baca* (A, O, EL, B) **Unit 1, Week 4:** *The Amazing Benjamin Franklin* (A, O, EL, B) **Unit 1, Week 5:** *The National Mall* (A, O, EL, B) **Unit 5, Week 3:** *Firefighting Heroes* (A, O, EL, B) **Unit 5, Week 4:** *Eunice Kennedy Shriver* (A, O, EL, B) **Unit 5, Week 5:** *The Fuel of the Future* (A, O, EL, B) **CLOSE READING COMPANION:** 15–20, 48–53, 154–159 **YOUR TURN PRACTICE BOOK:** 23–25, 33–35, 43–45, 223–225, 233–235, 243–245 **READING WORKSTATION ACTIVITY CARDS:** 19 **TEACHER'S EDITION: Unit 1:** T93V, T93W, T159D, T159I, T159P, T218, T225B, T225D–T225G, T225I–T225Q, T225T, T336 **Unit 2:** T159J, T159N, T159X, T159Y, T214, T225F **Unit 3:** T27X–T27Y, T93T, T159G, T159P, T214–T217, T225E **Unit 4:** T153F, T153K, T153N, T217M, T217P **Unit 5:** T89X–T89Y, T140–T141, T146–T147, T153D, T210–T211, T217A, T217B, T217E, T217G, T217K, T217N, T217P, T217R, T274, T328 **Unit 6:** T153I, T153L, T217J **www.connected.mcgraw-hill.com: RESOURCES** **Student Resources:** Comprehension Interactive Games and Activities **Teacher Resources:** Interactive Read Aloud Images
RI.3.2	Determine the main idea of a text; recount the key details and explain how they support the main idea.	**READING/WRITING WORKSHOP:** Unit 1: 89, 91 **Unit 3:** 219, 221, 235, 237 **LITERATURE ANTHOLOGY:** Unit 1: 91, 93, 97 **Unit 2:** 167, 185 **Unit 3:** 243, 247, 262, 265, 273 **Unit 4:** 339, 355, 357 **Unit 5:** 427,429, 451 **Unit 6:** 517, 543 **LEVELED READERS: Unit 1, Week 5:** *The National Mall* (A, O, EL, B) **Unit 3, Week 3:** *Destination Saturn* (A, O, EL, B) **Unit 3, Week 4:** *Inspired by Nature* (A, O, EL, B) **CLOSE READING COMPANION:** 53, 56, 57, 82, 83, 103, 115, 116 **YOUR TURN PRACTICE BOOK:** 43–45, 123–125, 133–135 **READING WORKSTATION ACTIVITY CARDS:** 9 **TEACHER'S EDITION: Unit 1:** T289C, T289D, T336 **Unit 3:** T154–T155, T159C, T159E, T159G, T159I, T159K, T159M, T159P, T173, T220–T221, T225C, T225G, T225J, T225L, T239, T336 **Unit 4:** T217C, T217J, T217N **Unit 5:** T153E, T208, T328–T329 **www.connected.mcgraw-hill.com: RESOURCES** **Student Resources:** Comprehension Interactive Games and Activities **Teacher Resources:** Graphic Organizers, Interactive Read Aloud Images, Skills Review
RI.3.3	Describe the relationship between a series of historical events, scientific ideas or concepts, or steps in technical procedures in a text, using language that pertains to time, sequence, and cause/effect.	**READING/WRITING WORKSHOP:** Unit 1: 70–75, 77 **Unit 4:** 304–307, 309 **Unit 5:** 390–393, 395 **LITERATURE ANTHOLOGY:** Unit 1: 74–91, 94–97 **Unit 2:** 172–185 **Unit 4:** 342–357 **Unit 5:** 432–451, 456–459 **Unit 6:** 540, 543 **LEVELED READERS: Unit 3, Week 4:** *Inspired by Nature* (A, O, EL, B) **Unit 4, Week 4:** *Future of Flight* (A, O, EL, B) **Unit 5, Week 5:** *The Fuel of the Future* (A, O, EL, B) **YOUR TURN PRACTICE BOOK:** 33–35, 183–185, 243–244 **READING WORKSTATION ACTIVITY CARDS:** 13 **TEACHER'S EDITION: Unit 1:** T220–T221, T225C, T225G, T225L, T225P, T251, T255 **Unit 3:** T159C–T159F, T159H–T159M, T216, T225C **Unit 4:** T212–T213, T217C, T217E, T217G, T217J, T217K, T217M, T217P, T231 **Unit 5:** T153C, T153I, T217M, T217Q, T276–T277 **Unit 6:** T217K, T217M, T217P, T217Q, T217S **www.connected.mcgraw-hill.com: RESOURCES** **Student Resources:** Comprehension Interactive Games and Activities **Teacher Resources:** Graphic Organizers, Skills Review

Reading Standards for Informational Text

Craft and Structure		McGraw-Hill Wonders
RI.3.4	Determine the meaning of general academic and domain-specific words and phrases in a text relevant to a *grade 3 topic or subject area.*	**READING/WRITING WORKSHOP: Unit 1:** 50–53, 66–69, 82–85 **Unit 2:** 130–133, 146–149 **Unit 3:** 200–213, 226–229, 242–245 **Unit 4:** 286–289, 300–303 **Unit 5:** 358–361, 372–375, 386–389 **Unit 6:** 430–433, 444–447 **TEACHER'S EDITION: Unit 1:** T146, T158, T174, T212, T214, T278 **Unit 2:** T159F, T159L, T159P, T159S, T212 **Unit 3:** T27Y, T146–T148, T159I, T159O, T170–T171 **Unit 4:** T142–T143, T164–T165, T217G, T217I, T217K, T228–T229 **Unit 5:** T142–T143, T217M, T228–T229, T270 **Unit 6:** T142, T206–T207, T228–T229 **www.connected.mcgraw-hill.com: RESOURCES** **Student Resources:** Comprehension Interactive Games and Activities, Vocabulary Interactive Games and Activities **Teacher Resources:** Graphic Organizers
RI.3.5	Use text features and search tools (e.g., key words, sidebars, hyperlinks) to locate information relevant to a given topic efficiently.	**READING/WRITING WORKSHOP: Unit 1:** 78, 92 **Unit 2:** 142, 158 **Unit 3:** 222 **Unit 4:** 310 **Unit 5:** 368 **Unit 6:** 440, 454 **LITERATURE ANTHOLOGY: Unit 3:** 265, 269 **Unit 4:** 356 **Unit 6:** 517 **CLOSE READING COMPANION:** 96, 161, 181, 182 **READING WORKSTATION ACTIVITY CARDS:** 16 **TEACHER'S EDITION: Unit 1:** T156, T174, T182, T186, T190, T192, T222–T223, T336–T337 **Unit 2:** T222–T223, T225D, T336–T337 **Unit 3:** T159F, T159G, T159K, T159L, T222–T223, T225F, T225K, T336–T337, T338–T341 **Unit 4:** T217I, T217K, T217P, T328–T329 **Unit 5:** T25W, T25X, T217M, T217W, T217X, T328–T329 **Unit 6:** T142, T150, T228–T229, T328–T329 **www.connected.mcgraw-hill.com: RESOURCES** **Student Resources:** Comprehension Interactive Games and Activities, Research and Inquiry **Teacher Resources:** Research and Inquiry
RI.3.6	Distinguish their own point of view from that of the author of a text.	**READING/WRITING WORKSHOP: Unit 2:** 134–139, 141, 150–155, 156 **Unit 5:** 362–365, 367, 376–379, 381 **LITERATURE ANTHOLOGY: Unit 2:** 146–167, 172–185 **Unit 3:** 240–255, 258–269 **Unit 4:** 326–339 **Unit 5:** 416–429, 432–451, 456–459 **LEVELED READERS: Unit 2, Week 3:** *The Race for the Presidency* (A, O, EL, B) **Unit 2, Week 4:** *Protecting the Islands* (A, O, EL, B) **Unit 5, Week 3:** *Firefighting Heroes* (A, O, EL, B) **Unit 5, Week 4:** *Eunice Kennedy Shriver* (A, O, EL, B) **YOUR TURN PRACTICE BOOK:** 73–75, 83–85, 223–225, 233–235 **TEACHER'S EDITION: Unit 2:** T154–T155, T159E, T159U, T173, T220–T221, T225M, T225N, T239, T240, T246–T248, T251, T252, T255, T256, T258 **Unit 5:** T148, T149, T153C, T153J, T153K, T153N, T167, T174, T175, T179, T183, T212–T213, T217T **www.connected.mcgraw-hill.com: RESOURCES** **Student Resources:** Comprehension Interactive Games and Activities **Teacher Resources:** Graphic Organizers, Skills Review

Integration of Knowledge and Ideas		McGraw-Hill Wonders
RI.3.7	Use information gained from illustrations (e.g., maps, photographs) and the words in a text to demonstrate understanding of the text (e.g., where, when, why, and how key events occur).	**READING/WRITING WORKSHOP: Unit 1:** 54–59, 70–75 **Unit 2:** 134–139, 150–155 **Unit 3:** 214–219, 230–235 **Unit 4:** 290–293, 304–307 **Unit 5:** 362–365, 376–379 **Unit 6:** 434–437, 448–451 **LITERATURE ANTHOLOGY: Unit 1:** 57 **Unit 3:** 255, 269 **Unit 6:** 517, 543 **READING WORKSTATION ACTIVITY CARDS:** 17 **CLOSE READING COMPANION:** 49, 58, 61, 70, 81, 89, 165, 181, 187,189 **TEACHER'S EDITION: Unit 1:** T156, T222, T225B, T225E **Unit 2:** T159D, T222, T225B, T225E, T225G, T225H **Unit 3:** T159E, T159G, T159K, T159L, T159O, T222 **Unit 4:** T153B, T153C, T153G, T217B–T217E **Unit 5:** T153F, T214, T215, T217C, T217M **www.connected.mcgraw-hill.com: RESOURCES** **Teacher Resources:** Graphic Organizers, Interactive Read Aloud Images, Research and Inquiry

Reading Standards for Informational Text

Integration of Knowledge and Ideas		McGraw-Hill Wonders
RI.3.8	Describe the logical connection between particular sentences and paragraphs in a text (e.g., comparison, cause/effect, first/second/third in a sequence).	**READING/WRITING WORKSHOP: Unit 1:** 54–59, 61, 77 **Unit 3:** 246–249, 251 **Unit 4:** 290–293, 295 **Unit 6:** 434–437, 439, 448–451, 453 **LITERATURE ANTHOLOGY: Unit 1:** 58–71, 74–91, 94–97 **Unit 2:** 146–167, 172–185 **Unit 3:** 272–275 **Unit 4:** 326–339, 342–357 **Unit 5:** 432–451, 465–459 **Unit 6:** 506–517, 520–543 **LEVELED READERS: Unit 1, Week 3:** *Judy Baca* (A, O, EL, B) **Unit 1, Week 4:** *The Amazing Benjamin Franklin* (A, O, EL, B) **Unit 4, Week 3:** *Life in a Tide Pool* (A, O, EL, B) **Unit 6, Week 3:** *Reach for the Stars* (A, O, EL, B) **Unit 6, Week 4:** *African Cats* (A, O, EL, B) **YOUR TURN PRACTICE BOOK:** 23–25, 33–35, 173–175, 273–275, 283–285 **READING WORKSTATION ACTIVITY CARDS:** 10, 11, 12, 13, 14, 15 **TEACHER'S EDITION: Unit 1:** T154, T225C, T225G, T225L, T225M, T225P **Unit 4:** T148–T149, T153C, T153D, T153E, T153G, T212–T213, T217C, T217G **Unit 5:** T217M, T217Q, T217U, T217V **www.connected.mcgraw-hill.com: RESOURCES** **Student Resources:** Comprehension Interactive Games and Activities **Teacher Resources:** Graphic Organizers, Skills Review
RI.3.9	Compare and contrast the most important points and key details presented in two texts on the same topic.	**LEVELED READERS: Unit 1, Week 3:** *Judy Baca* (A, O, EL, B) **Unit 2, Week 4:** *Protecting the Islands* (A, O, EL, B) **CLOSE READING COMPANION:** 21, 28, 99, 139, 146 **READING WORKSTATION ACTIVITY CARDS:** 18, 20 **TEACHER'S EDITION: Unit 1:** T173, T225T, T239, T303 **Unit 2:** T107, T159Z, T173, T239, T336 **Unit 3:** T93T, T107, T159R, T173, T303 **Unit 4:** T153N, T167, T231 **Unit 5:** T103, T167, T217V, T217X, T231, T295 **Unit 6:** T39, T103, T167, T231 **www.connected.mcgraw-hill.com: RESOURCES** **Student Resources:** Comprehension Interactive Games and Activities

Range of Reading and Level of Text Complexity		McGraw-Hill Wonders
RI.3.10	By the end of the year, read and comprehend informational texts, including history/social studies, science, and technical texts, at the high end of the grades 2–3 text complexity band independently and proficiently.	**READING/WRITING WORKSHOP:** These units reflect the range of text complexity found throughout the book. **Unit 1:** 86–89 **Unit 2:** 134–139 **Unit 3:** 230–235 **Unit 4:** 290–293 **Unit 5:** 348–351 **Unit 6:** 448–451 **LITERATURE ANTHOLOGY:** These units reflect the range of text complexity found throughout the book. **Unit 2:** 172–185 **Unit 3:** 240–255 **Unit 4:** 326–339 **Unit 5:** 432–451 **Unit 6:** 520–543 **LEVELED READERS: Unit 1, Week 3:** *Judy Baca* (A, O, EL, B) **Unit 3, Week 4:** *Inspired by Nature* (A, O, EL, B) **Unit 4, Week 3:** *Life in a Tide Pool* (A, O, EL, B) **Unit 6, Week 4:** *African Cats* (A, O, EL, B) **READING WORKSTATION ACTIVITY CARDS:** 22, 27 **TEACHER'S EDITION: Unit 1:** T156, T222, T225A **Unit 2:** T159A, T159W, T222, T225A, T225O **Unit 3:** T93S, T156, T159A, T222, T225A **Unit 4:** T150, T153A, T214, T217A **Unit 5:** T89W–T89Z, T150, T153A, T214, T217A, T278 **Unit 6:** T150, T153A, T214 **www.connected.mcgraw-hill.com: RESOURCES** **Student Resources:** Comprehension Interactive Games and Activities

Reading Standards: Foundational Skills

There are no standards for Print Concepts (1) or Phonological Awareness (2) in Foundational Skills for Grade 3.

Phonics and Word Recognition		McGraw-Hill Wonders
RF.3.3	Know and apply grade-level phonics and word analysis skills in decoding words.	
RF.3.3a	Identify and know the meaning of the most common prefixes and derivational suffixes.	**READING/WRITING WORKSHOP: Unit 2:** 143, 159 **Unit 3:** 223, 253 **Unit 4:** 283 **Unit 5:** 383 **YOUR TURN PRACTICE BOOK:** 77, 87, 118, 127, 128, 138, 147, 148, 167, 218, 237, 238, 248, 258, 268, 288, 298 **PHONICS/WORD STUDY WORKSTATION ACTIVITY CARDS:** 7, 9, 12 **TEACHER'S EDITION: Unit 1:** S17, S18,S28, T105, T243 **Unit 2:** T158, T159L, T159P, T224 **Unit 3:** T95, T110, T161, T174, T177, T182, T186, T191, T192, T226, T242–T243, T262 **Unit 4:** T89L **Unit 5:** T91, T106, T107, T217E, T217T, T219, T235 **Unit 6:** T26, T107, T235, T282 **www.connected.mcgraw-hill.com: RESOURCES** **Student Resources:** Phonics Interactive Games and Activities **Teacher Resources:** Decodable Passages
RF.3.3b	Decode words with common Latin suffixes.	**READING/WRITING WORKSHOP: Unit 3:** 223, 253 **YOUR TURN PRACTICE BOOK:** 127, 128, 147, 218, 248, 268, 288 **PHONICS/WORD STUDY WORKSTATION ACTIVITY CARDS:** 9 **TEACHER'S EDITION: Unit 2:** T158, T159P, T224 **Unit 3:** T95, T110, T159N, T161, T174, T177, T182, T186, T191, T192, T226, T242–T243, T262 **Unit 4:** T89L **Unit 5:** T91, T106, T107, T217E, T217T, T219, T235 **Unit 6:** T26, T91, T107, T219, T235 **www.connected.mcgraw-hill.com: RESOURCES** **Student Resources:** Phonics Interactive Games and Activities **Teacher Resources:** Decodable Passages
RF.3.3c	Decode multisyllable words.	**READING/WRITING WORKSHOP: Unit 1:** 63 **Unit 2:** 143, 159 **Unit 3:** 223, 239, 253 **Unit 4:** 269, 283 **Unit 5:** 341, 383 **Unit 6:** 413, 441 **YOUR TURN PRACTICE BOOK:** 27, 77, 87, 88, 98, 127, 137, 138, 147, 157, 167, 168, 188, 207, 208, 228, 237, 248, 257, 268, 277, 278, 288 **PHONICS/WORD STUDY WORKSTATION ACTIVITY CARDS:** 27 **TEACHER'S EDITION: Unit 1:** T28, T44, T45, T94, T110, T111, T176 **Unit 2:** T44–T45, T110–T111, T93L, T226, T227 **Unit 3:** T44–T45, T110–T111, T176–T177, T242 **Unit 4:** T90, T91, T170–T171, T219, T234–T235 **Unit 5:** T26–T27, T42–T43, T90–T91 **Unit 6:** T42–T43, T90–T91, T106–T107, T170–T171, T234–T235 **www.connected.mcgraw-hill.com: RESOURCES** **Student Resources:** Phonics Interactive Games and Activities **Teacher Resources:** Decodable Passages
RF.3.3d	Read grade-appropriate irregularly spelled words.	**YOUR TURN PRACTICE BOOK:** 298 **PHONICS/WORD STUDY WORKSTATION ACTIVITY CARDS:** 29 **TEACHER'S EDITION: Unit 1:** S31, T226 **Unit 2:** T160, T176–T177 **Unit 3:** T161 **Unit 4:** T218 **Unit 6:** T283 **www.connected.mcgraw-hill.com: RESOURCES** **Student Resources:** Phonics Interactive Games and Activities **Teacher Resources:** Decodable Passages

CORRELATIONS

CCSS

Reading Standards: Foundational Skills

Fluency		McGraw-Hill Wonders
RF.3.4	Read with sufficient accuracy and fluency to support comprehension.	
RF.3.4a	Read on-level text with purpose and understanding.	**READING WORKSTATION ACTIVITY CARDS:** 25, 26 **TEACHER'S EDITION: Unit I:** T48, T53, T58, TII2–TII4, TI6I, T334–T335 **Unit 2:** T29, T48, TII4, TI6I, TI80, T227, T246, T334–T335 **Unit 3:** T46, T49, T95, TII4, TI6I, T334–T335 **Unit 4:** T9I, TIIO, T326–T327 **Unit 5:** T27, T9I, TIIO, TI72, T326–T327 **Unit 6:** T46, T9I, TIIO, TI74, T238, T326–T327 www.connected.mcgraw-hill.com: **RESOURCES** **Student Resources:** Fluency Interactive Games and Activities
RF.3.4b	Read on-level prose and poetry orally with accuracy, appropriate rate, and expression on successive readings.	**YOUR TURN PRACTICE BOOK:** 3–5, 63–65, I33–I35, I73–I75, 2I3–2I5, 263–265 **READING WORKSTATION ACTIVITY CARDS:** 25, 26 **YOUR TURN PRACTICE BOOK:** 43–45, 63–65, II3–II5, I63–I65, 203–205, 253–255 **TEACHER'S EDITION: Unit I:** T29, T48, T95, TII4, TI27, TI6I, TI80, T227, T246, T334–T335 **Unit 2:** T48, TII4, T95, TI6I, TI80, T29I, T334–T335 **Unit 3:** T29, TII4, TI80, T227, T246, T29I, T334–T335 **Unit 4:** T27, T46, TIIO, TI74, T2I9, T238, T283, T326–T327 **Unit 5:** T46, TIIO, TI55, TI74, T2I9, T238, T326–T327 **Unit 6:** T46, TIIO, TI55, TI74, T238, T283, T326–T327 www.connected.mcgraw-hill.com: **RESOURCES** **Student Resources:** Fluency Interactive Games and Activities
RF.3.4c	Use context to confirm or self-correct word recognition and understanding, rereading as necessary.	**READING/WRITING WORKSHOP: Unit I:** 3I, 47, 93 **Unit 2:** III **Unit 3:** I9I **Unit 4:** 297, 3II **Unit 5:** 355, 369, 397 **Unit 6:** 455 **YOUR TURN PRACTICE BOOK:** 7, I7, 47, 57, I07, I77, I87, 2I7, 227, 247, 287 **READING WORKSTATION ACTIVITY CARDS:** 25, 26 **TEACHER'S EDITION: Unit I:** T224, T29I **Unit 2:** T27M, TI59I, TI59L, TI59P, TI59S, T225D, T225E, T225J, T225P **Unit 3:** T27E, T27K, T27Q, T27V, T93C, TI59I, T29I **Unit 4:** T89W, T2I7F, T2I7G, T2I7I, T2I7J, T2I7M **Unit 6:** TI55 www.connected.mcgraw-hill.com: **RESOURCES** **Student Resources:** Fluency Interactive Games and Activities

College and Career Readiness Anchor Standards for WRITING

The K-5 standards on the following pages define what students should understand and be able to do by the end of each grade. They correspond to the College and Career Readiness (CCR) anchor standards below by number. The CCR and grade-specific standards are necessary complements—the former providing broad standards, the latter providing additional specificity—that together define the skills and understandings that all students must demonstrate.

Text Types and Purposes

1. Write arguments to support claims in an analysis of substantive topics or texts, using valid reasoning and relevant and sufficient evidence.

2. Write informative/explanatory texts to examine and convey complex ideas and information clearly and accurately through the effective selection, organization, and analysis of content.

3. Write narratives to develop real or imagined experiences or events using effective techniques, well-chosen details, and well-structured event sequences.

Production and Distribution of Writing

4. Produce clear and coherent writing in which the development, organization, and style are appropriate to task, purpose, and audience.

5. Develop and strengthen writing as needed by planning, revising, editing, rewriting, or trying a new approach.

6. Use technology, including the Internet, to produce and publish writing and to interact and collaborate with others.

Research to Build and Present Knowledge

7. Conduct short as well as more sustained research projects based on focused questions, demonstrating understanding of the subject under investigation.

8. Gather relevant information from multiple print and digital sources, assess the credibility and accuracy of each source, and integrate information while avoiding plagiarism.

9. Draw evidence from literary and/or informational texts to support analysis, reflection, and research.

Range of Writing

10. Write routinely over extended time frames (time for research, reflection, and revision) and shorter time frames (a single sitting or a day or two) for a range of tasks, purposes, and audiences.

CCSS Common Core State Standards
English Language Arts
Grade 3

Each standard is coded in the following manner:

Strand	Grade Level	Standard
W	3	1

Writing Standards

Text Types and Purposes	*McGraw-Hill Wonders*
W.3.1	Write opinion pieces on topics or texts, supporting a point of view with reasons.
W.3.1a Introduce the topic or text they are writing about, state an opinion, and create an organizational structure that lists reasons.	**READING/WRITING WORKSHOP: Unit I:** 94 **Unit 2:** 128, 144 **Unit 3:** 254 **Unit 4:** 270, 284 **Unit 5:** 398 **Unit 6:** 414 **YOUR TURN PRACTICE BOOK:** 239, 249 **WRITING WORKSTATION ACTIVITY CARDS:** 13, 19 **TEACHER'S EDITION: Unit I:** T41, T293, T294, T295 **Unit 2:** T97, T99, T107, T163, T165, T173, T175, T183, T187, T193 **Unit 3:** T107, T239, T293, T295, T359 **Unit 4:** T29, T31, T38, T93, T103 **Unit 5:** T222, T223, T285, T287, T345, T347, T350 **Unit 6:** T29, T31, T103 www.connected.mcgraw-hill.com: RESOURCES **Student Resources:** Writer's Workspace, Inquiry Space: Opinion Performance Task
W.3.1b Provide reasons that support the opinion.	**READING/WRITING WORKSHOP: Unit I:** 94 **Unit 2:** 128, 144 **Unit 3:** 255 **Unit 4:** 271, 285 **Unit 5:** 398 **Unit 6:** 415 **YOUR TURN PRACTICE BOOK:** 79 **TEACHER'S EDITION: Unit I:** T293, T294, T295 **Unit 2:** T97, T99, T163, T165, T239 **Unit 3:** T293, T295, T353 **Unit 4:** T29, T31, T39, T93, T95, T103, T167, T175, T183, T187, T193, T346 **Unit 5:** T222, T223, T285, T287, T346, T352 **Unit 6:** T29, T31 www.connected.mcgraw-hill.com: RESOURCES **Student Resources:** Writer's Workspace
W.3.1c Use linking words and phrases (e.g., *because, therefore, since, for example*) to connect opinion and reasons.	**READING/WRITING WORKSHOP: Unit 4:** 284 **Unit 5:** 399 **Unit 6:** 428-429 **YOUR TURN PRACTICE BOOK:** 59, 119, 269 **WRITING WORKSTATION ACTIVITY CARDS:** 7 **TEACHER'S EDITION: Unit 3:** T131, T354 **Unit 4:** T93, T95 **Unit 5:** T285, T287, T343, T353, T361 www.connected.mcgraw-hill.com: RESOURCES **Student Resources:** Writer's Workspace
W.3.1d Provide a concluding statement or section.	**READING/WRITING WORKSHOP: Unit 2:** 145 **YOUR TURN PRACTICE BOOK:** 139, 189 **WRITING WORKSTATION ACTIVITY CARDS:** 12 **TEACHER'S EDITION: Unit 2:** T97, T99, T163, T165 **Unit 3:** T222-T223, T361 **Unit 4:** T352 www.connected.mcgraw-hill.com: RESOURCES **Student Resources:** Writer's Workspace

Writing Standards

Text Types and Purposes		McGraw-Hill Wonders
W.3.2	Write informative/explanatory texts to examine a topic and convey ideas and information clearly.	
W.3.2a	Introduce a topic and group related information together; include illustrations when useful to aiding comprehension.	**READING/WRITING WORKSHOP: Unit 1:** 64, 80 **Unit 3:** 224, 240 **Unit 4:** 298, 312 **Unit 5:** 370, 384, **Unit 6:** 442, 456 **YOUR TURN PRACTICE BOOK:** 129, 179, 229, 279 **WRITING WORKSTATION ACTIVITY CARDS:** 13, 14 **TEACHER'S EDITION: Unit 1:** T41, T107, T163, T165, T173, T229, T231, T239 **Unit 2:** T41, T107, T173, T229, T231, T239, T353, T359 **Unit 3:** T41, T107, T163, T165, T173, T229, T231, T239 **Unit 4:** T157, T158–T159, T190, T221, T223 **Unit 5:** T157, T158–T159, T182, T190, T221, T223 **Unit 6:** T157, T159, T182, T190, T221, T223, T246, T345, T350–T351 **www.connected.mcgraw-hill.com: RESOURCES** **Student Resources:** Writer's Workspace, Inquiry Space: Informative Performance Task
W.3.2b	Develop the topic with facts, definitions, and details.	**READING/WRITING WORKSHOP: Unit 1:** 80 **Unit 2:** 160-161 **Unit 3:** 224, 240 **Unit 4:** 298, 312 **Unit 5:** 370, 384 **Unit 6:** 442, 457 **YOUR TURN PRACTICE BOOK:** 19, 99, 299 **WRITING WORKSTATION ACTIVITY CARDS:** 2 **TEACHER'S EDITION: Unit 1:** T29, T31, T98, T99 **Unit 2:** T196, T229, T231, T360 **Unit 3:** T106, T163, T165, T196, T229, T231 **Unit 4:** T157, T159, T190, T221, T223 **Unit 5:** T157, T159, T221, T223 **Unit 6:** T157, T159, T221, T223, T352 **www.connected.mcgraw-hill.com: RESOURCES** **Student Resources:** Writer's Workspace
W.3.2c	Use linking words and phrases (e.g., *also, another, and, more, but*) to connect ideas within categories of information.	**READING/WRITING WORKSHOP: Unit 1:** 81 **Unit 4:** 299 **Unit 5:** 385 **YOUR TURN PRACTICE BOOK:** 39, 89 **WRITING WORKSTATION ACTIVITY CARDS:** 7 **TEACHER'S EDITION: Unit 1:** T29, T31 **Unit 2:** T64, T355 **Unit 5:** T221, T223 **Unit 6:** T157, T159, T346, T352 **www.connected.mcgraw-hill.com: RESOURCES** **Student Resources:** Writer's Workspace
W.3.2d	Provide a concluding statement or section.	**READING/WRITING WORKSHOP: Unit 1:** 65 **Unit 3:** 225, 241 **Unit 4:** 313 **Unit 5:** 371 **Unit 6:** 443, 457 **YOUR TURN PRACTICE BOOK:** 289 **WRITING WORKSTATION ACTIVITY CARDS:** 12 **TEACHER'S EDITION: Unit 1:** T163, T165 **Unit 2:** T228-T229, T361 **Unit 3:** T163, T165, T229, T231, T262 **Unit 4:** T221, T223 **Unit 5:** T157, T159 **Unit 6:** T157, T159, T221, T223, T347 **www.connected.mcgraw-hill.com: RESOURCES** **Student Resources:** Writer's Workspace
W.3.3	Write narratives to develop real or imagined experiences or events using effective technique, descriptive details, and clear event sequences.	
W.3.3a	Establish a situation and introduce a narrator and/or characters; organize an event sequence that unfolds naturally.	**READING/WRITING WORKSHOP: Unit 1:** T49 **Unit 2:** 112-113 **Unit 3:** 208 **Unit 4:** 326 **Unit 5:** 356 **Unit 6:** 428 **YOUR TURN PRACTICE BOOK:** 29, 169 **WRITING WORKSTATION ACTIVITY CARDS:** 4, 10 **TEACHER'S EDITION: Unit 1:** T31, T33, T64, T97, T99, T353, T359 **Unit 2:** T262 **Unit 3:** T55, T63, T97, T99 **Unit 4:** T345 **Unit 6:** T93, T95 **www.connected.mcgraw-hill.com: RESOURCES** **Student Resources:** Writer's Workspace, Inquiry Space: Narrative Performance Task

Writing Standards

Text Types and Purposes		McGraw-Hill Wonders
W.3.3b	Use dialogue and descriptions of actions, thoughts, and feelings to develop experiences and events or show the response of characters to situations.	**READING/WRITING WORKSHOP: Unit 1:** 32, 48 **Unit 2:** 112, 174 **Unit 3:** 192, 208 **Unit 5:** 342, 356 **Unit 6:** 429, 471 **YOUR TURN PRACTICE BOOK:** 9, 69, 169, 199, 219 **WRITING WORKSTATION ACTIVITY CARDS:** 1, 3, 4 **TEACHER'S EDITION: Unit 1:** T31, T33, T97, T99, T130, T353, T354, T360 **Unit 2:** T293, T295 **Unit 3:** T31, T33, T97, T99 **Unit 4:** T62, T126, T285, T287, T346, T351, T353 **Unit 5:** T126 **Unit 6:** T54, T93, T95, T126, T285, T287 **www.connected.mcgraw-hill.com: RESOURCES** **Student Resources:** Writer's Workspace
W.3.3c	Use temporal words and phrases to signal event order.	**READING/WRITING WORKSHOP: Unit 1:** 49 **Unit 2:** 112–113 **Unit 3:** 193, 209 **YOUR TURN PRACTICE BOOK:** 59, 119, 269 **WRITING WORKSTATION ACTIVITY CARDS:** 6 **TEACHER'S EDITION: Unit 1:** T97, T99, T163, T165, T196, T262, T360 **Unit 2:** T229, T231 **Unit 3:** T31, T33, T97, T99 **Unit 6:** T93, T95 **www.connected.mcgraw-hill.com: RESOURCES** **Student Resources:** Writer's Workspace
W.3.3d	Provide a sense of closure.	**READING/WRITING WORKSHOP: Unit 1:** 33 **Unit 2:** 112–113 **Unit 4:** 327 **Unit 5:** 343 **YOUR TURN PRACTICE BOOK:** 279, 289 **WRITING WORKSTATION ACTIVITY CARDS:** 12 **TEACHER'S EDITION: Unit 1:** T31, T33, T97, T99, T163, T165 **Unit 2:** T229, T231, T293, T295 **Unit 3:** T31, T33, T97, T99 **Unit 4:** T285, T287 **Unit 6:** T93, T95, T285, T287 **www.connected.mcgraw-hill.com: RESOURCES** **Student Resources:** Writer's Workspace
Production and Distribution of Writing		**McGraw-Hill Wonders**
W.3.4	With guidance and support from adults, produce writing in which the development and organization are appropriate to task and purpose. (Grade-specific expectations for writing types are defined in standards 1–3 above.)	**READING/WRITING WORKSHOP: Unit 3:** 254–255 **YOUR TURN PRACTICE BOOK:** 149 **WRITING WORKSTATION ACTIVITY CARDS:** 17, 20, 21, 22, 23, 24, 25, 26, 27, 28, 29, 30 **TEACHER'S EDITION: Unit 1:** T31, T32, T33, T97, T98, T99, T130, T163, T164, T165, T197, T229, T230, T231, T293, T294, T295 **Unit 2:** T31, T32, T33, T97, T98, T99, T123, T127, T129–T130, T163, T164, T165, T175, T178, T229, T230, T231, T293, T294, T295 **Unit 3:** T31, T32, T33, T46, T61, T93R, T109, T117, T121, T127, T163, T164, T165, T229, T230, T231, T293, T294, T295 **Unit 4:** T25T, T29, T30, T31, T62, T89T, T89Y, T93, T94, T95, T126, T157, T158, T159, T190, T217P, T221, T222, T223, T285, T286, T287, T238 **Unit 5:** T29, T30, T31, T62, T93, T94, T95, T157, T158, T159, T182, T221, T222, T223, T285, T286, T287 **Unit 6:** T29, T30, T31, T62, T93, T94, T95, T126, T157, T158, T159, T190, T221, T222, T223, T266, T285, T286, T287, T328 **www.connected.mcgraw-hill.com: RESOURCES** **Student Resources:** Writer's Workspace
W.3.5	With guidance and support from peers and adults, develop and strengthen writing as needed by planning, revising, and editing. (Editing for conventions should demonstrate command of Language standards 1–3 up to and including grade 3.)	**READING/WRITING WORKSHOP: Unit 1:** 33, 49, 65, 81, 95 **Unit 2:** 113, 129, 145, 161, 175 **Unit 3:** 193, 209, 225, 241, 255 **Unit 4:** 271, 285, 299, 313, 327 **Unit 5:** 343, 357, 371, 385, 399 **Unit 6:** 415, 429, 443, 457, 471 **TEACHER'S EDITION: Unit 1:** 65, T353–T356, T359–T362 **Unit 2:** T130, T262, T353–T356, T359–T362 **Unit 3:** T63, T130, T196, T262, T353–T356, T359–T362 **Unit 4:** T62, T126, T190, T345–T348, T351–T354 **Unit 5:** T62, T126, T190, T254, T345–T348, T351–T354 **Unit 6:** T62, T126, T190, T345–T348, T351–T354 **www.connected.mcgraw-hill.com: RESOURCES** **Student Resources:** Writer's Workspace

Writing Standards

Production and Distribution of Writing | *McGraw-Hill Wonders*

W.3.6 With guidance and support from adults, use technology to produce and publish writing (using keyboarding skills) as well as to interact and collaborate with others.

TEACHER'S EDITION: Unit 1: T302, T338–T341, T356, T362 **Unit 2:** T338–T341, T356, T362 **Unit 3:** T106, T238, T338–T341, T356, T362 **Unit 4:** T294, T330–T333, T348, T354 **Unit 5:** T330–T333, T348, T354 **Unit 6:** T102, T330–T333, T348, T354

www.connected.mcgraw-hill.com: RESOURCES
Student Resources: Writer's Workspace, Inquiry Space

Research to Build and Present Knowledge | *McGraw-Hill Wonders*

W.3.7 Conduct short research projects that build knowledge about a topic.

WRITING WORKSTATION ACTIVITY CARDS: 30
TEACHER'S EDITION: Unit 1: T40, T106, T172, T238, T338–T341 **Unit 2:** T40, T106, T172, T238, T338–T341 **Unit 3:** T40, T106, T172, T187, T238, T338–T341 **Unit 4:** T38, T102, T166, T230, T328–T329, T330–T333 **Unit 5:** T38, T102, T166, T230, T246, T330–T333 **Unit 6:** T38, T102, T328–T329, T330–T333

www.connected.mcgraw-hill.com: RESOURCES
Student Resources: Research and Inquiry, Writer's Workspace
Teacher Resources: Graphic Organizers, Research and Inquiry

W.3.8 Recall information from experiences or gather information from print and digital sources; take brief notes on sources and sort evidence into provided categories.

WRITING WORKSTATION ACTIVITY CARDS: 30
TEACHER'S EDITION: Unit 1: T27B, T27C, T27G, T27I, T27O, T40, T336–T337, T338–T341 **Unit 2:** T31, T33, T97, T99, T163, T165, T225F, T225G, T225I, T225K, T229, T231, T238, T293, T295, T336, T338–T341 **Unit 3:** T31, T33, T97, T99, T159G, T159K, T163, T165, T229, T231, T293, T295, T336–T337 **Unit 4:** T25B, T25D, T25E, T25G, T25J, T25P, T25Q, T29, T31, T89B, T93, T95, T157, T159, T221, T223, T285, T287, T346 **Unit 5:** T38, T328–T329 **Unit 6:** T29, T31, T93, T95, T102, T157, T159, T221, T223, T285, T287, T328, T330–T333

www.connected.mcgraw-hill.com: RESOURCES
Student Resources: Inquiry Space, Research and Inquiry, Writer's Workspace
Teacher Resources: Graphic Organizers, Research and Inquiry

W.3.9 (Begins in grade 4)

(Begins in grade 4)

Range of Writing | *McGraw-Hill Wonders*

W.3.10 Write routinely over extended time frames (time for research, reflection, and revision) and shorter time frames (a single sitting or a day or two) for a range of discipline-specific tasks, purposes, and audiences.

READING/WRITING WORKSHOP: Unit 1: 64–65 **Unit 2:** 112–113 **Unit 3:** 192–193 **Unit 4:** 298–299 **Unit 5:** 356–357 **Unit 6:** 428–429
WRITING WORKSTATION ACTIVITY CARDS: 20, 21, 22, 23, 24, 25, 26, 27, 28, 29, 30
CLOSE READING COMPANION: 3, 17,28, 30,33,36, 40, 43, 47, 51, 54, 57, 61, 63, 66, 69, 73, 76, 80, 83, 87, 90, 94, 96, 109, 116, 123, 129, 135, 142, 149, 156, 162, 168, 175, 182, 189, 195
TEACHER'S EDITION: Unit 1: T30, T41, T43, T51, T55, T61, T64, T96, T162, T228, T292, T338–T341, T342–T363 **Unit 2:** T30, T96, T109, T117, T121, T127, T128, T130, T162, T173, T228, T292, T338–T341, T352–T363 **Unit 3:** T30, T96, T162, T196, T225L, T220, T230, T231, T239, T241, T249, T253, T254, T261, T284, T338–T341, T352–T363 **Unit 4:** T95, T118, T119, T126, T158, T167, T330–T333, T344–T355 **Unit 5:** T28, T92, T156, T159, T179, T182, T190, T220, T222, T223, T231, T284, T330–T333, T344–T355 **Unit 6:** T28, T39, T62, T92, T126, T156, T190, T220, T246, T284, T330–T333, T344–T355

www.connected.mcgraw-hill.com: RESOURCES
Student Resources: Inquiry Space, Research and Inquiry, Writer's Workspace
Teacher Resources: Research and Inquiry

College and Career Readiness Anchor Standards for SPEAKING AND LISTENING

The K-5 standards on the following pages define what students should understand and be able to do by the end of each grade. They correspond to the College and Career Readiness (CCR) anchor standards below by number. The CCR and grade-specific standards are necessary complements—the former providing broad standards, the latter providing additional specificity—that together define the skills and understandings that all students must demonstrate.

Comprehension and Collaboration

1. Prepare for and participate effectively in a range of conversations and collaborations with diverse partners, building on others' ideas and expressing their own clearly and persuasively.

2. Integrate and evaluate information presented in diverse media and formats, including visually, quantitatively, and orally.

3. Evaluate a speaker's point of view, reasoning, and use of evidence and rhetoric.

Presentation of Knowledge and Ideas

4. Present information, findings, and supporting evidence such that listeners can follow the line of reasoning and the organization, development, and style are appropriate to task, purpose, and audience.

5. Make strategic use of digital media and visual displays of data to express information and enhance understanding of presentations.

6. Adapt speech to a variety of contexts and communicative tasks, demonstrating command of formal English when indicated or appropriate.

CCSS Common Core State Standards
English Language Arts

Grade 3

Each standard is coded in the following manner:

Strand	Grade Level	Standard
SL	3	1

Speaking and Listening Standards

Comprehension and Collaboration	McGraw-Hill Wonders
SL.3.1	Engage effectively in a range of collaborative discussions (one-on-one, in groups, and teacher-led) with diverse partners on *grade 3 topics and texts,* building on others' ideas and expressing their own clearly.
SL.3.1a Come to discussions prepared, having read or studied required material; explicitly draw on that preparation and other information known about the topic to explore ideas under discussion.	**READING/WRITING WORKSHOP: Unit I:** 28, 29, 44, 45, 60, 6I, 76, 77, 90, 9I **Unit 2:** I08, I09, I24, I25, I40, I4I, I56, I57 **Unit 3:** I88, I89, 204, 205, 220, 22I, 236, 237, 250, 25I **Unit 4:** I66, 267, 280, 28I, 294, 295, 308, 309 **Unit 5:** 338, 339, 352, 353, 366, 367, 380, 38I, 394, 395 **Unit 6:** 4I0, 4II, 424, 425, 438, 439, 452, 453 **CLOSE READING COMPANION:** I–I98 **TEACHER'S EDITION: Unit I:** T49, T53, T57, TII7, TII9, T123, T142, T214, T239 **Unit 2:** TII7, TI2I, TI27, TI42, T220, T239, T24I, T249, T253, T259 **Unit 3:** TI72, TI73, TI75, TI83, TI87, TI93, T208, T239, T24I, T249, T253, T26I **Unit 4:** T39, T74, T82, T86, TI02, TI03, TI67 **Unit 5:** TI0, T39, TIII, TII5, TII9, TI67, TI75, TI79 **Unit 6:** T47, T5I, T55, TI03, TIII, TII5, TII9, TI75 **www.connected.mcgraw-hill.com: RESOURCES** **Teacher Resources:** Build Background Videos
SL.3.1b Follow agreed-upon rules for discussions (e.g., gaining the floor in respectful ways, listening to others with care, speaking one at a time about the topics and texts under discussion).	**READING WORKSTATION ACTIVITY CARDS:** 24 **TEACHER'S EDITION: Unit I:** TI0, T76, T239 **Unit 2:** TI0, T76, TI62, T222 **Unit 3:** T76, TI06, TI07, TI72, TI73, T208, T209, T238, T239 **Unit 4:** TI0, T38, T39, TI02, TI03, T202, T230, T23I **Unit 5:** T74, TI03, TI66, T202, T203, T266 **Unit 6:** T74, TI38, T266 **www.connected.mcgraw-hill.com: RESOURCES** **Teacher Resources:** Build Background Videos
SL.3.1c Ask questions to check understanding of information presented, stay on topic, and link their comments to the remarks of others.	**TEACHER'S EDITION: Unit I:** TI8, T82, TI42, T2I8 **Unit 2:** TI4, T27Q, T27W, T40, T93I, TI59J, TI59N, TI73, T208, T340 **Unit 3:** TI0, T27I, T27V, T27X–T27Z, T93J, TI42, TI59H **Unit 4:** T89H, T89K, T89O, T89V, T89W, T89Y, T2I7D, T2I7H, T2I7I, T2I7J, T2I7M, T2I7R, T23I **Unit 5:** TI0, T23I **Unit 6:** TI38 **www.connected.mcgraw-hill.com: RESOURCES** **Student Resources:** Research and Inquiry **Teacher Resources:** Build Background Videos, Research and Inquiry
SL.3.1d Explain their own ideas and understanding in light of the discussion.	**CLOSE READING COMPANION:** 2, 9, I6, 23, 30, 35, 42, 49, 56, 65, 75, 82, 89, 96, I0I, I08, III, II5, II9, I22, I26, I3I, I34, I4I, I55, I74 **TEACHER'S EDITION: Unit I:** TI0, T76, T93B, TI07, TI73, T208, T222, T238, T340 **Unit 2:** TI4, T27B, T27F, T27L, T27N, T27P, T27X, T4I, TI59J, T225E, T225J **Unit 3:** TI59J, TI59L, TI73, T225H, T225I **Unit 4:** T25N, T25V, T39, T89H, T89O **Unit 5:** TI0, T28, TI02, TI04, TI38, TI39, TI67 **Unit 6:** TI66, T295, T332 **www.connected.mcgraw-hill.com: RESOURCES** **Teacher Resources:** Build Background Videos

Speaking and Listening Standards

Comprehension and Collaboration		McGraw-Hill Wonders
SL.3.2	Determine the main ideas and supporting details of a text read aloud or information presented in diverse media and formats, including visually, quantitatively, and orally.	**CLOSE READING COMPANION:** 40, 61, 127, 132, 193 **TEACHER'S EDITION: Unit 1:** T10, T12, T30, T78, T96, T144, T162, T208, T210, T228, T336 **Unit 2:** T10, T12, T30, T78, T96, T142, T144, T159Y, T162, T208, T210, T228, T336 **Unit 3:** T10, T12, T30, T78, T96, T142, T144, T159Y, T162, T172, T208, T209, T228, T302, T340 **Unit 4:** T12–T13, T28, T74, T76, T92, T156, T204, T220, T328 **Unit 5:** T10, T12, T28, T74, T76, T92, T140, T141, T156, T202, T204, T217W, T220, T230, T328 **Unit 6:** T38, T74, T76, T138, T140, T230, T328 **CLOSE READING COMPANION:** 40, 61, 127, 132, 193 www.connected.mcgraw-hill.com: **RESOURCES** **Student Resources:** Music/Fine Arts Activities **Teacher Resources:** Interactive Read Aloud Images, Music/Fine Arts Activities
SL.3.3	Ask and answer questions about information from a speaker, offering appropriate elaboration and detail.	**TEACHER'S EDITION: Unit 1:** T340, T342–T343 **Unit 2:** T41, T238, T302, T340, T342–T343 **Unit 3:** T41, T106, T107, T172, T173, T238, T239, T340, T342–T343 **Unit 4:** T166, T332, T334–T335 **Unit 5:** T38, T332, T334–T335 **Unit 6:** T39, T332, T334–T335 www.connected.mcgraw-hill.com: **RESOURCES** **Student Resources:** Research and Inquiry **Teacher Resources:** Research and Inquiry

Presentation of Knowledge and Ideas		McGraw-Hill Wonders
SL.3.4	Report on a topic or text, tell a story, or recount an experience with appropriate facts and relevant, descriptive details, speaking clearly at an understandable pace.	**TEACHER'S EDITION: Unit 1:** T18, T148, T340, T342–T343 **Unit 2:** T40, T107, T340, T342–T343 **Unit 3:** T40, T239, T340, T342–T343, **Unit 4:** T38, T332, T334–T335 **Unit 5:** T292, T332, T334–T335 **Unit 6:** T167, T230, T332, T334–T335 www.connected.mcgraw-hill.com: **RESOURCES** **Student Resources:** Research and Inquiry, **Inquiry Space:** Unit 2, Collaborative Conversations Videos **Teacher Resources:** Research and Inquiry
SL.3.5	Create engaging audio recordings of stories or poems that demonstrate fluid reading at an understandable pace; add visual displays when appropriate to emphasize or enhance certain facts or details.	**TEACHER'S EDITION: Unit 1:** T238, T340 **Unit 2:** T227, T291, T340 **Unit 3:** T238, T340 **Unit 4:** T102, T155, T166, T283, T294, T332, T334–T335 **Unit 5:** T27, T332, T334–T335 **Unit 6:** T27, T102, T332, T334–T335 www.connected.mcgraw-hill.com: **RESOURCES** **Student Resources:** Research and Inquiry **Teacher Resources:** Research and Inquiry
SL.3.6	Speak in complete sentences when appropriate to task and situation in order to provide requested detail or clarification. (See grade 3 Language standards 1 and 3 for specific expectations.)	**TEACHER'S EDITION: Unit 1:** T274, T342 **Unit 2:** T142, T173, T208, T303 **Unit 3:** T41, T107, T208 **Unit 4:** T167, T202 **Unit 5:** T138, T231, T332 **Unit 6:** T74, T167, T202, T230 www.connected.mcgraw-hill.com: **RESOURCES** **Student Resources:** Grammar Interactive Games and Activities, Research and Inquiry **Teacher Resources:** Research and Inquiry

College and Career Readiness Anchor Standards for LANGUAGE

The K-5 standards on the following pages define what students should understand and be able to do by the end of each grade. They correspond to the College and Career Readiness (CCR) anchor standards below by number. The CCR and grade-specific standards are necessary complements—the former providing broad standards, the latter providing additional specificity—that together define the skills and understandings that all students must demonstrate.

Conventions of English
1. Demonstrate command of the conventions of standard English grammar and usage when writing or speaking.
2. Demonstrate command of the conventions of standard English capitalization, punctuation, and spelling when writing.

Knowledge of Language
3. Apply knowledge of language to understand how language functions in different contexts, to make effective choices for meaning or style, and to comprehend more fully when reading and listening.

Vocabulary Acquisition and Use
4. Determine or clarify the meaning of unknown and multiple-meaning words and phrases by using context clues, analyzing meaningful word parts, and consulting general and specialized reference materials, as appropriate.
5. Demonstrate understanding of figurative language, word relationships, and nuances in word meanings.
6. Acquire and use accurately a range of general academic and domain-specific words and phrases sufficient for reading, writing, speaking, and listening at the college and career readiness level; demonstrate independence in gathering vocabulary knowledge when encountering an unknown term important to comprehension or expression.

CCSS Common Core State Standards
English Language Arts
Grade 3

Each standard is coded in the following manner:

Strand	Grade Level	Standard
L	3	1

Language Standards

Conventions of English	*McGraw-Hill Wonders*
L.3.1	Demonstrate command of the conventions of standard English grammar and usage when writing or speaking.
L.3.1a Explain the function of nouns, pronouns, verbs, adjectives, and adverbs in general and their functions in particular sentences.	**READING/WRITING WORKSHOP: Unit 1:** 65, 80 **Unit 2:** 112-113, 175 **Unit 4:** 270, 299 **Unit 5:** 343, 357, 399 **Unit 6:** 443 **Grammar Handbook:** 478-480, 481-486, 487-490, 491-492, 493-494 **TEACHER'S EDITION: Unit 1:** T151 **Unit 2:** T32, T65, T98, T99, T131, T177, T232 **Unit 3:** T34, T64, T100, T166, T197 **Unit 4:** T32, T68, T89D, T160, T190 **Unit 5:** T32, T33, T63, T97, T98, T160, T161, T190, T224, T225 **Unit 6:** T32, T33, T63, T96, T97, T160, T161, T191, T224, T225 www.connected.mcgraw-hill.com: **RESOURCES** **Student Resources:** Grammar Interactive Games and Activities
L.3.1b Form and use regular and irregular plural nouns.	**READING/WRITING WORKSHOP: Unit 2:** 129, 145 **Grammar Handbook:** 479-480 **YOUR TURN PRACTICE BOOK:** 38, 58 **TEACHER'S EDITION: Unit 1:** T227 **Unit 2:** T100, T130, T166-T167, T197 www.connected.mcgraw-hill.com: **RESOURCES** **Student Resources:** Grammar Interactive Games and Activities **Teacher Resources:** Music/Fine Arts Activities
L.3.1c Use abstract nouns (e.g., *childhood*).	**READING/WRITING WORKSHOP: Grammar Handbook:** 478 **TEACHER'S EDITION: Unit 2:** T34-T35, T65 www.connected.mcgraw-hill.com: **RESOURCES** **Student Resources:** Grammar Interactive Games and Activities **Teacher Resources:** Music/Fine Arts Activities
L.3.1d Form and use regular and irregular verbs.	**READING/WRITING WORKSHOP: Unit 3:** 193 **Unit 4:** 327 **Grammar Handbook:** 481-486 **TEACHER'S EDITION: Unit 1:** T111, T177 **Unit 4:** T32, T33, T63, T160-T161, T288-T289 www.connected.mcgraw-hill.com: **RESOURCES** **Student Resources:** Grammar Interactive Games and Activities **Teacher Resources:** Music/Fine Arts Activities
L.3.1e Form and use the simple (e.g., *I walked; I walk; I will walk*) verb tenses.	**READING/WRITING WORKSHOP: Unit 3:** 209, 225, 241 **Grammar Handbook:** 482-483 **TEACHER'S EDITION: Unit 2:** T111, T177 **Unit 3:** T34-T35, T100, T131, T166-T167, T197, T232-T233, T263 **Unit 4:** T160, T161 www.connected.mcgraw-hill.com: **RESOURCES** **Student Resources:** Grammar Interactive Games and Activities **Teacher Resources:** Music/Fine Arts Activities
L.3.1f Ensure subject-verb and pronoun-antecedent agreement.	**READING/WRITING WORKSHOP: Unit 5:** 371 **Grammar Handbook:** 483, 490 **TEACHER'S EDITION: Unit 2:** T151 **Unit 3:** T100, T101, T131, T166, T167, T197, T263 **Unit 4:** T32, T63, T288-T289 **Unit 5:** T32, T33, T97, T160, T161 www.connected.mcgraw-hill.com: **RESOURCES** **Student Resources:** Grammar Interactive Games and Activities

Language Standards

Conventions of English		*McGraw-Hill Wonders*
L.3.1g	Form and use comparative and superlative adjectives and adverbs, and choose between them depending on what is to be modified.	**READING/WRITING WORKSHOP:** Unit 6: 429, 456 **Grammar Handbook:** 492, 494 **TEACHER'S EDITION:** Unit 6: T96, T97, T161, T224, T225, T255 www.connected.mcgraw-hill.com: **RESOURCES** **Student Resources:** Grammar Interactive Games and Activities
L.3.1h	Use coordinating and subordinating conjunctions.	**READING/WRITING WORKSHOP:** Unit 1: 95 Unit 3: 254 **Grammar Handbook:** 476, 477 **TEACHER'S EDITION:** Unit 2: T222 Unit 4: T224-T225 www.connected.mcgraw-hill.com: **RESOURCES** **Student Resources:** Grammar Interactive Games and Activities
L.3.1i	Produce simple, compound, and complex sentences.	**READING/WRITING WORKSHOP:** Unit 1: 32, 48, 95 Unit 2: 160 Unit 3: 192, 254 Unit 4: 312 Unit 6: 415, 470 **Grammar Handbook:** 476, 477 **YOUR TURN PRACTICE BOOK:** 49, 109, 209, 259 **TEACHER'S EDITION:** Unit 1: T34, T63, T65, T100-T101, T129, T131, T166-T167, T195, T197, T232-T233, T261, T263 **Unit 2:** T63-T65, T260-T263 **Unit 5:** T30, T31, T54, **Unit 6:** T54, T61, T118, T125, T126, T190, T246, T253 www.connected.mcgraw-hill.com: **RESOURCES** **Student Resources:** Grammar Interactive Games and Activities
L.3.2	Demonstrate command of the conventions of standard English capitalization, punctuation, and spelling when writing.	
L.3.2a	Capitalize appropriate words in titles.	**READING/WRITING WORKSHOP:** Grammar Handbook: 498, 500 **TEACHER'S EDITION:** Unit 2: T35 Unit 3: T167, T233 Unit 5: T33, T97 www.connected.mcgraw-hill.com: **RESOURCES** **Student Resources:** Grammar Interactive Games and Activities **Teacher Resources:** Music/Fine Arts Activities
L.3.2b	Use commas in addresses.	**READING/WRITING WORKSHOP:** Grammar Handbook: 502 **TEACHER'S EDITION:** Unit 1: T356 Unit 2: T233 Unit 5: T33, T97 Unit 6: T33 www.connected.mcgraw-hill.com: **RESOURCES** **Student Resources:** Grammar Interactive Games and Activities
L.3.2c	Use commas and quotation marks in dialogue.	**READING/WRITING WORKSHOP:** Grammar Handbook: 504 **TEACHER'S EDITION:** Unit 3: T35 Unit 4: T97, T161 www.connected.mcgraw-hill.com: **RESOURCES** **Student Resources:** Grammar Interactive Games and Activities **Teacher Resources:** Music/Fine Arts Activities
L.3.2d	Form and use possessives.	**READING/WRITING WORKSHOP:** Unit 5: 385 Grammar Handbook: 480, 489 **TEACHER'S EDITION:** Unit 2: T161, T296-297, T327 Unit 4: T97 Unit 5: T224, T225, T255, T289 **YOUR TURN PRACTICE BOOK:** 78 www.connected.mcgraw-hill.com: **RESOURCES** **Student Resources:** Grammar Interactive Games and Activities **Teacher Resources:** Music/Fine Arts Activities
L.3.2e	Use conventional spelling for high-frequency and other studied words and for adding suffixes to base words (e.g., *sitting, smiled, cries, happiness*).	**YOUR TURN PRACTICE BOOK:** 18, 28, 38, 58, 68, 168, 218, 238 **PHONICS/WORD STUDY WORKSTATION ACTIVITY CARDS:** 24, 29 **TEACHER'S EDITION:** Unit 1: T46, T63, T112, T129, T178, T195, T244, T261 Unit 2: T45, T46, T112, T178, T195, T244 Unit 3: T46, T112, T130, T178 Unit 4: T44, T108, T172, T234, T254 Unit 5: T61, T98, T108, T125, T189, T236, T253 Unit 6: T44, T61, T108, T125, T170, T189, T234, T253, T302

Language Standards

Conventions of English		McGraw-Hill Wonders
L.3.2f	Use spelling patterns and generalizations (e.g., word families, position-based spellings, syllable patterns, ending rules, meaningful word parts) in writing words.	**READING/WRITING WORKSHOP:** Unit 4: 285 **YOUR TURN PRACTICE BOOK:** 8, 18, 28, 38, 58, 68, 168, 218, 238 **PHONICS/WORD STUDY WORKSTATION ACTIVITY CARDS:** 24 **TEACHER'S EDITION: Unit 1:** T36, T64, T102, T130, T170, T196, T166, T168, T234 **Unit 2:** T32, T65, T98, T99, T131, T177, T232 **Unit 3:** T36, T63, T102, T170, T196, T234, T300 **Unit 4:** T62, T96, T126, T190, T290 **Unit 5:** T34, T62, T98, T162, T190, T226, T254, T290 **Unit 6:** T62, T98, T126, T164, T190, T226 **www.connected.mcgraw-hill.com:** RESOURCES **Student Resources:** Grammar Interactive Games and Activities **Teacher Resources:** Music/Fine Arts Activities
L.3.2g	Consult reference materials, including beginning dictionaries, as needed to check and correct spellings.	**READING/WRITING WORKSHOP: Unit 1:** T38, T104, T170, T236, T302 **Unit 2:** T38, T104, T170, T236, T302 **Unit 3:** T38, T104, T170 **Unit 4:** T292 **Unit 5:** T36, T164, T228, T292 **Unit 6:** T36, T100, T164, T228, T292 **TEACHER'S EDITION: Unit 1:** T36, T102, T170, T234, T300 **Unit 2:** T36, T102, T170, T234, T300 **Unit 3:** T36, T102, T170 **Unit 4:** T290 **Unit 5:** T34, T226, T290 **Unit 6:** T34, T98, T162, T226, T290 **www.connected.mcgraw-hill.com:** RESOURCES **Student Resources:** Grammar Interactive Games and Activities **Teacher Resources:** Music/Fine Arts Activities

Knowledge of Language		McGraw-Hill Wonders
L.3.3	Use knowledge of language and its conventions when writing, speaking, reading, or listening.	
L.3.3a	Choose words and phrases for effect.	**READING/WRITING WORKSHOP: Unit 1:** 32–33, 48–49 **Unit 2:** 128–129 **Unit 4:** 284–285, 326–327 **Unit 5:** 356–357 **YOUR TURN PRACTICE BOOK:** 9, 69, 169, 199, 219 **TEACHER'S EDITION: Unit 1:** T96–T99 **Unit 2:** T96–T99, T130 **Unit 4:** T284–T287 **Unit 5:** T92–T95, T102 **Unit 6:** T284–T287, T294 **www.connected.mcgraw-hill.com:** RESOURCES **Student Resources:** Writer's Workspace
L.3.3b	Recognize and observe differences between the conventions of spoken and written standard English.	**READING/WRITING WORKSHOP: Unit 3:** 255 **TEACHER'S EDITION: Unit 1:** S35, T338, T354 **Unit 2:** T106 **Unit 4:** T102 **Unit 5:** T166 **Unit 6:** T166, T330–T333 **www.connected.mcgraw-hill.com:** RESOURCES **Student Resources:** Writer's Workspace

Vocabulary Acquisition and Use		McGraw-Hill Wonders
L.3.4	Determine or clarify the meaning of unknown and multiple-meaning words and phrases based on *grade 3 reading and content*, choosing flexibly from a range of strategies.	
L.3.4a	Use sentence-level context as a clue to the meaning of a word or phrase.	**READING/WRITING WORKSHOP: Unit 1:** 47, 93 **Unit 2:** 111 **Unit 3:** 191 **Unit 4:** 297, 311 **Unit 5:** 355, 369, 397 **YOUR TURN PRACTICE BOOK:** 17, 47, 57, 107, 177, 187, 217, 227, 247 **PHONICS/WORD STUDY WORKSTATION ACTIVITY CARDS:** 1, 2, 5, 11, 15 **TEACHER'S EDITION: Unit 1:** T26, T27N, T41, T92, T105, T172 **Unit 2:** T93S, T216 **Unit 3:** T26–T27, T27E, T93C, T159I, T212–T213 **Unit 4:** T152, T153F, T153I, T165, T216 **Unit 5:** T14, T36, T88–T89, T152–T153, T153E, T164–T165 **Unit 6:** T216–T217, T217I, T229 **www.connected.mcgraw-hill.com:** RESOURCES **Student Resources:** Vocabulary Interactive Games and Activities
L.3.4b	Determine the meaning of the new word formed when a known affix is added to a known word (e.g., *agreeable/disagreeable, comfortable/uncomfortable, care/careless, heat/preheat*).	**READING/WRITING WORKSHOP: Unit 2:** 143, 159 **Unit 3:** 223, 253 **Unit 4:** 283 **Unit 5:** 383 **YOUR TURN PRACTICE BOOK:** 77, 87, 127, 147, 167, 237 **PHONICS/WORD STUDY WORKSTATION ACTIVITY CARDS:** 9, 12 **TEACHER'S EDITION: Unit 2:** T158, T171, T224–T225 **Unit 3:** T95, T158–T159, T161, T171, T226, T234, T236–T237 **Unit 4:** T88–T89, T89L, T101 **Unit 5:** T14, T101, T153K, T153L, T165, T216–T217, T229 **Unit 6:** T26, T91, T165, T219, T229 **www.connected.mcgraw-hill.com:** RESOURCES **Student Resources:** Vocabulary Interactive Games and Activities

Language Standards

Vocabulary Acquisition and Use		McGraw-Hill Wonders
L.3.4c	Use a known root word as a clue to the meaning of an unknown word with the same root (e.g., *company, companion*).	**READING/WRITING WORKSHOP: Unit 3:** 239 **Unit 4:** 269 **Unit 5:** 341 **Unit 6:** 413, 441 **YOUR TURN PRACTICE BOOK:** 137, 157, 158, 207, 228, 257, 258, 277 **PHONICS/WORD STUDY WORKSTATION ACTIVITY CARDS:** 10, 13 **TEACHER'S EDITION: Unit 2:** T225K, T225N **Unit 3:** T159N, T224–T225, T225B, T225I, T225L, T237, T240 **Unit 4:** T24, T25B, T25P, T25T, T27, T155 **Unit 5:** T24, T37, T100, T155, T171 **Unit 6:** T24–T25, T27, T37, T100, T152–T153, T155, T165, T228 **www.connected.mcgraw-hill.com: RESOURCES** **Student Resources:** Vocabulary Interactive Games and Activities
L.3.4d	Use glossaries or beginning dictionaries, both print and digital, to determine or clarify the precise meaning of key words and phrases.	**TEACHER'S EDITION: Unit 1:** S27, T26, T39, T92, T93K, T105 **Unit 2:** T159I, T237 **Unit 3:** T26, T92, T237 **Unit 4:** T24, T216 **Unit 5:** T24, T88, T89I, T152, T217O, T280 **Unit 6:** T88, T216 **www.connected.mcgraw-hill.com: RESOURCES** **Student Resources:** Vocabulary Interactive Games and Activities
L.3.5	Demonstrate understanding of word relationships and nuances in word meanings.	
L.3.5a	Distinguish the literal and nonliteral meanings of words and phrases in context (e.g., *take steps*).	**READING/WRITING WORKSHOP: Unit 1:** 79 **Unit 2:** 127, 173 **Unit 3:** 207 **Unit 4:** 325 **Unit 6:** 427, 469 **YOUR TURN PRACTICE BOOK:** 37, 67, 97, 117, 197, 267, 297 **PHONICS/WORD STUDY WORKSTATION ACTIVITY CARDS:** 4, 6, 8 **CLOSE READING COMPANION:** 151 **TEACHER'S EDITION: Unit 1:** T93M, T224, T225H, T225K, T225M, T237 **Unit 2:** T92, T105, T113, T118, T122 **Unit 3:** T38, T92–T93, T93Q, T105 **Unit 4:** T25L, T89G, T89P, T89W, T217G, T217I **Unit 5:** T89Q, T89S **Unit 6:** T88–T89, T101, T142, T153A–T153B, T164, T292–T293 **www.connected.mcgraw-hill.com: RESOURCES** **Student Resources:** Vocabulary Interactive Games and Activities
L.3.5b	Identify real-life connections between words and their use (e.g., describe people who are *friendly* or *helpful*).	**READING/WRITING WORKSHOP: Unit 1:** 20–21, 68–69 **Unit 2:** 116–117, 148–149 **Unit 3:** 196–197, 212–213 **Unit 4:** 288–289, 302–303 **Unit 5:** 346–347, 360–361 **Unit 6:** 418–419, 460–461 **YOUR TURN PRACTICE BOOK:** 1, 21, 41, 101, 151, 181, 211, 241, 261, 291 **TEACHER'S EDITION: Unit 1:** T47, T76, T179, T208, T212, T245 **Unit 2:** T47, T76, T179, T245 **Unit 3:** T38–T39, T113, T146, T179, T212, T245 **Unit 4:** T10, T14, T78, T173, T235 **Unit 5:** T202–T203, T228–T229, T237 **Unit 6:** T36–T37, T78, T142–T143, T228–T229 **www.connected.mcgraw-hill.com: RESOURCES** **Student Resources:** Vocabulary Interactive Games and Activities **Teacher Resources:** Build Background Videos, Graphic Organizers
L.3.5c	Distinguish shades of meaning among related words that describe states of mind or degrees of certainty (e.g., *knew, believed, suspected, heard, wondered*).	**TEACHER'S EDITION: Unit 1:** T56, T171 **Unit 2:** T56, T105 **Unit 3:** T93M, T105 **Unit 4:** T101 **Unit 5:** T101 **Unit 6:** T229 **CLOSE READING COMPANION:** 17 **www.connected.mcgraw-hill.com: RESOURCES** **Student Resources:** Vocabulary Interactive Games and Activities
L.3.6	Acquire and use accurately grade-appropriate conversational, general academic, and domain-specific words and phrases, including those that signal spatial and temporal relationships (e.g., *After dinner that night we went looking for them*).	**READING/WRITING WORKSHOP: Unit 1:** 20–21, 36–37, 52–53, 68–69, 84–85 **Unit 2:** 100–101, 116–117, 132–133, 148–149, 164–165 **Unit 3:** 180–181, 196–197, 212–213, 228–229, 244–245 **Unit 4:** 260–261, 274–275, 288–289, 302–303, 316–317 **Unit 5:** 332–333, 346–347, 360–361, 374–375, 388–389 **Unit 6:** 404–405, 424–425, 432–433, 446–447, 460–461 **YOUR TURN PRACTICE BOOK:** 1, 11, 51, 61, 101, 111, 151, 161, 201, 211, 251, 261 **TEACHER'S EDITION: Unit 1:** T14, T38–T39, T80, T104–T105, T146 **Unit 2:** T93C, T104–T105, T212 **Unit 3:** T13–T15, T27Y, T146–T147, T159I, T172–T173 **Unit 4:** T14–T15, T36–T37, T142–T143, T153I, T164–T165, T217K **Unit 5:** T78–T79, T100–T101, T142–143, T164–T165, T228–T229 **Unit 6:** T36–T37, T44, T50, T54, T61, T100–T101, T206–T207